Intellectual Teamwork

**Social and Technological
Foundations of Cooperative Work**

Intellectual Teamwork

Social and Technological Foundations of Cooperative Work

Edited by

Jolene Galegher
University of Arizona

Robert E. Kraut
Carmen Egido
Bell Communications Research

LAWRENCE ERLBAUM ASSOCIATES, PUBLISHERS
1990   Hillsdale, New Jersey   Hove and London

Lawrence Erlbaum Associates, Inc., Publishers
365 Broadway
Hillsdale, New Jersey 07642

Library of Congress Cataloging-in-Publication Data
Intellectual teamwork : social and technological foundations of
  cooperative work / edited by Jolene Galegher, Robert Kraut, Carmen
  Egido.
      p.   cm.
  Includes bibliographical references.
  ISBN 0-8058-0533-8. — ISBN 0-8058-0534-6 (pbk.)
  1. Small groups.   2. Information technology—Social aspects.   3. Communication in small
  groups.   4. Cooperativeness.   5. Work groups.
I. Galegher, Jolene Rae, 1949–   . II. Kraut, Robert E.
HM133.I524 1990
302.3'4—dc20
                                                                                89-17047
                                                                                CIP

Printed in the United States of America
10 9 8 7 6 5 4 3 2

Contents

Part IV
Technology for Cooperative Work 405

List of Contributors

Mark Abel
US West Advanced Technologies
6200 South Quebec St., Suite 240
Englewood, CO 80111

Deborah G. Ancona
Sloan School of Management
Massachusetts Institute
of Technology
Cambridge, MA 02139

Daniel E. Atkins
Department of Electrical
Engineering and Computer Science
University of Michigan
Ann Arbor, MI 48109

Tora K. Bikson
The Rand Corporation
P.O. Box 2138
Santa Monica, CA 90406-2138

David F. Caldwell
Leavey School of Business
and Administration

Santa Clara University
Santa Clara, CA 95053

Aaron V. Cicourel
Department of Sociology
and School of Medicine
University of California, San Diego
La Jolla, CA 92093

Carmen Egido
Room MRE-2B299
Bellcore
445 South Street
Morristown, NJ 07960-1910

J. D. Eveland
The Rand Corporation
P.O. Box 2138
Santa Monica, CA 90406-2138

Tom Finholt
Department of Social
and Decision Sciences
Carnegie-Mellon University
Pittsburgh, PA 15213

Susan R. Fussell
Department of Psychology
Schermerhorn Hall
Columbia University
New York, NY 10016

John Gabarro
Harvard Business School
Cambridge, MA 02138

Jolene Galegher
Department of Management
and Policy
Harvill Building #76
University of Arizona
Tucson, AZ 85721

Barbara Gutek
Department of Management
and Policy
Harvill Building #76
University of Arizona
Tucson, AZ 85721

Edwin Hutchins
Institute for Cognitive Science
University of California
San Diego, CA 92093

Sara Kiesler
Department of Social
and Decision Sciences
Carnegie-Mellon University
Pittsburgh, PA 15213

Kenneth L. Kraemer
Graduate School of Management
University of California
Irvine, CA 92717

Robert M. Krauss
Department of Psychology
Schermerhorn Hall

Columbia University
New York, NY 10016

Robert E. Kraut
Room MRE-2E232
Bellcore
445 South Street
Morristown, NJ 07960-1910

Fred Lakin
Center for Design Research
Building 530 Duena Street
Stanford University
Stanford, CA 94305

George P. Landow
Institute for Research
in Information and Scholarship
Brown University
Providence, RI 02912

Joseph F. McGrath
Department of Psychology
University of Illinois at Urbana-
Champaign
603 East Daniel Street
Champaign, Il, 61820

Jay F. Nunamaker
Department of Management
Information Systems
University of Arizona
Tucson, AZ 85721

Gary Olson
Department of Psychology
University of Michigan
Ann Arbor, MI 48109

Alain Pinsonneault
Graduate School of Management
University of California
Irvine, CA 92717

Ronald E. Rice
School of Communication,
Information and Library Studies
Rutgers University
4 Huntington Street
New Brunswick, NJ 08903

Douglas E. Shook
Advanced Computing Systems
University of Southern California
Los Angeles, CA 90089

Lee Sproull
Department of Social
and Decision Sciences
Carnegie-Mellon University
Pittsburgh, PA 15213

Doug Vogel
Department of Management
Information Systems
University of Arizona
Tucson, AZ 85721

Preface

Most of the work that people do requires some degree of cooperation and communication with others—some kind of teamwork. This is true whether they are producing material products such as automobiles or intellectual ones, such as this book, a scientific theory or a strategic plan to govern a major corporation. Yet, as students of behavior in groups and organizations have observed, the difficulties of coordination and communication tend to counteract the benefits that come from collaborative work and decision making. Of course, many features of the complex organizations that play such an important role in contemporary society—hierarchy, formal rules and procedures, and cross-functional task forces, for instance—are, in fact, attempts to overcome those problems, and the study of organizational behavior is, in large part, an effort to understand the nature and influence of those mechanisms. But as that research reveals, the solutions these mechanisms provide are imperfect; despite people's best efforts, coordination systems fail, communication goes awry and, as a result, errors occur and important work is delayed.

Now, as a result of the efforts of computer scientists and engineers, a new category of tools to counter the difficulties associated with cooperative work is becoming available—multi-media electronic information systems that make it possible to transmit text, graphics, and video images across time and distance and to organize information in new ways. These new electronic tools are being deployed to solve traditional problems in communication and coordination. But, as some of the chapters in this book will show, these tools have not been as successful as their designers might have hoped, in part because they have not always been designed with the needs and goals of their human users in mind. The relevant social knowledge has not been as influential in the design of technology as it could be, for a number of understandable and possibly correctable reasons.

Our belief in organizing this book is that basic research on social processes can provide guidance to those creating technology for group work, and that the design of these tools presents a new challenge to social scientists. Our goal is to demonstrate the mutual relevance of social science and the design of information systems and to encourage better integration of those disciplines. We do so by bringing together in this volume the work of social scientists studying phenomena associated with work in groups and researchers developing tools to support such groups.

The book is divided into four sections that illustrate four themes: (1) That we know a substantial amount about the basic social processes underlying cooperative work that is relevant to the design of information technology; (2) That we can learn even more about the determinants of group effectiveness from studies of groups in situ; (3) That information technology has the potential to alter work group collaboration in interesting and sometimes useful ways; and (4) That an even newer generation of information technologies to support group work is on the horizon.

Our goals in this book are to entice more social scientists to orient their research around questions of practical interest to information system designers and to convince designers to seek out the knowledge about social and organizational behavior that would make their tools more useful. We believe that moving in these directions would lead to both richer and more detailed social science and more valuable and usable information systems. More broadly, our goal is to help provide a model to researchers and students of a truly interdisciplinary, applied social science.

The creation of an interdisciplinary endeavor is always a difficult task. Yet we believe that the better integration of social science and computer science—already starting in the fledgling field of computer-supported cooperative work—has the potential to benefit both disciplines, as well as the users of information technology. Although social scientists are fond of quoting Lewin's observation that nothing is as practical as a good theory, it is also true that nothing is as generative of good theory as good practical problems.

Jolene Galegher
Robert Kraut
Carmen Egido

1

Technology for Intellectual Teamwork: Perspectives on Research and Design

Jolene Galegher
University of Arizona

Robert E. Kraut
Bell Communications Research

Abstract

Intellectual teamwork is an increasingly important segment of white collar work, and information system designers are working to create technologies that will help groups perform more effectively. However, creating practical information technology requires not only technical expertise, but also an understanding of the social and behavioral processes that the technology is designed to support. Social science knowledge about groups and organizations could be extremely valuable in designing tools to help people communicate and structure their work, yet this knowledge is underused. This chapter presents reasons for that underuse and suggests that, to avoid reproducing these difficulties in new technological domains, social scientists should become actively and directly involved in design.

Most of the work that people do requires some degree of cooperation and communication with others—some kind of teamwork. In this book, we're particularly interested in intellectual teamwork and in the design of information systems to support it. The concept of intellectual teamwork embraces information intensive work of many kinds; it includes the formulation of corporate strategy, consultative medical diagnosis, and collaborative scientific research. It also includes the design and development of such diverse products as computer hardware and software, advertising campaigns and jointly authored magazine articles. The central image underlying these examples is one of individuals working together to produce or manipulate information; they illustrate that intellectual teamwork occurs in an enormous variety of tasks and settings.

The Soul of a New Machine, Tracy Kidder's (1981) entertaining account of the development of a new computer, provides a detailed portrait of a prototypical instance of intellectual teamwork. Kidder showed how the design ideas for Data General's new computer grew out of conversations between the engineers who had been recruited to the design team, and portrayed the importance of coordinating work, tracking progress and keeping records. He also demonstrated how individual involvement in the project was sustained by a combination of the intellectual challenges that the project presented and commitment to the group engendered by isolation, time pressure, and a sense of being part of a special mission. Finally, he showed how the group's ability to sustain itself and to carry out its mission depended on its success in representing its needs and achievements to other individuals and groups in the organization.

This account provides a rich source of evidence about the multidimensionality of group effectiveness. According to observers of group processes such as Hackman (1983) and McGrath (1984; chap. 2 in this volume), a group's effectiveness can be measured in terms of three criteria: its productivity; the extent to which it provides individual members with whatever social, material or intellectual rewards they are seeking; and its ability to sustain itself as a social unit over time. Their analyses reveal the complex interplay of skills, motivations, and organizational support required to complete a complicated project. This complexity creates particular difficulties in carrying out projects such as those previously described.

For instance, when complex tasks are partitioned among individuals, either because there is too much work for one person or because diverse kinds of expertise are needed, the added burdens of communication and coordination tend to counteract the productivity gains obtained by division of labor (Brooks, 1982). In addition to the difficulties that might arise from these structural factors, performance problems may result from social psychological processes. Conformity pressure may cause individuals in brainstorming groups to perform less effectively than they would have if they had been working alone; diffusion of responsibility and lack of ownership of a group product can cause individuals to put forth less effort to accomplish a group task than an individual task. Finally, members of a group may shut out relevant information to maintain group cohesion (Diehl & Stroebe, 1987; Janis, 1972; Latane & Nida, 1981). Social psychologists have come to refer to problems like these as "process losses" (Steiner, 1972).

Although these properties of groups and organizations are problematic for managers and supervisors who are concerned about productivity, and create frustration for individual workers as well, they present opportunities for computer scientists and software builders—the better mousetrap builders of the late twentieth century. In fact, both popular and scholarly writers (Dhar & Olson, 1989; Greif, 1988; Richman, 1987) have identified "technology for collaborative work" as an important focus of leading-edge information systems research, and there are many exciting developments occurring in this area at industrial and academic research labs around the country. These developments include computing and communication systems that are designed or can be used to support the sort of work already described. Many of them assume the presence of and familiarity with computers, but unlike software designed for word processing and data analysis they are intended to aid workgroups, project teams or whole organizations rather than to support the completion of specific tasks by individuals.

This realm includes both widely used, commercially available technologies and others that are almost unknown outside the narrow community of researchers whose work is represented here. The more familiar systems include: electronic mail, which permits users to send messages to each other via computer networks, providing a fast, low-cost alternative to surface mail and inter-office memoranda; computer conferences, which are the electronic equivalent of bulletin boards, permitting the development of on-line, asynchronous, multiperson discussions, the contents of which are available to all members of the conference; and audio and audio/video teleconferencing, which are designed to permit multiple, geographically dispersed users to hold meetings without the expense and inconvenience of travel. Some examples of the more exotic technologies are: group decision support systems, which are designed to improve the quality of group decisions by relying on computer software to guide deliberation and choice; hypertext software systems, designed to permit scholars and students to access and modify a common file, creating a network of linked, text and graphic entries and annotations on a common topic; and "virtual hallways," which combine audio and video technology to provide a continuous link between users at different sites as a way to overcome the barriers to informal communication imposed by distance.

These and other systems are described more fully in the following chapters; here, it is sufficient to note that all of these systems are intended to help people engaged in collaborative intellectual work communicate and structure their work. They differ on many dimensions including flexibility, expertise required to use them, ease of implementation, and cost. Taken together, they have the potential to provide people with the capacity to communicate across boundaries of time and distance and to increase the ease and effectiveness of their work.

Recently, these possibilities have elicited the interest of a small number of social and behavioral scientists whose theoretical interests include factors that affect human communication and the performance of groups and organizations. Simultaneously, the difficulty of developing systems that are appropriate to users' needs has prompted system builders to seek a more refined understanding of how people work together as a basis for design.

These parallel developments have led to the establishment of a new field of research called computer-supported cooperative work, drawing together the interests of these two communities. The aims of researchers in this field are to describe both the general features of collaborative intellectual work and the specific details of particular kinds of collaboration, to create technological systems that will improve the quality and efficiency of collaborative work and foster kinds of collaboration that would be impossible without advanced communication and computer support, and to assess the impact of these technologies on individuals, groups and organizations.

But these are very challenging goals, and there is currently a considerable gap between the state of our achievements in this area and the ends that we believe it is possible to attain. This book is based on the premise that careful understanding of collaborative intellectual work is crucial for the design of information technology to support that work. The goals of this introductory chapter are to describe some of the difficulties that have occurred as a result of failure to incorporate this understanding in the design of information systems, to identify factors that inhibit communication between systems designers and social and behavioral scientists, and to point out some of the difficulties that confront designers who seek to translate the wisdom of social science into system design. On the basis of this analysis, we argue for a new approach to system development, one in which behavioral researchers shift from reacting, as they do when they investigate the effects of technology, to being actively involved in design decisions, and in which systems developers seek this input as a way of insuring that designs are congruent with the intellectual and social processes they are intended to support.

DESIGN PROBLEMS IN TECHNOLOGY
FOR COOPERATIVE WORK

The history of experience with telecommunications and computer-based information systems contains many instances of expensive technological failures that are at least partly attributable to designs that do not mesh well with the social and behavioral systems in which they are to be used. We have reviewed these problems elsewhere (Galegher, 1987); here we present just two examples to give credence to our argument. The first concerns the long history of attempts to use telematics to improve communication among scientists and engineers. The goal of these attempts has been to capture the research literature of a discipline in computerized databases and to increase the scope of coverage, the number of researchers with access, the rapidity and accuracy of retrieval, and the ease of using retrieval systems. This goal continues to dominate thinking about the role of information technology in scientific communication. (See, for instance, the recent *Annals of the American Academy of Political and Social Science* [January 1988], devoted to discussions of scientific communication in the information age.)

But studies of the dissemination of scientific information and patterns of interaction among scientists (Crane, 1970; Garvey & Gottfredson, 1977; Garvey, Lin, & Nelson, 1970) suggest that these efforts may be too limited. These studies have shown that scientists rely heavily on informal communication within a network of scholars working on related topics to find out about new research. Through their informal networks, researchers in some disciplines know about 60% of the literature relevant to their specialty before it appears in published form. Their informal interactions help researchers learn which new research results are interesting and important enough to learn more about, and to learn this information before the research results become stale through publication delays. These long-standing behavior patterns imply that although computerized databases may be useful for archival purposes, they may not be the most effective way to broaden the distribution of scientific knowledge. In fact, almost twenty years ago, Crane (1970, p. 40) wrote, "Programmes for dealing with the 'information explosion' in science ought to be directed toward bringing relatively isolated scientists into contact with scientists who are the foci of communication networks. These individuals who sort, sift and channel information are more likely to be useful in orienting the activities of other scientists than computers which store vast quantities of information but are by their very nature unable to evaluate its potential relevance in terms of the sophisticated criteria required for developing new ideas in scientific research." Crane's observations imply that if information technology is to be useful in establishing links between working scientists, it must be designed to support rich communication between individuals, rather than to provide an electronic warehouse for scientific research.

A similar conclusion about the necessity to support rich communication may be drawn from the history of experience with teleconferencing. Egido (this volume) argues that teleconferencing, especially videoconferencing, has failed to live up to vendors' optimistic predictions of extensive reliance on these technologies as a way to reduce travel costs because particular features of the technology make conversation within teleconferences difficult and because eliminating travel to offsite meetings also eliminates the opportunities for informal interaction that executives value as a way of promoting themselves and their ideas. Of course, creating technologies that would support richer communication is not the solution for every design problem in this domain; rather, these two examples serve to illustrate the more general thesis that information system designs must somehow be appropriate for the tasks they are meant to support.

DILEMMAS IN LINKING SOCIAL SCIENCE
TO DESIGN

Why does technology fail to reflect what we know about social interaction in groups and organizations? We believe that problems like these stem, in part, from fundamental differences in the orientation of social scientists and technology designers. Social scientists are chiefly concerned with identifying regularities in human behavior. Their intellectual goal is to understand why humans behave as they do; their professional goal is to identify new research topics—areas of uncertainty about behavior that research could help reduce. On the other hand, design is fundamentally an engineering discipline; the goal is to find solutions to problems, not understanding for its own sake. Social scientists have information that is relevant to design, but rarely develop the practical import of their findings in ways that would allow designers to act on them. As a result, social scientists and designers who have much to say to each other nevertheless manage to talk past each other. Furthermore, these value differences have become enshrined in institutional structures—separate departments housed in different buildings, separate professional meetings, and separate journals. These various forms of isolation mean that it may take a long time for developments in one of these domains to be felt or have an influence in the other.

But even if designers were cognizant of all the relevant theory and research, translating these insights and observations into workable and useful information technology would be extremely difficult. Thus, we do not want to claim that linking theories of social behavior to the design of technologies to support social interaction is an easy, or even straightforward, enterprise. The difficulty stems not so much from the conceptual inadequacy of social and behavioral theories or the methodological inadequacy of the research (although such inadequacies certainly exist) as from the great complexity of the phenomena. For instance, as we noted earlier, workgroups and organizations have multiple goals and the importance of any one of them is likely to shift rapidly and, perhaps, unpredictably, over time; furthermore, the range of potential communication and information processing demands presented by even a few examples of intellectual teamwork is vast. These realities make designing information systems to support the multiple agendas and modes of communication that exist in complex social arenas a formidable task, indeed.

To illustrate this point in more depth, we consider the case of computerized group decision support systems (GDSSs). Behavioral research on individual and group decision making has clearly demonstrated that both cognitive biases and social constraints can and often do prevent people from behaving in ways that theories of rational choice predict. System developers have devoted considerable attention to improving decision processes by managing both the flow of data about the decision problem and the flow of communication among decision makers because of these problems and because of the importance of decision making in organizational life. (See Kraemer & Pinsonneault, chap. 14 and Vogel & Nunamaker, chap. 19 in this volume, for descriptions of these technologies and a review of research about their impact.)

Many of the features built into GDSSs are designed to improve decisions by reducing uncertainty; under uncertainty, the decision maker lacks the information needed to assess the likelihood of alternative outcomes given the choices. In principle, however, uncertainty can be reduced by gathering information relevant to the decision. For instance, a group of executives meeting to set prices on a line of consumer products would likely want to know about the sales history of similar products, the demographics of potential customers, manufacturing costs, and the like. In addition, they might want to attempt to predict the influence of a number of factors including price on consumer demand. Providing access to relevant databases and tools for building a model of consumer demand would help to reduce the decision makers' uncertainty about these issues, and the tools to achieve this uncertainty reduction can be made a part of a GDSS.

However, many organizational problems involve not only uncertainty, but also equivocality, uncertain preferences, and internal conflict over goals and values. Thus, decision making requires not only gathering data, but interpreting the problem, defining goals and strategies, and representing the decision effectively to internal and external constituencies. Under equivocality, decision makers may not know how to interpret the information they have at hand, or what information to gather to resolve the problems they face. Furthermore, decisions are often made by management teams, executive committees or task forces, so in addition to the information-processing problems resulting from equivocality and difficulties over goals, and the political problems that arise from differences in perspectives, there are communication problems that arise in the interaction among decision makers. In a situation of this sort, it will not be easy to gather data that are likely to lead to a decision about how to proceed, nor will it be easy to identify what constitutes a good decision. High equivocality means that decision makers are essentially involved in a process of generating shared interpretations of the problem, and enacting solutions based on those interpretations (Daft & Lengel, 1986; Weick, 1979). Thus, the processes involved are fundamentally social.

In situations characterized by high equivocality, decision makers prefer rich sources of information such as face-to-face meetings that allow them to test definitions of the problem and obtain feedback that tells them whether their views are shared (Daft & Lengel, 1986); this preference is inconsistent with the computer-based techniques of uncertainty reduction described earlier and also runs counter to the goal of decoupling the content of communication from the identity of the communicator that underlies the design of communication modes in some GDSSs (Vogel & Nunamaker, chap. 19 in this volume). To be sure, a preference for rich interaction does not indicate that it is an inherently superior communication mode, but considerable evidence indicates that it can be crucial in establishing a shared understanding of the problem confronting a group or team (Galegher, 1990; Krauss & Fussell, chap. 5 in this volume; Kraut, Egido & Galegher, chap. 6 in this volume) and may provide the framework within which organizational actors develop the consensus needed to carry out complex projects (Ancona & Caldwell, 1987; chap. 7 in this volume). Thus, this analysis suggests that, to the extent that decision makers confront equivocality rather than uncertainty, GDSS designers ought to insure that restricting or otherwise intervening in ordinary face-to-face discussion of problems does not diminish the quality of the group's decisions or impair its ability to implement solutions.

The distinction between decision making under uncertainty and under equivocality presents a problem for designers of GDSSs. For their work to be useful, system builders must be aware of the relationship between decision type (and many other contextual factors) and the characteristics of their designs. Different styles of group decisions are likely to require different types of technology to support them. A structured data-gathering, discussion and data analysis system may provide substantial benefit to decision makers operating in an uncertain environment by minimizing the likelihood that they have will sway each other from an optimal combination of information. But decision makers operating in an information environment characterized by equivocality may need to communicate in a more unstructured way to reach agreement. Real-world decision making, however, is typically not well-specified, stable, or orderly enough to permit decision makers to understand their situation and consciously adopt a suitable problem-solving approach. Rather, problems may contain elements of both uncertainty and equivocality, and are likely to present themselves at unpredictable times. Moreover, groups may lack awareness of the type of decision in which they are embroiled.

By revealing the variation that exists within what initially appears to be a single task domain (group decision making), this discussion illustrates the difficulties that designers face. This clarification supports the idea that the existing research on interpersonal, group and organizational functioning can usefully inform the design of some technology for cooperative work, but it also validates the related observation that applying this knowledge is not easy. The complexity we have discovered in what initially appeared to be a well-specified, unitary task implies that the tools needed to support the execution of this task are, in fact, contingent on many other factors.

PRESCRIPTIVE VERSUS PERMISSIVE TECHNOLOGY

Furthermore, our analysis illustrates that designers whose goal is to improve the functioning of human groups and organizations are confronted with a choice that is at once ideological and practical. On the one hand, they can design what might be called "prescriptive technology" whose structure is intended to correct human foibles. For example, the designers of some GDSSs have noted that one of the failures of group discussion is the social influence that inhibits the quantity of original ideas that the members would have generated had they been working in isolation. Their computer systems impose a model of group discussion in which individualistic idea generation precedes discussion and feedback from other group members (Vogel & Nunamaker, chap. 19 in this volume).

In contrast, what might be called "permissive technology" does not attempt to constrain or direct the behavior of its human users. Rather, the intent is to allow current practices to be extended into new realms in which they had previously been impracticable. For example, as we indicated earlier, much scientific knowledge is acquired by word-of-mouth rather than through the published research literature. As a result, the knowledge a scientist acquires is more haphazard than a model based on goal-oriented information searching would lead one to expect. One might turn to the computerized databases as a mechanism to make the dissemination of scientific knowledge not only broader, but more systematic as well. Designers could construct sophisticated information distribution systems that could target relevant scientific information to particular audiences. However, a more permissive approach would expand the current, inefficient, informal communication networks rather than replacing them. Relying on this approach to design, one might create communication links that allow researchers to "bump" into relevant others, independent of the physical distance that separates them (c.f., Abel, chap. 18 in this volume; Crane, 1970; Goodman & Abel, 1987; Kraut, Galegher, & Egido, 1987–1988; Root, 1988). Using such technology, researchers might place a request for information to the larger scientific community, for example, by posting a message on an electronic bulletin board, and receive in reply not only a relevant reference, but also an introduction to another researcher doing similar work.

This continuum between prescriptive and permissive technologies is well-illustrated by a comparison of generic electronic mail systems and a software product called the Coordinator TM. Electronic mail systems have been available in the United States since at least 1969, and by 1985 people were sending over 500,000,000 messages per year (Snyders, 1987). Electronic mail systems allow sending text messages and, in some experimental systems, graphics, pictures, spread-sheets, voice, and animated messages as well, from one individual to another or to a specified group of people (Olson & Atkins, chap. 16 in this volume). Most electronic mail systems provide only minimal structuring of messages. Typically, the system generates "From" and "Date" fields and may allow senders to complete a "Topic" and "Copy to" field. Both the topic field and the body of the message can be as varied as those in conventional, paper-based correspondence. Thus, electronic mail replicates, and perhaps even exacerbates, the difficulties in defining an audience, resolving ambiguity and the other flaws of much written communication (Kiesler, Siegel, & McGuire, 1984; Sproull & Kiesler, 1986). It has the benefit that written communication between individuals can take place across vast distances at a relatively rapid pace. For example, using electronic mail, messages and documents can move across the country in minutes rather than the days taken by the U.S. mail or even express mail services.

In contrast to the permissiveness of generic electronic mail, the Coordinator TM structures conversations taking place via electronic mail to remedy some problems in human communication. The Coordinator TM starts with observations drawn from linguistic analysis indicating that speech elements are used to perform social acts and a conviction, based on empirical evidence, that ambiguity as to the nature of a speech act in play is one of the causes of failure in using language to coordinate group-based, task-oriented activities (Winograd & Flores, 1987). To solve this problem, the Coordinator TM requires senders of messages to categorize the communicative intent of their messages, for example as an unstructured "conversation for possibilities" or a more structured "conversation for action." In a conversation for action, writers can indicate that their message is either an offer or a request. In a request, the writer is prompted to close a mail message with an "alert" to the recipient or by asking the recipient to "respond by," or "complete by," thus assigning a due date for fulfillment of the request. The recipient has a similar menu of response alternatives including "acknowledge," "promise," and "decline" that can be used to make the intent of the reply explicit (Flores, Graves, Hartfield, & Winograd, 1988).

As was the case with GDSSs, the choice between these approaches is both ideological and practical. In the ideological domain, the prescriptive approach is in tension with design and management philosophies that emphasize autonomy and workers' rights to make important choices about the ways in which they structure their work. By definition, technologies that structure and constrain the way individuals can communicate, make decisions, or otherwise perform their tasks reduce their autonomy. In the practical domain, embracing one or the other of these design philosophies has implications for the degree to which these technologies can actually improve the execution of cooperative work. A naive cost–benefit analysis of the value of systems for cooperative work must take into account the probability that a system will be used, the benefits derived from it if it is used, and the costs of using it, including the costs of transition.

Prescriptive technologies have the main benefit that if they are successful, they will remedy some flaws in current practice, whereas permissive technologies merely extend the status quo, with its attendant flaws. But to achieve these remedies, prescriptive systems must somehow change—whether modestly or substantially—established ways of carrying out tasks. Moreover, as previously discussed, they may reduce users' autonomy. These factors—the costs associated with changed procedures and loss of autonomy—may lower the probability of their use, regardless of their benefits if they are used. The likelihood that these costs will reduce the probability of use is especially high for discretionary and infrequent users— the people Cuff (1980) called casual users. People who use computer technology for substantial portions of their work day, such as airline reservationists, have little discretion about whether they use it, both because of their position in the organization and because the technology is essential for performing their jobs. Casual users, on the other hand, such as an executive using a GDSS or secretaries using electronic calendars, use the tools only occasionally and have substantial discretion about whether or not to use them. As a result, the benefits are likely to be diluted because of infrequent use and the costs are likely to be amplified.

MEETING IN THE MIDDLE: JOINING FORCES FOR MORE EFFECTIVE DESIGN

In the preceding discussion, we argued that social science knowledge about groups and organizations can provide useful guidance in the design of information systems for cooperative work, but integrating these two domains will not be an easy task. As we have seen, social scientists and designers inhabit different worlds, and translating social science generalizations into concrete advice for designers is often hampered by the complexity of the real world. Moreover, even if one knew precisely how to design technology to improve cooperative work, ethical considerations moderate the degree to which we would want to constrain or manipulate work groups and the difficulty of adopting new ways of working imposes practical limits on the benefits of attempts at social engineering.

One way to attempt to overcome these barriers is for social scientists to become actively involved as designers. We believe that successful design of technology for cooperative work requires both expertise in the underlying computer and communications technologies and expertise in the social and behavioral processes that the technology is designed to support. As we have suggested previously and as others have argued in the case of human-computer interaction more generally, the knowledge generated in research labs, or even in field studies, is often too abstract to be applied unambiguously in concrete circumstances. Social scientists working with designers can provide the translation needed between the abstract and the concrete and, using both formal and casual methodologies, can test whether the translation was successful.

This call for direct involvement by social scientists in the design and implementation of technology for cooperative work is not without precedent. Indeed, some interesting and successful technology, including some described in this book, has been jointly designed by social scientists and computer scientists. For example, social scientists' observations of problems in group deliberation and choice prompted the design of GDSSs and their recommendations for improving these processes formed the basis for the design of these systems. Although, as we illustrated previously, these systems still have problems, improvements to them will probably depend on better understanding of the strategies that groups use in making decisions and the design of flexible tools to support these strategies. Similarly, social scientists have been involved in the design of video technologies to support informal interaction (e.g., Goodman & Abel, 1987; Root, 1988), tools for distributing mail to those who would be interested in the topic (e.g., Malone, Grant, Lai, Rao, & Rosenblitt, 1987), and in tools to support communication among writers (e.g., Leland, Fish, & Kraut, 1988; Trigg, Suchman, & Halasz, 1986).

Despite the difficulties of integrating social science knowledge with technological design, we believe it is worth striving for this goal. There are strong precedents favoring greater involvement of social and behavioral scientists and technology designers in each others' worlds. Studies of the reciprocal influence of technology and social relations conducted in mining and manufacturing companies have enriched our understanding of organizational structure (Lawrence & Lorsch, 1970; Thompson, 1967; Trist, 1970; Woodward, 1958, 1965), and behavioral research about job characteristics that enhance workers' satisfaction and productivity has influenced the design of manufacturing technology (Morvat, 1984). This history of mutual benefit implies that similar advantages might accrue to scholars and designers whose interests intersect in the relatively new domain of information technology. A more refined understanding of the social and behavioral context in which the systems they build will be used might help technology designers avoid wasting resources on misdirected or flawed technologies such as those described earlier. For social scientists, the benefits of greater involvement in the design of information technology are perhaps less obvious, but Pelz (1967) showed that scientists who combine theory-guided basic research with work on applied projects are more effective and successful than those whose work lies exclusively in either domain. As many authors have observed, the confrontation of social theory and social reality can be illuminating to both.

OVERVIEW OF THE BOOK

The researchers and designers whose work is represented in this book met at a workshop in Tucson, Arizona, to examine and try to resolve some of these problems. The aim of that workshop was to expand communication between investigators concerned with fundamental problems in human interaction and social organization, system designers, and the few scholars whose expertise encompasses a portion of both these domains. This book captures and extends that effort to identify substantive overlap between social scientists studying phenomena underlying cooperative group work with researchers developing tools to support such groups. The chapters are arranged in four sections, each of which represents a segment of the theoretical, empirical and design work that constitutes the domain of technology for cooperative work.

The first section contains four papers that attempt to describe some fundamental properties of social behavior and social organization. Each paper takes up a different portion of this task, focusing on social units of different sizes and levels of permanence. McGrath's chapter (2) provides a theoretical analysis of the small group, the social unit that is the focus of discussion in many of the subsequent chapters. His discussion concentrates on two themes: the idea that group functioning is multidimensional and that the actions of individuals, groups and organizations have implications for outcomes on each of these dimensions, and the idea that the temporal sequence of behavior in groups is both a function and a determinant of group effectiveness. These themes then provide the foundation for a speculative discussion of the effects of information technologies that intervene in the temporal and social structure of behavior in groups. Gutek's chapter represents a more direct approach to understanding the relationship between the properties of workgroups and the utility of information technology. In keeping with our observations here, she argues that specifying the properties of both information technologies and groups in organizations is essential in creating an understanding of what works and what doesn't that can provide a basis for decisions about design and implementation. Seeking these regularities, she adopts a contingency perspective that provides a framework for directing and organizing empirical observations; much of her analysis focuses on establishing the conceptual clarity needed to support this empirical agenda.

In the next chapter, the unit of analysis shifts from workgroups to interpersonal interaction. Echoing McGrath's observation that group functioning is multidimensional, Gabarro describes both the affective and instrumental components of relationships with co-workers. He focuses on the stages through which work relationships move and the establishment of trust among members of a work team. A goal of his chapter is to identify the elements underlying personal relationships that also apply to work relationships. This analysis speaks to our concern about appropriate design by sensitizing us about the interrelatedness of performance and personal relationships. Chapter 5 also focuses on interpersonal interaction, but, rather than taking on the global analysis of interpersonal and group functioning as in the first three chapters, Krauss and Fussell concentrate on a specific problem in social interaction—the problem of establishing mutual knowledge, a fundamental necessity for cooperative work. Krauss and Fussell describe the results of a long series of elegant experiments designed to determine how variations in assumptions about the knowledge of one's listeners affect referential communication. Due to the centrality of mutual knowledge in the execution of cooperative work and the potential for disrupting communication associated with many information technologies, these findings have direct and important implications for the design of information technologies.

In the second section, each chapter presents an empirical description of a specific instance of intellectual teamwork. Although the types of tasks described and the research strategies used to generate these descriptions vary, these chapters have in common the goal of understanding the cognitive and social demands of a particular kind of collaborative intellectual work. This understanding then provides the basis for evaluating the utility of currently available information systems and for recommending design ideas for new technologies. Kraut, Egido and Galegher (chap. 6) describe scientific collaboration in academia and industry, emphasizing the role of physical proximity as a technology for promoting frequent, informal communication; the analyses indicate that this kind of communication both increases the likelihood of collaboration and aids its successful execution. These findings suggest features that information technology must have if it is to support intellectual teamwork among distributed workers. Ancona and Caldwell (chap. 7) describe patterns of interaction in new product teams, emphasizing that the effectiveness of a workgroup depends on its ability to obtain both moral and material support from other parts of the organizations in which it is embedded, as well as the manner in which the members work together. This observation implies that information technology that could help group members understand and communicate with stakeholders might play a useful role in the planning and execution of intellectual teamwork.

In the last two chapters in this section, Hutchins (chap. 8), studying oceanic navigation, and Cicourel (chap. 9), studying medical diagnosis, are both concerned about problems of coordination and communication in situations where the knowledge needed to carry out a highly consequential task is stored in several different heads. Their findings reveal an intricate interplay of the technical and social systems that sustain and control this interdependence. For instance, Hutchins claims that the opportunity for crew members to observe each other at work created by the physical layout of the control room aboard ship contributes to partial redundancy in their knowledge and thus to the maintenance of the group over time. This is a subtle and interesting argument that has implications for job design well beyond the scope of this book, but it also provides a foundation for some specific recommendations about the design of information technology. For instance, it suggests that technologies that allow users to observe each others' contributions (such as computer conferences and hypermedia systems) may provide a system for sustaining group memory independent of the presence of specific individuals in an organization. But, as Cicourel notes, divorcing information from its source may pose other problems; he argues that physicians rely heavily on their sense of who is and is not a reliable source of information in consultative diagnosis. This reliance on the trusted opinions of one's colleagues works against the likelihood that physicians will respond favorably to what is, perhaps, the leading information technology for medicine—computerized information retrieval systems and diagnostic tools. By decoupling diagnostic information from a trusted human source, the information retrieval system may inadvertently undermine its credibility.

In sum, the chapters in this section provide concrete examples of the abstract properties of interpersonal communication and social interaction described in the chapters in the first section. They emphasize the multidimensionality of group effectiveness and the interrelatedness of performance on these multiple dimensions. They also illustrate how naturally-occurring technologies such as physical proximity foster communication and make it possible for people to observe each other's personal qualities and professional skills. This technology provides a framework for the establishment of mutual knowledge, for constructing relationships with potentially helpful organizational allies, for achieving the redundancy in skills that sustains group performance, and for informally and unobtrusively assessing the intelligence and trustworthiness of potential collaborators and colleagues. Investigations like these are central to the broad agenda we have set ourselves; not only do they help to direct the design of information systems for particular kinds of tasks, but they validate the more general argument that empirical studies of cooperative work can provide a useful starting point for system design.

The third section contains five empirical investigations of experiences with technologies that have been available long enough and been used extensively enough to provide us with evidence about whether their potential to aid cooperative work has been fulfilled. For the most part, these technologies are designed to allow free-form communication without much structuring of messages: electronic mail, computer conferences, voice messaging, and video teleconferences. Only group decision support systems involve rules about how communication should proceed.

The authors of the first three chapters report studies showing the benefits of information technology that allows communication across space and time—computer conferencing, electronic mail, and voice messaging. Taken together, these chapters show that providing the capacity for asynchronous communication and for communication between individuals who would not otherwise encounter each other can enhance several aspects of group performance. Bikson and Eveland (chap. 10) report a field experiment using computer conferencing and electronic mail to support a task force writing retirement policy. Their study shows that computer-based communication can empower otherwise isolated people by providing them with the resources needed to accomplish their tasks, including access to information and other people. Finholt, Sproull, and Kiesler (chap. 11) examine the use of electronic mail in student work groups. Their research compares groups working on similar tasks, but using electronic mail to different degrees. Through content analysis and questionnaires, they provide a rich picture of how electronic mail is actually used to accomplish tasks. Frequent use of electronic mail improves intellectual collaboration, especially by making coordination among members easier. Rice and Shook (chap. 12) show that voice mail has advantages similar to those of electronic mail, and, in addition, provides a channel that makes it possible to communicate the emotional intensity of a message as well as its substantive content. Reflecting Gutek's discussion of "fit," these studies also demonstrate that, depending on their internal structure, the tasks they needed to perform, and the other communication means they had available to them, groups used electronic and voice mail in different ways to achieve their various goals.

On the other hand, the next two chapters reveal that experience with new technology to supplement or replace real-time meetings has been more problematic. Egido's (chap. 13) chapter reviews the literature on video conferencing, which supplements conference telephone calls among people at scattered locations with a visual channel. She argues that visual images of other participants in a meeting add little information and that the use of video teleconferencing for scheduled meetings ignores informal interaction through which much communication in organizations takes place. Nonetheless, she concludes by identifying some situations in which video-conferencing has been found to be useful, notably lecture-style presentations in which structured, one-way communication with a large audience is desired. Group decision support systems attempt not to replace, but to supplement, face-to-face meetings with computer-based tools for brainstorming, organizing information, voting, and the like. Kraemer and Pinsonneault's (chap. 14) review of the literature on group decision support systems takes a broad view of the technology and offers useful distinctions between systems with different features. Their analysis reveals a positive effect of GDSSs on decision quality, but they note that this conclusion is qualified by methodological shortcomings that make interpretation of these results ambiguous. By simultaneously summarizing and evaluating existing research, Kraemer and Pinsonneault provide a veridical, up-to-date portrait of the state of our knowledge about GDSSs and a launching pad for a new generation of research about their effects.

The last section, appropriately, treats more exotic technologies than the empirical reports in the previous section. Here, the emphasis is on new tools that might enable new kinds of cooperative work, rather than on the evaluation of established technologies. These technologies are at the cutting edge of system design; in most cases, their existence depends on high-speed computers with high-resolution screens, connected by high-speed networks. The first three chapters describe computer systems that allow groups to jointly author multimedia documents. Landow (chap. 15) describes a technology for tying together texts and graphics, commentaries, and personal notes that he argues enable new models of collaboration and authorship. Hypermedia software systems actively link chunks of text, pictures, graphics, voice recordings, and even video recordings in arbitrary ways, analogously to the marginalia, footnotes, personal annotations, and "see also" notations in scholarly works. Scholars and authors can weave their individual contributions into a context provided by original sources and other commentary and have that context immediately available to readers. Readers can append their own annotations or new reference material to already existing works. When used in an educational context, hypermedia encourages undergraduate students to move beyond passively soaking up what is already known about a particular topic to the more active, generative scholarly work typically associated with graduate education, thus increasing the value of their interaction with educational materials.

Olson and Atkins (chap. 16) describe software for jointly planning, writing, and submitting research proposals to funding agencies, to aid more traditional co-authorship. One problem with co-authorship of electronic documents is the diversity of equipment and formats used by different authors. With current computer technology, paper is the medium through which co-authors work on and revise each other's drafts and scotch tape is the tool they use to incorporate nontext objects like pictures or figures. In the system described by Olson and Atkins, text, outlines, graphics, and spreadsheets can be bundled in a single document, worked on in a unified way, sent to collaborators to be further refined, and then sent on to funding agencies, all in electronic form. Lakin (chap. 17) describes a different system to support coauthorship—a computer medium for performing text-graphics manipulations, that gives individuals and groups a quick and powerful sketching and writing editor and powerful processing capabilities to formalize sketches. The system that Lakin is building has the potential to allow people to move seamlessly between individual and group modes of work, between graphic and text work objects, and between casual and formal representations of objects. Although both chapters describe editors for multimedia documents, the two systems address different aspects of collaborative writing. Olson and Atkins's work addresses problems of diversity among collaborators using different systems, whereas Lakin's work aims at making a unitary, sleek and powerful editing system.

The next two chapters describe technology to support more interactive aspects of cooperative work. Abel (chap. 18) describes an old technology put to a new purpose. Bell Laboratories demonstrated the picture telephone in 1929 (Ives, 1930), and as Egido discusses in her chapter, since that time it has been used to augment standard single and multiparty telephone calls. Abel describes a case study in which video telephones were used to create permanent links between two geographically separated research labs to provide opportunities for informal interaction. This highly unstructured technology supported workgroups over several months of use. Abel reports that it was adequate to create a joint sense of place and culture, but just barely. It was less successful in supporting the detailed discussion on research tasks. On the other hand, Vogel and Nunamaker (chap. 19) describe a group decision support system designed to structure communication and decision processes in meetings of several hours duration. This system consists of multiple pieces of software, each of which is designed to support or steer a particular aspect of group decision making. Thus, it is permissive in that it allows user groups, working in collaboration with an experienced moderator, to select whatever computer tools might be appropriate for working on the problem at hand, but is prescriptive in that these tools attempt to guide users as they work through the decision process. This system has been used extensively in research and by groups of real-world decision makers, but as the authors point out, its features are continuing to change and grow as user reactions and more systematic research become available to define more clearly how technology can be used to reduce communication and information-processing problems in group decision making.

Taken together, then, the chapters in these four sections represent a broad sample of scholarly work relevant to the design and evaluation of technology for cooperative work. They demonstrate the relevance of high-level theories of social interaction and social organization, the value of empirical analyses of specific instances of intellectual teamwork, the effects of particular information technologies on the experiences and performance of users and, finally, they give us a hint of technologies that await us in the years ahead. Together they suggest to us the mutual benefit that could result from better integration of social science and technological perspectives on intellectual teamwork and illustrate the exciting work that is emerging in this new area.

REFERENCES

Ancona, D. F., & Caldwell, D. G. (1987). Management issues in new product teams in high technology companies. In D. Lewin, D. Lipsky, & D. Sockell, (Eds.)., *Advances in industrial and labor relations* (Vol. 4, pp. 199–221). Greenwich, CT: JAI Press.

Annals of the American Academy of Political and Social Sciences. (January 1988).

Brooks, F. B. (1982). *The mythical man-month: Essays on software engineering.* Reading, MA: Addison-Wesley.

Crane, D. (1970). The nature of scientific communication and influence. *International Sociology of Science Journal, 22,* 38–41.

Cuff, R. N. (1980). On casual users. *International Journal of Man-Machine Studies, 20,* 163–187.

Daft, R. L., & Lengel, R. H. (1986). Organizational information requirements, media richness and structural design. *Management Science, 32,* 554–571.

Dhar, V., & Olson, M. H. (1989). The role of value-based assumptions for design of collaborative work systems. In M. H. Olson (Ed.), *Technological support for work group collaboration* (pp. 33–50). Hillsdale, NJ: Lawrence Erlbaum Associates.

Diehl, M., & Stroebe, W. (1987). Productivity loss in brainstorming groups: Toward the solution of a riddle. *Journal of Personality and Social Psychology, 53,* 497–509.

Flores, F., Graves, M., Hartfield, B., & Winograd, T. (1988). Computer systems and the design of organizational interaction. *ACM Transactions on Office Information Systems, 6,* 153–172.

Galegher, J. (1987). *A proposal for a conference on technology and cooperative work.* Unpublished manuscript, University of Arizona.

Galegher, J. (1990). Intellectual teamwork and information technology: The role of information technology in collaborative intellectual work. In J. S. Carroll (Ed.), *Applied social psychology in organizational settings* (pp. 193–216). Hillsdale, NJ: Lawrence Erlbaum Associates.

Garvey, W., & Gottfredson, S. D. (1977). Scientific communication as an interactive social process. *International Forum on Information and Documentation, 2,* 9–16.

Garvey, W., Lin, N., & Nelson, C. (1970). Communication in the physical and social sciences. *Science, 170,* 1166–1173.

Goodman, G. O., & Abel, M. J. (1987). Communication and collaboration: Facilitating cooperative work through communication. *Office: Technology and People, 3,* 129–146.

Greif, I. (Ed). (1988). *Computer-supported cooperative work: A book of readings.* New York: Morgan Kaufmann.

Hackman, J. R. (1983). The design of work teams. In J. W. Lorsch (Ed.), *Handbook of Organizational Behavior* (pp. 315–342). Englewood Cliffs, NJ: Prentice-Hall.

Ives, H. E. (1930). Two-way television. *Bell Labs Record, 8,* 399–404.

Janis, I. L. (1972). *Victims of groupthink: A psychological study of foreign policy decisions and fiascoes.* Boston: Houghton Mifflin.

Kidder, T. (1981). *The soul of a new machine.* Boston, MA: Little, Brown.

Kiesler, S., Siegel, J., & McGuire, T. (1984). Social psychological aspects of computer-mediated communication. *American Psychologist, 39,* 1123–1134.

Kraut, R. E., Galegher, J., & Egido, C. (1987–1988). Relationships and tasks in scientific collaboration. *Human-Computer Interaction, 3,* 31–58.

Latane, B., & Nida, S. (1981). Ten years of research on group size and helping. *Psychological Bulletin, 89,* 307–324.

Lawrence, P. R., & Lorsch, J. W. (Eds.). (1970). *Organization structure and design.* Homewood, IL: Irwin & Dorsey.

Leland, M., Fish, R., & Kraut, R. (1988). Collaborative document production using Quilt. *Proceedings of the Conference on Computer-Supported Cooperative Work* (pp. 206–215). Portland, OR.

Malone, T. W., Grant, K. R., Lai, K., Rao, R., & Rosenblitt, D. (1987). Semi-structured messages are surprisingly useful for computer-supported coordination. *ACM Transactions on Office Information Systems, 5,* 115–131.

McGrath, J. E. (1984). *Groups: Interaction and performance.* Englewood Cliffs, NJ: Prentice-Hall.

Morvat, J. (1984). The problem solvers: Quality circles. In M. Robson (Ed.), *Quality circles in action.* Aldershot, UK: Gorver Publishing.

Pelz, D. C. (1967). Creative tensions in the research and development climate. *Science, 157,* 160–165.

Richman, L. S. (1987). Software catches the team spirit. *Fortune,* June 8, 125.

Root, R. W. (1988). Design of a multi-media system for social browsing. *Proceedings of the Conference on Computer-Supported Cooperative Work* (pp. 25–38). Portland, OR.

J. Snyders. Putting zip into e-mail. *Infosystems,* August 1987.

Sproull, L., & Kiesler, S. (1986). Reducing social context cues: Electronic mail in organizational communication. *Management Science, 32,* 1492–1512.

Steiner, I. D. (1972). *Group process and productivity.* New York: Academic Press.

Thompson, J. D. (1967). *Organizations in action.* New York: McGraw-Hill.

Trigg, R., Suchman, L., & Halasz, F. (1986). Supporting collaboration in NoteCards. *Proceedings of the Conference of Conference on Computer Supported Cooperative Work* (pp. 153–162). Austin, TX.

Trist, E. L., (1981). The sociotechnical perspective. In A. Van de Ven & W. F. Joyce (Eds.), *Perspectives on organization, design and behavior* (pp. 19–88). New York: Wiley.

Weick, K. E. (1979). *The social psychology of organizing.* Reading, MA: Addison-Wesley.

Winograd, T., & Flores, F. (1987). *Understanding computers and cognition: A new foundation for design.* Reading, MA: Addison-Wesley.

Woodward, J. (1958). *Management and technology.* London: Her Majesty's Stationery Office.

Woodward, J. (1965). *Industrial organization: Theory and practice.* London: Oxford University Press.

I BASIC SOCIAL PROCESSES

2

Time Matters in Groups

Joseph E. McGrath
University of Illinois, Urbana

Abstract

This chapter deals with some temporal features of group work, and with how those temporal matters are affected when technological tools are added. The first section deals with matters of temporal structure, such as stages of group development and phases of group task performance, treating those issues in terms of a new time-based theory of functional groups. The second section deals with matters of temporal patterning, giving special emphasis to entrainment processes. The third section considers an array of potential technological tools that can mediate and modify cooperative work in groups. Those tools are discussed in terms of how they might aid or hinder the temporal flow of communication and work in groups. That last section also poses some key questions for research.

The questions addressed in this book are, preeminently, matters of time: Groups develop and exist in a temporal context. Work is planned and carried out on real time schedules. Human behavior—at work and otherwise, alone and in groups—is temporally patterned in complex ways. And the introduction of technological tools, above all else, tampers with the time and space of it. So—to expand the pun of the title—this chapter will explore some temporal matters involved in the work of groups, and will try to show how such temporal matters do matter, both when people work together on common tasks, and when technological tools are added to the mix.

Issues regarding the temporal structure of group behavior have been raised at each of several levels of temporal scope. At the most macro level, the level of the "life cycle" of a group, temporal issues have been studied in the context of *developmental stages* of groups. Here, the key questions relate to whether there is a systematic sequence of structural–functional states through which groups of various kinds progress; that is, whether there is a general sequence of developmental stages for the "species": Group. That stage idea is embodied in Tuckman's (1965) description of four stages of group development, cleverly paraphrased as: "forming, storming, norming and performing." At a less macro level, the level of conduct of a concrete task or project, group researchers have asked whether groups exhibit a systematic series of problem-solving or task execution *phases.* That idea is embodied in the work of Bales and Strodtbeck (1951) on the phase sequence in single-session problem-solving groups, and related work on phase sequences in long-term groups (e.g., Landsberger, 1955; Psathas, 1960; Stock & Thelen, 1958).

At a still more micro level, the level of the group's ongoing interaction process, researchers have begun to ask questions about the rhythms or other temporal patterns by which groups synchronize their activities. That work is exemplified by studies dealing with patterning of sounds and silences in group conversations (e.g., Dabbs, 1983; Dabbs & Ruback, 1984; Jaffe & Feldstein, 1970; Warner, 1979, 1984, 1988), by studies analyzing temporal flow of the content of group interaction and mutual interpersonal influence (e.g., Gottman, 1979a, 1979b; Kerr, 1981), and by studies of internal and external influences on temporal patterning or synchronization of interaction (e.g., Kelly, 1988; Kelly & McGrath, 1985; McGrath & Kelly, 1986; McGrath, Kelly, & Machatka, 1984; Warner, 1979, 1984, 1988).

Both temporal structuring of the group's context (issues of stages and phases) and temporal patterning of the group's action (issues of synchrony) are important aspects of the study of groups, and both have implications for the effect of technology on work by groups. Therefore, the three sections of this chapter deal, respectively, with three clusters of temporal matters related to cooperative work. The issues of temporal structure, of stages and phases, are addressed in the first section, by means of a time-based theoretical perspective on what groups do and how they do it. The issues of temporal patterning, of synchrony, are the focus of the second section of the chapter, with special emphasis on entrainment processes. The third section considers how technology and time are likely to interact to affect communication in groups, and how we might modify some features of those technological tools so that they benefit, rather than disrupt, communication in groups.

The latter discussion, especially, will raise far more questions than it settles. For many issues, the impact of technological tools cannot be reckoned in any concrete way on the basis of current evidence. But the discussion of time and technology in the final section of the chapter, as well as the discussion of a number of temporal issues throughout the chapter, will both serve the twin objectives of this chapter: (a) to sensitize researchers to a number of important temporal issues involved in groups at work, including those that are influenced by use of new technologies; and (b) to provide a partial agenda for research that could increase our knowledge about those issues.

THE TEMPORAL STRUCTURE
OF WORK IN GROUP

In earlier treatments, both developmental stages and problem-solving phases were often construed as involving different specific types and patterns of activity in a fixed and more or less inexorable temporal sequence. But the temporal parameters of those phases were only crudely specified. For example, the time periods for Bales' problem-solving phases within a single "session" of a group's life were obtained by simply dividing up whatever period of time the group had worked on its problem into the desired number of temporally equal parts (e.g., dividing an hour-long group session into the initial, middle, and final 20 minutes segments). In many of the early studies on developmental stages in groups, the specification of time intervals for stages of group development was done in terms of successive meetings of the group, without much regard for comparability of the length and agenda of the various meetings of any one group, much less for comparability of those matters across groups. It is hard to replicate hypothesized temporal stages or phases based on such imprecisely specified temporal intervals—and even harder to refute them.

More recent work treats such stage and phase ideas more fully in their temporal contexts, and in considerably more sophisticated ways. Moreland and Levine (1988) used the stage idea in considering, simultaneously, both the temporal patterning of group development and the temporal course of socialization of members into a group. Wicker and King (1988) applied the stage idea in the context of the "life cycles of behavior settings." Both of these treatments try to tie down the temporal structure of group behavior with sharper definitions, and explore it within more elaborate relational nets.

Furthermore, Gersick's (1984, 1988) work has placed the question of the temporal structure of group action in a new light. She studied eight groups, each of which had a single mission and a predetermined life span, throughout their entire life course. The eight groups varied in life span from a few days to 14 weeks, but each had, from its "birth," a definite time deadline and an expected product (a report, a set of recommendations, a plan, etc.). Her most striking finding was the way every one of the groups made a major shift in what it did and how it did it at a point almost exactly halfway through its lifespan. However much progress a given group might have made vis-à-vis its task during the first half of its group life, each group had a more or less dramatic meeting at about the midpoint of its projected lifespan, and as a result changed the whole course and pattern of its activity. Before the midway point, many of the groups had seemed to flounder, or at least they did not seem to be moving efficiently toward their stated goals. After that midlife crisis, so to speak, each group moved fairly directly to an execution of the tasks that constituted project completion. This is a kind of phase movement, to be sure, but it is certainly a far cry from the kinds of temporal patterns implied in either Bales' or Tuckman's benchmark early works.

In the present context, one way to express Gersick's findings (and other studies of temporal patterning that will be discussed in the second section) is to say that the temporal patterning of group performance is relative to the task and to the time constraints under which the group is operating. In other words, there are temporal patterns in how groups go about their work, but those temporal patterns are not fixed in time in the sense that a given set of actions does not always last a certain number of minutes.

To take that dictum to heart and work through its implications, however, requires that we have a substantially different conception than we have had in the past about what groups are like, what group tasks are like, and how groups go about doing what they do. I have been trying to develop such a new formulation of groups, one that will let us deal more adequately with these and other time-based issues. Much of that new formulation is presented or implied elsewhere (e.g., Futoran, Kelly, & McGrath, 1989; McGrath, 1984, 1986, 1987; McGrath, Futoran, & Kelly, 1986). Here, I sketch only its key ideas, as a base for discussion of the stage/phase issues and other temporal matters in groups.

Outline of a Time-Based Theory of Functional Groups

In my time-based theory of functional groups, a group is regarded as an intact social system that carries out multiple functions while partially nested within, and loosely coupled to, surrounding systems (e.g., an organization). It is assumed that groups have similar partial inclusion and loose coupling relations with their components (members).

Multiple Functions

Groups are multifunctioned. They do things, and the things they do make contributions to the systems in which they are embedded, to their component parts, and to the group itself. The first of these, the group's contribution to its embedding systems, is here termed the group's *production function.*

The second, the group's contribution to its component parts, is referred to as the group's *member support function.* The third, its contribution to its own system viability, is labelled the group's *well-being function.*

The things groups do that make such contributions also cost—in time, energy, and other resources. Some of the costs accrue to the embedding system, some to the members, and some to the group itself. Therefore, we need to reckon the value of a group's activities in terms of its net contributions (gains relative to costs) to the embedding organization, to the members, and to the group itself. (These three functions are similar to the three criteria set forth in Hackman, 1985, for assessing the success of groups in organizations). These three functions are separable for analytic purposes, but are intimately intertwined in any concrete instance; all three functions are always being enacted to some degree.

Units of Group Activity

We can regard the group's activities at three partially nested levels: projects, tasks, and steps. A project is a mission. It involves a set of activities in the service of a goal(s), a set of actions intended to produce a given outcome (Little, 1983). Groups usually have multiple projects going on at any one time.

Projects consist of tasks, sets of activities instrumental to completion of a particular project. Task results have value as a contribution to the project, but little value standing alone. (Project results, on the other hand, are valued in themselves.) But any given set of tasks is merely one of many potential ways to carry out a given project.

Tasks, in turn, are made up of subsets of activities or steps, sequences of action that, when executed in the proper form and with appropriate timing, constitute completion of that task. Steps are identified in terms of what actions are to be done. Tasks are identified in terms of what their completion contributes, instrumentally, to the project(s) of which they may be a part. Projects are identified in terms of their purposes, that is, in terms of what outcomes or products are sought.

For the most part, researchers in the group area have studied steps and tasks but not projects. Indeed, group researchers seem not to have thought very much about groups as performing projects (that is, as achieving goals), but rather have thought of groups only as carrying out specifiable, repetitive tasks, often tasks assigned to them by management or by an experimenter. Notably, the now vast goal setting research literature (see Locke, Shaw, Saari, & Latham, 1981) deals almost entirely with goals that are a statement of intended production rate on such repetitive tasks, rather than goals in the broader usage given here. There is a need to study groups that are doing projects that extend over more meaningful periods of time, on which the constituent tasks are viewed as merely one possible set of instrumental activities that can accomplish the project mission. (Some of the research described in this volume by Kraut, Egido, & Galegher, chap. 6; Finholt, Sproull, & Kiesler, chap. 11; Bikson & Eveland, chap. 10; and Ancona & Caldwell, chap. 7 exemplify such studies).

At any one time, most groups in organizations are engaged in a messy array of projects, tasks, and steps, operating simultaneously. They are playing several games at once, against different opponents, so to speak. The efforts of various members on various projects must somehow be interwoven in time and place. Moreover, different projects make differential contributions to the group's various functions—production, support, well-being.

New technology can affect all three group functions, at all three levels. In regard to the production function, new technological means are likely to change the steps involved in many tasks. Such technological changes also often alter the sets of tasks by which some group projects can best be done. Moreover, new technologies sometimes open up possibilities for entirely new projects, missions that can help the group attain its long-run purposes but that were not possible or even conceivable within the limitations of the prior technology.

Furthermore, although technological changes are usually aimed at modifying the group's production function, they almost always have profound effects on the group well-being and member support functions as well. The distribution among group members of both access to the hardware portions of the new technology and of the expertise needed to use and understand the new systems may provide brand new dimensions of the distribution of status and power within a group—dimensions that correlate quite poorly with the prior status structure.

Nesting and Coupling

Groups are partially nested and loosely coupled systems. *Nesting* relations refer to the logical inclusion relations among different units within a system (members in work groups, groups in other organizational units such as departments, and so on). *Coupling,* on the other hand, refers to the efficient causal relations among the parts of a system. Both nesting and coupling have temporal implications, and both may be affected by the imposition of new technologies.

Individuals are partially nested within the groups of which they are members. When one says that certain persons are members of a certain group, one must keep in mind that they are, simultaneously, components in many other social units as well. Groups may also be partially nested in that a given group may have an overlapping relation within more than one larger unit of the organization within which they are embedded.

Coupling refers to the tightness of the causal and consequential relations within a system, the linkages by which an action of one part of a system does or does not have an impact on another part. The idea of loose coupling (Weick, 1976, 1982) suggests systems in which the causal connections themselves are inherently indirect and complex, indistinct and indeterminant, and perhaps temporally inconsistent. Here, I postulate that most work groups are loosely coupled systems in two senses: (a) The actions of individual group members are loosely coupled to one another, and (b) the behavior of the group as a unit is loosely coupled to the larger social units within which that group is embedded.

New technology may affect nesting relations by freeing group communication from the usual requirement of strict spatial and temporal contiguity. Usually it will also have major effects on coupling relations, especially on the temporal aspects of that coupling. The idea of social entrainment (discussed in some detail in the second section) has to do with the temporal coupling of behavior, among different parts of the group and between the group and its embedding systems.

Stages of Group Project Activity

Groups do projects in real time. Project activities involve a series of stages, but those stages should be regarded as a logical template for potential project activity, rather than as an endogenous set of inevitable developmental phases. There is a distinctive but parallel set of stages for activities related to the group's production function (often thought of as the group's task-instrumental activities), and for activities related to its member support and the group well-being functions (often considered, together, as the group's socioemotional or expressive or interpersonal activities). Generically, the stages of group activity are:

Stage I. A stage involving inception and acceptance of a project (goal choice)

Stage II. A stage involving solution of technical issues (means choice)

Stage III. A stage involving resolution of conflict, that is, of political issues (policy choice)

Stage IV. A stage involving execution of the performance requirements of the project (goal attainment).

Stages I and IV are always involved in the execution of any project; stages II and III may or may not be involved, depending on circumstances. The stages have somewhat different tones and titles with respect to each of the three functions, production, member support, and group well-being. The nature of the stages within each function, and of their relation to one another, are indicated in Figs. 2.1 and 2.2. I describe the four stages of the production function first, and then the parallel stages for each of the other two functions.

Stages of the Production Function

For the production function, Stage I, the project inception stage, poses for the group a production or achievement opportunity (and demand). This is the stage in which the particular project becomes one of the group's

Group Contribution Functions

Stages	Production	Member Support	Group Well-being
Inception (Goal Choices)	Production Opportunity Demand	Inclusion Opportunity Demand	Interaction Opportunity Demand
Problem Solving (Means Choices)	Technical Problem Solving	Position Status Attainments	Role Net Definition
Conflict Resolution (Political Choices)	Policy Conflict Resolution	Payoff Allocation	Power Distribution
Execution (Goal Attainment)	Performance	Participation	Interaction

FIG. 2.1.   Stages and functions.

PRODUCTION FUNCTION

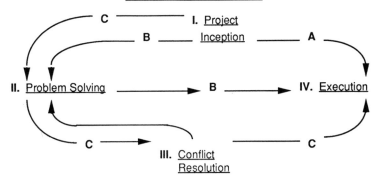

WELLBEING FUNCTION

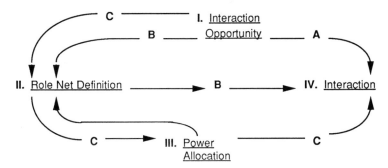

SUPPORT FUNCTION

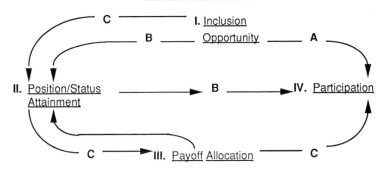

FIG. 2.2.   Paths through the project stages.

goals, priorities, or purposes. In general, groups acquire projects by one of three routes:

1. A member of the group proposes the project, which the group then decides to undertake.
2. An outside agent (such as the group's organizational superior, or an experimenter) assigns the project to the group, and the group then "decides" to accept it.
3. The project may be one that is in some sense indigenous to the group and its reason for existence, and/or a recurrent project of long standing for that group. The group undertakes such projects more or less automatically (unless it "decides" to change its raison d'etre or its past habits).

The inception stage involves several substages: acquisition of the goal or idea of the project; acceptance of that goal as one of the group's aims, and therefore acceptance of the project as having a certain priority for group attention, effort, and resources; and planning, at least at a general level, for conduct of the project. In general, Stage I involves a choice of goals and a consequent initial selection of a performance strategy.

There are three main alternative paths from inception to completion of a group project. If the activities required to achieve the project are straightforward, inception may lead directly to Stage IV, which is simply called execution. (See path A of Fig. 2.2). The execution stage refers to carrying out, in real time and space, the behaviors that are necessary and sufficient to attain the project goal(s). Stage IV involves goal attainment. Many projects need no intermediate stages (e.g., those that are recurrent and hence routine), and thus follow the relatively simple path A, which is the "default path" for work in groups.

Sometimes, however, direct attempts at execution of a project do not avail; it is not clear to the group just how the goal is to be attained. In such cases, the group needs to identify or construct a logically correct or best means for solution, or at least come to agreement on the procedures to be used. When the project poses such technical problems, the group's production function enters Stage II, the problem solution stage, which involves choices of means. When these choices of means have been made, the group can then go on to the execution stage (Stage IV) to complete the project by applying those chosen means. This is path B in Fig. 2.2. For path B, sometimes the problem-solving activities of Stage II are the heart of the matter, and Stage IV is pro forma once the correct procedure or appropriate algorithm has been determined.

Sometimes the activities involved in a group project require not so much the resolution of technical problems about means, but rather the resolution of either conflicting viewpoints or interests within the group. In such cases, after the inception of a project the group may attempt either to execute the task directly (i.e., Stage IV), or to deal with the project as if it were a set of technical problems to be solved (i.e., Stage II). However, it may find that a set of conflicting interests needs to be adjudicated before it can execute the project. In this case, the project enters Stage III, the conflict resolution stage. Here, the group must work through the conflicts of viewpoint or of interests and motives, and in so doing resolve conflicts of perspectives, value-orientation, goals, and outcome criteria within the group. If Stage II can be regarded as technical, Stage III can be regarded as political. With those issues settled, the group then moves the project to an execution stage (or, perhaps, back through a technical solution stage). This is Path C. For Path C, on some projects the resolution stage may be the heart of the matter, with the execution stage and even the technical solution stage pro forma or even trivial, once the political conflicts have been resolved.

The course of a project through these stages is not always as clear cut as indicated thus far. At the outset a group may not recognize that a project requires technical choices or resolution of conflicts, or both. Such groups may persist in trying to execute the project directly, without making those technical choices or resolving those conflicts. If so, the project will flounder in execution, eventually getting cycled back to appropriate earlier stages. Moreover, it is not always clear whether the problems or the conflicts have to be resolved first. Finally, actually working through the project may create new technical problems, or new conflicts, that were not there at the outset, and hence may require group action on the project to cycle back from the execution stage to some earlier stage. So projects often exhibit recurrent cycling of the production function among Stages II, III, and IV. For the sake of clarity, not all of those alternative loops are shown in Fig. 2.2.

Stages of the Group Well-Being and Member Support Functions

Stages of the group well-being and member support functions parallel those of the production function. For the well-being function, project stages reflect relations among group members. For the support function, project stages reflect relations between individual members and the group.

Consider Stage I, the inception of a project: This is an achievement opportunity (and demand) from the point of view of the group's production function. It is an interaction opportunity (and demand) from the point of view of group well-being. It is an inclusion/participation opportunity (and demand) from the point of view of the individual group member. It offers inclusion of that member in the group, in return for participation, loyalty, and commitment by that member to the group. All opportunities come tied to potential costs, risks, and dangers. Member participation in a group project always involves a balancing of interpersonal openness and closedness, of privacy and intimacy.

Consider Stage II, the technical stage of a project: This is a problem solution effort from the point of view of the production function. From the point of view of the group well-being function, it is a role net definition stage, in which the group must decide the technical staffing questions of who will do what, when, and with whom. These involve choices of interpersonal means. From the point of view of the member support function, it is a position or status attainment stage. In this case, attainment refers to both the self-selection and the group assignment aspects of how individuals fit into their positions, statuses, or roles within the group.

Consider Stage III, the political stage of a project: This is a conflict resolution activity from the point of view of the production function. From the point of view of the well-being function, it is a power allocation stage in which the group must resolve political issues of who controls the distribution of work and rewards. This involves the resolution of political issues of interpersonal status, power, and payoff. From the point of view of the member support function, it is a matter of allocation of payoffs and commitments. The individual's expected contributions to and payoff from the group must be negotiated and renegotiated as projects (and members) come and go.

Consider Stage IV, the execution stage of a project: This is an action or goal attainment stage from the point of view of the production function. From the point of view of the well-being function, it is an interaction stage, in which the group must carry out the concrete interpersonal activities that are involved in the group project performance process. From the point of view of the member support function, Stage IV is a matter of participation.

Concluding Comments

For productivity, well-being, and support functions, these four stages are not an inevitable sequence, but rather a set of logical relations that must be reckoned with. Not all group well-being activities have to deal with either role net definition or power allocation. Nor do all member support activities have to deal with new position/status attainments or payoff allocations. In some situations inception of a group project will lead directly to member participation, group interaction, and task execution. In other cases, project inception must be followed by activity involving the establishment or reestablishment of a role net definition and an allocation or reallocation of position/status attainments by individual members before participation, interaction, and task execution can be successful. In still other cases, inception must be followed by activity having to do not with the pattern of role differentiation and position/status attainment, but rather with the pattern of allocation of power, personal commitments, and payoffs, before participation, interaction, and task execution can be done effectively. As noted earlier, sometimes the group has to cycle back, to redirect its activities to some (logically prior) stage it had not adequately reckoned with, in relation to its group well-being function, its member support function, and/or its production function.

It should be expected that many group projects will require a three- or four-stage path, or an even more complicated recycling, for at least one function, even if it only requires a simple two-stage path for one or both of the other functions. Hence, there is often not a smooth, synchronized flow of all activities through a group's multifunction project stages. A researcher who is attending to only one function (e.g., the production function) may mistake such complexities of process for group performance inefficiencies, or in Steiner's (1972) pejorative term, "process losses."

The idea of process losses needs considerable translation to fit within the present multiple function, variable stage perspective. To be sure, there probably are some actions of groups that do not contribute positively to any, and contribute negatively to some, of the group's contribution functions. These would truly be process losses; they would be inefficient or wasteful actions from the point of view of all criteria of group success. But one cannot identify such "true" process losses by simply computing a task performance score and comparing it to some expected value based on a model that takes into account only the simple execution stage of the production function. One needs to examine comparable scores for support and well-being functions, based on appropriate theoretical models of those functions as well. It is not reasonable, from my perspective, to regard all group activity that is devoted to group well-being, to member support, and even to the solution of technical and political problems within the production function, as wasteful or as evidence of inefficiencies of process. Group process is much more complicated than can be reflected in a simple fit of a simple additive productivity model, as becomes evident in the next sections of this chapter.

In any case, these important but complex logical and temporal relations among the stages of each function, and among the three functions as well, are very likely to be modified by the introduction of new technology. By definition, new technology offers new technical choices for a range of tasks that groups might intend to carry out. But at the same time, such new technology might unwittingly introduce new political choices within the production function (e.g., the need to set priorities among projects, tasks, and members for access to the new technology). New technology is also likely to perturb the prior patterns of role definition, power, and payoff allocations within the group. Furthermore, some kinds of technology may free group members from the usual tight coupling of participation to spatial and temporal proximity; and at the same time it may modify the social psychological meaning of member inclusion in the group and the rewards and negative consequences that may flow from such inclusion. For example, for membership and participation in an electronic mail group, the idea of member inclusion and member support certainly implies a different set of social psychological conditions than membership, participation, and inclusion in a face-to-face work group, even if the frequency of participation is the same. Such effects of new technology on the structure of work in groups is discussed more systematically in the final section, after a further examination of the temporal patterning of work in groups.

THE TEMPORAL PATTERNING
OF BEHAVIOR IN GROUPS

Behavior in work groups shows many forms of complex temporal patterning, including some that are nonlinear and even nonmonotonic in temporal form. This section gives attention first to temporal aspects of the flow of work in groups, such as scheduling, synchronization, and time allocation, and then to the matching of "chunks" of time with "chunks" of work to be done. Much of the section deals with entrainment processes or patterns of synchronization—both the mutual synchronization, witting and unwitting, of group members' behavior with one another, and the synchronization of group behavior with ongoing events in the systems within which the groups are embedded.

The Flow of Work in Groups:
Timing, Timeliness, and Time Cost

Three generic temporal problems inherent in any collective action (and that are reflections of three major sources of stress in organizations) are temporal ambiguity, conflicting temporal interests and requirements, and scarcity of temporal resources (McGrath & Kelly, 1986; McGrath & Rotchford, 1983).

Organizational responses to these three inherent temporal problems can be characterized as scheduling, synchronization, and allocation, respectively. The parallel individual responses to those same problems can be identified as making temporal commitments, negotiating norms for behavior sequencing, and regulating the flow of task activity and interpersonal interaction. The "fit" (or misfit) between individual and organizational responses to these problems provides the potential for a set of residual problems for the system. Those residual problems are (a) the need to set and meet deadlines (the residual problem of the fit between organizational scheduling and individual commitment); (b) the need for dynamic team-work (the residual problem of the fit between the organization's efforts at synchronization and the sequencing norms adopted by the individual); and (c) the need to assure an adequate demand/capability match (the residual problem of the fit between the organization's allocation of temporal re-sources and the individual's regulation of the flow of task and other ac-tivities). These residual problems arise at the interface between individual and organization. Most often, that individual/organization interface occurs within the kinds of functional groups discussed here; hence, those interface problems get played out mainly in a group context (See McGrath & Kelly, 1986).

These three temporal issues also can be expressed in terms of three temporal criteria: timing, timeliness, and time cost. *Timing* has to do with whether the behaviors that individuals perform in order to carry out their tasks are synchronized (temporally coordinated), both within and between members and with other relevant sets of events or actions. *Timing* (or synchronization) is much involved with the entrainment processes dis-cussed later in this section. *Timeliness* has to do with whether a given set of actions, or a given task or project, is completed at a time appropriate to its scheduled deadline. Usually, deadlines are times at or before which some-thing must be done. Sometimes, however, timeliness has to do with whether a set of activities is completed within some temporal interval, neither too late nor too early. Thus, timeliness (or scheduling) is timing (or synchronization) at a more macrotemporal level. It, too, involves potentially complex entrain-ment processes. Time cost has to do with how much time a given task or project consumes. Time costs of a project can be calculated with reference to both hours of staff time (and other resources) used in the project, and in terms of calendar span elapsed from its launching until its completion. The former, staff time costs are often calculated in relation to some budgeted allocation of staff time and resources. The latter, calendar time costs are often evaluated in terms of completion by some overall deadline. Hence, time cost, too, is timing at an even more macro level.

These three time criteria are key elements in what might be called the "temporal infrastructure" of work in groups. And it is this temporal in-frastructure, more than anything else, that is both facilitated and perturbed by new communication technology.

The Time/Activity Match

Scheduling work entails fitting activities to periods of time. Melbin (1987) argued eloquently that time is a container into which we invest activities. In scheduling multiple projects in complex systems, it is vital to have as much flexibility as possible in regard to what bundles of activities can be done in what time periods. Two of the assumptions of the Newtonian conception of time, which dominates our culture and organizations within it, are (a) an atomistic assumption that time is infinitely divisible, and (b) a homogeneity assumption that all the "atoms" of time are homogeneous, that any one moment is indistinguishable from and interchangeable with any other. But these assumptions do not hold in our experience. Time is epochal, not homogeneous; a given hour of the day, day of the week, or month of the year is not like every other one. And for most practical purposes, different periods of time of equal duration are not infinitely divisible and interchangeable with one another.

Consider some examples in which time periods of equal duration but at different locations within a day, a week, or a year, cannot be indiscriminately interchanged with one another without cost. An hour-long meeting with one's child's teacher, for instance, may "cost" much more (in time and in opportunity costs) if it must be done midmorning on a workday than if it could be done that evening. Similarly, for many purposes, ten 1-minute work periods, scattered throughout the day, are not of equivalent productivity value to one 10-minute period of work from 9:15 to 9:25 A. M. Nor is the day before Christmas equivalent to February 17th for most retailers. A piece of time derives its epochal meaning, and its temporal value, partly in terms of what activities can (or must) be done in it.

Activities, too, cannot be divided into (or combined into) units of any arbitrary size without cost. Who would want to do laundry one garment at a time, or aggregate the dirty dishes over a full year? And what executive would schedule twelve 5-minute meetings, back to back in the same hour, and expect to fulfill that schedule? Space, facilities, sanitary considerations, and other matters of convenience, place substantial constraints on how much we can partition or aggregate any given activity, hence on how much time and which chunks of time we can effectively use to undertake and complete that activity.

Thus, both time and activities are "lumpy" and epochal in these and related ways, rather than smoothly divisible, aggregatable, and interchangeable. Work in groups is affected, dramatically, by at least three aspects of this time/activity match:

1. By the behavior versatility of the periods of time involved; that is, by the range of activities that can be done in them.
2. By the temporal flexibility of the activities involved; that is, by the range of times during which they can be done.
3. By the temporal modifiability of the activity bundles; that is, by the degree to which parts of the activities can be aggregated, or partitioned, into units of activity of different sizes, to fit the units of time that are available for their completion.

It should be noted that certain technological tools are designed in part to ease the constraints of the time/activity match in relation to communication in groups. For example, certain forms of computer conference arrangements permit so-called asynchronous communication among group members. This, in turn, loosens the limits of the time/activity fit, by permitting participants to use more time to insert more content, and to shift the time of their participation to a more convenient hour. The effects of this looser coupling of the time structure of communication may be quite complex. They are discussed in some detail in the final section of this chapter.

Social Entrainment

The term *entrainment* is borrowed from biological science, where it refers to the well-documented fact that some endogenous biological and behavioral processes are captured, and modified in their phase and periodicity, by powerful (internal or external) cycles or pacer signals. In the biological sciences entrainment applies to a plethora of physiological and behavioral processes in plants, animals, and humans. Here, the term *entrainment* is applied in a social psychological context, both at the macro level of broad social schedules (e.g., seasonal effects, rush hours, shift work effects), and at the more micro level of effects of time pressure on production rate and quality in work groups.

The idea of entrainment is not yet a familiar one for all social scientists, so a word of explanation is appropriate. To communicate the idea of entrainment, an analogy is often made to the somewhat more familiar action of tuning forks. If a tuning fork of a given pitch is set in motion, then placed near another stationary fork of about the same frequency (or a submultiple), the latter fork will begin vibrating more or less in synchrony with the former.

In the biological sciences, the classic cases most often used to exemplify entrainment processes are the circadian rhythms. All animals and plants have a number of physiological and biological processes that operate in rhythmic, periodic, or oscillatory forms. Among these are a set that operate with a periodicity of about 24 hours. (The two Latin words from which circadian is composed mean about and day). The processes that make up the set of circadian rhythms are endogenous oscillating processes. That is, they oscillate, on and off or high to low to high, naturally and without any external triggering.

Under ordinary conditions of life on earth, these processes become mutually entrained to one another; that is, they shift phase and frequency so that they oscillate in synchrony. Ordinarily, too, these processes all operate as a coordinated, mutually entrained bundle of biological processes with a periodicity of 24 hours, in synchrony with the day/night rotation of the planet. Under extraordinary conditions, however, when the light/dark and warm/cold variations of the day/night cycle have been surpressed by experimental means, these now "freerunning" rhythms shift to periodicities near but not exactly at the day/night 24-hour interval (hence the name, circadian). These freerunning rhythms tend to have a highly stable periodicity for any one individual—virtually a "signature"—but to vary from individual to individual. Jet lag—the discomfort that many people feel when they travel very rapidly across many time zones—reflects a decoupling of the mutually entrained rhythms of the circadian bundle. Furthermore, if freerunning continues long enough, the mutually entrained bundle tends to divide into two separate bundles—one with a periodicity much longer than 24 hours (sometimes exceeding 30 hours), and the other with a periodicity relatively nearer to 24 hours (e.g., between 23 and 24 hours). Furthermore, these two bundles are controlled by regulators ("clocks"?) located in different regions of the brain. For detailed and fascinating descriptions of these circadian rhythms see Moore-Ede, Sulzman, and Fuller (1982).

The idea of entrainment contains two kinds of synchrony:

1. The mutual entrainment of endogenous rhythms to one another, as occurs for the separate processes that make up the circadian bundle.
2. The external entrainment of such a rhythm or bundle, by powerful external signals or pacers (sometimes called zeitgebers or "time givers"), as occurs for the entrainment of the circadian bundle by the light and temperature signals contained in the day/night cycle of the planet.

Some researchers (e.g., Kelly & McGrath, 1985; McGrath & Kelly, 1986; Warner, 1979, 1984, 1988) have argued that both of these forms of synchrony operate for social psychological as well as biological processes, and that such social entrainment processes play an important role in the behavior of individuals and groups at each of many levels of social system operation. For example, Warner (1988) found mutual entrainment of speech patterns for interacting partners. Kelly and McGrath (1985) reported external entrainment, by time limit instructions, of group task productivity rate, features of group task product quality, and features of the content of group interaction (amount of evaluation of task contributions, amount of interpersonal content). These and other researchers (e.g., McGrath & Kelly, 1986; McGrath, Kelly, & Machatka, 1984) have argued that some of the effects of shift work on the worker have to do with entrainment of the non-work life to the work schedule and the consequent disentrainment of workers from the rhythms of daily living of the other people (spouse, family, friends) in their social networks.

Note that both forms of entrainment represent instances of loose coupling. The oscillating tuning fork induces but does not compel (in the sense of a tight mechanical linkage) the vibration of the nearby tuning fork that was initially at rest. The light and temperature changes of the day/night cycle induce but do not compel a shift in phase or periodicity of the bundle of circadian processes. So it is, as well, with instances of social entrainment. The time urgency contained in task instructions induces but does not compel changes in the group's rate and quality of task work, and in the rate and pattern of their interaction.

The research supporting the basic idea of social entrainment, some of which was noted earlier, merits further discussion. Kelly and McGrath (1985) found that the imposition of a task performance deadline (a part of the temporal context of the group) resulted in entrainment of the rate and quality of group task performance and of the pattern of group interaction process—effects not only on the initial trial but on later trials as well, when the deadlines had been changed. Groups who were assigned a tight time deadline early in their limited experimental "lives" continued to work at a fast rate (but with low quality, and with an interaction pattern that was highly task-focused) on later trials when in fact they no longer had the tight time deadline. Conversely, groups who began working against a less stringent time deadline continued to work at a slower rate (but with higher quality, and with an interaction pattern that was more interpersonally focused) on later trials when in fact they had shorter time deadlines.

Tasks of different types yield different patterns of entrainment effects, and those differences can be traced to what Kelly and colleagues (Kelly, 1988; Kelly, Futoran, & McGrath, 1988) called qualitative versus quantitative difficulty of the task. Under task conditions for which early trials yield an experience of qualitative difficulty, groups tend to slow down the rate at which they work on later trials (and may, thereby, increase the quality of that work). Under task conditions for which early trials yield an experience of quantitative difficulty, groups tend to speed up the rate at which they work on later trials (and generally reduce the quality of that work).

Entrainment processes operate within the group's communication pattern as well as in the group's productivity. Those same entrainment studies and others (e.g., Warner, 1984, 1988) show that the participation patterns of interacting group members tend to become mutually entrained to one another as they work together. This seems to hold for patterns of speech and silence, for patterns of nonverbal expression, and for features of the content of the interaction as well. As an example of the latter, Kelly and McGrath (1985) found that groups who begin work with stringent time deadlines (compared to groups that have more ample time in their early work periods) spend relatively less time in evaluations of proposed task ideas (agreements, modifications, disagreements), which might well affect the quality of the product. They also spend virtually no time in communication of interpersonal content, which might well affect both the member support and the group well-being functions. Furthermore, these interaction process effects carry over (as do the task product effects already discussed) even to later trials for which the time limits have changed.

Such nondeliberate and nonconscious synchronization of behavior of group members can occur in several forms. Sometimes synchronization requires out-of-phase alternation, as in human conversations. Sometimes it requires in-phase synchrony, as in the execution of many complex motor behaviors. The idea of mutual social entrainment of behavior between members of groups offers a new handle for exploring the interaction process itself. Furthermore, both mutual entrainment by members and entrainment by external pacers are central to the ways in which new technology may affect group process.

Stages, Functions, and Entrainment Processes in Group Interaction

Consider some implications of those entrainment effects in the flow of work in groups, if we regard groups as working in the multifunction, multistage project framework laid out in an earlier section. Suppose we observe a group that has acquired and accepted a project. Suppose that the group is a "task force" (McGrath, 1984), created for the purpose of executing that specific project. Suppose further that the intended primary focus of the project is on the production function. Nevertheless, because that group was created for the project and has no past history, it potentially has a lot of work to do in relation to its well-being and support functions (role net definition, position and status attainment, and perhaps power and payoff allocation). The project is presumably new to the members of that group, both collectively and distributively, so the group also has a lot of work to do in the problem-solving stage, and perhaps in the conflict resolution stage, of its production function. Thus, the project may call for a full cycle (that is, four-stage) treatment in the production function, as well as in the other two functions.

Now suppose, still further, that the group has imposed an artificial and stringent deadline. Presumably, group members will "work faster"—and, according to the Kelly and McGrath (1985) evidence, they are likely to produce a product at a poorer level of quality. Time pressure may induce such groups to try to go directly to the execution stage, even if the requirements of the project would normally have called for investment of some effort (and time) in technical problem solving. The Kelly and McGrath evidence also suggests that under such time pressure groups will eliminate much of the communication activity by which they evaluate one another's task ideas, and virtually all of the interpersonal or nontask aspects of their interaction. If so, then not only might the production function suffer in quality (because of the short shrift given to the technical solution stage, and to evaluation of task ideas), but the group is also likely to fare poorly on both its well-being and its member support functions because no time or communication activity has been devoted to these functions.

Conversely, the entrainment findings would suggest that a group, given a more than ample amount of time to carry out the same project, would indeed use up all the time available for it (as in Parkinson's notorious first law). But such groups might well spend some of that time "profitably," from a production function viewpoint, by moving the project through a technical problem-solving phase (and perhaps a conflict resolution phase as well). In any case, groups with ample time might deliver a product of higher quality in the end, if only because they pay more attention to evaluation of task contributions. Furthermore, the entrainment studies suggest that a group with such an "over supply" of time would put more attention and effort on the stages involved in the group well-being and member support functions (role definition, position/status attainment, power and payoff allocation, etc.). Hence, such a group might not only deliver a high-quality product on its initial assigned task, but in so doing might also position itself better to undertake other missions, of the same or even of different type.

The Gersick findings, discussed earlier, raise other interesting questions in the context of the entrainment findings. If groups with a fixed and known time deadline "take stock" and "redirect" half way through, what do groups with no time deadline (or with an indefinite one) do about these important matters? Many groups undertake projects without a specific deadline, but with the understanding that time is important, even crucial. For example, it may be clear that delay costs money—or even that the enemy may attack at any minute. Such groups are likely to work at the most rapid pace they can but to follow whatever strategy they happened to use at the outset. That is, they are likely to try to go directly to the execution stage, and to devote all their effort to the production function. Such "groups in crisis" might never make use of a midlife change in direction to improve strategy (that is, to carry out the technical solution stage), because time is always running out. This could lead to a consequent drop in quality on the production function (no communication about evaluation of the quality of ideas), and little or no attention to the well-being and support functions (no communication in the group about interpersonal matters). When groups work under such crisis conditions for extended periods of time, they are likely to produce low-quality work, and to be self-destructive social systems as well.

If the previous description is what happens when a group implicitly has an infinitely short time deadline, what happens when it implicitly has an infinitely long time to complete its project? That is, what if no time limit is given and the context makes it clear that the project does not have any time urgency (e.g., long-range planning activities)? Such a group might work at top quality on the project—if it worked on the project at all within any particular segment of time. Such a group might also spend considerable time and attention on the group well-being and member support functions. Assuming that such a time investment usually yields a net positive outcome on those well-being and support functions, such groups might become more attractive to their members (because of the strong member support function) and more effective and viable as a group—even if (or perhaps because) they did little or nothing during those early time segments to enhance the production function.

I do not mean to imply that if groups are given plenty of time they will always and inevitably turn out to be good groups, even in terms of their member support or group well-being functions, much less in terms of their production functions. The purpose, here, is to point out some new ways to look at these issues that are opened up by a temporal perspective, including the entrainment findings, along with a multifunction, multistage conception of groups at work.

In terms of the focus of this chapter, it is important to note that temporal patterning of interaction processes, in general, and entrainment processes in particular, play a dual role in relation to technological aids. On the one hand, they are key temporal features of group work that may get altered (for better or worse) by the introduction of technological tools. On the other hand, these same temporal processes are endogenous features of group communication that themselves either magnify or undo the intended effects of introduction of such technological tools. In the final section of this chapter, I examine these complex interactions of entrainment with endogenous communication processes when technological aids are introduced.

TECHNOLOGY AND TIME
IN GROUP COMMUNICATION

Much of what needs to be synchronized in groups is verbal and nonverbal communication. Any group's communication system is replete with key temporal features. Most technological tools are designed to alter the group's communication system one way or another. Consequently, most of those technological aids affect the temporal components of communication drastically.

We need to keep in mind that any particular communication system— whether or not it includes new technological aids—offers both possibilities for and potential constraints on communication in that group. We currently have at hand a spectrum of electronic devices—telephone, television, and computer—each usable in a variety of possible ways. We thus have a stunning array of potential new patterns of such constraints and possibilities for group communication, many of them never before contemplated much less realized in interperson communication. Many of these potential constraints and possibilities are temporal in character or have temporal consequences. Moreover, it is likely that any given use of a technological aid will alter the temporal features of that group's communication in both desired and undesired ways.

Stated in overly simplistic terms, then, this rich array of possibilities tempts us to ask: How can we manipulate channel and network links (telephone, television, computers, and so on) to help most, or to hinder least, the temporal flow of communication and work in groups? That question is infinitely easier to ask than to answer. It can be addressed in a limited fashion, though, by considering the advantages and limitations of communication in natural face-to-face situations compared to various kinds of electronically modified arrangements.

Communication in Groups

In any consideration of the effects of electronic interventions on group work it seems sensible to start with a discussion of the nature of direct, open, full-channel, so-called face-to-face communication, and view that kind of communication as the baseline case against which comparisons are to be made. Face-to-face communication may or may not be the best possible pattern, or the worst, for any given purpose. Rather, face-to-face communication is an appropriate baseline for comparison simply because we are used to having it available in almost all our human interactions—for better or worse.

Such face-to-face communication has a number of important features, many of them temporal in character, that affect the process and outcomes that are likely to result. It is important to keep in mind that those features—for example, time lags in response, differential participation of potential sources, certainty/uncertainty as to audience, and so on—are in themselves neutral, neither good nor bad. Rather, any one of those features will be advantageous in some communication circumstances and disadvantageous in others.

Features of Communication
in Face-to-Face Groups

There is a relatively vast literature on communication in face-to-face groups under more or less normal conditions. Unlike many other aspects of the group research literature, it shows a clear and robust pattern of results. Groups engaged in face-to-face communication exhibit a remarkably orderly pattern of communication, as if there were a rigorous set of norms or rules regulating that behavior.

First, across a wide range of sizes, types, and compositions of groups, there is a very orderly distribution of participation over time. There are few interruptions or times when more than one person is speaking. There are relatively few silences and those tend to be short.

Furthermore, there is a very orderly distribution of participation over group members. There is a positively skewed distribution of frequency (and duration) of acts across group members over any given block of time. That skew reflects a hierarchy—a status ordering—among group members. The skew increases with increases in the strength of the status ordering, as well as with increases in group size. Furthermore, the presence and strength of a status hierarchy, and the size of the group, have what might be called a "chilling effect" on contributions by low status members. That is, the larger the group, the lower the probability of contribution by the modal member; or, conversely, the larger the group, the larger the modal group of members that make few or no contributions.

Face-to-Face versus Written Communication Systems

This pattern can be contrasted with communication in groups that have various kinds of restrictions on their communication networks, modalities, or strategies. The literature is less abundant here, though still considerable (see Hesse, Werner, & Altman, 1987; Williams, 1977), at least for some communication systems. Results are also less robust, or at least less straight-forward and simple. It is clear, however, that there is a relatively complex pattern of shifts in features of the communication process that accompanies certain shifts in features of the communication structure.

The strongest contrast for which there is a solid body of evidence is between the face-to-face case and communications systems in which members of groups communicate with one another only in written form—as would be the case in what I later call on-line or synchronous computer conferencing (Hesse, Werner, & Altman, 1987; see later discussion). Some of the regularities found for face-to-face communication change when groups communicate only in written form. First, there is likely to be a more equal (less hierarchical) distribution of participation over members. That is, members are likely to participate without regard to status—, or, at least, low status members are more likely to participate. There is, you might say, a lessening of the "chilling effect" that status hierarchy and group size can have on contributions by low status members. But equal participation by all group members is not an unmixed blessing, especially because it is often the case that group members are far from equal in their potential for commu-nicating worthwhile contributions on a given issue. Nor is the anonymity of a message source that can be a part of such communication systems an unmixed blessing, and for the same reasons: It is often strategically valuable for group members to know the source of a contribution before reacting to it (Galegher, 1987, makes similar arguments).

Communication only by written means produces some other effects as well. There is a far less orderly flow of inputs over time. There are more anomalies in the transitions of floor turns, the smooth succession of "speakers." Depending on how the communication system is instrumented, these anomalies amount to delays or even denials of participation for some members. There are also longer, and far less predictable, lags between input and feedback.

These gross comparisons between face-to-face and one other rather constrained form of communication system hint at the complexity of the problem addressed here. There are many forms of technological aid that change the group communication pattern far less than the one examined here (synchronous computer conferencing), and some that change it far more. To consider as full a range of alternative forms as possible, and yet keep the complexity of matters manageable, the rest of this section is structured in the following way: First, I state as systematically but succinctly as possible the main features of communication in face-to-face groups that are relevant to the present issues. Second, I present a list of possible modifications of the face-to-face case by various technological means, ordered in terms of how drastically they alter the "normal" face-to-face communication process. That list is intended to be representative, not exhaustive; it is an ordered series of ideal types. I indicate which features of the face-to-face case are modified in each such ideal type. Those presentations imply a variety of effects on the communication process—some positive, some negative— that are associated with each of the modified communication systems. I close the section by trying to summarize some of the most important of those implications, both the good news and the bad.

Throughout this section, my emphasis is on the temporal features and consequences of communication systems. In furthering that emphasis, unfortunately, I may unintentionally overlook some other nontemporal features and consequences that are equally or more important.

Some Defacto Rules
of Face-to-Face Communication

Communication in face-to-face groups implies a set of at least two individual humans who are members of the communicating group. Each member is a potentially independent source of input. All members are, by definition, the targets of every input. All members are in the same place at the same time, all are known to one another, and the member who is the source of each message is known to all (i.e., neither members nor messages are anonymous).

Face-to-face groups are embedded within a full and open communication network. That is, each member is connected bidirectionally to every other member, via all modalities by which humans are capable of communicating with one another (sight, sound, olfaction, etc.). There is assumed to be zero time lag in message transmission and feedback response times.

Such face-to-face communication flows as if it were regulated by a strongly held set of cultural norms. These norms vary in detail from one culture (and subculture) to another. Within the dominant culture/subculture of our social system (the one that work organizations draw on), those norms about human communication include the following implicit rules:

Rule 1. Only one person can have the floor at any one time.

Rule 2. Someone must have the floor at all times, at least implicitly. There is, in effect, a "default speaker" at all times. Sometimes the default speaker is a continuing group leader; sometimes it is a host for the particular meeting; sometimes it is an issue protagonist (e.g., the person who asked for the meeting).

Rule 3. In the course of a discussion, the immediate prior speaker functions as default floor holder for a brief time after completion of his or her own contribution. Members act as if they need to have that person's permission, or at least his or her acquiescence, in order to take the floor. A speaker, therefore, can exercise some control over who the next speaker will be, as well as when the next speaker will take the floor.

Rule 4. Floor time is to be shared among group members, though not necessarily in an egalitarian way. Often, the floor sharing allocation is a hierarchically skewed distribution (e.g., a leader and followers; a presenter and audience).

Rule 5. Pause times between contributions are critical to smooth transitions. Because of rules 1 and 2 (that there be one and only one floor holder), pauses must not be either too short (risking interruptions) or too long (inserting silences).

Rule 6. Transitions between speakers are signalled by multiple cues, some verbal, some nonverbal (e.g., shifts of eye contact), and some paraverbal (e.g., lowering pitch and amplitude of voice). These signals are crucial for adjusting pause times, hence for upholding the norms about interruptions and silences and smooth transition between floor holders. These multiple signals use different modalities or communication channels; hence restrictions in communication systems reduce the redundancy normally available in these cases.

Rule 7. Participants assume that the audience for each contribution to the group's face-to-face communication is the set of all participants present, but only them. That is, they act on the assumption that all members are awake and attentive, and no one is surreptitiously eavesdropping.

Rule 8. Participants assume that the set of potential next speakers is the set of all participants present, but only them. That is, they act on the assumption that any one in the group can have the floor, and no outsiders will intrude.

Rule 9. The source of each communication input is known to all participants—there is no anonymity in face-to-face groups.

Rule 10. Participants assume that each input is logically and/or psychologically connected, either to the immediately preceding input or to other prior inputs, or else that it foreshadows future inputs. If there is not a connection to immediate or recent past inputs, it is assumed that the speaker will so inform the audience explicitly in the message.

A Classification
of Alternative Group Communication Technologies

There are a variety of forms in which technological aids can be used to modify normal face-to-face communication in groups (Galegher, 1987; Hesse, Werner, & Altman, 1987). Some of these involve video or audio communication systems; some involve computer communication systems.

Those modified communication systems can be arranged in a rough order of increasing drastic change from the face-to-face case. They fall into three sets. The first set are distance-spanning but time synchronous systems. These allow groups whose members are not all in the same place to "meet"—or at least to communicate. They buy that space-spanning advantage by restriction of modalities; but they retain the requirement that members are all acting in the same time. The second set are time-bridging or asynchronous systems. These retain the distance-spanning feature of the preceding set, but in addition relax the requirement that all members be sending and receiving in the same period of time. This time-bridging advantage is bought at a further cost in restriction of modalities. There is a third cluster of possibilities that are less pertinent in the present context but that are included for the sake of completeness of the comparison set. These are systems designed explicitly to be one-way communications. Some of them are on-line (e.g., a radio broadcast), whereas some are explicitly archival (e.g., a book). Neither expects feedback from recipients of the communication (See Fig. 2.3).

Synchronous Distance-Spanning Systems

The first main type of technologically altered group communication system alters the requirement that all group members must be in the same place, although they still retain the requirement that all be communicating in the same period of time:

TIME AND SPACE BOUND SYSTEMS (PROXIMAL & SYNCHRONOUS)

    Level 0:   Face-to-face groups

SYNCHRONOUS BUT DISTANCE-SPANNING SYSTEMS

    Level 1:   Closed circuit television

    Level 2:   Telephone conference

    Level 3:   "On-line" computer conference

ASYNCHRONOUS, TIME-BRIDGING & DISTANCE-SPANNING SYSTEMS

    Level 4:   Asynchronous computer conference

    Level 5:   Electronic mail

ONE-WAY COMMUNICATION SYSTEMS

    Level 6:   Broadcasts (concurrent, one-way)

    Level 7:   Archival (tapes, letters, books)

FIG. 2.3. Alternative technologies for communication in groups.

Closed Circuit Television Conferencing with Audio.   These represent a major restriction of modalities, though we often fail to recognize that fact. They eliminate communication in all sensory modalities (e.g., olfaction, tough, taste) except the visual and auditory channels. Sometimes such systems also lose some nonverbal cues because of limitation of cameras and positions. Such systems may or may not impose any substantial transmission or response lags, although hookups over long distances could do so at least on the audio channel.

Telephone Conferencing.   In addition to the constraints imposed in the closed-circuit video case, telephone conferencing loses all nonverbal cues and is likely to lose some paraverbal information as well. Telephone conferencing also can have substantial transmission and response lags if long distances are involved.

On-Line Computer Conferencing (perhaps including a simultaneous chat mode). This refers to communications systems in which the participants operate in so-called synchronous communication mode via computer. In addition to the restrictions already listed for the video and audio cases, such computer conferencing may be limited to two or a very few members, especially if they are using a truly simultaneous or chat mode rather than a form involving synchronous communication limited to one "speaker" at a time. In either case, such systems can involve substantial transmission and response lags. These systems also give up all nonverbal and paraverbal information, as well as the other sensory modalities.

Furthermore, such systems extract a high time cost per word for messages, because typing is much slower than talking even for the best of typists. Users often attenuate this cost by sending messages in cryptic and abbreviated forms. Using such condensed transmissions runs the risk of loss of information that is carried in the syntactical forms of the written or spoken language when used in standard form. There is also a potential loss of connotative information that is carried in the style of full-form written communication. This is less of a problem in this level than it is likely to be for the asynchronous computer conferencing mode to be discussed later.

An even more serious problem involves procedures for changing speakers that are not fully developed for such systems, either in a formal structural sense or in the sense of strong regulatory norms. Hence, turn taking often becomes highly chaotic, with many interruptions and silences. Of course, simultaneous input in a true chat mode by-passes the turn taking idea—but it does so by drastically restricting the number of participants and by violating the natural communication pattern of one and only one speaker at a time.

Asynchronous, Time-Bridging Systems

The second main class of technologically altered group communication system relaxes the time-synchrony requirement as well as that for place-sharing.

Asynchronous Communication Conferencing. In addition to all of the restrictions of modalities indicated for the preceding systems, these systems also relax the "same time" constraint as well as the "same place" requirement. These systems involve communication in written form, via computer, but with various participants choosing to receive and send at times of convenience to them (as in electronic mail, see below). Consequently, this kind of communication system inserts extensive and highly unpredictable lags in feedback, and it totally eliminates all of the nonverbal and paraverbal channels as well as the other sensory modalities. Furthermore, as in the synchronous version of computer conferences, asynchronous

computer conferencing systems increase time cost per word, thereby encouraging cryptic and abbreviated messages and the potential loss of syntactical and connotative information as discussed in the case of on-line computer conferencing. The problem is even more serious here than in the
preceding, synchronous case. From several studies discussed in the literature reviews cited here (see Galegher, 1987; Hesse et al., 1987), users of
this form of communication system apparently also complain about losing
information regarding the temporal order of messages when the messages
arise from more than one source; but that does not seem to me an inevitable
or insurmountable problem.

Such communication systems can accommodate a virtually unlimited
number and variety of participants, although they also can be used with
restricted and predetermined networks. Message sources are anonymous
unless some form of signature system is imposed—and that anonymity can be
either an advantage or a disadvantage in communication depending on the
nature of the task and what participants assume about the expertise of various
participants. The potential audience is also unknown unless a restricted net is
used. In any case, the actual audience for any given message is totally
unknown until and unless feedback is received. Furthermore, who the next
speaker will be, when the next input will occur, and whether or not it will be
connected to the current input, is unknown to and totally out of the control
of the current speaker. The more "open" the system is made, regarding time,
place, source, and recipient, the more "chaos" there can be in the flow of
information.

Electronic Mail.   This communication system contains all of the restrictions and features of asynchronous computer conferencing as previously
described. In addition, there is a reduction in the normative force on the
recipient of a message to provide feedback, a reduction in the normative
constraints on length and number of messages that one source sends, a
reduction in normative constraint on the range of permissible topics of
messages, and no normative requirement for connectedness between messages. All of these add up to an increase in volume of information received,
and a reduction in control of when, how much, and what kind of information
is received. That is to say, from the point of view of the receiver there is an
increase in the level of chaos, or a reduction in the degree of structure, of the
communication process.

One-Way Communication Systems

This class of technologically altered group communication systems is
really not group communication at all; rather it is a one-way communication
of one to many. It is included for completeness.

Broadcasts: One-Way, Concurrent Communication Systems. These systems are, in order of increasing restriction of channels: telecasts, radio broadcasts, computer bulletin boards, and memos. They share all of the restrictions of the preceding systems. In addition, they virtually preclude feedback or insure a long delay; they can make the source quasi-anonymous and the audience totally unknown. There is no communication process flow (that is, there is no turn taking, no next speaker, no connectedness of messages, and so on). Those features are totally constrained.

Archival Forms of Communication.   These also are not group communication, and are not intended to draw response. They include, in order of increasing restriction of channels: video tape, audio tape, computer files or tapes, and printed products such as books, magazines, journals, and newspapers. These share all of the restrictions affecting the preceding communication forms, and have the additional feature of being intended to be "timeless"—that is, to continue to be both available and useful on into the indefinite future.

Summing Up: The Good, the Bad, and the Hopeful

All of the preceding material adds up to some good news and some bad news for people interested in using technological aids to improve group communication. It also implies some questions amenable to research, that can help us reap some of the potentially good effects and avoid some of the potentially bad ones.

We can begin a summing up by asking: Do technological aids alter the temporal aspects of communication in groups? The answer, it would seem, is a loud and definite "yes." The effects appear to be both powerful and pervasive, and they contain both positive and pernicious consequences for group behavior.

We can continue that summing up by posing three further questions, which serve as the basis of the following discussion:

1. What are the effects of technologically produced changes in network, modality, and channel configurations on information transmission in groups?

2. What are the effects of such technological changes on the timing of communication activity, hence on synchronization/entrainment processes in those groups?

3. What are the effects of such technological changes on the sequence of stages by which groups do their work—not only the stages of the production function, but also those of the member support and group well-being functions?

Technology and the Flow of Information

As group communication systems are altered by technological means, and thereby moved along the continuum implied by the classification system of the preceding section, there are two concomitant changes in the channel/modality configuration of that system. On the one hand, there is a progressively more constrained use of channels and modalities. At the same time there is a progressively less constrained definition of who, where, when, and what will enter into that communication network. So, use of electronic means opens up the who/what/when/where of it and simultaneously closes down the how (modality) of it.

This is both good and bad news. On the negative side, virtually any restriction of communication modality or channel affects the breadth and redundancy of cues available for smoothing the flow of communication (e.g., for signaling change of speaker). Such reductions make it harder to follow the normative rules about communication on which we all depend. In information theory terms, they thereby both reduce the redundancy of cues needed to regulate flow, and increase the potential chaos or noise in the communication system.

Furthermore, such technological aids to communication have asymmetrical effects on sender and receiver. For example, asynchronous communication systems are more loosely coupled systems than face-to-face groups. This loose coupling provides a liberating effect for the sender—it relaxes the constraint on the who/where/when of participation in the network as a sender. At the same time, from the point of view of each receiver in the net, that loose coupling largely removes the constraints on amount and sequencing of incoming information; hence it provides a less orderly, more chaotic, less predictable flow of information for the receiver. So, although such technological changes free the sender with respect to time and place, for the receiver they reduce redundancy and increase noise—that is, they increase uncertainty.

On the other hand, the so-called asynchronous communication systems permit meetings or at least discussions to be held among sets of people who are not all in the same place and not even all "in" the group at the same time. Indeed, the gains from being able to communicate across different time periods sometimes seem to the participants to be more important than the gains from communication over spatial distances (Eveland & Bikson, 1986; Galegher, 1987).

The gains to be had from such asynchronous communication systems (asynchronous computer conferences in the earlier discussion) seem to be offset by losses arising from several other features of the communication process in such systems: The resulting overload of information for the receiver; uncertainty about audience; frustration from lack of response to one's contributions; and confusion about source and sequence of other's communications (see Galegher, 1987; Hesse et al., 1987).

This is a more favorable balance sheet than it might seem at first glance. The time bridging gains cannot be gainsayed, so to speak; they inhere in the nature of the system. On the other hand, the losses just ennumerated seem capable of elimination or reduction by rather straightforward means. Asynchronous computer conferences can be run using signature systems to identify contributors. They can select and delimit participants, and make the audience nonanonymous. They can generate an agreement among participants to read and react to all contributions by some predetermined deadline. They can include an agreement on upper and lower limits of input by each participant, and thereby generate any distribution of "floor time" among members that they wish.

Note that none of these efforts to make asynchronous computer conferences more effective involve any hardware development at all, and they require relatively little in development of software in conventional senses. Rather, they require social contracts among the participants. That is, they require the deliberate creation of the very kinds of social norms that apparently arise spontaneously in natural face-to-face groups, and that are very powerful and effective devices for regulating face-to-face communication in those groups.

We certainly need research in this area to explore these matters. For example, it seems likely that there are substantial differences in the cue value of various channels or modalities. We need to know which ones are most valuable. We also need to develop techniques for inserting effective turn-taking information into some of the reduced-modality communication systems. As already noted, such techniques are more likely to involve social rules agreed on by participants, than to involve costly hardware or complex software.

Thus we need major research efforts to invent and test means for more effective use of currently available technological tools, not new electronic devices as putative aids to communication in groups. Those inquiries should seek ways of offsetting the inherently adverse effects that such technological aids apparently have on the group communication process when they are used in their natural states. As already noted, effective means for making current technology more "group friendly," so to speak, are more likely to involve rules regulating procedures of use—operational algorithms if you will. I prefer to call those rules social system norms.

Synchrony and Timing
Between Communication Partners

The timing of contributions to a flow of communication is sort of the other side of the coin from the time/activity match. It is the match of bursts of sending and bursts of receiving across partners. Those two can match up well or poorly across the two (or more) partners in a communication system. Making communication asynchronous is again a two-edged sword: It eliminates cues and makes the mesh harder to achieve; it also stretches the time scale so that required coordinations are not so fine-grained, and hence are easier to accomplish.

In earlier parts of this chapter I have argued that normal face-to-face communication in groups involves strong entrainment (or other temporal patterning) across communication partners—and that multiple, redundant channels, back channels, and other features of the communication system operate to produce the patterned synchrony. Some technological tools reduce the redundancy of cues, because they eliminate some of the channels or modalities (e.g., nonverbal and paraverbal channels) through which the cues that structure these entrainment processes can flow. Those technological tools thereby disrupt the attainment of synchrony or entrainment between communication partners.

There is further bad news about timing. Many kinds of electronic interventions introduce time lags both in message transmission and in feedback response. We have little empirical evidence about the effects of such lags on the communication process in groups. But we do know that some researchers in human engineering areas have deliberately introduced such transmission and response lags as a means for inducing stress. Hence, it seems like a good bet that the introduction of such time lags will not turn out to have extremely positive effects on communication in groups. The question of transmission and response lags is directly related to entrainment issues as well. It seems likely that transmission and response lags can be major factors leading to desynchronization among otherwise mutually entrained features of the communication process.

Certainly this area calls for empirical research. Moreover, this is one clear example of how we can use electronically modified communication systems to do more effective basic research on some features of communication in normal or unaided systems. The experimental study of such lags offers a means for learning, at one and the same time, both about fundamental temporal processes in groups and about the impact of technological aids on those processes.

There is a need, for example, for a systematic set of studies (probably laboratory experiments) that are designed to explore the consequences of changes in various temporal features of communication, and to identify the limits of those changes beyond which the communication process is seriously altered or breaks down altogether. It is easy to visualize a series of parametric experiments to study such communication lags in relation to entrainment processes. Such studies would insert transmission lags of different temporal durations and patterning into the communication system for members of groups engaged in tasks requiring collaboration, presumably using electronic equipment to carry out the interventions. Such a series of experiments could identify the "range of entrainment" (Moore-Ede et al.,

1982) of such transmission and response lags beyond which mutual entrainment processes (i.e., cross member synchronization) break down—and, one would presume, beyond which effective group performance deteriorates, as well.

Stages and Functions of Group Work

Communication by technological means may also strip away affect and interpersonal content in the group's communication activity. This is likely to affect the group's work in two ways. First, it is likely to reduce the amount of attention given to Stage II and Stage III of the group's production function—for better or worse, depending on the circumstances. That is, groups placed in the more constrained communication environments of the systems that are heavily mediated by technological aids are likely to attempt direct execution of projects with whatever strategy gets implemented at the outset. That conjecture poses at least two direct implications for group work in such communication systems. First, if groups working in such technologically aided systems tend to attempt direct execution and avoid technical problem-solving and conflict resolution activities, then those systems are likely to work much better for tasks in which Stages II and III (technical problem-solving and conflict resolution) are relatively unimportant and/or already resolved. This in turn implies that such systems will work best for already-established groups doing relatively routine and well-practiced tasks, for which they already have a well-established division of labor and allocation of payoffs. Such an implication would hardly make technological aids for group work the high road to increased creativity in groups! But these implications must be regarded now as merely hypotheses—though testable ones, inviting future research.

There is a second implication of the conjecture that groups in which communication is mediated via highly technological systems will deemphasize Stages II and III of the production function: If so, then very early inputs by group members will have a disproportionate influence on the group's problem-solving strategy. In fact, there already is evidence of such a disproportionate influence of early contributions to the group in normal face-to-face groups that are not blessed (or cursed) with technological aids. The line of argument developed here would suggest that such disproportionate influence of early actions would be increased for groups with technologically aided communication systems. That suggestion, too, is a hypothesis both worthy of and amenable to test.

Along with these potential effects of added technology on how groups do the stages of their production function, there is a parallel set of potential effects on the group's attention to its other functions. Specifically, the depersonalization effects of technological devices may reduce the amount of attention that the group pays to all stages of the group well-being and member support functions. This could have major deleterious effects on the accomplishment of truly collaborative work in groups.

Collaborative work—in anything but the most trivial sense of two people who just happen to be doing some task together—implies that there is more or less long-term cooperative work on a broad band of activities (i.e., projects) among the same collaborators. This would be exemplified by joint authors of a book, by co-investigators of a substantial research project, or by partners in a joint business. But if success requires the broad and deep cooperation of the same collaborators over a long time period, by definition they need to put forth some effort, early on, to address successfully those tough and tenacious interpersonal questions implied in the stages of the member support and group well-being functions: What will I get out of it; what will it cost me; whose ox is to be gored and whose ax is to be ground; how much stroking will I have to do to get appropriate responsiveness from my partners; and the like? If the presence of technological tools increases the chances that these questions cannot (or at least do not) get addressed, it may at the same time increase the chances that the collaborative effort will not flourish over a long period of time.

A number of tactics might help reduce the problems created by a neglect of member support and group well-being functions, and of the middle stages of the production function as well. For example, we might create work groups initially on a face-to-face basis, and then when they are established (in the sense of the functions and stages discussed here) add the technological tools to their armamentarium. Alternatively, we might try to create large working groups of communicators, using technologically mediated communication systems (such as electronic mail networks) at the outset but dealing only with routine communication matters. Then, let interest-based subgroups emerge from that large network to become continuing collaborative groups, using multiple communication systems—including the face-to-face option—as their collaboration becomes more lasting and less topic specific.

Concluding Comments

The conjunctures put forth on these latter issues imply considerably more complicated questions for research, and intervention possibilities that pose considerably more difficult operational problems. Nonetheless, these suggestions for future study, along with the hypotheses and suggested research approaches offered in earlier parts of this chapter, provide a partial agenda for research that can help us make best use of the technological possibilities we currently face, as well as those we may acquire in the near future. This review should also make it clear that the proper questions to ask do not involve discovering the perfect mix of electronic and human means that will deliver a communication system that is all things to all communicators. Rather, our hope lies in the formulation and pursuit of the kinds of research questions noted throughout this summary, most of them having to do with social psychological processes rather than electronic innovations. Research along those lines of inquiry can (and I believe should) be designed so that it helps us learn about effective uses of technological tools in groups at the same time as it will contribute to our basic knowledge about group process and performance—especially about those time matters in groups on which this chapter has focused.

ACKNOWLEDGMENTS

Work underlying preparation of this paper was supported, in part, under National Science Foundation grants BNS 85-06805 and BNS 87-05151.

I want to thank Jolene Galegher for her very helpful advice and editorial review of several earlier drafts of this paper.

REFERENCES

Bales, R. F., & Strodtbeck, F. L. (1951). Phases in group problem solving. *Journal of Abnormal and Social Psychology, 46,* 485–495.

Dabbs, J. (1983). *Fourier analysis and the rhythm of conversation* (ERIC Document Reproduction Service No. ED 222 959).

Dabbs, J. M. Jr., & Ruback, R. B. (1984). Vocal patterns in male and female groups. *Personality and Social Psychology Bulletin, 10,* 518–525.

Eveland, J. D., & Bikson, T. K. (1986). Evolving electronic communication networks: An empirical assessment. *Proceedings of the New York University Symposium on Technological Support for Work Group Collaboration,* New York, NY, May 21–22, 1987.

Futoran, G. C., Kelly, J. R., & McGrath, J. E. (1989). TEMPO: A time-based system for analysis of group interaction process. *Basic and Applied Social Psychology, 10,* 211–232.

Galegher, J. (1987). *A Proposal for a Conference on Technology and Cooperative work.* Tucson, AZ: Department of Management and Policy, University of Arizona.

Gersick, C. J. G. (1984). *The life cycles of ad hoc task groups: Time, transitions, and learning in teams.* Unpublished doctoral dissertation, Yale University.

Gersick, C. J. G. (1988). Time and transition in work teams: Toward a new model of group development. *Academy of Management Journal, 31,* 9–41.

Gottman, J. M. (1979). Detecting cyclicality in social interaction. *Psychological Bulletin, 86,* 81–88.

Gottman, J. M. (1979). *Marital interaction: Experimental investigations.* New York: Academic Press.

Hackman, J. R. (1985). Doing research that makes a difference. In E. E. Lawler, A. M. Mohrman, S. A. Mohrman, G. E. Ledford, T. G. Cummings & Associates (Eds.), *Doing research that is useful for theory and practice.* San Francisco, CA: Jossey-Bass.

Hesse, B. W., Werner, C. M., & Altman, I. (1987). *Temporal aspects of computer-mediated communication.* Salt Lake City, UT: University of Utah.

Jaffe, J., & Feldstein, S. (1970). *Rhythms of dialogue.* New York: Academic Press.

Kelly, J. R. (1988). Entrainment in individual and group behavior. In J. E. McGrath (Ed.), *The social psychology of times: New perspectives* (pp. 89–110). Newbury Park, CA: Sage Publications.

Kelly, J. R., Futoran, G. C., & McGrath, J. E. (1988). *Entrainment and experienced difficulty: Temporal patterns in task performance.* Unpublished manuscript.

Kelly, J. R., & McGrath, J. E. (1985). Effects of time limits and task types on task performance and interaction of four-person groups. *Journal of Personality and Social Psychology 49,* 395–407.

Kelly, J. R., & McGrath, J. E. (1988). *On time and method.* Newbury Park, CA: Sage Publications.

Kerr, N. L. (1981). Social transition schemes: Charting the group's road to agreement. *Journal of Personality and Social Psychology, 41,* 684–702.

Landsberger, H. A. (1955). Interaction process analysis of the mediation of labor-management disputes. *Journal of Abnormal and Social Psychology, 51,* 552–558.

Little, B. R. (1983). Personal Projects: A rationale and method for investigation. *Environment and Behavior, 15,* 273–309.

Locke, E. A., Shaw, K. N., Saari, L. M., & Latham, G. P. (1981). Goal setting and task performance: 1969–1980. *Psychological Review, 90,* 125–152.

McGrath, J. E. (1984). *Groups: Interaction and performance.* Englewood, NJ: Prentice-Hall.

McGrath, J. E. (1986). Studying groups at work: Ten critical needs for theory and practice. In P. Goodman, & Others (Eds.), *Designing effective work groups* (pp. 362–391). San Francisco, CA: Jossey-Bass.

McGrath, J. E. (1987). *Toward a time based theory of functional groups* (Tech. Rep. No. 87-1). Urbana, IL: University of Illinois at Urbana-Champaign, Department of Psychology.

McGrath, J. E., Futoran, G. C., & Kelly, J. R. (1986). *Complex temporal patterning in interaction and task performance: A report of progress in a program of research on the social psychology of time* (Technical Report 86-1). Urbana, IL: Research Program on Social Psychology of Time.

McGrath, J. E., & Kelly, J. R. (1986). *Time and human interaction: Toward a social psychology of time.* New York: Guilford Press.

McGrath, J. E., Kelly, J. R., & Machatka, D. E. (1984). The social psychology of time: Entrainment of behavior in social and organizational settings. In S. Oskamp (Ed.), *Applied social psychology annual* (Vol. 5, pp. 21–44). Beverly Hills, CA: Sage Publications.

McGrath, J. E., & Rotchford, N. (1983). Time and behavior in organizations. In L. Cummings & B. Staw (Eds.), *Research in organizational behavior* (Vol. 5, pp. 57–101). Greenwich, CT: JAI Press.

Melbin, M. (1987). *Night as frontier.* New York: Free Press.

Moreland, R. L., & Levine, J. M. (1988). Group dynamics over time: Development and socialization in small groups. In J. E. McGrath (Ed.), *The social psychology of time: New perspectives* (pp. 151–181). Newbury Park, CA: Sage Publications.

Moore-Ede, M. C., Sulzman, F. M., & Fuller, C. A. (1982). *The clocks that time us.* Cambridge, MA: Harvard University Press.

Psathas, G. (1960). Phase movement and equilibrium tendencies in interaction process in psychotherapy groups. *Sociometry, 23,* 177–194.

Steiner, I. D. (1972). *Group process and productivity.* New York: Academic Press.

Stock, D., & Thelen, H. A. (1958). *Emotional dynamics and group culture: Experimental studies of individual and group behavior.* New York: New York University Press.

Tuckman, B. W. (1965). Developmental sequence in small groups. *Psychological Bulletin, 63* (6), 384–399.

Warner, R. M. (1979). Periodic rhythms in conversational speech. *Language and speech, 22,* 381–396.

Warner, R. M. (1984). *Rhythm as an organizing principle in social interaction: Evidence of cycles in behavior and physiology.* Unpublished manuscript.

Warner, R. M. (1988). Rhythm in social interaction. In J. E. McGrath (Ed.), *The social psychology of time: New perspectives* (pp. 63–88). Newbury Park, CA: Sage Publications.

Weick, K. E. (1976). Educational organizations as loosely coupled systems. *Administrative Sciences Quarterly, 21,* 1–19.

Weick, K. E. (1982). Management of Organizational Change among Loosely Coupled Elements. In P. S. Goodman & Associates (Eds.), *Change in organizations: New perspectives on theory, research and practice.* (pp. 375–408). San Francisco, CA: Jossey-Bass.

Wicker, A. W., & King, J. C. (1988). Life Cycles of behavior settings. In J. E. McGrath (Ed.), *The social psychology of time: New perspectives* (pp. 182–200). Newbury Park, CA: Sage Publications.

Williams, E. (1977). Experimental comparisons of face-to-face and mediated communication: A review. *Psychological Bulletin, 84,* 963–976.

3

Work Group Structure and Information Technology: A Structural Contingency Approach

Barbara A. Gutek
University of Arizona

Abstract

Structural contingency theory, which suggests that, to be effective, an organization or work group must fit its technology to the structure of its tasks, can be used to guide research on computer use in cooperative work. In this chapter, I explain structural contingency theory, provide some examples of findings which support the theory, and critique each of the theory's four key concepts: technology, structure, effectiveness, and fit. Finally, I use it as a framework for analyzing the influence of information technology on work group effectiveness by providing examples of issues suggested by structural contingency theory that I am currently studying.

The world of information technology encompasses not one but many specific technologies that can be used for a broad range of tasks and functions. It does not follow, however, that any information technology is equally useful for any kind of work. Indeed, implicit in many of the chapters in this book is the assumption that particular kinds of computer systems are more appropriate for some tasks than others. If this is true, it follows that information technology needs to fit or match the needs of its users. When its users are individuals working in groups, the technology needs to be "in synch" with the tasks the group is trying to accomplish.

What could be gained by achieving a fit or match between tasks of the work group and type or configuration of information technology? Lack of fit between information technology and group tasks often leads to under-utilization of the technology. It is not uncommon to hear managers say that they installed some new system, but "nobody used it." Rather than conclude that the system did not match the tasks of the group, managers conclude that information technology is a worthless luxury and become wary of the next attempt to bring a computer system into their workgroups. Thus, the first—but not the only—benefit of a good match between technology and work group structure is greater use of the technology. Greater effectiveness in the form of more carefully revised text or better records of transactions and greater efficiency in the form of more transactions per hour or greater volume of output may also result from a good fit between work group tasks and information technology. Work groups that require communication within the work group or between the work group and other work groups may be able to collaborate more effectively when they use a computer system that fits their task structure. Finally, people in work groups may be more satisfied with their technology and jobs if their computer systems fit their work needs.

These speculations about the fit between computer systems and work group needs are consistent with the tenets of structural contingency theory, an influential theory in organizational studies. In fact, Drazin and Van de Ven (1985) contended that "structural contingency theory has dominated the study of organizational design and performance in the past 20 years" (p. 514). In its most general form, structural contingency theory suggests that, to be effective, an organization must conform to its context. Three types of context have been studied: environment, size, and technology.

Structural contingency theory has guided studies of firms and agencies, as well as subunits such as divisions, departments, work groups, or task teams within them. This versatility is valuable to students of technology as it means that the structural contingency framework can be used to study the fit between a work group's technology and the structure of its tasks or a firm's technology and its structure. In this chapter, I consider the value of structural contingency theory as a framework for analyzing the influence of information technology on work group effectiveness. As in previous research with Bikson (e.g., Bikson & Gutek, 1983; Bikson, Gutek, & Mankin, 1987; Gutek, Bikson, & Mankin, 1984), I define a work group as a collection of employees having at least one level of supervision; that is, a direct supervisor, whose tasks involve some common information-related process or product (See McGrath, chap. 2 in this volume, for an alternate, complementary definition of group.) Implicit in this definition of work group is the notion of cooperative work. A work group involves coordinated work where the group members are, at a minimum, coacting, and, more probably, actively collaborating or cooperating with some or all other members of the group.

STRUCTURAL CONTINGENCY THEORY

Structural contingency theory has been around for almost 30 years (Burns & Stalker, 1961; Lawrence & Lorsch, 1967; Perrow, 1970; Woodward, 1965), well before information technology made substantial inroads into white-collar work. Thus, structural contingency theory was not developed to account for computer use in organizations, but emerged through the study of manufacturing firms as a general theory, applicable to many organizations, structures, and technologies.

Structural contingency theory can be viewed as being about two different relationships or outcomes. The first relationship is between the organization's technology and its structural characteristics. Particular technologies fit (or do not fit) the organization's structure; for example, a decentralized organization calls for a different configuration of technology than a highly centralized organization. The second relationship is between this "fit" and the organization's effectiveness. According to the theory, those organizations that achieve a good fit between technology and structure will be more efficient or effective than those organizations or work groups whose technology and structure are mismatched. Although some investigators are silent about how fit is achieved, others have made explicit claims about the causal order in the relationship between technology and structure. However, these claims tend to contradict each other. Some (e.g., Aldrich, 1972) suggest that structure is causally prior to technology, that is, technology adapts to structure, but others contend that structure must adapt to technology and technology is causally prior (cf. Carter, 1984; Pfeffer & Leblebici, 1977). These differing views about causal priority are referred to as, on the one hand, the structural or organizational imperative and, on the other hand, the technical or technological imperative (Collins, Hage, & Hull, 1988; Gutek, Bikson & Mankin, 1984; Markus & Robey, 1987).

In support of structural contingency theory, researchers found that organizations can achieve effectiveness through different technology-structure combinations. For example, Van deVen, Delbecq, and Koenig (1976) found that as task uncertainty increased, mutual work adjustments through horizontal communication channels and group meetings increased. From their findings, they concluded that perceived task uncertainty and workflow interdependence (measures of technology) were associated with different modes of coordination (a measure of structure). Schoonhoven's (1981) study of 17 hospital operating rooms revealed symmetrical and non-monotonic interactions among technology, structure, and effectiveness. In conditions of high uncertainty (technology), decentralization (structure) had a negative effect on severe morbidity (effectiveness). When uncertainty was low, increased decentralization and destandardization resulted in lower effectiveness. Also studying hospital units, Argote (1982) found that programmed means of coordination (structure) made a greater contribution to organizational effectiveness under conditions of low-input uncertainty than high-input uncertainty (technology). Another application of structural contingency theory was Carter's (1984) study of computers in newspaper organizations. In her study, characteristics of computer technology were related to organizational structure, but the relationship was contingent on the size of the organization.

Over the years, several investigators have summarized the research on structural contingency theory, including Fry (1982), who reported a consistent relationship between routinization of technology and structure within work groups, but only at the subunit (e.g., work group, department) level. He concluded that routine technology was associated with highly centralized and highly formalized structure within organizational subunits. These studies and reviews illustrate how organizational research has been guided by structural contingency theory. However, they also illustrate how difficult it is to summarize the corpus of findings except in a broad, general way—that is, the relationship between technology and structure is, in turn, related to effectiveness— because structural contingency theory is so broad and general.

There is a second difficulty in summarizing the findings of research testing structural contingency theory because, as the previous sample of studies shows, the concepts are measured in different ways in the various empirical investigations. There is no standard format for measuring technology or structure, so comparing any two studies based on structural contingency theory can be like comparing apples and oranges. These difficulties imply that the framework of structural contingency theory is probably more useful to the study of information technology than the specific operational definitions, instruments, or scales used in previous organizational research.

By definition, a structural contingency framework involves four concepts: technology, structure, effectiveness, and fit. In the following paragraphs, I discuss each of the concepts, both as it has been measured in previous organizational research and as it might be used in the study of information technology in cooperative work groups. In this discussion, I evaluate the merits of these concepts and review both theoretical and empirical criticisms of each. It becomes obvious that despite its popularity, structural contingency theory has been subject to much criticism having to do with how to define and measure the key elements, as well as how to test the contingency aspects of the theory (cf. Carter, 1984; Drazin and Van de Ven, 1985; Fry and Schellenberg, 1984; Schoonhoven, 1981; Tosi and Slocum, 1984). Nevertheless, I hope to show that, despite its flaws, researchers can use the structural contingency framework to provide some insight into decisions about technology design, organizational design, and implementation and use of information technologies.

TECHNOLOGY

To use structural contingency theory to study computer systems, the researcher must define the key attributes of the technology and decide how to measure them. The correlation between these measures and measures of structure indicates how well the technology matches structure. Unfortunately, the first generation studies of social and organizational effects of information technology do not reveal much about how the important properties of these systems should be defined and measured. Many of these studies either compare computer-using groups with nonuser groups or compare work groups before and after they acquire a computer system. In these studies, computer systems are treated as global entities rather than as bundles of attributes. It is the information system in its entirety rather than its particular characteristics that has been of interest to researchers. The impact of a desktop publishing system as a global entity may be a topic of study, for example, whereas the key aspects of the desktop publishing system that determine the observed effects have not been studied. (But see both McGrath, chap. 2 and Kraemer and Pinsonneault, chap. 14 in this volume for examples of efforts to identify salient properties of information technology.)

The choice of research designs used in the first generation of studies on information technology—comparison group, posttest designs, or pre- and postdesigns—serve to aid and abet researchers in treating computer systems as global entities rather than bundles of attributes. In research parlance, technology is manipulated, not measured. The research designs do not require investigators to delineate or measure key elements of the computer system, thus researchers learn relatively little from these studies about key attributes of computer systems, although they may speculate about them. For example, Zuboff (1988) observed cases of computer systems in organizational contexts and speculated that the abstractness and symbolism of computer work are the key attributes responsible for many of the effects she observed.

In defining key aspects or categories of computer systems, researchers will not get much assistance from organizational researchers, in part because of differences in the way technology is defined. Researchers studying information systems are likely to focus on the tools themselves, for example, "PCs connected by a LAN"; "a mainframe environment with dumb terminals" (Markus, 1986), whereas organizational researchers tend to view technology as the process by which work is done (cf. Rousseau, 1979; Rousseau & Cooke, 1984) and would include lecturing or presenting case material as the technology of the classroom or behavior modification as the technology of a therapy clinic.[1] This difference in focus raises questions about whether the categories of work processes defined by organizational researchers are useful for researchers interested in information technologies. For instance, Woodward (1965) sorted manufacturing technologies into three categories—small batch, assembly line, and automated process—but it is not yet clear whether or how these categories capture the tasks and tools found in information intensive work.

Related to this distinction is the assumption of many proponents of structural contingency theory that all organizations and organizational units such as work groups have a technology. By defining technology as workflow or the process by which work gets done, organizational researchers have committed themselves to the notion that all organizational units have a technology. A faithful parallel of organizational technology applied to information systems could mean broadening the definition of information technology to including pencils and yellow pads. Such an exercise may or may not be useful in understanding cooperative work. In some chapters in this book (i.e., Kraut, Egido & Galegher, chap. 6; Hutchins, chap. 8), the authors take a broad view; their analyses encompass whatever means the workers they are studying use to communicate and accomplish their tasks. However, if the research is concerned with computer use in cooperative work, the researcher may prefer to reject the assumption that all organizational units have an information technology, and focus instead on variations in the properties of these systems (Kraemer and Pinsonneault, chap. 14; Vogel & Nunamaker, chap. 19; Lakin, chap. 17; Olson & Atkins, chap. 16).

Another reason why organizational research is not of much assistance to researchers interested in using a structural contingency framework for studying information technology concerns the measurement of technology. If technology is defined differently in organizational theory and information science, it is not surprising that technology is also measured differently. Organizational researchers, for example, rarely measure physical aspects of the technology like its size, weight, speed of operation, or physical location but instead either categorize types of technology (batch, assembly-line, or automated [Woodward, 1965]; intensive, mediating, or long-linked [Thompson, 1967]) or measure "key aspects" of the technology, for example, task predictability and work-flow predictability (Comstock & Scott, 1977), task variability, and uncertainty (Perrow, 1970). These key aspects

---

[1]Technology also has been defined more concretely as a tool used to do work (Tornatzky et al., 1983).

of technology are often measured by workers' evaluations of their own situation (e.g., "there is variety in my work" [Fry & Slocum, 1984]). This variation in measures means that it is very difficult to compare the various findings from research based on structural contingency theory because what may be measured as technology in one study is quite different from what is measured as technology in another study.

The problem created by the lack of commonality in technology measures is compounded by the fact that measures of technology are frequently confounded with other, separate concepts. For example, a statement like "there is variety in my work" has been used as a measure of technology (Fry & Slocum, 1984), but sometimes is treated as a job characteristic (an aspect of structure) or job attitude (often viewed as an outcome measure). Thus, measures of technology are frequently confounded with either the concepts of structure or effectiveness (see Rousseau & Cooke, 1984 for a discussion).

In sum, although the structural contingency notion that technology should be measured is probably worthwhile, organizational researchers have produced a very abstract definition of technology, the usefulness of which has not yet been demonstrated in the study of computerized cooperative work. In addition, they have not produced a common set of reliable or valid measures that could readily be borrowed by researchers studying information technology. The delineation of key aspects or important physical properties of information technology remains to be done (but see Strassman, 1985; Zuboff, 1988).

STRUCTURE

According to structural contingency theory, an organizational unit should match its technology to its structure, and, as is the case with technology, structure must be measured and the way structure is defined determines the way it is measured. As used in theory, organizational structure is defined somewhat differently than it is in research. For example, in their open systems theory of organizations, Katz and Kahn (1978) defined structure as cycles of activity, suggesting a dynamic quality associated with tasks that are accomplished. As used in research, organizational structure is considered to be relatively stable or static, "the enduring characteristics of an organization" (James & Jones, 1976, p. 76).

In particular, researchers sometimes classify organizations according to structure in much the same way as they classify organizations according to their technology, using a global "enduring characteristic" to categorize organizations. Most frequently, organic organizations or groups are compared with mechanistic organizations or groups (Burns & Stalker, 1961). In mechanistic organizations, authority, control, and communications are organized hierarchically, whereas in organic firms, networks of authority, control, and communications are organized as networks. Presumably an organization becomes mechanistic or organic in response to its context, that is, environment, technology, and size.[2]

Besides creating a typology of organizational structure (mechanistic versus organic), organizational researchers have also delineated dimensions of structure. The following six are most frequently cited as enduring characteristics of organizations, in other words, dimensions of structure: (a) specialization, that is, the number of different work activities performed by a work unit; (b) centralization of authority and decisionmaking; (c) formalization of rules and procedures, (d) configuration, that is, number of hierarchical levels and units; dispersion of work group in space; or distribution of people along key dimensions such as sex, educational level, administrative/nonadministrative, age, exempt/nonexempt; (e) standardization of procedures; (f) interdependence of organizational units or tasks (Indik, 1968, James & Jones, 1976; Sathe, 1978).

Although the previous list is illustrative of "relatively enduring properties" of organizations, it is not an exhaustive list of possible dimensions of organizational structure. Some or all of this set of dimensions may be useful in the study of computer-using work groups, but it may also be necessary to consider other dimensions such as the distribution of computer expertise or norms about time within the group or organization. What constitutes an appropriate pace of work, the extent to which workers have autonomy over their use of time, the extent to which work done in one department must be sequenced with the work of another department—norms about time in a workgroup—constitute relatively enduring characteristics of the unit that are likely to affect and be affected by the use of computers (McGrath, chap. 2 in this volume; Schriber & Gutek, 1987).

Finally, although there are more commonly used measures of dimensions of structure than measures of dimensions of technology, they come with some potential problems. Most notable is the fact that the same concept measured "objectively" and "subjectively" taps different aspects of the concept (Sathe, 1978). For example, formalization of rules and procedures can be ascertained by asking employees in an organizational unit about their perceptions of the formalization of rules and procedures or by counting some externally verifiable entity such as the number of rules or the number of pages in the organization's rules and procedures manual. In an examination of objective and subjective measures of three dimensions of structure, Sathe (1978) found only a weak relationship between objective and subjective measures.

---

[2]Within organizational research, the early use of mainframe computers in organizations sparked some controversy over the issue of whether computers (i.e., mainframe computers) would centralize or decentralize authority in organizations (Whistler, 1970).

In sum, although the structural contingency notion that structure should be measured is worthwhile, organizational researchers have not produced a common set of reliable or valid measures that can be readily used to study computerized work groups. Although key dimensions of structure have been identified and measured, a slightly or substantially different set of dimensions of structure may be relevant to a structural contingency perspective on information systems. The investigator must also decide whether objective or subjective measures of structure are more appropriate in his or her research.

EFFECTIVENESS

Effectiveness is as multidimensional as technology and structure. Classically in organizational research, effectiveness (overall survivability) is contrasted with efficiency (the ratio of inputs to outputs), one component of effectiveness (Katz & Kahn, 1978). Colloquially, efficiency and effectiveness are often contrasted in the following way: knowing how to do a task versus knowing which task to do.

In the case of computer use in work groups, effectiveness may encompass many dimensions. For example, where computer use is discretionary, use might be viewed as a component of effectiveness (Bikson & Gutek, 1983). A system is hardly effective if no one uses it. User satisfaction, too, may be viewed as a component of effectiveness.[3] Efficiency and productivity can be measured objectively as in volume of sales, number of forms filled, lines of code written, or subjectively as worker or supervisor perception of individual or group productivity. It seems likely, though, that measures of effectiveness will always have to be tailored to the group or organization being studied, which makes both comparative analyses and generalizations about the influence of particular technologies problematic.

FIT

The concept of fit is implicit in commonsense notions about the acquisition of information technology. Organizations want to buy, and vendors want to sell, information technology that "meets the needs" of the purchaser, that is, matches or fits the tasks that are done by the work group acquiring the technology. The general notion of fit is also treated explicitly or implicitly in discussions of computer systems (cf. Kling & Iocono, 1988; Laudon &

---

[3]Satisfaction is sometimes used as an indicator of effectiveness and satisfaction and productivity are frequently both assumed to be outcomes of the same conditions despite the fact that in repeated reviews of the literature, job satisfaction and productivity are unrelated (average r = approx. 14) (Brayfield & Crockett, 1955; Iaffaldano & Muchinsky, 1985).

Laudon, 1987). Yet the concept of fit, match, or "meeting the needs," as used in everyday discussion of computing in organizations, is fuzzy at best.

Within organizational research, fit has been an imprecise notion, but several investigators have recently attempted to clarify this concept (see Drazin & Van de Ven, 1985; Fry, 1982; Fry & Schellenberg, 1984; Gutek, Sasse, & Bikson, 1986). Fry (1982) distinguished between congruence and contingency. Many studies measure only the *congruence* or association (fit) between structure and technology and do not measure effectiveness. Studies of congruence are relatively simple as far as measurement and analysis are concerned; any statistical measure of relationship will do. In addition, congruence studies include measures of structure and technology only.

Studies involving *contingency* are more complex than studies of congruence both because they involve more concepts—fit and effectiveness as well as technology and structure—and because statistical analyses are more complex. Fry (1982) suggested that assessing contingency is a two-stage process consisting of (a) an assessment of the relationship between structure and technology that yields a measure of fit, and (b) an assessment of the relationship between fit and effectiveness. Trying to construct a measure of fit can become quite complicated and quite remote from the original measures of structure and technology. Fit is usually a "synthetic" variable (Barker & Barker, 1984) that is created from an analysis of the relationship between technology and structure. For example, in one set of analyses, Drazin and Van de Ven (1985) used the residuals from a regression line to create deviation scores for each organizational unit and used the deviation scores as an indicator of fit. Other examples of the way fit has been operationalized are deviations from mean scores and interaction terms in moderated regression analyses. (For discussions about measures of fit see Collins, Hage, & Hull, 1988; Drazin & Van de Ven, 1985; Fry, 1982; Gutek, Sasse, & Bikson, 1986).

The difficulty of measuring fit as a concept independent of structure, technology, and effectiveness leads to an interesting question. Should the concept of fit be independent of the concept of effectiveness, or is fit simply another term for effectiveness? That is, is a work group that has achieved a good fit between its computer system and work group structure, by definition, an effective work group? Can a work group achieve a good fit and still be ineffective? Research findings show that when fit is measured by a synthetic variable, the work group can be ineffective, even if its structure and technology match (cf. Drazin & Van de Ven, 1985; Gutek et al., 1986). Nevertheless, perhaps loose, imprecise wording of structural contingency theory has led researchers down a blind alley searching for the elusive measure of fit, which may be simply another term for effectiveness. Structural contingency theory can be stated without reference to fit, for example: certain structure-technology combinations lead to greater effectiveness than either particular structures or technologies alone.

A most intriguing alternative to creating a synthetic indicator of fit is to treat fit as an interaction term in an analysis of variance or moderated regression design (see for example, Drazin & Van de Ven [1985] and Majchrzak, Mosher, & John [1986]). This conceptualization of fit also is consistent with the following wording of structural contingency theory: under conditions of structure A, one kind of information system is associated with work group effectiveness, whereas under conditions of structure not-A, another kind of information system is associated with work group effectiveness. Stated more simply, the relationship between information system and work group effectiveness is moderated by (i.e., varies with) work group structure.

In sum, several recent attempts to make structural contingency theory more precise have been reasonably successful. But although the theory and concept of fit have been clarified, this clarification has greatly complicated the way fit is measured. As an alternative to creating these complex two-step analysis procedures involving synthetic variables, I suggest researchers consider treating the concept of fit as linguistic baggage that unnecessarily complicates our efforts to understand the relationships among work group structure, technology, and effectiveness. This problem can be avoided by restating structural contingency theory and omitting the term *fit* altogether.

WHERE TO FROM HERE?

Although we have an accumulating body of research on the effects of computerization in workgroups, we know relatively little about the particular characteristics of information systems that lead to the various effects. Structural contingency theory provides an alternative framework that can move us beyond our current state of knowledge. Although the general notion of structural contingency theory, that the relationship between technology and effectiveness is contingent on a work group's structure, is implicit in many studies, an explicit use of the framework leads to new issues and areas of study. In the previous sections, I explained structural contingency theory, provided some examples of findings supporting the theory, and critiqued each of the theory's four key concepts.

Among the many criticisms leveled against studies of technology based on structural contingency theory are the following: (a) the concept of technology is abstract and imprecise; (b) measures of technology vary from study to study; (c) some measures of technology are confounded with measures of structure; (d) measures of structure vary considerably from study to study; (e) the concept of fit is used loosely; it is measured in different ways and analyzed using various procedures with different underlying assumptions; (f) effectiveness is difficult to measure; (g) the theory itself is worded so imprecisely that very different (and inconsistent) analysis models have been used to test the same theory.

Clearly structural contingency theory is flawed, but a flawed theory may be better than no theory. Although structural contingency theory makes few specific predictions, it does provide a perspective to guide research. I have recently undertaken a 2-year investigation of effectiveness in computer-using work groups, relying on the perspective provided by the contingency approach.[4] In planning this research, structural contingency theory has proven to have considerable heuristic value. First, because the structural contingency perspective relates technology to structure, it leads the re-searcher away from studying one type of computer system or one type of work group and toward a broad sample of computer systems and work groups. Our sample consists of 89 computer-using groups in over 40 public and private sector organizations. Furthermore, the contingency perspective helps the researcher to think about which aspects of the technology and work group structure are likely to be important to the particular issue he or she wishes to address. Its flexibility and generality make it as useful today as a framework for studying computer-using groups as it was 30 years ago when it was used as a framework for studying textile manufacturing. As today's information systems develop and their key attributes change, researchers can study the influence of new sets of attributes, while still using the same general framework. Of the various issues relevant to computer-using cooperative work groups, I give priority to the following issues suggested by structural contingency theory.

First, consistent with the contingency framework's emphasis on key at-tributes of technology, I would like to delineate some of the key psychologi-cal dimensions of work group computing. What are the aspects of informa-tion technology in use that are important for understanding work group effectiveness? By information technology in use, I mean computer systems as configured for use in particular work groups. These may or may not conform to any vendor's notion of what his or her system "in use" should be like. In previous research we found that most computer-using work groups had partially or totally customized systems, designed to meet their own needs and goals (Bikson, Gutek, & Mankin, 1987). In our current research, we are interested in abstract features of computer systems; for example, intensiveness, the ratio of hardware, software, and applications to people in the group; complexity, that is, the number of types of components and number of different components; or specialization, that is, the number of tasks or functions for which the computer system is used by members of the work group. We hope to be able to identify patterns of computer charac-teristics (e.g., intensive, complex, highly connective, unspecialized) and

---

[4]Supported by National Science Foundation grant # IRI-87-14768.

characterize work groups according to pattern of computer attributes. We also examine the extent to which abstract characteristics of computer systems relate to specific hardware and software features.

In addition, what are the characteristics of work group structure that are likely to combine with computer characteristics to affect effectiveness? We are interested, for example, in the specialization and interdependence of tasks within the work group. This includes the uniformity or diversity of tasks within the work group and within individuals. We are interested, for example, whether or not everyone within the work group performs the same task (as is the case in reservations or order entry department) or almost everyone performs different tasks (as, for example, in a small law office) and whether an individual performs the same tasks all the time (as is the case of order entry) or whether each individual performs many different tasks throughout the day (as in the case for most engineers or secretaries). Studying the structure of tasks also includes the kind and number of tasks performed within the work group, the predictability of tasks in the workgroup, and interdependence of tasks within and across work groups.

With McGrath (chap. 2 in this volume), we are interested in the structure of time in work groups and expect norms about time to affect the relationship between characteristics of computer systems and work group effectiveness. We use some previously developed measures (Schriber, 1986; Schriber & Gutek, 1987) to assess norms about schedules and deadlines, work pace, punctuality, sequencing, autonomy of time use, and the like. The norms of time relate to three commonly cited aspects of structure: standardization, centralization, and formalization.

Another example of structure we are studying comes under the label of configuration. We are interested in the distribution of people within the work group along dimensions such as sex, race, education level, age, and exempt versus nonexempt status, both as these relate to type of information system available to the work group and as configuration of work group and configuration of technology together affect work group effectiveness. Here we are interested not only in the sex, age, and exempt status of work group members, but the work group composition as well. In previous research, we found that type of computer system and computer use varied by occupation and by sex (Gutek & Bikson, 1985). Lower level work groups and female-dominated work groups had older, less complex systems than professional/managerial groups and work groups populated by men rather than women. In the current project, we expect work groups with many women will have computer systems that differ, for example, in intensity, complexity, specialization, or connectivity from computer systems in male-dominated work groups when other confounding factors (like occupation) are held constant.

We are also studying the dispersion of work groups in time (one versus several shifts; uniform hours versus flexible hours) and space (see also Kraut, Egido, & Galegher, chap. 6 in this volume; McGrath, chap. 2 in this volume). It appears that spreading a work group across multiple physical locations (e.g., several floors of a building, several buildings, or several geographical sites) is no longer a rarity and may be associated with particular configurations of computer systems and tasks. In fact, certain computer attributes may allow an MIS department or personnel department, for example, to disperse employees among the departments or divisions they serve rather than keep them in one geographical location removed from their customer or constituent groups.

The third priority is pursuing the concept of fit to see if it is necessary to understanding the relationships among technology, structure, and effectiveness or whether it is, in fact, linguistic baggage that can be dropped from the statement of structural contingency theory. This will be done by using different analysis strategies that include and exclude both direct and synthetic measures of fit. The results of the various analyses will provide information about the usefulness of fit. We will be able to determine whether we can explain work group effectiveness with attributes of technology and structure alone, or whether the inclusion of an indicator of fit greatly improves the predictability of work group effectiveness.

In sum, although the structural contingency framework has many shortcomings as a theory, as a heuristic framework, it has considerable merit. It has led me, for example, to a series of intriguing issues about computer-using work groups that I would not otherwise be addressing. As such, structural contingency theory is one of many conceptual frameworks used in behavioral, social, and organizational research that can direct and guide research about information technology in cooperative work groups (see also McGrath, chap. 2; Krauss & Fussell, chap. 5; and Gabarro, chap. 4 in this volume). In return, research on computer-using work groups may contribute to refining and delimiting the boundaries of structural contingency theory.

ACKNOWLEDGMENTS

I would like to thank Jolene Galegher whose editorial efforts and skill improved my chapter substantially.

REFERENCES

Aldrich. H. E. (1972). Technology and organization structure: A re-examination of the findings of the Aston Group. *Administrative Science Quarterly, 19,* 26–43

Argote, L. (1982). Input uncertainty and organizational coordination in hospital emergency units. *Administrative Science Quarterly, 27,* 420–434.

Barker, H. R., & Barker, B. M. (1984). *Multivariate analysis of variance (MANOVA): A practical guide to its use in scientific decision making.* Tuscaloosa, AL: University of Alabama Press.

Bikson, T. K., & Gutek, B. A. (1983). *Advanced office systems: An empirical look at utilization and satisfaction* (N-1970/NSF). Santa Monica, CA: Rand Corporation.

Bikson, T. K., Gutek, B. A., & Mankin, D. A. (1987). *Implementing computerized procedures in office settings.* (R-3077-NSF/IRIS) Santa Monica, CA: Rand Corporation.

Brayfield, A. H., & Crockett, W. H. (1955). Employee attitudes and employee performance. *Psychological Bulletin, 52,* 396–424.

Burns, T., & Stalker, G. M. (1961). *The management of innovation.* London: Tavistock.

Carter, N. M. (1984). Computerization as a dominant technology: Its influence on the structure of newspaper organizations. *Academy of Management Journal, 27,* 247–270.

Collins, P. D., Hage, J., & Hull, F. M. (1988). Organizational and technological predictors of change in automaticity. *Academy of Management Journal, 31,* 544–569.

Comstock, D. E., & Scott, W. R. (1977). Technology and the structure of subunits: Distinguishing individual and workgroup effects. *Administrative Science Quarterly, 22,* 172–202.

Drazin, R., & Van de Ven, A. H. (1985). Alternative forms of fit in contingency theory. *Administrative Quarterly, 30,* 514–539.

Fry, L. W. (1982). Technology structure research: Three critical issues. *Academy of Management Journal, 25,* 532–552.

Fry, L. W., & Slocum, J. (1984). Technology, structure and workgroup effectiveness: A test of a contingency model. *Academy of Management Journal, 27,* 221–246.

Fry, L. W., & Schellenberg, D. (1984). *Congruence, contingency and theory building: An integrative perspective.* Unpublished manuscript, University of Washington, Seattle.

Gutek, B. A., & Bikson, T. K. (1985). Differential experiences of men and women in computerized offices. *Sex Roles, 13,* 123–136.

Gutek, B. A., Bikson, T., & Mankin, D. (1984). Individual and organizational consequences of computer-based office information technology. In S. Oskamp (Ed.), *Applied Social Psychology Annual* (Vol. 5, pp. 231–254). Beverly Hills, CA: Sage Publications.

Gutek, B. A., Sasse, S. H., & Bikson, T. K. (August 1986). The fit between technology and work group structure: The structural contingency approach in office automation. In B. A. Gutek (chair), *Technology: Its meaning, measurement, and impact in the age of computerized work.* Symposium presented at the annual Academy of Management Convention, Chicago, IL.

Iaffaldano, M. T., & Muchinsky, P. M. (1985). Job satisfaction and job performance: A meta-analysis. *Psychological Bulletin, 97*(2), 251–273.

Indik, B. P. (1968). The scope of the problem and some suggestions toward a solution. In B. P. Indik & F. W. Berrien (Eds.), *People, groups and organizations* (pp. 3–26). New York: Teachers College Press.

James, L. R., & Jones, A. P. (1976). Organizational structure: A review of structural dimensions and their conceptual relationships with attitudes and behavior. *Organizational Behavior and Human Performance, 16,* 74–113.

Katz, D., & Kahn, R. L. (1978). *The social psychology of organizations* (2nd ed.). New York: Wiley.

Kling, R., & Iocono, S. (1988). L'informatisation du travail de bureau et l'organization du travail [Desk top computerization and the organization of work]. *Journal Technologies de l'Information et Societe, 1,* 57–90.

Laudon, K., & Laudon, J. (1987). *Information systems and organizations.* New York: Macmillan.

Lawrence, P. R., & Lorsch, J. W. (1967). *Organizations and environment.* Boston: Harvard Business School, Division of Research.

Majchrzak, A., Mosher, P., & John, R. (August 1986). *Technological change and structural contingency theory.* Paper presented at the Academy of Management conference, Chicago, IL.

Markus, M. L. (August 1986). *Information technology in organization and management theory research.* Paper presented at the Annual Meeting of Academy of Management, Chicago.

Markus, M. L., & Robey, D. (1987). *Information technology and organizational change: Causal structure in theory and research.* UCLA Graduate School of Management Information Systems Working Paper No. 5-87.

Perrow, C. (1970). *Organizational analysis: A sociological view.* Belmont, CA: Wadsworth.

Pfeffer, J., & Leblebici, H. (1977). Information technology and organizational structure. *Pacific Sociological Review, 20*(2), 241–261.

Rousseau, D. M., & Cooke, R. (1984). Technology and structure: The concrete, abstract, and activity systems of organizations. *Journal of Management, 10*(3), 345–361.

Rousseau, D. M. (1979). Assessment of technology in organizations: Closed versus open systems approaches. *Academy of Management Review, 4*(4), 531–542.

Sathe, V. J. (1978). Institutional versus questionnaire measures of organizational structure. *Academy of Management Journal, 21,* 227–238.

Schoonhoven, C. B. (1981). Problems with contingency theory: testing assumptions hidden within the language of contingency "theory." *Administrative Science Quarterly, 26,* 349–377.

Schriber, J. B. (1986). *An exploratory study of the temporal dimensions of work organizations.* Unpublished doctoral dissertation, Claremont Graduate School.

Schriber, J. B., & Gutek, B. A. (1987). Some time dimensions of work: The measurement of an underlying aspect of organization culture. *Journal of Applied Psychology, 72,* 642–650.

Strassman, P. (1985). *Information payoff: the transformation of work in the electronic age.* New York: Free Press.

Thompson, J. D. (1967). *Organizations in action.* New York: Wiley.

Tosi, H., & Slocum, J. (1984). Contingency theory: some suggested directions. *Journal of Management, 10,* 9–26.

Tornatzky, L. G., Eveland, J. D., Boylan, M. G., Hetzner, W. A., Johnson, E. C., Roitman, D., & Schneider, J. (1983). *The process of technological innovation: reviewing the literature.* Washington, D.C.: National Science Foundation, Division of Industrial Science and Technological Innovation, Productivity Improvement Research Section.

Van de Ven, A., Delbecq, A., & Koenig, R. (1976). Determinants of modes of coordination within organizations. *American Sociological Review, 41,* 332–338.

Whisler, T. L. (1970). *The impact of computers on organizations.* New York: Praeger.

Woodward, J. (1965). *Industrial organization: Theory and practice.* London: Oxford University Press.

Zuboff, S. (1988). *In the age of the smart machine: The future of work and power.* New York: Basic Books.

4

The Development
of Working Relationships*

John J. Gabarro
Harvard University

Abstract

Human relationships are crucially important in work situations, especially among managers. This chapter presents a brief overview of the existing literature on working relationships and describes their characteristic development and the ways in which they are similar to or different from social and intimate personal relationships more generally. While working relationships develop over time, they are less adequately characterized by stage paradigms than are intimate relationships. Because working relationships generally exist to accomplish tasks while social relationships are not, task achievement, task instrumentality and task-specific competence are especially important in work relationships, while affect and self-disclosure are less important. The chapter concludes with methodological and substantive implications for research

Human relationships are a fact of life for people of every occupation, situation, rank, and status, but they are an especially critical and pervasive aspect of a manager's life. The executives who were the subject of Mintzberg's now-classic study of managerial work spent 78% of their working time interacting with others, and as much as 50% of that time in interactions with subordinates (Mintzberg 1973, pp. 39–45). More recent studies by Stewart (1982) and Kotter (1982) provide further support for the importance of two-person ("dyadic") relationships in managerial work. Kotter found that developing a network of interpersonal relationships was critical to a general manager's ability to formulate and implement an agenda and

---

*Originally appeared as: John J. Gabarro, "The Development of Working Relationships," in HANDBOOK OF ORGANIZATIONAL BEHAVIOR, Lorsch, ed., c1987, pp. 172–189. Reprinted by permission of Prentice Hall, Inc., Englewood Cliffs. New Jersey.

that the quality of these relationships was a key determinant of managerial effectiveness (Kotter 1982, chaps. 2, 3, 4). Similarly, Liden and Graen (1980) found that subordinates reporting good relationships with superiors were better performers, assumed more responsibility, and contributed more to their units than those reporting poor relationships. The importance of interpersonal relationships as an aspect of management is documented in study after study of managerial behavior, regardless of national culture or type of management job.[1] Indeed, Weick (1969, p. 57) has argued that from a social-psychological point of view, relationships are the principal means through which organizations are controlled. Most experienced managers would agree.

Any manager regardless of position, is dependent on subordinates, peers, and superiors for his or her unit's performance. This dependency is especially important for general and upper-level managers because they typically cannot be experts in all of the functions that report to them and thus must rely on the competence of subordinates and others. Moreover, the greater the size or complexity of a manager's organization, the more difficult it is for him or her to influence all of the key variables directly, regardless of how good the company's information, control, and reward systems are. Thus much of the work of managing complex organizations occurs in the individual relationships that make up the networks described by Kotter and others.

Given the importance of these relationships, it is surprising that relatively little research has focused on the topic of how working relationships actually develop in organizations and what behaviors lead to effective relationships (Wortman & Linsenmeier, 1977). There are some notable exceptions to this generalization, such as the early work of Hodgson, Levinson, and Zaleznik (1965) on the executive role constellation; Levinson's (1964, 1968) work on the psychodynamic aspects of superior-subordinate relations; and Gabarro's (1978, 1979) research on the development of managerial working relationships. But relatively little research within organizational behavior has focused explicitly on the development of two-person relationships as such. Most of the research that has addressed the topic of working relationships has done so within the context of broader processes, such as managerial work, group behavior, or leadership.

This chapter presents a brief overview of the existing literature on working relationships and compares their characteristic development with that of other types of social relationships. It draws on two literatures relevant to the development of two-person working relationships. The first is the liter-

---

[1]Mintzberg (1973, nn. 103–4), for example, cites studies conducted by Stieglitz (1969) on non-U.S. executives; Inkson et al. (1970) on English and U.S. executives; Stewart (1967) on British executives; and Dubin and Spray (1964) on U.S. executives.

ature on the broader topic of relationship formation, which has focused almost exclusively on social and intimate relationships rather than on task-based relationships. The second is the much smaller literature within organizational behavior that has dealt with aspects of task-based relationships. Viewing the topic from these two perspectives allows us to deal with the conundrum that although "relationships are relationships," as Weick (1969) has put it, task-based relationships are likely to differ from social relationships because they are subject to different situational and contextual forces (Wortman & Linsenmeier, 1977; Triandis, 1977).

Any interpersonal relationship involves both some degree of interaction between two people and some degree of continuity between successive interactions (Hinde, 1977; Swensen, 1973). The term *working relationship* is used here to mean an interpersonal relationship that is task-based, non-trivial, and of continuing duration. Working relationships like social relationships develop over time and can vary in their stability, mutuality, and efficacy (Gabarro, 1978). Although working relationships have not been studied as a substantive area of inquiry, the more general topic of relationship formation in social and intimate relations has been treated extensively. The topic occupies a significant place in the literatures on interpersonal attraction and two-person relationships. Accordingly this review will begin with these more general literatures.

Several conceptual and methodological problems are inherent in studying and describing interpersonal relationships of any kind. The most basic of these problems is that although they can be defined in terms of dyadic characteristics, such as shared meaning, content of interaction, "quality," patterning of behavior, and context (Hinde, 1979), relationships are themselves the consequence of interactions amongst individuals and are heavily permeated by the effects of individual personality and predispositions (Sullivan, 1953; Carson, 1969, Hodgson, Levinson, and Zaleznik, 1965). Moreover the processes involved in the evolution of a relationship are multifaceted (Huston, 1974) and involve different levels and types of behavior. Triandis (1977), for example, has differentiated among attributive, affective, and overt behaviors, while Huston (1974) has distinguished among evaluative, cognitive, and behavioral components. Altman and Taylor (1973) have described the relevant processes as consisting of internal subjective processes (including expectations, attribution processes, and evaluative judgments) and overt behaviors, which they define as including verbal and nonverbal behaviors and the use of objects and space. Altman has further argued that the process of relationship formation is sufficiently complex, in terms of the variables that influence it over time, that the phenomenon should be studied from a social-ecological point of view (Altman, 1974, 121–25).

A final question that arises in discussing relationship formation is what distinguishes a "developed" relationship from a partially developed one. As Hinde (1979) has pointed out, even the distinction between "interaction" and "relationship" is by necessity somewhat arbitrary. The question is a particularly difficult one because most theoretical descriptions of the development of relationships include not only a temporal dimension but also hierarchical dimensions of mutuality and pair relatedness (Levinger, 1974) and commitment (Secord & Backman, 1964).

These problems are further compounded when we focus our attention on working relationships as a substantive category. All of the research and theory on the general topic of relationship formation strongly indicates that the situational and role-related factors that distinguish working relationships from social ones are likely to make a difference in their development.

This chapter obviously cannot examine in depth all of the processes and issues just described. It is possible, however, to address some of these questions one at a time, beginning with a discussion of the dimensions along which relationships develop as indicated by the general literature on social relationships. Then, after considering the stages that characterize relationship formation and the underlying social processes that drive it, we can turn to working relationships as a substantive category and explore the issues involved in their development in more detail.

DIMENSIONS ALONG WHICH RELATIONSHIPS DEVELOP

Although scholars differ in their definitions of a developed relationship, there is a remarkable degree of convergence in the literature on the dimensions that characterize the development of relationships. Several of these dimensions are summarized in Table 4.1, which draws heavily on the integrative review of Altman and Taylor (1973) and to a lesser degree on those of Levinger and Snoek (1972) and other authors referenced in Table 4.1. Let me briefly describe each of these dimensions as characteristics, while postponing my discussion of the underlying processes, such as social exchange, that move relationships along the various dimensions.

The first three dimensions listed in Table 4.1 are perhaps the most frequently cited as characteristics of mature, stabilized relationships: the *degree of self-disclosure* present in a relationship; the degree and richness of *knowledge that each party has of the other;* and the ability of both parties to *predict and anticipate each other's reactions and responses.* It is no accident that these three characteristics are interrelated. The higher the level of mutual self-disclosure in a relationship, the greater the knowledge base each

TABLE 4.1

Summary of Dyadic Dimensions Among which Relationships Develop

From	To
OPENNESS AND SELF-DISCLOSURE[1,2,3,4,6]	
Limited to "safe," socially acceptable topics	Disclosure goes beyond safe areas to include personally sensitive, private, and controversial topics and aspects of self
KNOWLEDGE OF EACH OTHER[2,4,5,6]	
Surface, "biographic" knowledge; impressionistic in nature	Knowledge is multifaceted and extends to core aspects of personality, needs, and style
PREDICTABILITY OF OTHER'S REACTIONS AND RESPONSES[2,4,5,6]	
Limited to socially expected or role-related responses, and those based on first impressions or repeated surface encounters	Predictability of other's reactions extends beyond stereotypical exchange and includes a knowledge of the contingencies affecting the other's reactions
UNIQUENESS OF INTERACTION[1,2,5]	
Exchanges are stereotypical, guided by prevailing social norms or role expectations	Exchanges are idiosyncratic to the two people, guided by norms that are unique to the relationship
MULTIMODALITY OF COMMUNICATION[1,2]	
Largely limited to verbal channels of communication and stereotypical or unintended nonverbal channels	Includes multiple modalities of communication, including nonverbal and verbal "shorthands" specific to the relationship or the individuals involved; less restrictiveness of nonverbal
SUBSTITUTABILITY OF COMMUNICATION[1,2]	
Little substitution among alternative modes of communication	Possession of and ability to use alternative modes of communication to convey the same message
CAPACITY FOR CONFLICT AND EVALUATION[1,2,3,5]	
Limited capacity for conflict; use of conflict-avoidance techniques; reluctance to criticize	Readiness and ability to express conflict and make positive or negative evaluations
SPONTANEITY OF EXCHANGE[1,2,3]	
Interactions tend to be formal or "comfortably informal" as prescribed by prevailing social norms	Greater informality and ease of interaction; movement across topical areas occurs readily and without hesitation or formality; communication flows and changes direction easily

(Continued)

TABLE 4.1
(*continued*)

From	To
SYNCHRONIZATION AND PACING[1,2]	
Except for stereotyped modes of response, limited dyadic synchrony occurs	Speech and nonverbal responses become synchronized; flow of interaction is smooth; cues are quickly and accurately interpreted
EFFICIENCY OF COMMUNICATION[1,2]	
Communication of intended meanings sometimes requires extensive discussion; misunderstandings occur unless statements are qualified or elaborated	Intended meanings are transmitted and understood rapidly, accurately, and with sensitivity to nuance
MUTUAL INVESTMENT[2,7]	
Little investment in the other except in areas of role-related or situation interdependencies	Extensive investment in other's well-being and efficacy

[1]Altman and Taylor 1973, 129–36.
[2]Levinger and Snoek 1972; Levinger 1974, 100–109.
[3]Jourard 1971.
[4]Hinde 1979, 133–134.
[5]Swensen 1973, 105–6, 455, 230–37.
[6]Triandis 1977, 191–93.
[7]Second and Backman 1964.

person has of the other; the more extensive this knowledge base, the easier it is for each party to anticipate the other's responses and reactions correctly. Even without extensive self-disclosure, two people will get to know each other better (and therefore predict each other's reactions better) simply through the residual personal learning that results from the repeated interactions that occur in sustained relationships.

The next three dimensions noted in Table 4.1 are also manifestly related to how well both parties know each other and are to some degree a natural product of cumulative and sustained interaction. *Uniqueness of interaction* is the extent to which exchanges are idiosyncratic to a dyad and guided by norms unique to the relationship, as compared with the more stereotypical exchanges that occur in casual relationships, which tend to be guided by prevailing social norms (Altman & Taylor, 1973) or by role expectations (Kelvin, 1970). *Multimodality of communication* refers to the number of modalities of communication that are available and used by a dyad, including verbal and nonverbal shorthands specific to the relationship. The general finding has been that mature and stable relationships are characterized by greater multimodality than casual or less intense relationships. *Substitut-*

ability of communication concerns a dyad's ability to use alternate modes of communication to convey the same message. Such substitutability is a characteristic of mature, developed relationships, because it requires considerable mutual knowledge and experience to develop a shared repertoire of meanings and ways of expressing those meanings.

The next three dimensions listed in Table 4.1 can also be seen as parts of a related constellation. A dyad's *capacity for conflict and evaluation* refers to the readiness and ability of two people to express conflict and to make positive or negative evaluations of each other. Although this capacity requires more than the mere passage of time and sustained interaction, it is more likely to be found in developed relationships than in those involving surface encounters (Levinger, 1974), in which social norms prescribe the polite avoidance of conflict and criticism (Altman & Taylor, 1973). *Spontaneity of exchange* refers to the informality and ease of interaction characteristic of a relationship and the ability of a dyad to move across topical areas readily (Altman & Taylor, 1973; Levinger, 1974). This type of spontaneity seldom occurs between people whose relationship remains at a superficial level, because it assumes a high degree of shared meaning and interpersonal comfort. *Synchronization and pacing* refers to the degree to which verbal and nonverbal responses are coordinated, the smoothness of interaction, and the extent to which cues are quickly and accurately interpreted. All three of these characteristics presume a depth of familiarity and mutual knowledge that is seldom found in casual acquaintanceships, and it should not be surprising that they become more prevalent as a relationship grows in importance and experience.

Efficiency of communication refers to the degree to which intended meanings are transmitted and understood with rapidity, accuracy, and sensitivity to nuance. Again, it is not surprising that as a relationship develops, its efficiency of communication increases. Progress along this dimension is presumably closely related to progress along the other nine dimensions. For example, a high degree of substitutability and multimodality of communication cannot help but increase the efficiency with which two people can exchange meanings. Similarly the development of norms and shorthands unique to a relationship, a capacity for conflict, spontaneity, and synchronization all help two people communicate more quickly and accurately.

Finally, *mutual investment* refers to each party's interest in the other's well-being and efficacy. This dimension derives principally from the work of Levinger and Snoek (1972), who directly relate it to several of the other dimensions already discussed, as well as to underlying dynamics of social exchange.

Before proceeding further, it is useful to underscore several observations concerning the characteristics we have just reviewed. First, they are not pure dimensions, because they are closely interrelated and appear to emerge from common underlying processes, such as social exchange, evaluation, and attribution, which have not yet been discussed. Second, these dimensions are progressive in nature and are treated as such in the literature (see Altman & Taylor, 1973). They are progressive even when the nature of the relationship is pathological, and increased movement along such dimensions as mutual investment and uniqueness and synchrony of interaction can result in destructive outcomes for one or both parties (Carson, 1969; Lidz et al., 1957; Lidz & Fleck, 1960). Third, as will be discussed later, progression along these dimensions is moderated by three general classes of factors, which Altman and Taylor (1973) term *individual factors, situational context*, and the *outcomes of the exchange* for each party.

Although the dimensions just described are based almost exclusively on research conducted on dyads of a social and intimate nature, they have face validity and relevance for task-based relationships, at least at a descriptive level. Everyday observation would suggest that individual working relationships differ from each other along these dimensions and progress along these dimensions as they develop. Moreover, barring underlying psychodynamics of a pathological nature, progression along these dimensions should enable the two parties to work better together, if only because of the increased efficacy of exchange that characterizes more developed relationships.

STAGES IN THE RELATIONSHIP-FORMATION PROCESS

Implicit in the dimensions just reviewed is progression not only of a qualitative nature but also of a temporal and cumulative nature as well. A number of authors have suggested that relationships typically progress through stages as they develop. Although Hinde (1971, 1979) has argued that such stages cannot be distinguished by observable discontinuities and that any definitions of stages are likely to depend on arbitrary criteria, he also suggests that it can be useful to describe changes in a relationship as involving a succession of stages (pp. 289–90). Stage paradigms of the relationship-formation process have been postulated by several researchers. Simmel (1950), for example, implied a progression through stages of casual acquaintanceships, friendships, reciprocated love, and established dyads; Newcomb (1961) postulated differences in stages in terms of balance theory; Kerckhoff and Davis (1962) described differences in terms of similarity and complementarity of attitudes; and Murstein (1977) postulated stages in terms of stimulus, value comparison, and role compatibility. This review, however, will focus only on the three stage paradigms that figure most prominently in the literature on relationship formation (see, for example, reviews in Hinde, 1979; Huston, 1974; Swensen, 1973; Triandis, 1977).

These three are Secord and Backman's (1964) reciprocal-exchange-stage paradigm, which is heavily based on Thibaut and Kelley's (1959) work; Levinger and Snoek's (1972) and Levinger's (1974) pair-relatedness model; and Altman and Taylor's (1973) social-penetration model. Table 4.2 describes these stage paradigms in terms of both the stages postulated and the underlying processes thought to move relationships through these stages.

TABLE 4.2
Major Stage Paradigms of the Relationship-Formation Process

I. Reciprocal exchange paradigm (Secord & Backman 1964; Thibaut & Kelley 1959)

Stages or levels of relationship	*Underlying processes*
1. *Sampling*: Selection process by which a person chooses another with whom he will have a more involved relationship; requires propinquity; appearance, attractiveness, similarity are used to evaluate potential payoffs.	The "motor" for both the formation and termination of the relationship is each party's desire to *maximize personal outcomes.* Each person's comparison level (Thibaut and Kelley 1959) and comparison level of alternatives change over time with experience and learning, and therefore the evaluation of payoffs is evolutionary.
2. *Bargaining*: Each party tests and negotiates to see if "a more permanent trading relationship would be to mutual advantage." In a sense, this starts the moment two people begin to interact; rewards come from ease of interaction, similarity of values, and complementarity of needs.	
3. *Commitment*: Relationship becomes more central and, in social and romantic relationships, intimate. Each party forgoes relations with others to engage in relationship with the other party.	
4. *Institutionalization*: Formal ratification of the commitment takes place (if deep and appropriate). Legal, symbolic, or other ratification and mutual acknowledgment of the commitment occurs.	

II. Mutuality and pair-relatedness paradigm (Levinger & Snoek 1972; Levinger 1974)

Levels of relationship	*Underlying processes*
1. *Unilateral Awareness*: (Level 1) Other is seen entirely in terms of external characteristics. Attraction based on perception of favorable and *potentially* rewarding attributes (expected favorable outcomes before	Dyads develop through stages of increasing *mutuality* of rewarding exchanges. Processes include 1. *Mutual Disclosure*: Disclosure of selves and sharing of significant attitudes, feelings, and experiences re-

---

(*Continued*)

TABLE 4.2
(*continued*)

extended interaction occurs). Knowledge of each other is superficial.

2. *Bilateral Surface Contact*: (Level 2)
Interactions primarily superficial and
stereotyped; defined by socially determined roles. Relationships typically segmented in that they deal
with partial aspects of living; attraction based on *actual* reward-cost
outcomes and expected future outcomes. Variables are important at this
stage, not necessarily so for later
stages. Knowledge of each other is
partial.

3. *Mutuality*: (Level 3) A continuing
evolution toward greater shared
meanings; attraction is based on the
satisfactions of levels 1 and 2 and
also on unique dyad emotional investments, interdependencies, and
mutuality of need satisfactions. Partners possess shared knowledge of
each other and assume responsibility
for furthering each other's outcomes.
Both parties share private norms for
regulating their association.
(Advanced level 3) The prior history
of the pair's interactions serves to increase the "number of its actual and
potential joint behavior repertoires."

sult in a "spiral of shared
assumptions."

2. *Mutual Investment*: As a relationship
unfolds, each party takes increasing
pleasure in the other's satisfaction.
Mutual investment includes learning
how to accommodate each other's
responses and preferences. The deeper the relationship, the larger the
cargo of joint experiences, shared
feelings, and behavior coordination.

III. Social-penetration paradigm (Altman & Taylor 1973)

Stages of social penetration

1. *Orientation*: Interactions are stereotyped in nature; exchanges lack
breadth, depth, or richness. Information exchanged at superficial level.
Little open evaluation, criticism, or
expression of conflict; indirect techniques used for conflict avoidance.
Interactions limited to outer, public
areas of personality. "Social actors
scan one another and communicate
according to conventional formula."

2. *Exploratory affective exchange*: Interpersonal behavior is still at periphery of self. Relations flow more
smoothly and are more relaxed.

Underlying processes

1. *Social penetration involves* (1) *overt
interpersonal behaviors,* (2) *internal
subjective processes* (including attribution, assessment) which pre-
cede, accompany, and follow overt
exchange. Interactions are "critiqued"
to see if further contact or penetration is worth pursuing.

2. Penetration is a systematic, orderly
process of mutual self-disclosure,
which proceeds gradually from superficial to deeper areas of
personality.

3. The rate and stage of penetration
varies as a function of interpersonal

TABLE 4.2
(*Continued*)

Commitments are limited or temporary.

3. *Full affective exchange*: Both parties know each other well; fairly extensive history of association; exchange more spontaneous; considerable interpersonal synchrony, permeability, and substitutability; readiness to make positive and negative evaluations; increased uniqueness in patterns of communication. Knowledge of intermediate levels of each other's self; many barriers to intimacy down, but exchange still retains restrictedness and caution.

4. *Stable exchange*: Achieved in only a few relationships. Exchanges involve richness, spontaneity. Parties know each other well and can readily interpret and predict feelings and probable behavior of other; considerable knowledge and dialogue involving core areas of personality.

rewards and costs (absolute magnitude and reward/cost ratio), both immediate and expected.

4. Depenetration is the reverse process and is also systematic.

5. The process is moderated by personal characteristics of the two people involved, outcomes of exchange, situational context.

The Reciprocal-Exchange Model

Secord and Backman (1964) postulated that social relationships can progress through four stages, which they called *sampling, bargaining, commitment,* and *institutionalization* (see Table 4.2). Their view of the underlying social processes that account for progress through these stages is based on social-exchange theory. A relationship's progress through these stages, they argue, will depend on each person's ability to maximize personal rewards in the relationship as compared with external alternatives. A relationship will develop if doing so increases personal outcomes, given each person's internal comparison level and comparison levels of alternatives (Thibaut & Kelley, 1959). They further argue that each person's comparison levels will change over time and that the evaluation of payoffs is evolutionary in nature.

Mutuality and Pair-Relatedness

Levinger and Snoek (1972) see the potential evolution of relationships in terms of three levels of pair relatedness, which are in turn based on the degree of mutuality present in a relationship (see Table 4.2). Like that of

Secord and Backman, their model is based on social-exchange theory (Homans, 1950, 1961; Thibaut & Kelley, 1959) in that dyads are seen as developing through stages of increasingly rewarding mutual exchanges. However, Levinger and Snoek go well beyond the simple concept of rewards and costs and describe mutual self-disclosure (Jourard, 1959) and mutual investment in a common bond as important underlying processes that move a relationship through these stages. Thus their stage paradigm goes significantly beyond the social-exchange paradigms of Secord and Backman (1964) and Thibaut and Kelley (1959).

Social-Penetration Model

Perhaps the most inclusive, integrated, and detailed stage paradigm of the relationship-formation process has been presented by Altman and Taylor (1973) (see Table 4.2). They postulate four stages of social penetration, which involve increasing degrees of mutual knowledge, openness, uniqueness of exchange, spontaneity, synchrony, and substitutability. Although they emphasize that any attempt to categorize the social-penetration process into clearly delineated stages is artificial their four stages differ markedly in their central activities, exchanges, and characteristics. They see the social-penetration process as including both overt interpersonal behaviors and internal subjective processes (including attribution, assessment, and expectations), which take place before, during, and after exchanges. Interactions are "critiqued" over time to see if further penetration is worth pursuing.

Altman and Taylor define social penetration as a systematic and orderly process of mutual self-disclosure, which proceeds gradually from superficial to deeper areas of exchange involving more central aspects of each person's personality. In this respect, their view of the underlying dynamics is similar to Levinger and Snoek's. Similarly, they also view the rate and stage of social penetration as a function of interpersonal rewards and costs (in terms of absolute magnitude and reward/cost ratio), both immediate and expected.

Altman and Taylor's social penetration model is quite inclusive and extends to aspects of personality and self. Like Levinger and Snoek, they believe the development of a relationship is closely related to self-disclosure and the breadth and depth of each person's knowledge of the other. Critical to their conception of the social-penetration process, however, is the degree of access each person has to core aspects of the other's personality. They visualize both disclosure and access in terms of a "breadth" dimension (how many aspects of one's personality become known to the other), a "breadth-frequency" dimension, and a "depth" dimension (disclosure of central versus peripheral aspects of self). In these terms, the social-penetration process proceeds toward greater depth, breadth, and interconnectedness, resulting in greater vulnerability and access to "socially undesirable" characteristics as well as greater understanding of the whole personality. A surface relationship would tend to be segmented (low breadth) and peripheral (low depth), while a more advanced relationship would be characterized by mutual disclosure and knowledge of a broader, deeper, and more interconnected nature.

Commonalities

These three stage models have several important underlying similarities. The first is that early stages largely involve interactions that are socially "safe" or stereotypical, concerning topics that are routine, superficial, or prescribed by role expectations. Commitment tends to be tentative; knowledge of the other is superficial and segmental; and the focus of each party's concerns tends to be principally unilateral rather than bilateral. In contrast, later stages are characterized by richer and more penetrating exchanges, more commitment to the other and to the relationship itself, and finally greater permanence and stability.

Underlying Processes

The three stage paradigms are all rooted in social-exchange theory in that movement from one stage to another is based on the prospect that greater social penetration, mutuality, or commitment will be, on balance, more rewarding. All three models also presume the presence of what Altman and Taylor have described as internal subjective processes, such as attribution, the development of expectations, assessment, and evaluation. Finally, several common overt processes are involved in moving from one stage to another. These include selective self-disclosure, exploration, testing, and negotiation.

In their shared view of the direction of movement and the underlying processes, the three stage models are readily applicable to the development of working relationships. It is not clear, however, that the *particular configurations* of the stages postulated by these authors are as applicable to working relationships as they are to social and intimate relationships. Let us now turn our attention to working relationships as a substantive category to explore these differences and their implications in more detail.

WORKING RELATIONSHIPS AS A SUBSTANTIVE TYPE

One should not draw too sharp a line between working relationships and social relationships. Working relationships are, after all, a form of social relationship; they employ social modalities, develop between two social beings, and exist in organizational contexts that are themselves social structures. For these reasons we will treat them as a substantive type of social relationship. Nonetheless, it also seems clear that working relationships are not the same as purely social or intimate relationships. The stage paradigms reviewed in Table 4.2 do not apply easily to most working relationships, except as they pertain to their purely personal aspects. A key question thus is what characteristics of working relationships distinguish them from other types of social relationships.

Interpersonal Setting and Relationship Goals

An important factor affecting the development of any relationship is the behavioral setting itself (Barker, 1968; Wicker, 1972) and the expectations that people bring to it as an interpersonal setting (McCall, 1974). Interpersonal settings have been described in terms of a number of dimensions. These include such contextual cues as time, space, and objects (Athos & Gabarro, 1978) and place, imagery, and nonverbal clues (McCaskey, 1978). Altman and Taylor (1973) have argued that the purpose of a relationship is itself a basic aspect of the interpersonal setting. They cite earlier work by Bennis et al. (1964) in which interpersonal settings are defined in terms of relationship goals, that is, the purposes inherent in why a given relationship is formed in the first place. Using this definition, Bennis et al. identified four different types of relationships that act as interpersonal settings: (1) relationships formed to fulfill themselves (such as love, friendship, and marriage); (2) those formed for self-confirmation or situational definition; (3) those formed to influence or bring about change; and (4) those formed to focus on task achievement. Although working relationships often meet two or more of these goals simultaneously, their primary purpose is usually the achievement of a task, and the wider setting is typically an organizational or task-based context. Because of their distinctive purpose and interpersonal setting, several factors are much more important in working relationships than in purely social ones. These factors include task and task instrumentality, the degree of affect, the role of competence, the nature of self-disclosure, and the importance of role.

Task and Task Achievement. One result of the centrality of the task dimension is that the social component of a working relationship is less important than it is in an intimate relationship (Triandis and Davis 1965; Goldstein and Davis 1972). In terms of underlying social-exchange dynamics, the principal rewards and costs concern task achievement. Similarly, although the affective component is important to all relationships, it is less so in task-based, formal relationships than in purely social ones (Triandis 1977). In part, this is because people seek out other interpersonal settings to attain other kinds of rewards (McCall 1974) and form working relationships principally to focus on task completion.

Task Instrumentality.   When task attainment is the basis for a relationship, people can be expected to value attributes in the other that are consistent with task accomplishment (Wortman & Linsenmeier, 1977). Research by Wall and Adams (1974) and others shows clearly that in task-based dyads, a person's ability to perform effectively influences a number of interpersonal outcomes, including the other person's willingness to grant autonomy, the development of trust, and the other person's evaluation—all of which are important to the relationship-formation process. Similarly, other research has shown that successful task performance is a basis for both liking and attraction (Farris & Lim, 1969) and satisfaction and cohesion (Staw, 1975).

Conversely, some research on working relationships also suggests that some conventional sources of interpersonal attraction are less important in working relationships than they are in social or intimate relationships. In a three-year longitudinal study of the evolution of managerial relationships, Gabarro (1978) found that initial liking and attraction were not predictive of the longer-term strength of the relationship. Other more instrumentally relevant attributes, such as judgment, competence, and task consistency, were far more important to the development of a working relationship and its resulting quality, but these attributes did not emerge until after the two parties had worked together for some time. Gabarro also found that if a superior or subordinate was an effective working partner, managers would overlook social traits that they would have considered undesirable in a personal relationship (Gabarro, 1978, 290–92).

Elsewhere, I have referred to the task-based instrumentality found in managerial relationships as a "pragmatic imperative," arguing that it shapes interactions profoundly but not always with the best outcomes (Gabarro 1980).[2] The pragmatic imperative influences how a relationship develops

---

[2]In using the expression *pragmatic imperative* I am calling attention to the desire of managers to focus on aspects of causality that are instrumentally relevant in achieving the ends they are most concerned with, i.e., creating effects that contribute to task attainment and personal and organizational performance. But in a more basic sense *all* relationships are pragmatic in that people see their situations and act upon them in ways that help them attain what they want or what they think is important (Lecky, 1945). Part of this pragmatism in everyday life is that people tend to perceive their situations in ways that simplify them so they can focus on what is *salient* to them, just as managers do in their own particular setting. The need for this selective simplification is a recurrent theme in virtually every school of psychology and social psychology, and the concept of the pragmatic imperative as a variable in human interaction is an old and pervasive one. Weick (1969, p. 67) explicitly describes the predominant orientation of the human actor as pragmatic and identifies this pragmatism as the essential determinant of what a person attends to and what meanings he makes of his experiencing. Thus, in using the term *pragmatic imperative,* I am only highlighting an essential aspect of all human interaction in managerially specific terms.

and what is valued in it. It has particular implications for competence and for the nature of self-disclosure in working relationships.

Competence. Task-specific competence plays a much greater role in the development of working relationships than it does in purely social ones. Considerable research suggests that competence has a direct effect on the development of both interpersonal trust and influence (see the review by Walton et al., 1968; Bachman, 1968; Wall & Adams, 1974; Gabarro, 1978, 1979; Schwarzwald & Goldenberg, 1979). Demonstrated competence has also been found to influence liking and interpersonal evaluation in working relationships (Lowin & Craig, 1968; Farris & Lim, 1969; Fromkin, Klimoski, & Flanagan, 1972) as well as how much a person is willing to invest in a relationship (Gabarro, 1978). Thus competence can be expected to be a very powerful personal attribute in the development of working relationships.

SELF-DISCLOSURE

In all three of the major stage paradigms reviewed earlier, self-disclosure, especially of a personal or intimate nature, figures prominently both as a characteristic of a relationship and as an underlying process involved in the development of relationships. The limited work that has been done on the role of self-disclosure in working relationships suggests that disclosure about self is less important than openness concerning task or organizational issues (Gabarro, 1978), but that openness concerning task-related issues is quite critical (Gaines, 1980; Sgro et al., 1980). Current research also suggests that interpersonal trust as related to openness is a two-factor variable comprising a person-specific, attitudinal factor, which is broad-based and stable, and a situation-specific factor, which is less stable and is situationally contingent (Archer, 1979; Scott, 1980). Indeed, Gabarro (1978) found examples of working relationships that were perceived by both parties as highly effective and satisfying but that involved very little disclosure of a personal or intimate nature. This should not be surprising, because working relationships are, in Altman and Taylor's (1973) terms, segmental in nature: they do not necessarily involve all aspects of a person's life. Disclosure of one's intimate thoughts and feelings is not as important to the development of a working relationship as openness about variables that directly influence the relationship. In fact, personal disclosures may have a negative effect if seen as inappropriate (Jones & Gordon, 1972; Derlega & Grzelak, 1979; Wortman et al., 1976) or poorly timed (Jones & Archer, 1976).

Role as a Factor

If task instrumentality is an important consequence of the purposive nature of working relationships, the presence of organizational roles is an equally important aspect of their interpersonal setting (Biddle & Thomas, 1966).

Roles and role expectations are part of the context of all social interaction, but they are even more pervasive and are more explicitly defined in working relationships, particularly when they occur within or across organizational hierarchies. Most working relationships develop between people by virtue of their roles. In this respect, people begin with an institutionalized role relationship, often before they have begun to develop an actual working relationship. For example, superiors and subordinates begin their interactions with a "ratified role relationship," which is the final stage in the Secord and Backman paradigm of relationship development (see Table 4.2). In a perverse way, they are at stage 4 before they have begun the activities that Secord and Backman describe as occurring in earlier stages. The operational question for such a dyad is not whether to get "married," but rather how to make the marriage work (Gabarro & Kotter, 1980).

A second consequence of roles in hierarchical organizations is that the distribution of power in working relationships tends to be far clearer and more asymmetric than in relationships of a purely social and voluntary nature. Asymmetry in power has a negative effect on self-disclosure and the development of trust (Walton et al., 1968; Walton, 1969) unless such self-disclosure is legitimized by role-related social norms, such as those pertaining to relationships with psychiatrists, physicians, social workers, and priests (Derlega & Grzelak, 1979). Thus working relationships are likely to develop in a more guarded and monitored fashion than those described in the general literature on relationship formation. On the other hand, work by Tedeschi (1974) and others suggests that asymmetry in power can sometimes be a basis of attraction if a foundation of trust or credibility exists.

A final and rather direct way in which role definitions can affect the development of working relationships is that people's reactions to each other and the attributions they make about each other are clearly influenced by role expectations (Davis, 1973; Guiot, 1977; Triandis, 1977). Guiot has argued convincingly that attributions about intention and behavior are made quite differently if one is viewed "in role" rather than "*qua persona,*" and that behavior that leads to the attribution of sincerity or trustworthiness "*qua persona*" will not lead to the same attribution if a person is seen "in role." Guiot further argues that because of this distinction many findings in the attribution literature are not applicable to role-based situations.

Salient Differences

As the preceding discussion makes clear, working relationships differ from more purely social relationships in a number of ways that are likely to influence their development. First, they are more *segmental* in nature than intimate or personal relationships. Both the mutuality of exchange and the breadth of that mutuality can be expected to be narrower and less inclusive than in personal relationships; relationship development is more likely to involve depth of mutual understanding concerning task-related issues rather than breadth along a fuller range of issues. Second, *openness* concerning task-salient issues can be expected to be more important than self-disclosure per se. Third, specific *competencies* that are task relevant will be an important influence on attributions, liking, and evaluation. Finally, *role definitions* can be expected to temper openness, trust, and self-disclosure as a working relationship progresses and, all other things being equal, retard the degree of social penetration that is likely to occur (Altman & Taylor, 1973).

THE DEVELOPMENT OF WORKING RELATIONSHIPS

With these differences in mind, let us now turn our attention to the question of how working relationships develop. Although the particular configurations and content of the stages summarized in Table 4.2 do not fit working relationships easily, the underlying processes and directionality of these paradigms do have applicability if we consider the differences just reviewed as moderating variables. For example, working relationships clearly evolve toward the greater shared meanings of Levinger and Snoek's pair-relatedness model, though this development may not occur along all of the dimensions described in Table 4.2. The underlying process of self-disclosure is also applicable if we consider self-disclosure in terms of task-relevant openness. The related notion of a "growing spiral" of shared assumptions also applies if we construe it in terms of assumptions salient to task. Similarly the process of mutual investment has manifest applicability in terms of mutual accommodation and investment in common goals, if not along the other dimensions shown in the figure. The same argument can be made about the directionality of Altman and Taylor's stages of orientation, exploration, and stabilized exchange, if one views progression as occurring segmentally in terms of depth.

We can expect therefore that working relationships that develop beyond role-specified surface encounters will progress along the dimensions summarized in Table 4.1 and with the directionality of movement indicated in Table 4.2. Thus for a working relationship to develop effectively, we can expect that mutual understanding and richness of knowledge will increase, and that the nature of this mutual knowledge will move from being general and impressionistic to specific and concrete. The underlying processes of expectation formation, attribution, assessment, and evaluation will operate in the development of working relationships just as they do on other types of relationships. Finally, we can expect that task-relevant openness will play a role analogous to that of self-disclosure in intimate relationships, and depth of mutual investment will not occur unless doing so is on balance more rewarding (or less costly) than not doing so.

Although little field-based research has been done on the actual development of working relationships, there is some evidence suggesting that the development of mutual expectations is an important factor influencing both the effectiveness of working relationships (Liden & Graen, 1980; Baird & Wieting, 1979) and how satisfying they are (Klimoski & Hayes, 1980; Valenzi & Dessler, 1978). These findings are similar to those reported in the leadership literature suggesting that the structuring of expectations is the single pattern that contributes positively to productivity and satisfaction (Stogdill, 1974).

The findings of the longitudinal study cited earlier are consistent with these findings. In a three-year study of the evolution of managerial relationships. Gabarro (1978, 1979) found that over time, expectations about performance, goals, and each party's role became not only more mutual but more concrete and specific as well. Interestingly, the exceptions to this pattern were either relationships that involved relatively little interdependence or ones in which one or both parties were dissatisfied with the relationship once it became stabilized. In the latter cases, Gabarro concluded that these were relationships in which insufficient openness, testing, or exploration had occurred.

The findings of this study also suggested, however, that individual relationships varied greatly in the rate at which mutuality and concreteness of expectations developed. Because of the small sample (thirty-three president/vice-president dyads in four sites) it was not possible to identify why this variation occurred. One can, however, postulate a number of reasons why some relationships develop more quickly or with greater depth than others, including differences in personal style, variations in interdependency, the relative performance of the subordinate's unit (e.g., poor performance would create greater interaction and scrutiny), and proximity (a subordinate located five hundred miles away is not likely to interact as often with his or her superior as one on the same floor).

Just as mutual expectations tended to become more specific over time, Gabarro also found attributions about such interpersonal variables as trust and influence became more differentiated with continued interaction. In early stages, attributions of the other's trustworthiness were typically general and impressionistic, while at later stages they were quite differentiated and specific, for example, "His sense of the market is excellent but he's consistently too optimistic [on sales forecasts]" (Gabarro, 1979, p. 12). On the basis of cross-time interview comparisons, Gabarro identified several dimensions along which attributions of trust were differentiated; these fell into two broad groups: character-based sources of trust (trust in the other's integrity, motives and intentions, consistency of behavior, openness and discreteness) and competence-based sources of trust (trust in the other's functional or specific competence, interpersonal competence, and "general business judgment") (Gabarro, 1978, pp. 295–98). Also identified were several dimensions along which attributions of influence were differentiated in terms of both positional and personal bases.

In comparing the evolution of these relationships over the three years of the study, Gabarro postulated a four-stage model of the development of working relationships: (1) orientation and impression formation; (2) exploration; (3) testing and working through; and (4) stabilization. Table 4.3

TABLE 4.3
Stages in the Development of New Working Relationships:
Characteristics, Tasks, and Issues

Stage	Characteristics	Major Tasks	Issues and Questions
I. Orientation: Impression formation	Brief period, perhaps lasting the first several weeks. Mutual sizing up beginning with first impressions, and continuing with more extended and less stereotyped interactions. Trust is impressionistic and undifferentiated Personal influence not yet developed.	Deal with the question of the other's motives. Exchange an initial set of expectations at a general level concerning objectives, roles, and needs. Develop initial understanding of how both parties will work together in the future.	How competent, reliable, and open is the other person? What are the other's concerns, motives, and intentions? How open and forthright to be with the other person?
II. Exploration: Beyond impressions	Longer period than Stage I, perhaps lasting the first several months. General and tentative expectations of Stage I become more specific and concrete. Rapid learning to search out the other's important assumptions and expectations, and to communicate one's own. Both parties begin to assert their personal identities, styles, and values.	Explore in more detailed and concrete terms other's expectations about goals, roles, and priorities. Surface and clarify differences in expectations. Explore and identify questions and sources concerning trust in terms of motives, competence, consistency, and openness. Explore and identify questions and	How much can the other person be trusted in terms of integrity, motives, competence, judgment, and consistency of action? How safe is it to be open with the other person in terms of problems or differences of opinion? What is the other person's credibility and decisiveness?

TABLE 4.3
(*Continued*)

Stage	Characteristics	Major Tasks	Issues and Questions
	Leads to confirmation or rejection of initial impressions.	sources concerning influence in terms of positional and personal attributes.	
III. Testing: Testing and defining the interpersonal contract	A long period, perhaps six months to a year in duration, but could be longer. Testing concerning minimal expectations, areas in which trust exists, and limits of each person's influence on the other are tacitly and overtly tested. As a result, limits of the evolving interpersonal contract are defined for better or for worse.	Test the mutuality of expectations, and the bases and limits of trust and influence. Work through and negotiate basic unresolved differences. Assess the degree to which mutual accommodation is possible, and whether the costs of achieving it are acceptable. Define stabilized set of expectations concerning each other's role, and the bases for trust and influence in the relationship.	To what extent is the situation (e.g., environment, structure, culture) rather than the other person the cause of the difficulties in the relationship? How long should the testing continue? How to know when enough is enough? How to insure an adequate testing to avoid a superficial and unsatisfactory relationship, without pressing too hard and risking unnecessary or unproductive confrontation?
IV. Stabilization	Interpersonal contract becomes defined Little further effort goes into learning about or testing each other. Aspects of the relationship such as expectations, trust, and influence undergo lit-	If events or episodes lead to negative feelings (e.g., conflict over a decision, slight, or oversight), take steps to repair the damage. Insure that the relationship continues to be productive, adaptive, and satis-	Is the interpersonal contract appropriate given changes in the individuals or the situation? How to keep the interpersonal contract viable in the face of major individual and situational changes?

(*continued*)

TABLE 4.3
(*Continued*)

Stage	Characteristics	Major Tasks	Issues and Questions
	tle additional changes. Major event or change needed to destabilize the relationship.	fying as the needs of the situation and the parties change. If a major episode (e.g., one party's actions violate the level of trust built up) or a significant environmental change destabilizes the relationship, rework the earlier stages of the relationship-building process from the point of regressions.	

Reprinted from V. Sathe, *Culture and Related Corporate Realities* (Homewood, Ill.: Irwin, 1985), by permission.

presents Sathe's (1985) overview of these stages, which summarizes the interpersonal tasks, issues, and dilemmas characteristic of each stage. The model is quite similar in many respects to those presented by Altman and Taylor and by Secord and Backman. The important difference is that the stages presented in Table 4.3 are described in terms of archetype issues that emerge with continued interaction rather than in terms of the "goodness" of a relationship. Gabarro postulated that management dyads progress through these stages regardless of the quality of their relationships, unless one party quits or is fired before the relationship becomes stabilized. For this reason, some working relationships that reached the stabilization stage were seen by one or both parties as not fully effective or satisfying (Gabarro, 1979, pp. 9–17.

Using a "contract" metaphor (Lawless, 1972; Levinson, 1968; Thomas, 1976), Gabarro postulated that managers go through these stages in the process of forming a unique interpersonal contract. He also argued, however, that a relationship's effectiveness is not determined by whether a dyad progresses through these stages, but rather by how well the dyad deals with the archetypical problems and dilemmas presented by each stage. Thus, unlike the stage paradigms reviewed earlier, Gabarro's stages are defined simply by the interpersonal tasks and issues that emerge with sustained interaction. It should be clear, however, that working relationships could also be configured in terms of stages defined along hierarchical dimensions of mutuality or other qualitative aspects of relationships, which would be more directly analogous to the stage paradigms of Altman and Taylor and Levinger and Snoek.

Despite these differences, the general directionality of Gabarro's stages is essentially the same as that described in the Secord and Backman and Altman and Taylor stage paradigms. Moreover, the content and process issues described as characterizing each of the stages in Table 4.3 require the same types of exploration, openness, and reward/cost assessments as those described by Altman and Taylor and Levinger and Snoek, as well as the implicit testing and negotiating described by Secord and Backman. Indeed Table 4.3 implies that these interpersonal processes must occur if a working relationship is to develop effectively. Otherwise the relationship will stabilize at a relatively superficial level.

THE DEVELOPMENT OF MUTUAL EXPECTATIONS

Working relationships vary in their mutuality, efficacy, and intensity. Some stabilize at a relatively superficial level of exchange, others at rather deep levels of mutuality and synchrony. For purposes of this discussion, the development of working relationships has been seen as a progression from role-specified surface encounters to a greater degree of mutual exchange and task-related efficacy. The process involves both temporal dimensions (such as the sequential phases shown in Table 4.3) and qualitative dimensions (such as those summarized in Table 4.1). An implicit assumption has been that when the work of two people makes them highly dependent on each other, it is desirable to develop a relationship that is mutual and robust enough to be rewarding and effective.

How can this process be facilitated? Several implications can be drawn from the work we have just reviewed. The first is that developing a robust working relationship takes time. The internal subjective processes of attribution, expectation formation, and assessment, described earlier as underlying the relationship formation process, all occur over time, are interactive, and typically involve extended sequences of interactions (Altman, 1974). To accelerate or influence the process (i.e., actually "develop" a working relationship rather than let it evolve) will require purposive "interpersonal work." Identifying and dealing with important differences of opinion, for example, requires emotional energy and action, as well as a level of awareness, of self and other, that does not occur naturally for most people.

A second implication is that the development of mutual expectations plays a key role in this process. In terms of task instrumentality and effectiveness, the relevant areas of mutuality in expectations concern (1) expectations about what the task is and what the outcomes of the joint endeavor should be; (2) expectations about how the two parties should actually work with each other (which include assumptions abut process as well as responsibility); and (3) expectations about how the two people work singly and independently on the joint task. Thus the task-salient aspects of mutuality include not only expectations about outcomes but also about interpersonal processes involving interdependence, autonomy, and individual influence, which are in turn affected by each person's assumptions about trust and power within a relationship (Argyris, 1962; Barnes, 1981; Deutsch, 1962; Jacobson, 1972).

Both the general literature on relationship formation and the field-based research reviewed earlier suggest that the development of mutual expectations requires a great deal of exploration, testing, and negotiation of individual expectations. These processes occur at both tacit and overt levels of behavior. It also requires considerable internal subjective work by each party, involving attributional processes, the formation and revision of individual expectations, and evaluative processes of the type described by social exchange theorists. To work actively toward developing shared expectations therefore requires a clear communication of initial expectations, where possible, and the exploration and testing of any difference in expectations. Exploration is also required when it is not clear to one or both parties what should be done or how to proceed (as is often the case at the outset of a joint endeavor). Finally either tacit or overt negotiation of differences is required before mutual expectations can be formed.

Although mutual expectations are sometimes negotiated or clarified as a result of critical and occasionally dramatic events, they are more typically worked out over time during a succession of routine interactions, such as *ad hoc* encounters, meetings, progress reviews, and discussions of task-based problems (Gabarro, 1978). Thus much of the work of developing mutual expectations will appear to be routine, invisible, or tacit, except where differences in initial expectations are clear.

The difficulty involved in clarifying, exploring, testing, and negotiating expectations will depend on the *a priori* differences between the two people involved. In this respect, working relationships are no different from purely social relationships, in which similarities in values and attitudes affect the ease with which further mutuality can develop (Berscheid & Walster, 1969). Considerable evidence suggests that the more similar two people are in background and attitudes, the easier and more satisfying a task-based relationship will become (Wexley et al., 1980; Ross & Ferris, 1981; Posner & Munson, 1979; Weiss, 1978). The literature on organization theory also suggests that differences in functional backgrounds result in different cognitive orientations concerning task achievement and different attitudes toward structuring, which are themselves natural sources of conflict (Lawrence & Lorsch, 1967; Lorsch & Allen, 1973). Thus we can expect that differences in social attitudes and values as well as functionally based task predispositions will influence the amount of interpersonal work needed to develop an effective working relationship. This will be especially true in early stages, when initial expectations are "traded" and explored, and in later stages when mutual expectations are tested and negotiated.

Most of the research on working relationships (as well as much of the work done on the dynamics of task-based groups) suggests that openness in the confrontation of differences can make the outcomes of these processes more effective. The dilemma, of course, is that although openness tends to be reciprocated (Chaikin & Derlega, 1974), some threshold amount of interpersonal trust is needed before it seems safe to be open with another person (Rubin, 1975), especially where differences involve emotionally charged issues. No doubt this is why people "test" apparent differences incrementally and why modeling of openness by one or both parties is seen by many scholars of two-person relationships as a major explanation of why two people become more open over time (Bandura, 1977). In working relationships, it seems clear that the superior or the higher-status member of the dyad is in the safer position to model such behavior (Gabarro, 1979; Levinson, 1968).

The process of developing mutual expectations is further complicated by the reality that often one or both parties do not know what they want at the outset of a working relationship. One's expectations often do not become clear until after one has had some experience working with another person. In this respect, most differentiated expectations result from a process that Weick (1979) has called "retrospective sense-making" involving the "reflective glance." Much of the work of developing mutual expectations is therefore episodic and iterative. Even if early agreement on initial expectations is easily attained, subsequent renegotiation is needed as relationships develop. Several large U.S. corporations, such as General Electric and Exxon, have used "assimilation meetings" to facilitate the clarification and negotiation of mutual expectations between newly assigned managers and their new subordinates. These meetings have been very effective in clarifying initial expectations, developing a basis of trust, and accelerating the process by which initial mutual expectations are agreed upon. Experience with these interventions suggests, however, that subsequent meetings are needed after six to eight months to deal with issues that neither party could anticipate at the outset.

The development of mutual expectations is an extended process. Concrete differentiation of these expectations takes time and requires interpersonal work. As for the development of influence and trust, one-time interventions are insufficient (Scott, 1980). The research reviewed in this chapter, however, suggests that greater attention on the part of one or both parties can greatly influence the success and effectiveness of this process, and that certain interventions of the type just described can help focus and accelerate the process. My own belief is that they also legitimize the confrontation and resolution of differences early in the relationship-formation process, thereby making it easier and safer for both parties to be open with each other as the relationship develops.

IMPLICATIONS FOR FURTHER RESEARCH

The development of working relationships is a vital aspect of organizational life. Nevertheless, although a large number of scholars trained in social psychology have recently entered the field of organizational behavior, it remains a neglected area of inquiry.

The thinness of existing research applicable to understanding how working relationships develop has at least three implications for further work. The first is that more research is needed on the development of working relationships as a substantive area of knowledge. The second is that more field-based work is needed so that working relationships can be studied in context. The third is that more work of a longitudinal nature is needed because the development of working relationships is an evolutionary social phenomenon.

Substantive Area of Inquiry

Research on phenomenal causality of behavior within two-person relationships is a strong tradition within social psychology, dating back to the early 1930s. This tradition has included work on interpersonal perception as well as phenomenal causality, and has yielded several major theories, including balance theory, other consistency theories, exchange theories, and, most recently, attribution theory. Yet for our purposes, this impressive body of knowledge has two significant limitations. First, although these theories are potent in their general explanatory power, they are of less value in predicting behavior and outcomes in *specific types of relationships*. This is not because they are poorly constructed theories. Rather, it is because they are so general that they cannot be usefully applied unless one first understands the situational context and purpose of a relationship. As Levinger (1974, p. 117) has pointed out in a critique of exchange and reinforcement theories, the strengths of these theories are simultaneously their weaknesses: "that which explains everything explains nothing; the 'laws' of [such theories] must be moved toward greater specificity and their elements differentiated." What is salient in a relationship obviously depends in part on its nature and context (From 1957; Tagiuri, 1969; Jones & Thibaut, 1958). Situational forces are sufficiently complex and variable in and of themselves that one cannot understand what is important to two people in a relationship without understanding the context and how it impinges on the people involved (Kerckhoff, 1974). For example, attribution theory is clearly germane to the question of how two managers make attributions about each other in forming working relationships. But it is not very useful in understanding how working relationships develop unless one understands what traits, dispositions, behaviors, and contextual entities are salient to managers in their working relationships.

Indeed, several theories emerging from the literature on phenomenal causality—most notably attribution theory, cognitive-dissonance theory, and exchange theory—have been taught for some time in most graduate business schools and are included in most current textbooks on organizational behavior. Yet practicing managers seldom use these concepts to inform their decisions. I suspect that one reason for this disjunction between theory and practice is the lack of situationally grounded substantive theory. The importance of this gap between general and substantive theory has been pointed out by Wortman and Linsenmeier (1977) in their review of research on interpersonal attraction and ingratiation and its applicability to organizational settings. They note that the importance of competence and power in working relationships significantly affects the extent to which existing theory and findings are useful in predicting outcomes, and they conclude that considerably more research is needed on the particular "vicissitudes of the phenomena in organizational settings" before existing research on interpersonal attraction and ingratiation can be applied to the substantive issues and problems of organizational and managerial behavior (p. 173).

Clearly, certain basic underlying dynamics of relationships transcend situational settings. But the manifestation of these dynamics and the particular contextual factors that affect them vary from setting to setting. Further work of an integrative and substantive nature is needed to learn how these processes take place between people within organizations.

Field-Based Longitudinal Research

As we attempt to learn more about the development of working relationships, there is a great need for field-based, longitudinal research. Very little research so far has focused on how "natural," working relationships evolve over time. By natural relationships, I mean real, ongoing relationships as they exist in everyday life. Most research on relationship formation has involved "synthetic" relationships created for purposes of laboratory experimentation.[3] Such synthetic relationships are by their very nature

---

[3]See, for example, Swensen's (1973) review of various approaches to the study of interpersonal relations and the data and methods employed within these approaches (pp. 144–47). There are, of course, some exceptions to this generalization, especially in regard to social exchange theory (pp. 245–56).

carefully constrained, controlled, and short-lived (as brief as thirty minutes; typically no longer than a couple of hours). Usually the person with whom the subject interacts in the relationship is a confederate of the experimenter, so that even if the subject's reactions are "natural" those of the confederate are not.

Obviously laboratory experimentation has many advantages, the principal one being that it enables the researcher to focus on specific variables under controlled conditions. Most of the advances in attribution theory and interpersonal attraction have been based on such work. But the results of laboratory research have only limited applicability to our understanding of the dynamics of developing relationships. Natural relationships are ongoing and evolutionary in nature, and people's interactions are less constrained than in a laboratory setting. In real relationships people are free to seek additional information, and, more important, they are able to "proact" on each other over time. As Weick (1979) and others have pointed out, people learn from their actions and the consequences of their actions and make cause-effect attributions in terms of past history (Jones & Goethals, 1972). Laboratory subjects are really objects, in the literal sense of the word, because they are one of the variables being manipulated and their ability to proact is severely constrained. In real relationships people are both subjects and objects. They can seek more information, act, and learn from their actions, and they do this over time (Bugental, 1969, 1978). To my knowledge, little empirical research within organizational behavior has focused on the development of natural working relationships and on how attributions change or develop over time as two people work together.

A related limitation of much of the work on relationship formation in general is that it is largely devoted to the verification and development of general theory (or what Glaser & Strauss [1967] and others have called formal theory). Thus, although some of it has dealt with specific aspects of behavior, the resulting findings are still at a very general level of abstraction and thus of limited utility in substantive areas such as working relationships. Unfortunately, this is particularly true of research on attribution, which is a central aspect of the relationship-formation process.

In stressing the need for more field-based longitudinal research and for more substantive theory, I do not wish to reinforce further the polarity that currently exists between field-based, middle-range theory and laboratory-based general theory. Clearly, further substantive research on the topic needs to be informed by existing formal theory, and conversely the development of more grounded, substantive theory cannot help but inform and articulate the larger base of general theory.

ACKNOWLEDGMENTS

The author gratefully acknowledges the assistance of Colleen Kaftan for her insights and help in reviewing the basic literature on relationship formation.

REFERENCES

Altman, I. (1974). The communication of interpersonal attitudes: An ecological approach. In T. L. Huston (Ed.), *Foundations of interpersonal attraction* (pp. 121–142). New York: Academic Press.

Altman, I., & Taylor, D. A. (1973). *Social penetration: The development of interpersonal relationships.* New York: Holt, Rinehart and Winston.

Archer, R. L. (1979). Role of personality and the social situation. In G. J. Chelune (Ed.), *Self-disclosure* (pp. 28–58). San Francisco: Jossey-Bass.

Argyris, C. (1962). *Interpersonal competence and organizational effectiveness.* Homewood, IL: Dorsey Press.

Athos, A. G., & Gabarro, J. (1978). *Interpersonal behavior: Communication and understanding in relationships.* Englewood Cliffs, NJ: Prentice-Hall.

Bachman, J. G. (1968). Faculty satisfaction and the dean's influence: An organizational study of twelve liberal arts colleges. *Journal of Applied Psychology, 52,* 55–61.

Baird, J. E., Jr., & Wieting, G. K. (1979). Nonverbal communication can be a motivational tool. *Personnel Journal, 58,* 607–625.

Bandura, A. (1977). *Social learning theory.* Englewood Cliffs, NJ: Prentice-Hall.

Barker, R. (1968). *Ecological psychology: Concepts and methods for studying the environment of human behavior.* Stanford CA: Stanford University Press.

Barnes, I. B. (1981). Managing the paradox of organizational trust. *Harvard Business Review, 59,* 107–116.

Bennis, W. G., Schein, E. H., Berlew, D. E., & Steele, F. I. (1964). *Interpersonal dynamics.* Homewood, IL: Dorsey Press.

Berscheid, E., & Walster, E. (1969). *Interpersonal attraction.* Reading, MA: Addison-Wesley.

Biddle, B. J., & Thomas, E. J. (1966). *Role theory: Concepts and research.* New York: Wiley.

Bugental, J. F. T. (1969). Someone needs to worry: The existential anxiety of responsibility and decision. *Journal of Contemporary Psychotherapy, 2,* 41–53.

Bugental, J. F. T. (1978). Intentionality and ambivalence. In A. G. Athos & J. J. Gabarro (Eds.), *Interpersonal behavior: Communication and understanding in relationships.* Englewood Cliffs, NJ: Prentice-Hall.

Carson, R. C. (1969). *Interaction concepts of personality.* Chicago: Aldine.

Chaikin, A. L., & Derlega, V. J. (1974). *Self disclosure.* Morristown: NJ: General Learning Press.

Davis, M. S. (1973). *Intimate relations.* New York: Free Press.

Derlega, V. J., & Grzelak, J. (1979). Appropriateness of self-disclosure. In G. J. Chelune (Ed.), *Self-disclosure* (pp. 151–176). San Francisco: Jossey-Bass.

Deutsch, M. (1962). Cooperation and trust: Some theoretical notes. In *Nebraska Symposium on Motivation* (pp. 275–319). Lincoln, NE: University of Nebraska Press.

Dubin, R., & Spray, S. L. (1964). Executive behavior and interaction. *Industrial Relations, 3,* 99–108.

Farris, G. F., & Lim, F. G., Jr. (1969). Effects of performance on leadership, cohesiveness, influence, satisfaction, and subsequent performance. *Journal of Applied Psychology, 53,* 490–97.

From, F. (1957). The Experience of Purpose in Human Behavior. Paper read at Fifteenth International Congress of Psychology, Brussels.

Fromkin, H. L., Klimoski, R. J., & Flanagan, M. F. (1972). Race and competence as determinants of acceptance of newcomers in success and failure work groups. *Organizational Behavior and Human Performance, 7,* 25–42.

Gabarro, J. J. (1978). The development of trust, influence, and expectations. In A. G. Athos & J. J. Gabarro (Eds.), *Interpersonal behavior: Communication and understanding in relationships.* Englewood Cliffs, NJ: Prentice-Hall.

Gabarro, J. J. (1979). Socialization at the top: How CEO's and their subordinates evolve interpersonal contracts. *Organizational Dynamics, 3,* 2–23.

Gabarro, J. J. (1980). The evolution of managerial working relationships. Working Paper, Harvard University International Senior Management Program Center, Vevey, Switzerland.

Gabarro, J. J., & Kotter, J. P. (1980). Managing your boss. *Harvard Business Review, 58,* 92–100.

Gaines, J. H. (1980). Upward communication in industry: An experiment. *Industrial Relations, 33,* 929–942.

Glaser, B., & Strauss, A. L. (1967). *The discovery of grounded theory: Strategies for qualitative research.* Chicago: Aldine.

Goldstein, M., & Davis, E. E. (1972). Race and belief: A further analysis of the social determinants of behavioral intentions. *Journal of Personality and Social Psychology, 22,* 346–355.

Guiot, J. M. (1977). Attribution and identity construction: Some comments. *American Sociological Review, 42,* 692–704.

Hinde, R. A. (1971). Some problems in the study of development of social behavior. In E. Tobach, Aronson, L. R. Aronson, & E. Shaw (Eds.), *The biopsychology of development* (pp. 411–432). New York: Academic Press.

Hinde, R. A. (1977). On assessing the bases of partner preferences. *Behavior, 62,* 1–9.

Hinde, R. A. (1979). *Towards understanding relationships.* London: Academic Press.

Hodgson, R. C., Levinson, D. J., & Zaleznik, A. (1965). *The Executive Role Constellation.* Boston: Division of Research, Graduate School of Business Administration, Harvard University.

Homans, G. (1950). *The human group.* New York: Harcourt, Brace and World.

Homans, G. (1961). *Social behavior: Its elementary forms.* New York: Harcourt, Brace and World.

Huston, T. L. (1974a). *Foundations of interpersonal attraction.* New York: Academic Press.

Huston, T. L. (1974b). A perspective on interpersonal attraction. In T. L. Huston (Ed.), *Foundations of interpersonal attraction* (pp. 3–28). New York: Academic Press.

Inkson, J. H. K., Schwitter, J. P., & Hickson, D. J. (1970). A comparison of organizations structure and managerial roles: Ohio, U.S.A., and the Midlands, England. *The Journal of Management Studies, 7,* 347–363.

Jacobson, W. D. (1972). *Power and interpersonal relations.* Belmont, CA: Wadsworth.

Jones, E. E., & Archer, R. L. (1976). Are there special effects of personalistic self-disclosure? *Journal of Experimental Social Psychology, 12,* 180–193.

Jones, E. E., & Goethals, G. R. (1972). Order effects in impression formation: Attribution context and the nature of the entity. In E. E. Jones, D. E. Kanouse, H. H. Kelley, R. E. Nisbett, S. Valins, & B. Weiner (Eds.), *Attribution: Perceiving the causes of behavior* (pp. 27–46). Morristown, NJ: General Learning Press.

Jones, E. E., & Gordon, E. M. (1972). Timing of self-disclosure and its effects on personal attraction. *Journal of Personality and Social Psychology, 24,* 358–365.

Jones, E. E., & Thibaut, J. W. (1958). Interaction goals as bases of inference in interpersonal perception. In R. Tagiuri & L. Petrullo (Eds.), *Person perception and interpersonal behavior* (pp. 151–178). Stanford, CA: Stanford University Press.

Jourard, S. M. (1959). Self-disclosure and other cathexis. *Journal of Abnormal and Social Psychology, 59,* 428–431.

Jourard, S. M. (1971). *Self-disclosure: An experimental analysis of the transparent self.* New York: Wiley-Interscience.

Kelvin, P. (1970). *The basis of social behavior: An approach in terms of order and value.* London: Holt, Rinehart & Winston.

Kerckhoff, A. C. (1974). The social context of interpersonal attraction. In T. L. Huston (Ed.), *Foundations of Interpersonal Attraction* (pp. 61–78). New York: Academic Press.

Kerckhoff, A. C., & Davis, K. E. (1962). Value consensus and need complementarity in mate selection. *American Sociological Review, 27,* 295–303.

Klimoski, R. J., & Hayes, N. J. (1980). Leader behavior and subordinate motivation. *Personnel Psychology, 33,* 543–555.

Kotter, J. P. (1982). *The general managers.* New York: Macmillan.

Lawless, D. J. (1972). *Effective management: A social psychological approach.* Englewood Cliffs, NJ: Prentice-Hall.

Lawrence, P. R., & Lorsch, J. W. (1967). *Organization and environment.* Boston: Harvard Business School.

Lecky, P. (1945). *Self-consistency: A theory of personality.* New York: Island Press.

Levinger, G. (1974). A three-level approach to attraction: Toward an understanding of pair relatedness. In T. L. Huston (Ed.), *Foundations of interpersonal attraction* (pp. 99–120). New York: Academic Press.

Levinger, G., & Snoek, J. D. (1972). *Attraction in relationship: A new look at interpersonal attraction.* Morristown, NJ: General Learning Press.

Levinson, H. (1964). *Emotional health in the world of work.* New York: Harper & Row.

Levinson, H. (1968). *The exceptional executive.* Cambridge, MA: Harvard University Press.

Liden, R. C., & Graen, C. (1980). Generalizability of the vertical dyad linkage model of leadership. *Academy of Management Journal, 23,* 451–465.

Lidz, T., Cornelison, A., Fleck, S., & Terry, D. (1957). The intra-familial environment of schizophrenic patients: II. Marital schism and marital skew. *American Journal of Psychiatry, 114,* 241–248.

Lidz, T., & Fleck, S. (1960). Schizophrenia, human integration, and the role of the family. In D. D. Jackson (Ed.), *The etiology of schizophrenia* (pp. 323–345). New York: Basic Books.

Lorsch, J. W., & Allen, S. A. (1973). *Managing diversity and interdependence.* Boston: Harvard Business School.

Lowin, A., & Craig, J. R. (1968). The influence of level of performance on managerial style: An experimental object-lesson in the ambiguity of correlational data. *Organizational Behavior and Human Performance, 3,* 440–458.

McCall, G. J. (1974). A symbolic interactionist approach to attraction. In T. L. Huston (Ed.), *Foundations of interpersonal attraction* (pp. 217–231). New York: Academic Press.

McCaskey, M. B. (1978). Place imagery and nonverbal cues. In A. G. Athos & J. J. Gabarro (Eds.), *Interpersonal behavior: Communication and understanding in relationships.* Englewood Cliffs, NJ: Prentice-Hall.

Mintzberg, H. (1973). *The nature of managerial work.* New York: Harper & Row.

Murstein, B. I. (1977). The stimulus-value-role (SVR) theory of dyadic relationships. In S. Duck (Ed.), *Theory and practice in inter-personal attraction* (pp. 105–127). London: Academic Press.

Newcomb, T. M. (1961). *The acquaintance process.* New York: Holt, Rinehart and Winston.

Posner, B. Z., & Munson, J. M. (1979). The impact of subordinate-supervisor value consensus. *Akron Business and Economic Review, 10,* 37–40.

Ross, J., & Ferris, K. R. (1981). Interpersonal attraction and organizational outcomes: A field examination. *Administrative Science Quarterly, 26,* 617–632.

Rubin, Z. (1975). Disclosing oneself to a stranger: reciprocity and its limits. *Journal of Experimental Social Psychology, 11,* 233–260.

Sathe, V. (1985). *Culture and related corporate realities.* Homewood, IL: Irwin.

Schwarzwald, J., & Goldenberg, J. (1979). Compliance and assistance to an authority figure in perceived equitable or nonequitable situations. *Human Relations, 32,* 877–888.

Scott, C. L., III. (1980). Interpersonal trust: A comparison of attitudinal and situational factors. *Human Relations, 33,* 805–812.

Secord, P. F., & Backman, C. W. (1964). *Social psychology.* New York: McGraw-Hill.

Sgro, J. A., Worchel, P., Pence, E. C., & Orban, J. A. (1980). Perceived leader behavior as a function of the leader's interpersonal trust orientation. *Academy of Management Journal, 23,* 161–165.

Simmel, G. (1950). *The sociology of Georg Simmel* (K. H. Wolff, Trans.). New York: Free Press of Glencoe.

Staw, B. M. (1975). Attribution of the 'causes' of performance: A general alternative interpretation of cross-sectional research on organizations. *Organizational Behavior and Human Performance, 13,* 414–32.

Stewart, R. I. (1967). *Managers and their jobs.* London: Macmillan.

Stewart, R. I. (1982). *Choices for the manager: A guide to managerial work and behavior.* Englewood Cliffs, NJ: Prentice-Hall.

Stieglitz, H. (1969). *The Chief Executive—And His Job,* (Personnel Policy Study No. 214). New York: National Industrial Conference Board.

Stogdill, R. M. (1974). *Handbook of leadership.* New York: Free Press.

Sullivan, H. S. (1953). *The interpersonal theory of psychiatry.* New York: Norton.

Swensen, C. H., Jr. (1973). *Introduction to interpersonal relations.* Glenview, IL: Scott, Foresman.

Tagiuri, R. (1969). Person perception. In G. Lindzey & E. Aronson, (Eds.), *Handbook of social psychology,* Vol. 3, 395–449, Reading, MA: Addison-Wesley.

Tedeschi, J. T. (1974). Attributions, liking, and power. In T. L. Huston (Ed.), *Foundations of interpersonal attraction* (pp. 193–215). New York: Academic Press.

Thibaut, J., & Kelley, H. H. (1959). *The social psychology of groups.* New York: Wiley.

Thomas, R. (1976). Managing the psychological contract. In P. Lawrence, L. Barnes, & J. Lorsch (Eds.), *Organizational behavior and administration* (pp. 465–888). Homewood, IL: Irwin.

Triandis, H. C. (1977). *Interpersonal behavior.* Monterey, CA: Brooks/Cole.

Triandis, H. C., & Davis, E. E. (1965). Race and belief as determinants of behavior intentions. *Journal of Personality and Social Psychology, 2,* 715–725.

Valenzi, E., & Dessler, G. (1978). Relationships of leader behavior, subordinate role ambiguity, and subordinate job satisfaction. *Academy of Management Journal, 21,* 671–678.

Wall, J. A., & Adams, J. S. (1974). Some variables affecting a constituent's evaluations of and behavior toward a boundary-role occupant. *Organizational Behavior and Human Performance, 2,* 290–308.

Walton, R. E. (1968). *Social and psychological aspects of verification, inspection, and international assurance.* Lafayette, IN: Purdue University Press.

Walton, R. E. (1969). *Interpersonal peacemaking: Confrontations and third-party consultation.* Reading, MA: Addison-Wesley.

Weick, K. E. (1969, 1979). *The social psychology of organizing.* (2nd Edition, 1979). Reading, MA: Addison-Wesley.

Weiss, H. M. (1978). Social learning of work values in organizations. *Journal of Psychology, 63,* 711–718.

Wexley, K. N., Alexander, R. A., Greenawalt, J. P., & Couch, M. A. (1980). Attitudinal congruence and similarity as related to interpersonal evaluations in manager-subordinate dyads. *Academy of Management Journal, 23,* 320–330.

Wicker, A. W. (1972). Processes which mediate behavior-environment congruence. *Behavior Science, 17,* 265–277.

Wortman, C. B., & Linsenmeier, J. A. W. (1977). Interpersonal attraction and techniques of ingratiation in organizational settings. In G. Salancik & B. M. Staw (Eds.), *New directions in organizational behavior* (pp. 133–178). Chicago: St. Clair Press.

Wortman, C. B., Adesman, P., Herman, E., & Greensburg, R. (1976). Self-disclosure: An attributional perspective. *Journal of Personality and Social Psychology, 33,* 184–191.

5

Mutual Knowledge and Communicative Effectiveness

Robert M. Krauss
Susan R. Fussell
Columbia University

Abstract

For people to communicate effectively, they must solve the mutual knowledge problem. That is, they must develop some idea of what their communication partners know and don't know in order to formulate what they have to say to them. Speakers come to conclusions about their partners' states of knowledge through a number of mechanisms—by listening to what they themselves have just said, by making inferences about the partners' state of knowledge from their category membership, or by relying on direct and backchannel feedback from their partners. This chapter describes experimental research illustrating these proposition and draws implications from this research for communication technology to support cooperative work.

It is hardly more than a platitude to observe that all cooperative work is mediated by some form of communication, but, platitude or not, there are few situations in which people can work cooperatively without a means of coordinating their efforts. Coordination of effort requires that information be exchanged among the cooperating individuals, and the exchange or transfer of information makes up a large part of what we mean by communication. The explosion in the development of communications technology that has occurred over the last quarter century or so has raised questions about (a) the kinds of information that must be communicated in order that different sorts of work can be accomplished, and (b) the communication modalities that can more or less efficiently transmit these different sorts of information.

This chapter reviews some research on the social psychology of communication, and speculates about its relevance for the study of technology and cooperative work. The focus of the review is what we call the *mutual knowledge problem*. The mutual knowledge problem derives from the assumption that to be understood, speakers must formulate their contributions with an awareness of what their addressee does and does not know. Effective communication, in Roger Brown's (1965) felicitous phrase, "requires that the point of view of the auditor be realistically imagined" (p. 342). Thus, communicating parties are faced continuously with the task of constructing their common cognitive environment—that is, ascertaining and representing the information that they and the other participants can (and will) assume to be known to all.

In this chapter, we review research that examines how communicators deal with some of the consequences of the mutual knowledge problem. Where possible, we try to examine converging lines of evidence, but our review of the literature is selective and speculative. We first attempt to formulate the mutual knowledge problem in a coherent way and set it in a conceptual framework. We then describe the relevant research findings. Finally, we speculate on the ways that various communication technologies might interact with the mutual knowledge problem.

Communication and Mutual Knowledge

For the purposes of this discussion, we regard communication as a process by which knowledge that resides in one or more people comes to be represented in one or more others. Certainly the transfer of knowledge is not the only thing that happens in communication, and for certain purposes it may not be the most useful way of thinking about the process. Below we refer briefly to some other dimensions of communication that may be important for cooperative work. Underlying the knowledge transfer view of communication is the assumption that any communicative act rests on a base of mutual knowledge or, as it is referred to by Clark and his colleagues, "common ground" (Clark & Carlson, 1982; Clark & Marshall, 1981).[1] The two terms will be used interchangeably. Mutual knowledge is knowledge that the communicating parties both share and know they share.[2] It is assumed that

---

[1]We are following the usage of Ekman and Friesen (1975) and distinguishing between acts that are *informative* (i.e., that serve as a basis for some inference about the actor) and those that are *communicative* (i.e., that are intended by the actor to convey information). The distinction gets somewhat fuzzy around the edges, but something like it is necessary when one talks of the role of mutual knowledge in communication. Informative acts do not presume mutual knowledge or, indeed, knowledge of any sort.

[2]As Clark and his colleagues have made clear, the condition of mutual knowledge is considerably more complex than this, at least in its abstract form. Logically, in order for X (some item

we can only tell someone about something he or she does not know by making use of something he or she does know. In the most trivial sense this is obviously true. For the purpose of writing this chapter, we have assumed that the reader either understands English or will have it translated, and that the reader is aware that we have made this assumption. Hence, the body of knowledge that constitutes "the ability to understand English" can be assumed to be mutually known.

But beyond this triviality, we have made a great many other assumptions about what the reader does and does not know, and to a substantial degree our ability to communicate effectively is dependent on the accuracy of these assumptions. For example, the next paragraphs describe referential communication tasks, a technique used in many social psychological studies of communication. We are aware that some of our readers will, but many will not, be familiar with such tasks. The next paragraph, then, reflects our assumption about the distribution of a certain kind of knowledge in the likely readers of this chapter, and represents an effort to ensure that the existence of the common ground on which the subsequent discussion will depend. Among the questions to be addressed are how this accounting is accomplished—how people go about determining, correctly or incorrectly, what is mutually known between them and their conversational partners—and the consequences this has for communication.

Referential Communication Tasks

Now for the adumbrated paragraphs. A great many social psychological studies of communication have employed what has come to be called a "referential communication task," and because the use of such procedures is so pervasive it is appropriate to say a few words about their strengths and limitations. A referential communication task presents communicators with a fairly elementary problem. It requires that one of them formulate a message about something (typically a visual stimulus of some sort) that will enable another person to select that thing from among a set of similar things. The thing that is described or characterized in the message is termed the *referent* and the things from which the referent is distinguished are called the *nonreferents* or the *nonreferent array*. The particular description or characterization of the referent contained in the message is often called the

---

of information) to be "mutually known" by persons A and B, it is necessary but not sufficient that A and B know X. A must also know: that B knows X, that B knows that A knows X, that B knows that A knows that B knows that A knows X, and so forth; and similarly for B. As Clark (1985) pointed out, the form of the problem is an infinite regress and therefore has no solution. Precisely how people deal with this formally unsolvable problem is a matter of some interest. Sperber and Wilson (1986) provided a thoughtful discussion of whether this is in fact a real problem for communicators. We briefly address this issue later.

referring expression. For example, in such a task one person (the "speaker"[3]) might be asked to describe a picture of a face to another person (the "listener") who, having heard the description, would attempt to select that picture from a set of similar pictures.

Reference is a fundamental function of language, and in large part is the ability of language to represent referentially the objects, events, and relations of experience that makes it so powerful a tool in communication. Referential communication tasks attempt to simulate, under controlled circumstances, the process of reference that occurs in natural settings. A very large number of experiments, investigating a wide variety of substantive issues, have been run using variants of this procedure and it would serve no useful purpose to try to review them here, but there are some noteworthy aspects of the procedure.

First, the task permits the investigator to index objectively and quantitatively the adequacy of communication—that is, how well the speaker's communicative intention has been implemented or, if you will, the effectiveness of the communication that has taken place. It is the speaker's goal (by the rules of the experiment) to formulate a referring expression that will allow the listener(s) to distinguish the referent from the nonreferent; the listener's success in doing this is a reasonable way to assess the effectiveness of the communication that has taken place.[4] This is no small thing. When we ask whether people do a better job of communicating face-to-face than over a telephone, or whether having a graphics capability makes remote conferencing more efficient, we are implicitly asking about the effectiveness of communication. The problem is how communicative effectiveness should be assessed. For example, it seems intuitively reasonable to ask someone a question like "How effectively did A communicate his ideas to you?" and such a question, asked under the appropriate circumstances, will elicit a reply, but it's not completely clear how the responses should be interpreted. In general, the literature seems to indicate that the best predictor of how effective or satisfactory communicative interaction will be judged is how much the person judging got to talk. People seem to feel that the most satisfactory or effective interactions are ones in which they talked a lot. However, most of us have found that the correlation between how much people talk and how effectively they communicate is closer to zero than to

---

[3]To facilitate communication, we refer to the individuals who initiate message as "speakers" and "encoders" and to message recipients as "listeners," "hearers," "addressees," and "decoders" regardless of the particular mode of communication in the experiment we are discussing. We also use the term "overhearer" to refer to someone who receives a message intended for someone else, even when those messages are written and delayed in time.

[4]This, of course, assumes that the participants are cooperating with the experimenter, that they understand what they are supposed to do, and so forth. In normal circumstances, these are not unreasonable assumptions.

unity. A referential communication task is not the only way to assess objectively the adequacy of communication, but it is at least one way and it is a way that has been used a lot.[5]

In addition, a referential communication task has the advantage that it constrains what the participants talk about. Unless the participants stray from their assignment, the topical domain is defined by the task, and this allows the investigator to do two things. First, it becomes possible to make comparisons among different communicators without being concerned that observed differences in performance are accounted for simply by differences in what they are talking about. Second, it permits the investigator to vary properties of the referent array in a systematic way, and thus assess effects of "topic" (using the term in this loose sense). We discuss some experiments in which this is done. Finally, the messages generated in referential communication tasks can be removed from their original context and transmitted to parties other than those for whom they were intended, allowing the investigator to assess, for example, the extent to which messages are individuated for their intended recipients, and how such individuation affects their ability to be understood by others.

However, along with these advantages go some significant drawbacks. These grow out of the fact that such tasks are, at best, a model of one kind of communication situation, and results obtained from their use should be generalized to other kinds of situations only with great caution. By their nature, referential communication tasks focus the participants narrowly on the transmission of specific kinds of information, and this heavily constrains what they can do. Typically the participants' speech lacks the texture of conversation, and at times their exchanges take on the mechanical, depersonalized quality of interactions with a directory assistance operator. The interaction of experimental subjects is socially situated in a curious institution called "the psychological experiment." Like all social situations, this one has its own rules, and the rules may not be the same as the ones that apply in other situations. A Martian observing the behavior of subjects in a referential communication task, and believing it to be typical of human communicative exchanges, would probably conclude that human communication is a one-sided, mechanical process, lacking affect, variety, playfulness, or conflict. Indeed, some of the very qualities that make linguistic communication the versatile and effective tool that it is (i.e., the subtle, flexible and creative ways in which language can be employed) are effectively disabled by the nature of the task.

Although not all that we know about the relation of mutual knowledge to communicative effectiveness is based on research using referential commu-

---

[5]We discuss some experiments that use other techniques to determine the effectiveness of communication.

nication tasks, a good deal of it is, and when thinking about the results of these studies, it probably is a good idea to keep clearly in mind the limitations of this method.

Mechanisms in the Establishment of Mutual Knowledge

We argue that there are three interrelated sets of mechanisms that communicators employ to establish the condition of mutual knowledge in their interactions.[6]

Direct Knowledge

The first set of mechanisms depends on personal knowledge of other individuals, more specifically knowledge of what particular other people know. So if you told a friend that you had seen the movie *Fatal Attraction* and were scared out of your wits by it, this information could be considered to be common ground between you and your friend. Of course, it is not necessary to say something in order for it to be mutually known. If you and your friend were physically copresent at some event (and mutually know this), you could assume that the salient aspects of that event were also part of your common ground.[7]

Direct knowledge, especially of habitual behaviors, often makes it possible for the speaker to extrapolate from what is directly known to draw inferences about what has a high probability of being known. Given that you and a colleague mutually know that you both read the *Wall Street Journal* every morning, and the fact that a story on the XYZ company (in which you both have a special interest) was prominently featured on the front page of the *Journal* that morning, the story's contents can be assumed to be mutually known without direct knowledge. Similarly, a dedicated Yankee fan can begin a conversation with another fan by saying "What are we going to do about George?" secure in the knowledge that his partner will be able to locate the particular incident (e.g., firing the manager, publicly criticizing a player, etc.) that constitutes the appropriate interpretive context for his remark about the team's owner.

---

[6]This account is based largely on the theoretical argument of Clark and Marshall (1981), although we have partitioned the variables somewhat differently.

[7]Two people are mutually copresent if they mutually know that they both were there—that is, each both knows that the other was there and knows that the other knows that, and so forth. Obviously not all aspects of an event at which two people were copresent can reasonably be assumed to be mutually known, only those that are above some threshold of saliency.

Category Membership

A second set of mechanisms derives from the fact that individuals can often be assigned to social categories, and such category membership often predicts individual knowledge. So, for example, it is reasonable to assume that a person belonging to the occupational category "New York City taxi driver" knows that with a few exceptions, the even-numbered streets in Manhattan are one-way eastbound and the odd-numbered streets are one-way westbound. Similarly, it is reasonable to assume that a person belonging to the category "average, normal American teenager" knows that "Dead Kennedys" refers not to a former president and attorney-general who were brothers, but to a now-defunct punk rock group. Of course, category membership is not a perfect predictor of knowledge. Doubtless there are some teenagers who have no idea who the "Dead Kennedys" are, and with increasing frequency one encounters New York taxi drivers whose knowledge of local geography barely goes beyond "the Bronx is up and the Battery's down." Nevertheless, group or category membership is often a very good indicator of what, at a minimum, an individual can be expected to know.

Interactional Dynamics

A third set of mechanisms for ascertaining common ground grows out of the dynamics of the interaction process itself. One way of characterizing this is in terms of what Clark and Marshall (1981) called the "linguistic copresence heuristic." In the course of a conversation, anything said at time T can be assumed to be mutually known at time $T + 1$.[8] In this way, individual knowledge is transformed incrementally into mutual knowledge. But the linguistic copresence heuristic, applied in so bald and mechanistic a fashion, fails to capture the flexibility and richness of human communication that accounts for much of its effectiveness. It portrays the process as one in which participants alternate in producing discrete messages, interacting in much the same way as parties using e-mail. Conversation (and similar interactive forms) permits communicators to formulate messages that are tightly linked to the immediate knowledge and perspectives of the individual participants, because it affords the participants moment-to-moment information on each others' understanding.

One of the devices by which this is accomplished is what Yngve (1970) and others called messages transmitted in the back channel. The brief vo-

---

[8]As with the other heuristics described by Clark, some measure of qualification is in order. Surely it is not the case that one expects his conversational partner to remember everything that was said in the course of a long conversation, but just how to characterize in a formal way what is and is not reasonable to expect another to remember is not a simple job.

calizations, head nods and shakes, facial expressions, and so forth, produced by the participant who at that moment is nominally in the role of listener, are a rich source of information about the state of the common ground. Such information permits the formulation of messages that are extremely efficient because they are based on a reasonably precise assessment of the hearer's current knowledge and understanding. There is a fair amount of research that goes to this point, some of which is reviewed later.

LISTENER EFFECTS
ON MESSAGE FORMULATION

What evidence is there to indicate that communicators do indeed take the informational status of a listener into account when they formulate messages? We have done several studies that speak to this point.

Self Versus Others

Perhaps the simplest sort of distinction in informational status that one can make is between oneself and others. Although it seems obvious that not everything we know is familiar to others, the speech of young children does not consistently take this into account (Glucksberg, Krauss, & Weisberg, 1966; Krauss & Glucksberg, 1969). An experiment by Krauss, Vivekenanathan, and Weinheimer (1968) investigated whether people formulated different messages depending on whether they themselves or another person were the intended recipient. Underlying the experiment were two assumptions: First, because not everything one knows can be assumed to be mutually known by some other person, messages formulated for the self should be different from those formulated for others. Second, the smaller amount of common ground one shares with another person should be reflected in the effectiveness of communication. In the experiment, undergraduate women were asked to name each of a set of 24 colors under one of two conditions. Half of our subjects were asked to give each color a name that would enable the subject herself at some later time to select the named color from a large array of colors. We called this the nonsocial naming condition. The remainder of our subjects were instructed to give each color a name that would enable some other female undergraduate to select the named color. We called this the social naming condition. Then, about 2 weeks later, all subjects returned to the laboratory, and tried to match each of a large number of color names to the color that had elicited it. One-third of the names were those the subject had given herself 2 weeks earlier; we call these *own names.* Another third were *social names*—that is, those of another subject from the social naming condition. The remaining third were *nonsocial names*—those of another subject from the nonsocial naming condition.

The results of the experiment are shown as the bars on the left side of Fig. 5.1. We take as our criterion of communication effectiveness the accuracy with which a message permits a receiver to select the designated color. It becomes evident that the most effective messages were those whose source was the subject herself. However, among those messages whose source was another person, those intended for another person (i.e., produced in the social naming condition) communicated more effectively than those intended for the source herself (i.e., produced in the nonsocial naming condition). In formulating messages for themselves, our subjects were able to exploit the extensive common ground available, to employ arcane or idiosyncratic knowledge that one could not reasonably assume another person would have available. For example, they likened the stimulus colors to the color of objects familiar to them—the paint in a particular room, or an automobile seatcover. However, subjects whose task it was to formulate messages for others could not employ this strategy, and were forced to rely on the standard English color lexicon or to refer to the colors of commonly known objects.

Despite the fact that the experiment yielded informative results, it seems clear in retrospect that colors are not the best kind of stimulus material to use in this sort of experiment. As in many languages, English has a rich and highly differentiated lexicon of color terms. By combining terms and using standard

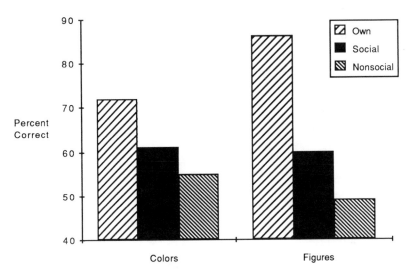

FIG. 5.1. Recognition accuracy based on Own, Social, and Nonsocial messages. (Data from Krauss, Vivekananathan & Weinheimer, 1968; Fussell & Krauss, 1989.)

modifiers like *light, dark, bright,* and so forth a communicator has available a broad range of conventional referring expressions. Much of this conventional lexicon is in common ground. Hence, the need to invent expressions is small, and we would expect this to minimize differences in recognition accuracy.

Recently, we replicated this experiment (Fussell & Krauss, 1989) using as stimuli drawings of nonsense figures; some examples are shown in Fig. 5.2. Unlike colors, these stimuli have no well-established conventionalized names and, for this reason, require that communicators closely monitor the common ground they share with the message recipient. This has important consequences for both the form of messages and the adequacy of communication. We used the same procedure as in the previous study, with only two changes: we substituted a set of 30 nonsense figures for the colors, and we used both males and females as subjects.

As the bars on the right side of Fig. 5.1 indicate, we reproduced the overall results of the previous experiment: Communication is most accurate when sender and receiver are the same person. When the source is someone else, communication is significantly more accurate if the message was originally intended for another person (the social condition) rather than the sender him- or herself (the nonsocial condition). But as we anticipated, the differences among the three conditions are greater for the figures than for the colors. As the histogram shows, with one's own names, identification accuracy is higher for the nonsense figures than it was for the colors (about 86% versus 74%, respectively). However, it is not simply the case that figures are easier to encode than colors. With another person's messages, accuracy is lower for figures than for colors (about 50% versus 57%).

A lexical analysis of messages in the two conditions yields some insight into the differences in language responsible for the differences in recognition accuracy. Nonsocial messages were less than half as long as social messages, and they were considerably less stereotyped and more diverse

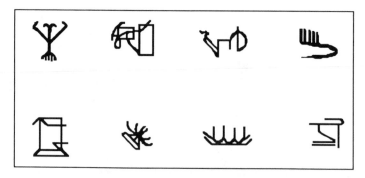

Fig. 5.2. Some of the "nonsense figures" used as stimuli.

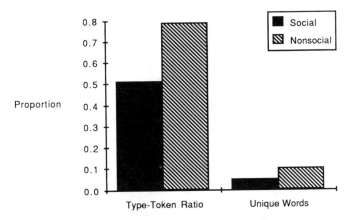

FIG. 5.3. Lexical properties of Social and Nonsocial messages. (Data from Fussell & Krauss, 1989.)

lexically. For each subject, we computed two indices of lexical diversity: (a) *Type–Token Ratio* (TTR)—the ratio of the number of different words used in a speaker's messages (types) to the total number of words (tokens). The higher the TTR, the greater the lexical diversity of the speaker's messages; (b) *Unique Words*—the proportion of words in a subject's messages that were not found in any other subjects' messages. Figure 5.3 shows the results of this analysis. On both the TTR and the unique words measures, nonsocial messages were significantly more diverse than social messages.

We hypothesized that these lexical differences resulted from different strategies adopted by senders in the two conditions. There appeared to be three strategies our describers used in characterizing the nonsense figure stimuli. One was to describe them analytically, in terms of their geometric elements—as a collection of lines, arcs, angles, and so forth. A second is to describe them in terms of the objects or images they suggest—for example, a "Picasso nude" or a "skinny crayfish." We termed the former type of characterization a *literal description,* and the latter kind a *figurative description.* A third strategy, which seemed neither literal nor figurative, was to characterize a figure in terms of a familiar symbol—specifically a number or letter of the alphabet. We called this a *symbol description.*[9] We coded each of our describers' messages for the type of description it contained.

As one would expect, figurative messages tended to be shorter than literal

---

[9]The symbol descriptions were quite diverse in form, and probably do not represent a distinctive naming strategy. Some were holistic ("capital G" to describe a whole figure), whereas others were rather analytic ("E, backward 4, and angle"). The symbol description category reduces the heterogeneity of the other two categories.

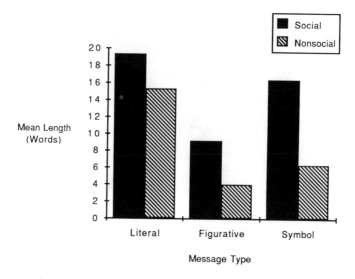

FIG. 5.4.   Mean description length by message type and describing condition. (Data from Fussell & Krauss, 1989.)

ones—it takes fewer words to say what something looks like than to list its geometrical elements and describe their spatial arrangement—and this was true for both social and nonsocial describers. As Fig. 5.4 shows, symbol descriptions, which contain both literal and figurative elements, fell midway in length between those two types of messages. We would expect social describers to use more literal descriptions than nonsocial describers, because one can reasonably assume the geometric elements that make up a literal description to be familiar to virtually all college students, and hence part of common ground. Figurative descriptions, however, can be more problematic. If the addressee is unfamiliar with the object the stimulus is being likened to, or cannot see how the figure resembles it, communication will fail. Figurative descriptions are efficient where common ground exists, but if one cannot be sure that it does, it is safer to employ the literal description strategy. As Fig. 5.5 reveals, the preponderance of our describers' messages are figurative. However, social describers produce more literal descriptions and fewer figurative descriptions than nonsocial describers. The proportion of symbol descriptions is just about identical in the two conditions.

In order to examine the relationship between common ground and communicative effectiveness, we categorized each figurative description in terms of the primary concept or image it employed,[10] and then divided our

---

[10]Typically this was the head noun. For descriptions that used two equally weighted nouns, the first noun was taken as primary.

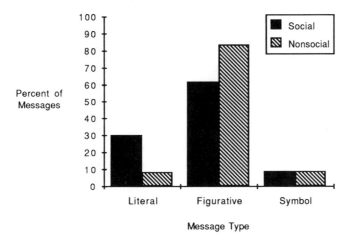

FIG. 5.5.   Proportion of literal, figurative and symbol-based descriptions in the two describing conditions. (Data from Fussell & Krauss, 1989.)

messages into those in which the primary concept was *shared* (i.e., occurred in seven or more descriptions of a given stimulus) and those in which it was *idiosyncratic* (i.e., occurred in fewer than seven descriptions). We then examined the relationship between message type and communication effectiveness, with the figurative descriptions divided into those whose primary concept was shared or idiosyncratic. As Fig. 5.6 shows, subjects using their own descriptions were about equally accurate regardless of the type of

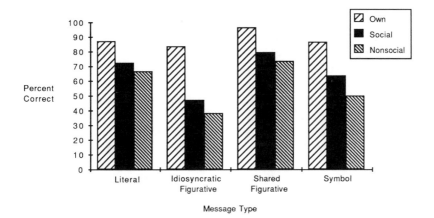

FIG. 5.6.   Percent of correct identifications from Self, Other-Social and Other-Nonsocial messages for four message types. (Data from Fussell & Krauss, 1989.)

message it was.[11] However, accuracy of performance using the descriptions of others did depend on message type. Subjects were most accurate using literal descriptions, next most accurate with figurative descriptions (with the shared and idiosyncratic categories combined), and least accurate with symbol descriptions. But for figurative messages, the accuracy resulting from shared and idiosyncratic descriptions differs markedly. Shared-figurative descriptions are about as good as literal descriptions, whereas the idiosyncratic-figurative descriptions are considerably worse. Note also that the shared-figurative descriptions generated in the nonsocial naming conditions elicit the same percentage of correct identifications as those generated in the social naming condition.

Friends versus Strangers

The distinction between self and other is rather a rudimentary one (although George Herbert Mead contended that it is the distinction on which all further differentiations of the social world are based), but can it be shown that we differentiate between message recipients when one them is not ourselves? Using the same experimental paradigm, we recruited pairs of subjects who identified themselves as friends (Fussell & Krauss, in press). Then we had each label the nonsense figures so that his or her friend could identify them. A couple of weeks later, we had all our subjects return and try to identify the nonsense figures on the basis of three types of names: the names that the subject him- or herself had generated (we call these *own names*), the names the subject's friend had generated (we call these *friend's names*), and the names that a randomly selected other subject had generated for his or her friend (*stranger's names*). As Fig. 5.7 illustrates, the three types of names produced differences in how accurately a receiver could identify the nonsense figures. As in the previous experiments, subjects were most accurate using names they themselves had generated. But, using names formulated by some other person, they were more accurate using names formulated specifically for them (i.e., *friend's names*) than they were using names formulated for some other person (i.e., *stranger's names*). Although the margin of difference between the friend's and stranger's names conditions is small— only about 5% —it is reliable statistically.

These results provide stronger support for the common ground hypothesis than the relatively narrow margin of difference between the friend and stranger conditions would lead one to conclude, because the experimental situation was one that would minimize the likelihood of finding such differences. Our subject population was quite homogeneous and shared considerable background knowledge; all were undergraduates enrolled in the

---

[11]This was true for describers in both in the social and nonsocial describing condition.

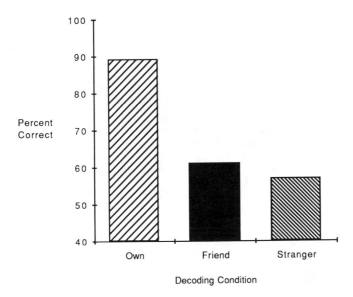

FIG. 5.7. Identification accuracy for Own, Friend's, and Stranger's names. (Data from Fussell & Krauss, in press.)

same introductory psychology course. Theoretically, the common ground between two randomly selected subjects would be considerable. In addition, most of the friendships in our study were of quite recent vintage and relatively superficial; some of our subjects did not even know their "friend's" last name. Few of our pairs were true intimates. That we should have found any differences under such unfavorable circumstances suggests that our subjects were quite skillful in exploiting the common ground that existed between themselves and their addressee. In an experiment in which subjects knew each others really well (for example, married couples) or in which there was substantial diversity in background knowledge (for example, subjects from different cultural backgrounds), we would expect to find considerably larger differences.

In our experiment, subjects could infer the addressee's knowledge from their shared memberships in the Columbia student community, the population of 18–21 year olds, American society, and so forth. They did not need to rely heavily on their private common ground (i.e., knowledge that was both mutually known and exclusive to this pair), and many probably did not. This may be the reason that messages for friends are so similar to those for "another student," and also why the difference in identification accuracy between friends' and strangers' messages is relatively small. In situations that accentuate privately shared knowledge and/or restrict the use of community common ground, messages for a friend should be much better understood by

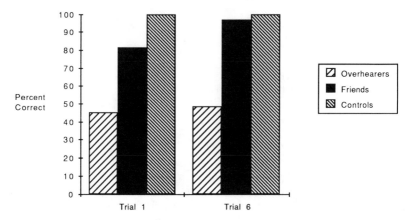

FIG. 5.8. Accuracy of Friends, Overhearers, and Controls. (Data from Clark & Schaefer, 1987.)

that friend than by others. Clark and Schaefer (1987) demonstrated this, using an interactive (conversational) version of the referential communication task in which one member of a pair of student friends tried to refer to a series of pictures of campus scenes in such a way that their friend could identify the correct pictures, but another student overhearing the description could not. As Clark and Schaefer noted, this task should be impossible for unacquainted pairs of students. Their results are summarized in Fig. 5.8. Friends' accuracy is high relative to that of overhearers, and the accuracy of the latter group does not improve appreciably over six trials. Presumably the overhearers' failure to show improvement is a consequence of their inability to build up common ground with the speaker.

The results demonstrate that subjects are able to distinguish between private and community-wide knowledge, although with less-than-perfect success, because overhearers could interpret almost half of the messages.[12] The results also shed some light on the contents of privately shared common ground. The kind of knowledge subjects used to construct their messages concerned events at which both were present, their habitual activities, similarities between depicted items and other mutually known things, and mutually known locations. Nevertheless, it was more difficult to construct messages based solely on private knowledge than to use the shared lexical terms for the depicted entities that are common ground in that community. Subjects run in a control condition, in which content did not have to be

---

[12]It may also have been the case that subjects were aware their messages utilized community-wide knowledge but were unable to think of knowledge shared with their friend that would have helped him or her locate the referent.

hidden from the overhearer, identified the correct pictures with virtually perfect accuracy from the very first trial.

Common Ground and Category Membership

In communicating with friends, we are likely to have direct and detailed knowledge of the information we share with our intended recipient. But frequently we communicate with individuals whom we have never met before, and about whom we know only that they are members of certain communities or social categories. Is there any evidence that senders make differentiations among receivers when all they have available is knowledge of the recipient's community membership? A study by Douglas Kingsbury (1968) suggests that they do. Kingsbury stopped randomly selected male pedestrians in downtown Boston and asked for directions to Jordan Marsh, a well-known local department store about six blocks away. To a third of the people he stopped he said "Can you tell me how to get to Jordan Marsh?" To another third, he prefaced his question with "I'm from out of town." To the remaining third, he asked the unprefaced question, but employed what he called a rural Missouri accent. He covertly tape-recorded their responses.

Kingsbury transcribed these responses and performed a variety of analyses on them. We discuss only two: the two number of words in the respondent's directions, and the number of places enroute to the destination referred to by the respondent. As is shown in Fig. 5.9, when Kingsbury prefaced his question with "I'm from out of town," he received longer and more detailed responses than he did to the unprefaced question. In a sense, this is not particularly surprising. By the maxim of relevance, when Kingsbury prefaced his question by stating that he was from out of town, he was implicitly indicating something about the information he lacked.[13] It is more surprising that the rural Missouri accent—exotic even in cosmopolitan Boston—produced results quite similar to the explicit statement. It seems reasonable to assume that respondents assigned the questioner to a category of persons who lack certain kinds of local information, and they inferred this from his speech.

The results of Kingsbury's field experiment, and a laboratory study by Isaacs and Clark (1987) to be discussed later, suggest that speakers make inferences about what their addressees are likely to know from the social categories to which they belong. But we are a long way from understanding in detail how this process works. Just how does a speaker who believes or suspects that an addressee is a member of a particular social category establish the boundaries of that person's category-related knowledge? It seems reasonable to expect a member of the category "New Yorker" to know

---

[13]For example, one would not say, "I'm from out of town. Can you tell me the time?"

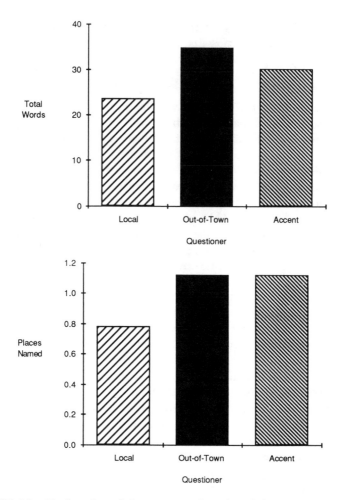

FIG. 5.9.   Number of words in response and number of places named as a function of questioner condition. (Data from Kingsbury, 1968.)

the location of such landmarks as the Empire State Building or St. Patrick's Cathedral, and less reasonable to expect that person to be familiar with such arcanae as the Woolworth Building or the Museum of Colored Glass and Light. But it is not clear how these expectations are formed.

There is, by now, an extensive social psychological literature on the process by which perceivers make attributions about the predispositions of others based on behavioral or categorical information (see, for example, Cantor, Mischel, & Schwartz, 1981; Hastie, 1982; Markus & Zajonc, 1985; Taylor & Crocker, 1981), but this research has been concerned almost exclusively with predispositions that derive from motivational state or personality type. Still, whereas people may infer from the fact that someone is a librarian that he or she is likely to be introverted (Snyder & Cantor, 1979), this certainly does not exhaust the inferences that can be drawn from this bit of categorical information. Librarians can reliably be assumed to know certain things that nonlibrarians may or may not know, and certainly communicators utilize such assumptions when they formulate messages. In research currently underway, we are investigating the ways speakers utilize categorical information about their addressees in formulating messages.

THE COORDINATION OF MEANING

Most of the research discussed thus far has not involved interaction between speaker and addressee.[14] The methodological reasons for doing this are probably obvious, but it is a mistake to assume that a static simulation can capture the essential character of interactive phenomena. We can write letters that will communicate to their addressees and prepare talks that we later deliver to audiences at scientific meetings, but such messages are different in significant ways from those we transmit in conversation.[15]

The messages transmitted in conversation—or utterances, as we are more accustomed to calling them—differ from the kinds of messages subjects formulate in our static simulations in a variety of ways. First, the addressee can participate in the formulation of an utterance in a way that the target of the communication in a static simulation cannot. In the latter situation, the addressee does contribute to the formulation of the message to the extent that his or her characteristics help define the common ground on which the message rests. Even if the target is some vague other person, the speaker must make some assumptions about what he or she knows. The assumption may be quite general (e.g., that the recipient will know the referent of the word

---

[14]Even in the Kingsbury study, the interactive component was negligible. The questioner's behavior was programmed as much as possible to keep conditions constant across subjects.

[15]The mutual knowledge problem, as posed by Clark and Marshall, may be more a logical than a practical problem for communicators in face-to-face interaction. Sperber and Wilson (1986) argued that the establishment of common ground is neither necessary for communication, nor practically feasible. Mutual knowledge is a necessary condition for communication only if we demand that communication be error free—that the meaning the listener comprehends is precisely the one the speaker intended. Certainly there are circumstances in which the parties will strive to achieve this, and on such occasions they will go to great lengths to establish what is mutually known. As the current (as of the time of this writing) Senate debate on the ratification of the SALT Treaty demonstrates, complete mutual understanding is difficult to achieve, even by professionals skilled in the language of diplomacy. But in most everyday communication situations, such precision is unnecessary. The consequences of misunderstanding are minor, and the dynamics of conversation provide a mechanism by which important misunderstandings can be detected and repaired.

indigo or will not know what an inductorium looks like), but without some such assumptions the speaker would have no reason for differentiating between messages for his or her own use and message directed at another person. In conversation, however, the addressee is free to respond directly—to ask questions, to paraphrase, to seek clarification.[16] Moreover, work by Kraut and his colleagues (discussed later) and Duncan and Fiske (1977) suggests that people routinely utilize a signalling system in face-to-face interaction whose function it is to make sure the interacting parties are coordinated with respect to meaning. In such situations the meaning of an utterance seems more akin to something that is arrived at collaboratively by the participants, rather than a property of messages that is encoded by the speaker and decoded by the listener (Clark & Wilkes-Gibbs, 1986; Krauss, 1986, 1987).

The Evolution of Referring Expressions

An examination of the development of referring expressions yields some insight into the process by which participants collaborate in the formulation of meaning. Frequently we need to refer to something lacking a name or whose name we do not know. For example, one of us recently went to a local hardware store and asked for "one of those things with springs at both ends that keeps the roll of toilet paper from falling out of the holder." When the clerk returned with the object he had requested, out of curiosity he asked what the thing was actually called. She replied, "We just call it the thing with springs at both ends that keeps the roll of paper from falling out of the holder."[17] Although this referring expression will get you the object you want, it is unlikely that so unwieldy a name would be used for anything that was referred to frequently. As Zipf (1935) demonstrated, in languages there is a systematic negative relationship between the frequency with which a word is used and its length. The process appears to be a dynamic one. Lengthy terms that enter the language and then achieve currency are shortened to a more manageable length. Thus photographers call *hypothiosulfate of soda solution* "hypo," *random access memory* is referred to as "RAM" by computerists, and on rainy nights we stand on street corners and vainly try to find a "taxi," not a *taximeter cabriolet.*

---

[16]Such referential strategies as try-markers—combining a declarative utterance with a rising intonation to signal that the addressee may be unfamiliar with the thing being referred to (Sacks & Schegloff, 1979)—require feedback from the listener, and thus are restricted to interactional contexts. These forms of reference are reviewed by Clark and Wilkes-Gibbs (1986).

[17]One of us has made a modest and unsystematic effort to learn the name for this object, without success. Most of the people queried say that the thing has a name and that they once knew it, but are unable to think of it at the moment.

The process by which descriptions of innominate objects are transformed into referring expressions illustrates some of the dynamic factors involved in the development of common ground (Carroll, 1985). Imagine that two people have to communicate on a series of occasions about nonsense figures that have no names and do not bear a close resemblance to anything in particular. Typically, on successive references, a name for the nonsense figure evolves in a reasonably orderly way. The process is illustrated in Fig. 5.10. On their first reference to one of these stimuli, most people use a long and rather unwieldy referring expression that is more like a description than a name. But over the course of successive references, typically this phrase is shortened to one or two words. Often the referring expression that the pair finally settles on is not one that, by itself, would evoke the stimulus. Its use presumes the mutual knowledge that has accrued over the course of its development. In the example shown in Fig. 5.10, it is unlikely that *Martini,* by itself, would direct an uninitiated listener to the correct figure. Similarly, few people who try to hail taxis are aware that the term they use derives etymologically not from the vehicle but from the meter that calculates the cost of the trip by measuring the distance traversed.

It was our hypothesis (Krauss & Weinheimer, 1964) that this process of shortening was heavily dependent on back-channel responses transmitted by the receiver. Without the information contained in such responses, we speculated, a sender could not confidently assume the receiver would be able to understand the message and, in order to prevent errors, would maintain a relatively high level of redundancy. In effect, the back channel

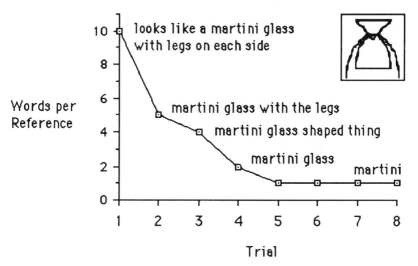

FIG. 5.10.   Illustration of shortening of referring expression over successive references.

responses serve to establish what is and is not in common ground. If our hypothesis was correct, then reducing the amount of back-channel information should affect the rate at which the sender shortens the referring expressions for the nonsense figures. We designed an experiment in which we could compare the performance of dyads using bidirectional circuits (on which the receiver as well as the sender could transmit) with dyads using unidirectional circuits (on which only the sender could transmit). Curves representing the average number of words in the first, second, and subsequent references to the figures in the two experimental conditions are shown in Fig. 5.11. Preventing the sender from receiving back-channel responses produced a flatter curve, compared with the situation in which such responses were available to the sender (Krauss & Weinheimer, 1966). That is, in the absence of back-channel responses, the names used to refer to the stimuli were shortened at a much slower rate.

It is not necessary to eliminate back channels entirely in order to demonstrate the extent of communicators' dependence on them for formulating efficient referring expressions. A similar, albeit somewhat less dramatic, result can be achieved simply by inserting a delay loop in the circuit, and thereby temporally displacing the back-channel response. We used three delay intervals: zero delay, 0.6 second delay, and 1.6 second delay. As Fig. 5.12 shows, a delay of 1.6 seconds is sufficient to disrupt the ability of the sender to refer efficiently to the strange stimuli, despite the fact that the back-channel response is eventually transmitted (Krauss & Bricker, 1966). Something very much like this condition is familiar to most of us. Satellite circuits often involve appreciable propagation times experienced by the user as transmission delay. Many people find talking on such circuits frus-

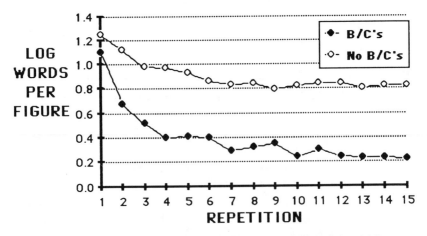

FIG. 5.11.   Changes in length of referring expression as function of availability of back-channel responses. (From Krauss & Weinheimer, 1966.)

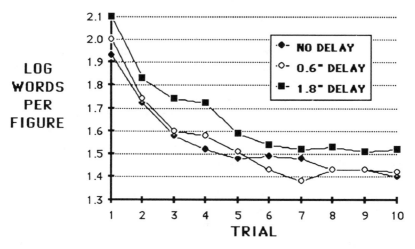

LOG
WORDS
PER
FIGURE

FIG. 5.12.   Change in length of referring expression as function of delay interval. (From Krauss & Bricker, 1967.)

trating and feel the delay affects the quality of their communication, although we know of no research to this point.

Of course, in everyday face-to-face communication, a variety of visible signals also convey back-channel information—smiles, head shakes and nods, and the like. Visible back channels can compensate for the absence of vocal information (Krauss, Garlock, Bricker & McMahon, 1977). With visible information available, the effect of delayed transmission of verbal information is completely mitigated.

It seems clear that a speaker's ability to formulate efficient messages is critically dependent on information about the receiver's understanding. In the absence of such information, the sender cannot confidently assume that the message is being correctly understood and, in an apparent effort to avoid misunderstanding, transmits messages that are highly redundant. The process is so dependent on this information that displacing the back-channel response by a brief interval of time is sufficient to produce a measurable effect.

Expertise and the Development of Mutual Knowledge

In our experiments, subjects typically are equally knowledgeable (or equally ignorant) about the topical domain that is the focus of their interaction—that is, the nonsense figures. In real-life interactions, however, it is more often the case that participants know different amounts about the topic under discussion, and this fact must be taken into account as they formulate their contributions. Isaacs and Clark (1987) simulated this process with a referential communication task in which picture postcards of New York City land-marks were used as stimuli. By varying whether describer and listener were very familiar with New York (experts) or were unfamiliar with it (novices), Isaacs and Clark could examine how the participants adjusted to their partners' knowledge state. As shown in Fig. 5.13, the general shape of the curves for the number of words used to describe the postcards over trials looks remarkably similar to those obtained for subjects describing nonsense figures: lengthy initial descriptions are shortened over the course of suc-cessive references. But the curves' intercepts were a function of the novice–expert status of the dyad. Experts describing to experts consistently used the briefest referring expressions and, overall, novices communicating to novices used the longest. The two other kinds of dyads (expert to novice and novice to expert) fell between these extremes.

Examination of the strategies communicators used gives further insight into the process by which each participant adjusted to his or her partner's knowledge state. Isaacs and Clark (1987) classified the communications into those that used proper names to refer to the landmarks, those that referred by describing the landmarks, and those that combined names and descriptions. As Fig. 5.14 indicates, proper names were used by describers in expert–expert dyads at a consistently high rate across the six trials, whereas the rate for novice–novice dyads was quite low. Conversely, the rate of descriptions is high for dyads in which both participants are novices and low for those in which both are experts. This is not entirely surprising. If both participants have the requisite expertise, it is both simpler and more

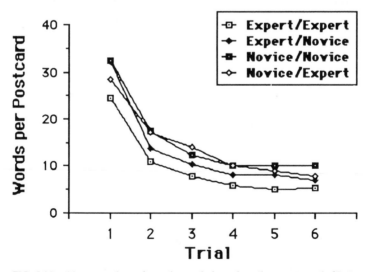

FIG. 5.13.   Mean number of words needed to describe a postcard. (Esti-mated from Isaacs & Clark, 1987.)

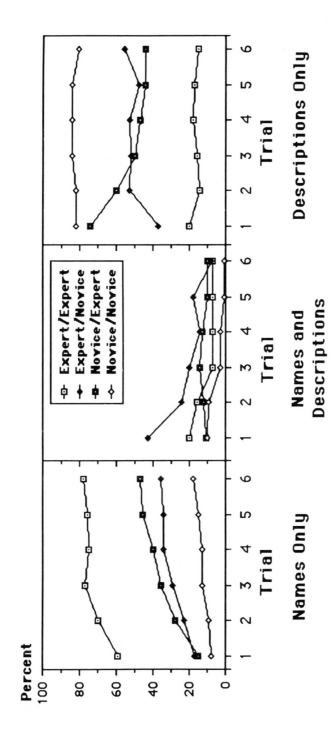

FIG. 5.14. Percent of references by Name Only, Name and Description, and Description Only in the four dyad types. (Data from Isaacs & Clark, 1987.)

reliable to designate a landmark by its name ("Washington Square Park" "World Trade Center") than to try to describe it in a way that would differentiate it from other possible candidates; members of novice–novice dyads are considerably less likely to know the proper names of the landmarks. When a novice is paired with an expert, the strategy that is employed appears to depend on who is in which role. Initially in both novice-to-expert and expert-to-novice dyads relatively few references that consist exclusively of names are used, but experts communicating to novices tend initially to use a relatively high proportion of references that combine names and descriptions and a relatively low proportion of references that are descriptions only. In contrast, novice to expert dyads initially rely mainly on descriptions. What is happening is easier to see in Fig. 5.15, which plots the frequency of all references in which names are used, combining the names only and the names and descriptions. A naming strategy initially is predominant in expert-to-novice dyads, but declines over successive trials. On the other hand, in novice-to-expert dyads a describing strategy is initially employed, but over successive reference use of the naming strategy increases, presumably reflecting the tutelage of the expert addressee. At least in this situation, the process seems to be shaped to a greater extent by the knowledge state of the addressee than of the speaker. Subjects did not know their partner's knowledge state before they began interacting, and according to Isaacs and Clark relatively few specifically announced whether or not they were familiar with New York, so this information had to be inferred from the others' responses. Nevertheless, it appears that relatively little in the way of response was necessary to allow speakers to reach a conclusion about their partners' familiarity with New York City.

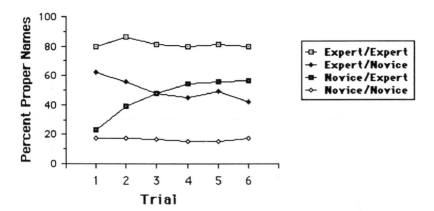

FIG. 5.15. Percentage of descriptions using a proper name on the first postcard. (Data from Isaacs & Clark, 1987.)

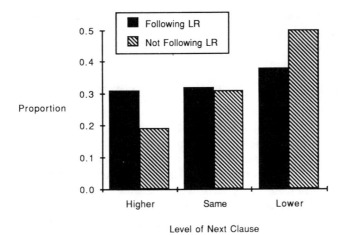

FIG. 5.16.   Relation of clause's level to the level of the preceding clause for clauses that did or did not follow a listener response (LR). (Data from Kraut & Lewis, 1982.)

Effects of Listener Responses on Semantic Content

Kraut and his associates examined in greater detail some of the mechanisms by which listener responses affect the semantic content of a speaker's messages. Their work has the additional advantage of having employed an experimental situation that is more similar to natural conversation than the referential communication tasks used in the work discussed previously. In one study, Kraut and Lewis (1982) examined how back-channel responses affected the hierarchical relations of successive clauses in the speech of people responding to questions about their personal history and opinions. Using a scheme based on Grimes' (1975) analysis of rhetorical predicates, they classified each clause in terms of whether it was at a higher, lower, or the same level as the preceding clause. Their results are summarized in Fig. 5.16. Clauses that followed a listener response were more likely to be at a higher level than the preceding clause, compared to clauses that did not. Conversely, clauses that did not follow a listener response were more likely to be at a lower level than the preceding clause, compared to clauses that did not.

In a second study, Kraut, Lewis, and Swezey (1982) had speakers relate the plot of a cowboy movie they had just seen to a listener, who then took a set of objective tests to determine the extent of his or her knowledge of the movie. Listeners were allowed to respond in a normal fashion to the speaker, but for each listener there was a yoked control (an "eavesdropper") who heard everything the speaker said but was unable to interact with him or her. On a variety of measures it was shown that a listener's knowledge of the movie's plot was superior to that of the eavesdropper, despite the fact that both had access to the same information.

Modality Effects on Communication Effectiveness

From the proceeding it would seem reasonable to assume that the more information the communicating parties have access to, the more effective their communication will be. Plausible as that conclusion may seem, it does not appear to be generally true. For example, other things being equal one might expect messages that conveyed visual as well as verbal information would communicate more effectively than messages that conveyed only verbal information. However, the literature provides little support for such an expectation. In an extensive review, Short, Williams, and Christie (1976) found very few studies that reported differences of any kind between communication using channels carrying only vocal information and communication using audio-visual channels (see also Williams, 1977). As surprising as it may seem, the differences that are found are not always in the direction one would expect.

As part of a study that is still in progress, speakers were videotaped describing nonsense figures like those in Fig. 5.2 either face-to-face to listeners seated across a table from them or over an intercom to listeners located in another room. These descriptions were then played, either in a normal picture plus sound (audio-video) version, or a sound-only (audio-only) version, to a new set of listeners who tried to identify the figures being described. Not surprisingly, the availability of visual information made little difference in terms of listeners' accuracy for Intercom describers. Given that their listeners couldn't see them, speakers sensibly encoded the necessary information verbally. More surprising is the fact that the availability of visual information was no more helpful for Face-to-Face decoders, and that overall, the performance of our Face-to-Face describers was slightly less good than that of the Intercom describers. The data is shown in Fig. 5.17. Note that the accuracy rate for the two intercom conditions is higher by a small (but statistically reliable) margin than the Face-to-Face conditions.[18] Even with stimuli as graphic as these, visual information seems to have no unique value. Our impression is that face-to-face describers tended to overestimate the usefulness of visual information[19], and gave rather sketchy verbal descrip-

---

[18]While mean performance is better in the Audio-Visual condition than in the Audio-Only condition, this difference does not approach significance.

[19]Some face-to-face speakers seemed not to appreciate that their listeners were seeing a mirror image of the shapes they drew in the air or formed with their hands. With stimuli that were bilaterally asymmetrical, this could be quite confusing.

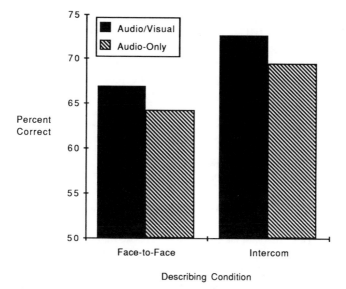

FIG. 5.17.   Accuracy of communication of Face-to-Face and Intercom descriptions presented in Audio-Only and Audio-Video versions.

tions. Intercom describers, because they were unable to utilize visual information, seemed to put more effort into the formulation of their verbal messages. We are still working on the analysis of the messages in the two describing conditions to try to understand the ways in which the two kinds of descriptions differ.

IMPLICATIONS FOR TECHNOLOGY AND COOPERATIVE WORK

It seems reasonable to assume that communication is a necessary condition for cooperative work to be accomplished, and that technology makes a variety of kinds of communication possible. The work discussed here has examined one function of communication—information exchange. Certainly this is an important function, but it's probably a good idea for those of us who work in this area to remind ourselves periodically that it is not the only purpose that communication serves and, in many situations, it may not be the most important one (Higgins, 1981). People communicate for a variety of reasons, and a technology that optimizes the efficiency of information exchange may be less than optimal insofar as the other functions are concerned. The research reviewed here has focused on a problem that communicators have to deal with—the need to establish what is mutually known in order that messages can be formulated, and the meaning of messages can be constructed, with this taken into account. In this section we pose some questions suggested by this work.

First, does the determination of mutual knowledge pose a problem for people working cooperatively? Our own experience attending conferences suggests that the amount of time devoted to such activities as establishing definitions, describing the background and history of issues, and so forth— tasks directed primarily at establishing common ground—is a function of the number of disciplines represented at the conference. Workers within the same disciplinary area (e.g., social cognition) are likely to have direct knowledge of one another, either from interactions at previous meetings or from having read each others' publications. But even without this, membership in the category of psychologists who study social cognition identifies a vocabulary and a body of information that can be assumed to be mutually known. Although it is possible that an anthropologist knows what "misattribution" or "the availability heuristic" refer to, it cannot safely be assumed.

Kraut, Egido and Galegher (chap. 6 in this volume) suggest that achieving a shared understanding of a research question is a difficult process typically requiring a number of face-to-face meetings for resolution. Certainly there are a number of reasons why face-to-face meetings are particularly helpful at this critical stage in the development of a research collaboration, but one of them might be that it is easier to construct a body of mutual knowledge in such settings.

One would expect the establishment of common ground to be particularly problematic when two or more groups of individuals, who had previously worked together intensively, are brought together to work on a common task. In such situations, each group is likely to have developed its own "miniculture," with a distinctive vocabulary and mutually known body of information.

In addition, in what ways might technology interact with the mutual knowledge problem? Consider a continuum that has, at one extreme, face-to-face interaction between two coworkers who share an office and, at the other extreme, a message and response on a computer bulletin board. In the former situation, coworkers have a variety of informational sources (e.g., knowledge of their interactional histories, the constraints of the situation, and the dynamic mechanisms of interaction, etc.) to draw on in formulating what is mutually known. In the latter situation, only the information available in the message and response are available.[20] It would be instructive to examine the

---

[20]Actually, strangers communicating via a computer bulletin board mutually know *something* about each other—they mutually know that they are able to use a computer bulletin board. It follows from this that each is a member of the class of people who know how to (and do) use computer bulletin boards. Very likely other sorts of knowledge is correlated (or perceived to be correlated) with membership in this category.

strategies people employ in an effort to establish common ground in such situations.

We have observed that bulletin board users will often quote the message they are responding to, and the messages preceding that message, which sometimes results in a summary version of the history of the interaction.[21] On issue-oriented bulletin boards where views on controversial issues are aired, contributors may preface a statement of their opinion with information about themselves. We assume that the personal information is intended to provide the interpretive context in which they wish their opinion statement to be understood.[22] On information-oriented bulletin boards, it is not un-

---

[21]Note, for example, the following. The inequality marks indicate the order of the previous contributions, with $<<<$ the first, and the unmarked contribution the most recent:

From: SOURCENAME

Newsgroups: rec.sport.baseball

Subject: Re: Bench clearing brawl

References: $<3159@Portia.Stanford.EDU>$

$>>>$I just saw a good brawl in today's Giants/Cards game in St. Louis.

$>>>$Will Clark was sliding into second where Oquendo was trying to turn a double play. Clark slid right over and past the bag, tying up Oquendo. Ozzie Smith came into the tie up, and Oquendo then kicked Clark lightly while Clark was still on the ground. Clark got up and pushed Oquendo, but Ozzie clubbed Clark from behind, an all-time cheap shot from an all-time all-star like Smith.

$>>$Well, first of all, he didn't slide past the bag. He wound up with his right knee practically on the bag. It was a good (albeit hard) slide. He was

$>$Whoa! I watched the replay of Clark's slide, and if he had tried to slide like that to steal second, he'd have ended up in left field. He started sliding barely 5 feet away from the bag. Hard slide, yes. Good slide, no.

But he wasn't trying to steal second. He was trying to slide in to break up the double play. In this case a hard slide *is* a good slide.

[22]For example;

From: SOURCENAME

Newsgroups: soc.culture.jewish

Subject: "Tolerance" and Conservative arrogance

In article PRIORSOURCE writes:

$>$This "holier than thou" attitude I see of some Orthodox Jews is really annoying. . .

As a "Orthodox" Jew, I will agree with you here. I put Orthodox in quotation marks because although I have most of the outward attributes of an Orthodox Jew (kosher home, tzizit, yamulke, etc.), I suspect that certain other members of the Orthodox community would look at me askance (at least—"pillory" might be the better term) for some of my more radical beliefs, e.g., I think that what Eliezer Berkovits says about non-Orthodox conversions in _ Not in Heaven _ is perfectly senesible. Actually, I am in sympathy with what Conservative Judaism ought to be. What it is is another matter.

common for novices to declare their beginner status before asking questions or seeking advice.[23] We make no claims for the representativeness of these observations, but it does not seem unreasonable to view these devices as strategies on the part of message sources to construct the common ground necessary to interpret their messages correctly.

Communication technologies make possible a variety of kinds of "mediated" (i.e., not face-to-face) communication. In so doing, these technologies also may disembody communicators by reducing to a minimum the information they have about those with whom they interact. Some of the consequence of electronic mail and similar kinds of mediation have been studied by Kiesler and Sproull (Kiesler & Sproull, 1986; Siegel, Dubrovsky, Kiesler & McGuire, 1986; Sproul & Kiesler, 1986).

Moreover, should a distinction be drawn between the informative and other functions of communication? A department chairman faced with the unpleasant task of informing a junior colleague that the department had voted not to recommend tenure would probably go to the colleague's office to bring the bad news, rather than using the phone. Certainly the information can be conveyed adequately over the phone, but somehow it seems an inappropriate way to do it—too impersonal and too little concerned with the person's well being. Although such considerations may be unimportant insofar as information exchange is concerned, as McGrath (chap. 2 in this volume) points out, they are significant determinants of group effectiveness.

Although it has been difficult to demonstrate clear performance effects

---

In fact, if there was any single moment which convinced me that I was to become an Orthodox Jew it would be when the Orthodox Rabbi at my college Hillel told the members of the kahal that they shouldn't be impolite to the non-Orthodox Jews who met at the same time. "If you're so convinced you're right," he said, "then you should behave in a manner that will make others want to emulate you. Being impolite to them is not such a manner."

[GOES ON TO LENGTHY DISCUSSION OF ISSUES]

[23]For example:

From: SOURCENAME

Newsgroups: rec.food.cooking

Subject: Chicken recipes desperately needed.

This summer is the first time I have actually been on my own and now that I have to cook for myself, I see the problems arising. Don't get me wrong, I love to cook. The problem is coming up with new things to try. I recently took my veal parmigian recipe and made it with chicken breats, since I could find no veal in this small town.

My question is, what things can be done with chicken, besides frying and baking. Since chicken is always easy to find, and usually cheap I was hoping someone could suggest new and wild ways to prepare it.

Thanks for any help.

attributable to communication modality (Short et al., 1976; Williams, 1977), the difference between talking face-to-face and over a telephone has well-documented psychological consequences. According to Rutter (1987), who provided an extensive review of this literature, the absence of visual information that occurs in telephonic communication, and presumably in many other kinds of mediated interaction (Sproull & Kiesler, 1986), reduces the richness of the social cues available to the participants, increasing the social distance that separates them and causing them to adhere closely to prescribed task roles. One need not accept Rutter's theoretical analysis of the effects of mediated communication, but it does seem to be the case in a variety of situations that the discussions of subjects communicating via telephone are more task-oriented and contain less personal content than those of people performing the same task face-to-face. One might conclude from these studies that from the point of view of cooperative work, mediated communication has substantial advantages because it seems to promote task-oriented communication. However, it would be unwise to assume that the depersonalization that seems to occur in mediated communication is without cost, especially when long-term cooperative relations that must be responsive to strain are involved (cf. McGrath, chap. 2 in this volume).

Furthermore, are there ways in which technology can reduce the difficulty of formulating what is mutually known? Professors often suggest that before going on job interviews in academic departments, graduate students should spend a bit of time learning about the people they will be meeting with by skimming some recent articles or looking them up in some standard reference source. Part of this is in the service of an ingratiation strategy, but most job candidates also find it easier to talk informatively to someone about their own work if they have some idea with what that person is likely to be familiar and unfamiliar.

Are there ways in which communicators can access information about the people with whom they interact that would make it easier to achieve common ground? The notecard system described by Trigg (this volume) suggest one technology that might aid in this process.

Finally, the research and theoretical ideas discussed here for the most part are relevant to messages that are, in terms of the distinction drawn by Ekman and Friesen (1969), "communicative." What can be said about messages that are "informative"—in other words, that serve as a basis for inferences we make about others but that are not necessarily intended to serve that function. A great deal of information in face-to-face interaction is derived from such things as tone of voice, facial expression, appearance, and so forth. These information sources can be controlled to some extent, but not completely. Some mediated communications systems might be thought of as a filter that acts to eliminate such information. To what extent do these information sources contribute to cooperative work, and what provision (if any) ought to be made to make them accessible?

REFERENCES

Brown, R. (1965). *Social psychology.* New York: Free Press.

Cantor, N., Mischel, W., & Schwartz, J. (1982). Social knowledge: Structure, content, use, and abuse. In A. Hastorf & A. Isen (Eds.), *Cognitive social psychology* (pp. 33–72). New York: Elsevier North-Holland.

Carroll, J. M. (1985). *What's in a name?* New York: W. H. Freeman.

Clark, H. H. (1985). Language use and language users. In G. Lindzey & E. Aronson (Eds.), *Handbook of social psychology* (3rd ed., Vol. 2, pp. 179–231). New York: Random House.

Clark, H. H., & Carlson, T. B. (1982). Speech acts and hearers' beliefs. In N. V. Smith (Ed.), *Mutual knowledge* (pp. 1–36). New York: Academic Press.

Clark, H. H., & Marshall, C. E. (1981). Definite reference and mutual knowledge. In A. K. Joshi, I. Sag, & B. Webber (Eds.), *Elements of discourse understanding* (pp. 10–63). New York: Cambridge University Press.

Clark, H. H. & Schaefer, E. F. (1987). Concealing one's meaning from overhearers. *Journal of Memory and Language, 26,* 209–225.

Clark, H. H., & Wilkes-Gibbs, D. (1986). Referring as a collaborative process. *Cognition, 22,* 1–39.

Duncan, S., & Fiske, D. (1977). *Face-to-face interaction: Research, methods, and theory.* Hillsdale, NJ: Lawrence Erlbaum Associates.

Fiske, S. T., & Taylor, S. E. (1984). *Social cognition.* New York: Random House.

Ekman, P., & Friesen, W. V. (1969). The repertoire of nonverbal communication: Categories, origins, usage, and coding. *Semiotica, 1,* 49–98.

Fussell, S., & Krauss, R. M. (1989). The effects of intended audience on message production and comprehension: Reference in a common ground framework. *Journal of Experimental Social Psychology, 25,* 203–219.

Fussell, S. R., & Krauss, R. M. (in press). Understanding friends and strangers: The effects of audience design on message comprehension. *European Journal of Social Psychology.*

Glucksberg, S., Krauss, R. M., & Weisberg, R. (1966). Referential communication in nursery school children: Method and some preliminary findings. *Journal of Experimental Child Psychology, 3,* 333–342.

Grimes, J. (1975). *The thread of discourse.* The Hague: Mouton.

Hastie, R. (1981). Schematic principles in human memory. In E. T. Higgins, C. P. Herman & M. P. Zanna (Eds.), *Social cognition: The Ontario Symposium* (Vol. 1, pp. 39–88). Hillsdale, NJ: Lawrence Erlbaum Associates.

Higgins, E. T. (1981). The 'communication game': Implications for social cognition and communication. In E. T. Higgins, C. P. Herman & M. P. Zanna (Eds.), *Social cognition: The Ontario Symposium* (Vol. 1, pp. 343–392). Hillsdale, NJ: Lawrence Erlbaum Associates.

Isaacs, E. A., & Clark, H. H. (1987). References in conversation between experts and novices. *Journal of Experimental Psychology: General, 116,* 26–37.

Kiesler, S., & Sproull, L. (1986). Response effects in the electronic survey. *Public Opinion Quarterly, 50,* 243–254.

Kingsbury, D. (1968). Manipulating the amount of information obtained from a person giving directions. Unpublished Honors Thesis, Department of Social Relations, Harvard University.

Krauss, R. (1986). Cognition and communication: A social psychological perspective. *Psychological Journal* (USSR), 7, 37–49.

Krauss, R. M. (1987). The role of the listener: Addressee influences on message formulation. *Journal of Language and Social Psychology, 6,* 81–97.

Krauss, R. M., & Bricker, P. D. (1966). Effects of transmission delay and access delay on the efficiency of verbal communication. *Journal of the Acoustical Society, 41,* 286–292.

Krauss, R. M., Bricker, P. D., McMahon, L. E., & Garlock, C. M. (1977). The role of audible and visible back channel responses in interpersonal communication. *Journal of Personality and Social Psychology, 35,* 523–529.

Krauss, R. M., & Glucksberg, S. (1969). The development of communication: Competence as a function of age. *Child Development, 40,* 256–266.

Krauss, R. M., & Weinheimer, S. (1966). Concurrent feedback, confirmation and the encoding of referents in verbal communication. *Journal of Personality and Social Psychology, 4,* 343–346.

Krauss, R. M., & Weinheimer, S. (1967). Effects of referent similarity and communication mode on verbal encoding. *Journal of Verbal Learning and Verbal Behavior, 6,* 359–363.

Krauss, R. M., & Weinheimer, S. (1964). Changes in the length of reference phrases as a function of social interaction: A preliminary study. *Psychonomic Science, 1,* 113–114.

Krauss, R. M., Weinheimer, S., & Vivehananthan, P. S. (1968). "Inner speech" and "external speech": Characteristics and communication effectiveness of socially and nonsocially encoded messages. *Journal of Personality and Social Psychology, 9,* 295–300.

Kraut, R. E., & Lewis, S. H. (1982). Feedback and the coordination of conversation. In H. Sypher, & J. Applegate (Eds.), *Cognition and communication.* Hillsdale, NJ: Lawrence Erlbaum Associates.

Kraut, R. E., Lewis, S. H., & Swezey, L. (1982). Listener responsiveness and the coordination of conversation. *Journal of Personality and Social Psychology, 43,* 718–731.

Markus, H., & Zajonc, R. B. (1985). The cognitive perspective in social psychology. In G. Lindzey & E. Aronson (Eds.), *Handbook of social psychology* (Vol. 1, pp. 137–230). New York: Random House.

Rutter, D. (1987). *Communicating by telephone.* Oxford, England: Pergamon Press.

Sacks, H., & Schegloff, E. (1979). Two preferences in the organization of reference to persons in conversation and their interaction. In G. Psathas (Ed.), *Everyday language: Studies in ethnomethodology* (pp. 15–21). New York: Irvington.

Short, J., Williams, E., & Christie, B. (1976). *The social psychology of telecommunications.* Chichester, England: Wiley.

Siegel, J., Dubrovsky, V., Kiesler, S., & McGuire, T. (1986). Group processes in computer-mediated communication. *Organizational Behavior and Human Decision Processes, 37,* 157–187.

Snyder, M., & Cantor, N. (1979). Testing hypotheses about other people: The use of historical knowledge. *Journal of Experimental Social Psychology, 15,* 330–342.

Sperber, D., & Wilson, D. (1986). *Relevance: Communication and cognition.* Cambridge, MA: Harvard University Press.

Sproull, L., & Kiesler, S. (1986). Reducing social context cues: Electronic mail in organizational communication. *Management Science, 32,* 1492–1512.

Taylor, S. E., & Crocker, J. (1981). Schematic bases of social information processing. In E. T. Higgins, C. P. Herman, & M. P. Zanna (Eds.), *Social cognition: The Ontario Symposium* (Vol. 1, pp. 89–134). Hillsdale, NJ: Lawrence Erlbaum Associates.

Williams, E. (1977). Experimental comparisons of face-to-face and mediated communication: A review. *Psychological Bulletin, 84,* 963–976.

Yngve, V. H. (1970). *On getting a word in edgewise.* Papers from the sixth regional meeting of the Chicago Linguistics Society.

Zipf, G. K. (1935). *The psychobiology of language.* New York: Houghton-Mifflin.

II FIELD STUDIES
OF COLLABORATIVE WORK

6

Patterns of Contact and Communication in Scientific Research Collaboration

Robert E. Kraut
Carmen Egido
Bell Communications Research

Jolene Galegher
University of Arizona

Abstract

In this chapter, we describe the influence of physical proximity on the development of collaborative relationships between scientific researchers and on the execution of their work. Our evidence is drawn from our own studies of scientific collaborators, as well as from observations of research and development activities collected by other investigators. These descriptions provide the foundation for a discussion of the actual and potential role of communications technology in professional work, especially for collaborations carried out a distance.

For many people, the word *scientist* conjures up an image of a white-coated figure, working alone in a laboratory with mysterious instruments and substances. But, as scientists know, science is a fundamentally social process. Examinations of patterns of authorship in the sciences reveal that collaborative research is increasing in many disciplines. In psychology, for example, the mean number of authors per published article rose from 1.5 in 1949 to 2.2 in 1979 (Over, 1982). And, in 1981, over 65% of articles in a sample of six social psychology journals were jointly authored (Mendenhall, Oddou, & Franck, 1984). Nevertheless, there is little research that examines the reasons for the increase in the proportion of research that is published collaboratively, or, more importantly for our purposes, the work processes and problems that differentiate collaborative from solo research.

Yet this evidence of coauthorship means that science is a social activity not only in the sociology of science sense that researchers are connected in networks defined by their intellectual lineage and common interests (cf., Crane, 1976; Garvey & Gottfredson, 1977; Menzel, 1962), but also in the sense that their day-to-day work involves frequent and consequential interaction with other people—colleagues, students, and research assistants. The development of new ideas for scientific research, the execution of research tasks and the preparation of formal research reports have all become processes involving extensive social interaction, accompanied by all the complexity that characterizes other kinds of interpersonal relationships. But, with the notable exceptions of Pelz and Andrews (1966) and Allen (1977), we have little information about the ways in which social processes affect the process of doing science.

This is unfortunate because, in addition to their importance to science itself, research collaborations are an important social and organizational phenomenon. They are somewhat unusual in the realm of work relationships in that they are mainly voluntary and both their duration and their focus are determined by the participants. But this kind of work relationship may be becoming more important outside of academic settings as corporate restructuring minimizes vertical differentiation between employees and as the proportion of "knowledge workers" in the workforce increases. We believe that scientific collaboration provides a model of the way professionals in many fields construct intellectual products. Thus, understanding these relationships is important because they represent a distinctive work process, one that appears to be characteristic of many kinds of professional work.

Finally, to connect our interest in collaboration to the theme of this book, the study of research collaboration may help to specify the technological needs of cooperating work groups, as well as the limits on this technology. So far, improvements in technology do not seem to have caused or even facilitated the increase in the frequency of collaboration that we have reported. With the important exception of improvements in the quality and cost of telecommunications transmission, information technology has not evolved to meet the needs of collaborating research scientists. The trends already noted, however, suggest that opportunities to test and implement technologies supporting collaborative research are proliferating and seem likely to grow more in the years ahead. The premise of this chapter is that understanding the nature of collaborative work relationships can help to make those efforts a success.

Of course, collaborative success is a multidimensional concept; it includes (a) productivity—collaborations that produce an abundance of high-quality research products, (b) longevity—collaborations that last through multiple research projects, and (c) enjoyment—collaborations in which the process of working together is at least minimally pleasant (Hackman, 1987). Moreover, collaborative research relationships differ along at least three important dimensions (Hagstrom, 1965); these variations influence the criteria by which collaborations should be judged and place the observations we present later in context. First, collaborative research may involve a traditional, small-scale project such as an empirical investigation in social psychology or large-scale projects, common for example in particle physics. Second, collaborations differ depending on whether the substance of the research involves a theoretical science, such as mathematics, or an empirical science, such as biology or psychology. The former are characterized by collaborations among equals, with little division of labor, whereas the latter are characterized by more explicit exchange of services and more substantial division of labor. Finally, participants in a collaborative relationship may be peers or near peers, such as university faculty members, or researchers of unequal status, such as faculty members and their graduate students or paid assistants. Although this difference has important implications for many aspects of collaboration, it is not particularly relevant to our interest in technological support; thus, we leave the examination of status influences for a future paper. Here, we present the data we have gathered regarding small, "traditional science" collaborations, primarily in the empirical sciences. The goal of this chapter, then, is to examine some of the factors—especially patterns of contact and communication—that affect the likelihood that a collaborative relationship will develop and that it will be successful and to assess the implications of our findings for the design of technology to support collaborative work.

Our analysis of what brings researchers together and leads them to have successful collaborations draws on several sources of evidence, including data on the research and development process collected by us and by others and extrapolations from relevant literature in social psychology and organizational behavior. Our own data collection consists of three studies: (a) an interview study involving semistructured, hour-long, telephone interviews with one member of each of 90 research collaborations in social psychology, computer science, and management science, in which the respondents provided detailed information about the unfolding of a single collaboration; (b) a survey study in which 66 psychologists described the production and their evaluations of a sample of their published articles; and (c) an archival study in which personal, organizational, and geographic variables were used to predict who would work with whom among 93 members of a large research and development organization. We describe our methods and present portions of our data as they become relevant in the upcoming discussion.

ADVANTAGES AND DISADVANTAGES OF COLLABORATION

Both our own data and the prior literature provide mixed evidence about why researchers work together and the advantages and disadvantages of doing so. We learned from our interviews that researchers become involved in collaborative relationships for a variety of reasons. As Hagstrom (1965) suggested, combining resources to accomplish a project is a major reason.

Our interviews suggest that these resources are both material (e.g., grant money, research assistants, labor, computer time) and intellectual (e.g., substantive knowledge and methodological skills). Moreover, people collaborate because collaboration changes the process of research for them in desirable ways. For many of our respondents, working with another person was simply more fun than working alone. They also believed that working with another improved the quality of the research product, because of the synthesis of ideas it afforded, the feedback they received from each other, and the new skills they learned. In addition to these two major motives, a number of our respondents collaborated primarily to maintain a preestablished personal relationship. In a relationship threatened by physical separation, the collaboration provided a reason for keeping in touch. Finally, some researchers collaborated for self-presentational or political reasons, because they believed that working with a particular person or being in a collaborative relationship per se was valuable for their careers. Of course, these motives are not mutually exclusive, and in most cases respondents cited a combination to explain whey they chose to collaborate.

These professed motivations for collaboration all imply that it has a positive influence on the research process. Through collaboration scientists are able to tackle problems that they are incapable of working on alone because of limitations on their resources, skills, or time. They have more fun doing the work, and their reputations improve in the process. But there is considerable evidence from research on various aspects of group performance that would lead one to be skeptical about claims of unalloyed benefits from research collaboration. In particular, our knowledge of process losses stemming from conformity effects (Janis, 1972), social loafing (Latane, Williams, & Harkins, 1979), and difficulties in coordinating activity (Steiner, 1972), as well as evidence that group problem-solving processes such as brainstorming are not necessarily superior to individual efforts (Dunnette, Campbell, & Jaastad, 1963; Lewis, Sadosky, & Connolly, 1975) cast doubt on this proposition. Direct evidence relevant to these claims is sparse because the prior literature on scientific collaboration has not examined questions of quality; the only relevant study we found is Presser (1980). His analysis of acceptance rates in one social psychology journal for a single year suggests that collaborative articles are better than solo ones; for this journal, articles with multiple authors received higher evaluations from reviewers and higher acceptance and conditional acceptance rates than solo-authored articles.

We attempted to gather additional data about collaborative processes and products by surveying researchers who had moved into or out of jobs at one of the top departments of psychology in the United States between 1980 and 1983. We were able to locate the current mailing addresses of 95 of the 98 psychologists whose names were given to us by 30 university departments, and we sent each of these authors a questionnaire containing titles, publication dates and authorship information about the articles they had published between 1975 and 1986. These titles, which were drawn from *Psychological Abstracts,* included all of their solo articles and up to two randomly selected collaborative articles for each year during this period. We oversampled solo articles, because about 75% of the articles published by these authors were coauthored. For each article, respondents reported project start and end dates, how far their offices were from that of their principal coauthor, and how frequently they communicated with that coauthor. They also rated their satisfaction with various aspects of the research relationship, with the work process, and with the article itself. Sixty-six (69%) of the authors completed these questionnaires.

The results of our survey lead to a somewhat less favorable view of collaborative research than either Presser's data or the endorsements presented by many of our interviewees. For instance, among the authors in this study, having a collaborative research style did not lead to greater overall productivity. Some authors tended to be productive by writing more—both collaborative and noncollaborative articles (r (total collaborative $\times$ total solo articles) = .33; N = 66; p < .01),—but those who wrote a higher proportion of collaborative articles were no more productive than those who wrote a higher proportion of solo articles (r (proportion collaborative $\times$ total articles) = .20; p > .10).[1] Thus, the reported claim that one can "get more articles out" by working collaboratively does not seem to be supported by these data.

We also examined respondents' evaluations of solo and collaborative articles and the production process. These questions were presented in an ipsative format (i.e., compared to an author's own corpus) and respondents reported their evaluations on five-point Likert-scales where 1 meant that a particular article was worse than average on a specified dimension for that respondent, a 3 meant that it was typical of the respondent's work, and a 5 meant it was better than average for that respondent. Table 6.1 shows the results of the comparison of these evaluations for 57 respondents who had published at least one solo article (M = 3.6) and one collaborative article (M = 12.7).

In general, these psychologists rated their solo-authored articles more highly than their collaborative works, both in terms of outcome and process. In particular, they thought manuscripts they wrote alone were better (i.e., clearer, more ingenious and of better quality; p < .05) and the work they represented was more important (i.e., more central to the field and of higher theoretical and empirical quality; p < .10). They also thought it was easier to

---

[1]Although these correlations both seem small and similar to each other, they are influenced by outliers. Computing robust correlations by dropping the most extreme respondents raises the correlations between solo authored and collaboratively authored articles, but lowers the correlations between proportion of collaborative articles and total productivity. For example, dropping the most extreme 20% of respondents raises the former correlation to .57, but lowers the latter to .07.

TABLE 6.1
Differences Between Solo and Collaborative Research

Outcome	Solo Mean	Collaborative Mean	t	r
Satisfaction with publication	3.9	3.7	−2.02	−.26**
Satisfaction with research process	3.9	3.7	−1.45	−.19
Perceived importance of work	3.4	3.2	−1.7	−.22*
Ease of scientific & technical tasks	3.2	3.0	−1.54	−.20
Ease of managerial tasks	3.8	3.1	−4.41	−.53***
Years to complete project	1.6	1.7	+.34	+.06
Citations within 3 years	6.3	5.8	−0.61	−.08

*$p < .10$
**$p < .05$
***$p < .01$

handle the managerial work of research (e.g., supervising assistants, handling paperwork, meeting deadlines, coordinating information; $p < .001$) when working alone, and no harder to handle the scientific and technical tasks (i.e., refining hypotheses, devising methods, applying statistics, or expressing ideas; $p < .15$). More objective measures of research quality also fail to show that collaborative articles are superior to solo articles. For example, both solo and collaborative articles took about 19 or 20 months from planning to writing a draft for publication and both garnered about six citations in the *Social Science Citation Index* within three years of their publication. Finally, a stylistic analysis of manuscripts from a different sample of researchers showed no differences in readability between single and multiauthor publications. In sum, we do not find much evidence that collaborative research is more advantageous to either the researcher or science.

Given these outcomes, one might wonder why so many researchers work collaboratively and why the proportion of collaborative scientific research has been increasing. As Beaver and Rosen (1979a,b) argued, both the increased professionalism and the increased empiricism of science is associated with greater collaboration. In psychology the ease or feasibility of working in one way versus the other may depend on the nature of the project. The work involved in executing an empirical project is more amenable to division of labor than the work involved in producing a theoretical article. Thus, we might argue that one reason for the high proportion of collaborative articles in our sample and for the general increase in collaborative psychological work noted earlier is the way psychology has become an increasingly empirical discipline, with current practice differing substantially from say, Freud, William James, and more recently, Piaget.

This apparent relationship between empiricism and collaboration can be seen as part of a larger trend—the increasing sophistication—including specialization, professionalization, and institutionalization of scientific activity. Over time, science has changed from a lonely, sometimes speculative, intellectual pursuit carried out by individuals such as the isolated, white-coated figure portrayed in the earlier description to a highly professionalized, heavily funded and, in some fields, more rigorous, activity carried out within a highly complex social system. This change is both required by and a determinant of changes in the kinds of research questions scientists undertake.

To understand more about how the institutionalization of science contributes to the occurrence of collaborative research, and, in particular, about how specific collaborative relationships arise, we turn now to an examination of the role of physical proximity as a determinant of who collaborates with whom. We argue that professionalization and institutionalization result in groups of scientists being colocated; this physical proximity, in turn, makes it possible for scientists to find research partners and to carry out their research work in efficient ways. In the following section, we focus on the role of proximity in the process of partner selection among scientific collaborators and describe ways in which proximity aids in the execution of research tasks.

PHYSICAL PROXIMITY:
THE FRAMEWORK FOR SCIENTIFIC COLLABORATION

In an earlier work (Kraut, Galegher, & Egido, 1988), we reported that physical proximity helps scientists avoid or minimize many of the problems that arise in the process of conducting research—meeting partners, defining problems, planning projects, supervising coworkers and subordinates—and may influence the probability of repeated collaboration. In this section we treat the role of physical proximity in more detail by examining its effects on the collaborative process and the mechanisms by which it has its effects.

As noted before, the process of selecting a research partner is in many ways analogous to the process of choosing a mate, with combinations of mutual benefit, personal and intellectual compatibility, and ease of contact all influencing whether a pair of potential partners decide to work together. In this process, simple proximity is especially important. As Hagstrom (1965) noted in his study of 96 university faculty and other scientists, "spatial propinquity often leads to collaboration since it is likely to lead to informal communication" (p. 122). In our interview data, this general phenomenon is illustrated by a husband and wife pair who discussed research possibilities in the bathtub and a former pair of housemates whose research plans emerged over the breakfast table. More frequently, researchers in the same academic department decided to work together following informal discussions over lunch or coffee.

Interesting as they are, these stories do not permit us to assess the systematic effect of propinquity on the likelihood of collaboration. To do so requires a different type of data than either our own or Hagstrom's interview studies provide—data that include information about pairs who did not collaborate as well as those who did. We obtained these data by looking at the relationship between propinquity and collaboration among research scientists and engineers in a large industrial, research, and development laboratory. These data show that within the laboratory, proximity is associated with research collaboration.

The research component of this research and development company consists of approximately 500 PhD and MS-level researchers in the physical, engineering, computer, and behavioral sciences. The organizational structure consists of three hierarchical levels (laboratories, with approximately 125 members each; departments with approximately 30 members each; and groups with approximately 7 members each). The laboratories are located on two campuses, located approximately 40 miles apart. Each building consists of several floors, with several wings per floor. We selected a sample of 93 researchers, all those who had published at least two internal research reports in 1986 and 1987. At least one of these reports had a coauthor, and the other was either a solo-authored report or had a coauthor not included in the first report. For each of the 4,278 unique pairings of the 93 researchers in the sample, we obtained data on four measures:

1. Collaboration: Data on whether that pair published at least one internal research report together were obtained from a company-maintained database of internal publications.

2. Organizational proximity: Proximity on the organizational chart was coded 1 if the pair were in the same group, 2 if they were in the same department, 3 if they were in the same laboratory, and 4 otherwise.

3. Physical proximity: Using the organizational phone book, which listed office addresses with codes for building, floor, and corridor, we computed a rough measure of physical proximity. Offices were coded 1 if they were on the same corridor of the same building, 2 if they were on same floor of the same building, but different corridor, 3 if they were on different floors of the same building, and 4 if they were in different buildings.

4. Research similarity: For each pair, we computed an index of the similarity between the publications of one member and those of the other member on which the first individual was not a coauthor. This index is based on the assumption that authors who share research interests will have written reports containing similar concepts and that abstracts of these reports contain sufficient detail to demonstrate this similarity. The research similarity index is based on information retrieval techniques developed to identify semantic similarity in large text sources (Deerwester, Dumais, Fur-

TABLE 6.2
Distance Between Offices and Probability of Research Collaboration

Office Location	Actual Collaborations	% of Actual	Potential Collaborations	% of Potential
Same corridor	25	46	243	10.3
Same floor	20	36	1038	1.9
Different floors	5	9	1736	.3
Different buildings	5	9	1261	.4

nas, Landauer, & Harshman, in press). Basically, the similarity of a pair of abstracts is a function of the proximity of the concepts they contain in a semantic space.[2]

Table 6.2 shows the association of collaboration with distance between potential collaborators' offices, without controlling for any other variables.

The data clearly show that pairs whose offices were close to each other were more likely to collaborate (Yules Q for the 2 × 2 table comparing same corridor and floor to different floor or building = .82; $p < .001$).[3] Eighty two percent of collaborations occurred among researchers with offices on the same floor, even though these constituted only 12% of potential collaborative pairs.

Mechanisms Underlying the Relationship Between Proximity and Collaboration

To explain the association between proximity and the likelihood of research collaboration, we present data from our studies of collaboration and from the more general literature on propinquity in the social science research literature. This evidence is organized around two general explana-

---

[2]Lynn Streeter and Susan Dumais suggested this approach, and Karen Lochbaum aided us by writing computer programs for this analysis. The analysis starts with a large matrix representing the number of times each of 7,100 terms appears in each of the 4,000 abstracts of research reports from the company. This matrix is reduced to a large number of orthogonal dimensions using singular value decomposition, so that terms that are similar in meaning appear as neighbors in the space. The centroid of the words in each author's abstracts was used to represent his or her work in this multi-dimensional space. In comparing any two researchers, we use only those abstracts in which the other was not a co-author (i.e., solo authored work or collaborative work with other co-authors). The research similarity between two authors is the cosine or product moment correlation between the 100 dimensional vectors representing each author. A cosine of 1.0 (a 0 degree angle) would indicate that the two authors' papers are on top of each other in the space.

[3]Yules Q is a measure of association for 2 × 2 tables with unequal marginals. It is -1 if the least frequent variable never co-occurs with the more frequent variable. 1 if it always co-occurs, and 0 if there is no relationship between variables.

tions—colocation of similar others and the availability of frequent, high-quality, low-cost communication as a mechanism to facilitate the development of ideas and the execution of collaborative tasks. After dismissing the hypothesis that this relationship is entirely a consequence of the fact that individuals with similar interests are colocated, we discuss the impact of informal communication on both social and mechanical aspects of collaboration.

The Influence of Colocation

One explanation, bordering on artifact, is that researchers who are similar to each other in important ways also have their offices close to each other. It is true that both in academia and in industry researchers whose offices are close together are likely to share common organizational goals and to have research interests in common. In a university, for example, members of an academic department are likely to be colocated, and subspecialities within the same department often have offices on the same floor, corridor, or in the same wing of a building. It is possible that this similarity in research interests, not the fact of proximity, is sufficient to lead to research collaboration. Indeed, in our research and development sample, researcher pairs in the same department were more likely to work together than those in different departments (52% of 294 of the pairs in the same department versus .7% of the 3,984 pairs in different departments; Yule's Q = .88). Moreover, those with similar research interests as defined earlier were more likely to work together (3.3% of pairs in the top quartile of similarity versus .3% of those in the bottom quartile; Yules Q based on a median split of similarity = .74).

But the effects of propinquity on research collaboration cannot be completely explained by organizational proximity and similarities in research interests among those who are close to each other. In a logit analysis holding constant organizational proximity and research similarity, physical proximity has an independent effect on research collaborations. Table 6.3 shows

TABLE 6.3
Numbers of Research Collaborations by Organizational and Physical Proximity

	Organization			
	Same Department		Different Department	
Office Location	Pairs	% Collaborating	Pairs	% Collaborating
Same floor	271	10.3	909	1.87
Different floors	23	4.3	1708	.29
Different buildings	0	NA	1261	.40

the association of collaboration and physical proximity holding constant the organizational proximity between potential collaborators (i.e., whether they were in the same or different departments). Our sample did not include enough pairs of researchers who were in the same department but sufficiently far apart to analyze the effects of physical distance within a department. We did, however, have enough variation in physical distance among researchers in different departments to examine this relationship. Table 6.3 shows that among researchers in different departments, pairs of researchers who were on the same floor as each other were about six times more likely to enter into research collaboration than pairs on different floors or in different buildings.

Clearly, even among researchers in different departments, having offices on the same hallway increases the likelihood of research collaboration. Instead, what appears to be important is the opportunity for unconstrained interaction provided by proximity.

The Importance of Informal Communication

Most often, naturally occurring, informal contact and communication provide the opportunity for potential collaborators to learn about each other, and also serve as the framework within which collaborative tasks are accomplished. To illustrate the importance of these opportunities, we describe three properties of informal communication and show how these properties affect collaborative work and collaborative relationships.

Communication Frequency. The major mechanism through which proximity has its impact on the likelihood of research collaborations and on their longevity is through its impact on frequency of communication. Even if we consider technologically mediated communication such as telephone (Mayer, 1977) and computer mail usage (Eveland & Bikson, 1987), the frequency of communication between any two people is a strong function of their geographical proximity. What holds true in the world of residential phone service and corporate mail networks holds true in the research world as well. As our interviews and those conducted by Hagstrom indicate, the informal contact that results from frequent opportunities for communication often leads to collaboration. In his sample of industrial research and development engineers, Allen (1977) showed a striking logarithmic decline in communication frequency with distance between potential communicators. For example, in Allen's data, about 25% of engineers whose offices were next door to each other (less than 5 meters apart) talked to each other about technical topics at least once a week; if their offices were 10 meters apart, this figure drops below 10%. After this sharp decline, the curve asymptotes at approximately 30 meters, so that engineers, 30 meters apart and those several miles apart had approximately the same low probability of talking to each other at least once a week.

Our own data show a similar phenomenon even among collaborators already working together. In our survey study of collaboration among psychologists, we asked our respondents to indicate the distance between their own offices and those of the primary coauthor for each of their collaborative articles and to estimate the frequency of their communication with this coauthor when initially planning the project and when planning the journal article itself. Distance was measured on a seven-point, semilogarithmic scale, where a 1 meant that offices were next door, a 4 meant that they were in different floors of the same building, and a 7 meant they were in different states. Communication frequency was measured on a seven-point semilogarithmic scale, where a 1 meant that the collaborators communicated multiple times per day, a 4 meant that they communicated about once per week, and a 7 meant that they communicated less than once a month. Physical proximity was strongly related to frequency of communication during both the planning stage and the writing stage of the research process, as shown in Fig. 6.1. It demonstrates, for example, that researchers who have offices next door to each other have approximately twice as much communication as those whose offices are simply on the same floor.

As a result of this frequent interaction, researchers who are situated near each other are likely to come to like each other more. According to Zajonc (1968), merely being in contact with a person or object increases one's liking

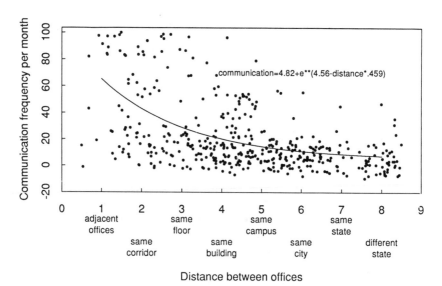

FIG. 6.1.   Communication frequency as a function of physical distance.

for it, perhaps by reducing the inherent dislike people have of the unfamiliar. In addition, because one is likely to have to deal with neighbors in the future, the human tendency to like those with whom we anticipate future interaction (Darley & Berscheid, 1967) and to feel in a unit relation with them (Heider, 1958) may also come into play. If, in turn, people are more likely to want to work with people they like, then the opportunity for frequent interaction is likely to have a strong influence on the likelihood of collaboration.

Quality of Communication

In addition to increasing the likelihood of informal communication through increased contact, proximity increases the quality of communication. By high-quality communication, we mean two-way interactions involving more than one sensory channel. The opportunity for interactions of this type is especially important during the initiation and planning stages of a project, when the need for a rich communication modality is strongest.

Our interview data provide evidence of how high-quality informal communication brings researchers with diverse backgrounds and interests together. In the typical situation, a common focus for collaborative projects was constructed from the preexisting interests and expertise of the participants. One example of this sort of relationship is a social psychologist who sought a collaborative relationship with a cognitive psychologist to develop an ill-specified project in social cognition. He said, "the idea was still very fuzzy. We often eat lunch together, so there are many informal opportunities to raise issues and discuss them . . . it was in one of those informal settings, at lunch, or after lunch sometime, I brought up the issue the broad outlines of things, little things meshed and she recommended I read a particular paper." These informal conversations eventually grew into a collaborative project that joined the interests of these two researchers. It seems unlikely that one could have predicted the occurrence of a collaborative relationship between these two individuals, but, in this case, and in many others, the opportunity for high-quality, informal interaction led to a productive relationship. In sum, our data suggest that high-quality informal communication is important because it allows researchers to develop common interests with their neighbors.

Drawing again on our interviews, we learned that discussions of this type tend to merge into more focused conversations about specific projects. According to our respondents, the initial task-level activity in a collaborative relationship usually consists of multiple face-to-face discussions, occurring frequently over the course of days, or, more typically, weeks or even months. Our survey data support this observation; they indicate that when collaborators are most intensively planning their work, they meet almost daily (M

= 27 times per month). These discussions are the most intensely interactive aspect of the entire research process and, according to the researchers, the most intellectually exciting and rewarding aspect as well. At a later stage of project development, when collaborators are planning the writing of their research reports, we observed a similar reliance on frequent face-to-face communication. Although actual writing is most often a solitary activity, our survey respondents report meeting 17 times per month while planning these documents. Although frequent, this is significantly less than during initial project planning ($p < .001$).

The intense, highly interactive meetings that characterize planning work generally take place in offices or conference rooms and, typically, the only technologies involved are paper, pencils, and blackboard. Most often, the participants do not prepare for these meetings in any formal sense. There is little reliance on prewritten documents or diagrams as a basis for the discussion; instead, collaborators seem to value the opportunity for spontaneous, informal, and unstructured exchange of ideas. The participants talk, argue, interrupt, write equations, draw sketches, and modify both their own and their partners' work. Participants may take notes in order to have a record of important observations or issues that arise in the conversation or to remind themselves of things to do—articles to read, people to contact, purchases to make—but there is usually no explicit effort to make a formal record of the proceedings. In listening to reports of these conversations, one has the sense of high energy levels and a high level of concentration on the serious, substantive intellectual questions involved. Current communication technology available to most researchers does not allow the intensity of interaction nor the spontaneous exchange of notes and documents that are typical of these face-to-face meetings. Thus, quality problems are likely to arise because research partners are unable to engage in rapid-fire conversation or are unable to obtain the feedback they need to adjust their communications to fit their partners' information needs (Krauss & Weinheimer, 1967; Kraut, Lewis, & Swezey, 1982).

Cost of Communication

A third important feature of communication with one's research partners is cost. Some costs are obvious; if one's research partners are not colocated, the costs of collaboration will have to include the expense of plane tickets and phone calls. More importantly, they are also likely to include the burden of having only intentional, structured interactions via a restricted modality within an already existing relationship. But proximity makes it possible to explore new relationships, and to supervise and sustain progress by providing the low-cost communication necessary to assess compatibility, to catalog what has been done, to alert partners to minor problems, and to enforce guilt.

Being situated near a pool of potential collaborators provides a low-cost opportunity for a researcher to discover the qualities of another that might make him or her a desirable collaborator. This increased awareness of the attributes of one's neighbors allows one to choose partners judiciously, lowering the risk of selecting an inappropriate collaborator. Later on, low-cost communication and the opportunity for quick and easy access to a partner are crucial for collaborators' joint supervision of the project and each other's work. For most of our researchers, project management was extremely informal, with the supervision of subordinates and coordination with peers occurring during casual hallway and lunchroom conversation as often as through formal, scheduled meetings. These "on the fly" interactions are impossible in collaborations over a distance.

Proximity also allows collaborators to share even small decisions. Many of the sticking points in conducting research are minor. They consist of questions like: Should I change the wording of a question in a questionnaire? At what points should we break the program into modules? While working alone, one would simply make a decision. When working with a collaborator, researchers often want to consult with each other on such points, if only to preserve the balance of control they and their partners share in the project. Distance raises the personal costs of communication, so that short messages become uneconomical. As a result, distance cuts down on nags and feedback, which are both crucial to accomplishing collaborative activities. Many interviewees reported frustration at the slowness of working with collaborators who were in different locations. For instance, in describing problems in finishing up projects at a distance, one researcher said, "[This] was the first project that I had done long distance and it certainly made it more time consuming. I was used to being able to walk down the hallway from my office to [my collaborator's] office to talk to him about a problem . . . [In the long distance collaboration] we either relied on the mail going back and forth or even phone conversations and that just wasn't as satisfactory as talking face-to-face . . . It took a long time, and I wasn't used to having that much of a lag for the turn-around . . . I was used to being able to make it much faster."

In sum, having multiple opportunities for high-quality, low-cost interactions makes it possible for potential collaborators to find each other and to manage their work efficiently. Without these opportunities for informal communication, collaborations don't get started, and if the opportunity for informal communication declines, collaborative work typically slows down, becomes more burdensome and, sometimes, comes to an end.

Limits on the Influence of Proximity

Although physical proximity provides people with the opportunities for informal interaction that are important to the initiation of collaboration and managing the work, according to our survey data it does not seem to be associated with either the likelihood of continuing to collaborate with a particular coauthor after an initial project or with the collaborators' satisfaction with their work and the process of producing it—at least not within the normal restricted range of distances from which researchers choose their collaborative partners. However, this null finding may be a function of our methodology, because we do not have estimates of the distance between collaborators after they broke up, and we do have evidence that many collaborations break up if the partners move apart. Our interviews are replete with cases in which a successful collaboration stopped because one partner moved away. For instance, one researcher reported that although he and his former partner often generated ideas for new projects over cocktails at annual conventions, the plans never came to fruition because they never had the opportunity to have the "second conversation" needed to build the idea into a real project (Kraut et al., 1988).

Our survey data indicate that these outcome measures are associated with the pleasantness of the interpersonal relationship between the collaborators, thus we intend to explore the determinants of longevity and satisfaction by discussing collaborative relationships as relationships in a future study. We believe that examining scientific collaboration from this perspective will offer substantial insight into the social psychology of science, a largely unexplored territory. Here, our interest in technology leads us to focus on using the description of collaborative processes that we have already presented as a basis for making recommendations about how technology might make these processes easier and more efficient, especially for collaborators working at a distance. We think it is likely that such technology would also indirectly aid the maintenance of the personal relationships that apparently sustain collaborative work by increasing the opportunities for frequent, high-quality, low-cost communication.

IMPLICATIONS FOR TECHNOLOGY FOR COLLABORATIVE WORK

The previous discussion has natural implications for the design of technology to aid collaborative work. In the following paragraphs we revisit some of the functions that proximity plays in research collaborations and recast them as requirements for group communications technology. We argue that current research in this area concentrates too heavily on the computer support of work-related activities performed once a collaborative effort is underway and directly related to the successful completion of work products. Furthermore, many computer technologies aim to structure these work tasks in ways that fundamentally alter the collaborative process. According to our view, communications technologies that allow more free-form interaction in real-time and time-shifted modes to augment and even to substitute for physical proximity are likely to yield greater benefits. As we discuss later, the aim should be specifically to increase the frequency and quality and to decrease the cost of interactions among potential collaborators who are working across barriers of place and time.

The spate of recent workshops and conferences devoted to the subject reflects the growing interest in refocusing research and development in information technology to address the needs of multiperson work teams, particularly distributed work terms. At least three general classes of tools are needed to support these teams: (a) communication tools to facilitate both planned and unplanned real-time and delayed interactions among collaborators, (b) coordination and management tools to minimize the overhead inherent in multiperson work, and (c) task-oriented tools designed to facilitate the completion and integration of specific work products, whether individually or jointly executed.

Most of the research activity in technologies to support work groups has concentrated on a small part of this range, either on enhancements to formal face-to-face meetings with the explicit goal of structuring interaction or on highly task-specific applications. Thus, technologies such as teleconferencing, group decision support systems (e.g., Kraemer & King, 1986; Vogel & Nunamaker, chap. 19 in this volume), group outlining systems (e.g., Cognoter—Foster, & Stefik, 1986), and group drawing programs (Lakin, chap. 17 in this volume) are designed to facilitate formal meetings among coworkers. Moreover, they often often fix on narrow, albeit important, aspects of these meetings. Tools like collaborative writing systems (Olson & Atkins, chap. 16 in this volume; Fish, Kraut, Leland, & Cohen, 1988) support specific tasks within the total work process. As such they support only a minor portion of the communicative activities that occur in the course of a cooperative work effort.

In the following discussion, we use our knowledge of the functions that proximity serves in research collaborations to define basic requirements that communication technologies must meet to support research collaboration, or for that matter, any cooperative intellectual work that spans months and is at least partially based on a sustained personal relationship among the members of a work group. We believe that these functions translate into two fundamental requirements for communication technology: high quality and low personal cost. Although high quality at low cost is a marketing platitude that has been applied to automobiles, hot dogs, and dishwashers, it applies with special meaning to communications technology. By low cost we mean that the communications medium should be so ubiquitous that a potential user need make no planned effort to use it. That is, the behavioral cost to the actual user would be low, even though the financial cost to users or the organization supporting them may be high. As we said earlier, high quality means that the communication system allows users to transmit all of the information they need to exchange rapidly. Typically, this will mean a two-way (or N-way) communication link involving more than one sensory channel. We expand on these requirements in the following sections.

Low-cost Interactions

As discussed earlier, frequent, informal, and, at times, unplanned contact provides a mechanism for both bringing together potential partners as well as for maintaining existing collaborative relationships. Indeed, we believe the lesson of the J-shaped relationship between distance and communication frequency lies in the fact that much useful communication between research partners is not planned and would not occur if it had to be planned (see Abel, chap. 18 in this volume). During the initiation of a collaboration, proximity allows low-cost contact that provides potential collaborators with the opportunity not only to make contact with each other but to discreetly assess and develop their mutual compatibility before committing to work together. Opportunities for spontaneous communication are especially important in the preplanning stages of a research collaboration, when potential partners are playing with ideas and surreptitiously assessing each others' desirability as a research partner. Once they become committed to working together, frequent communication holds together the threads of a collaborative relationship over time. During the execution of the work, proximity plays a crucial role in project management and mutual supervision between collaborators. The frequent, low-cost communication that proximity permits enables collaborators to provide each other with both subtle prods and status information through casual interactions. Also, quick and easy access to a partner permits sharing of major and even minor decisions and, thus, creates the sense of ownership that keep participants committed to a project. Finally, and perhaps most importantly, throughout the collaborative process as a whole, proximity supports a convivial personal and working relationship by building a consensus of views and interests and maintaining shared knowledge about the project and about the local culture in which it is embedded.

To maintain this level of communication in the absence of proximity requires technology that makes communication cheap, frequent, and spontaneous enough that collaborators can be in touch as easily as if their offices were next door to each other. The technology must allow not only frequent but informal and unplanned interactions as well; many of the interactions that make up this feedback over time are damaged by intentionality and simply would not occur if they must be willfully initiated. This goal of adding a random component to communications is at odds with the traditional goal of communication technology from the courier to the telegraph, from the telephone to electronic mail, which has been to support intentional, planned communication. In point-to-point communication systems (as opposed to broadcast systems), senders have to have a recipient in mind before they initiate communicative activity. For example, they dial the phone number before they talk.

However, this approach to communication technology is not inevitable. The concept of an electronic hallway or sidewalk where people in different locations can meet spontaneously was raised at least as early as 1975 (Thompson, 1975). The recent experiment at Xerox to provide an omnipresent video connection between two of its research facilities (Goodman & Abel, 1987; Abel, chap. 18 in this volume) is one of the few innovations in the use of communications technology that takes this concept seriously. This pioneering experiment is unique in that it created an environment that encouraged unplanned interactions mediated by technology over considerable geographic distance. Usage data indicated that over 70% of the interpersonal communication between the two sites was casual, drop-in style interaction of less than 5 minutes in duration and that these interactions would likely not have occurred in the absence of a continuous video link. Participants' experiences suggest that having this video link was marginally adequate to promote a shared context and culture that supported joint work across the two locations.

Unfortunately, the communications technology in the Xerox experiment was limited, both by the state-of-the-art in commercial video equipment and by the high financial costs of transmitting the huge amount of information that comprises moving video images. As a result the two locations were linked only by a single channel for slow scan video, two lines for audio connections and an additional one for data. Participants felt that this was inadequate to support crucial aspects of cooperative work, such as project initiation, delicate negotiation, and detailed joint work that required shared graphics (Abel, chap. 18 in this volume). The logistics of switching the limited video resource became burdensome, and in any case, was not sufficient to match the quality of the spontaneous interactions that physical proximity provided within a work site. We deal with some aspects of these deficiencies in the technology in a later section, but can presage the discussion by noting that more sophisticated communications technology may more adequately solve some of the problems solved naturally by proximity.

Although the Xerox experiment attempted to use communications technology to duplicate the effects of physical proximity, one can go beyond mere duplication by using communications technology to create virtual environments that are impossible in the physical world. In the physical world an office can only be surrounded by a few others along a corridor. Even in a better, less linear office arrangement that minimizes average separation among co-workers we are still limited by the two-dimensionality of physical layouts. And in the real world, the inhabitants of those offices are as likely to be there because of accident, seniority, or bureaucratic inertia rather than careful planning.

To overcome the limitations of physical proximity, we can imagine video hallways or other communications technologies that would provide virtual proximity to a larger or more appropriate set of colleagues. Also, unlike physical office arrangements, which are not even as flexible as the organizational structures that support their inhabitants, such electronic hallways are potentially reconfigurable to accomodate organizational changes, changes in personal work interests, or other changes that might affect the collaborative compatibility of a particular set of people.

High-Quality Real-time Interactions

Just as proximity supports low-cost communication, it also supports high-quality interaction. For example, during the idea generation stages that occur at the beginning of a project, when collaborators plan the execution of the work, and later when they plan the documentation of the project, proximity enables the intense, highly interactive, face-to-face sessions that are the cornerstone of the collaborative process.

As our interviews and the Xerox experiment suggest, these intensive meetings require communications tools sophisticated enough to permit high-quality interactions. At a minimum these communication tools must allow participants to exchange whatever information they bring with them to the discussion or create during the course of a meeting itself. Some of this material might be text, on paper or in computer files. Other material might be graphical, ranging from handwritten notes, to figures, photographs, or annotations of already exchanged documents. Currently, commercial video cameras and monitors do not provide sufficient resolution to allow the exchange of this textual and graphical material.

In addition, participants in these meetings must be able to jointly see, point to, and modify these text and graphics objects. Just as one participant in face-to-face meetings might point to headings on a blackboard or paragraphs on a page for the other participants', they must be able to do so in a technology mediated meeting.

Most importantly, however, the technology to support planning and other types of intensely interactive meetings must support the backchannel and other feedback mechanisms that participants in a meeting use to accomodate the informational needs and processing capacities of listeners as well as the dynamic evolution of speakers' conversational goals (Kraut & Higgins, 1984). When people communicate in ways that allow them to assess their partners' view of the world and of their own speech and to use this information to change their conversational tactics, their communication becomes more effective and efficient than it might be when this feedback is lacking (Krauss, Garlock, Bricker, & McMahon, 1977; Kraut, Lewis, & Swezey, 1982; Krauss & Weinheimer, 1966, 1967).

The role of dynamic feedback between communicators in facilitating smooth and efficient exchange of information explains at least in part users' frustration with teleconferencing systems that provide inadequate half-duplex audio (i.e., to reduce audio feedback, only one person can talk at a time) in exchange for the hands-free convenience. Similarly, the lack of real-time feedback may provide a partial explanation for the dissatisfaction with some forms of asynchronous computer communication systems. In a computer conference, for instance, participants enter comments, perhaps about very complex topics, without knowing exactly who they are writing to and without being able to ascertain whether any listener has understood what they are saying. Without the capacity to obtain immediate feedback, authors may find it difficult to tailor their communications so that they are readily understandable to other readers. If readers do not understand a particular entry, they may be unlikely to follow it up or to respond in a way that seems directly relevant; this process of inadequate encoding and unresponsiveness may then produce the frustration about lack of responses described by Tombaugh (1984). Given this dynamic, it is easy to see why it has proven to be difficult to get people to use computer conferences on a regular basis (Johansen, 1987).

Conclusions

In this section we did not attempt to exhaustively catalogue technology that would support research collaborations nor even to list all of the available communication technology. Rather, we have focused our attention on the two major functions currently fulfilled by physical proximity. We drew implications from these functions about two styles of communications technology that we believe could provide the foundation for technologies supporting cooperative work. Omnipresent video might provide the low-cost and therefore frequent and spontaneous interactions crucial to initiating collaborations, monitoring and coordinating the project, and maintaining a smooth personal relationship. Multimedia meeting tools might provide the high-quality communication to support planning and review. Although many other specific tools have been proposed and could be built to support particular tasks that occur frequently, most are likely to build from these two foundations.

REFERENCES

Allen, Thomas J. (1977). *Managing the flow of technology.* Cambridge, MA: MIT Press.
Beaver, D. B., & Rosen, R. (1979a). Studies in scientific collaboration: Part II. Scientific co-

authorship, research productivity and visibility in the French scientific elite, 1799–1830. *Scientometrics, 1,* 133–149.

Beaver, D. B., & Rosen, R. (1979b). Studies in scientific collaboration: Part III. Professionalization and the natural history of modern scientific co-authorship. *Scientometrics, 1,* 231–245.

Crane, D. (1976). The nature of scientific communication and influence. *International Sociology of Science Journal, 22,* 38–41.

Darley, J. M., & Berscheid, E. (1967). Increasing liking as a result of the anticipation of personal contact. *Human Relations, 20,* 29–40.

Deerwester, S., Dumais, S. T., Furnas, G. W., Landauer, T. K., & Harshman, R. (in press). Indexing by latent sematic analysis. *Journal of the American Society for Information Science.*

Dunnette, M. D., Campbell, J. P., & Jaastad, K. (1963). The effect of group participation on brainstorming effectiveness for two industrial samples. *Journal of Applied Psychology, 47,* 30–37.

Eveland, J., & Bikson, T. (1987). Evolving electronic communication networks: An empirical assessment. *Office: Technology and People, 3,* 103–128.

Feldman, M. (1987). Electronic mail and weak ties in organizations. *Office, Technology and People, 3,* 83–102.

Fish, R., Kraut, R., Leland, M., & Cohen, M. (1988). Quilt: A collaborative tool for cooperative writing. In R. B. Allen (Ed.), *Proceedings of the ACM Conference on Office Automation Systems* (pp. 30–37). New York: Association for Computing Machinery.

Foster, G., & Stefik, M. (1986). Cognoter: Theory and practice of a Colab-orative tool. *Proceedings of the Conference on Computer-Supported Cooperative Work.* New York: Association for Computing Machinery.

Garvey, W., & Gottfredson, S. D. (1977). Scientific communication as an interactive social process. *International Forum on Information and Documentation, 2,* 9–16.

Goodman, G. O., & Abel, M. J. (1987). Communication and collaboration: Facilitating cooperative work through communication *Office: Technology and People, 3,* 129–146.

Hackman, J. R. (1987). The design of work teams. In J. W. Lorsch (Ed.), *Handbook of organizational behavior,* (pp. 315–342). Englewood Cliffs, NJ: Prentice-Hall.

Hagstrom, W. O. (1965). *The scientific community.* Carbondale, IL: Southern Illinois University Press.

Heider, F. (1958). *The psychology of interpersonal relations.* New York: Wiley.

Janis, I. L. (1972). *Victims of groupthink.* Boston: Houghton Mifflin.

Johansen, R. (1987). A user view of computer-supported teams: What are they? *Proceedings of the NYU Symposium on Technological Support for Work* Group Collaboration, New York.

Kraemer, K., & King, J. L. (1986). Computer-based support for group decision support: Status of use and problems in development. *Proceedings of the Conference on Computer-Supported Cooperative Work.* New York: Association for Computing Machinery.

Krauss, R. M., & Weinheimer, S. (1966). Concurrent feedback, confirmation and the encoding of referents in verbal communication. *Journal of Personality and Social Psychology, 4,* 343–346.

Krauss, R. M., & Weinheimer, S. (1967). Effect of referent similarity and communication mode on verbal encoding. *Journal of Verbal Learning and Verbal Behavior, 6,* 359–363.

Krauss, R. M., Garlock, C. M., Bricker, P. D., & McMahon, L. E. (1977). The role of audible and visible back-channel responses in interpersonal communication. *Journal of Personality and Social Psychology, 35,* 523–529.

Kraut, R. E., Galegher, J., & Egido, C. (1988). Relationships and tasks in scientific collaboration. *Human-Computer Interaction, 3,* 31–58.

Kraut, R. E., & Higgins, E. T. (1984). Communication and social cognition. In R. S. Wyer, Jr. & T. K. Srull (Eds.), *Handbook of social cognition* (Vol. 3, pp. 87–127). Hillsdale, NJ: Lawrence Erlbaum Associates.

Kraut, R. E., Lewis, S. H., & Swezey, L. W. (1982). Listener responsiveness and the coordination of conversation. *Journal of Personality and Social Psychology, 43,* 718–731.

Latane, B., Williams, K., & Harkins, S. (1979). Many hands make light the work: The causes and consequences of social loafing. *Journal of Personality and Social Psychology, 37,* 822–832.

Lewis, A. C., Sadosky, T. L., & Connolly, T. (1975). The effectiveness of group brainstorming in engineering problem solving. *IEEE Transactions on Engineering Management,* EM-22, 119, 124.

Mayer, M. (1977). The telephone and the uses of time. In I. Pool (Ed.), *The social impact of the telephone.* Cambridge, MA: MIT Press.

Mendenhall, M. Oddou, G., & Franck, L. (1984). The trend toward research collaboration in social psychological research. *Journal of Social Psychology, 122,* 101–103.

Menzel, H. (1962). Planned and unplanned scientific communication. In B. Barber, & W. Hirsch (Eds.), *The sociology of science* (pp. 417–441). Glencoe, IL: Free Press.

Over, R. (1982). Collaborative research and publication in psychology. *American Psychologist, 37,* 996–1001.

Pelz, D. C., & Andrews, F. M. (1966). *Scientists in organizations.* New York: Wiley.

Presser, S. (1980). Collaboration and the quality of research. *Social Studies of Science, 10,* 95–101.

Steiner, I. D. (1972). *Group process and productivity.* Orlando, FL: Academic Press.

Thompson, G. B. (1975). An assessment methodology for evaluating communications innovations. *IEEE Transactions of Communication, 23,* 1045–1054.

Tombaugh, J. W. (1984). Evaluation of an international scientific, computer-based conference. *Journal of Social Issues, 40,* 129–144.

Zajonc, R. B. (1968). Attitudinal effects of mere exposure. *Journal of Personality and Social Psychology* (Monograph Supplement, Part 2), 1–27.

7

Information Technology and Work Groups: The Case of New Product Teams

Deborah G. Ancona
Massachusetts Institute of Technology

David F. Caldwell
Santa Clara University

Abstract

Advances in computing and communications capabilities are becoming widely available to groups to help them to do their work. The development of these systems has primarily grown out of new technologies and not from an understanding of the assignments groups are asked to complete. We believe that an in-depth understanding of the complex tasks that groups are frequently assigned is necessary to realize the full capabilities of new technologies. In this chapter, we focus on groups which face the highly interactive and complex task of developing new products and present a description of the activities in which these teams engage and move from that data to suggest how information technology might better be used to support the work of those teams.

THE CHANGING ROLE
OF GROUPS IN ORGANIZATIONS

Today, task forces and project teams are performing tasks that might formerly have been either handled through an organization's formal structure or assigned to individuals. Whether it is the establishment of product development teams at General Motors or Proctor and Gamble, quality circles at Lockheed, or groups to implement new manufacturing strategies in the aerospace industry (Kazanjian & Drazin, 1988), the use of teams is expanding rapidly (Goodman, 1986). Teams are believed to increase individual commitment and performance, thus shortening the time necessary to bring

173

a new product to market and thereby increasing competitiveness (Hackman & Walton, 1987; Kanter, 1986). Groups are also formed out of necessity; as products and technologies become more complex, what once could have been done by an individual may now require the input and experience of several individuals. Similarly, because important decisions involve many constituencies, the use of teams broadens participation in decision making, thus increasing commitment to the decision (c.f. Coch & French, 1948; Janis & Mann, 1977).

Although groups have always been an important tool for accomplishing organizational goals, the form and usage of groups differs from the past. One area of difference is in the increased amount of authority and responsibility granted to the team (Galbraith, 1982; Kanter, 1983). In response to international competition and the accelerating pace of technological and market change, organizations have attempted to become more flexible and adaptable. One way to do this is to push decision making down the organizational hierarchy, assigning the freedom and responsibility to respond to threats and opportunities to task forces and project teams. However, when group projects and goals are generated from within rather than assigned from above, the group bears a special burden; because it lacks administrative approval for its actions, it must work to find support for its ideas within the organization.

In addition, the use of groups is changing in how individuals are assigned to them. Rather than permanently assigning individuals to work groups with a fixed task or set of tasks, the norm is often to assign individuals to work part-time on multiple projects. These groups are usually temporary and have membership that changes over time; they are made up of individuals who must work closely together for a short period of time while simultaneously carrying on other individual or group work, and maintaining commitments and loyalties to other parts of the organization.

Furthermore, cross-functional composition or orientation differentiates the new form of groups from others. To respond to competitive challenges, organizational units often have to be more closely coupled than in the past, sometimes even working in parallel to complete assignments spanning traditional organizational units (Clark & Fujimoto, 1987). Thus, individual work group members must interact extensively with non-team members. The group can no longer be seen as a bounded unit; rather it must be viewed as an open system interacting with other groups and individuals in the organizational environment.

At the same time as the use and form of organizational groups is changing, advances in computer science and information technology offer new techniques that can influence the processes and performance of a group. In recent years not only have large numbers of employees acquired access to computers, but the ability to connect computers has created the potential for altered patterns of communication and coordination. For instance, tele-conferencing allows for multiple individuals in geographically dispersed locations to hold meetings, group decision support systems have been de-signed to enhance the decision-making ability of groups through pro-cedures that structure the weighting of alternative solutions (Kraemer & King, 1986), and CAD/CAM systems can be used to help people display and manipulate technical information more effectively in face-to-face meetings. Finally, as the other chapters in this volume indicate, "groupware" of vari-ous kinds is continually being developed to support collaborative work (Abel, chap. 18; Lakin, chap. 17; Landow, chap. 15; Olson & Atkin, chap. 16 in this volume).

These new technologies may significantly affect the way group members work with each other and with other parts of the organization. What is less clear is whether the nature and role of these new technologies will depend solely on the intuitions of systems designers or will be guided by a coherent theory of how people must coordinate their activities to complete group tasks (Malone, 1987).

DEVELOPING MORE COMPLETE THEORIES
OF GROUPS

To keep pace with these changes, conceptual analyses of groups need to take into account the specific things groups must do and how group mem-bers must interact with individuals outside the group to complete their assignments. This contrasts with the more typical approach of relying on simple models of group tasks and focusing exclusively on interactions with-in the group.

An understanding of the specific task a team must perform can lead to the development of a fuller model of group process and allow for a more complete definition of team performance (Goodman, Ravlin, & Schminke, 1987) than is normally used, therefore eliminating many of the conflicting findings common in group research (c.f. Gresov, 1988). We contend that only group research that begins with a clear understanding of the team's task can lead to useful theories of coordination that can guide the develop-ment of improved information technologies.

Teams and task forces must both draw resources from and give back to the organization the results of their efforts, thus we believe that models of group activities must include both the things team members do with one another and those things that are done with people outside the group. This approach contrasts with many theories of groups that focus almost ex-clusively on the processes and activities occurring inside the group. There is a long history of lumping the critical activities of a group into those related to accomplishing the task and those contributing to the maintenance of the group (Philip & Dunphy, 1959; Schein, 1988). Research growing out of this tradition has led to a good understanding of individual behavior in groups (c.f. McGrath, 1984), communication among group members (Putnam, 1986), the phases groups go through (Tuckman, 1965; Gersick, 1988), and how groups make decisions (c.f. Bettenhausen & Murnighan, 1985). It has not, however, led to a clear understanding of how groups deal with others, including how the group obtains the resources necessary to complete its task and gains support for the results of its efforts.

Recently, a number of studies have started to explore communications between work groups and the environment in which they exist and to examine the impact of these communications on group performance. For example, in investigations of research and development laboratories, the amount of external communication with other parts of the organization has been positively related to performance (Allen, 1984; Katz & Tushman, 1981; Tushman, 1977, 1979). Bringing information into the group is only one way the group interacts with other groups. In an earlier paper (Ancona & Caldwell, 1988), we described a broad model of the types of activities in which groups engage to manage their dependencies with others, including how the group defines its membership, how the group manipulates the permeability of its boundary, and how the group attempts to obtain information and resources from its environment.

These observations have led us to conclude that theories of groups in organizations would be more useful if they incorporated information about the group's task and consider both internal processes and the way the group deals with others. Furthermore, we posit that if information technologies are to be used to improve the performance of highly complex teams, they must be designed with a clear understanding of the communications and task activities that take place within the group as well as those between group members and outsiders. To provide a part of that foundation, we describe part of our observations of new product teams, one exemplar of the type of group now assuming increasing importance in organizations.

These teams are responsible not only for the specific technical design of a product, but also for coordinating the numerous functional areas and hierarchical levels that have information and resources necessary to make the new product a success. Team members may be assigned to the team full-time or may be only part-time participants. Similarly, members may remain on the team from inception to finish, or may terminate membership after some portion of the task is completed. Given these characteristics, the new product team provides an ideal model of the ad hoc task group, and is therefore a useful model for thinking about how information technology might be used to assist teams who must manage dependencies on other organizational entities to carry out a complex collaborative task.

In the remainder of this chapter, we describe the task of the new product team and some of the activities through which these teams complete their work, concentrating on how the team interacts with others to complete its assignments. We then outline how information technology might be designed to help these groups carry out their work.

THE TASK OF THE NEW PRODUCT TEAM

Our observations about the complex tasks faced by new product teams are based on data drawn from a study of the product development process in high technology companies. The conclusions we present are based on data collected during interviews with the managers of new product teams at seven corporations in the computer, integrated circuit, and analytical instrumentation industries. We interviewed 34 new product team managers whose teams were at various stages of the product development process. The interviews were semistructured and ranged from 1 to 8 hours, with an average length of approximately 3 hours. We asked each manager to describe, in detail, the activities he or she and the other members of the team carried out, both within and outside the group; we asked each to discuss shifts in team activities over the product development process and to describe stumbling blocks that impeded progress. In addition, we interviewed four managers who were responsible for supervising multiple teams. These managers were asked to describe patterns they had observed and differences between teams. The interviews were taped and transcribed, and the transcriptions were evaluated to identify patterns of activity and transitions in the product development process. In addition, 15 new product team members were asked to keep a log in which they described their interactions as they worked to complete their tasks. This sample is neither representative nor large enough to test specific hypotheses. Rather, our goal is to describe the task and processes of the new product team, thereby augmenting the normative literature with observations from the field.

For most of the teams we studied, the new product team managers described a general pattern in which two events served to divide the process and direct the new product team's activity. We refer to these events as transition points because they mark major shifts in the activities of team members; they divide the product development process into three phases that we label: creation, development, and diffusion. The first transition point represents a shift from a "possible product" to "definite product." The second involves a transfer of the technology and product ownership from the new product team to others in the organization. For many teams, these transitions represent major challenges to the viability of the group.

Our interviews suggest that each phase and transition point requires different patterns of team functioning and different patterns of interaction with outsiders on the part of the new product team. We illustrate the nature of these phases and transition points with excerpts from several of our interviews and summarize a wider range of activities found across the teams.

The Creation Phase

The first thing I did was to go to talk to lots of people to find out what they thought the product was and how to get there. This was at the technical level, what are the details, not just global suggestions. I started out with the guy who brought me here, he sent me to see someone else, and so it went that I came to talk to a lot of high- and middle-level people. The interviews were open-ended but I pushed and maybe even taught them a few things about their concept; what it meant to produce the product they envisioned. So I gained knowledge about details of what the product ought to be, who the players were, what they did, and what they wanted.

It's not exactly clear how the whole thing got started, but then it seldom is. There were these two other projects going on, but they weren't doing too well. So, about a year ago the Product Committee decided to start this new project. We started out by having a meeting with the two old project teams, and members of the top corporate and division management. This was May and we were supposed to have this wonder machine ready to ship by January. After the two former leaders were signed up for the project I pulled in two more key people and had an initial meeting. This was the core of the group. We added a few more people and then spent a couple of weeks frittering about, reading stuff, deciding if the product was feasible. People were saying 'no way it can happen' and I was busy setting things up so we'd have a place to live. We moved in and launched into work.

In this early phase, our interviewees typically reported that they talked frequently with people outside the team. The topics of most of these interactions fell into one of three categories: collecting information or resources, modeling the organizational environment, and building links with other groups. They collected technical information about what was and was not feasible and what the latest innovations had been, market information about what products were selling well and what the competition was doing, and political information about who did or did not support the project. In addition to collecting information, they attempted to create models of how other groups would respond to the product. This included forecasts of top management's response to the product concept or potential "snags" that might occur in the future. Finally, team leaders' reports suggest that the new product teams also developed communication links with other groups who did not have information or resources currently needed by the team. Many of these contacts were undertaken in anticipation of a later phase, when the cooperation and support of the target groups would be needed. In other cases, these efforts to build communication links involved trying to shape outside opinion to make it more favorable towards the team.

However, not all of the new product teams' activities were externally oriented; there was a great deal of interaction among team members as well. Product definition was a clear priority, particularly the process of moving from a very general idea to a specific design plan. One manager described this phase as "playing in the sandbox"; members were occupied with exploring various ideas and determining feasibility (See Kraut, Galegher, & Egido, 1987–1988 for a similar description of intellectual play in the project initiation phase of collaborative research.). This preceded the difficult job of selecting the best of the alternatives that had been examined.

During this phase, the membership of the team stabilized, and internal patterns of interaction developed and began to formalize. At this time the task of the group is one of defining the product, determining its feasibility, and organizing to become a working team.

Possible to Definite Project: A Transition Point

The design review was set up to make sure we weren't going off in crazy directions. All of R&D was invited, quite a few showed up. We had answers to most of their questions, and we got lots of helpful input. We were official now, they had given us the OK. We went back to work.

The first sell was to the R&D staff. We had decided what we wanted to do and we had to get them to agree, the VPs had to sign off. We're spending their money, we have to meet their needs to keep getting resources. We got lots of comments. Then we had to present our responses to their comments at another meeting with a broader audience. We were seeking the blessing of top management.

Management just couldn't all get together and decide which chip they were going to use. It was debated and changed and debated and we couldn't really get working. The cost and time to delivery got out of control. We had to scrap the whole thing and most of the team left the company.

Our interviews suggest that the first transition point occurs just prior to the major portion of the development phase and involves a shift from recognition of potential feasibility to commitment to one new product idea. This entails movement from low-cost effort with minimal organization support to major capital investment and support from top management. In our sample there was usually some formal, organizationally imposed, design review that forced the new product team to present and defend its design. Even when this was not the case, there was usually informal organizational pressure about this time to brief top management and get their support. Team leaders describe spending a great deal of frenzied time and activity preparing for these reviews, be they formal or informal.

Three of our interviewees reported difficulties with this transition. Two described teams that failed to get agreement with and the support of other groups and could not progress. The third described a team whose members could not agree among themselves about certain technical issues. These groups could not built both internal and external consensus on project specifications, hence they could not move from the process of deciding what the product should be to deciding how to actually make the product. Our interviewees generally reported a shift in activities in the teams that successfully completed this transition point. The general task of the team moved from defining the new product idea, determining feasibility, and gaining support for it to actual product development.

Development

There was a lot of coordinating to do. I wanted to make sure they had ordered the components and the printed circuit boards. George was the liaison to manufacturing, but I needed to check on things once in awhile. As time went on there was so much to watch over that we decided to bring in three people from manufacturing. They helped with the components decisions: which could be obtained, did they have the right performance specs. At this point we also started meeting with people outside the group to provide a status update. We had representatives from purchasing, larger manufacturing areas, production planning, diagnostics and marketing. We informed them of progress and changes and published the meeting minutes on-line so everyone could access them. We also kept the Product Committee informed.

By November the top committee was getting panicky: they were nice, but they were nervous. I tried hard to protect the team from the pressure, but the rest of the company was like a pressure cooker. Some of the team even had to come in during Christmas time. The machine just wasn't working and everybody felt as though we'd failed, even though we'd done the impossible. Still we were late to Manufacturing and everyone was scared.

Several rules are in place now, such as minimizing new technology so that this thing gets out in time. Now for every piece of the product we have a plan and every Monday morning people had to report on where they are with respect to this plan. I'm in the middle of two ends of a problem. From above I get major direction and goal setting, like we really don't want to deliver in February but in December, and then Monday mornings I get reality.

I decided to house us in an isolated building. This was a novel task, there were lots of new people, and we were going to be going hard and fast. That kind of intensity has to be isolated. Besides, if people aren't together the project isn't going to turn out as good as it could have. People who are working have two things to do. One is they have to do the operating system for the project. The other is they have to stay in touch with the rest of the organization, so they are torn. I want people to make project optimizations not local ones.

Many of our interviewees described the type of dilemma illustrated in the final quotation. The development stage requires that the team focus much of its effort internally, on technical issues. However, team leaders also reported that substantial efforts were needed to maintain and build relationships with other groups.

In this phase, the team needs to spend its time on technical development; therefore, it cannot be constantly interrupted. An important dilemma that team leaders talked about is how much separation there should be between the team and the rest of the organization. Specifically, should the team obtain separate facilities or perhaps even physically isolate itself from the rest of the organization? Isolation allows the team to focus on technical innovation and speed but may make it difficult for the team to carry on transactions with other functional groups. Within the group, this stage requires the highest need for close coordination among team members and most teams appear to work out routines and methods for accomplishing this.

Isolation allows the group to shift its activities. During the development phase, the team must move from product definition to setting goals and schedules for actual development. For this to be done, inputs from others regarding their priorities and suggestions for the product design need to be restricted unless market or competitive information radically changes. This restriction may be difficult to maintain because other functional groups may view the product as a concept that is open to constant change and updating (Dougherty, 1987). Isolation can facilitate information restriction. Groups that are unable to restrict this information may lose valuable time and suffer reduced effectiveness. The potential importance of this isolation was illustrated in that two of the three of the team leaders who informed us that their teams failed at this stage, reported continually changing work goals and schedules in response to new information and inputs to be the cause of the failure.

Although, during this stage, the group's priorities change to managing its internal activities, our interviews indicate that in the development stage there is still a need to manage team activities and relations with others. The focus of the team is on using the resources and information previously obtained to develop the product, yet the group must begin to coordinate with other functional groups to ensure that they will provide components and take over the product at the agreed on time. During this time, top corporate management needs to be informed of the product's progress as well.

Technology Transfer: A Second Transition Point

Then we had this big fight. Manufacturing said let's build it and make repairs later: Engineering said let's hold it. I was in the middle. Manufacturing yanked these people out. I was in a tenuous position. I wanted the product to stay with the team to get the bugs out but the product committee and the rest of the organization were going crazy. We had made a deal with some customers. There were huge pressures to get it over to manufacturing.

DECLARATION OF IMPATIENCE: A time has come, we believe, to call a halt to product XX engineering and ship the product. We believe it is time to say IT'S DONE!!! Put the unfinished business on the shelf for product 2XX. This product already is the best on the market, by far, and the momentum of things to come will insure that it stays that way. BUT NOT IF IT DOESN'T SHIP! We sell the customer on evolution, not on a solution for all men, for all time, now. Get on with the final game. NO MORE DEVELOPMENT!!! (Memo sent to a new product team by one team leader)

A second transition point normally occurs somewhere during the testing phase. In most cases, technological problems have been assessed and a prototype exists and has been tested. The transition consists of moving from team ownership of the product to more general organizational ownership. Our interviewees report a change similar to what Quinn and Mueller (1963) called a technology transfer point, where the emphasis moves from developing the technology to passing information, enthusiasm, and authority to use that technology to other groups in the organization. Our interviewees report that this transition will not occur if the group is either unwilling to relinquish the product or unwilling to continue to work on the product when it has passed into the hands of others.

This was a difficult transition for all the teams described to us. Problems ranged from members who were unwilling to transfer the product to others, to less committed team members who began work on other projects, leaving the project before a smooth transition to manufacturing occurred. For most teams, this transition signaled a decrease in the isolation and commitment of team members. Many interviewees reported a shift in team activities from internal team decisions to "selling" the product idea to other groups.

Diffusion and Ending

The team now has a whole different form. Those who are helping manufacturing are spending most of their time in New Hampshire at the factory. That is a small subset of the original team. Some of the team members are busy going over documentation and support products. There are still a lot of other groups that have to come through for us to make this product shine. Then there were quite a few people who left when their part of the project was done. There are a few who have stayed on along with some new people to work on the third generation. This is sort of a transition from one team to another.

At this point, the team wasn't meeting much. People didn't seem to know what to do. It was the end of an intense group. People were burnt out. People were zombies. People weren't ready to start over. They hadn't recovered. Maybe I should have been doing some career planning but that's not really what I wanted to do. People were lost but the product was great. I sent all my people on vacation.

Our interviewees reported that during the diffusion phase the external activities of their teams dramatically increased as members began transferring technical data as well as a sense of ownership to other groups that must manufacture and market the new product. The necessity of transferring product ownership causes some obvious difficulties for a team. Some interviewees reported that the nature of the second stage of the development process, particularly if the team has isolated itself, caused teams to develop a very impermeable boundary. Although the isolation this boundary created may have been important in facilitating the internal decision making and group cohesiveness necessary during the second stage, it occasionally made the product transfer difficult.

The team leaders reported that variability of individual involvement in completing the product was high at this stage. The key issue was keeping those members needed to finish up the project committed to it, while moving those whose efforts were no longer needed on to other activities. A number of team leaders mentioned that balancing these responsibilities was difficult. Maintaining motivation was difficult because the major product development decisions had already been made and what remained was completing product details and transferring the product to other groups.

Dominant Task Activities Within Phases

In sum, our interviews suggest that new product teams follow a pattern as the product development process proceeds. We found three phases of activity: creation, development, and diffusion. Each phase can be described in terms of a dominant task requirement, and each of these task requirements demands different patterns of interaction among team members and between the team and outsiders.

During the creation phase the team must obtain the information and resources it will need initially and in the future. The main task requirement for the team at this time is *exploration*. Teams must determine what resources are available to them, what the product can and should be, and what the other areas of the organization want the product to be. In addition, teams must explore the technologies available for building the product and the markets it might serve at this time. Exploration inside the team involves getting to know other team members, determining who has particular skills, and who can be trusted.

Teams then face a difficult transition as they move from exploration of numerous alternatives, to commitment, to a specific product design. The dominant task requirement following this transition is the efficient *exploitation* of the information and resources the team has collected. To develop the product in the form that was agreed on, the team must solve technical problems and learn to operate efficiently. Externally the team moves from gathering information and determining others' expectations for the new product to coordinating, keeping others informed, and building relationships with the groups that will receive the team's output.

Following a second transition, the emphasis for the team becomes that of *exportation* of its product to others. As the team transfers ownership of the product to others, the emphasis on smooth, efficient internal operations declines and the emphasis on external relations characteristic of the creation phase recurs. To make the development process a success, the team must export not only the product, but a sense of excitement and commitment to the other groups who will be responsible for marketing, manufacturing, and servicing the new product. Thus, in this stage, the team shifts to working intensively with members of these other groups.

Two general conclusions can be drawn from our interviews. First, product development demands a complex pattern of group activities and interactions that change over time and what is necessary for the group to do at one time is detrimental to accomplishing the task at another. Moreover, a model of the group process of the new product team requires an understanding of both the interactions among the team members and how the group members deal with outsiders. We believe that clear, complete models of group behavior can facilitate the design of effective information technologies.

ISSUES
IN DESIGNING INFORMATION TECHNOLOGIES
THAT FIT GROUP TASK REQUIREMENTS

The task requirements of exploration, exploitation, and exportation require different patterns of interaction both among team members and between the team and outsiders. Therefore, information technology to support groups, such as new product teams, must facilitate very diverse patterns of interaction. To aid the group with internal and external task requirements, and with shifting from one type of activity to another, information technology must have a great deal of flexibility. As the interactions required of team members change, computer-based communication and decision support systems must facilitate adaptation to the new set of demands. If they do not, they may disrupt the group's progress by encouraging it to retain familiar modes of working that are no longer appropriate. We draw out the implications of our observations for the design of computer applications to support these varied tasks. However, we hasten to point out that our expertise is in the analysis of social behavior; thus, our ability to make detailed recommendations in this domain is limited. This shortcoming on our part only serves to emphasize the central theme of this book—that behavioral scientists and systems designers live in separate worlds and that many more researchers who speak both languages are needed to bring the worlds closer together.

Exploration

One key aspect of exploration is modeling, or creating a picture of the external environment including predictions of where resources can be found, who supports the team's efforts, and what expectations others hold for the team. There are a number of ways that information technology could potentially be applied to helping the group model its environment. For example, a program could be developed to supply the team with organization charts showing relevant parts of management, manufacturing, marketing, and other functional areas. Team members could then work together to mark in some way those people who have relevant resources, those who support the team and those who do not, and to define others' expectations of the product. Perhaps most importantly, members could also mark those individuals whose views are currently unknown by the team. This mapping process could then automatically generate responsibility charts that would structure the group to fill in gaps of knowledge, direct it to plan meetings with outsiders who need to be encouraged to help, or help it decide which expectations it can realistically meet. Although not yet commercially available, the Stakeholder Identification and Assumption Surfacing Tool described by Vogel and Nunamaker (chap. 19 in this volume) is a useful prototype of this sort of software.

Exploration also involves exploring ideas and possibilities for the new design. Computer applications could help the team keep track of its ideas, increase creativity, and evaluate its work. For example, one of the teams in our study was struggling to decide how compatible with other computers the computer they were designing had to be. Information technology could provide a structure to list current options, and to prompt brainstorming of additional ideas. Team members and outsiders could then be asked to set criteria for choosing among the options. Prompts would be programmed to assure that issues of manufacturability, commercial potential, and finance would be considered. This setting of criteria might also point out areas where more information about the options would need to be gathered.

Then team members and outsiders would be asked to rate each option and the ratings would be displayed to present areas of agreement, areas of disagreement, high-scoring and low-scoring options. After discussion of the data the process could be repeated until consensus built around one option. Later, this same process could be used to get feedback from external groups on the design.

Exploitation

During the development stage the primary task requirement is exploitation of information and resources to achieve efficient internal operations. Information technology could facilitate coordination among group members, forecasting of schedule delays, and external reporting of team progress. By focusing on internal progress and coordination, this technology could help the group shift its emphasis away from exploration.

Some of the teams in our study designed their own PERT charts to track what each team member had to have ready at a particular time; this procedure is very complex and could easily be simplified by generic scheduling programs. Systems dynamics modeling has been developed that will forecast the impact on commercialization schedules of a delay in the production of a major component. Providing team members with this capability would both help them to forecast revised schedules, and communicate the enormous effect that an early slippage can have later in the process. Finally, electronic mail systems could be used to facilitate communication within the group and to supplement current modes of coordination with those outside the group.

Exportation

The final set of tasks requires the team to export ownership of the product to those responsible for manufacturing, selling, marketing, and servicing the new product. This exportation is difficult because the team is often competing with other teams for organizational resources and these other groups do not understand or feel committed to the product. Information technology can aid in product transfer both by preparing other groups for the new product in advance of the transfer date and by facilitating the actual exchange. Tools such as computer conferencing and electronic mail can allow the team to regularly brief other groups during product development and build the knowledge and support of other groups well in advance of the exportation of the product. Such systems could be designed to prompt team members to update other groups on specific topics and at regular intervals.

Information technologies can also facilitate the direct exchange of the product. At a simple level, CAD/CAM might be used to distribute pictures of the product and ease the communication of technical details across functional barriers. The development of expert systems to aid in the documentation of the new product would be of greater value. By partially automating this task, such aids could reduce delays in the new product transfer due to late or incomplete documentation.

Group Theory and Information Technology

If information technology is to improve group performance while maintaining favorable group dynamics, care must be taken in how the systems are designed and used. We argue that the design of information technology can benefit from an in-depth understanding of behavior in groups; in particular, we claim that information technology designs must be based on an adequate consideration of external, as well as internal interactions, and the shifts in group task over time.

Many of the recent developments in information technology have been designed with an internal perspective on the group; that is, they are aimed at improving the processes and interactions among group members. Although this is an extremely valuable goal, such systems may have the unintended consequence of diminishing the group's interactions with outsiders. Two examples may illustrate how this can develop. We were told of one team that developed programs and languages for use on a local area network among team members that were incompatible with a broader organizational network. Although this system facilitated and simplified communication among the team members, it made communication with nonmembers relatively more difficult.

The second example has to do with systems designed to enhance group decision making. Systems have been developed to improve group decisions by reducing individual biases, speeding up the process, and facilitating interactive decision making—in short, by helping the group improve its internal processes. Although extremely useful under many circumstances, such decision aids may lead group members to view themselves as a closed system. If this happens, the group may not work to ensure that information is obtained from external sources and outsiders become committed to what the group produces. Clearly, applications need to be developed to encourage teams to model their dependence on the external organization and to develop ways to meet that dependence.

Also important to accomplishing the group task is correctly mapping out changing task demands. Most information technology has the advantage that it lowers the cost of communication and coordination. Under many circumstances this enhances task accomplishment. For certain tasks, however, the unfiltered flow of information, which is useful for a certain period, becomes disruptive as requirements change. One of our interviewees described a team that failed because it was unable to commit to a single design idea. The team would constantly rethink decisions in response to new information, preventing the team from making systematic progress. In this case, the team leader continued to seek input from other groups and use it to redefine the product. If individuals are not sensitive to the information needs of a team, an information system may allow and even encourage the transmission of more data than the team can process. This may become the equivalent of electronic "junk mail."

For all of the benefits of information technology, we must also realize its limitations. Given the myriad tasks the team must perform, information technology can only support and improve on the performance of some. The use of electronic or conferencing systems may aid in the communication of relatively unambiguous information. However, if such systems become the primary communication vehicle, the team may reduce its ability to obtain the kind of information communicated through subtlety and nuance. Our data suggest that successful teams are those that are able to build support from others in the organization and ensure the products they create fit the organization's product strategy. Team leaders indicate that accomplishing these goals is frequently a function of a long-term relationships team members have established with others, the ability of the team leader to "read" the support others are willing to provide the team, and the ability of team members to negotiate with outsiders. Current information technology applications do not have the capacity to allow for such multifaceted exchanges, yet they need to be carried out.

As the responsibilities given to teams change and broaden, information technologies provide great opportunities for improving performance. However, to realize the potential of these new technologies, their designers must carefully match the capabilities of the technology to the tasks. If this is to happen, new models of group behavior and a clear understanding of the task of the group are necessary. The results of our study of new product teams illustrates the complex nature of the tasks teams will increasingly face. In the case of new product teams, models of effective behavior must describe not only how team members should interact, but also how team members must deal with outsiders. This suggests that if information technologies are to improve this type of team's performance, they must be designed to both improve the group's decision making and enhance group members' interactions with nonmembers.

ACKNOWLEDGMENTS

Support for this research was provided by the Center for Innovation Management Studies, Lehigh University. We thank Jolene Galegher for her comments on an earlier draft of this chapter.

REFERENCES

Allen, T. J. (1984). *Managing the flow of technology: Technology transfer and the dissemination of technological information within the R & D organization.* Cambridge, MA: MIT Press.

Ancona, D. G., & Caldwell, D. F. (1988). Beyond task and maintenance: External roles in groups. *Group and Organization Studies, 13,* 468–494.

Bettenhousen, K., & Murningham, J. K. (1985). The emergence of norms in competitive decision-making groups. *Administrative Science Quarterly, 30,* 350–372.

Clark, K. B., & Fujimoto, T. (1987). Overlapping problem solving in product development. Cambridge: Harvard Business School Working Paper 87-048.

Coch, L., & French, J. R. P. (1948). Overcoming resistance to change. *Human Relations, 1,* 512–533.

Dougherty, D. (1987). *New products in old organizations: The myth of the better mousetrap in search of the beaten path.* Unpublished doctoral dissertation, Sloan School of Management, MIT.

Galbraith, J. R. (1982). Designing the innovating organization. *Organizational Dynamics,* Winter, 5–25.

Gersick, C. J. (1988). Time and transition in work teams: Toward a new model of group development. *Academy of Management Journal, 31,* 9–41.

Goodman, P. (1986). The impact of task and technology on group performance. In P. Goodman (Ed.), *Designing effective work groups* (pp. 120–166). San Francisco, CA: Jossey-Bass.

Goodman, P., Ravlin, E., & Schminke, M. (1987). Understanding groups in organizations. In B. M. Staw, & L. L. Cummings (Eds.), *Research in organizational behavior* (Vol. 9, pp. 121–174). Greenwich, CT: JAI Press.

Gresov, C. (1988). Exploring fit and misfit with multiple contingencies. *Administrative Science Quarterly,* forthcoming.

Hackman, J. R., & Walton, R. E. (1986). Leading groups in organizations. In P. Goodman (Ed.), *Designing effective work groups* (pp. 72–119). San Francisco, CA: Jossey-Bass.

Janis, I. L., & Mann, F. (1977). *Decision making: A psychological analysis of conflict, choice, and commitment.* New York: Free Press.

Kanter, R. M. (1983). *The change masters: Innovation for productivity in the American corporation.* New York: Simon & Schuster.

Kanter, R. M. (1986). The new workforce meets the changing workplace: Strains, dilemmas, and contradictions in attempts to implement participative and entrepreneurial management. *Human Resource Management, 25,* 515–539.

Katz, R., & Tushman, M. (1981). An investigation into the managerial roles and career paths of gatekeepers and project supervisors in a major R & D facility. *R & D Management, 11,* 103–110.

Kazanjian, R. K., & Drazin, R. (forthcoming). An empirical test of a stage of growth progression model. *Academy of Management Journal.*

Kraemer, K., & King, J. (1986). Computer-based systems for group decision support: Status of use and problems in development. *Proceedings of Conference on Computer-supported Cooperative Work,* Austin, TX, December 1986.

Kraut, R. E., Galegher, J., & Egido, C. (1987–1988). Relationships and tasks in scientific collaboration. *Human-Computer Interaction, 3,* 31–58.

Malone, T. W. (1987). Modeling coordination in organizations and markets. *Management Science, 33,* 1317–1332.

McGrath, J. F. (1984). *Groups: Interaction and performance.* Englewood Cliffs, NJ: Prentice-Hall.

Philip, H., & Dunphy, D. (1959). Developmental trends in small groups. *Sociometry, 22,* 162–174.

Putnam, L. L. (1986). Conflict in group decision making. In R. Y. Hirokawa, & M. S. Poole (Eds.), *Communication and group decision making.* Newbury Park, CA: Sage Publications.

Quinn, J. B., & Mueller, J. A. (1963). Transferring research results to operations. *Harvard Business Review, 41* (January–February), 44–87.

Schein, E. H. (1988). *Process consultation: Its role in organization development* (Vol. 1). Reading, MA: Addison-Wesley.

Tuckman, B. W. (1965). Developmental sequence in small groups. *Psychological Bulletin, 63,* 384–399.

Tushman, M. (1977). Special boundary roles in the innovation process. *Administrative Science Quarterly, 22,* 587–605.

Tushman, M. (1979). Work characteristics and subunit communication structure: A contingency analysis. *Administrative Science Quarterly, 29,* 82–98.

8

The Technology of Team Navigation

Edwin Hutchins
University of California, San Diego

Abstract

Large ships are navigated by a team of people working with a specialized set of tools. This chapter looks first at the nature of the tools and the navigation task and argues that the tools do not amplify the cognitive abilities of the team members, but instead transform what are normally difficult cognitive tasks into easy ones. It then considers the division of labor among the members of the navigation team and the techniques by which they coordinate their work activities. The progress of various team members through the career cycle of navigation practitioners produces an overlapping distribution of expertise that makes it possible for the team to achieve training and job performance in a single activity.

NAVIGATION TECHNOLOGY

Step aboard any modern ship and you will find yourself surrounded by an incredible mixture of technologies. Systems of levers, cables, and pulleys that Leonardo daVinci would have understood perfectly dominate the deck, while just inside a metal hatchway are sophisticated electronic systems whose design and operation are fully understood by only a handful of people in the world. Similarly, the technology of the navigation suite is an odd mixture of old and new. Every functional chart house contains a collection of artifacts in which one can see the long tradition of the practice of navigation at sea. In a typical hour of navigation work, a modern navigator is likely to use technological devices whose basic designs vary in age from a few years to several centuries.[1]

At all times while a naval vessel is underway, a plot of its past and projected movements is maintained. Day and night, whenever a ship is neither tied to a pier nor at anchor, navigation computations are performed. In a long passage, the navigation activities may be continuously performed for weeks or even months on end. Most of the time the work of navigation is conducted by one person working alone, but when a ship leaves or enters port, or operates in any other environment where maneuverability is restricted, the computational requirements of the task may exceed the capabilities of any individual and the navigation duties are then carried out by a team of individuals working together.

This chapter considers the technology involved in a navigation task called *piloting,* which is the principal method of navigation when ships are moving in restricted waters. Technologically, this is a particularly conservative practice. The gyrocompass is the most advanced piece of technology involved, and the principles of its operation were well worked out by the end of the First World War. The other technological devices, a telephone circuit for communication among members of the navigation team, a telescopic sight, ballpoint pens and log books, pencils and plotting tools, and the Mercator projection chart are hardly what anyone would consider examples of high technology.

Yet there is something about these tools that keeps them in use in this important endeavor in spite of the introduction of more advanced technologies around them. Without doubt, much of the piloting task could easily be automated with existing computer technology, and I am frequently asked, but find myself unable to answer, why the navigation team and its old tools have not yet been replaced by perhaps a single navigator using an electronic chart. The pursuit of an answer to that question would doubtless lead us to consider who wants such a change, how technology needs are recognized and promoted, who pays for the development of new technology, what other tasks have more urgent technological needs, what resources are available to proponents of competing schemes, and so on. Such an exercise would likely demonstrate once again that technological change is as much a social as a technical process. Instead of speculating on why this technology has not yet been overtaken by "something better," it seems more productive to look closely at how this existing technology is actually used.

I argue first that the old technologies that survive here constitute a different kind of advanced technology. The altitude of a technology might

---

[1]In what is perhaps the ultimate technological contrast, I once saw a junior officer take latitude and longitude coordinates from a satellite navigation computer, and roughly plot the ship's position on a chart using the span of his fingers as a measurement tool.

not be measured only in terms of the sophistication of the inner workings of the device hardware, but also in terms of the extent to which the device renders an important problem easy to solve. I then show that the use of these tools supports a distribution of knowledge among the members of the navigation team that makes the system very robust in the face of individual component failures.

Piloting is a specialized task that, in its ordinary operation, confronts a limited set of problems, each of which has a well-understood structure. The problem that confronts a navigator is usually not to figure out how to do the processing of the information in order to get an answer. That has already been worked out. Rather the problem, in most instances, is simply to use the existing tools and techniques to process the information that is gathered by the system and to produce an appropriate evaluation of the ship's situation or an appropriate recommendation about how the ship should proceed in order to get where it is supposed to go. This task therefore differs from many that are considered by other chapters in this volume inasmuch as it is a well-understood, narrowly bounded task that is performed in a technological environment that has been evolving for hundreds of years.

NAVIGATING LARGE SHIPS

Guiding a large ship into or out of a harbor is a difficult task. Ships are massive objects; their inertia makes them slow to respond to changes in propeller speed or rudder position. Because of this response lag, changes in direction or speed of ships must be anticipated and planned well in advance. Depending on the characteristics of the ship and its velocity, the actions that will bring it to a stop or turn it around, for example, may need to be taken tens of seconds, or even minutes, before the ship arrives at the desired turning or stopping point. Aboard naval vessels, a continuous plot of the position of the ship is maintained to support decisions concerning its motion.[2] An officer called the conning officer is nominally responsible for the decisions about the motion of the ship, but for the most part the conning officer does not make such decisions. Usually, such decisions are actually made by the navigation team and passed to the conning officer as recommendations, such as "Recommend coming right to zero one seven at this

---

[2]Such complete records are not always kept aboard merchant vessels and are not absolutely essential to the task of navigating the ship in restricted waters. It is possible for an experienced pilot to eyeball the passage and make judgments concerning control of the ship without the support of the computations that are carried out on the chart. Aboard naval vessels, however, such records are always kept for reasons of safety primarily, but also for purposes of accountability so that if there should be a problem, the ship will be able to show exactly what it was doing and where it was at the time of the mishap.

time." The conning officer considers the recommendation in the light of the ship's overall situation, and if the recommendation is appropriate, will act on it by giving orders to the helmsman, who steers the ship, or to the leehelmsman, who controls the ship's engines.[3]

The navigation activity is event-driven in the sense that the navigation team must keep pace with the movements of the ship. Unlike many decision-making settings, when something goes wrong aboard ship, quitting the task or starting over from scratch are not available options. The work must go on. In fact, the conditions under which the task is most difficult are usually the conditions under which its correct and timely performance is most important.

In this chapter I consider the members of the navigation team together with the team's social organization and the tools of the navigation trade as a system of socially distributed computation. In particular, I consider the roles of people and technological devices in the computations that constitute the navigation task.

Position Fixing by Visual Bearings

In order to plan the motions of the ship, the navigation team must establish the position of the ship and compute its future positions. The most important piece of technology in this task is the *navigation chart*. A navigation chart is a specially constructed model of a real geographical space. The ship is somewhere in space and to determine or "fix" the position of the ship is to find the point on the appropriate chart that corresponds to the position of the ship in the world.

The simplest form of position fixing, and the one that concerns us here, is position fixing by visual bearings. For this one needs a chart of the region around the ship, and a way to measure the direction, conventionally with respect to north, of the line of sight connecting the ship and some landmark on the shore. The direction of a landmark from the ship is called the landmark's bearing. Imagine the line of sight in space between the ship and a known landmark. Although we know that one end of the line is at the landmark and we know the direction of the line, we can't just draw a line on the chart that corresponds to the line of sight between ship and landmark because we don't know where the other end of the line is. The other end of the line is where the ship is and that is what we are trying to discover.

Suppose we draw a line on the chart starting at the location of the symbol for the landmark on the chart and extend it past where we think the ship is, perhaps off the edge of the chart if we are really unsure. We still don't know

---

[3]On older ships, of the sort aboard which this study was conducted, the leehelmsman operates a device called the engine order telegraph, which indicates the desired engine speed to personnel in the engineroom who actually control the engines directly by operating valves that admit high pressure steam to the propulsion turbines.

just where the ship is, but we do know it must have been somewhere on that line when the bearing was observed. Such a line is called a line of position. If we have another line of position, constructed on the basis of the direction of the line of sight to another known landmark, then we know that the ship is also on that line. If the ship was on both of these lines at the same time, the only place it could have been is where the lines intersect. Each line of position thus provides a one-dimensional constraint on the position from which the landmark was observed. The intersection of two lines of position uniquely constrains the location from which the observations were made. In practice, a third line of position with respect to another landmark is constructed. The three lines of position form a triangle and the size of the triangle formed is an indication of the quality of the position fix. It is sometimes said that the anxiety of the navigator is proportional to the size of the fix triangle.

The Fix Cycle

The necessity for continuously plotting the ship's position, projecting the future track, and preparing to plot the next position is satisfied by a cycle of activity called the fix cycle. If the ship is near enough to land to take visual bearings on terrestrial landmarks, yet on a heading that will not soon bring it near shallow water or other dangers, the cycle may be completed at a leisurely pace of say once every half hour.[4] When the ship is in restricted waters, however, it may be necessary to complete the cycle on one-minute intervals. Under these conditions, no single person could make all of the observations and do all of the computations required to complete the cycle in the amount of time available.

The Fix Cycle in Sea and Anchor Detail.   When the ship is operating in restricted waters, the work of the fix cycle is distributed across a team of six people.[5] The duty stations of the members of the team in the configuration called *sea and anchor detail* are shown in Fig. 8.1 as elliptical shapes. We can follow the fix cycle by following information through the system.

New information about the location of the ship comes from the bearing takers on the wings of the ship (positions 1 and 2 in Fig. 8.1). They find landmarks on the shore in the vicinity of the ship and measure the bearings of the landmarks (direction with respect to north) with a special telescopic sighting device called an alidade. The true north directional reference is provided by a gyrocompass repeater that is mounted under the alidade. A

---

[4]Once the ship is out of sight of land, position fixes are made using a number of techniques beyond the scope of this chapter. These include radar, celestial, loran, omega, and satellite navigation.

[5]On other ships, and on this ship in different circumstances, the team may be somewhat larger or smaller depending on the availability of qualified personnel.

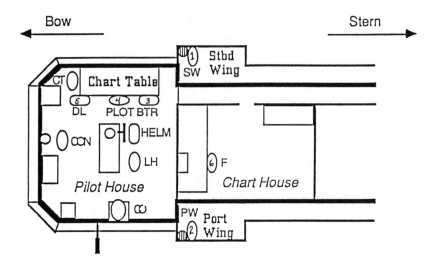

FIG. 8.1.   Watchstander positions for sea and anchor detail.

prism in the alidade permits the image of the gyrocompass scale to be superimposed on the view of the landmark. (An illustration depicting the view through such a sight is shown in Fig. 8.2.) The bearing takers read the measured bearings and then report them over a telephone circuit to the bearing timer-recorder.

The bearing timer-recorder (position 3 in Fig. 8.1) stands at the chart table inside the pilothouse. This person talks to the bearing takers out on the wings and writes the reported bearings in a book called the *bearing log,* which is kept on the chart table.

The plotter, (position 4 in Fig. 8.1) plots the bearings that are reported by the bearing takers. This person normally has no direct communication with the bearing takers, but is either told the bearings by the bearing timer-recorder, or reads them out of the bearing log. From the perspective of the plotter, the bearing timer-recorder is an information buffer. In order to make a high-quality fix, the bearings should be observed as quickly and as nearly simultaneously as possible. It takes much longer to plot a line of position than it does to make the observation of the bearing, so the activities of the plotter and the bearing takers have different distributions in time. The activities of the bearing timer-recorder not only provide a permanent record of the observations made, they permit the bearing takers and the plotter to work, each at their most productive rates, without having to coordinate their activities in time. The bearing log is thus a technology that is used to "ease the constraints of time/activity match" (McGrath, chap. 2 in this volume).

In addition to plotting the ship's position, the plotter also projects where the ship will be at the time of the next few fix observations. This requires a knowledge of the heading and speed of the ship. The plotter normally reads these from the deck log, which lies on the chart table to his left.

The keeper of the deck log (position 5 in Fig. 8.1) maintains the deck log in which all events of consequence for the ship are recorded. All commands given by the conning officer to the helmsman (HELM in Fig. 8.1) concerning the course to steer, and all orders to the leehelmsman (LH in Fig. 8.1) concerning the speed to order from the engineroom are recorded.

When the projected position of the ship has been plotted, the bearing timer-recorder consults with the plotter to decide which landmarks will be appropriately situated for the next position fix, and assigns the chosen landmarks to the bearing takers by talking to them on the phone circuit. In choosing landmarks, the plotter and the bearing timer-recorder are looking for a set of three landmarks such that the lines from the three landmarks to the projected position of the ship intersect at reasonably steep angles. If the lines from any pair intersect at a shallow angle, then a small angular error in either one will move their point of intersection (one corner of the fix triangle) considerably, and add uncertainty to the fix. If the angles of the

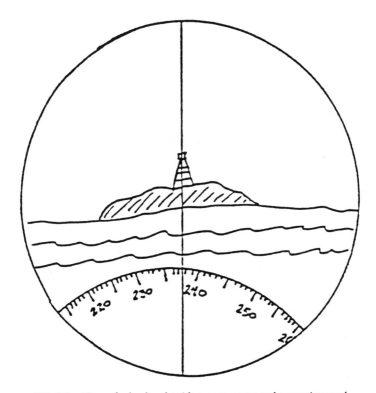

FIG. 8.2.   View of a landmark with gyrocompass scale superimposed.

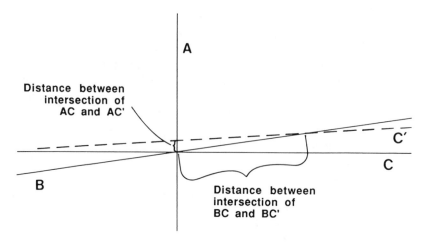

FIG. 8.3.   Effects of errors of different sizes on the accuracy of the fix.

intersections of the lines of position are steep, then small errors in the observations themselves will have small effects on the locations of the intersections (see Fig. 8.3).

The bearing timer-recorder uses a wristwatch to time the fix intervals, and about 10 seconds before the next fix time, calls out "Standby to mark." This alerts the bearing takers that they should find their landmarks and aim their telescopic sights at them.

In a room just aft of the pilothouse sits another member of the team called the fathometer operator (position 6 in Fig. 8.1). This individual uses an instrument called an echo sounding depth finder or fathometer and is connected on the phone circuit with the bearing takers and the bearing timer-recorder. When the timer-recorder gives the "Standby to mark" signal, the fathometer operator reads the depth of water under the ship from the fathometer display and reports it to the bearing timer-recorder. This is recorded in the bearing log, and is later compared with the depth of water indicated on the chart at the plotted position. This comparison provides an additional check on the quality of the position fix.

At the time chosen for the fix observations, the bearing timer-recorder says "Mark," and the bearing takers observe and report the bearings of the landmarks they have been assigned. Thus the cycle begins again.

TECHNOLOGIES OF REPRESENTATION

How shall we think about the roles of technology and the people in this task performance? We are accustomed to thinking about technological systems as amplifiers of information-processing abilities or as intelligent intermediaries or agents who are also involved in the task performance. These are common metaphors for information-processing system design and they carry with them ways of thinking about the relations of people to technology that may prevent us from seeing the full range of possibilities (Hill, 1988; Hutchins, 1988). Looking in detail at this task has led me to think about the role of technology in cooperative work in a different way.

Problem Solving as Re-representation

In his seminal book, *The Sciences of the Artificial,* Herbert Simon (1981) said "Solving a problem simply means representing it so as to make the solution transparent" (p. 153). Of course, the meaning of "transparent" depends on the properties of the processor that must interpret the representation. Still, it is a powerful point, and although Simon had theorem proving in mind when he made it, it is also true of many other kinds of problem solving. The practice of moving a problem from one domain to another and solving it there has been an important technique in mathematics ever since Descartes' introduction of coordinates, a domain into which many problems have been moved and in which many solutions become apparent.[6] Gauss proved that a 17-sided regular polygon can be constructed with a straightedge and compass (the last previous regular polygon construction proof having come 2,000 years earlier), by using the knowledge that quadratic equations can be solved with straightedge and compass and showing that the construction of the 17-sided polygon was tantamount to solving a series of quadratic equations (Stewart, 1977). As useful as Cartesian coordinates are, many problems in relative motion that seem difficult in Cartesian coordinates become trivial when expressed in polar coordinates. Many instances of "Aha!" insight occur when a problem expressed in one way is re-represented in another in which the answer is literally staring the problem solver in the face (Gardner, 1978).

Four Ways To Do Distance/Rate/Time Problems

To get a better feel for how the way a problem is represented can change what is required of the problem solver, let us consider just one computation in the fix cycle. Suppose the plotter has just plotted a fix and needs to compute the ship's speed based on the distance the ship has moved in the interval of time that elapsed between the current fix and the previous one.

In particular, suppose the two fix positions are 1,500 yards apart and three minutes have elapsed between the fix observations.

---

[6]Modern navigation is still exploiting Descartes' insight. The chart itself is a carefully constructed coordinate space in which the solutions to many navigation problems become apparent.

Now, we are going to consider the cognition required of a task performer doing this task under four different conditions. Each of these is a real possibility.

Condition 1: The task performer has the following resources: paper and pencil, knowledge of algebra, knowledge of arithmetic, knowledge that there are 2,000 yards in a nautical mile and 60 minutes in an hour, and knowledge of the equation D = RT.

Condition 2: The task performer has the same resources as in condition 1, except that instead of a paper and pencil, the task performer has a four-function pocket calculator.

Condition 3: The task performer has either a three-scale nomogram of the sort shown in Fig. 8.4, or a nautical slide-rule of the sort shown in Fig. 8.5 and the knowledge required to operate whichever tool is present.

Condition 4: The task performer has no material implements at all, but knows how to use what navigators call the "three-minute" rule.

It is impossible to specify in advance just how any particular person will actually do this task in any of these conditions, but if the person actually uses the resources in the ways they are intended to be used, it is not difficult to determine what is likely to be involved.

In Condition 1, the task performer will first have to use the knowledge of algebra to manipulate the formula $D = RT$ to the form $R = D/T$ so that rate can be solved for directly from the given values of D and T. Then, the distance in yards will have to be converted to the equivalent number of miles using the knowledge of the number of yards in a mile and the knowledge of arithmetic. The time in minutes will have to be converted to the equivalent number of hours using the knowledge of the number of minutes in an hour and, again, arithmetic. The distance measure must be divided by the time measure, arithmetic again, to get the rate. Of course, these things can be done in a different order; for example, the division could come before either of the unit conversions, or between them, but in any case all these things must be done in order to solve the problem.

The reader may want to try it as an exercise just to get a feel for the sort of work involved. I estimate that this problem would tax the abilities of many navy navigation practitioners. Not because the arithmetic is difficult, but because it is necessary to figure out what to do and how the various things that are done fit together to produce the desired solution. One may be perfectly capable of doing every one of the component subtasks in this problem, but fail completely for lack of ability to organize and coordinate the various parts of the solution with each other.

In the calculator version, the procedures for doing the arithmetic opera-

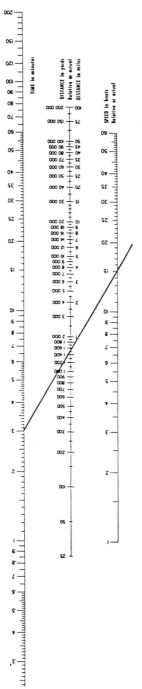

FIG. 8.4. Three-scale nomogram.

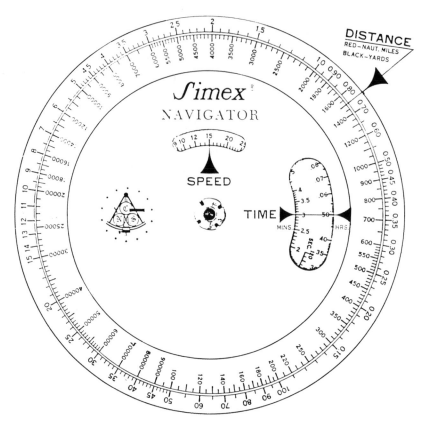

FIG. 8.5.   Nautical slide rule.

tions of division and multiplication are restructured so that instead of constructing a pattern of symbols on a piece of paper and decomposing the problem to a set of operations on single-digit arithmetic arguments, values are keyed into the calculator and operator buttons are pushed. Also, depending on the order in which the steps are taken, it may be necessary to remember a previous result and enter it into a later operation after other operations have intervened. I think that this version of the task would also tax the abilities of many navigation practitioners, because the hard part is not doing the arithmetic but in deciding how to coordinate the arithmetic operations with each other. These tools give no support for that part of the task.

   The paper and pencil condition and the calculator condition are alike in that they utilize completely general computational engines. The knowledge of the equation for distance, rate, and time and the knowledge of the constants required for the unit conversions are specific to the task, but they provide little help in structuring the actions of the task performer. As a result, the procedures for doing the computation are complex. When we write them out at even the shallow level of detail previously given, we find that they contain many steps. If we actually got down to counting each symbol written on the paper or each key press on the calculator as a step (not an unusually detailed level for a cognitive analysis), we would find that they each run to many tens of steps.

Now consider the cognition required of the task performer in Condition 3. To use the nomogram, one finds the value of the time on the time scale and makes a mark there. One finds the value of the distance on the distance scale and makes a mark there. Then one draws a line through those two marks with a straightedge and reads the value of speed, in the desired units, where the line drawn intersects the speed scale. Now you may complain that the fact that these scales are already constructed in terms of the units set by the problem gives this condition an unfair advantage over the first two conditions. But that is part of the point. This is a very frequently occurring problem, and the nomogram is a tool designed specifically to make its solution easy. The use of the nautical slide-rule is very similar. It, like the nomogram, is a medium in which multiplication and division are represented as alignments of logarithmic scales. One aligns the distance index with the desired distance on the distance scale (could be yards or miles, both are represented side by side), aligns the elapsed time index with the desired time on the time scale (either minutes or hours, both are present side by side), and having done that the speed index will point to the speed in knots on the speed scale.

Having the scales in the units as set by the problem is helpful because it eliminates the need to convert one kind of unit into another, but it is more important to note that the knowledge of algebra is not required for this condition of the task. The nomogram and slide-rule transform the task from one of computation planning—figuring out what to divide by what—to one of simple manipulation of external devices. In the first two conditions, all that stands between the task performer and the nonsensical expressions $R = DT$ and $R = T/D$ is a knowledge of the syntax of algebraic transformations. When using the nomogram or the slide-rule, the structure of the artifacts themselves obviate or lock out such relations among the terms. The relations $D = RT$, $R = D/T$, and $T = D/R$ are built into the structure of the nomogram and slide-rule.[7]

The task performer still needs to know something, but the knowledge

[7]Looking at the nomogram, we see that the time and speed scales flank the distance scale on either side of it. A line drawn between any point on the speed scale and any point on the time scale intersects the distance scale at a point that is the averaged sum of the logarithm of the time and the logarithm of the speed. Sums of logarithms are products, so the very construction of the nomogram constrains the relationships among the terms to be of the correct type. Similarly, the slide-rule is constructed such that the distance reading is the angular sum of the logarithm of the speed and the logarithm of the time.

that is invoked to solve the problem with these tools is less complicated, and less general, than the knowledge required with the paper and pencil or calculator versions. A good deal of what needs to be done can be inferred from the structure of the artifacts themselves. They constrain the organization of action of the task performer by completely eliminating the possibility of certain syntactically incorrect relationships among the terms of the computation. Compared with Conditions 1 and 2, one may be reluctant to say that the answer was actually computed by the task performer in Condition 3. It seems that much of the computation was done by the tool used by the performer, or by the designer of that tool. The person somehow could get by doing less because the tool did more. But before we go that far, let us consider the task in Condition 4.

Where Condition 3 utilized specialized external artifacts, Condition 4 utilizes a specialized internal artifact. Since three minutes is one-twentieth of an hour and 100 yards is one-twentieth of a mile, the number of hundreds of yards (twentieths of a mile) a ship travels in three minutes (a twentieth of an hour) is its speed in nautical miles per hour. Thus, a ship that travels 1,500 yards in three minutes has a speed of 15 nautical miles per hour. In order to "see" the answer to the problem posed, the navigator need only imagine the number that represents the distance travelled in yards, 1500, with the last two digits removed: 15. The representation in which the answer is obvious is simply one in which the images of the characters that make up the numbers are manipulated.

Now the reader may really cry "foul play." "It's a special example with ginned-up numbers that permits this trick to be used," you say. In fact, this is not an unusual problem for a navigator. The most common interfix interval is three minutes precisely because this rule is so simple and so easy to use. The navigation team is capable of performing the fix cycle on two-minute, or even one-minute, intervals, but three minutes is more common—not because it meets the needs of the ship better than the other intervals, but because it meets them well enough, and it makes this computation so convenient.[8]

What are these tools contributing to the computations? It has now be-

---

[8]The nautical slide-rule and nomogram are normally only used when the ship is away from land and the fix intervals are much longer than three minutes. When the cycle is performed on the shorter intervals of one or two minutes, speed is normally computed by conversion to the three minute standard. For example, if the ship travels 800 yards in two minutes, it would travel 1200 yards in three minutes, so its speed is 12 knots. And finally, regardless of the speed of the ship, as long as both the speed and the fix interval are constant, there is no need to recompute ship's speed to project the ship's position for the next fix. The distance traveled during the next interval will be the same as that covered in the last interval, so it can simply be spanned with dividers and laid on the projected track line without even determining its actual distance.

come commonplace to speak of technology, especially information-processing technology, as an amplifier of cognitive abilities. Cole and Griffin (1980) showed, however, that the appearance of amplification is an artifact of a commonly assumed perspective. When we concentrate on the product of the cognitive work, cultural technologies, from writing and mathematics to the kinds of tools we have considered here, appear to amplify the cognitive powers of their users. Using these tools, people can certainly do things they could not do without them. When we shift our focus to the process by which cognitive work is accomplished, however, we see something else. Every complex cognitive performance requires the application of some number of component cognitive abilities. Computing speed from distance and time with the calculator involves many component subtasks; remembering a symbolic expression, transforming the expression, determining which quantities correspond to which terms of the expression, mapping the expression to operations on the calculator, finding particular calculator keys, pressing the keys, and so forth. The application of these abilities must be organized in the sense that the work done by each component ability must be coordinated with that done by others. If we now consider doing the same task with the nomogram or with the three minute rule, we see that a different set of abilities is enlisted in the task. None of the component cognitive abilities has been amplified by the use of any of the tools. Rather, each tool presents the task to the user as a different sort of cognitive problem requiring a different set of cognitive abilities or a different organization of the same set of abilities.

There are two important things to notice about the computational technology of the piloting task. First, the existence of these specialized tools and techniques is evidence of a lot of cultural elaboration directed toward avoiding the use of algebraic reasoning and arithmetic. In fact, there is more than I have presented here. The problem could also have been solved by looking up the speed in a table of distances, rates, and times. We can only surmise that these are things that people are not good at.

Moreover, these tools and techniques permit the task performer to avoid doing algebraic reasoning and arithmetic by replacing those activities with aligning indices with numbers on scales, or imagining numerical representations and making simple transformations. Rather than amplifying the cognitive abilities of the task performers, or acting as intelligent agents in interaction with them, these tools transform the task the person has to do by mapping it into a domain where the answer or the path to the solution is apparent.

Perhaps this should also give us a new sense of expert systems. Clearly, a good deal of the expertise in the system is in the artifacts, both the external implements and the internal strategies; not in the sense that the artifacts are themselves intelligent or expert agents, but because the act of getting into coordination with the artifact constitutes an expert performance by the person. These tools permit the people using them to do the tasks that need to be done while doing the kinds of things the people are good at: recognizing patterns, modeling simple dynamics of the world, and manipulating objects in the environment (Rumelhart, Smolensky, McClelland, & Hinton, 1986). At this end of the technological spectrum at least, the computational power of the system composed of person and technology is not determined primarily by the information-processing capacity internal to the technological device, but by way the technology exploits the cognitive resources of the task performer.

Propagation of Representational State Across External Media

Let us return now to the execution of the whole fix cycle by the navigation team. In light of the preceding discussion, we can now see the activity of the team differently. Each technological system involved provides a representation of the information about the relation of the ship to the world. When bearing takers align the hairline in the alidade sight with a landmark on the shore, they have imposed a representational state on the alidade in which the hairline also crosses the gyrocompass scale at a particular point. When they read that bearing and speak it into the phone, they have moved the representation of the bearing from the domain of the gyroscope scale to the domain of spoken words. When bearing timer-recorders write the bearing in the book, they impose a new representational state on the bearing book. The information is moved to the domain of written numbers. When plotters read the bearing and align the index of the plotting tool with its scale, they move the information to still another domain. And, when they plot the bearing, they move the information to a domain in which it can be integrated with other information of the same type to form a position fix. That is, drawing the line of position imposes a representational state on the chart. It is still a representation of the bearing of the landmark, but now it is in a medium in which its relationship to other lines of position establishes a position of the ship.

The chart is the domain in navigation where the representation of information about the relation of the ship to its surroundings becomes interpretable. It is the domain where it is easy to "see" the answer to the question, "Where is the ship?" The written entries in the bearing log provide a complete specification of the position of the ship with respect to the landmarks on the shore, but it is not easy to see the answer in those entries, nor is it easy to perform the subsequent computations required by the task in the representation as it appears in the bearing log. The task of the navigation team, therefore, is to propagate information about the directional relationships between the ship and known landmarks across a set of technological systems until it is represented on the chart. Between the situation of the ship in the world and the plotted position on the chart lies a bridge of technological devices. Each device (alidade, phone circuit, bearing log, etc.) supports a representational state, and each state is a transformation of the previous one. Each transformation is a trivial task for the person who performs it, but, placed in the proper order, these trivial transformations constitute the computation of ship's position.

THE COORDINATION OF HUMAN ACTIVITY

In the previous section, we saw the work of the members of the navigation team as the propagation of representational state across a number of media until it arrived on the chart. To accomplish this, the various activities that go into the navigation task must be coordinated with each other. At the beginning of the chapter, I noted that the fix cycle is executed by an individual working alone when the ship is not in restricted waters. This fact provides us with an opportunity to contrast the means of solving the coordination problem in the two work configurations.

The job of the solo watch stander is more difficult than the task facing any member of the navigation team because the lone task performer must not only operate all of the devices, but must also coordinate the use of each device with the uses of the others. The problems of coordination in the solo performance concern the control of the sequence of actions required to do the job. Recall that controlling the sequence of steps was just the problem faced by the navigator trying to compute the ship's speed from distance and time using paper and pencil or a calculator. In that case, the problem of sequence control was eliminated by the design of specialized tools on which the task is performed in a single step. For the lone watch stander doing the entire piloting task, the sequential control problem cannot be eliminated, but it is solved, as in many other military tasks, by a different sort of artifact, a procedure. A procedure is a plan for sequential action, and the task performer is expected to learn the procedure and use it as a guide in organizing his actions.

Coordination of Action in the Team Performance

When the navigation task is performed by the team, the coordination among the actions of the members of the team is not achieved by following a master procedure. Instead it emerges from the interactions among the members of the team.

Consider the bearing taker. This person coordinates his or her activity with the (timing) behavior of the timer-recorder. Upon hearing "Standby to mark" the bearing taker finds the landmark, and then waits for the "mark" signal. Upon hearing that, he or she reads and reports the bearing of the designated landmark. The bearing taker has thus delegated the control of some aspect of his or her own behavior to the timer-recorder. This person has delegated the control over some other aspects of his or her behavior to the device with which he or she interacts. The bearing taker reads the value that appears where the hairline crosses the gyrocompass scale. His or her behavior is nicely constrained by the two coordination activities. The bearing timer-recorder can only attend to one bearing report at a time, thus the two bearing takers must coordinate their reports. If one hears that another is already in the process of reporting a bearing, the first person must wait until the phone circuit is clear to make a report.

When a bearing taker reports a bearing, the timer-recorder coordinates his or her (recording) behavior with the bearing taker. Other activities are on hold while the timer-recorder attends to and records (perhaps doing both simultaneously) the bearing. The plotter waits for the first bearing to appear in the bearing log book and plots it while the other are being reported. By the time the plotter is ready for the second bearing, it is usually already recorded in the log, so it can be read and plotted.

In the team performance configuration, in the place of an executive we find an interrelated set of functional units. Each team member does a part of the job only when certain conditions appear in the task environment. Coordination among the activities of the team members arises because some of the conditions for each team member's actions are produced by the activities of the other members of the team.[9]

The Metronome of Execution

As we saw earlier, taking fixes at regular intervals greatly simplifies the computations involved in projecting the position of the ship at the next fix time. For this reason and others, the initiation of the fix cycle is carefully timed. This results in a remarkable periodicity in the performance of this task.

The coordination of the whole system with the meter of time is accomplished when the timer-recorder coordinates with a wristwatch and the others coordinate with the timer-recorder. The timer-recorder's coordina-

---

[9]This aspect of the coordination of the activities of the team could be well modeled by a production system in which each team member would be modeled as a set of productions and the working memory of the system would model the environment to which they respond and in which they produce states for each other.

tion with the watch requires a maintained (a) vigilance to the watch, and (b) a test of when it is time to take another round. For the latter, the time-recorder must have a procedure for determining when the next round should fall and a way of determining when that time has been reached. Lack of vigilance, owing to the appropriation of attention by other tasks, may cause the timer to miss a mark. The plotter, who shares the physical environment of the timer apparently sometimes participates in that task redundantly and has been observed to comment, "Isn't it about time for a round?"

Coordination by Mutual Constraint

Notice that in the group performance mode, the sequence of actions to be taken need not be explicitly represented anywhere in the system. If participants know how to coordinate their activities with the technologies and people with which they interact, the global structure of the task performance will emerge from the local interactions of the members. The structure of the activities of the group is determined by a set of local computations rather than by the implementation of the sort of global plan that appears in the solo performer's procedure. In the team situation, a set of behavioral dependencies are set up. These dependencies shape the behavior pattern of the group. Similar effects have been observed by Kraut, Galegher, and Egido (1987-88) in their study of the distribution of labor among scientific collaborators.

Nominal and Real Divisions of Labor

In ideal conditions, the nominal division of labor depicted in the preceding sections is a reasonable description of what people do. But such conditions rarely prevail. Most of the time, there are small problems being encountered and solved, small errors being committed and corrected, and little bits of interaction structure being broken and repaired. In these more usual conditions, the nominal division of labor is routinely violated. Let me illustrate this with three brief examples.

Sometimes, bearing takers are not able to find the landmarks they have been assigned to observe. In the following exchange, the starboard bearing taker needs additional information to resolve an ambiguity. Here, SW is the starboard wing bearing taker and B is a qualified watch stander working as bearing timer-recorder.

SW: (Is it)The one on the left or the one on the right?
B: The one on the left, O.K.?
SW: Yah, I got it.

In this case, the bearing timer-recorder is called on to do part of the bearing taker's job of identifying the landmark. When the confusion or lack of knowledge is more profound, it is simply impossible to communicate enough information over the phone circuit, and someone has to go in person to the wing and do more of the bearing taker's job. A little later in the same exit from port, the starboard bearing taker was unable to find the north end of the 10th Avenue terminal. The plotter P, who is also the most qualified and highest ranking member of the team, went onto the wing to point it out. On the wing, P put his arm over SW's shoulders and aimed his body in the right direction.

P: The north one, all the way up.

SW: O.K.

P: If you can't see the light, just shoot the tangent right on the tit of the, the last end of the pier there.

SW: O.K., that pier, where those two . . .

P: Yah, all the way at the end.

SW: Alright.

P: There should be a light out there but if you can't see the light out there at the end of the pier (when we get in position), just shoot the end of the pier.

In the previous example, it was the bearing timer-recorder who temporarily left his duties to take on those of the bearing taker. This time it is the plotter.

At one point during an entry to port, the plotter was called away from the chart table for a consultation with the ship's captain just at the beginning of a fix cycle. When the bearings had been reported, the bearing timer-recorder reached over and set the index of the plotting tool to the first reported bearing. Upon returning a few seconds later, the plotter found that someone had done the first step of the plotting job.

This type of helping action occurs frequently. If they did not, if each individual was required to produce flawless performance entirely alone, the system would grind to a halt everytime any member of the team was unable to do his or her part of the job. Not only are members of the team responsible for their own jobs, they seem also to take responsibility for all parts of the process to which they can contribute.

The discussion of the coordination of action showed the people to be a sort of connecting tissue that holds the hardware of the technological systems together. The devices do not communicate with each other, it is the people who move the information from one device to another in performing the task of navigation.[10] Here we have seen that the flexibility and robustness of the system stems from the ability of this connecting tissue to adapt to changing circumstances. Sometimes the changing circumstances are consequences of problems in the connecting tissue itself (e.g., when a team member is unable to do his job), and sometimes it is a consequence of problems with the hard technology. In all cases, the management of the deployment of human resources, the on-line negotiation of the distribution of labor, is essential to the operation of the system. If the distribution of labor was fixed, the system would surely fail whenever one of its components failed.

The distribution of labor can only be negotiated if the distribution of knowledge and ability is at least partially redundant. In the organizational literature, this has been called "redundancy of function." Emery and Trist (1973) argued that such redundancy is necessary for the operation of adaptive, self-regulating systems in variable environments. Morgan (1986) called such systems "holographic" because "capacities relevant for the functioning of the whole are built into the parts" (p. 99). These notions raise the issue of the need to negotiate the division of labor, but do not address the issues of the way that negotiation proceeds or the conditions under which it can work. Emery and Trist (1973) and, later, Stratton and Flynn (1980) saw values as the coordinating mechanism among functionally redundant units. As noted earlier, members of the team seem to take responsibility for doing whatever they know can be done to ensure the timely propagation of information through the system. But values can only provide the disposition to act. To actually help, one must be aware of the need to help.

PRODUCTION AND REPRODUCTION
IN COOPERATIVE WORK

The movement of people through careers or the fact of mortality more generally forces human systems to solve two problems at once. They must both produce whatever they produce, and, if they are to endure, they must reproduce themselves at the same time. The need to reproduce the system itself involves parts of what McGrath (chap. 2 in this volume) called the "support function," the system's contribution to its component parts, and the "well being function," the system's contribution to its own viability. As

---

[10]As an antidote to rampant anthropomorphisms in artificial intelligence, Michael Cole often stressed the idea that people do not communicate with machines, rather their communication with other people can be mediated by machines. In this setting perhaps we could say that the devices do not communicate with each other, except when their communication with each other is mediated by people.

people leave the system, replacement expertise must somehow be created. Sometimes this reproductive function is delegated to special institutions like schools, but much of what needs to be known is, and perhaps can only be, acquired in the work place.[11]

An Overlapping Distribution of Knowledge

The flexibility and robustness of the system described in the previous section is made possible by the overlapping distribution of knowledge and ability across the members of the team. This distribution of knowledge that is so important to the synchronic operation of the team is a consequence of the way the system replicates itself.

Knowledge in cooperative tasks is frequently assumed by analysts to be partitioned among individuals in an exhaustive and mutually exclusive manner such that the sum of the individuals' knowledge is equal to the total required, and there is little or no overlap. Consider the knowledge required to perform just the input portion of the basic fix cycle. This requires the knowledge of the bearing takers, the bearing timer-recorder, and the plotter. We could imagine designing an experiment along these lines by training up a person to perform each of these roles and then putting them in interaction with each other. This assumes no history for the participants except that they are each trained to do a particular job. This would result in a distribution of knowledge as shown in Fig. 8.6. Here the knowledge required to do each job is represented by a region in the pie.

It is certainly possible to organize a functional system along these lines, but in fact, outside of experimental settings, this is a very rare knowledge distribution pattern because it is very vulnerable to breakdown. If, for any reason, one of the members of the team is unable to perform, the whole system will fail. At the other end of the knowledge distribution spectrum, one can imagine a system in which everyone knows everything about the task. This is the pattern called for by Emery and Trist (1973) and by Morgan's (1986) "holographic" conception, but it too is a rare pattern, because if acquiring the knowledge costs anything at all, this pattern will be very expensive to produce. More commonly, there is substantial sharing of knowledge between individuals with the task knowledge of more expert performers completely subsuming the knowledge of those who are less experienced. Splitting the task into coordinated fragments permits relatively less skilled people to contribute to task performance.

In many human systems, as people become more skilled they move on to

---

[11]Cicourel, (chap. 9 in this volume) discusses aspects of medical knowledge that can only be acquired in the practice of medicine in a social setting characterized by a distribution of expertise similar to the one described here.

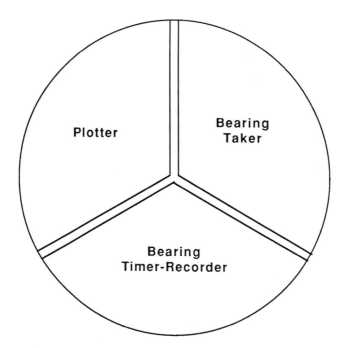

FIG. 8.6.   Distribution of knowledge among individuals assuming no interaction and no history of experience in each other's jobs.

other roles in the task performance group, making way for less skilled people behind them and replacing the more expert people before them who advance or leave the system. This is what we observe in the case of the development of navigation skills aboard ship. The bearing taker knows how to do that job, but because of the interaction with the bearing timer-recorder, the person also knows something about the timer-recorder's job (see Fig. 8.7a). The bearing timer-recorder knows how to do that job, but also knows all about being a bearing taker, having once held that job. Furthermore, the timer-recorder knows a good deal about the activities of the plotter because they share the chart table. What the bearing timer-recorder knows is shown in Fig. 8.7b. Finally, a competent plotter knows how to plot, but also knows everything the bearing timer-recorder and bearing takers know having worked both those jobs before advancing to plotting. What the plotter knows is shown in Fig. 8.7c. The distribution of knowledge that is the sum of these individual expertises is shown in Fig. 8.7d. Thus, this movement through the system with increasing expertise results in a pattern of overlapping expertise, with knowledge of the entry-level tasks most redundantly represented and knowledge of expert-level tasks least redundantly represented.

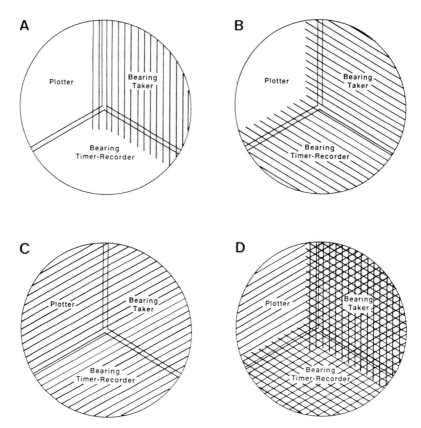

FIG. 8.7.   Overlap in the distribution of knowledge as a result of interaction between individuals and experience in each other's jobs.

The Horizon of Observation

Let us refer to the outer boundary of the portion of the task that can be seen or heard by each team member as that person's horizon of observation. The scope of the horizons of observation of the members of a work group is important for two reasons. First, lines of communication and limits on observation of the activities of others have consequences for the knowledge acquisition process. This is so because they define the portion of the task environment available as a learning context to each task performer. As Hackman (1987) argued, making some parts of a joint task more visible to other participants permits group members to educate each other. Second, as already noted, the awareness of the need for help is often a prerequisite for help. The extent to which a system can benefit from the functional redundancy of its parts will depend on the extent to which the parts are aware of needs for redundant functioning. Technology has a key role here because the horizons of observation of the members of the work group are often defined by technology.

Open Interactions

The physical arrangement of tools and work stations together with the local ethos of work can affect the horizon of observation, and thus the opportunities to learn, of members of the team. Here is an example of a learning event that was enabled by the fact that the plotter, the bearing timer-recorder, and the keeper of the deck log all share the same work space.

On a previous at sea period, D, the deck log keeper had served as bearing timer-recorder, but D's performance there was less than satisfactory. That is the job that was next in line for him, however, and D was anxious to acquire the skills required to perform the job. One of the most important aspects of the bearing timer-recorder's job is knowing when particular landmarks will be visible to the bearing takers on the wings. One complication of this judgment is the fact that a large convex mirror is mounted outside the pilot house windows just in front of the port wing bearing taker's station. The mirror is there so that the commanding officer, who sits inside the pilot house, can see the part of the flight deck that lies aft of the pilot house. Unfortunately, the mirror obstructs the port bearing taker's view forward and the bearing timer-recorder must be able to judge from his position at the chart table whether or not the port wing bearing taker's view of a chosen landmark will be blocked by the mirror.

The plotter, P, the bearing timer-recorder, B, and D, were all standing at the chart table. The ship had just entered the mouth of the harbor and the team was running the fix cycle on two-minute intervals. The previous fix taken at 36 minutes after the hour, called "time 36," was complete, and P had just finished plotting the dead reckoned track out through times 38 and 40. B indirectly solicited P's assistance in deciding which landmarks should be shot for the next round of bearings. D stood by, watching what B and P were doing. All of the pointing they did in this interchange was to the chart itself.

1. B: Last set still good? O.K. Ballast Point, light Zulu.
2. P: Here's (time) 36 [pointing to the DR position on the chart]
3. B: So it would be that [pointing to light Zulu], that [pointing to Bravo Pier] . . .
4. P: One, two, three. Same three. Ballast Point, Bravo. And the next one . . .
5. B: (Time) 40 should be, Ballast Point . . .

6. P: Front Range, Bravo.
7. B: And Balla . . .
8. D: He may not be able to see Front Range.
9. B: Yah.
10. P: Yah, he can. Once we get up here [pointing to the ship's projected position for the next fix].
11. B: Yah. Up there O.K.
12. P: Down here [pointing to ships current position] he can't. It's back of the mirror, but as you come in it gets enough so that you can see it.

Because what B and P are doing is within D's horizon of observation, D has a chance to see how the landmarks are chosen. Furthermore, the fact that the decision about which landmarks to shoot is made in an interaction opens the process to D in a way that would not be the case if a single person were making the decision alone. In utterance 8, D raises the possibility that the port wing bearing taker may not be able to see the landmark. Three days earlier, on another sea and anchor detail, D had made the same suggestion about the mirror blocking the port wing bearing taker's view and P had agreed. In the present circumstances, however, D's caveat is inappropriate. B and P have already anticipated the problem raised by D, and they jointly counter D's objection, each building on what the other has said. Clearly, if D did not share the work space with B and P or if there was a strict division of labor such that people did not monitor and participate in the actions of their fellows, this opportunity for D to have even peripheral involvement in that task that will someday be his would be lost. Furthermore, D's horizon of observation is extended because the decision making about landmarks is conducted as an interaction between B and P.

Open Tools

However, being in the presence of others who are working is not always enough by itself. In the previous example, we saw that the fact that the work was done in an interaction between members opened it to other members of the team. In a similar way, the design of tools can affect their suitability for joint use or for demonstration and may thereby constrain possibilities for knowledge acquisition. The interaction of a task performer with a tool may or may not be open to others depending on the nature of the tool itself. The design of a tool may change the horizon of observation for those in the vicinity of the tool. The navigation chart is an explicit graphical depiction of position and motion so it is easy to see certain aspects of solutions. The chart representation presents the relevant information in a form such that much of the work can be done by perceptual inferences. The work a chart does is performed on its surface—all at the device interface, as it were—but watching someone work with a chart is much more revealing of what is done to perform the task than watching someone work with a calculator or a computer.

The openness of a tool can also affect its use as an instrument in instruction. When the bearing timer-recorder chooses a set of landmarks that result in lines of position with shallow intersections, it is easy to show, on the chart, the consequences of such actions and the nature of the remedy required. Figure 8.8 shows a fix that resulted from landmark assignments made by the bearing timer-recorder. Bearings off to the side of the ship rather than ahead or astern are called *beam* bearings. After plotting this fix and observing how it came out, the plotter scolded the bearing timer-recorder.

C: What did you take a bunch of beam bearings for? Why ain't you shooting up there [points out the front window of the bridge] some

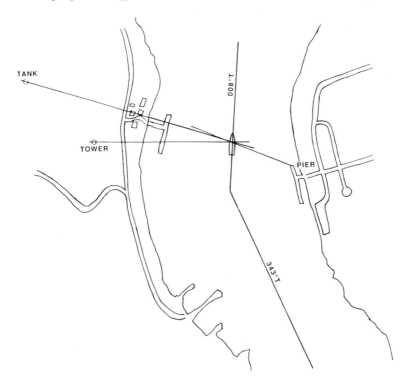

FIG. 8.8.   Fix based on "beam" bearings resulting in shallow intersections of the lines of position.

place? Look what you did! [points to the chart] You shot three beam bearings. You shot three beam bearings. You better tell 'em to shoot from up ahead some place.

Once the fix was plotted of course, it was easy for the bearing timer-recorder to see the nature of his error. Imagine how much more difficult it would be to explain the inadequacy of the landmark assignment if the lines of position were represented as equations to be punched into a calculator, rather than as lines drawn on the chart.

CONCLUSION

When we consider the activities of the navigation team in any particular navigation exercise, the costs associated with the added burdens of communication and coordination in the socially distributed form of this task could be seen, following Steiner (1972), as process losses for the system. Clearly, there is a good deal of inefficiency in the coordination of the activities of the various team members with each other. One can argue, even in the particular instance, that some of the losses are compensated for by the increased information-processing speed that comes with parallel task performance. After all, that is why the task is done by a team when the time pressures are great. Still, the costs are high. McGrath (chap. 2 in this volume) has argued, however, that we must take a broader perspective in which we consider not only the production function of group activity, but the support and well-being functions as well. Our concern should not be simply for the efficiency of any particular performance of the task, but for the quality of the performances of many tasks across a span of time on the scale of an individual team member's career. From this perspective, we see that some of what appear as losses in particular instances are in fact investments in future performances. Some of these costs are payment for the maintenance of a base of expertise that is periodically threatened by the departure of an experienced member of the team.

Let me now recapitulate the main points of the argument. I have tried to show that in the world of large ship piloting, the technological devices are better seen as media for representation than as amplifiers or surrogates for cognitive abilities. The central computations of the navigation tasks are accomplished by the propagation of information across representations and representational media. There is a nominal division of labor among the members of the team that is supposed to ensure the timely propagation of information, but the need to violate the mandated division of labor in order to avoid breakdowns arises frequently. The negotiation of the division of labor that permits the system to respond robustly to failures of individual team members requires an overlapping distribution of expertise; that is, some level of functional redundancy. In addition to satisfying its production function, the system must also reproduce itself, and its mode of reproduction, as reflected in the career trajectories of the individual group members, both replaces lost expertise and maintains the desired functional redundancy. The space through which the career trajectory passes, the jobs that the members do, and the opportunities to learn in those jobs are all defined in large part by the properties of the technology. Many tools in this setting are open tools in the sense that their use in public and observable in its details by other members of the team. These open tools provide many learning contexts.

The observations I have presented here should not be taken as either claims that the current ways of doing things are optimal, or as arguments against the automation of the tasks of ship navigation. The existing system of ship navigation is problematic in many respects and very probably could be improved by technological innovations. I have tried to show that the robustness of the system in the face of component failures is dependent on the openness or public nature of much of the work of the navigation task. For example, the detection of error requires access to errorful performance and the correction of error requires a functionally redundant distribution of knowledge. There is a danger because the public nature of work that creates these required conditions seems particularly vulnerable to the introduction of high-tech solutions to the narrowly conceived production problem. Although some promising work on computer support for collaborative work is now underway (see Lakin, chap. 17; and Landow, chap. 15 in this volume; and CSCW, 1986, 1988), the typical high-tech widget is still a single operator system where the interaction between user and device is a private world of activity. Rather than an argument against automation, take this to be a call for expanded design criteria.

The low technology system examined here incorporates ways for operators to learn their jobs while working, redundant means for the detection and the correction of error, and possibilities for adaptation and continued functioning in the face of failures of component parts. It would be unfortunate indeed if these clearly desirable features were overlooked and left behind in the pursuit of an efficient automated means of fostering productivity.

ACKNOWLEDGMENTS

The research on which this chapter is based was supported by the Independent Research program of the Navy Personnel Research and Development Center, San Diego, by the Personnel and Training Research programs, Psychological Sciences Division, Office of Naval Research, under Contract No. N00014-85-C-0133, and by a fellowship from the John D. and Catherine T. MacArthur Foundation. The views and conclusions presented in this chapter are those of the author and should not necessarily be interpreted as representing the official policies, either expressed or implied, of the sponsoring agencies.

REFERENCES

Cole, M., & Griffin, P. (1980). Cultural amplifiers reconsidered. In D. R. Olson (Ed.), *The social foundations of language and thought* (pp. 343–364). New York: Norton.

CSCW. (1986). *Proceedings of the conference on computer supported cooperative work.* Austin, TX: Microelectronics & Computer Technology Corporation.

Emery, F. E., & Trist, E. L. (1973). *Towards a social ecology.* New York: Plenum.

Gardner, M. (1978). *Aha! insight.* New York: W. H. Freeman.

Hill, W. C. (March 1988). *The mind at AI: Horseless carriage, mousetrap, card trick, clock* (Internal report). Austin, TX: Microelectronics & Computer Technology Corporation.

Hackman, J. R. (1987). The design of work teams. In J. W. Lorsch (Ed.), *Handbook of organizational behavior* (pp. 315–342). Englewood Cliffs, NJ: Prentice-Hall.

Hutchins, E. (1988). Metaphors for interface design. In M. M. Taylor, F. Neel, & D. G. Bouwhuis (Eds.), *The structure of multimodal dialogue* (pp. 26–44). Amsterdam: North Holland.

Kraut, R. E., Galegher, J., & Egido, C. (1987–88). Relationships and tasks in scientific collaboration. *Human-Computer Interaction, 3,* 31–58.

Morgan, G. (1986). *Images of organization.* Beverly Hills, CA: Sage Publications.

Rumelhart, D., Smolensky, P., McClelland, J., & Hinton, G. (1986). Schemata and sequential processes. In J. McClelland, & D. Rumelhart (Eds.), *Parallel distributed processing: Explorations in the microstructure of cognition* (Vol. 2, pp. 7–57). Cambridge, MA: MIT Press.

Simon, H. (1981). *The sciences of the artificial* (2nd ed.), Cambridge, MA: MIT Press.

Steiner, I. D. (1972). *Group process and productivity.* New York: Academic Press.

Stratton, W. E., & Flynn, W. R. (1980). Ecological theory and organization development. In T. G. Cummings (Ed.), *Systems theory for organization development* (pp. 307–322). New York: Wiley.

Stewart, I. (1987). Gauss. In *Scientific genius and creativity: Readings from Scientific American* (pp. 40–49). New York: W. H. Freeman.

9

The Integration of Distributed Knowledge in Collaborative Medical Diagnosis

Aaron V. Cicourel
University of California, San Diego

Abstract

Medical diagnosis is widely understood to be an intellectually complex task, but, in this chapter, it is also shown as the product of a complex social process involving individuals who vary in status and area of expertise. The author reveals this social component by examining the discourse that occurs as medical experts evaluate clinical evidence in order to arrive at a satisfactory diagnosis and treatment plan. This discourse shows how diagnoses arise out of social interaction as physicians exchange observations and assess their credibility. Because physicians learn to assess the value of medical information on the basis of its association with a trusted human source, information systems designed to aid medical decision making must somehow incorporate evidence of the their own credibility.

OVERVIEW

The delivery of appropriate medical care depends on establishing an accurate diagnosis, but in many cases, obtaining information that could specify the cause of a patient's symptoms is a complex, iterative task. The diagnostician must integrate data about a patient from a variety of sources including laboratory and radiological reports and physical and medical histories. All of this information must then be evaluated in terms of the physician's medical knowledge base. The large number of decision making studies in this domain (see Kleinmuntz, 1986, for an article that presents an analysis of the issues and review of major research streams) indicates that researchers have long recognized the cognitive complexity of this task. A diagnosis, however, can be not only cognitively, but also socially complex. In many cases, a diagnosis involves obtaining and evaluating the opinions of a number of individuals who may differ in their areas and levels of expertise.

In principle, it should be possible to overcome both of these types of complexity and reduce the resulting uncertainty by formalizing the diagnostic process. Indeed, awareness of these problems and of the extreme difficulty of keeping up with developments in the growth of medical knowledge, together with more general evidence of systematic errors and biases in human judgment (Tversky & Kahneman, 1974), has prompted efforts to rationalize the diagnostic process by introducing expert systems and other computer-aided information retrieval processes (Kleinmuntz, 1986). These systems are designed to increase the validity and reliability of medical decision making. Although such systems have considerable promise, they have not become widely accepted as part of the standard armamentarium of medical practice.

In this chapter, I suggest that one of the obstacles to formalizing the diagnostic process through increased reliance on computer-based information systems is that physicians typically assess the adequacy of medical information on the basis of the perceived credibility of the source, whether the source is the patient or another physician. For example, physicians often refer to patients as "good or bad historians"; a good historian is treated as a reliable source of information about his or her own health, but the reported symptoms of a bad historian may be viewed with some skepticism. Similarly, advice from physicians who are perceived as "good doctors" is highly valued, whereas advice from sources perceived as less credible may be discounted. Of course, clear evidence as well as widespread agreement about who is or is not a good historian or a good doctor, are conditions that are not easily met. Yet, the source of a medical opinion remains a powerful determinant of its influence. I suggest that one of the difficulties associated with more systematic approaches to diagnostic decision making is that the sources of the information obtained—individual patients and physicians— have not been foci of attention in the conceptualization and implementation of these systems.

In the case to be described in this chapter, I examine the discourse processes involved in discussions between physicians and between physicians and other health care providers as a way of showing how the social context provides the ground for the development of medical diagnoses and how the perceived value of medical information is related to the perceived credibility of the source. By calling attention to aspects of the social system that produces medical diagnoses, it may become possible to improve efforts to systematize these decisions through the development of information retrieval technology and expert systems.

DISTRIBUTED COGNITION: THROUGH THE WINDOW
OF SOCIAL DISCOURSE

The idea of socially distributed cognition refers to the fact that participants in collaborative work relationships are likely to vary in the knowledge they possess (Cicourel, 1974; Schutz, 1964) and must therefore engage each other in dialogues that allow them to pool resources and negotiate their differences to accomplish their tasks. The notion of socially distributed cognition (Hutchins, 1985) is analogous to the idea of distributed computing (Chandrasekaran, 1981; Gomez & Chandrasekaran; 1981; Smith & Davis, 1981; Wesson, Hayes-Roth, Burge, Stasz, & Sunshine, 1981). In automated systems, distributed problem solving refers to the cooperative solution of problems by a decentralized and loosely coupled collection of knowledge sources located in different processors. A central assumption is that the knowledge sources must cooperate to solve a problem because no one source has enough information to do the job. Hutchins (1985) argues that the social and temporal organization of cognitive activity outweigh the frequent preoccupation with individual intelligence or cognition in accounting for performance in a variety of domains. His remarks bear repeating because they clarify the proposition that organizations can have an important influence on a group's use of cognitive strategies. The above work suggests that to create a satisfactory account of differential human performance, researchers must shift their focus from the cognitive properties of individuals to on-line studies of groups in natural settings.

Medical decision making in university hospitals is an example of socially distributed cognition that is carried out through the medium of task-relevant discourse. As I noted earlier, automated systems designed to aid in this task do exist; however, the modeling in automated medical diagnostic systems underrepresents the distributed nature of clinical knowledge in these settings. To reveal how medical knowledge is distributed and how this distribution affects the diagnostic process, I have examined the discourse that occurs between physicians, medical students and other medical experts in university teaching hospitals. In these settings, participants in diagnostic conferences (or, more informally, physicians conferring with each other) engage in spontaneous and structured discourse as a way of assessing and revealing competence and of establishing or sustaining individual niches in the group. An individual's performance in these exchanges is a way of demonstrating competence to others and simultaneously affects the cooperative work processes needed to realize the group's implicit and explicit goals. Participants in these groups vary in status, and that variation, along with a pervasive contest atmosphere that can exist are key aspects of these interactions.

Although laboratory and field studies of work in groups often implicitly involve the communication processes underlying cooperative decision making and work productivity, these studies often take work-related discourse for granted, rather than examining it directly. This oversight may be due to the difficulty of developing appropriate measures of how authority structures and policies are revealed in discourse, but this aspect of the institutional setting needs to be taken into account. It informs the participants, and can inform the researcher as well, about the intentions, motives, beliefs and distributed knowledge involved in cooperative problem solving.

THE INSTITUTIONAL CONTEXT OF MEDICAL DECISION MAKING

The hospital context permits us to see the way institutionalized settings can frame local activities. For example, group-derived norms can channel people with particular titles and presumed competencies, responsibilities and entitlements into certain physical spaces at particular times to engage in particular tasks (Cicourel, 1987a). The social and physical setting not only shapes activities but also permits emergent processes of talk that create a narrow, locally organized sense of context that is negotiated over the course of the interaction. The content and style of what is or is not said in this local discourse can affect problem solving; for instance, the experiences that participants acquire by working together and by reported or perceived reputational assessments can lead to beliefs about the distribution of knowledge that can, in turn, influence who is consulted. Thus, the result of this local discourse is that, in addition to the distribution of knowledge attributed to individuals because of their official titles and duties, there is an implicit or assumed distribution of knowledge that can diverge from the organizational conditions of decision making by official titles and duties.

Another important aspect of institutionalized settings is the existence of different substantive and social domains. For instance, medical institutions have both horizontal and vertical structures, particularly in teaching hospitals where there are attendings or specialists with considerable autonomy at the top of a vertical structure that can include a division, clinic or ward. Communication is framed and guided by these organizationally defined status and role relationships and by expectations that are locally emergent and managed. Because of their varying positions in this structure individuals are likely to have differential access to evidence, and to experience differential support and resistance from other personnel in their efforts to communicate within and across these domains.

The day-to-day functioning of teaching hospitals is especially dependent on interpersonal networks (Granovetter, 1972, 1974, 1976, 1983). These networks reflect the status and interpersonal relationships between physicians and between physicians and other health care providers and create a foundation for the enactment of distributed problem solving. For instance, although radiological and laboratory evidence may be examined independently of the actions pursued by technicians or other experts, physicians routinely consult other physicians or experts about particular patients and their radiological and laboratory tests. The strength of these ties can influence the consultation process and will mirror both distributed cognitive strategies and the status and interpersonal relationships that motivate the process.

Finally, institutionalized health care delivery systems rely on a variety of technologies for computing, communicating and transforming information. For example, the patient's chart often combines technical reports and a large body of seemingly chaotic written material. Different health care actors, employing different information-gathering techniques, contribute to the chart; this information may be used not only in planning subsequent treatment for the patient, but may also be retrieved for studying individuals and groups of patients categorized by similar symptoms and/or illnesses. The interpretations by health care personnel of the materials assembled in a chart reflect a complex set of professional and social relationships and attributions about the distribution of cognitive skills.

LOCAL CLINIC ORGANIZATION AND AUTHORITY

The allocation of tasks associated with diagnosing and treating patients in outpatient clinics in particular medical specialties reveals the structure of authority relations in more detail. Students and residents examine a patient's chart and then engage the patient in an exchange that will produce information about his or her medical condition. In teaching hospitals, novices and attendings can be differentiated according to their expertise in such tasks. Novices take more time to interview a patient and conduct a physical examination and the kinds of information elicited will vary considerably. These interviews and examinations provide the basis for diagnostically relevant inferences and the creation of treatment plans—exercises that are relentlessly enacted (sometimes under much stress) on several occasions a day.

However, the subordinate status of students and house staff means that their decisions must be directly or indirectly monitored; designated experts must be aware of their activities. This monitoring normally includes routinely interrogating novices, but its intensity can vary depending on local ecological constraints. That is, because monitoring requires intermittent communication under circumstances where time is at a premium, cases are likely to differ in the extent to which they are reviewed by senior physicians. In general, however, the organization of teaching hospitals encourages and requires a kind of contest atmosphere in which the communicative and medical competence of novices and experts can be subjected to routine scrutiny. The student or resident's account about the patient to the attending can be described as an asymmetrical power relationship in which both parties know that the outcome of the diagnosis and treatment plan proposed by the novice will be assessed critically by the attending.

It is the attending's responsibility to teach the residents and students how to deliver quality health care. The resident and student are expected to interview the patient, do a physical examination and reach a tentative diagnosis and plan of treatment. Nurses mediate between attendings or chief residents and other residents and students by familarizing themselves with aspects of the patient's chart, taking the patient's temperature, blood pressure, weight, and pulse before medical personnel conduct a history and physical examination. The nurse often asks patients why they are seeing the attending and can then present this information to the student and resident to help them orient themselves to the case. The attending interacts with the House Staff and patient to assess the diagnosis and treatment plan and to ask the residents and students about the adequacy of their assessment and possible alternative diagnoses and plans. The attending's assessment of the House Staff will include their general appearance, the medical terms they use and the kinds of reasoning that appear to have influenced the choices made by students and residents.

Hospitals and clinics differ in the extent to which particular areas are reserved for an attending or chief resident. For instance, the two hospital clinics I studied differed in terms of the responsibilities assumed and implemented by staff members who differed in status. At one hospital, attendings were usually present because a part of their earnings could be affected if they could not see each patient personally. The attending is responsible for the patient's medical outcome and can be held legally liable for the actions of the residents and students. At the other hospital, it is possible for a chief resident to be responsible for a clinic's activities, but normally an attending is actively involved in the daily round of duties.

In a given clinic, say, one in pediatrics, infectious diseases, or general surgery, we can view several examining rooms as units of a temporally designated self-contained system. Patients are distributed into rooms by nurses who may leave patients' charts on the outside of the door. These small, local units communicate with others in the sense that the medical student, intern, or resident who enters the small room returns to an expert who may be a fellow, the chief resident or attending. The expert visits the local units to confirm or disconfirm the assessments of the novices. Each local unit is also self-contained in the sense that the chart becomes a source of computation that must be linked to communication between the patient, the novice and expert. For the local unit to reach a state of equilibrium, information must be elicited from the patient, there must be coordination between a novice and expert and a written account must be entered into the chart. Thus, several types of messages are generated by the local unit that result in selectively written accounts of this unit's problems. The chart eventually returns to the nurses' station as part of the clinic's goal of achieving equilibrium for a designated temporal period.

The clinic, in a teaching hospital, then, is not only an arena in which health care is delivered, but also a setting for training future physicians. The goals of these hospitals include exposing medical students and residents to an organizationally structured environment and to a variety of complicated technologies which expand the range of potential diagnostic and treatment procedures. However, they also include exposing the novice to a complex network of interpersonal relationships within which he or she also acquires tacit knowledge which must be integrated with the declarative knowledge found in lectures, textbooks, journal articles and the patient's medical chart.

Despite this reliance on technological artifacts and the services of others, the practice of medicine also involves individual actions that become associated with the individual physician in a highly personal sense. The skills and knowledge necessary to carry out these actions thus create a power base over House Staff and patients. The work environment, therefore, is a miniaturized system of social stratification. Moreover, the sociocultural conditions that permit this system to emerge and sustain itself always override the official goals or objectives of the institutionalized work setting.

To show how a medical unit such as a clinic or ward is linked to other units and the technological artifacts necessary for primary medical care, I will describe briefly a selective aspect of the microbiology laboratory. The lab is an essential part of modern health care delivery and illustrates the cooperation, understanding and background knowledge that individuals in a collaborative work setting must differentially share and negotiate to accomplish their objectives. The particular features of the laboratory described here may differ from what might be found in other teaching hospitals in the United States, but the nature of the collaboration necessary typifies the kinds of organizational and interpersonal processes that must occur if the work is to be realized.

HIERARCHY AND COOPERATION IN A TEACHING HOSPITAL LAB

As the description of authority relations above suggests, teaching hospitals can be natural laboratories for the study of authority derived from expertise grounded in scientific training, clinical experience and credentials that require certification by professional associations (Bourdieu, 1981; Freidson, 1970a, 1970b). Weber's (1968, p. 941) work on domination can be invoked to clarify the way authority and power influence social action in this setting. According to Weber, the professional's ability to create and influence social action can be seen as power derived from special knowledge and the ability to employ this knowledge in ways that enhance one's power over others. In teaching hospitals, the attending's medical knowledge is seldom challenged by patients, students, residents or other hospital personnel. The physician's power stems from the ability to create "objective" representations of a patient's mental and physical condition.

There were several types of novices and experts associated with my research with infectious disease professionals, including medical students, residents, one or more infectious disease attendings and a pathologist who directed (or, in one hospital) rotated through the microbiology laboratory. Interns could be included when discussions occurred on the wards, but they were not present in the clinics and laboratory activities I observed. Nurses, for the most part, were not directly involved in the cases I examined but did perform the kinds of activities noted earlier.

A unique type of interaction between the infectious disease attending (IDA) and pathology attending (PA) existed in the two hospitals in which I conducted my study. They routinely exchanged views about particular cases and met regularly at laboratory rounds each morning at 11:00 A.M. and also formed part of a larger group of specialists that met each week at teaching or grand rounds. This collaboration provided an opportunity for infectious disease attending and pathology specialists to exchange ideas about areas of medicine that overlap while making use of their complementary clinical and basic science knowledge and experiences. In the case of teaching rounds, many more experts can be included, making it possible for different physicians to establish informal and formal relationships with other experts.

A number of infectious disease cases are seen by referral from other services. For the most part, personnel associated with the subspecialty of infectious diseases see cases by consultation requests from particular services such as surgery, a trauma or burn unit, medicine, and so on. If routine cultures are taken, the infectious disease personnel will often become aware of patients suspected of infection fairly early, especially if the attending physician asks for a consultation. The infectious disease expert (IDA) worked closely, in my study, with personnel from microbiology, virology and histology laboratories, actively seeking out reports on organisms found in patients.

The hospital microbiology laboratories with which I am familiar require special procedures, and are densely populated with technological artifacts that can greatly expand the health professional's ability to solve medical problems. For example, making smears of specimens on glass slides (except for blood cultures) for immediate microscopic examination can provide quick answers about a patient's condition. The information can then be entered into a computer database on all patients with infectious diseases that clinicians can access. The database permits the laboratory to monitor individual patients and also obtain aggregated data across patients by date, demographic characteristics, medications prescribed and organisms identified over different periods of time.

In addition to these computerized data bases, there are also many other technologies that are routinely associated with the detection of disease. An obvious example is the use of radiological films for the detection of many different kinds of pathological conditions. Thus, the work practices of people in a teaching hospital are of special interest to researchers who study the role of information technology in cooperative work settings. But consideration of the nature of these technologies and how they are used also reveals the limitations of current diagnostic tools and the importance of individual and distributed cognition in medical decision making.

In particular, the distinction posed by Hutchins (chap. 8 in this volume) between technologies whose information processing capacity is internal to the device and technology that exploits the cognitive resources of the task performer is relevant to an understanding of the role of medical technologies in the diagnostic process. In most cases, the information yielded by the technologies commonly employed in the practice of medicine must be evaluated or interpreted by a human actor or actors to be clinically relevant. Thus, in the present study we see that even when the information revealed by a particular test or examination is unequivocal, the clinical relevance of those findings is still a matter of judgment on the part of the physician(s).

For instance, knowing the source of a specimen permits the microbiology laboratory to plant specimens into different media, based on knowledge about what organisms could grow from a particular source. The procedure for planting specimens into cultures according to the possible pathogens that can grow from a source amounts to a decoupled diagnostic technique in which the information processing capacity is internal to the device, but the clinical relevance of the findings must be determined and converted into action by the attending physician individually or in consultation with other medical experts. Perceptions of the patient's condition are therefore contingent on several possible technologies or sources of information that accrue from a socially distributed information processing system to produce a cooperatively assembled knowledge base, which ultimately comes back to the attending physician for judgment and action. The following empirical description provides an example of this process.

THE ORGANIZATIONAL ASPECTS OF MEDICAL DIAGNOSIS

The daily lab rounds are the occasion for reviewing cultures on different patients for the past twenty-four hour period. The meeting takes place in a crowded room that is part of a suite of rooms that make up the microbiology, virology and histology laboratories (See Fig. 9.1). For the purposes

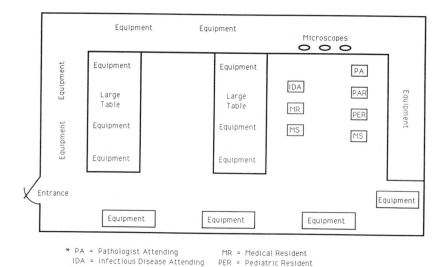

* PA = Pathologist Attending   MR = Medical Resident
 IDA = Infectious Disease Attending   PER = Pediatric Resident
 PAR = Pathology Resident   MS = Medical Student

FIG. 9.1.   Schematic View of a Part of a Microbiology Laboratory

of the present chapter, I focus on one of the hospitals in which I conducted my research.

The group that meets each day can vary somewhat, but normally the infectious disease attending (IDA) and pathology attending (PA) are present as well as a medical resident, one or two pathology residents, one or more pediatric residents or training fellows, and one or two fourth year medical students on a month-long rotation. The somewhat cramped corner of the room in which the meeting occurs will have at least one microscope and often one or more extensions so that more than one person can examine a slide. In addition to the cultures available, there will be a slip of paper on each patient that indicates what organism or organism(s) have been found or are suspected. The pathology resident may assist the (PA) in organizing and providing information on the laboratory findings. The medical and pediatric residents will provide information on the patients they have seen. The residents often use small index-like cards on which they have written information about a patient, such as age, weight, race and/or ethnicity, blood pressure, pulse, specific problems, and the results of routine tests about the patient's blood gases, urinanalysis, and the like. The IDA and PA specialists may also supply information on the patient.

The PA is the primary expert here and orchestrates the discussion. The IDA will often share the verbal space that emerges. The IDA and PA specialists have offices in another part of the hospital with their own small labs for their personal research activities. These offices are on the same hall and the different IDAs are likely to see the PA frequently over the course of a day and week. The collaborative relationship and physical proximity that exists between the IDAs and PA in the hospital described here is similar to the role of physical proximity in the development of collaborative relationships between scientific researchers reported by Kraut, Egido, and Galegher (chap. 6 in this volume). As these authors note, proximity facilitates frequent interaction and allows individuals to develop a sense of each other's competence and the opportunity to share information at low cost.

In both hospitals studied, there is continual collaborative work between the IDA and pathology experts in the labs. Residents become part of these exchanges throughout their rotation in infectious disease or pathology. The IDAs supervise and monitor both patients and novices and are responsible for structuring the clinical care rendered by the group. The director of the labs monitors the activities of the pathology residents and other technical personnel.

The contest and assessment aspects of teaching hospitals are evident during lab rounds. Residents are expected to summarize the relevant information pertinent to particular patients and thereby reveal their ability to describe a patient's problems succinctly. Both medical students and residents may be called upon by the pathologist to identify an organism microscopically and, perhaps, to describe its morphology and microbiological characteristics and its clinical relevance for treating the patient. The novice's acquisition and display of professional competence, therefore, is subject to constant tacit and formal scrutiny. The novice's ability to reason clinically and link her or his thoughts to what is known about an organism and its clinical manifestations and basic science characteristics reproduces and will reflect the confrontational and cooperative aspects of the health care system.

As this description suggests, cooperative work does not mean the absence of conflict or differences in the views of participants. Nor do differences mean that the way participants present themselves to others need be viewed always as "unpleasant" or "tense" despite the perception of such states of affairs by those involved in collaborative work. In teaching hospitals, a wide range of behavioral displays can be observed. In short, attributions of an interpersonal and professional nature and concerns about someone's competence are normal aspects of all work settings and need to be included as part of the modeling of distributed cognitive systems.

ROUTINE DISCOURSE IN A HOSPITAL MICROBIOLOGY LAB

The case discussed in Fig. 9.2 has been presented elsewhere (Cicourel, 1987a, 1987b). The patient under review is a 48-year-old white female with a chief complaint upon admission to the hospital of "swelling of the left eye" and a primary diagnosis of "periorbital cellulitis" and described as a "right-

FIG. 9.2.   ID Resident's oral history to ID Attending.

1	A:	. . . about Mrs. Price.
2	R:	All right. [Phoebe, Price? Phoebe P. Price?]
3	A:	We don't know the middle initial.
4	R:	(laughs) She's [a] 48 year old uh . . white lady with a history
5		of alcohol abuse, chronic pancreatitis, seizure disorder,
6		ventral hernias, type 2 diabetes melitis for 2, 3 years, now
7		on insulin and a history of gout, too, who five days, ago,
8		last Sunday night, six days ago, uh felt a bug bite she
9		thought on her eye,⌈on her left eye.
10	A:	⌊During
11		the night, or during the day?
12	R:	During the night, and swatted, what she thought was a bug,
13		off of her nose. I don't know what it was, but in any case,
14		shortly thereafter she started having nausea and vomiting,
15		and noted uh fever with rigors (shaking), [she said?] she
16		got quite warm, and didn't take her temperature, but she
17		was, warm. [the narrative continues for another 24 lines]

A: = I.D. attending
R: = I.D. resident

upper-lid abscess with periorbital cellulitis." According to my informants, the patient could be described as having an infected, swollen-shut left eye that is highly inflamed, with purplish coloring of the skin around the eye that was attributed to blood seeping into the skin. My observations revealed someone whose left side of the face was swollen, including the eye and ear, with pus oozing out of the area of the eyelids.

Prior to the speech event recorded in Fig. 9.2, the medical ID resident and I visited the nurses' station where the patient's chart was kept. The medical resident (MR) examined the chart and explained the patient's various problems. We then went to the ward where the MR conducted a medical history and examined the patient's eye and facial condition. In other publications noted earlier, I examine aspects of the present case in some detail. Here, I wish to move quickly to the material in Fig. 9.2 to call the reader's attention to the way the attending and MR interact about a specific case. The exchange is not only typical of the way teaching hospitals function, but is at the heart of sustaining the production of physicians.

The attending topicalizes the discussion by referring to the patient by name in line 1 of Fig. 9.2, and the MR's response ("All right") could be seen as a confirmation that the topic is appropriate. The bit of humor exhibited by the MR seemed to me to be in keeping with what I observed to be an exchange that was always amiable. The remarks by the MR in lines 4–9 are typical of the kind of oral medical history residents are expected to give an attending after interviewing a patient for the first time. The patient's age, racial or ethnic status, past and current illnesses are crisply outlined for the attending. In lines 7–9, the MR begins a long narrative about the symptoms or signs that brought the patient to the attention of physicians at the university hospital. The narrative continues after the attending asked for a temporal clarification about the alleged "bug bite." The MR, in lines 12–17, begins to describe some of the patient's symptoms. I have arbitrarily cut short his descriptive details about further symptoms because they do not contribute new information to the present analysis.

The MR's long narrative about the patient's current problems includes many details about blood pressure, the results of her blood tests, the presence or absence of other clinical problems and the medications she was being given for a suspected infection. The MR reports on a number of conditions that allude to the inclusion or elimination of possible illnesses or diseases. The MR's participation in a training program requires cooperation between the MR and the attending. The details and general inferences exhibited by the MR allow the attending to assess the MR's ability to describe a medical case appropriately and to include information that is relevant to an understanding of a differential diagnosis and a plan of treatment. The resident is also expected to link clinical information about the patient to clinical and basic science research on the particular illness or disease that is attributed to the case.

The training program of which the MR is an integral part demands the kind of presentation depicted in Fig. 9.2. Existing status differences require the attending to assess the resident's performance and this evaluation can influence the resident's future status. The attending's expertise is highly evident throughout all of their discourse as is documented elsewhere. The material presented in Fig. 9.3 reveals aspects of differences in expertise that the MR and attending exhibit in such encounters. In lines 46–52, the somewhat confusing discourse refers to a prior occasion in which the attending had counseled the house officers about a particular fungal agent (mucor). The MR was letting the attending know that he had become sensitive to this type of fungus. The reference to mucor was not relevant for the present case but could be seen as an effort by the MR to impress the attending with his awareness of an area of concern to her.

The attending is referring to an actual case of mucor that is to be presented to the medical mortality conference that is held regularly and is another occasion for the assessment of house officers. The reader should note that in lines 52–53, the attending's remark "We're gonna present that case" occurs in a context where considerable knowledge about local circumstances is required to understand this cryptic deictic expression. The case in point has nothing to do with the discussion of the patient with an infected eye, but the ambiguous referent becomes linked to the present case by another deictically ambiguous referent when the attending states (lines 54–55), "So

FIG. 9.3.   ID Resident and Attending discussion of patient: Knowledge base differences.

46	R:	Uh the other worry I guess was mucor, but . . [A: (?)
47		screaming and shouting] after all your screaming and
48		shouting. [A: yeah.] Did you scream and shout at
49		them poor house officers?
50	A:	└No I didn't shout at them,
51		but I mean I've I've said to everybody that they
52		should definitely recognize uh mucor, clinically. We're
53		gonna present that case to, eh, uhm, at medical
54		mortality conference as well. [R: Uh huh] So this
55		will be a nice contrast with that.
56	R:	└I hope it's a nicer conference than
57		the one yesterday uh what uh, so clinically how would
58		you differentiate, between, mucor and a bacterial . .
59		cellulitis.
60	A:	Well, uh one of the ways, obviously, is to look uh
61		right away and see if you see uh [R: (?)
62		microscopically] any pus that you can stain and if
63		there's something in it that's heavy, and that was
64		the point we wanted today to have that slide [R: It's
65		there] It's there.
66	R:	Oh, it's 117-H.
67	A:	Up there. Okay. And so if you see a heavy something that
68		would be one way of telling, if you see heavy bacteria,
69		although it won't rule out mucor. Another thing, is that
70		with mucor yo you, you may have severe compromise in
71		vision, and apparently her vision is fine.
72	R:	└No, no
73		double vision, no
74	A:	└ that doesn't, yeah, and

this will be a nice contrast with that." The pedagogical implications of the proposed contrast are not explained immediately, and the MR at first refers back to the earlier medical mortality conference before topicalizing the clinical differences (lines 58–59) "between, mucor and a bacterial . . . cellulitis," thus clarifying the earlier deictic expressions.

The response by the attending in lines 60–65 begins to explain the difference between a particular bacterial organism and fungal agent. The exchange, therefore, can be viewed as a clear instance of collaborative teaching in which the MR topicalizes the exchange after having first described the patient with cellulitis. The topic of mucor refers back to an earlier meeting and a different patient's problem about which the attending had been anxious to tell the house staff. The remarks in Fig. 9.3, however, are clearly not self-evident. Understanding the exchange presupposes knowledge associated with several semantic domains within medicine and microbiology. Terms like *mucor* and *bacterial cellulitis* do not activate a specific image but do activate semantic domains with images that bear a family resemblance to each other or a number of descriptive morphological and molecular biological and biochemical properties. The medical oral history of Fig. 9.2, therefore, became an occasion for the MR to show the attending his sensitivity to an issue that was perceived as important to the attending and at the same time obtain additional knowledge about the two patients and their respective problems.

The exchange between the MR and attending in Fig. 9.3 continues for another 30 or so lines of which I have only shown another 9 lines. The discussion takes place in the microbiology lab while making use of a standard reference text in microbiology. Both parties are fully aware of the didactic nature of the discourse, but the teaching aspects of the speech event are not couched in obvious authoritarian or power-laden terms. The exchange is informal and, to my perception, quite amiable. The discussion is typical of the work conditions that occur in teaching hospitals. Technical artifacts are available and made use of when necessary. The status differences are marked primarily by who receives requests for information. The MR, as the novice, tries to insert information he has obtained from the patient as a means of revealing that he has been responsible in his duties.

The attending's remarks in lines 61–63 of Fig. 9.3 ("... and see if you see uh [R:microscopically] any pus and that you can stain and if there's something in it that's heavy ...") are not likely to be self-evident to the reader but are stated as if the MR should find them to be obvious. The instructional format seems designed to include the MR as an inside member while simultaneously providing him with the information to support his membership in the professional exchange. In lines 67–71, the attending underscores the importance of seeing "... a heavy something ... if you see heavy bacteria ..." and also provides a key clinical sign; "... you may have severe compromise in vision ..." The reference to the patient's vision, therefore, can be translated into action on the occasion of a medical history with a patient with suspected mucor. The attending's remarks seek to clarify differences between a bacterial and fungal infection by calling the MR's attention to two recent cases they have both seen.

The didactic exchange between the MR and the attending is not designed to resolve the patient's diagnostic condition but does contribute to its understanding. Another institutionalized meeting occurred not long after the aforementioned speech event and in the same location—the microbiology lab. The occasion was the lab rounds noted earlier where house officers and attendings meet each day to discuss new cases from the past 24 hours. Fortunately for my research, the patient with cellulitis was discussed. The occasion is not only a teaching event, but a necessary and routine aspect of health care delivery. The pathology and ID attendings negotiate a differential diagnosis and treatment plan but as part of a clinical teaching and practice context in which there is an opportunity for the house staff to be questioned about their understanding or lack of knowledge about the case.

As in all work settings, the participants must learn specific details about the relationship between authority and expertise. The materials found in Fig. 9.4 reveal a typical conversation between several physicians. This type of exchange was observed on many occasions during the years in which I conducted my research. The reader has no way of knowing who the three participants are and their respective authority and knowledge about the topic at hand. Identifying PA, IDA, and MR as three physicians and noting they are in a medical facility enables the reader to follow the dialogue, especially if a medical dictionary is consulted. The exchange in Fig. 9.4 cannot be understood or treated as valid unless the participants, the research analyst and reader can assume or believe in the credibility of each speaker. Both novices and experts in such settings develop a sense of the preferences for different sources of information under perceived conditions of high to low equivocality and the kind of consensus desired or dissensus that can be tolerated.

Beginning with line 1, the reference to "the same one (we?) (ya?) did yesterday?" implies a setting in which some task or activity has been done on a previous occasion. The remark by the IDA in line 3 seems to tell us that a different person is involved, but says nothing about the problem until line 5. The opening line contains a question by the PA that topicalizes an unidentified but particular type of object that others present seem to recognize as part of a subset of a general category.

The terms employed in lines 5, 7, 11, 17, 19, 28, 32, 34, 35, and 41 of Fig. 9.4 presuppose considerable knowledge about medicine and the pathological conditions associated with a particular type of infection that is called "group A strep." The opening line by the PA can be seen as appropriate when it is known that he is the ranking expert of the group vis-a-vis the patient's pathological condition.

The case of Mrs. Price was of interest to the attendings because she was found to have low blood pressure and group A strep, but the attribution of "shock" was never documented. In lines 9–12 of Fig. 9.4, the IDA refers to a complex problem; the patient who may have been in shock but where no bacteremia was present. The present case, however, confirmed bacteremia but could not document the existence of shock. In lines 23–24, the PA returns to this problem by noting that the patient's shock was ambiguous. The exchange is of special interest to the two attendings because such cases can have implications that can be extended to basic issues in clinical medicine and research.

FIG. 9.4. Discourse during microbiology lab rounds.

1	PA:	(?)(low voice level) Is this the same one (we?)
2		(ya?) did yesterday?
3	IDA:	No. This is the eye lady.
4	PA:	(?)
5	IDA:	Cellulitis
6	PA:	Oh.
7	IDA:	With group A strep . . in shock
8	PA:	In shock. (Slight rise in voice level) How about that.
9	IDA:	I[t?] was gonna be more interesting if she didn't
10	MR:	⌊I'm(?)
11	IDA:	have bacteremia but (laughing and voice level
12		increasing) now she's had bacteremia so
13	MR:	⌊There's a little, there's
14		little (voice level increases) problem with that
15		that I'll, will go into more as far
16	IDA:	Yeah.
17	MR:	how much shock she really was in.
18	IDA:	⌊was in, right.
19	MR:	compared to what [abrupt shift] she's a liver lady,
20		you know, an' I don't know what her blood pressure sits
21		at. It may not be real high to start with.
22	IDA:	⌊Right. ⌊Right.
23	PA:	So she didn't have peripheral, evidence of shock
24		really? Just a low blood pressure.
25	MR:	⌊No, she wasn't, she wasn't ever clamp, you
26		know
27	PA:	Uh huh
28	MR:	clamped down or flushed or anything
29	PA:	OK
30	MR:	I can . . and, and she doesn't
31		[abrupt shift] one thing that argues
32		against a lot of neuropathy, you know, from diabetes, for
33		one, she's only had it for three years, but two, you know,
34		her neuro exam an' her an' her peripheral vascular exams.
35		is really normal, is normal sensory, good pulses distally,
36		and stuff, and I just have a hard time.
37	PA:	Yeah
38	MR:	there'd be a lot of sy-sympathetic, you know
39	PA:	Right
40	MR:	phone calls.
41	IDA:	Have they got sinus films on her yet?

(Each dot between words = one second)

During lab rounds, slides (and petrie dishes directly) are examined under a microscope and then discussed by those present in the lab as part of
the health care process and the training of novices. The IDA may provide a
few initial remarks about the patient but the MR is expected to fill in many
of the clinical details needed for clarifying the relationship between the
patient's symptoms and the laboratory findings. In addition, the pathology
resident often is asked to participate in the discussion.

The PA and IDA are expected to provide authoritative information about
the pathological and clinical aspects of each case and although there is often
an overlap in their knowledge about such matters, there is also a division of
labor. The attendings listen attentively to the novices when they are asked
to say something about the patient's condition. The language employed by
the novices (e.g., lines 19–36) becomes an important source of information
about their understanding of a case and the ability to make appropriate
inferences.

Medical teaching settings then, typify the interpenetration of technology
and collaborative work. The patterns of interaction described in this paper
can be found in all work settings; an individual's status and reputation give
credibility to her or his comments and provide the warrant for assessing the
adequacy of the observations and conclusions of novices. Novice and expert
are constrained and guided by their general and local knowledge of social
structure; this structure provides the framework for the distributed cognition associated with the pursuit of medical health care goals. The tacit
cultural regularities that frame and guide verbal and nonverbal local interaction influence the way status differences and a differential distribution of
knowledge permeate medical teaching about diagnostic problem solving
and treatment plans.

The cultural and organizational regularities and contingencies are conditions that impose limits on the acceptability or usefulness of technologies
when the latter possess properties that are inconsistent with the usual way
of doing things. Computerized databases designed to aid diagnostic decisions often lack sufficient information about the local ecological and clinical
conditions under which diagnostic activity occurs despite claims that such
expert systems can reduce the diagnostic workup dramatically. A key factor
here is the reasoning employed when a medical history is taken and subsequently written into a patient's chart.

CONCLUSION

In the present chapter, I have made a number of observations about the
value of different technologies in the practice of medicine within teaching
hospitals. For example, computerized databases designed to aid diagnostic

decisions are evident in the settings I observed, as well as laboratory analyses that attain a decoupled status once their sources are known. The analysis of blood or tissue cultures, to cite one important laboratory procedure, is a well-known case.

I have been critical of attempts to employ computer-aided diagnosis through the use of expert systems because such systems often lack sufficient information about the local ecological and clinical conditions under which diagnostic activity occurs despite claims that such systems can reduce the diagnostic workup dramatically. What needs to be added to medical expert systems are the kinds of reasoning employed when a medical history and physical examination are taken and particular inferences and hypotheses are subsequently written into the chart.

The obstacles to the creation of useful data bases and expert systems for medical diagnosis can be mitigated by paying more attention to the way the initial communication process between physician and patient activates overlapping but distributed cognitive resources for the task at hand. These resources help the physician to bring into being a frame to which memory elements from different clinical experiences and knowledge of basic science concepts can be recruited (Kahneman & Miller, 1986). These retrieved elements interact with local knowledge conditions to create hypotheses about diagnostic possibilities.

The case of Mrs. Price illustrates the collaborative nature of training and diagnostic reasoning in a medical setting. Knowing which participants are experts or novices is essential in order to understand the discussion between the MR and IDA about the clinical signs that can be linked to the patient's infectious left eye. The discussion between the MR and IDA implies differences in the way information is elicited from patients and the adequacy of its content. Further, the expert must assess the extent to which the novice has understood and made adequate use of the information in reaching a diagnosis and plan of treatment.

In the present case, the very low blood pressure of the patient when she first entered the hospital alerted two medical attendings to the possibility of bloodstream infection (the release of toxins in the blood). The risk is septicemia or microbial agents in the bloodstream that can result in bacteremic shock. In a separate interview with the IDA, she explained that when the patient arrived at the hospital "everybody thought her blood pressure was pretty low and they thought she was in shock . . ." The key issue for the medical team was determining if the patient was in shock and the low blood pressure was the primary clinical sign that was used. The clinical picture, however, was confusing because of no prior information on the patient's blood pressure and the patient's age and chronic liver disease.

The resident's questions in Fig. 9.3 seemed motivated by a desire to understand the attending's reasoning but the clinical signs were ambiguous and did not admit of an unequivocal assessment of the case. The case proved equivocal in other respects because of the confusion over whether the patient had ever been bitten by an alleged spider or had developed an infection in her eye that had perhaps started in the throat and worked its way up to the sinuses and then into the eye.

By the time the case reached lab rounds (Fig. 9.4), there was enough bacterial evidence to confirm the treatment that had been started earlier after the initial examination of a preliminary gram stain and before detailed laboratory tests had been conducted. The exchange in Fig. 9.4, therefore, served both didactic and health care functions and enabled the attendings to make a fairly conclusive diagnosis and validate an existing treatment plan. But the case also included some unanswered questions about how the patient might have encountered the microbial agent in question and in particular, it was never clear that the patient had been in shock. Finally, the case was of sufficient interest to the two attendings to have the patient presented at teaching or grand rounds that occur each week and frequented by a large number of attendings and house staff. The goal was to find adequate evidence for the possible existence of shock and the source of the infection.

In earlier sections of the chapter, I implied that the research analyst should develop an ethnographically driven cognitive and sociolinguistic methodology for the kind of field research described herein. The research analyst, as part of her or his analysis, must consult informants who can provide interpretations of the discourse and technological activities associated with work tasks. For example, verbal and written exchanges about different types of laboratory cultures and radiological films used to infer illness or disease and prescribe appropriate courses of action.

The work setting examined briefly in this chapter includes several problem solving tasks and an institutionalized division of labor that formally specifies the kinds of knowledge background or expertise associated with persons occupying particular positions. In addition, there are the organization goals of training qualified future physicians and diagnosing and treating patients successfully. The success of the system requires feedback from several actors and monitoring and assessing the activities of the house staff and other attendings even when judgments are not challenged directly.

Different individuals collaborate in a teaching hospital and acquire different yet overlapping cognitive representations of the environments in which they must interact with each other and various technological artifacts. Received knowledge is activated continuously and is simultaneously subject to modification in situations where a high premium is placed on inductive procedures and the credibility of novices and experts. The conditions that can trigger inductions or deductions are contingent on noisy elicitation procedures in which variable circumstances of uncertainty and facticity coexist. Although medical experts in clinical settings rely on different types of technology and technical assistance in constructing a differential diagnosis and plan of treatment, these activities are contingent upon the social organization of health care facilities and especially upon socially structured communication processes. For example, the organization of vertical and horizontal authority structures can create social barriers to the implementation of theoretically valuable expertise and technology. Interpersonal relations and the credibility of experts, technicians and patients can both facilitate and block effective collaborative work relationships.

ACKNOWLEDGMENTS

I am grateful to anonymous readers for their helpful criticisms and to Jolene Galegher for helpful editorial suggestions and advice during revisions of two drafts of this chapter. I want to thank Dr. Charles Davis and Dr. Elizabeth Ziegler for their support and encouragement and their generous advice, suggestions and patience with a naive voice in their midst.

REFERENCES

Bourdieu, P. (1981). The specificity of the scientific field. In C. Lemert (ed.), *French sociology.* New York: Columbia University Press, pp. 257–292.

Chandrasekaran, B. (1981). Natural and social system metaphors for distributed problem solving: Introduction to the issue. *IEEE Transactions on Systems, Man and Cybernetics, Vol. SMC-11,* 1–5.

Cicourel, A. V. (1974). *Cognitive sociology: Language and meaning in social interaction.* New York: Free Press.

Cicourel, A. V. (1987a). The interpenetration of communicative contexts: Examples from medical encounters. *Social Psychology Quarterly, 50,* 217–226.

Cicourel, A. V. (1987b). Cognitive and organizational aspects of medical diagnostic reasoning. *Discourse Processes, 10,* 347–367.

Freidson, E. (1970a). *Professional dominance: The social structure of medical care.* New York: Atherton.

Freidson, E. (1970b). *Profession of medicine: A study of the sociology of applied knowledge.* New York: Dodd, Mead.

Gomez, F., & Chandrasekaran, B. (1981). Knowledge organization and distribution for medical diagnosis. *IEEE Transactions on Systems, Man and Cybernetics, Vol. SMC-11,* 34–42.

Granovetter, M. (1972). The strength of weak ties. *American Journal of Sociology, 78,* 1360–1380.

Granovetter, M. (1974). *Getting a job.* Cambridge, MA: Harvard University Press.

Granovetter, M. (1976). Network sampling. *American Journal of Sociology, 81,* 1287–1303.

Granovetter, M. (1983). The strength of weak Ties: A network theory revisited. In R. Collins (Ed.), *Sociological theory.* San Francisco: Jossey-Bass, pp. 201–233.

Hutchins, E. (1985). *The social organization of distributed cognition.* Unpublished manuscript, University of California at San Diego.

Kahneman, D., & Miller, D. T. (1986). Norm theory: Comparing reality to its alternatives. *Psychological Review, 93,* 136–153.

Kleinmuntz, B. (1986). The scientific study of clinical judgment in psychology and medicine. In H. R. Arkes & K. R. Hammond, (Eds.), *Judgment and decision making: An interdisciplinary reader.* Cambridge: Cambridge University Press.

Schutz, A. (1964). *Collected papers II: Studies in social theory.* The Hague: Nijhoff.

Smith, R. G. & Davis, R. (1981). Frameworks for cooperation in distributed problem solving. *IEEE Transactions on Systems, Man, and Cybernetics, Vol. SMC - 11,* 61–70.

Tversky, A. & Kahneman, D. (1974). Judgment under uncertainty: Heuristics and biases. *Science, 185,* 1124–1131.

Weber, Max. (1968). Economy and society: An outline of interpretive sociology, 3 Vols. (G. Roth & C. Wittich, Eds.). New York: Bedminister Press.

Wesson, R., Hayes-Roth, F., Burge, J. W., Stasz, C. & Sunshine, C. A. (1981). Network structures for distributed situation assessment. *IEEE Transactions on Systems, Man and Cybernetics, Vol. SMC-11,* 5–23.

III

EXPERIENCES WITH TECHNOLOGY FOR COOPERATIVE WORK

10

The Interplay of Work Group Structures and Computer Support

Tora K. Bikson
J. D. Eveland
The Rand Corporation

Abstract

When members of task groups communicate through computers instead of traditional means, much about the group could change: group structure, intensity of communication, interaction across physical barriers, and the work process. This chapter probes these issues by reviewing a year-long field experiment among active workers and retirees planning a company's retirement policy. The study shows many effects of computer communication. Among other findings, the study shows that computer communication can help reduce barriers to social interaction in distributed work groups and can broaden leadership roles.

How are task groups affected, if at all, by access to computer-based communication capabilities in addition to conventional communication media? What happens when the infrastructure for shared work is built on cables, microprocessors, and screens along with corridors, meeting rooms, and blackboards? How, if at all, does networked information technology affect group structures and interaction processes?

On the one hand, it has been proposed that the diffusion of interactive information technologies will permit rapid and widespread exchange, overcoming barriers to group interaction and promoting more egalitarian task processes (e.g., Hiltz, 1985). On the other hand, these technologies have also been said to impair the social properties of communication and encourage counternormative or counterproductive interactions (e.g., Sproull & Kiesler, 1986).

Although these kinds of issues were raised in the 1960s (see review in

Laudon, 1977), the need for answers has become pressing in the 1980s. Two trends—the decentralization of mainframe environments and the networking of microcomputers—have stimulated a demand for group-level software; new generations of tools (e.g., hypertext media, group decision support systems, messaging protocols designed for coordination) are rapidly emerging to fill the need. Although technical expertise is now focusing on the domain of cooperative work support, it is equally important to bring to this arena the perspective of behavioral research—if only because the determinants of successful task collaboration are likely to be as much social as they are technological in nature (Bikson & Eveland, 1986).

This presentation reviews current multidisciplinary field research efforts undertaken by The RAND Corporation. Ranging from case study to field experiment, their aim is to understand the interplay between work group structures and the computer-based technologies that support them.

RESEARCH QUESTIONS

A number of questions about the ways electronic information media may influence work groups—their structures, patterns of individual interaction, experiences of task and social involvement—have recurred in research efforts with quite different aims and methods. Among them are the following:

- When work groups get access to computer-based media for handling information and communication tasks, do their structures change? Do they move closer to or further from formally established organizational structures? Do group positions (e.g., leader roles, assistant roles) stay the same or change?
- Do computer-supported groups overcome physical barriers to interaction (e.g., space or time constraints)? Do they overcome preexisting social barriers (e.g., status differences)? Do they form tight clusters ("electronic islands") or are they overlapping and not sharply defined ("loose bundles")?
- How if at all do networked information technologies affect the amount or density of interaction in a group? How do they affect extent of members' integration within a group? Or centralization across a group?
- How do these new technologies affect social communication among group members? How do they affect group members' perceptions and evaluations of the work process? Do these media supplant or supplement other means for exchanging information and coordinating group tasks?

In addressing these questions, this discussion relies most heavily on a year-long field experiment designed to provide and support electronic versus conventional interaction media for two otherwise identical task groups (see also Bikson & Goodchilds, 1988; Eveland & Bikson, 1988). However, we also draw on findings from a number of other projects, including a large cross-sectional study of 55 work groups making use of computer-based tools in private sector organizational settings (Bikson, 1987; Bikson, Gutek, & Mankin, 1987); a development project to design, implement, and track a message-handling system intended to cohere with hypothesized organizational needs and structures (Eveland & Bikson, 1987); and two case studies examining new information technology introduced into multiple work groups in single organizations (Bikson, Stasz, & Mankin, 1985; Stasz, Bikson, & Shapiro, 1986).

Although each research activity examined project-specific hypotheses, they share conceptual definitions of major terms and make use of a common set of guiding assumptions. That general framework was developed in broad-based literature reviews (Bikson, Gutek, & Mankin, 1981; Bikson & Eveland, 1986) and successfully applied in studies with quite diverse research designs and methods.

RESEARCH FRAMEWORK

All the projects previously cited, for example, assume that the work group is the critical unit of analysis for understanding the nature and effects of new interactive technology. They look secondarily at the overall context in which groups are embedded and at individual differences among group members. For the most part they do not examine occupational strata (e.g., managers, clerical workers) because these are groups only in the statistical sense.

The projects further suppose that any interactive technology introduced into a work group will be—borrowing from Kling and Scacchi (1982)—more like a web than like a discrete entity. While reinforcing our behavioral focus on groups rather than individuals, this tenet leads to a technical focus not on highly specific electronic tools but on the broader interactive environment of which the tools are a part. That environment, we believe, should be modeled generically as an information–communication system. For example, its major components can be regarded as messages, or chunks of content (which may be composed from text, numbers, images, graphics, and so on, and may be operated on with content-appropriate electronic tools); senders, who compose, manipulate, and transmit the contents; and receivers, either another individual(s) or the same individual at another time, who may interact with the retrieved contents as they choose.

What happens, then, when a web of interactive technology is introduced into a work group? The result, we believe, is a sociotechnical system in the traditional sense: work groups are "directly dependent on their material means and resources for their output" (Trist, 1981; cf. Bikson & Eveland, 1986; Johnson et al., 1985; Pava, 1983; Taylor, 1987). That is to say, individuals become interdependent not only on one another but also on the technology for accomplishing their tasks. Although the avenues for group work and the means for managing it may have multiplied, new challenges are introduced along with the technology that preexisting social structures may be ill-prepared to handle.

Finally, we expect as a consequence to observe the mutual adaptation of social and technical systems. That is, new interactive media will be modified and extended to fit user contexts even as work groups are changing their task behaviors and social structures to incorporate the technology (Bikson & Eveland, 1986). The term *interplay* in the title of the chapter intends to capture the reciprocal influence of task groups and computer systems over time. With the guiding assumptions outlined, it is next appropriate to define their basic terms and review some key findings.

WORK GROUPS

The notion of a work group is a familiar one, but it is often presupposed rather than defined. For purposes of the research described here, we found it helpful to rely on the generic conception of a "work unit" from traditional organizational research. Trist (1981), for example, defined primary work units in the following way: "These are the systems that carry out the set of activities involved in an identifiable and bounded subsystem of a whole organization, such as a line department. . . . They have a recognized purpose, which unifies the people and activities."

If this characterization is amended so that the work unit's activities primarily involve the generation, transformation, or transmission of products of the kind described earlier (chunks of informational content), it yields a reasonable starting definition of the types of task groups we have studied (groups of "information workers" or white-collar workers).

We operationalized this definition to emphasize both the complexity and the organization of work units. That is, following Rousseau (1983), we targeted study groups of four or more persons, representing at least two different status or occupation categories, whose activity is related by products or by task processes (Bikson & Eveland, 1986; Bikson & Gutek, 1983; Bikson, Gutek, & Mankin, 1987; Gutek, Bikson, & Mankin, 1984; Talbert, Bikson, & Shapiro, 1984).

Work groups, then, comprise multiple individuals acting as a bounded whole in order to get something done (cf. Dunham et al., 1986; Kraut, Galegher & Egido, 1987–88). So construed, they are inherently cooperative, where that term designates the requirement to coordinate interdependent events to accomplish an acknowledged goal; it does not imply the absence of competition or conflict among group members. A work group's purpose or goal, in turn, may well involve a number of multiperson tasks and task cycles; its activities are expected to persist over time and to survive membership changes (cf. McGrath, 1984). Finally, we have emphasized missions—what groups do—for identifying and understanding them. In the phrase *work group, work* and *group* get equal stress (Akin & Hopelain, 1986).

Applying this construct in the large cross-sectional research project already cited, we found it an appropriate unit of study.[1] We learned, first, that work groups can be recognized and classified on the basis of what they do—their mission or purpose within the broader organizations to which they belong. For instance, some groups in an organization have a function that is primarily managerial (e.g., the comptroller's office, the personnel department), whereas others have predominantly professional functions (e.g., marketing research, product development) or supporting roles (e.g., payroll processing, inventory control). A four-fold typology comprising management/administration, technical professional, text-oriented professional, and support groups resulted (Bikson & Gutek, 1983).

More importantly, we learned that a host of other differences accompany these differing organizational roles, so that group work should not be treated as a unitary phenomenon. For example, we observed substantial differences in size and internal structure associated with work group type. Although average group size was 10 in the cross-sectional study, management/administration groups tended to have fewer members and support groups, more members. Interestingly, both these group types were significantly more centralized than either type of professional group (Bikson & Gutek, 1983), a finding that reappeared in network analyses of communication data generated in our electronic mail design and development project (Eveland & Bikson, 1987). In contrast to previous studies that interpret

---

[1]Supported by a grant from the National Science Foundation, the study explored how well conceptions of technological innovation from previous research could inform and explain successful implementation of computer-based procedures in diverse white-collar settings. Over 500 white-collar employees, representing 55 work groups in 26 different manufacturing and service organizations, participated in the project. Data were obtained from employee surveys, managerial interviews, archival records, and observation. The research is reported in detail in Bikson, Gutek, and Mankin (1987) and summarized in Bikson (1987). For convenience, this research is often cited as the "cross-sectional" study throughout the presentation.

centralization as a function of group size (e.g., Crowston, Malone, & Lin, 1986), our research suggests that internal structure is more influenced by group type than by size.

Not surprisingly, we found characteristic sets of information handling activities distinctive of each type of group. An activities checklist employed in the cross-sectional study showed, for instance, professional groups do a great deal of writing and rewriting or analysing and reanalysing; by contrast, management/administration groups create forms and distribute information, whereas support groups fill in forms and process information. On the other hand, the same checklist revealed some common activities. For example, although writing original material is most prevalent in text-oriented professional groups. two-thirds of the employees in our cross-sectional study ($N=531$) have occasion to do it from time to time as a part of regular task processes. Similarly, although management/administration group members spend a higher proportion of time in oral communication than others, almost everyone reports oral communication to be a non-negligible part of group work. And over half of all group members have some sort of information files to maintain.

COMPUTER SUPPORT

From an empirical look at work groups and the activities their missions subsume, then, it seemed our view of the supporting technology might be an apt one: a highly generic information-communication environment in which more specialized applications are embedded as needed to carry out particular group tasks. Within such a framework, computer systems are seen as instrumental in relation to group goal accomplishment. That is, from this perspective, computer systems are taken quite literally as information "tools," in accord with accepted definitions of tools as means for extending the capability of individuals, work groups, or organizations (Bikson & Eveland, 1986; Tornatzky et al., 1983).

The research we have undertaken targets interactive computer systems that can support multiple functions and that are appropriate for use by all the members of a work group. (This is not to claim that every function of the system is appropriate for all the members but only that some subset is appropriate for each of them.) This conceptualization of work group technology is quite broad and is satisfied operationally by widely varied configurations of hardware, software, and communications media. It leaves system architecture unconstrained—technology webs may be constituted from microcomputers, minicomputers, mainframes, or combinations of these. Candidate systems might range from personal computers communicating via the manual transfer of floppy disks to powerful intelligent workstations linked by broadband networks.

The systems involved in our research fall somewhere between these extremes, although it must be acknowledged that they fall closer to the low-tech end of the distribution. Nonetheless, what we found when we examined interactive systems supporting group work were technologies—with an emphasis on the plural. In the large cross-sectional study we observed considerable variety among electronic tools in use; even within work units, the technology tends to be a loosely configured and changing collection of hardware, software, I/O devices, and communications capabilities acquired from multiple sources (Bikson, Gutek, & Mankin, 1987).

Our data corroborate the conclusion drawn by Kraut, Galegher, and Egido (1987–88): There is no single technology that adequately supports the collaborative process; groups rather need and make use of a "rich palette" of computer-based tools, typically involving more than one vendor's products. We should add that often they do so in spite of rather than because of technology planning processes. In fact, our case studies (e.g., Stasz, Bikson, & Shapiro, 1986; Bikson, Stasz, & Mankin, 1985) illustrate why and how, even when organizational policies dictate use of a single vendor or uniform product line, work groups will find a way to incorporate diversity.

There are, however, patterns in the diversity and one way to find them is by looking at arrays of computer-based tools in relation to work group types (Gutek, Sasse, & Bikson, 1986). Considering both hardware and software, for example, we learned that professional group types have the richest palettes and are perhaps best situated to take advantage of newly emerging tools for the support of collaborative work. Management types, in contrast, more often have access to microcomputers and to individual productivity tools; their slower start with connectivity (and concomitant lack of experience with shared hardware, software, or databases) may put them at a disadvantage socially and technologically in attempting to incorporate group-level tools. Support groups, on the other hand, have likely had only too much prescribed sharing; very often they operate in mainframe environments with relatively rigid systems not initially designed to support multi-function interactive use (Bikson & Gutek, 1983). These patterns are probably overdetermined. That is, they are influenced by history (the time at which different kinds of computer-based tools emerged in the market-place), by industrial sector, by availability of economic resources and technical expertise, by local opportunity, and by corporate policy—making causal questions about the interplay of work groups and computer support quite difficult to examine.

THE INTERPLAY

Reviews of research literature on technological innovation in varied domains led us to construe the relationship between new systems and extant social settings as one of reciprocal influence (see, for example, Bikson, 1980; Bikson, Gutek, & Mankin, 1981; Bikson, Quint, & Johnson, 1984). A close look at studies of successful implementation corroborates a view of that process as one of mutual adaptation (Bikson & Eveland, 1986). In particular, in examining the interplay between work group structures and computer support, we expected to observe users modifying or reinventing their electronic tools, creating new tasks or altering old ones, and changing work structures and processes as a result.

Although such mutual adaptation should be observable in most work groups that successfully incorporate new technologies into their task repertoires, we expected it to be most evident among groups whose computer support includes electronic communication. First, high levels of intragroup communication have been associated with task group success regardless of type of task (McGrath, 1984). Moreover, communication is an established predictor of the diffusion of innovations in general (Bikson, Quint, & Johnson, 1984); in our cross-sectional study, the availability of electronic communication is a significant predictor of a work group's acceptance and use of computer technology (Bikson, Gutek, & Mankin, 1987). Most important, the capacity of electronic information technology to integrate data processing, text processing, and communication within a single user-accessible framework is what is fundamentally different about computer-supported work groups. It enables the sharing and coordination of multiperson tasks in ways quite different from those that characterize work group structures and processes that rely on more conventional media (Eveland & Bikson, 1987).

For these reasons we have made electronic communication capability the focus of field research aimed at understanding the interplay between work group structures and computer support. A major project was carried out at RAND to develop, introduce, and track an electronic messaging system—RANDMAIL—among users previously familiar with computers but new to electronic mail.[2] One goal of the project was to learn whether electronic media can overcome physical and social barriers to enable col-

---

[2]RANDMAIL is a message-handling system designed to be coherent with and to enhance existing organizational communication processes at RAND. For 18 months after its introduction, message header data (to, from and cc nodes plus date/time) were captured on two unix-based minicomputer host machines. The 69,000 message headers logged represented 800 individual sender and/or receiver nodes. Nodes were linked with organizational characteristics (e.g., department, occupation, office location) to help interpret results generated by network analyses. This research, supported by an internal grant from the RAND Corporation, is reported

laboration among individuals who otherwise would not be able to work together (cf. Feldman, 1986).

We found that at RAND people rarely used electronic messaging to contact people who are spatially out of reach. On the contrary—except for interactions between East and West coast offices of RAND—we found spatial distance to be negatively associated with electronic interaction. On average, people sent about 45% of their messages to others in their immediate physical vicinity (Eveland & Bikson, 1987). Borrowing Orr's (1986) phrase, we seem to find "electronic hallways," but they appear in the main to parallel the spatial ones. On the other hand, we learned that alleviating temporal barriers with asynchronous messaging may be much more important than is often realized. Sending patterns revealed striking differences in the ways individuals within groups distribute their interactions over the work day.

Data regarding electronic links and social divisions were harder to interpret. For instance, in spite of what is often said about the difficulty of communicating across disciplinary lines, we observed very high levels of interdisciplinary interaction. Moreover, department-based communication clusters became more open and permeable over the 18-month logging period. A counterinstance was provided by examining communication patterns in relation to work group types (professional research groups, management groups, and support groups). Here we found professional research groups to be relatively close to one another in the context of the total communication space; management groups are also relatively close to one another and most central in the organizational communication space; and there is very little communication between professional and management groups. Support groups tend to be at the periphery of the communication space, not interacting with one another or with other types of groups. The pattern is a robust one that shows no change over the course of the research.

In sum, data provided by this study together with evidence from other field research projects lead us to think that electronic communication systems do become embedded in the infrastructure of work and augment multiperson tasks as sociotechnical theory suggests. Electronic mail is more a general information-communication vehicle than it is a substitute channel (e.g., for when the person is spatially out of reach or hard to get by phone). But interactive linkages between work messages, work media, and workers make constraints of both time and space more manageable, especially by letting individuals queue their tasks and proceed at their own pace within a group context.

---

in Eveland and Bikson, 1987. For convenience, it is referred to throughout as the "RANDMAIL" study.

In consequence, such systems probably expand the potential for participation in multiple groups, allowing for collaborative work across a broader base of potential members. We find evidence for this conclusion in the increased interactions, within RAND, between disciplines. We also noted increased lateral interaction in our case study sites, even when it was specifically against organizational policy at the time; the organization's rules had to be altered in response (Stasz & Bikson, 1986). Thus the hypothesized interplay between social structures and technical support seems both theoretically justifiable and empirically plausible. However, causal relationships are hard to disentangle, especially when intact groups have incrementally acquired communications technology. To explore more systematically the interplay between work group structures and computer support, we undertook the field experiment reported in detail in the following sections.

AN EXPERIMENTAL COMMUNICATIONS PROJECT

Although we believed we learned a great deal from the projects reviewed earlier, we sought to extend the findings by using a more powerful research design. For instance, the RANDMAIL project allowed us to control type of communications hardware and software as well as its relationship to other computer-based tools; but it did not permit us to evaluate the extent to which network structures and interaction patterns that emerged over time were influenced by the new technology in comparison to ongoing social relationships, task differences, and other factors. It could not reveal how, if at all, computer-supported work group structures and processes differed from those that would be observed in groups similar in other respects but employing standard interaction media.

We decided, then, that we needed to carry out a field experiment—a procedure that would allow us randomly to assign group members to computer-based versus traditional support in the completion of identical work goals, as well as to design and control the introduction of new information and communications technology. An effective design, it seemed to us, should also have the following characteristics:

- If individuals are expected to become familiar with new information technology, accomplish a meaningful goal, and in the process have an opportunity to form or reform work structures and social relations, it would require an intervention of at least a year's time.
  Furthermore, if individuals in both the "electronic" and "standard" conditions were to participate in a year-long effort, a strong mission focus was essential—the goal for group activity and the role of communication would have to be highly motivating.

- And, for noncolocated individuals to agree to take part (and to continue their participation) in randomly assigned groups, they should be selected from a common "community"; that is, they should come from a common social environment, share some concerns, and have some reason to think they might want to work with one another (cf. Bikson, 1980; Markus, 1987).
- Last—and definitely not least—we need to find a funding source willing to support a rather costly experiment of this sort!

Given these constraints, the experiment we eventually developed had as its basis a task force on the transition to retirement, funded by a nonprofit organization whose two programmatic interests are aging/adult development and social uses of media.[3]

Field Procedures

From one of the older and larger corporations in the greater Los Angeles area, we recruited volunteers to take part in a year-long effort focused on the transition to retirement—thinking about it, planning for it, and adjusting to it in a time when U.S. policies and organizational practices are also undergoing change.[4] The letter of solicitation told prospective participants, in part:

The unusual and, we hope, exciting aspect of the study is that we are looking to you as someone directly involved to provide the issues and explore their implications. What do you envision as the goods and bads, the major unknowns, the unexpected pitfalls and delights, in retirement planning today? We ask you to consider joining us and other . . . colleagues in this effort.

We are forming two retirement Task Forces, and the charge to each is straightforward. Members, half retired and half actively employed, will work together over the course of a year. Their task will be to consider, deliberate, probe, and develop a set of recommendations about preretirement planning—recommendations that can be addressed to persons nearing retirement, to organizations (including but not limited to [yours]), and to professionals involved in preretirement planning. To realize this goal, the Task Force participants may meet, form subgroups, correspond, work hard, play a little, or whatever you decide will best accomplish our joint purpose.

---

[3]This research project, still underway, was made possible by a grant from The John and Mary R. Markle Foundation, for whose support we are deeply indebted.
[4]We are grateful to the Los Angeles Department of Water and Power for providing the organizational context for this project and for giving the research effort its continuous, willing and able cooperation.

Additionally, members of one of the two Task Forces will have the option of communicating with each other and conducting their business with the aid of computers. Each member of this electronic group will have access to a micro-computer. Because we are interested in the possible advantages and disadvantages of ELECTRONIC communication compared with more STANDARD media, we will randomly appoint Task Force volunteers to either group. We want you to consider participating whether or not you have used a computer before.

The project enrolled 79 members, all of them middle- to upper-level professionals or managers with prior problem-solving or decision-making responsibility on the job (all male). Mean age was 62 for the retired and 60 for the employed participants; those who were retired had done so in the past four years, and those who were employed were all currently eligible to retire. At an initial in-person meeting, the following explanation for the research was presented.

WHY RETIREMENT? Retirement is dramatically different today from what it was even a few years ago. Now it is a transition that can occur any time over about a 30-year age span and will involve a host of personal, familial, social, and professional decisions.

WHY YOU? Since retirement has changed so much, there are no established "experts." The expertise lies with the people who are experiencing the new preretirement planning environment and its effects. Moreover, each side in the transition to retirement has something to offer to and learn from the other. By working together, exchanging information, sharing problems and solutions, they are likely to generate a good model for preretirement planning in a changing environment.

WHY THE 2-GROUP APPROACH? Two Task Forces have been formed, exactly alike in all respects but one. The "electronic" Task Force will use computers for exchanging information while the other will rely on more traditional methods of interaction. The use of two such groups allows researchers to address an as-yet unresolved issue: whether or not computers will facilitate communication among people not located in the same place but trying to work jointly on a task.

TABLE 10.1
Design

	Computer	No Computer
Retired:	$n = 20$	$n = 20$
Not Retired:	$n = 20$	$n = 19$

After this explanation, conditions were assigned, with subjects distributed into the four cells of the design as illustrated.

Prior computer experience was much the same across conditions. About half in each task force had had some sort of contact with batch-processing mainframe computers at work, and about a quarter had tried using a small home computer (typically for games). None had ever used computer-based communications.[5] An open-ended item at the end of the initial interview asked subjects why they had agreed to participate in the project. In both conditions a similar pattern emerged: Retirees were interested in giving information and employees were interested in getting information about the transition to retirement; the task force topic itself was a strong incentive. The other often-mentioned motivation was curiosity about research procedures. Access to the technology was infrequently cited as an incentive—only 10% of the standard group and 5% of the electronic group mentioned they were interested in computers.

To enable these groups to get underway, we scheduled two start-up meetings for each task force, held about a month apart. Each of these gatherings was chaired by a clinical psychologist with expertise in organizational development and group facilitation. The first meeting provided an opportunity for collecting consent forms, announcing the assignment to experimental conditions, and brainstorming about retirement issues that the task force might address in its work. At the second meeting, these issues were prioritized and grouped; then the general charge to the task force was discussed in more detail and the membership devised organizational arrangements and procedures for fulfilling it. Figure 10.1 represents some of the issues generated by the task forces at their initial meetings; it also gives the major categories into which the issues were classified.

Initially, the structure of the two task forces was much the same. Both groups had the same charge, generated highly overlapping issues, and approached the question of working arrangements in very similar ways. That is, each divided the basic mission into smaller issue areas suitable for attention by subgroups. Although the names of the subdomains differed somewhat between the two task forces, their orientations were quite congruent; each eventually settled on six (as shown in Fig. 10.1). The subgroups in turn elected chairs, with the set of six chairs forming a task force steering committee. With a structure in place, the participants were to be on their own.

Subgroup membership was by self-selection in both task forces, with

---

[5]Although computer experiences at work were the same for retirees and employees, a higher proportion of retirees in the two task forces reported having tried video games as well as home computer games. We interpreted this as a reflection of the more general finding that retirees pursue a greater variety of nonwork activities than their still employed peers (see Bikson & Goodchilds, 1988).

Initial retirement issues generated by the task forces.

Health	Sexuality
Finances	Letting go of the job
Understanding and timing requirement	Attitudes toward retirement
	Housing, relocation
Family adjustment	Mortality, religion
Time management and use	Continuing education
Self-impact	Community resources, information
Recreation, hobbies, leisure	
Social adjustment	Part-time work, volunteer work

Issue Categories Devised
to Organize Task Force Work

Health
Finances
Use of time
Family and social adjustment
Self esteem
Retirement planning processes

FIG. 10.1.   Approach to Retirement Issues

individuals choosing to associate with a topic area they found most interesting, felt most knowledgeable about, or considered most problematic. In both task forces as well, each subgroup's membership was roughly constituted half and half of workers and retirees—in the standard task force by design, in the other by happy accident. That is, the standard group spent considerable effort getting the right balance of employees and retirees in each subgroup while making sure that everyone's preferences were accommodated. No participant became a member of more than one, so that each group enrolled about 6 or 7 people. In the electronic task force, by contrast, about half the participants chose to participate in more than one subgroup; the size of the groups varied from 6 to 15, averaging 10 or more. It is important to stress that this difference in subgroup patterns was not imposed by the experimenters, but was generated by the participants themselves. Apparently the members of the electronic task force thought that their technology would allow them to work on as many topics as interested them. To be sure, not every member participated in all subgroups to the same extent, but there was a much broader range of involvement than in the standard group.

Succeeding sections of this chapter compare social structures and processes over time for the two task forces, describe the pattern of electronic interaction that emerged within the electronic condition, and discuss participant assessments of task force activity.

WORK GROUP STRUCTURES AND PROCESSES

A general theme of the hypotheses motivating this research was that the processes, patterns, and structures of interaction among participants would be significantly affected over the life of the project by the nature of the technology available. That is, the sociotechnical system created and maintained by the interplay between the electronic task force and its computer network would evolve differently from that created and maintained by the interplay between the standard task force and its more conventional work technology (meeting rooms, blackboards, telephones, paper mail). Untangling the effects of technology on a social process over time from the effects of other factors such as individual predilection and group history is always, of course, an inherently difficult task. However, we believe that an experimental design with random assignment is the best methodological technique available for making plausible causal inferences in such complex circumstances. When such a procedure shows differences as profound and systematic as those we portray here, and when the findings are consistent with conclusions drawn from quite different research methods such as those represented in the projects previously described, we believe it is reasonable to assume that the technology itself has exerted substantial influence.

To permit a detailed mapping of the "social space" of each task force as well as the patterns developing within in, a portion of every interview addressed the nature and extent of relationships among respondents. These standardized inquiries used as stimulus materials a set of participant ID cards—laminated photos with names for each task force member.[6] Re-

---

[6]Many of the sociometric measures used in this research were derived from the four rounds of questionnaires. At each time point, respondents were shown pictures (with names) of each of the other participants. They were asked first to indicate how well they "knew" the person (scaled as "know well," "know a little," "don't know"). "Know a little" was defined as "recognize by name or by face." If they "knew" the person at all, they were then prompted for whether they had had any "contact" with the person in the last two weeks, where contact was defined to include in person interaction (meetings, casual conversation, other contexts), phone calls, memos or electronic mail. If a contact was reported, they were asked if the purpose of the contact was "chance," "social," "general business," or "task force business" (more than one response was acceptable). In addition, at the last interview respondents were also asked how the contact took place—by "scheduled meeting," "unscheduled face-to-face encounter," "telephone," "written letter/memo," or (for the electronic group), "electronic mail."

spondents sorted the ID cards and answered a number of questions about each familiar name or face. From such items, we constructed three measures reflecting varying degrees of interpersonal attachment:

1. recognition, reflecting other task force members with which a subject is familiar at least by recognizing the name or face;
2. knowing, or reciprocal acknowledgment between pairs of subjects in the task force that they know each other somewhat or very well; and
3. contact, or having been in touch with any of the other task force members (in person, by phone, by memo, and/or by computer) in the past 2 weeks.

At baseline (i.e., prior to the experiment) subjects on average "recognized" over a third of the other members of their task force, but "knew" only about 10% of them. Very few instances of actual contact were reported.

We found virtually no differences between the two experimental groups on these measures. Members of the standard task force tended to be slightly more widely recognized and better known, which we interpreted as a reflection of their higher status in the parent organization (differences were not statistically significant). Much stronger differences, however, were observed as a function of work situation (employed versus retired) across the two task forces; measures of recognition and knowing, and especially of contact, were lower for retirees than for those still employed. Retirees in both electronic and standard groups were relatively peripheral in the social space defined by relationships among task force members. These initial differences had been expected in part because retirees are no longer a part of the official social structure of work and in part because they are geo-

---

The three attachment measures were constructed from 40 by 40 matrices summarizing the knowledge degree and contact responses. Each matrix had the individuals as both row and column headers. Each row represented the answers of a given individual; each column, the people with whom that attachment was being reported. For "knowledge," values could range from 0 (no knowledge) to 2 (know well). For contact, values were either 0 (no contact) or 1 (contact). The matrices were initially not symmetric, because it was not necessarily the case that the two parties would agree on their connection.

The matrix of "recognition" relationships was constructed as a symmetric matrix by allowing the relationship between two people to be coded as "1" if either person reported knowing the other even a little ("0" otherwise). The matrix of "knowing" relationships was constructed by coding as "1" only if BOTH parties reported knowing the other "well." The contact matrix was merely made symmetric; that is, a contact was presumed to exist if EITHER party reported it. There were thus a minimum of three matrices of relationships given careful analytic attention for each task force for each of four time periods. Matrices reflecting the purposes of contacts were also constructed, but are not reported in detail here. Finally, for time 4, five matrices were also constructed reflecting the contacts through different media, by coding as "1" if a contact was reported and a given medium was mentioned.

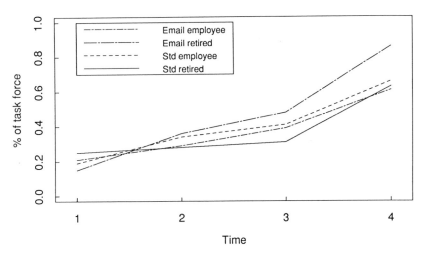

FIG. 10.2.   Name/face recognition by other task force members.

graphically distant from their former work colleagues as well as from one another.[7]

As the experiment progressed, the percentage of potential social relations represented by actual social relations, or the "density" of the social space, increased over time for both task forces.[8] Figure 10.2, for instance,

---

[7]The proportion of the population with whom a given individual is in contact provides a contact-based "integrativeness" index. In both task forces the integrative index for retirees averaged about .08. This percentage contrasts with about .12 for electronic employees and about .20 for standard employees. An analysis of variance shows the only significant difference to be that due to employee-retiree status ($F=15.87, p<.001$); neither condition nor interaction effects are significant.

[8]The structural indices used in social analyses were largely constructed from the matrices described in Note 3. The "density" of a network of interconnections summarized in a matrix is simply the proportion of actual relationships reported relative to the total possible (in a 40×40 matrix, this would be 780, or ($N(N-1)/2$). If everyone were connected to everyone else, the index would be "1.0"; if there were no relationships, it would be "0" (Knoke & Kuklinski, 1982).

"Integrativeness" and "betweenness" are indices relating to an individual's position relative to others in the network (matrix). Integrativeness is related closely to density, and is simply the proportion of others in the network to whom one is connected. Betweenness is a related but distinct concept reflecting one's centrality in a network; specifically, it measures the proportion of all the links between network members that pass through a given person (Freeman, 1976). It is an approximate measure of power/control vested in a given person. Both measures reflect higher values for a person the more significant his/her participation in the network might be. Scalar values for each individual in the network were calculated for each matrix and time period, and used in correlation and regression analyses. The satisfaction and involvement measures used in these analyses were derived from questionnaire items that used a five-point scale from high to low.

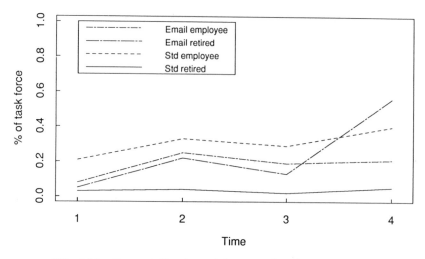

FIG.   10.3.   Contact with other task force members (prior two weeks).

shows changes in recognition density; for all groups, name or face recognition increased by time 4 to well over 50%. The increase is most striking for the electronic retirees, who went from recognizing less than 10% of their group at baseline to over 90% by the project's end. Figure 10.3 shows the changes in actual contacts between task force members (contact reports over the 2-week period prior to each interview). Again, electronic retirees evidence greatest overall change, with contact density increasing to over 50%.[9]

A repeated measure analysis of variance confirms the significance of these trends. The largest main effect, not surprisingly, is for time (recognition: $F=22.4$, $p<.001$; contact: $F=28.5$ $p<.001$). For recognition density, task force condition (electronic versus standard) is also an important source of variation ($F=9.9$, $p<.01$); and the three-way interaction of work status with condition and time is significant as well ($F=3.5$, $p<.05$). For contact density, both experimental condition ($F=3.9$, $p<.05$) and the retiree versus employee difference ($F=18.9$, $p<.001$) are sources of main effects; the condition by status interaction term is also significant ($F=15.6$, $p<.001$). These findings provide striking evidence that interactive information media can help reduce barriers to social interaction in distributed work groups.

Examining the patterns of interaction within and among subgroups of the

---

[9]Figure 10.3 shows declines in actual contacts between time 2 and time 3. The time 3 interviews were conducted in the fall; informal comments to interviewers suggest that vacation schedules had reduced the extent of participation in the period prior to the fall interviews.

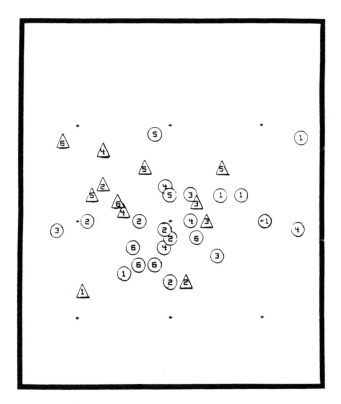

FIG.   10.4.   Contact relationships in standard group - Time 1.

two larger groups provides more information about the interplay between work processes and computer support. For illustrative purposes, Figures 10.4 and 10.5 show "contact maps," or spatial representations of the patterns of contact at baseline for the two task forces.[10] In these contact maps, space can be interpreted as social distance; for instance, symbols near the edges of the map represent task force members who are relatively peripheral in the sense of being associated with few other participants on the relationship dimension used to construct the space. We have used triangles

---

[10]The "network maps" or "sociograms" were constructed by decomposing the various matrices through multidimensional scaling, resulting in a two-dimensional representation of the more complex matrix (Rogers & Kincaid, 1981). In these "maps," people more central to the network tend to be closer to the center, whereas those less involved tend to be toward the periphery. People who interact with each other, and with others in similar ways, tend to be closer together in clusters on the map. For most purposes, visual inspection of the map is enlightening. For more rigorous analyses of social structure, there are tests for clustering and group formation; this stage in our analysis is still under way at this reporting.

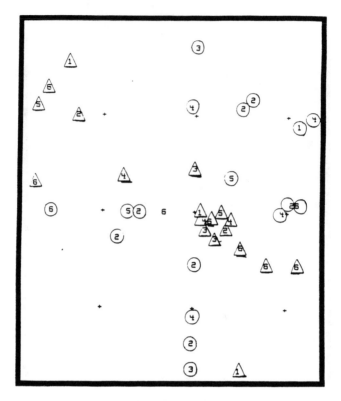

FIG.   10.5   Contact relationships in electronic group - Time 1.

to stand for retirees and circles to stand for employees, with numbers inside
the symbols indicating the subgroups to which they belong. As is evident by
inspecting the distribution of symbols in these two figures, subgroup members show no particular tendency to cluster at the beginning of the project
year. That is, there is no evidence that individuals chose to join particular
issue-oriented groups because of existing contacts with others in the group.
And in both tables, the relatively peripheral position of the retired members
is apparent.

By time 2, 3 months later, patterns of contact have shifted substantially
(see Figures 10.6 and 10.7). In the standard task force, several of the subgroups had formed relatively well-defined clusters, reflecting a tendency for
the participants to communicate much more with one another than with
others in the larger group. In the electronic task force, by contrast, the map
shows much less sharply defined subgroup clusters, probably reflecting
overlapping subgroup memberships.[11] These patterns, like sociometric

---

[11]Contact maps for times 3 and 4 are generally similar to those for time 2.

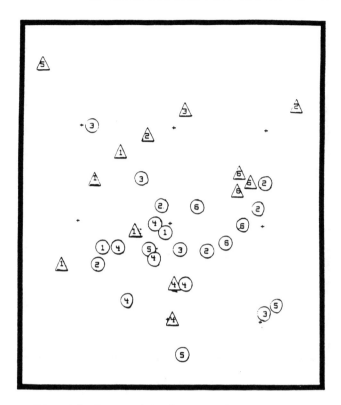

FIG.   10.6.   Contact relationships in standard group - Time 2.

findings from the study of RANDMAIL (Eveland & Bikson, 1987), suggest that electronic media facilitate lateral interaction and participation in multiple work teams.

These structural differences are associated with differences in overall levels of contact experienced by task force members during the project year. Figure 10.8 shows the number of people with whom an average task force member reported contact at each time period. Again, there is a strong interaction effect for work status and experimental condition over time. At baseline, employees in both task forces reported contacts with five to six others on average; retirees reported contacts with one to two. For the standard group, both levels remain essentially static across the experiment, with retiree contacts actually declining somewhat. For the electronic group, employee contacts also remain basically stable, but retiree contacts increase dramatically. This leads to a theme that will characterize much of the rest of this chapter: The standard task force remained predominantly the preserve of the employees during the period of the experiment, whereas interactions

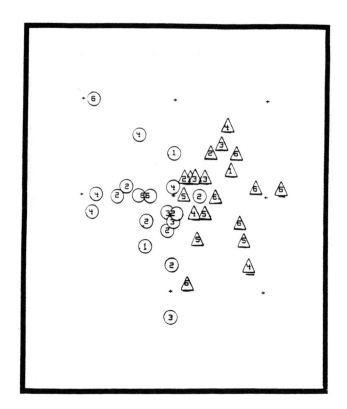

FIG. 10.7. Contact relationships in electronic group - Time 2.

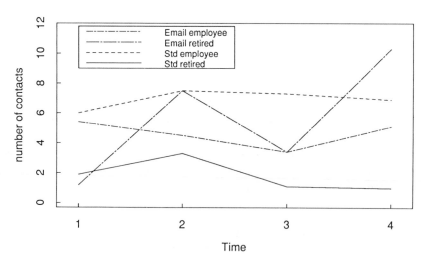

FIG. 10.8. Average number of contacts per group member at each time period.

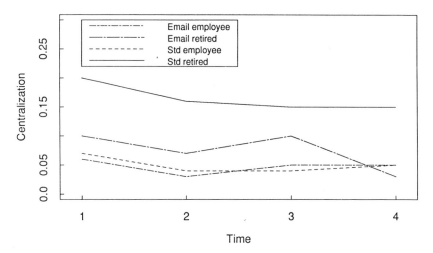

FIG.   10.9.   Centralization indices for contact networks.

in the electronic task force, starting from the same point, became increasingly the domain of the retirees.

Besides differences in level of contact, the experimental conditions appear to have supported other differences in social roles and processes. For example, the two task forces varied in the degree of centralization that characterized their communication networks.[12] Figure 10.9 shows the changes in centralization indices for both task forces. In each, employee members' interactions show a slight tendency toward increased centralization over time. The high centralization scores for retirees in the standard condition reflect their overall lower level of participation as well as the role of a small number of key individuals in this task force. Retirees in the electronic task force, by contrast, finish the project in a significantly less centralized position than when they began. In general, centralization reflects both participation and distribution of control; it is clear that the electronic task force completed its work in a considerably more participative mode than the standard group.

Likewise, the standard task force experienced significantly greater stability of leadership roles during the experiment than did the electronic group. This finding is supported by examining "betweenness" measures, where betweenness is taken to represent the relative centrality of a person in a network.[13] Table 10.2 provides intercorrelations among "betweenness"

---

[12]Centralization is the extent to which group communications are concentrated in relatively fewer group members.

[13]The results of these and other analyses that make comparisons between groups at one or more points in time rely on an analysis of variance treating experimental condition (standard

TABLE 10.2
Continuity of Leadership Structure

	Pearson Correlations	
	Standard	*Electronic*
Time 1 to Time 2	.47	.19
Time 2 to Time 3	.69	.28
Time 3 to Time 4	.57	.21

scores obtained for the four time periods.[14] A repeated measures analysis of variance shows significant effects for experimental condition ($F=7.7$, $p<.01$) and for work status ($F=33.9$, $p<.0001$), as well as for the interaction of task force condition with time ($F=4.6$, $p<.01$). In the standard task force, the betweenness scores at each time point are significantly predicted by the betweenness scores at the preceding point (F's range from 11.5 to 18.6, $p<.01$). In the electronic group, this is not the case; at any point, betweenness scores are not significantly associated with the previous period's scores.

For heuristic purposes, we explored these results by looking at leadership roles, arbitrarily defining the five most central individuals in each task force at each period as the "leadership cadre" for the contact network at that point in time. Summing over the four time periods, then, there are a total of 20 possible leadership slots for each task force. In the standard group, 13 people fill those 20 leader positions, with 7 repeating the role at more than one time period; all but one are employees. In the electronic group, there are 16 leaders, 4 of whom are repeaters; 7 are employees, 9 retirees. These analyses confirm the view that in the computer-supported task force, leadership roles are more broadly shared over time; and they are

vs. electronic) and work status (retired vs. employed) as 2-level independent variables. These variables are crossed unless an analysis is explicitly restricted to a subset of subjects (e.g., experimental participants only or retirees only). When the same dependent variable is measured at multiple time points, a repeated measures analysis of variance is employed with time added as a repeated factor; number of levels for the repeated factor depends on how often a particular measure was collected.

Whether a one-way, two-way or repeated measures design is used, the same conventions are employed to represent significance of statistical tests summarized in tables:

$$t \quad .05 < p < .10$$
$$* \quad p < .05$$
$$** \quad p < .01$$
$$*** \quad p < .001$$

[14]Because of high skewness in betweenness scores, logs of raw scores were used to generate the correlations reported in Table 10.2.

much less dominated by employees than are leadership roles in the standard condition.

In general, then, we see an emergent pattern characterized by initial similarity of task force social structures and work processes, followed by increasing differentiation. The standard group shifts toward less participation (particularly by retirees), greater centralization, and more stable leadership; the electronic group shows broadening participation, with retirees holding a majority of leadership roles and a fluctuating leadership pattern related to functional needs. It seems clear that the technology supplied to the electronic group enabled a much richer and more dense interaction structure than could be supported by the technology available to the standard group; and each group's task definition, work processes, and accomplishments are in turn influenced by such infrastructures.

The technology was also presumably useful for helping the electronic task force overcome physical barriers to work group interactions. Whereas the preceding discussion emphasizes the social properties of interactions, it is important to take their spatiotemporal context into account. As noted, a frequently cited characteristic of interactive information media is their ability to enable people to work together at widely separated physical locations and on different time schedules. The RANDMAIL research summarized earlier (Eveland & Bikson, 1987) tended to corroborate this view, and the task force experiment further substantiates it. In particular, we find that members of the standard task force conducted a relatively high percentage of their business via communication routes that relied on proximity and chance, making it difficult for retirees to participate; electronic task force members, by contrast, used modes that encouraged or at least enabled retiree participation.

The use of different communication modes at different times depends partly on personal preferences and partly on situation and task characteristics. No single mode is likely to be effective in all circumstances. As we have explained, both task forces had access to a full range of meeting, correspondence, and telephone capabilities, with computer-based communication provided in addition to the electronic group. In the last interview, sociometric questions were modified to include, after each reported contact, an item tapping the manner of contact. Table 10.3 shows the number of contacts reported in the 2 weeks prior to the last interview as a function of mode of contact.[15]

---

[15]Questions about media involved in each contact were asked only at time 4. Table 10.3 shows the number of actual contacts reported as using each medium; a few contacts were reported as using more than one medium, and are logged here as separate contacts. The maximum possible number of contacts in any one cell is $(N(N-1)/2)$, or 780 for the 40 individuals in each group.

TABLE 10.3
Frequencies of Different Types of Contacts in Standard
and Electronic Groups

	Standard	Electronic
Scheduled Meetings	36	220
Unscheduled Meetings	116	84
Telephone	23	41
Letters/Memos	2	8
Electronic Mail		55
Total	178	408

For the standard group, in the last period surveyed, contacts most often took the form of unscheduled meetings; not surprisingly, retirees tended to be out of the unscheduled meeting loop, because these almost always occurred at the workplace. Retirees participated in only 12% of the unscheduled meetings reported by standard task force members, and in 25% of those reported by electronic group. For electronic task force members, by contrast, contacts tended to be primarily in the form of scheduled meetings, with less reliance on unscheduled meetings and relatively heavy use of electronic mail. Retirees took part in 75% of the scheduled meetings reported by electronic task force members, whereas their counterparts in the standard group participated in 19% of the scheduled meetings reported. Moreover, in the electronic group, retirees accounted for about 80% of the electronic mail that was sent.[16] Although we do not have communications channel data for the three earlier time periods, we do have data on the purposes of reported contacts in each period that are suggestive of similar interaction modes. Table 10.4 shows the percent of contacts in each task force at each time period that were reported as being chance contacts (rather than scheduled for any reason).[17] These data indicate that throughout the field experiment the standard task force was characterized by significantly higher levels of chance contact. On the other hand, although the

---

[16]The electronic task force set up a series of scheduled in-person meetings at the end of the study to coordinate preparation of their final report. This emphasis on scheduled meetings is probably not representative of the entire period of work. Electronic mail in this final phase of work was also heavily used to schedule and coordinate formal meetings as well as to share results of data analyses and circulate draft sections of text for members' review and comment.

[17]For both task forces, chance contacts were almost exclusively a mode available to employees; anywhere from 92% to 100% of chance contacts involved employees, depending on the time period.

TABLE 10.4
Percent of Contacts Attributed to Chance

	Time 1	Time 2	Time 3	Time 4
Task Force:				
Standard	41%	32%	33%	55%
Electronic	53%	24%	26%	12%

electronic task force started out with approximately the same levels of chance contacts, it quickly came to rely on methods other than chance to carry out its work; by time 4, it reported less than one-fourth the percentage of chance contacts in the standard task force.

If, as these data suggest, electronic communication media effectively alleviate the otherwise centrifugal effects of physical distance on social network participation, we should expect to see quite different patterns of relationships between distance and interaction for members of the two task forces. In fact, the differences we observed are rather striking. Table 10.5 presents the rank-order correlations between the integrativeness measure of participation in the contact network at each of the four data collection periods and the physical distance of each of the retirees from the corporate headquarters (where all the employees were located.)[18] As the table shows, participation is strongly and negatively correlated with distance for the standard retirees; that is, the farther away they live, the less they take part. For the electronic retirees, participation is somewhat negatively correlated with distance at time 1 (before most of them were on-line). Subsequent time periods are characterized by a somewhat positive or at least neutral relationship between distance and participation. It is evident that, whatever else electronic tools did for this task force, they permitted retirees who were physically distant from the workplace to be centrally involved with each other and with work group activity.

Evidence about electronic tools and temporal barriers to interaction can be examined only within the electronic condition. For members of the electronic task force, the logging of message header data (further details given elsewhere) provided a way to determine when different types of

---

[18]The distance metric used was rather crude, being simply a measurement of linear distance on a map from the retiree's home address to the workplace. For ordinal purposes, however, this measure is probably adequate. More complete measures incorporating actual driving times would, of course, give a finer-tuned picture. Average distances from the workplace are practically the same for retirees in both task forces.

TABLE 10.5
Correlations Between Integrativeness and Physical Distance

	Time 1	Time 2	Time 3	Time 4
Task Force:				
Standard	−.62	−.42	−.61	−.66
Electronic	−.14	.25	.49	.09

people preferred to do on-line work. Figure 10.10 shows the number of messages sent by time of day by the different types of participants (it should be recalled that the subgroup chairs in this task force were all retirees). Retirees in general and steering committee members in particular differ notably from employees. The employees tend to come into the office early and log on (the 7 to 8 A.M. peak), and then to check in again just after lunch. They do not stay in the office after 5 P.M., at least not to do computing.[19] The retirees, by contrast, rise later, eat a later lunch, and often sign on again after dinner for an evening session. The chairs, in fact, do a lot of their work in the evenings. These differences, although not intrinsically surprising, confirm that people use electronic communications in ways that suit their own schedules, potentially overcoming temporal barriers to group work.

THE STRUCTURE
OF THE ELECTRONIC NETWORK

As we explained, the research project retained a log of the headers of all network messages exchanged among electronic task force participants over the project year. This log included the sender's ID, the receiver's ID, the message date and time, and—if the message was a reply—the date and time of the original message. Topic lines were not retained, to protect the confidentiality of communications.[20] These data comprise a rich source of information about the structure of the electronic network and the on-line behavior of its participants.

Table 10.6 summarizes the messaging dataset. During the project year, 4,091 messages were sent by the 40 people taking part in the electronic network.[21] Given the use of various "aliases" (multiple recipients addressed

---

[19]It is worth noting that the computers for employees were all located at the office, whereas those for the retirees were in their homes. Whether the employees would have exhibited retireelike work patterns if their machines had been differently located is an open question.

[20]Advance consent to message header logging was obtained prior to the start of the project.

[21]This figure does not include messages sent by project staff to task force members, either as originals or replies; they were routed through another host and were not logged.

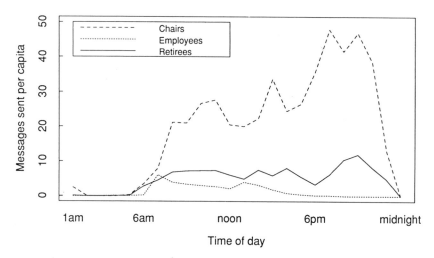

FIG.   10.10.   Messages sent by retirees, employees and committee chairs by time of day.

by a single name that expands into a distribution list), this number translates into 15,528 messages received. About 40% of these messages were sent point-to-point, sometimes to multiple addresses; and about 30% were messages to project staff, either for computer assistance or for substantive purposes (e.g., submitting interim reports).

These messages were not evenly distributed across task force members. As several other studies have reported (cf. Eveland & Bikson, 1987), approximately 25% of the people accounted for about 75% of the messages sent. The 10 "high senders" in this case included the 6 subcommittee chairs

TABLE 10.6
Total Message Traffic Over Project Year

Messages Sent			*Messages Received*
1745	To Individuals		
	1160	To Single	1160
	585	To Multiple	1746
1266	To Staff		1266
1080	To Aliases		11590
	434	To Task Force Alias	
	407	To All Chairs	
	239	To Force	
4091	Total Messages Sent		
	Total Messages Received		14496

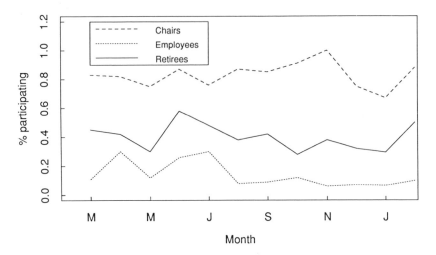

FIG.   10.11.   Percent of retirees, employees and committee chairs who sent at least one e-mail message per month.

(all retirees); and only one employee emerged as a heavy sender. Figure 10.11 shows percent of participation (i.e., percent of members who sent at least one message) during each project month, by employment status. Retirees averaged nearly 50% participation each month; employees averaged closer to 20%, dropping to only about 10% during the last months.

Numbers of messages sent, on average, by individuals in these three categories exhibit a similar pattern. Figure 10.12 shows that on average, chairs sent four to five times as many messages per month as other participants. Of course, as Figure 10.13 indicates, chairs also received considerably more messages than other people; much of this information was apparently exchanged among themselves. Figure 10.13 also shows that, whereas retirees tended to send more messages than employees, they tended to receive just about the same number.[22] In our first electronic mail study (Eveland & Bikson, 1987), we found that users divided quite early into heavy and light senders, with heavy senders getting heavier and light senders, lighter. Figure 10.14 contrasts sending patterns for the 10 "high users" with those of the remaining 30 electronic network members. Here, too, such a pattern is observed: high users get off to a fast start initially and their usage increases over time; light users start slow and change little over time. The consistency of these trends suggests that they should be taken into account in implementation and training plans for electronic communication systems.

---

[22]This table is based on the 15,000+ expanded-alias message set.

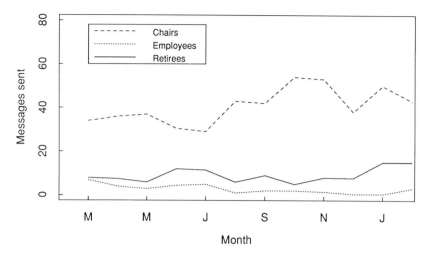

FIG. 10.12.   Messages sent per capita by retirees, employees and committee chairs.

As we suggested earlier, operating an electronic network is labor-intensive and adequate "humanware" is crucial to its performance. Figure 10.15 summarizes the distribution of messages to project staff, by month. After an initially high level of sending during the training and early learning period (March and April), messages fell off—only to rise again in June as the due date for an interim report approached. Staff messages rose again in October

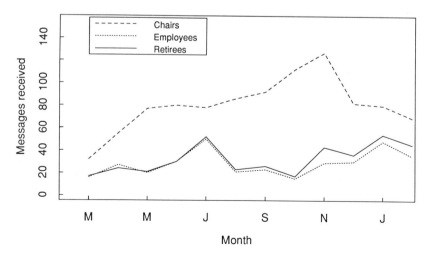

FIG.   10.13.   Messages received per capita by retirees, employees and committee chairs.

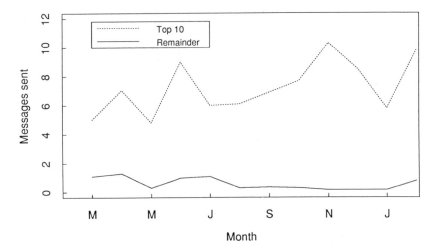

FIG. 10.14.   Average number of messages sent per week by high and low users.

and November, as task force members were learning to use a database program to analyse survey data they had collected. Not surprisingly, subcommittee chairs were the predominant generators of staff inquiries, although those who took on the main burden of data analysis made their share of inquiries as well. The low level of employee inquiries is probably attributable to the fact that relatively few of them undertook anything particularly unusual or risky with the system—and also to the availability of within

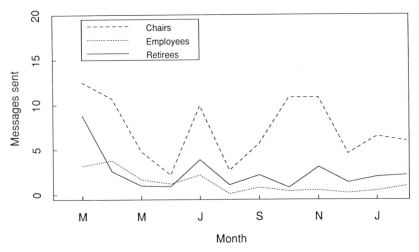

FIG.   10.15.   Per capita messages sent to staff by retirees, employees and committee chairs.

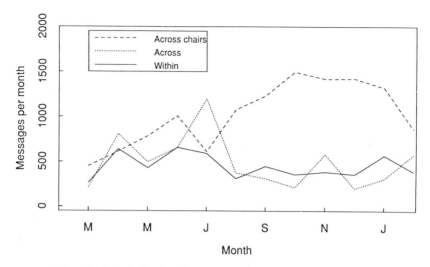

FIG. 10.16. Distribution of messages within and between task groups.

group expertise. Toward the end of the project year, a number of members of the electronic task force had become highly proficient users of the system and its documentation and were able to extend help to others who needed it.

Earlier we described how both experimental task forces organized their work into manageable domains: six committees tackled distinct retirement issue areas. Figure 10.16 shows the distribution of messages within and between the six domain-specific task groups. It is interesting to note that two-thirds or more of the messages per month were sent across task group lines, and also that a large part of the cross-task communication was carried out by subgroup chairs. Other members tended to send about as many messages to the 10 (or so) members of their own subgroups as they sent to the 30 other individuals who belonged to different subgroups.

The availability of logged data for the electronic task force also provides an opportunity to examine the relationship between computer-based communication and overall contact (structured self-report data). In general, we expected total reported contacts to exceed electronic contacts—and it would not have been surprising to obtain reports of contact between people who do not exchange electronic messages. However it is quite surprising to find the reverse. Table 10.7 shows the proportions of contacts that are associated with the exchange of electronic messages.[23] The first part of

---

[23]These data are from time 4; however, similar patterns exist in each of the preceding time periods. The proportions are based on the 780 contacts possible among a group of 40 people. The first two parts of the table are based on the expanded message set; the third part are based on the point-to-point limited message set.

TABLE 10.7
Relationship Between Log of Electronic Messages
and Recall of Message Exchange

Any Contacts	Any Electronic Messages		Completed Message Loops		Completed Point-to-Point Loops	
	Yes	No	Yes	No	Yes	No
Yes	.03	.16	.02	.18	.01	.18
No	.08	.72	.05	.75	.006	.79

this table shows that if we look at all messages exchanged, about 8% of the individuals reported having no contact with people with who they had in fact exchanged electronic communication. If we look only at "message loops" (i.e., messages that have received an answer), the proportion in this category drops to about 5%. Further restricting the definition of what constitutes an "exchange" to a message loop that is addressed to only one person rather than a group and that is answered results in largely, although not entirely, eliminating this category.[24] In any event, we believe that the question of just what it is about an electronic exchange that defines it as a contact from the participant perspective is an interesting one. The issue is significant particularly in terms of the presumed ability of logging systems to capture the electronic message exchange. Although logging systems can capture message traffic, the question remains what has actually been measured in social interaction terms. Certainly the exchange of messages is not to be equated with contact as perceived by the messagers. The issue of the relationship between perceived contact and electronic message exchange, we believe, deserves further investigation.

OUTCOMES

Besides wanting to understand how access to a networked computer system might influence group structures and interactions, we also sought to learn what effects it might have on participants' perceptions and evaluations of task force activity. For this purpose, we relied chiefly on structured interview questions directed toward a number of outcome areas for participants in both experimental conditions.

---

[24]The overall contact matrix and the "all loops" matrix correlate at only .03. The point-to-point electronic loop matrix and the overall contact matrix correlate at .15 (not statistically significant).

The Computer Experience

For members of the electronic task force we obtained a great deal of objective usage data. However, as the previous discussion points out, such information needs to be supplemented with an account of users' experiences. Electronic task force members were asked at three points in time, starting with the first interim interview, to give their impressions of the task force computer. After being told that "some people love computers, others hate them, and still others are neutral," each was asked to indicate how the computer experience seemed to him using 5-point rating scales. Responses to the six adjectival scales are summarized in Table 10.8 (where 1 = "not very" and 5 = "very" in reference to the experience represented by each); they were treated as outcomes in repeated measures analyses of variance with employment status serving as the independent factor.

The two positive adjectives, *fun* and *gratifying,* show similar patterns (not surprisingly, because their average correlation for the three periods is .71). Retirees' ratings start out and remain very positive, whereas em-

TABLE 10.8
Impressions of Computer Use

	Mean Ratings			F	F
	Time2	*Time3*	*Time4*	*(status)*	*(time)*
Fun:[a]					
Retirees	4.4	4.5	4.4		
Employees	3.7	3.5	4.0	5.0*	n.s.
Gratifying:					
Retirees	4.6	4.3	4.4		
Employees	3.4	3.6	3.7	9.4**	n.s.
Challenging:					
Retirees	4.5	4.5	4.8		
Employees	3.9	3.8	4.4	8.0**	4.8**
Intimidating:					
Retirees	2.3	2.9	3.15		
Employees	2.4	2.7	2.6	n.s.	3.76*
Frustrating:					
Retirees			3.3		
Employees	2.8	2.8	2.7	n.s.	n.s.
Disappointing:					
Retirees	1.7	1.9	1.9		
Employees	2.1	2.3	2.0	n.s.	n.s.

Note: All ratings were made on 5-point scales where 1 = not very and 5 = very for each adjective.

[a]Time × status, the interaction term, yields a value of F = 3.2, <.05. No other interactions in the analyses summarized were statistically significant.

ployees' subjective reactions are less positive initially and improve over time. These data suggest that, for our sample, the computers were not experienced as novelties or gadgets whose interest value would diminish over the year. Neither did their capacity to challenge or intimidate wear off; rather, both dependent measures exhibit a significant effect for time. Mean ratings are higher among retirees (significantly so for the 'challenge' scale), who were the most vigorous users, and increase as use increases for both groups. We interpret these findings to mean that the more the task force tried to do with its computers, the more impressive it found them. Happily the members were not in the main disappointed by their efforts, although they were accompanied by an intermediate and consistent level of frustration throughout.

At the last interview, in addition to gathering users' impressions, we asked them to judge the effectiveness of computer-based communication in three ways: electronic mail as a medium for exchanging information with another individual(s); aliases and bulletin boards for distributing and receiving information among small groups of people; and large electronic networks for general information exchange among great numbers of people.

At the end of the project year, as shown in Table 10.9, electronic task force members gave high effectiveness ratings to each type of computer-based communication in relation to different information exchange needs. These ratings are not significantly intercorrelated, an outcome that would seem to substantiate the conclusion from logged data that the three communication vehicles are used and experienced in quite different ways.

The Task Experience

To explore the comparative effectiveness of computer-based and conventional media for carrying out group work, we asked members of both task forces to evaluate their efforts. After a series of items about specific activities,

TABLE 10.9
Effectiveness of Computer-Based Communication for Different Types of Information Exchange (Means and Correlations)

	Among Small Groups	Among Large Groups
Among individuals (mean = 4.3)	r = .30	r = .14
Among small groups (mean = 4.4)		r = .03
Among large groups (mean = 4.5)		

Note: Effectiveness was rated on a 5-point scale where higher numbers mean greater effectiveness.

TABLE 10.10
Evaluations of Work Group Performance Across Time

	Means:		
	Time.2	Time.3	Time.4
1. How well has your task force done its work?			
Retirees			
Electronic	2.8	3.2	3.7
Standard	3.5	3.4	3.3
Employees			
Electronic	2.8	2.9	3.8
Standard	3.7	3.6	3.4
Condition: F = 2.99^t	Time: F = 5.53**	Condition x time: F = 13.7***	
2. How well has your study group done its work?			
Retirees			
Electronic	2.8	3.1	3.6
Standard	3.5	3.1	3.0
Employees			
Electronic	2.7	2.8	3.6
Standard	3.7	3.6	3.5
Condition: F = 3.24^t	Time: F = 2.51^t	Condition x time: F = 10.82***	

Note: Higher numbers mean better performance ratings.

two general questions were raised: how well has your study group(s) done its work; and how well has your task force done its work? As before, responses were obtained using five-point scales and subsequently examined in repeated measures analyses of variance. Results for the two analyses—whose patterns are quite similar—are summarized in Table 10.10.

After three months' work, members of the standard task force give their work higher performance ratings whether the evaluation targets subgroups ($F=11.9$, $p<.001$) or the group as a whole ($F=20.4$, $p<.001$). But by the end of the project year, the situation is reversed; electronic members give higher evaluations to their subgroups ($F=2.84$, $.05<p<.10$) and their task force ($F=3.89$, $p<.05$). The net effect is the very strong time-by-condition interaction reported in Table 10.10, a function of increasingly positive accomplishment judgments on the part of the electronic group.

The pattern is not difficult to interpret. Standard task force members tackled their shared charge immediately, whereas their counterparts in the electronic condition put most of their energy into learning to use the computer system and initially made little headway toward their substantive goal. After mastering the basics, however, they turned more of their efforts to the

TABLE 10.11
Perceived Effect of Experimental Condition Across Time

	Means:		
	Time.2	Time.3	Time.4
Retirees			
Electronic	3.9	4.0	4.6
Standard	3.1	2.9	2.7
Employees			
Electronic	3.3	3.5	3.9
Standard	3.8	4.1	3.7

Condition: $F = 7.58***$
Condition × status: $F = 16.51***$
Condition × time: $F = 10.32***$
Note: Higher numbers mean the condition is perceived as more helpful.

task itself and—with the electronic tools at their disposal—were able to make great progress.

Early in the process, several participants in both task forces suspected that electronic information media might be as much a hindrance as a help—especially for employees whose job commitments made it difficult to set aside time for both learning and task force work. Informal comments to this effect led the research team to include in interview protocols a direct question about the influence of experimental condition on task force performance (see Table 10.11).

These judgments, like the data in Table 10.10, show a significant time-by-condition effect. Over time, members of the electronic task force become increasingly convinced that their experimental assignment helped them accomplish their work, whereas standard task force members become less certain that their assignment was advantageous. More illuminating, however, is the very strong interaction of experimental condition with work status. Retirees in the electronic condition and employees in the standard condition give their experimental assignments relatively high marks. Assignments were just the opposite initially for employees in the electronic condition and retirees in the standard condition; with time, however, condition assessments by electronic employees show substantial improvement, whereas standard retirees judge themselves by far the most disadvantaged.

The Retirement Experience

As we have explained, a basic requirement for this field experiment was to design the research around a real purpose for bringing into interaction a collection of individuals who are not colocated and who may not know one

TABLE 10.12
Anticipated Contact With Retired Task
Force Members

	Means*
Retirees	
Electronic	2.8
Standard	0.1
Employees	
Electronic	0.8
Standard	0.0

Condition: $F = 20.49$, $p < .001$
Status: $F = 7.68$, $p < .01$
Condition $\times$ status: $F = 6.66$, $p < .01$
Note: Means represent average number of individuals named as new contacts with whom respondents expect to remain in contact after the experiment.

another but who could probably benefit by being in communication. In particular, we supposed that people who have retired might suffer from the loss of contact with colleagues with whom they had developed meaningful social relationships. If so, providing an avenue for staying in touch with work friends could be an interesting and positive experience. Concomitantly we believed that those still employed but nearing retirement might benefit from involvement with already-retired peers; research literature suggests they are worried about the transition and uncertain about what it entails. These hypotheses assume that interaction among role incumbents on either side of the retirement transition will have positive effects for both.

For purposes of understanding the broader potential influence of computer-based media, they direct attention to comparisons between experimental conditions on outcome variables related to the retirement experience itself. To address the first question—will task force interactions create social ties among retirees and between them and their still-employed counterparts—we asked subjects during the exit interview to tell us who, among people they met on the task force, they think they will continue to see socially. Responses were coded for employment status and counted; the results are summarized in Table 10.12. Between-conditions comparison yielded a strong effect, with those in the electronic task force significantly more likely to stay in contact with retirees ($F=20.49$, $p<.001$). Although the dependent measure represents expectation and not necessarily reality, the direction of effect suggests electronic communication may be able to maintain social ties between retirees and their colleagues.[25]

---

[25]A follow-up grant from the John and Mary R. Markle Foundation will allow to reinterview participants in a year's time to learn more about the fate of electronically maintained social ties.

TABLE 10.13
Expectations About Retirement

	Means:	
	Time. 1	Time. 4
Retirees		
Electronic	3.6	3.6
Standard	3.9	3.9
Employees		
Electronic	3.6	4.2
Standard	3.2	3.5

Time: $F = 4.48^*$
Time $\times$ status: $F = 5.57^*$
Condition $\times$ status: $F = 3.23^t$
Note: The higher the number, the more the
respondent looks forward to retirement.

To address the second question—whether task force interactions will ameliorate employees' views of retirement—we asked employees during both the first and last interviews whether or not they looked forward to retirement. Responses, gathered on a 5-point scale (1=not very much, 5=very much), yielded a positive effect for time ($F=4.48$, $p<.05$); these data are summarized in Table 10.13. We interpreted this to mean that communication with retirees had improved employee attitudes toward retirement (the constancy of retirees' responses to the same question helps rule out history and other potential confounds). Moreover, the effect interacted with experimental condition, being strongest for those in the electronic task force ($F=3.23$, $.05<p<.10$). Computer-based interactions, then, seem a viable avenue for the communication of attitudes and values.

DISCUSSION

In the beginning of this chapter, we reviewed some themes drawn from previous RAND research on computer-based work that guided the design of the field experiment and framed the questions it would attempt to address. We should begin by underscoring that we are reporting here less on a single study than on a longer-term program of study directed generally at interactive information technology in user contexts; the field experiment is only one part of a set of projects that employ multiple methods and diverse research subjects in order to converge with greater confidence on common conclusions. It is appropriate now to discuss what we think we have learned about this area and the implications of the findings.

Experience with the field experiment—both informal and analytic—reinforces the value of the work group as a critical unit of study and supports the operationalization borrowed from previous organizational research. That definition emphasizes the complexity of the structure of groups, and entails embedded levels of analysis. That is, for some questions (e.g., effects of communication medium on attitudes), the individual is the required analytic unit. Individual behavior is, of course, influenced by group membership, and for some analyses the primary work group is an appropriate focus of study (e.g., questions about relative amounts of within-group and between-group communication). But the behavior of primary groups such as the issue-oriented subcommittees of the experimental task forces can be interpreted only in the context of the larger social space in which they are embedded. Using a research design that embeds individuals within complex groups located in a larger social space for purposes of working together over a period of time also permits observing the ways leadership roles, group structures, and interaction patterns evolve and change.

As noted, the experimental design provided an opportunity to observe the creation and evolution of new sociotechnical systems in these social spaces. Although field studies provide a rich context, it is only by introducing technology in a controlled environment under the rules of behavioral science experimentation that causal inferences about the interaction of technology and social structure can most reliably be made. The strikingly divergent courses taken by two initially similar groups provided with different technologies to support their work illustrates the intimate interplay over time of tools, task definitions, and group procedures and practices. Technology quickly becomes not an exogenous force acting on groups, but rather part of the web of interpersonal and task interactions. Over time, the tools are in fact "enacted" by those who use them, shaping and shaped by the experiences of group participants without a high degree of self-consciousness. Neither the initial expectations of system developers nor the preconceptions of users reliably predict how such sociotechnical systems evolve in practice.

The consequences for group processes and structures are dramatic, and begin to appear almost immediately in response to their differing work technologies. Electronically supported groups develop a richer communications structure with less hierarchical differentiation, broader participation, and more fluctuating and situational leadership structures. This appears in turn to be associated with greater feelings of involvement in the task and greater satisfaction and identification with group products. The electronic technology substantially weakens the constraints posed by time and space that accompany conventional group work tools. Employees and retirees tend to use the computer on different time schedules apparently reflecting lifestyle differences, and can interact through the asynchronous medium without having to be on the same schedules. Conventional media (particularly informal/unscheduled meetings) tend to disadvantage those physically distant from the central locus of the work; by contrast, electronic media allow direct access to that locus irrespective of physical distance.

These experimental findings converge with those from our earlier field studies in interesting ways. In particular, we have consistently observed the ability of electronic technology to reinforce communication patterns across lateral groups, facilitating communication across disciplines and organizational status barriers, and supporting multiple group memberships. Time becomes significantly less of a barrier to such interactions, and physical space becomes more a reflection of how people choose to position themselves than a strict limit on their ability to work together. In office settings people who work together are likely to locate their work spaces proximally. Physical adjacency certainly can create task interactions, but it is also true that the electronic medium can compensate for the very long distances that are often true barriers to interaction. Distances within buildings can often be harder to span conceptually than distances across the city or across the country.

In any case, it is evident that the electronic infrastructure is not a simple substitute for in-person contact, telephone calls, print correspondence, or any other more conventional medium. Rather, as our experiment illustrates, messaging establishes a quite distinct avenue for exchange whose nature is yet unclear. The communication role of electronic office technology cannot be understood outside of the context of its role in supporting information work generally, including text and data processing and information storage and access. The electronic environment is a rich context in which doing work and sharing work become virtually indistinguishable, and the frequency and spontaneity of interactions equally facilitate task and social exchange. In fact, far from replacing other media, electronic media add a new dimension to their usability by improving the efficiency of direct contacts, providing easy access to shared data, and allowing more efficient production of print documents. As the functionality of electronic tools improves and they become increasingly integrated with adjuncts such as voice messaging, fax, and related advances we expect to see this trend toward multimedia interaction through a single computer-based infrastructure to expand and improve in effectiveness. In the meantime, the use of even relatively low-technology systems of the sort we employed seems promising not only for work group support but also for the communication of affect and the establishment and maintenance of durable social ties.

However, humanware requirements are substantial. Electronic technology to support group work is not self-enacting, but rather requires significant investments of time and energy in learning ways to use the tools to best advantage, both on the part of individuals and work groups. The bounds of participation in and potential control over the group task are set less by preexisting position and status and more by capacity to master and leverage the tools. The less centralized the technology, the potentially broader the ability to bring new people into participation. In the experiment, the retired group had significantly more time and energy resources to master the tools, and thus gradually assumed effective direction of the group. By contrast, in the conventionally supported group with its technology largely centered at corporate headquarters, the employee group retained mastery of the tools. Neither pattern was inevitable or inherent in the technology, but was rather a function of the way the groups evolved.

Creating and maintaining an electronically supported group requires the willingness of the participants to invest resources in a learning period characterized by relatively low output and relatively high consumption of outside assistance. However, as mastery of the tools is gained, output rises quickly and makes up for—and may surpass—the learning period lag. Each new tool requires a similar learning phase. Thus, tolerance for a less even pace of group production appears to be necessary in making effective use of electronic technology in work groups.

In sum, this entire line of research to date has the burden that electronic tools can constitute a significant component of the "means of production" for information-intensive work groups. Supplementing and extending other aspects of group production and coordination methods, these new tools provide a set of resources that are likely to be differentially available to group members, at least initially. It is the ability to make effective humanware investments in mastering the technology that sets limits on how these resources will be used and how group structures, processes, and control balances will be affected. It is inevitable that electronic information tools will affect what work groups do and how they do it, but there is nothing at all inevitable about specific directions those changes will take. The important point for participants in the process of information technology implementation and use is to recognize that the tools will affect how tasks are defined and the ways in which they are addressed, and proactively to develop strategies for using the new resources to meet collective as well as individual needs and interests. Organizational and technological dynamics will reshape the system; whether this shaping satisfies the participants or simply whipsaws them is in significant measure up to the participants themselves.

Although we have learned a good deal about how computer-supported cooperative work tools shape and interact with task definitions and task demands, there is a lot left to learn, particularly about longer-term outcomes and what strategies will facilitate the achievement of positive outcomes for work groups at varied organizational levels. These strategies must be worked out within the context of what makes task collaboration succeed (McGrath, 1984; McGrath & Altman, 1966):

- High skill, high ability in group members
- Good group training, lots of group experience
- Autonomy, participative decision making, cooperative work conditions
- Mutual liking—group members value one another's task and social attributes, hold one another in esteem, accord themselves high status
- High level of intragroup communication

The studies we have reported show that computer support can do much to enhance the last of these characteristics—and interacts interestingly with the others as well. There is a great deal to learn about how new technology affects these characteristics required for successful teamwork. There is a need for research of many forms: observational studies, laboratory experiments, and field experiments are all possible and all have much to contribute to our evolving understanding. The general phenomenon of technology in work groups is more important than the particular technology involved. The challenge is both to recognize that sociotechnical systems based on interactive information technology are not bound to any predeterminable pattern but can be shaped in many different ways, and develop research and intervention strategies that reflect both the constraints and opportunities in these new fluid social environments.

REFERENCES

Bikson, T. K. (1980). *Getting it together: Gerontological research and the real world.* The RAND Corporation, P-6447.

Bikson, T. K. (1987). Understanding the implementation of office technology. In Robert Kraut (Ed.), *Technology and the Transformation of white collar work* (pp. 155–176). Hillsdale, NJ: Lawrence Erlbaum Associates. (Also N-2619-NSF, The RAND Corporation.)

Bikson, T. K., & Eveland, J. D. (1986). *New office technology: Planning for people.* New York: Pergamon.

Bikson, T. K., & Goodchilds, J. D. (1988). *Experiencing the retirement transition: Managerial and professional men before and after.* The RAND Corporation, WD-4055-MF.

Bikson, T. K., & Gutek, B. A. (1983). *Advanced office systems: An empirical look at utilization and satisfaction.* The RAND Corporation, N-1970-NSF.

Bikson, T. K., Gutek, B. A., & Mankin, D. A. (1987). *Implementing computerized procedures in office settings: Influences and outcomes.* The RAND Corporation, R-3077-NSF.

Bikson, T. K., Gutek, B. A., & Mankin, D. A. (1981). *Implementation of information technology in office settings: Review of relevant literature.* The RAND Corporation, P-6697.

Bikson, T. K., Quint, B. E., & Johnson, L. L. (1984). *Scientific and technical information transfer: Issues and options.* The RAND Corporation, N-2131-NSF.

Bikson, T. K., Stasz, C., & Mankin, D. A. (1985). *Computer-mediated work: Individual and organizational impact in one corporate headquarters.* The RAND Corporation, R-3308-OTA.

Crowston, K., Malone, T., & Lin, F. (1986.) Cognitive science and organizational design: A case study of computer conferencing. *Proceedings of the conference on Computer-Supported Cooperative Work* (pp. 43–61). Austin, TX.

Eveland, J. D., & Bikson, T. K. (1987). Evolving electronic communication networks: An empirical assessment. In *Office: Technology and people* (pp. 103–128). Amsterdam: Elsevier Science Publications.

Eveland, J. D., & Bikson, T. K. (1988). *Work group structures and computer support: A field experiment.* ACM Transactions on Office Information Systems, 6(4), 354–379.

Feldman, M. (1986). Constraints on communication and electronic messaging. *Proceedings of the Conference on Computer-Supported Cooperative Work* (pp. 73–90). Austin, TX.

Freeman, L. (1976). A set of measures of centrality based on betweenness, *Sociometry, 40,* 35–41.

Gutek, B. A., Sasse, S. H., & Bikson, T. K. (1986). The fit between technology and workgroup structure: The structural contingency approach and office automation. *Proceedings of the Academy of Management,* Chicago, IL.

Gutek, B. A., Bikson, T. K., & Mankin, D. A. (1984). Individual and organizational consequences of computer-based office information technology. In S. Oskamp (Ed.), *Applied social psychology annual* (Vol. 5, pp. 231–254). Beverly Hills, CA: Sage.

Hiltz, S. R. (1985). *Online communities: A case study of the office of the future.* Norwood, NJ: Ablex.

Kling, R., & Scacchi, W. (1982). The web of computing: Computer technology as social organization. *Advances in Computers, 21,* 2–60.

Knoke, D., & Kuklinski, J. H. (1982). *Network analysis.* Beverly Hills, CA: Sage Publications.

Kraut, R., Galegher, J., & Egido, C. (1987–88). Relationships and tasks in scientific research collaborations. *Human Computer Interaction, 3,* 31–58.

Laudon, K. C. (1977). *Communications technology and democratic participation.* New York: Praeger.

Markus, M. L. (1987). Toward a "critical mass" theory of interactive media: Universal access, interdependence and diffusion. *Communication Research, 14* (5), 491–511.

McGrath, J. E. (1984). *Groups: Interaction and Performance.* Englewood Cliffs, NJ: Prentice-Hall.

McGrath, J. E., & Altman, I. (1966). *Small group research.* New York: Holt, Rinehart & Winston.

Orr, J. (1986). Narratives at work—story telling as cooperative diagnostic activity. *Proceedings of the Conference on Computer-Supported Cooperative Work* (pp. 62–72). Austin, TX.

Rogers, E., & Kincaid, D. L. (1981). *Communication networks: Toward a new paradigm for research.* New York: Macmillan.

Sproull, L., & Kiesler, S. (1986). Reducing social contest cues: Electronic mail in organizational communication. *Management Science, 32* (11), 1492–1512.

Stasz, C., & Bikson, T. K. (1986). Computer-supported cooperative work: Examples and issues in one federal agency. *Proceedings of the Conference on Computer-Supported Cooperative Work* (pp. 318–324). Austin, TX.

Stasz, K., Bikson, T. K., & Shapiro, N. Z. (1986). *Assessing the forest service's implementation of an agency-wide information system: An exploratory study.* The RAND Corporation, N-2463-USFS.
Tornatzky, L. G., Eveland, J. D., Boylan, M. G., Hetzner, W. A., Johnson, E. C., Roitman, D., & Schneider, J. (1983). *The process of technological innovation: Reviewing the literature.* Washington, DC: National Science Foundation.

11

Communication and Performance in Ad Hoc Task Groups

Tom Finholt
Lee Sproull
Sara Kiesler
Carnegie Mellon University

Abstract

Ad hoc groups are an important way for organizations to respond to rapid changes in the environment and to nonroutine situations. These groups face significant obstacles to high performance, however, including communication and coordination difficulties. This chapter explores ways in which computer-mediated communication technology can reduce these difficulties. We propose that more computer mail use can help ad hoc groups exchange information more efficiently, better schedule group activities, partition work more successfully, increase participation in group communication—and therefore, to do better than groups that do not use computer mail as much. A set of communication and coordination hypotheses are examined using data collected from seven software development teams. Groups that frequently used computer mail outperformed those that did not. Further, it is shown that use of computer mail changes the pattern of work, not just the output of work. The chapter speculates on the larger organizational implications of new technology, including the possibilities for collaboration beyond the limits of current experience and theory.

Collaborative work in organizations is frequently accomplished and managed in small work groups, either formal work groups or ad hoc groups. The formal work group has relatively permanent membership, ongoing tasks, and routinized reporting relationships within the organization. Members typically work in close proximity. Over time they elaborate personal relationships, divisions of labor, norms, and routines for communication to support their work. They learn to work together by doing work together.

They draw on a repertoire of information sharing and communication routines such as distribution lists, route slips, regularly scheduled meetings in regularly available rooms, and routine reporting requirements to support their work. Over time, skills and information of group members become more group-specific and norms more implicit. There is less communication on how to work together and more on the work itself. These processes improve coordination and increase commitment to the group.

Despite these advantages, some kinds of work are best performed in ad hoc groups. Such groups are convened for a particular purpose, consist of members who otherwise would not work together, and disband after completing their assigned task. Ad hoc task groups range from a search committee choosing a new college president to a blue ribbon panel, such as the Challenger commission. Ad hoc groups permit an organization to respond rapidly to changes in the environment and to nonroutine problems by calling on expertise regardless of where it resides in the organization. They reflect a strategy for overcoming organizational inertia induced by structure and routine. But bypassing structures and routines also creates three major communication problems: (a) Group members might not work in the same physical location and must communicate over a distance; (b) Group members' status, authority, and expertise with respect to each other is ambiguous. Absence of prior social structure means group members must develop new structures for sharing information, for example, norms or rules for reporting progress and division of labor; (c) Task goals are likely to be relatively short-term, so the emphasis is on efficient learning and task completion rather than on gradual socialization and group development.

How does a group organize itself and learn quickly, particularly when group members are geographically and organizationally dispersed? The question we address in this chapter is how communication and communication technology affect the performance of these groups. We describe an empirical study of ad hoc work groups. Then we discuss some more general research and management issues having to do with communication in organized collaborative work.

Previous experimental research suggests that the productivity of an ad hoc task group will depend on the information resources it has and how it puts those resources to use. Many ad hoc task groups are much less productive than the competencies of their individual members would suggest (Hackman & Morris, 1975; Steiner, 1972). That is, although the group has good information resources, it does not use them effectively. For example, brainstorming groups produce fewer ideas, even fewer good ideas, than the individual members of these groups produce working alone (Diehl & Stroebe, 1987). Problem-solving groups usually perform better than their average member, but not at the level of their most competent member (Rohrbaugh, 1979).

It is conventionally understood that group productivity is hampered by what are called *process losses* or, alternatively, *transaction costs*. Process losses or transaction costs derive from the inability of group members to communicate efficiently, and also from certain social pressures that emerge in groups. One mundane but ubiquitous transaction cost is the time taken to distribute information among group members. For example, in brainstorming groups, people spend time listening to others and telling others their ideas. This decreases the time each group member might spend generating original ideas. In geographically-dispersed groups, the cost of information exchange includes the time it takes to travel to and from meetings, the time for a written memorandum to be distributed to others, and, once people meet, the time to schedule more meetings.

A related transaction cost is the time and effort the group must spend coordinating its work, along with the extra work that arises from inefficient coordination. Groups may decide to partition their project and distribute tasks to individual members (McGrath, chap. 2 in this volume). This is a good coordination device, but the tasks must be merged at some point. Groups may decide to work collectively, but this leads to new transaction costs. Pressures for consensus can reduce the effectiveness of individual members who have distinctive expertise. Most groups make decisions preferred by the majority of their members and by high status members, reducing the influence of group members who hold minority opinions or low status, even when they are competent (Davis, Kerr, Atkin, Holt, & Meek, 1975; Berger, Fisek, Norman & Zelditch, 1977). Also, working together can reduce group members' sense of control over their own work, an effect leading to "motivation losses." One of these is the "I'll not be a sucker" reaction, whereby the group member reduces his or her effort in the expectation others are doing the same (Yamgishi & Sato, 1986).

If an ad hoc group has a difficult task that has to be completed under a close deadline, transaction costs are magnified. Time pressures and complexity increase the load on the group members, saturating them with more task and role demands, including communication demands, than they can easily handle (Shaw, 1964; Shaw, 1978; McGrath, 1984). Moderate levels of saturation may be positive in that group members feel challenged. But heavy saturation can lead to chaotic interdependence, reducing individuals' feelings of autonomy and ability to contribute effectively, and increasing the likelihood of motivation and coordination losses.

Recent developments in computer-mediated communication technology may be particularly helpful to ad hoc task groups confronting physically dispersed members, lack of information-sharing routines, and short-term deadlines. Computer-mediated communication technology uses computer text-processing and communication tools to provide high-speed information exchange. Anyone with a computer account can create and send information to anyone who has an account on that computer or on any other to which it is connected through a computer network. The networked computers might be in the same building and connected via a local area network, or in different states, countries, or continents, and connected by long distance telecommunications. The most common application and the one we focus on in this chapter is computer mail. Depending on software sophistication, the sent information can be a message, document, computer program, statistical data, or even a collection of organized messages—a computer discussion or digest. At the recipient's convenience, he or she can read the information, edit it, save it, delete it, move it to another computer file, forward it to other people, combine it with other computer mail, and/or reply to the sender. At the sender's convenience, he or she can share information, select the audience for a message, combine and edit old messages to generate new information, and send messages seeking new information.

Computer communication has several characteristics that may make it particularly useful for ad hoc groups. First, it overcomes physical barriers to communication; the sender and the receiver do not have to be in the same place to communicate. Furthermore, it is asynchronous; the sender and the receiver do not have to coordinate their communication as they would, for example, in a telephone conversation or videoconference. Moreover, computer mail can be sent to several people as easily as to one person, or even to a group as a whole. A list of people's names and computer addresses, sometimes called a distribution list (DL), is given a name—such as "Red Team" or "Vacation Project." A sender mails one communication to the group name, then the computer automatically sends the communication to every person whose name and address are on the distribution list. Senders do not have to specify the names and addresses of group members in order for them to receive their messages. Computer communication allows relatively efficient communication over distances. It is both asynchronous and fast, thus it can be used to report progress and divide tasks as they evolve rather than waiting for a face-to-face meeting. All-group mail is as easy to send as mail to one person, and it increases the ease of sharing information held by individual members.

Our study of computer mail in ad hoc software development teams allowed us to observe how this technology was used by these groups. One hypothesis we examined was whether improved group performance was related to use of computer mail. In line with our argument that computer mail can reduce transaction costs, we predicted that groups that used computer mail in their work would be more productive than groups that did not use computer mail as much. One simple advantage of using computer mail might be to do some tasks faster and more easily that would otherwise have to be done in face-to-face meetings. For example, to schedule a meeting, a manager needs to have information about other peoples' schedules and then must announce the meeting time and place after scheduling it. The manager might use computer mail to collect and disseminate this scheduling information, as needed, rather than take up time in group meetings to plan other meetings. It is conceivable a manager could use this technology to design more intricate schedules or to demand more group meetings. But we thought the opposite would happen in groups with heavy deadline pressures. We expected a substitution effect whereby necessary tasks done by computer mail would offset the same tasks done face-to-face, by telephone, and in hard-copy memoranda. Therefore we hypothesized that total communication would not increase when groups used computer mail; rather, that more computer mail would lead to less use of other kinds of communication.

Another way computer mail might reduce transaction costs is by allowing the groups to partition their work more efficiently than they might do otherwise. Many tasks that groups do are best done by a subset of one or more members. If the best programmer writes a piece of code, in effect the whole group has written the code, but without wasting the time of the other group members (McGrath, 1984). Groups sometimes avoid partitioning tasks, or implement the strategy badly, because of the transaction costs arising from having to keep track of people's progress, encouraging them to do their work, collecting finished jobs, communicating to others how the work is going, making group members feel they are part of a group activity, and merging individual or subgroup products with the group product. This array of transaction costs effectively limits groups to partitioning only as much work as will not fatally threaten the cohesiveness and coordination of the group. Computer mail could enlarge the domain of partitionable work. Certain coordination and morale-boosting functions could be performed by computer mail rather than in face-to-face interaction. For example, through the mail system, group members could tell each other about their individual progress and find out about how others are doing; this should increase both coordination and cohesiveness.

Notice that we are referring not just to improved coordination of partitioned work, but to a group working in a new way, offloading more work onto parts of the group and using computer mail as an electronic link between individual activity and the group. The implication of this is not only that less time will be spent in meetings, but also that some of the penalties for working in groups will be reduced. By partitioning the work but keeping others informed, people would have greater control over and responsibility for their own work. Competent individuals might capture more of the problem solving. Perhaps the advantages would be seen most in socially heterogeneous groups where status generalization and conformity effects can reduce the effectiveness of highly competent people.

We did not expect groups using computer mail to divide their work to the degree that they would never meet together. A group would need to address certain questions face-to-face. For example, in the software teams we studied, final decisions as to the overall design of the project and plans for presenting these designs to the client might best be done in a meeting. Conventionally, people think that important decisions need to be made face-to-face. As we have seen, the actual evidence shows that decisions arising from group action can be narrow-minded and inefficient. On the other hand, when decisions have important implications for the future or when they need active support by every member of the group, we want the decision-makers to be sensitive to all the information available and to personify this sensitivity in face-to-face discussion (see in particular (Daft & Lengel, 1986) on the role of information "richness"). Computer mail discussion probably cannot substitute for the personal and symbolic value of meetings. Moreover, because computer mail reduces social context cues (Sproull & Kiesler, 1986), it leads to difficulties in resolving conflicts of ideology or interest. Previous experiments (Siegel, Dubrovsky, Kiesler & McGuire, 1986) show that when a demand for consensus is placed on groups having a difference of opinion, the computer-mediated groups have more difficulty reaching consensus than face-to-face groups.

In addition to investigating how groups might use computer mail to reduce transaction costs, we examined another issue having implications for productivity, that is, how would people organize computer communications to one another? For example, would one person run things? Would people send only one-to-one messages? Would the groups use the group distribution list? As templates against which to observe our teams, we used some models of interaction developed in experimental research nearly four decades ago (Bavelas, 1948; Leavitt, 1951; Shaw, 1959). One distinctive pattern of communication studied in this early work on "communication nets" is the so-called wheel pattern, more accurately called the "spoke and hub" pattern. People in the spoke and hub pattern communicate only with one central member; all information passes through this central person, the "hub" of the wheel. Many studies have shown that the spoke and hub gets information to people faster and more accurately than other ways of organizing information exchange. It is particularly useful for relatively simple tasks where the central person is the most competent member of the group and can collect all the information needed to solve the problem. However, the spoke and hub pattern becomes ineffective when the problem is highly complex, or the group is very large, or when competencies are distributed throughout the group. In that case, the central person can become overwhelmed with information at the same time the group members bombard him or her with requests for information.

An alternative form that is very efficient is the *circle* whereby members of a group communicate with adjacent members of the group, but no one person is central. Whereas the spoke and hub pattern represents the utmost in centralization, the circle represents extreme decentralization. The early experiments showed that the circle is very advantageous when competence is evenly distributed through the group, and the information to be handled is too complex or burdensome for one central person. The circle allows tasks to be taken on by people who will actually do the work, and it allows decisions to flow to the person or persons who are best suited to make them. Participants like this decentralized organization because it gives them more autonomy, and also more information.

All of the early experiments on communication structures were conducted with groups that communicated with one another selectively and simultaneously by, for example, passing hard-copy messages to one another. They were also one-time trials. Conditions are quite different in a computer communication system being used to support an on-going group task. In particular, although all users of such a system are completely interconnected, the flexibility of these connections allow groups, at different times, to create structures that meet their functional needs. This is an important distinction between these systems and the crude lab apparatus employed in the earlier studies. It suggests, further, that there are limits to the application of the structural metaphors from these experiments. That is, a system which at one point assumes a functional pattern resembling a spoke and hub, and at another point assumes a functional pattern resembling the circle form cannot really be said to possess the characteristic shape of either of these patterns. Instead, modern communication systems seem to produce amalgamated forms. For example, computer mail might support both a spoke and hub functional form, advantageous for coordinating, and more circular functional forms, advantageous for sharing information. Or it might support any combination of functional forms between these extremes. Informally, we have observed this pattern; working groups in the ARPANET, for instance, often have a moderator or chair who helps keep order and coordinates individual work with the group's needs, while other members of the groups send mail to each other frequently.

If groups used computer mail along with meetings and other forms of communication, this behavior would in effect diversify the channels available for communication. We thought this diversification might result in an improved attitude on the part of people who do not have a good chance to talk in meetings, either because these interactions are dominated by others or because they are reluctant to communicate face-to-face. Having an opportunity to "talk" via computer mail might increase the motivation of these group members, and might offset some of the group motivation losses that commonly arise when people have interdependent relationships but cannot or do not participate fully in the group's work. A previous study of a city government (Huff, Sproull, & Kiesler, 1988) found that the more computer mail people sent to others, the more committed they felt to the city organization. This relationship held especially strongly among shift workers; people who had little opportunity to participate in face-to-face decision making of the organization. Receiving mail was found to be unrelated to commitment, which suggests that simply receiving information is not especially motivating. These data suggest that providing a supplementary channel to have a say can have positive motivational results on members of a group.

In summary, we offer the following ideas in respect to the performance and work of ad hoc groups.

1. Ad hoc groups that use computer mail will perform better than groups that do not.

2. The more computer mail a group uses, the less it will use other kinds of communication, but this tradeoff will stop short of complete substitution.

3. All groups will partition work and use computer mail to coordinate this work. Therefore, coordinating messages will be an important component of computer mail content.

4. Ad hoc groups will not use computer mail to make substantive consensus decisions. Therefore, consensus forming messages will not be an important component of computer mail content.

5. Computer mail will allow the most competent group members to coordinate work they do independently, while maintaining contact with the remainder of the group.

6. Ad hoc groups will use amalgamated communication structures to organize their computer communications.

7. Some people who do not talk in face-to-face meetings will use computer mail. Participating in group discussions via this alternative medium may be associated with higher commitment and better performance for these people than for people who are low-rate participants in both media.

METHOD

Software Development Teams

The data for this study were collected from seven software development teams at Carnegie Mellon University in the fall of 1986. The teams consisted of two managers and from five to eight programmers and documenters. All were seniors in a required upper-division information systems course. The sole activity of the course was to design and build a working computer-based information system for a real client. Each team was assigned a different software development project. Projects included a work scheduling system requested by the director of university administrative services, a marketing database requested by the director of a charitable organization serving 68 agencies in the greater Pittsburgh area, and a course advising system requested by a dean's office. The teams were given an average of $3,000 to purchase equipment and software, as well as unlimited access to the university's networked professional workstations for development purposes. The task was to design, build, and test a working information system, to the client's specification and satisfaction, within a period of 3 months. A typical project was PC-based, could process between 200 and 2,000 data records, and required about one person year of effort to complete. Each student's grade in the course was based on the client's evaluation of the quality of the group's work, which could be modified one letter grade higher or lower by fellow group members' evaluations of each student's contribution to that work.

Past studies of group communication have examined communication in laboratory problem-solving groups, such as mock juries, in primary groups, such as friendship networks or families, in organizational work groups, and in therapy groups. The groups in this study were much like other ad hoc work groups, except that members were not permanent employees of an organization and were relatively inexperienced. Like the situation in many organizational groups, membership in the seven software development teams was not completely voluntary. A course instructor assigned students to teams, and recruited the managers based on a variety of criteria, including skill level, leadership ability, and prior performance. The group members did have a say in their assignments. One criterion for group assignment was the preference ranking of projects and fellow group members completed by each student. The teams in this study were given great latitude to determine both how they would produce their systems and divide their work among members. These teams were newly constituted for this task; they had not worked together as a group before. However, through participation in the same academic program, they did share common experience in previous courses, common skills, and information.

The overall task for each team was the production of a working computer-based information system for the team's client. To meet this goal, each team had to complete many different tasks. Teams had to negotiate contract terms with their clients. These included system specifications, performance criteria, and resource support. Teams had to acquire needed resources. This involved contact with hardware and software suppliers, dealings with university and client purchasing departments, and delivery and set-up of purchased equipment. Teams had to write code and documentation for their systems. This involved reliability and security checking, debugging, and testing of programs and instructions. Teams also had to train users of the system. Finally, at several points during the course each team had to present progress reports to clients, and make group presentations before the other groups.

Certain characteristics of the teams made them ideal candidates for studying group communication. First, group members were locally dispersed. That is, all members lived on or near the university campus, but they did not have assigned offices and it was not trivial for groups (or subgroups) to meet together (i.e., members could not just stroll down an office hallway to confer with fellow members). Second, and most important, the nature of the groups' tasks demanded extensive group communication. Teams had to schedule their work. The 3-month deadline was a non-negotiable term of every contract. Groups struggled to set appropriate interim deadlines to ensure steady progress. The complexity of the overall task demanded task decomposition into manageable units, such as documentation tasks, programming tasks, debugging tasks, and training tasks. Groups had to decide which members would be responsible for each of these subtasks and had to coordinate activity among members working on parallel tasks. Team members required regular feedback on progress by other team members. Groups had to build and maintain cohesion and commitment despite heavy workloads and high deadline pressure. This involved praise, team parties, and other forms of morale boosting.

Each team had a regularly scheduled meeting time during the week. Each team member also had access to the university's computer mail system and unlimited account allocations for using computer mail. Each student was given a directory with all students' telephone numbers, addresses, and computer mail addresses. Distribution lists (DLs) were established for all groups.

Measures

Four kinds of data were collected. First, we gathered archival background information on each study participant. This included prior performance (grade point average up to the period of the study and class rank), number of computer science courses taken[1], and project preferences. We then administered questionnaires at the beginning and end of the 3-month period. The initial questionnaire contained items to assess likely degree of participation in the group. General level of likely participation was assessed by seven 7-point Likert scales which revealed level of motivation. Likely face-to-face participation was assessed by a measure of shyness adapted from the Stan-

---

[1]There was no variance in this measure so it was dropped from subsequent analyses.

ford Shyness Survey (Zimbardo, 1977) and, in addition, twenty 5-point Likert scales were used to calculate McCroskey's Personal Report of Communication Anxiety (PRCA) Index for each team member (McCroskey, 1970).[2] Likely computer mail participation was assessed by measuring prior computer mail experience and computer access. The final questionnaire contained four 10-point Likert scales to measure level of commitment to the group (adapted from Mowday, 1979), seven 7-point Likert scales to measure perceived quality of communication within the group (adapted from O'Reilly and Roberts, 1976), and five 5-point Likert scales to measure perceived quality of coordination within the group (adapted from Georgeopolous & Mann, 1962). The final questionnaire also contained an open ended item to determine each student's prior information system employment experience.

We also collected communication data from each participant for the entire period. At 1-month intervals, we observed face-to-face meetings in each team. During these observations we audiotaped the meeting discussion for later content analysis, and monitored participation patterns using a sampling technique of recording the name of the group member speaking at the start of each minute. At these 1-month intervals, participants were also asked to report phone calls to and from other members, memos sent to or received from other members, face-to-face interactions with other members, and computer mail messages sent to or received from other team members. All project-related computer mail sent by team members was also collected for the 3-month period.

Finally, we collected project evaluations from the clients, and individual performance evaluations from each member's teammates at the end of the semester.[3] The project performance measure was obtained from the average of five 10-point Likert scales that clients used to evaluate their team's performance. These five scales were: (1) How well did the project team communicate with you; (2) How well did the project team solve or alleviate problems; (3) How much effort do you think the project team put into the project; (4) How professional were the team's presentations; and (5) How useful has this project and its development been to you. The individual performance measure was obtained from the average percent contribution to group performance assigned to a given individual by the other group

[2]We dropped the PRCA from the analysis because it was correlated highly with measured shyness, $r_p = .59$. Here, and elsewhere in the paper, Pearson correlations will be noted by r_p, while Spearman correlations will be noted by r_s.

[3]The clients did not participate in the selection of team members or managers, were not involved with this study, did not complete their evaluations jointly with the course instructors, and were equally blind to team member qualifications beyond the same general presentation made to all clients that the groups would be competent to perform the specified system implementation.

members, where the total percent contribution across all members had to equal 100%.

RESULTS

Background Characteristics and Performance

Team member background characteristics across teams are summarized in Table 11.1. Prior to the project, the average team member had a grade-point average between a B− and a B, had information system related employment experience, was highly motivated, was not shy, and was male. The average team member did not own a computer, was not a computer science major, sent or received one computer mail message per day, had easy access to the university computer mail system, and found that system easy to use. Means separation tests using the Tukey–Kramer criterion showed no significant difference among teams on any of these background characteristic variables. We examined the relationship between the average background characteristics of members within teams and group performance, the average evaluation score assigned to each team by their client. Prior performance, the average grade point average for each group, was positively related to group performance ($r_s = .47$, n = 7). Level of computer ownership in each group, the percentage of group members that owned computers, was also positively related to group performance ($r_s = .35$, n = 7). There were no other high correlations with the group performance measure.

Communication and Performance

Table 11.2 summarizes communication behavior and group performance. The first four rows represent the self-reported mean weekly communication behavior per member in each team. These categories recorded self-reports of total communication behavior for each medium (e.g., messages sent and received, phone calls made and received). The fifth row represents the average number of computer messages sent and received per week that we collected from each member of the team. Although team members provided mail voluntarily and we cannot know if they failed to provide any significant proportion of it, we estimate we retrieved essentially all of it.[4] It is interesting that almost all of the group members underestimated the amount of mail

---

[4]We base this estimate on two indicators. 1) No message in our sample alluded to any other message that we did not also have. 2) At least one member in each group gave us his or her entire mail file for the sampling period (including many messages totally unrelated to this project). Because every group member received the same all-group mail, a complete file from one group member allowed us to reconstruct the all-group files for every group member.

TABLE 11.1

Background Characteristics of Group Members

Characteristic	Group 1 (n = 8)	Group 2 (n = 7)	Group 3 (n = 9)	Group 4 (n = 8)	Group 5 (n = 7)	Group 6 (n = 7)	Group 7 (n = 10)
Prior performance (High = 4.0, Low = 0)							
Mean	2.69	2.97	2.91	2.79	2.64	2.95	2.46
STD	0.64	0.57	0.39	0.55	0.44	0.59	0.32
% information system related employment experience (percentage of group with experience)							
	100	86	56	63	86	86	70
Motivation (1–7, highly motivated = 7.0)							
Mean	5.84	6.25	6.17	6.00	6.32	6.43	6.03
STD	0.80	0.60	0.99	0.35	0.51	0.19	0.66
Shyness (1–14, not at all shy = 14)							
Mean	9.62	10.33	9.11	12.25	13.43	9.71	8.62
STD	4.87	3.78	4.40	2.55	0.53	4.46	4.53
% female membership (percentage of females in group)							
	13	43	44	38	43	43	30
% computer ownership (percentage of computer owners in group)							
	13	43	0	50	29	0	10
% non-CS majors (percentage of non-CS majors in group)							
	100	100	100	100	100	100	100
Sent (e-mail messages per week, prior to course)							
Mean	3.00	5.43	3.22	10.62	15.14	3.14	2.90
STD	3.12	8.7	2.95	10.41	24.5	2.04	2.42
Rcvd (e-mail messages per week, prior to course)							
Mean	3.75	4.43	3.11	11.50	14.43	3.14	4.30
STD	3.28	5.47	1.76	14.50	24.8	1.95	3.02
Ease of system access (1–7, very easy = 7.0)							
Mean	6.00	5.14	5.89	5.50	5.50	6.14	5.40
STD	0.93	2.04	0.33	1.60	1.64	1.07	0.97
Ease of system use (1–7, very easy = 7.0)							
Mean	6.00	4.86	6.00	5.87	5.14	5.71	5.20
STD	0.93	1.46	0.50	0.83	1.68	0.49	0.92

they exchanged. This recalls a phenomenon we noted in another study, the perceived ephemeral quality of computer mail (Sproull & Kiesler, 1986). Rows 6 through 8 represent subsets of the total mail collected, reporting the average amount of dyadic (or one-to-one) mail sent per member (row 6), the average amount of group mail sent per member (row 7), and the average total amount of mail sent per member (row 8).

TABLE 11.2
Mean Weekly Group Communication Behavior and Group Performance

Communication Behavior	Groups						
	Grp 1 (n = 8)	Grp 2 (n = 7)	Grp 3 (n = 9)	Grp 4 (n = 8)	Grp 5 (n = 7)	Grp 6 (n = 7)	Grp 7 (n = 10)
1. Face-to-face, Self-report (interactions per week per member)	5.6	12.4	9.2	5.6	5.7	11.9	14.9[a]
2. Phone, Self-report (interactions per week per member)	1.1	7.4	4.0	0.6	2.1	4.3	8.6[b]
3. Hardcopy memo, Self-report (memos sent and received per week per member)	1.5	1.5	2.3	0.7	0.3	2.7	3.0
4. Computer mail, Self-report (messages sent and received per week per member)	6.4	3.3	2.7	2.7	6.9	2.8	0.1[c,d]
5. Computer mail, collected (messages sent and received per week per member)	12.0	4.1	3.9	7.2	6.9	3.0	0.0[e,f]
6. Dyadic computer mail sent, collected (dyadic messages sent per week per member)	2.3	1.1	0.9	1.7	1.3	0.4	0.0
7. Group computer mail sent, collected (all-group messages sent per week per member)	0.8	0.2	0.2	0.4	0.4	0.3	0.0
8. Total computer mail sent, collected (all messages sent per week per member)	3.1	1.3	1.1	2.1	1.7	0.7	0.0
9. Group performance (1 = worst performance, 10 = best performance)	9.4	9.4	9.2	9.0	8.6	8.4	6.9

Notes: (all entries rounded to nearest .1)

[a]Group 7 is significantly different from Groups 1, 4, and 5 according to the Tukey-Kramer criterion.

[b]Group 7 is significantly different from Groups 1, 4, and 5 according to the Tukey-Kramer criterion.

[c]Group 7 is significantly different from Groups 1 and 5 according to the Tukey-Kramer criterion.

[d]Groups 3, 4, 6, and 7 are significantly different from Group 5 according to the Tukey-Kramer criterion.

[e]Group 7 is significantly different from Groups 1, 4, and 5 according to the Tukey-Kramer criterion.

[f]Group 1 is significantly different from Groups 2, 3, 6, and 7 according to the Tukey-Kramer criterion.

Means comparison tests using the Tukey–Kramer criterion showed significant differences across groups' communication behavior in the face-to-face, phone, and computer mail modalities. Particularly interesting is the difference between Group 7 (high face-to-face, high phone, low computer mail) and Groups 1 and 5 (low face-to-face, low phone, high computer mail). The last row shows each team's performance.

To evaluate the relationship between group communication and group performance, we carried out a correlation analysis, summarized in Table 11.3. Two computer mail measures ("dyadic computer mail sent, collected ⟨dyadic message sent per week per member⟩" and "computer mail, collected ⟨messages sent and received per week per member⟩") were strongly related to the group performance measure ($r_s = .67$, n = 7; $r_s = .67$, n = 7). The other computer mail measures ("computer mail, self-report ⟨messages sent and received per week per member⟩" and "group computer mail sent, collected ⟨all-group messages sent per week per member⟩") were also positively related to the performance measure ($r_s = .44$, n = 7; $r_s = .40$, n = 7). The non-computer mail communication measures ("face-to-face, self-report ⟨interactions per week per member⟩," "phone, self-report ⟨interactions per week per member⟩," "hardcopy memo, self-report ⟨memos sent and received per week per member⟩") were all negatively related to group performance. Further, all of the computer mail measures were negatively related to the measures of traditional communication behavior. That is, groups that used computer mail did not simply increase their volume of communication using other media.

TABLE 11.3
Correlation Matrix for Group Performance and Average Group
Weekly Communication Behavior

	1	2	3	4	5	6	7
1. Face-to-face (self-report)	—						
2. Phone (self-report)	1.00	—					
3. Hardcopy memo (self-report)	.79	.62	—				
4. Computer mail (self-report)	−.34	−.34	−.67	—			
5. Group computer mail sent (collected)	−.86	−.86	−.75	.61	—		
6. Dyadic computer mail sent (collected)	−.86	−.86	−.86	.60	.89	—	
7. Computer mail (collected)	−.86	−.86	−.86	.60	.89	1.00	—
8. Group performance	−.36	−.36	−.41	.44	.40	.67	.67

Note: n = 7, all entries are r_s.

What were the contents of the computer mail? By way of example, we describe three kinds of mail that could be interpreted as coordinative in function: messages related to scheduling meetings, task assignment, and status reports. All managers who used computer mail sent messages to their group announcing or reiterating the time and place of an upcoming meeting (see A:1). (Sample messages, with names changed to pseudonyms, are displayed in Fig. 11.1). Some managers also used mail more interactively to solicit information about when people were available for meetings and to negotiate meeting times. A second use of mail was to announce or reiterate task assignments for individuals or subgroups (see A:2). A subset of assignment messages served as advance organizers for face-to-face meetings, telling people what they should have done before the meeting or what they should be prepared to do in the meeting. We have suggested earlier that computer mail allows the removal of some necessary but mundane tasks, like scheduling meetings, from the face-to-face domain. These advance organizer messages suggest that computer mail may also contribute to the productivity of face-to-face meetings by increasing the probability that people have "done their homework" before the meeting. A third use of mail was to give status reports either to the manager or to the group as a whole (see A:3). Groups used computer mail both to implement and to monitor their performance strategies (Hackman, 1987).

To understand systematically what group members talked about when they met face-to-face and sent computer mail we examined all of the meeting transcripts and computer messages. We devised six categories of interactions to describe mail and meeting contents: scheduling, task assignment, reports of work status, problem solving (or decision making), social-emotional interactions such as morale boosting, and a miscellaneous category. Based on these content categories, we developed a detailed coding guide and used it to train two coders. Working independently, they analyzed each transcript and each set of computer messages and obtained 79% agreement, which produced inter-coder reliability of .68 using Scott's pi (Scott, 1955). The coding unit for computer mail was the message and, for face-to-face interaction, a meaningful turn of at least five words.[5] We do not assume, of course, that these different coding units are comparable; we are interested in the pattern and distribution of content within each medium.[6]

Figure 11.2 shows our findings, group by group. The pattern indicates

---

[5]A message or utterance could contain more than one content category. In cases of multiple categories, each category was given an appropriate fractional weighting (.5 for each category if two were present; .33 if three were present; and so on).

[6]The message and the turn are naturally-produced units. Alternatively we could have used a mechanistic unit such as the same arbitrary number of words or sentences for coding both messages and transcripts. This would have produced apparently comparable data at the price of grossly distorting and obscuring the differences across media.

A: 1
Announcing a Meeting

Date: Thu 28 Aug 86 10:45:52-EDT
From: Horatio Nelson ⟨HN03@TB.CC.CMU.EDU⟩ {manager}
Subject: Meeting Update
To: Group:

I have arranged a meeting with Robert {client} from 12:30 to 1:00 today. Anyone who can is free to attend. A summary of the meeting and details about next week will follow later today.

Horatio

A: 2
Task Assignment

Date: Thu 25 Sep 86 18:35:51-EDT
From: OP12@TD.CC.CMU.EDU   {manager}
Subject: update
To: PROJECT: ;

In lieu of the meeting this week, here's what needs to be going on at this point:

1) everyone—make sure that you have interviewed your UW people by Wednesday. Technically, by then we have to meet and pull together out of the interviews what everyone would like from the system, and what we can feasibly do. If you ABSOLUTELY can't do it by then, then by Thursday or Friday, NO LATER. When you interview them, (or call to set up the interview, introduce yourself and the system, explain what Claudia has already suggested, and what Timothy wants, and ask them what information not already wanted by Timothy or Claudia would be helpful to them in their decision making process, specifically what kinds of statistics—if they can be that specific.) Claudia's wishes are explained in clause 7 of the contract and Timothy wants info for DataMate. Make sure you write down carefully what they want, since you'll be the only one there, and most likely we won't have the chance to meet with them again. If you need help, or can't make your interview see if someone else would be willing to go in your place.

2) everyone—i assume you got the message from Olson—hardware is being delivered tomorrw (Friday) to Social Science. ANYONE who can be there to supervise the setting up PLEASE GO !!! (I have to be at SteelCo. tomorrow, so I can't do it.) It's at 2 in PH 208. You should go back and reference Olson's message for the details.

3) Kai, Lynn, Max {group members}—you should continue to work on the data dictionary for Datamate. No rush at this point but there's a lot that has to be done, i know.

4) Anne {member}, Nancy {assistant manager}—finish setting up appointments with the chairmen and exec. directors. Let me and Dylan {member} know if you need people to go to interviews. Anne, the Gantt chart is a last priority, but if you have time . . .

5) I have a copy of the R:Base programming manual that Kai found for us. Anyone who wants to start looking at it let me know. I've read a couple chapters, and it doesn't look too bad.

FIG. 11.1.   Sample Messages. (Note: Identities have been changed in these messages).

6) Next meeting is our regular meeting on Wednesday, tho i'll be in touch. Call me—if you have questions or problems.

Oliver Perry

A: 3
Task Accomplishment

Date: Thu 4 Sep 86 15:19:35-EDT
From: JJ76@TD.CC.CMU.EDU   {manager}
Subject: End of week reports
To: Our-group: ;

Though I basically know what everyone has done all week it is probably a good idea to get in the habit of sending weekly reports. So . . . , if you would, please try and send them to me by tomorrow morning. Thanks.

John (jj76@td)

Date: Sun, 21 Sep 86 23:38:18 edt
From: nimitz@andrew.cmu.edu (William Nimitz)   {member}
To: jj76@andrew.cmu.edu (John P. Jones)   {manager}
Subject: End Of Week Report 9-14-86
CC: nimitz@andrew.cmu.edu (William Nimitz)

John-
A synopsis of the weeks effort;
Worked on producing slides for the probdef presentation.
Worked with Dreux on the presentation outline and text.
Well thats realy about it, Idon't realy know what else to add.

William

Date: Tue. 16 Sep 86 10:46:03 edt
From: caroline@andew.cmu.edu (Caroline Shea)   {member}
To: jj76@andrew.cmu.edu (John P. Jones)   {manager}
Subject: Re: some tasks for me

John,
    A weekly meeting time might be difficult for me since my schedule is based on when other people want to meet. (like bosses and stuff). How about if we set Monday afternoons at 1:30 aside? I haven't had a meeting scheduled for that time slot in a few weeks.
    I'm disappointed in what I've accomplished in the last week—nothing! And it's not because I didn't work on anything. I spent most of last week working on adding some important menu items. and trying to get the cut and paste work. None of it worked. and I had to take much of it back out because some things quit working. I also tried to add a panel using the Layout manager and the program core dumped on me. Tom has been real busy and hasn't had the time to give me assistance. but I hope to spend some time with him this week. . I guess my weekly report could say that I continued to review the code that exists and noted the modules that need to be modified in order to get some work items accomplished. (vague enough?)

FIG. 11.1. (*Continued*)

Are you free tomorrow morning? If so, let's get together to talk about some tasks for you.

A: 4
Performance Monitoring

Date: Sun 21 Sep 86 21:37:04-EDT
From: KD03@TD.CC.CMU.EDU   {manager}
Subject: Presentation
To: am4f@TD.CC.CMU.EDU   {member}

Alfred,
    Seeing as you have yet to pick up the report, I assume you have done nothing this weekend with regard to the presentation. The report is still sitting in my slot in the UCC, so you can pick it up when you get a chance. I suggest you start soon—I have a feeling it is more work than you think,
                    Katie
PS. check your mail on TC

FIG. 11.1. (*Continued*)

that some relationship between communication content and communication medium was present. That is, the proportion of electronic communication devoted to scheduling and task assigning messages was higher than the proportion of face-to-face utterances devoted to these topics, while the proportion of face-to-face utterances devoted to problem solving was high-

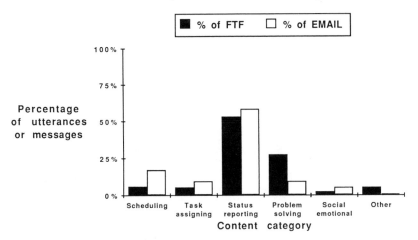

FIG. 11.2.   Message content by medium for each group.

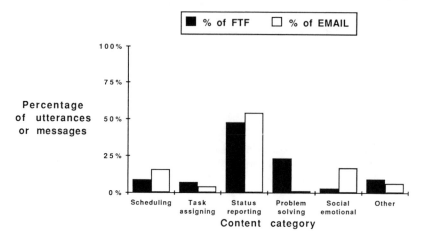

FIG. 11.2.   (*Continued*)

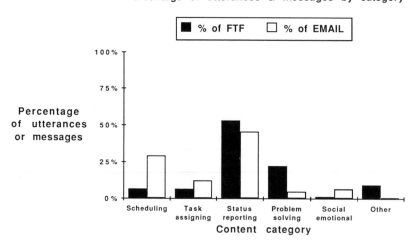

FIG. 11.2.   (*Continued*)

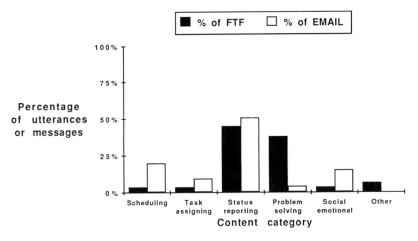

FIG. 11.2. (*Continued*)

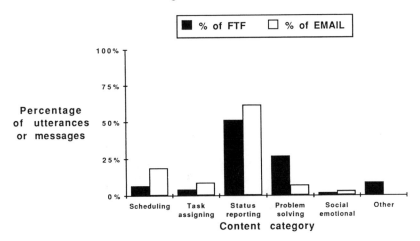

FIG. 11.2. (*Continued*)

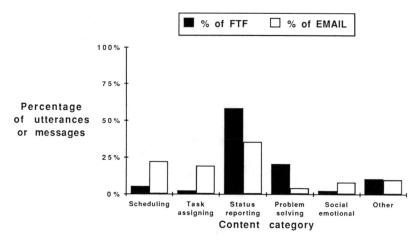

FIG. 11.2. (*Continued*)

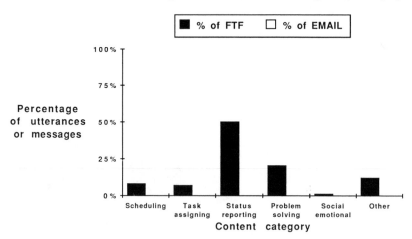

FIG. 11.2. (*Continued*)

TABLE 11.4
Summary of Logit-Model Analysis for Communication Content

Model/Source	Marginals Fitted	L^2	df	p
Null/total	GM, C	284.01	55	< .0001
Due to group	GM, GC	47.79	25	< .01
Due to medium, given group	GM, MC, GC	193.93	5	< .0001
Due to interaction	GMC	42.98	25	< .01

er than the proportion of computer mail messages in this category. To test these relationships we conducted a logit analysis of the coding data with content category as the dependent variable and group and medium as the independent variables.[7]

Table 11.4 presents the goodness-of-fit results for a series of models we fitted to the data. To control for any differences in category distribution due to group we examined the group effect model first. Although this model did not fit well (residual $L^2 = 236.2$, df = 30), the group term did make a slight contribution to better fit over the null model (component $L^2 = 47.79$, df = 25). Next we fit a model with the group and medium effects. Adding the medium term produced a large improvement in the fit to the data (residual $L^2 = 42.98$, df = 25), and the contribution of medium was clearly significant ($L^2 = 193.24$, df = 5). However, this model still did not offer a good description of the data. The medium X group interaction term offered a modest contribution to overall fit (component $L^2 = 42.98$, df = 25). Given these results we estimated logit coefficients from the group and medium model, and from the saturated model.[8]

Table 11.5 presents the coefficient values from the medium and group effect model, and the saturated model. Most notable was the strong relationship between scheduling communication and computer mail ($\lambda = .52$, z-score = 6.1), and between task assigning communication and computer mail ($\lambda = .33$, z-score = 3.3). We also found a strong relationship between problem solving communication and the face-to-face medium ($\lambda = .86$, z-

---

[7]Because we did not assume that the computer mail coding units and the face-to-face units were comparable the values in the cells in the three dimensional table described by category, medium, and group were the percentage of each group's messages or utterances that fell into a particular category. Note that this assumption constrains the marginal total for Group X Medium (i.e., using the percentages fixes the total for each medium, by group, at 100; see Fienberg (1980) pp. 95–97 for details on the analysis of fixed margin tables). Therefore, all analyzed logit models included this term.

[8]In general we tried to follow the model selection strategies outlined in (Fienberg, 1980) and (Kennedy, 1983).

TABLE 11.5
Lambdas, and Tests on Lambdas for Two Models
Fitted to the Communication Content Data

Content Category Variable	Selected Logit Model		Saturated Model	
	Mail	FTF	Mail	FTF
Scheduling				
λ	.52	−.52	.60	−.60
z-score	6.11	−6.11	6.44	−6.44
Task assigning				
λ	.33	−.33	.39	−.39
z-score	3.36	−3.36	3.55	−3.55
Status reporting				
λ	−.06	.06	−.00	.00
z-score	−1.17	1.17	−0.07	0.07
Problem solving				
λ	−.86	.86	−.82	.82
z-score	−9.66	9.66	−8.23	8.23
Social/emotional				
λ	.56	−.56	.57	−.57
z-score	4.62	−4.62	4.34	−4.34
Other				
λ	−.49	.49	−.75	.75
z-score	−4.34	4.34	−4.19	4.19
Total				
λ	0.00	0.00	0.00	0.00

Note: The lambda values are estimates for coefficients in a logit equation where the dependent variable is the log-odds ratio of the percentage of messages/utterances in a given category to the percentage of message/utterances not in a given category. Therefore, the magnitude and sign of the lambdas indicate the degree to which type of medium contributes to this log-odds ratio for the models examined.

score = 9.7). These results offered evidence that the groups we examined did have different communication content patterns across the face-to-face and computer mail mediums. Combined with the earlier investigation of the various models, where we found that there was not a strong effect for group on category, we concluded that the groups were selecting communication medium in part, based on the nature of the information they needed to exchange. Groups used computer mail more to attend to coordination issues, such as scheduling meetings and they used face-to-face interaction to attend to consensus-forming issues, such as problem-solving.[9]

---

[9](Kraut et. al., chap. 6 in this volume) report results consonant with ours. Although they do not look explicitly at computer mail, they find that consensus-forming among research collab-

In the preceding discussion, we suggested that using computer mail might have helped the software development teams in several ways. First, it provided a fast vehicle to do work that would be done more slowly in group meetings or by telephone. Also, it provided a way to coordinate the work of group members. These findings were related to the group as a whole. We also wondered if all group members used mail in the same way or if more than one mail-use pattern could be detected. For instance did high and low performing members use mail in the same way? High performers might use one-to-one mail to communicate heavily among themselves, and not so much with low performers. High performers might also use all-group mail to share solutions with low performers. This implies emergence of an in-group within the mail system. We also wondered if managers and non-managers used mail in the same way. Managers might use one-to-one mail to communicate heavily with non-managers in order to monitor, prod, or schedule them (e.g., see A:4, Fig. 11.1). Managers might also use all-group mail to broadcast announcements to the group, while non-managers might primarily use one-to-one mail to reply to one-to-one mail or all-group mail from the managers. This implies a functional pattern resembling the stylized features of the spoke-and-hub shape. Alternatively, in addition to the above, non-managers might broadcast their own announcements via all-group mail and use one-to-one mail to communicate extensively with other non-managers. This implies the mixed forms characterized earlier as an amalgamated pattern.

To examine these issues, we looked first at computer communication among high performing group members, those who received the top individual evaluations, and low performing group members, those who received lower individual evaluations. Table 11.6 shows the results of this analysis for both one-to-one mail and all-group mail. Groups 3, 4, and 5 had a higher than expected volume of high performer to high performer one-to-one computer mail, under a model of proportional sending and receiving.[10] Note also that communication from low performers to low performers was not as frequent as expected. One-to-one communication from low to high performers, and from high to low performers was greater than expected only in Group 3. In each of these three groups there was a higher than expected volume of all-group mail sent by high performers. Together, these results are consistent with the emergence of expert in-groups in computer mail. In particular, the data suggest that one-to-one mail may have been used

orators occurs mostly in extended face-to-face meetings to plan the project and to plan the report. Most interim coordination occurs in brief hallway conversations which, according to our research, could be performed instead by computer mail.

[10]So did Group 1. The heavily skewed distribution of members on the performance variable, however, casts doubt on the significance of this result for this group.

TABLE 11.6

Patterns of Sending and Receiving of Computer Mail Between High
and Low Performing Team Members

	Group					
	1	2	3	4	5	6
High performers	7	2	3	5	4	4
Low performers	1	5	6	3	3	3
One-to-one mail						
High to high	89.4	5.7	22.9	64.3	72.8	31.3[a]
	76.6	8.2	11.1	39.1	32.7	32.7
High to low	7.9	26.1	36.1	14.6	16.0	21.9
	11.0	20.4	22.2	23.4	24.5	24.5
Low to high	2.8	39.7	32.5	19.9	8.6	43.8
	11.0	20.4	22.2	23.4	24.5	24.5
Low to low	0.0	28.4	8.4	1.2	2.5	3.1
	1.6	51.0	44.4	14.1	18.4	18.4
Total	100.0	100.0	100.0	100.0	100.0	100.0
	100.0	100.0	100.0	100.0	100.0	100.0
	(n = 216)	(n = 87)	(n = 83)	(n = 171)	(n = 81)	(n = 32)
Chi-square for goodness of fit, one-to-one computer mail (df = 1)						
Receive	4.2	12.3	18.3	34.4	19.6	4.2
Send	18.7	0.5	24.7	19.7	33.3	0.2
All-group mail						
High to group	100.0	66.0	84.0	86.0	95.0	88.0
	88.0	28.0	33.0	63.0	57.0	57.0
Low to group	0.0	34.0	16.0	14.0	5.0	12.0
	12.0	72.0	67.0	37.0	43.0	43.0
Total	100.0	100.0	100.0	100.0	100.0	100.0
	100.0	100.0	100.0	100.0	100.0	100.0
	(n = 88)	(n = 23)	(n = 19)	(n = 44)	(n = 41)	(n = 26)
Chi-square for goodness of fit, all-group mail (df = 1)						
Send	13.6	71.7	117.6	22.7	58.9	39.2

Note: Group 7 did not use computer mail
[a]top number is the actual percentage, bottom number is the expected percentage.

by high performers to concentrate work, while all-group mail was used to
share the results of this work. Group 2 was unusual, relative to the other
groups, because of the high volume of communication initiated by low
performers. Low to high, low to low, and all-group mail sent by low performers were all frequent in this group, while high to high, and all-group

mail sent by high performers were less frequent than in other groups. This may have been a reflection of an in-group emerging along lines other than expertise.

We also examined the pattern of computer mail use for managers and non-managers in each group. Table 11.7 shows the results of this analysis for

TABLE 11.7
Patterns of Sending and Receiving of Computer Mail
Between Managers and Non-Managers

	Group					
	1	*2*	*3*	*4*	*5*	*6*
Managers	2	2	2	2	1	2
Non-managers	6	5	7	6	6	5
One-to-one mail						
Manager to	50.5	5.7	10.8	4.7	0.0	12.5[a]
manager	6.3	8.2	4.9	6.3	2.0	8.2
Manager to	30.0	26.1	39.8	31.0	32.1	34.3
non-manager	18.8	20.4	17.3	18.8	12.2	20.4
Non-manager to	18.1	39.8	39.8	39.2	37.0	46.9
manager	18.8	20.4	17.3	18.8	12.2	20.4
Non-manager to	1.4	28.4	9.6	25.1	30.9	6.3
non-manager	56.3	51.0	60.5	56.3	73.5	51.0
Total	100.0	100.0	100.0	100.0	100.0	100.0
	100.0	100.0	100.0	100.0	100.0	100.0
	(n = 216)	(n = 87)	(n = 83)	(n = 171)	(n = 81)	(n = 32)
Chi-square for goodness of fit, one-to-one mail (df = 1)						
Receive	218.2	12.3	38.8	32.4	34.2	14.9
Send	355.6	0.5	38.8	10.4	21.0	5.3
All-group mail						
Manager to	100.0	66.0	89.0	52.0	79.0	85.0
group	25.0	28.0	22.2	25.0	14.0	28.0
Non-manager to	0.0	34.0	11.0	48.0	21.0	15.0
group	75.0	72.0	77.7	75.0	86.0	72.0
Total	100.0	100.0	100.0	100.0	100.0	100.0
	100.0	100.0	100.0	100.0	100.0	100.0
	(n = 88)	(n = 23)	(n = 19)	(n = 44)	(n = 41)	(n = 26)
Chi-square for goodness of fit, all-group computer mail (df = 1)						
Send	300.0	71.7	271.4	38.9	350.8	161.0

Note: Group 7 did not use computer mail.
[a]top number is actual percentage, bottom number is expected percentage.

both one-to-one and all-group mail. Note that in each group one-to-one communication among non-managers was never as frequent as expected under a model of proportional sending and receiving, while one-to-one communication among managers in Groups 2, 3, 4, and 6 conformed roughly to the expected frequencies (Group 5 also conformed, but there was only one manager in this group). One-to-one communication from managers to non-managers and from non-managers to managers exceeded expected levels. And finally, the frequency of all-group mail sent by managers was higher than expected in each group, while the frequency of all-group mail sent by non-managers was less than expected. These data strongly suggested the presence of spoke-and-hub-like functional communication patterns in the groups. However, there was some indication of other functional communication structures. For example, the presence of modest levels of one-to-one communication among non-managers, and the sending of some all-group mail by non-managers indicated the weak presence of amalgamated patterns in Groups 2, 4, and 5.

Finally, we looked at whether people who got an opportunity to talk via computer mail but not face-to-face had higher individual performance, higher reported group commitment, higher perception of group cohesion, and

TABLE 11.8
Average Within Group Correlations for Low
and High Face-to-Face Communicators

	Low (n = 6)	High (n = 6)
Computer mail sending with:		
Commitment	.82	.71
Individual performance	.16	.85
Cohesion	.22	−.36
Coordination	.41	−.53
Openness	.17	.04
Accuracy	.04	.18
Responsiveness	.30	−.12
Face-to-face talking	.09	.79
Face-to-face talking with:		
Commitment	−.01	.59
Individual performance	.52	.74
Cohesion	−.16	−.43
Coordination	.53	.38
Openness	.16	−.75
Accuracy	−.02	.46
Responsiveness	.14	−.54

Note: All table entries are Pearson correlation coefficients computed from the average of the Fisher transformed, within groups correlations. Group 7 did not use computer mail.

more positive evaluation of group communication than nontalkers who did not use the mail system. Table 11.8 summarizes the results of this analysis. The table entries are the correlation coefficients for the average of the Fisher transformed, within group correlations for high face-to-face communicators and low face-to-face communicators across the six groups that used computer mail. The high VS. low distinction was created by dividing the participants in each group at the median level of face-to-face participation, measured by our observations of group meetings. For frequent face-to-face communicators, talking and computer mail sending were very positively related ($r_p = .79$, n = 6). For low face-to-face communicators, talking and computer mail sending were unrelated ($r_p = .09$, n = 6). This suggests, then, that the relationships between communication behavior and individual performance (talking $r_p = .52$, mail $r_p = .16$), communication behavior and reported commitment (talking $r_p = -.01$, mail $r_p = .82$), and communication behavior and perceived coordination (talking $r_p = .53$, mail $r_p = .41$) were more positive for computer mail users relative to non-users among low face-to-face participators. This is consistent with a view of computer mail creating new communication opportunities for people traditionally left out of group interaction—and as a result, expanding the scope of group participation.

DISCUSSION

We have shown in this study that a computer mail system can influence the productivity of ad hoc task groups or project teams. In particular, we found a strong relationship between levels of computer mail use and group performance. Further, we established that in these groups increased computer mail use was associated with reduced amounts of other communication, such as face-to-face meetings, phone conversations, and hardcopy memoranda. Also, we showed a strong association between information content and communication medium, with a high proportion of non-status reporting computer mail devoted to coordinating messages and a high proportion of non-status reporting face-to-face interaction devoted to consensus formation. These results suggest that the use of computer mail did change the output of group work by streamlining communication and by matching information efficiently to the most appropriate medium.

In the beginning, however, we argued that the use of computer mail would influence the pattern of group work as well as the output. Along these lines, we showed that in many groups the highest performing individuals appeared to use one-to-one computer mail to form electronic ingroups—and used all-group mail to maintain contact with the entire group. We found that managers in every group sent the majority of all-group mail, and that the majority of one-to-one mail was exchanged between managers and non-managers. However, we also found weak evidence of one-to-one traffic among non-managers and of all-group mail sent by non-managers. These results indicate that the use of computer mail did alter the pattern of group work by facilitating the formation of constructive in-groups and by creating the opportunity for new functional communication structures, although the nature of manager to non-manager interaction in these groups suggests that members experimented with these structures, rather than using them extensively. Finally, we showed that there were individual consequences of computer mail use, including positive relationships between mail use and individual evaluation, between mail use and commitment to the group, and between mail use and perception of coordination by low face-to-face communicators.

This study had several shortcomings that should be noted. First, despite the real-world conditions, team members were still students in an information system course. Although team members were highly motivated and talented, they were not professional software designers. Nor were their leaders professional managers. In addition, the number of teams studied was small. Moreover, our measures of non-computer mail communication relied heavily (although not entirely) on self-report. We cannot be sure that these measures were an adequate substitute for more behavioral measures.

We cannot definitively rule out two competing explanations for our findings: (a) "computer ability" in the group was responsible both for the volume of computer mail, and (b) the quality of group performance with no direct link between mail and performance. There were differences across groups in prior performance and computer ownership. A second alternative explanation is that good managers might have been responsible for both volume of computer mail and quality of group performance with no direct link between mail and performance. The course instructors emphasized the importance of using available communication channels. Good managers might have decided to use computer mail extensively simply to comply with this recommendation. By virtue of superior managerial ability good managers might also have been better at organizing their groups, motivating lazy team members, and dealing with clients. Under this scenario, high group performance stems from these latter factors, and the relationship between computer mail use and performance is spurious. However, if this were the case, the good managers would also have to explicitly decide to reduce their groups' volume of noncomputer communication, and decide to use computer mail for coordination messages, with no expectation that these decisions would affect group performance. There probably was a relationship between managerial ability and volume of group computer mail, but we believe it was straightforward; that is, good managers determined how to exploit the technology to benefit the group directly.

Despite its shortcomings, we feel this study represents a somewhat different approach to research on organizational communication than has been taken in the past. Researchers need to learn much more about the broad spectrum of communication behavior and technology in organizations today. Traditional studies of processes that involve communication such as "participation" and "implementation" have deep roots in American social science and business, but refer to highly circumscribed phenomena (e.g., union-management relations). The conditions that gave rise to theories about these processes have changed enormously. In part motivated by technological advances, work is more cognitive, workers are better educated and more autonomous, decision making is more elaborate, organizations are larger, more geographically dispersed, and more complex, and most employees communicate in more groups, over a broader range of topics, people, and locations than they did in the past. Recent studies of how people actually communicate with others to do group or collaborative work, such as Hannaway's (1989) study of managers and Kraut, Galegher, and Egido's (1988) study of research collaborators, suggest that we have much to learn about how different kinds of people actually work together in the course of doing different tasks. The absence of strong theory in this area is indicative, we think, of the paucity of interesting data.

One reason for the infrequency of behavioral studies of organizational communication, of course, is that collecting the data is a highly labor-intensive occupation, and it is likely to be intrusive as well. Our use of the computer mail system to collect data on-line suggests a new development in this respect; we and others are trying to develop ways to collect communication data for research purposes automatically, unobtrusively, and in a manner that produces analyzable data (Blackwell, 1987; Huff, 1988; Mackay, 1988; Sproull, 1986). These techniques will not only allow us to collect data that have been too costly to collect in the past (e.g., to monitor the number of others people communicate with), but also to collect new kinds of data and to look at organizations from new perspectives. For example, most studies of group work involve only one or very few groups. We recently finished a study of electronic groups in an organization where many employees belonged to 30 or more groups (Finholt & Sproull, 1989). This raises some new issues such as what membership in groups means to members of organizations—how it affects their attachment to the organization, their knowledge of the organization, and their influence in the organization.

In recent years, the introduction of computers and computer networks have opened a door to more flexible ways of doing work. For example, the Manufacturers Hanover Trust has linked many of its employees world-wide on an electronic network. The network allows people and groups to interact according to their function or product as well as within their home department or geographic location. Potential advantages in terms of an organization's ability to adapt to a rapidly changing environment, to overcome parochialism, and to increase organizational learning are apparent. For instance, when a product manager in Hong Kong can ask for advice from a product manager in Frankfurt, the result is likely to be more shared expertise. As these two people exchange information about their work, and involve others with similar concerns, the electronic group becomes an information buffer available to anyone on the system who sends mail to one of the group members, or to the group as a whole. The group becomes an information system that is up-to-date and responsive.

In conventional patterns of group work, people alternate periods of work alone with periods of face-to-face meetings. During alone time, each person concentrates on his or her piece of the project. During meeting time people discuss overall project goals and are reminded of the way the pieces must fit together. They share progress and problems. While in meetings, people cannot make progress on their individual tasks. This can frustrate people who say, "I spend all my time in meetings and never get any work done." While working alone, the group becomes less salient. This can create performance gaps when individuals stray from group guidelines or schedules. Computer mail can change this pattern by connecting people to the group while they are alone. People send and read mail at their own convenience but when they do so every group message makes the group salient to each recipient. Because members do not have to wait for meetings to report problems or discoveries, they can share status reports on a daily or even hourly basis. Thus members (or subgroups) can work independently but in mutual awareness of other members and tasks.

Also in conventional patterns of group work, in-group formation necessarily leads to out-groups, who experience reduced interaction, information, motivation, and often, lower performance. Computer mail can change this pattern by supporting in-groups without out-groups. Expertise in-groups can form via one-to-one computer mail. But via all-group mail that expertise can be shared with all group members. Similarly when groups communicate only or primarily in face-to-face meetings, only one person at a time can talk. But adding computer mail means that more people and different people can contribute. Our findings and observations about new patterns of group work mesh nicely with a concern for more sophisticated theory about group processes (McGrath, chap. 2 in this volume).

Will computer communication foster new forms of collaborative work? Today it is hard to imagine the possibilities. As is suggested by our own use of the classic wheel and circle metaphors in this chapter, we tend to think about the uses and impact of new technologies in terms of old technologies. When the telephone was first introduced, its developers imagined it to be an improved telegraph on which managers might broadcast orders to employees. They adopted the telephone, but they did not comprehend its implications. When the Xerox photocopier was first introduced, analysts forecast a quite limited market for it because they thought it would be used to make copies only at the point of origin as was the case with all previous copying technologies. Today we are only beginning to perceive the possibilities of computer communication; many people still regard it as a glorified answering machine. But we have shown that it has the capacity to support new forms of group behavior. A new technology, of course, does not compel new kinds of behavior. The culture and imagination of people encountering the technology are just as important as the technology itself in determining how it is developed and used.

Most of the interesting examples of collaborative systems using computer networks come from the engineering and scientific communities. Still, these examples may suggest what lies in our future. A major programming language, COMMON LISP, which was developed in large measure with the computer mail system of the ARPANET, exemplifies one possible direction. This long-distance project consisted of dozens of people in many universities and research laboratories all over the country who carried out the work over a period of 30 months using computer mail. As one of the participants described what happened, "design decisions were made on several hundred distinct points, for the most part by consensus and by simple majority vote when necessary. Except for two one-day face-to-face meetings, all of the language design and discussion was done through the ARPANET. . ." (Steele, 1984, p. xi). This example suggests that in evaluating the impact of technology on collaborative work we should not constrain our thinking to present-day versions of group interaction or collaborations. Whether someday ordinary members of organizations will be able to collaborate like the COMMON LISP developers did, is anybody's guess. As researchers, we should use our skills of observation to learn not only how technology affects old ways of working together, but also how it will stimulate new ways of doing so.

ACKNOWLEDGMENTS

The research reported in this paper was supported by the System Development Foundation, the National Science Foundation Graduate Fellowship program, and NSF Grant ASC8617695. The paper was written while Tom Finholt was a Research Intern, and Professors Sproull and Kiesler were Visiting Scientists, at the Xerox Palo Alto Research Center. Helpful comments were provided by Jolene Galegher, Bob Kraut, Pat Larkey, and Robyn Dawes. Special thanks to Treva Fombry, Michael Gallo, Laura Haburay, Erin McGinley, Drew Waegel, and Diane Watson who assisted with the transcription and content coding.

REFERENCES

Bavelas, A. (1948). A mathematical model for group structure. *Applied Anthropology, 7,* 16–30.

Bavelas, A. (1950). Communication patterns in task-oriented groups. *Journal of the Acoustical Society of America, 22,* 725–730.

Berger, J., Fisek, M. H., Norman, R. Z., & Zelditch, M. (1977). *Status characteristics and social interaction.* New York: Elsevier.

Blackwell, M. (1987). Electronic observations of computer user behavior. In Kiesler, S., & Sproull, L. (Eds.), *Computing and change on campus* (pp. 70–89). New York: Cambridge University Press.

Daft, R. L., & Lengel, R. H. (1986). Organizational information requirements, media richness and structural design. *Management Science, 32,* 554–571.

Davis, J. H., Kerr, N. L., Atkin, R. S., Holt, R., & Meek, D. (1975). The decision process of 6- and 12-person juries assigned unanimous and 2/3 majority rules. *Journal of Personality and Social Psychology, 32,* 1–14.

Diehl, M., & Stroebe, W. (1987). Productivity loss in brainstorming groups: Toward the solution of a riddle. *Journal of Personality and Social Psychology, 53,* 497–509.

Fienberg, S. E. (1980). *The analysis of cross-classified data.* Cambridge, MA: MIT Press.

Finholt, T., & Sproull, L. (1989). Electronic groups at work. *Organization Science.*

Georgeopolous, B. S., & Mann, F. C. (1962). *The community general hospital.* New York: Macmillan.

Hackman, J. R. (1987). The design of work teams. In Lorsch, J. (Ed.), *Handbook of organizational behavior* (pp. 315–342). Englewood Cliffs, NJ: Prentice-Hall.

Hackman, J. R., & Morris, C. G. (1975). Group tasks, group interaction process, and group performance effectiveness: A review and proposed integration. In L. Berkowitz, (Ed.), *Advances in experimental social psychology* (pp. 47–100). New York: Academic Press.

Hannaway, J. (1989). *Managers managing: The workings of an administrative system.* New York: Oxford University Press.

Huff, C. (1988). The online voyeur: Promises and pitfalls in the observation of electronic communication. Unpublished manuscript, Carnegie Mellon University, Pittsburgh.

Huff, C., Sproull, L. S., & Kiesler, S. (1988). Computer communication and organizational commitment: Tracing the relationship in a city government. *Journal of Applied Social Psychology,.*

Kennedy, J. J. (1983). *Analyzing qualitative data: Introductory log-linear analysis for behavioral research.* New York: Praeger.

Kraut, B., Galegher, J., & Egido, C. (1987–88). Relationships and tasks in scientific research collaboration. *Human Computer Interaction, 3,* 31–58.

Leavitt, H. J. (1951). Some effects of certain communication patterns on group. *Journal of Abnormal and Social Psychology, 46,* 38–50.

Mackay, W. (1988). More than just a communication system: Diversity in the use of electronic mail (p. 344–353). *Proceedings of CSCW '88, Portland, OR September 1988.* New York, ACM.

McCroskey, J. C. (1970). Special reports: Measure of communication-bound anxiety. *Speech Monographs, 37,* 269–277.

McGrath, J. E. (1984). *Groups: Interaction and performance.* Englewood Cliffs, NJ: Prentice-Hall.

Mowday, R. T. (1979). Measurement of organizational commitment. *Journal of Vocational Behavior, 14,* 224–247.

O'Reilly, C. A., & Roberts, K. H. (1976). Relationships among components of credibility and communication behavior in work. *Journal of Applied Psychology, 61,* 99–102.

Rohrbaugh, J. (1979). Improving the quality of group judgment: Social judgment analysis and the Delphi technique. *Organizational Behavior and Human Performance, 24,* 73–92.

Scott, W. A. (1955). Reliability of content analysis: the case of nominal scale coding. *Public Opinion Quarterly, 19,* 321–325.

Shaw, M. E. (1959). Some effects of individually prominent behavior upon group effectiveness and member satisfaction. *Journal of Abnormal and Social Psychology, 59,* 382–386.

Shaw, M. E. (1964). Communication networks. In Berkowitz, L. (Ed.), *Advances in experimental social psychology* (Vol. 1, pp. 111–149). New York: Academic Press.

Shaw, M. E. (1978). Communication networks 14 year later. In Berkowitz, L. (Ed.), *Group processes* (pp. 351–361). New York: Academic Press.

Siegel, J., Dubrovsky, V., Kiesler, S., & McGuire, T. (1986).Group processes in computer-mediated communication. *Organizational Behavior and Human Decision Processes, 37,* 157–187.

Sproull, L. S. (1986). Using electronic mail for data collection in organizational research. *Academy of Management Journal, 29,* 159–169.

Sproull, L. S. & Kiesler, S. (1986). Reducing social context cues: Electronic mail in organizational communication. *Management Science, 32,* 1492–1512.

Steele, G. L., Jr. (1984). *Common LISP: The language.* Bedford, MA: Digital Press.

Steiner, I. D. (1972). *Group process and productivity.* New York: Academic Press.

Yamgishi, T., & Sato, K. (1986). Motivational bases of the public-goods problem. *Journal of Personality and Social Psychology, 50,* 67–73.

Zimbardo, P. (1977). *Shyness: What it is, what to do about it.* Reading, MA: Addison-Wesley.

12

Voice Messaging, Coordination, and Communication

Ronald E. Rice
Rutgers University

Douglas E. Shook
University of Southern California

Abstract

What are the conditions under which users will take advantage of sophisticated communication systems to enhance their coordination and collaboration? Voice mail systems include both simple answering machine
functions and more sophisticated, communication-oriented features such
as sending messages directly or with a time delay to other users, forwarding messages, diverting on-going calls for later retrieval, and broadcasting
messages to a distribution list. This chapter examines voice mail use in
several divisions of a nationwide insurance company. Users report that
voice mail was useful for time-delayed communication and for retaining
affect in delayed communication. Workers used sophisticated communication features most in complex, nonroutine jobs. In more complex jobs, the
communication behavior of peers strongly influenced the degree to which
workers used voice mail, while in less complex, more routine jobs, the
communication behavior of one's supervisor predicted the use of voice
mail.

Day after day the corporate claims division of the nationwide insurance
company studied in this chapter must provide quick service, interpret ambiguous information, overcome obstacles such as telephone tag and scheduling meetings, as well as coordinate communication among members of
work units and between divisional boundaries and with large client organizations. This particular division handles inquiries and claims dealing with
policies in commercial areas (theft, fire, commercial auto, etc.). Internal and
external auditors assign claims according to the claimants' various policies.

The primary customers are the independent agents; however, some policyholders also call if a claim is pending. Telephone traffic is very heavy. The claims office uses two call sequencers, with four administrative assistants answering the calls in order after the sequencer releases the call (if the caller has not hung up by then; the average time on hold is 5.75 minutes). The assistants then relay messages to six outside adjusters. Supervisors also leave assignments for the adjusters through the assistants. The adjusters are required to call in twice a day for messages. When they do establish contact, which is not easy because often the lines are tied up by other adjusters calling in, they leave their phone number for customers to call with questions. However, adjusters generally have to gather information about a claim before they can answer. This preparation often requires in-depth research, involving a series of communications among supervisors, adjusters, and file processors, often to resolve questions and problems for which there are no clear policy answers. A supervisor may delegate a portion of this problem to one or more subordinates, and occasionally has to meet with the group working on the problem—perhaps even calling in the adjuster—to resolve particularly unclear issues.

As this example illustrates, many tasks facing large organizations demand a variety of individual talents and skills, involve multiple sequences of actions and decisions, and involve multiple departments or external organizations. Additionally, during basic research, new product development, initiation of new projects or approaches, and so forth, it is common for personnel to be organized around projects, or to work together on various portions of organizational tasks (Burgelman & Sayles, 1986; Katz & Tushman, 1979; Keller, 1986). Thus the abilities to exchange the right information, to communicate rapidly and effectively among several interdependent people, and to foster shared interpretations of ambiguous situations, are critical for effective group and organizational performance (Goodman & Abel, 1987). Thus much information work requires coordination and collaboration.

Computer-mediated communication systems, especially text-based systems such as electronic mail and computer conferencing, have gained a foothold in American organizations and have provided considerable opportunities for research (Hiltz & Turoff, 1978; Kiesler, Siegel, & McGuire, 1984; Rice, 1980, 1987; Rice & Associates, 1984). More complex, but less accessible, systems include group decision support systems, electronic blackboards, intelligent information retrieval systems, groupware systems, and other systems described in this book.

In this chapter, we consider how voice mail systems can facilitate coordination and collaboration of organizational work. We describe what voice mail is, its market, and its applications. We particularly distinguish between the use of voice mail for answering or messaging. Use of voice mail for its messaging capabilities, we argue, is not only best understood in the context of shared tasks and managerial coordination, but also is likely to foster greater communication benefits than its use only for voice answering. We therefore develop a theoretical model for assessing the influence of these contexts on the use of voice mail, and for predicting some of the potential communication outcomes of voice mail. We provide both qualitative and quantitative evidence of these relationships based on a longitudinal study in a multisite insurance organization, and discuss the implications of these results.

VOICE MAIL: DESCRIPTION, MARKET, AND APPLICATIONS

Many of the systems designed to support collaborative work are still in the prototype stage, or are still too expensive for wide diffusion. Many media are currently available, however, for maintaining interactive, location- or time-independent communications: cellular car phones, personalized answering services, voice mail, answering machines, beepers, and electronic mail. Related accessible applications include linking cellular telephones to voice mail, combining databases with voice mail via audiotex, and paging clients on the basis of voicemail calls (Ruprecht & Wagoner, 1986).

Voice mail (VM) is a computer-aided telephone system capable of storing and forwarding digitized spoken messages. VM systems combine computer storage and processing with the conventional abilities of a private branch exchange (PBC), a Centrex switch, or even a personal computer with an add-on board and large harddisk storage. Each user has a voice mailbox and an ID number. Users may record and send messages directly and asynchronously to another user's mailbox. Users may also store incoming messages for reference, forward messages to other users, record and store a message for future delivery, broadcast a single message to a number of users, trigger a "rollover" function that diverts conventional incoming calls from one's telephone extension into the voice mailbox, change the greeting message, control the volume and speed of messages, or use an on-line directory of names to find another user's voice mailbox. Due to its natural and accessible interface—the nearly ubiquitous touch-tone telephone—VM could have a wider appeal than text-based computer-mediated communication systems—which require users to have access to, and type on, computer terminals—for many applications.

VMX, Inc. installed the first major commercial VM system at 3M Corporation in May 1980. Approximately 500 systems were sold to U.S. businesses in 1984 (Henricks, 1985). By early 1985, 9 of the top 30 Fortune 500 companies used voice message systems (Matthews, 1985). At Eastman Kodak alone there are more than 16,000 users (Paznik, 1987). VM market revenues grew from approximately $30–50 million in 1983, to $300 million in 1985, and are expected to grow to $500 million in 1988 and $1 billion in 1990 (Chevreau, 1986; Crawford, 1986; Goldstein, 1986; Hafner, 1986; Kondo, 1985; Pollack, 1985). The market is particularly likely to pick up in the next few years because a Computer III inquiry ruling allows the local telephone operating companies to offer VM services (Moore, 1986).

VM systems offer a wide range of possible benefits and applications due to the reduction of constraints on traditional telephone communication—as well as other communication, such as staff meetings or memos (Beswick & Reinsch, 1987; Parker, 1987; Rice, 1987; Stewart, 1985). For example, consider the problem of telephone tag: only one in five land-to-mobile calls is typically connected on the first attempt; only one in four business calls is successfully completed on the first attempt (Fennel, 1986; Pfeiffer, 1986); three-quarters of telephone calls require only a one-way drop of information, whereas half of all calls contain content not related to the explicit purpose of the call (Town, 1983). Reinsch and Beswick (1988) found, based on telephone diaries kept by 350 employees for a week-long period prior to implementation of voice mail, that the respondents, on the first try, did not successfully complete 38% of their internal phone calls or 25% of external calls, and 32% of all their calls were repeat attempts or return calls.

While potentially reducing many of the problems associated with conventional telephone communication, VM, however, introduces some constraints of its own, such as technical incompatibility across systems, unanswered messages, inability to produce a written record, insufficient computer memory to store long messages or messages for long periods of time, security, incomplete adoption by a user population, and so forth.

This study analyzes how VM may support coordination and collaboration in organizational work. Central to our argument is the conceptual distinction between two categories of VM use:

Voice answering is the interception, receipt, and storage of messages until the receiver is prepared to hear them. In a VM system, this function occurs when an outside client calls intending to reach and talk to an organizational representative who is away from the telephone or busy. The VM system simply records the message, much like an answering machine. The intended receiver listens to the recording when convenient, and responds as appropriate, often by another telephone call or a memo. Telephone answering is particularly appropriate for organizational tasks characterized by (a) large or bursty call volumes, (b) fairly predictable messages, (c) the need to allocate some time for uninterrupted work to prepare for a return call, and (d) the need to capture relatively routine information without providing feedback. In the example that started this chapter, voice answering could resolve some of the problems such as leaving messages requesting information, assigning claims cases, and checking for clients' calls.

Voice messaging is the intentional use of the system for asynchronous communication, employing capabilities for processing the communication such as forwarding, distribution lists, prioritizing, speed browsing of messages, and so forth. Voice messaging is particularly appropriate for organizational tasks characterized by (a) exchanging information among a group of employees, (b) the involvement of persons who are hard to reach because they are mobile or work in different time zones or shifts, (c) broadcasting small amounts of information to many people, (d) requiring only asynchronous information exchange, perhaps in response only to another message, or (e) the need to store messages as reference material or for future delivery. Generally, voice messaging facilitates the coordination and management of complex or collaborative communication activities among a number of users. In the example, voice messaging could resolve some of the problems such as maintaining the customer's original explanation of the problem along with the supervisor's delegation of the task to several subordinates by distributing both in one message, or by a sequence of interactions among several employees that resolve an ambiguous policy decision but avoids having to schedule and wait for a meeting.

THEORETICAL FRAMEWORK FOR IDENTIFYING
INFLUENCES AND OUTCOMES OF VOICE MAIL USE

Although it would be simple to provide examples of VM uses for voice answering and voice messaging, we feel that it is more insightful to develop a theoretical framework that predicts the influences on VM use and on communication outcomes. Hypothesized relations supported by our empirical study may then be applied to other situations where computer-mediated communication systems may support coordination and collaboration.

Organizational Structure and Task Environments

The general theoretical foundation of the present research is contingency theory (Burns & Stalker, 1961; Galbraith, 1973; Lawrence & Lorsch, 1967; Perrow, 1972; Thompson, 1967; Woodward, 1956). Gutek's introductory chapter provides a rich and detailed review and critique of this theoretical approach, so we mention only those aspects most relevant to our analyses of VM use and outcomes. Contingency theory argues that organizational structure is, to a large degree, an artifact of the interaction of an organization's legal incorporation, markets, constraints, problems, technology, and environments. Environments create tasks that require the organization to process different amounts and kinds of information. Effective organizational performance depends on a good fit between the organization's structure, its processing and communication capabilities, and these task requirements.

An organization adapts its structure to environmental requirements by creating horizontally and vertically differentiated units.

Horizontal differentiation creates work units particularly well-suited for, or specialized in handling, a given set of tasks. To successfully meet task demands, individuals must communicate in concert with others performing similar or interdependent tasks that have similar information-processing requirements; appropriate structures bring these individuals together. Thus communication activities of others in an individual's work unit should in some way influence the individual's communication activities. Furthermore, before a communication medium or system can support the coordination of, or the interaction among, interdependent organizational workers, there must be a "critical mass" of users, that number of adopters that both increases the value of the system and reduces the costs of learning how to use the system sufficiently to motivate enough others to use the system so that all may perform their tasks (Markus, 1987; Rice, Grant, Schmitz, & Torobin, in press).

Vertical differentiation creates structures (i.e., the organizational hierarchy) that coordinate the various horizontally differentiated units, with supervisory-subordinate relations based on authority and responsibility as the basis for information flows both up and down the organization (Fayol, 1949). Insofar as superiors attempt to coordinate the work unit members through their communication activities, and insofar as subordinates have less discretion in choosing to respond or not, a superior's communication activities should directly influence the subordinate's communication activities.

Organizational task environments have been categorized into two primary dimensions: the relative number of exceptions to routine procedures one encounters during the performance of daily responsibilities, and, given these exceptions, the analyzability of the search for information necessary to cope with the exceptions (Perrow, 1972). As the number of exceptions increases, and as the analyzability of these exceptions decreases, the organization must increase its coordination of information and communication flows in order to perform well. Increased coordination of workflows may involve increased amounts of communication, but, more importantly for the present research, may require changes in the type and direction of communication.

In modern organizations, computer-based information systems are new ways to support this differentiation and coordination (Huber, 1984). With respect to VM, the distinction between increased amount and changed type of communication corresponds to the difference between voice answering and messaging.

Media Characteristics and Communication Tasks

The derived, and more specific, theoretical foundation of this study is the hypothesized relationship between media characteristics and task demands, known under the conceptual labels of social presence and information richness.

Until recently, the possibilities for communication channels have been categorized into (a) face-to-face or (b) mediated (typically meaning broadcast mass media such as radio, television, newspapers, and other print media). Although there has been some social science research on the use and impacts of the telephone (Pool, 1977; Short, Williams, & Christie, 1976), generally the telephone has not received much attention even though (and perhaps because) it lies on the boundary of these two categories.

Each communication channel within these two traditional categories operates under a broad range of constraints, such as the number and type of senses involved (vision, hearing, touch, etc.), whether users must use the medium simultaneously, be in the same place, need to know the exact address of a recipient, must use a sequence of different media, can send the same message to multiple people at the same time, can process the message (such as storing, forwarding, editing, retrieving), can access the medium from a variety of places, can obtain or provide rapid feedback, and so forth (Rice, 1987). With the convergence of computers and telecommunications, new media have reduced or created different patterns of constraints. The conventional telephone, for example, has an intermediate level of constraints, whereas computer-based VM has fewer constraints—in some ways fewer than face-to-face communication. So although VM is not face-to-face communication, it may have more potential for supporting coordination of organizational work than channels traditionally categorized as "mass media."

In spite of the potential reductions in communication constraints that new media may provide, some media theories tell us that the influence of any medium partially depends on how well the characteristics and constraints of the medium (such as VM) fit the task's information-processing and communication requirements (such as coordination). This fit is related to the extent to which a medium can convey *social presence* (Short, Williams, & Christie, 1976) or *information richness* (Daft & Lengel, 1986).

Social presence is the degree to which a communication medium conveys the actual physical presence of the participants communicating. Social presence is a perceived attribute of a medium that is dependent on the context of the communication as well as on the intrinsic characteristics of the medium. It is most frequently measured either by a set of semantic differentials (such as warm and cold, personal and impersonal, precise and ambiguous), or more explicitly, by statements about the appropriateness of different media for a range of common organizational communication tasks (such as exchanging information, resolving disagreements, or getting to know someone).

Daft and Lengel (1986) proposed that communication channels differ in the extent to which they are rich in information, that is, are able to bridge different frames of reference, make issues less ambiguous, or provide opportunities for learning in a given time interval, thus influencing task and organizational performance. They extend the question of task-medium fit to organizational hierarchies, arguing that because higher-level managers spend more time making strategic decisions and reducing equivocality from environmental inputs, they must use more information-rich media in order to perform well. Trevino, Lengel, and Daft (1987), for example, found that a small sample of managers reported that they would be more likely to use rich media such as face-to-face communication for low analyzable tasks, meetings and written memos for symbolic purposes (such as indicating an official communication), and information poor media such as electronic mail for overcoming situational constraints.

Channels high in social presence or information richness, such as face-to-face communication or video conferencing, can convey motion, distance, and paralinguistic cues, as well as denotative content. Channels such as a business memo or a computer printout are categorized as low in social presence or information richness. The telephone and electronic mail typically have been categorized as being somewhere in the middle of these continua (Rice & Love, 1987; Rice & Shook, 1990; Short et al, 1976, p. 71).[1] VM, because it provides both the cues of spoken communication with the processing and transmission capabilities of computer systems, may well provide both considerable information richness/social presence and the ability to overcome situational constraints. Thus, it may be quite appropriate for supporting coordination and collaboration, tasks that require sequences of interactions and may not be easily analyzed.

HYPOTHESES ABOUT RELATIONSHIPS AMONG VM USAGE, MEDIA CHARACTERISTICS, STRUCTURAL EFFECTS, AND TASK ENVIRONMENT

We attempt to assess the validity and utility of the theoretical model developed elsewhere by testing the following hypotheses:

---

[1]We should note that although the social presence literature has provided considerable empirical evidence, there has been little empirical testing in the information richness literature, despite considerable theoretical elaboration. One of the main contributions of the

VM and Media Characteristics

H1. VM can reduce situational constraints.

H2. VM can provide information rich communication.

VM, Structural Effects, and Task Environment

H3. VM can better support the coordination of organizational tasks when there is a critical mass of other users.

H4a. A work unit's use of VM will positively influence individual work unit members' use of VM (horizontal differentiation effect).

H4b This relationship will be stronger in less analyzable task environments.

H5a. A supervisor's VM usage will positively influence subordinates' usage (vertical differentiation effect).

H5b. This relationship will be stronger in less analyzable task environments.

VM, Outcomes and Task Environment

H6a. The use of VM will lead to an improved ability to distribute and to obtain information.

H6b. This relationship will be stronger in less analyzable task environments.

H6c. This relationship will be stronger when individuals use VM more for messaging than for answering.

H7. These relationships will occur when controlling for effects of innovativeness, hierarchical level, and organizational tenure (see Shook, 1988 for a full discussion of these influences; our purpose here is simply to control for these as alternative explanations).

Figure 12.1 portrays the relationships implied by hypotheses H4–H7.

SAMPLE AND SITE

A large insurance organization in the process of pilot testing a voice mail system provided the setting for the study. The sample included approximately 550 organizational members in sites at three cities who were tar-

---

present research is to provide a rigorous test of some of the implications of information richness theory.

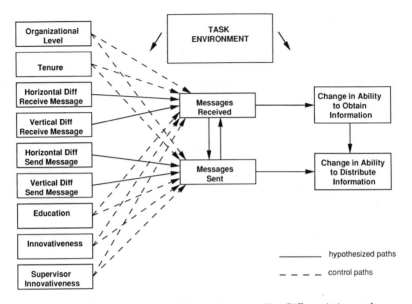

FIG. 12.1.   Theoretical Model of Voice Messaging Use, Differentiation, and Communication Performance. Higher Use of Messaging, and Greater Improvements in Dependent Variables, are Predicted for Less Analyzable Task Environments. Greater Improvements in Dependent Variables are Predicted for Those Who Use the System More for Messaging Than for Answering.

geted as potential users of the VM system and thus would receive voice mailboxes (accounts). Respondents included organizational members from all hierarchical levels and a wide variety of areas of expertise (e.g., sales, management, clerical, technical, legal services, administrators, etc.).

The initial rationale for this pilot VM implementation was to solve communication problems experienced by field agents who had difficulty contacting headquarters personnel who were often away from their desk. Twenty locations in the Northeast (out of the approximately 300 field office locations nationwide and the home office) were initially selected that involved some of the 10 applications previously identified as having communication needs appropriate for VM. Final sites and applications were selected on the basis of which applications they performed and their willingness to become involved in the pilot. They included: Claims processing, marketing, and employee benefits in one field office; marketing, two classes of claims processing, and administration in another field office; and corporate audit, litigation, telecommunications, and corporate technology planning in the home office.

The VM systems were not networked across the three cities, but all of the organization's buildings within a city location had access to the same system. Only a small portion of our respondents had access to an IBM PROFS system for electronic mail, but use was minimal. A dedicated telephone toll line existed between two of the locations, but inspection of the monthly telephone records kept on microfiche showed that the number of calls was negligible.

DATA COLLECTION AND MEASURES

Data collection included self-report questionnaires administered 1 month before (T1) and 5 months after (T2) implementation of the VM system, computer-monitored VM usage data collected weekly (see Rice & Borgman, 1983), archival information such as organizational charts, five focus groups consisting of five managers each (conducted during the end of the second data-collection period), and responses to open-ended questions on the questionnaires. The number of cases from the questionnaire data for each variable ranged from 227 to 326, except for two change-in-performance variables, with $N = 120$ cases in common between T1 and T2.

Questionnaire measures included (a) a standardized four-item scale measuring task analyzability (Withey, Daft, & Cooper, 1983), divided into high and low analyzable task environments by dichotomizing the scale at the mean; (b) change in two performance variables—ability to get information, and ability to distribute information—computed by subtracting responses at time 2 from responses at time 1; (c) a standardized 10-item individual innovativeness scale (Hurt, Joseph, & Cook, 1977); (d) simple ordinal measures used as indicators of organizational level according to a ranking provided by our organizational contact; (e) education; (f) tenure; (g) self-report measures of the number of messages sent and received per day; and (h) the percentage use of the system as an answering machine compared to usage of the system for voice messaging. Table 12.1 provides statistical descriptions and sample items for these measures.

Computer-monitored VM usage measures (based on 6,400 data points) were divided by the number of weeks (mean 12.5, minimum 2, maximum 21) since the respondent first used the system, and then normalized to enable use of parametric statistics. The quantitative analyses use only those respondents who had nonzero computer-monitored usage data.

To represent the influence of vertical differentiation in VM usage, we created two new variables for each subordinate that were equal to the number of (normalized) VM messages sent and received by the subordinate's superior.

We identified respondents as horizontally undifferentiated (members of a work unit) if they reported to the same superior. For the variables representing the influence of horizontal differentiation in VM usage, the means of

TABLE 12.1
Descriptive Statistics and Sample Items of Variables

Variable	M	S.D.	Cronbach's Alpha Reliability
Size of work units	4.7	3.1	
Mean task analyzability	2.9	.9	.79
sample items:			
"clear known ways to do work"			
"rely on established practices"			
from 1 (very little extent) to 5 (very great extent)			
Change in "able to get the information I need from others on time"	.4	1.6	
from 1 (strongly agree) to 7 (strongly disagree)			
Change in "can distribute information to groups of people quickly and easily"	.1	1.9	
from 1 (strongly agree) to 7 (strongly disagree)			
Innovativeness	5.6	.8	.81
sample items:			
"skeptical of new ideas"			
"challenged by ambiguities"			
from 1 (strongly agree) to 7 (strongly disagree)			
Organization level	3.7	2.0	
from 1 (management) to 7 (secretarial/clerical)			
Education	3.1	1.2	
from 1 (high school) to 5 (graduate school)			
Tenure	10.6	8.5	
years at the organization			
Percent use of VM for messaging	28%	33%	
Mean messages sent per day:			
484 voicemail box holders	1.1	3.2	
290 who ever used VM*	1.8	4.0	
Mean messages received per day:			
484 voicemail box holders	1.2	2.0	
290 who ever used VM*	1.5	3.2	
Self-reported voice messages sent and received per day	6.6	5.5	

*Although the mean computer-monitored usage appears low, even when just considering users, usage patterns are highly skewed: 190 of the 484 voice mailbox account holders never sent a message even though they may have received messages, and the maximum number of the two (normalized) VM variables for all subordinate members of a work unit were computed, then multiplied by the number of persons in the work unit. For each individual, the value of that individual's VM usage measure (messages sent and messages received) was subtracted from this product, and this difference was divided by $n - 1$. The resulting value measures average (normalized) VM usage within a user's horizontally differentiated work unit.

QUALITATIVE RESULTS

Overcoming Constraints

VM can overcome situational constraints inherent in using the telephone, which not only requires both communicators to use the medium at the same time, but also generally involves the transformation of the communication content across several media (such as writing a message slip, copying that to a calendar, mentioning the information to another person, writing the information onto a memo, calling back to confirm, etc.) (Rice & Bair, 1984). For example, the average call holding time in the example that began this chapter dropped from nearly 6 minutes to less than 1 minute after VM was implemented.

In response to the open-ended questionnaire item, "For what specific applications or opportunities could voice messaging be especially useful?", the two most common categories of responses were "During travel, lunch, breaks, after hours" ($N = 39$, 18.9%) and "Avoid telephone tag" ($N = 11$, 5.3%). Focus group comments provided other evidence of the ability of VM to overcome some communication constraints:

> "Well, before it was a real pain because you had to sit there and write, listen to the phone conversation and make your notes while you were doing that, then make your instruction notes and then sent them on. So we had to write all that stuff down."

messages sent per day was nearly 40. Furthermore, they are very similar to usage figures reported from other systems: (a) in an integrated voice and text system, 86 users who had been on the system for a year sent .4 voice messages/person/day (Nicholson, 1985); (b) 350 users who had been on a voice mail system for three months sent 1.3 messages/person/day (Reinsch & Beswick, 1988); and (c) in three companies reported by Paznik (1987), the number of messages sent per person per day (although based upon monthly figures) was approximately 1.4, and the number of messages received was 2.7.

"You bet. Hang on a minute. Pete, pick up on line one. If Pete's not there and I know that the case is going to go to him, I can record the message [with voice mail]. Hang on a minute, let me get the recorder on. I can record the message and then I can leave the recorded message to Pete's line."

"I like the group distribution system where my immediate staff's on it . . . instead of before, I had to dictate out an action slip to my secretary, she would have to type it out, she would have to get copies and then physically hand deliver these things."

With VM, one can avoid maintaining, indexing, and retrieving written messages, while using the timing function to place that information in a more meaningful context:

"Dick does a good job on his thing, just a quick four line message. I'd rather get it over the voice, through the phone, than have to read another daily memo and wade through ten piles of stuff to get to the memo that really means something to you . . . Yea, you just throw it on the floor and stuff it in your briefcase, and then you get home and you say, oh four hours ago."

"One of the biggest problems I have is handwritten notes all over the office and some aren't even on the desk, they get on the floor, in the file cabinets, filed away with someplace else, and you have no idea what you've been doing for the day. Being able to leave a message triggers what you called about and I really like that because at my age senility has set in."

Once the communication can be captured by voice mail, it then can be processed according to individual and organizational needs: "That concept of capturing information, you know, in voice, and then being able to move it around, is something that we've found to be really [valuable]."

Information Richness

A major concern in a service-oriented industry such as insurance is the need to maintain personal contact with customers. Therefore, the use of VM raises the question of whether the medium is sufficiently information-rich, say compared to face-to-face or even to the regular telephone with its real-time communication. Indeed, in response to the open-ended questionnaire item, "How might voice mail affect the company's relationship with customer or agents?", two relevant categories of response were "May create 'customer only a number' atmosphere" ($N = 39$, 19.2%), and "Impersonal, but efficient" ($N = 9$, 4.3%). However the second and third most frequent categories of response were "Customer relations improved; better contact" ($N = 15$, 7.2%) and general positive impacts ($N = 10$, 4.8%). With respect to internal use of VM, a typical initial response pointed out that communication is less rich if it is mediated, but that initial opinion can change: "In some cases, I physically see the person calling my mailbox, leaving a message, or I'm sitting in my office and, at first I would try to figure out the reasons why they don't like talking to me. But, after getting used to that, I found that it was a very effective means of communication."

VM can provide the information richness of audio communication as well as overcome constraints inherent in both face-to-face communication and other mediated communication such as written notes:

"So my responsibility right now is take the message, call Pat, or call whomever the contract is assigned to and say, okay, here's what they wanted, get back to them. Now the sense of urgency is gone because it's now a written message. It's no longer a telephone message. The sense of urgency has suddenly been degraded and they say, well I've got these other four things to do and all of a sudden, that answer may come out two or three days later. Because they didn't hear the guy, and as much as I may tell them, boy, he was pounding on his desk, I could hear him . . . But if I could do as John said, let me record this message . . . , and if I could at least record the message and I said, number one, listen to what this guy is saying, and not only Pat, but Mike or Vicky or whomever, and let them get the message."

". . . doing business is not just cold passing around of information, it's a sense of what's this person going to do, what's this person committed to? You know, what this person can buy, how's this person going to react to what we're doing here. That's how we do business."

Communication, Coordination, and Critical Mass

VM can support the management and coordination of work, through delegation of tasks, broadcasting of information, and timely handling of communication. In response to the open-ended questionnaire item, "What did you like best about using voice mail?", the most frequent category of response was "More information; better prepared for return call" ($N = 20$, 9%). Other relevant response categories were "Having 24-hour access" ($N = 11$, 5%), and "Higher rate of answered calls" ($N = 8$, 3.6%). Focus group participants elaborated:

"The ability to move messages is what's important. Especially me when I'm trying to run an organization from out of town.

Messages, yea. And what happens with the new work is that I can assign the new work from wherever I am by simply taking that telephone call that comes into me where somebody says I have a problem with my message, my set of instructions, and assign it to whomever is best qualified to handle the case without ever having to write anything down. And getting it done in a hurry."

"I think that transmittal of phone calls that come in, taking that message and being able to send it to another person and saying, here, this is for you, you should be handling this. This delegation thing that John was talking about. Saying, okay, this guy called about this [its] your area to handle, you handle it, then it's done, it's almost done now—you don't have to write it."

"And, quite frankly, some very successful implementations of voice messaging systems . . . are . . . not used in a telephone answering mode at all, but rather they're used to communicate information more quickly."

Respondents were quite explicit about the need for a critical mass of users to make the voice mail system more valuable, especially the messaging capabilities:

"If all the departments were on voice messaging and everybody was familiar with it and we had fluent use of it all the time, I could see easily that it should be able to cut down our acceptance of information and data and also our sending out the questions and information that we need in order to respond."

"Almost overnight, you get on the phone, you've got the group distribution list and all of your key contacts and your key departments and they know about them immediately and at least can start thinking about it even before they get some documentation in the mail."

"Rick, you pointed out that some of the key people you need to interact with aren't on the system, so therefore, you wind up using it as an answering service."

The increasing complexity of information work requires increased coordination, which VM can facilitate:

"Before proposal preparations got so complicated, you had to tap into the expertise of other departments, we used to do a lot more internally, but the business has gotten so complicated that we need to ask other people to help us out."

"Within our area, in development of proposals, insurance proposals, where a marketing strategy, there has to be constant communication both between the field office and within our unit. So, it's really in the exchange of information and communication, we use it as a true mailbox voice messaging service, not as an answering machine. And that's an important distinction."

"It's not the telephone tag of that external person trying to get hold of Rick or John, it's the telephone tag of your [representative] in Milwaukee trying to get hold of you or of your analyst down in the other department that doesn't know you're not at your desk cause you're in a meeting, needing to pass that information to help you get that account."

VM can be combined with other media to increase the ability to manage and coordinate work:

"It is not part of the session, but we've put cellular phones in each of their cars so that while they're traveling from one agent to another, they can ring up their mailbox, see how many messages they have. (Are you finding that they leave you messages like, this is what's happening in this agency, so you have a better sense of what's happening in their work, rather than just where they are?) Yea. No question about that."

QUANTITATIVE RESULTS

Overall Results

Shook (1988) provided detailed descriptions of items, scales, correlations, and tests of specific models. For the purposes of this chapter we simply describe the most relevant results of structural equations models based on the hypothesized model in Fig. 12.1, as tested by LISREL, a maximum-likelihood structural equation modeling program. We report results from the overall model, from separate models for high and low analyzable environments, and from separate models for high and low use of voice messaging (versus voice answering).

The overall model pictured in Fig. 12.1 had a nonsignificant chi-square statistic (28.85, $p = .26$), indicating that the associations proposed by the model were not significantly different from the observed associations. The adjusted goodness of fit index was .81, and the coefficient of determination was .87. The overall model explained from 60% to 79% of the variance in the two usage variables (sending and receiving voice messages), and nearly 40% of the variance in the two performance variables (change in distributing and obtaining information).

Horizontal differentiation was a strong and significant predictor of sending messages and a moderate predictor of receiving messages; number of messages sent by a respondent's work unit significantly predicted the numbers of messages sent by the respondent, and the same held for number of messages received.

Considering vertical differentiation effects, the influence of a superior's VM usage on the respondent's VM usage was significant, but reversed from the paths specified in the theoretical model presented in Fig. 12.1: number of messages sent by the superior predicted number of messages received by the subordinate, and number of messages received by the superior predicted number of messages sent by the subordinate. These results describe an organizational process of parallel communication within work units, but sequential communication across vertical differentiation as determined by the superior's communication activities.

Ignoring the structural effects, the number of messages a respondent sent weakly but significantly predicted the number of messages the respondent received, but receiving messages had no significant effect on sending messages.

The number of messages received significantly predicted the change in ability to obtain information, and indirectly predicted the change in reported ability to distribute information, through the number of messages sent. An improved ability to obtain information predicted an improved ability to distribute information.

With respect to the hypothesized control variables, lower organizational level directly predicted improved ability to obtain information. Innovativeness directly and positively predicted improved ability to obtain information, and positively predicted number of messages received, but negatively predicted number of messages sent. Supervisor's innovativeness negatively predicted number of messages sent. Education and tenure did not independently predict either number of messages sent or received or the two performance variables.

The Effect of Task Environment on the Relationships Between VM Usage and Performance

Different Usage in Different Task Environments

Separate analyses were performed for those individuals in positions with high task analyzability and those individuals with low task analyzability. Simple t-tests between low and high analyzable environments showed that voice messaging was used more heavily in less analyzable environments (33% compared to 23%, $p<.01$, $N = 252$). The number of computer-monitored voice messages sent per day was not significantly different, though higher (1.40 versus 1.17), whereas the number of voice messages received per day was significantly greater in low analyzable task environments (1.54 compared to 1.09, $p<.05$). Thus, in low analyzable task environments, respondents used VM more, and used it more for messaging.

Influences on Usage in Low Analyzable Task Environments

The average number of VM messages sent by one's workunit strongly predicted the number of messages sent by the respondent. The number of messages received by one's work unit also predicted the number of messages received by the respondent, but the relationship was less powerful. Higher education predicted the number of messages sent, and innovativeness predicted fewer number of messages received. Number of messages sent was a powerful predictor of number of messages received. Supervisor's usage (vertical differentiation effect) did not significantly affect a respondent's VM usage in this task environment. Approximately 70% of the variance in each VM use variable was explained by the model for low analyzable task environments.

Influences on Usage in High Analyzable Task Environments

The number of messages sent by one's supervisor (vertical differentiation effect) strongly predicted the number of messages received by the respondent. The number of messages sent by one's work unit predicted the number of messages sent by the respondent. Innovativeness also predicted number of messages sent. 76% of the variance in number of messages received, and 36% in number of messages sent, was explained by the model for high analyzable task environments.

Improved Ability to Obtain and to Distribute Information in Different Task Environments

Several models were used to examine differences between improved ability to obtain and distribute information in high and low analyzable task environments. As predicted, use of VM for messaging in high analyzable task environments did not predict changes in either ability. In line with our speculations about the fit of VM characteristics with task demands and potential benefits, using the system as an answering machine had no significant effect on changes in the ability to obtain or to distribute information. The use of VM for messaging, however, explained 23% of the improved ability to obtain information, and 26% of the improved ability to distribute information in low analyzable environments. Thus, when tasks require rich information or greater social presence because they are easily analyzable, the use of VM for messaging leads to improvements in the ability to get and distribute information. In more routine environments, the messaging capabilities of VM provide no additional benefits. Use of VM primarily for answering does not improve either of these communication activities.

DISCUSSION

Table 12.2 summarizes the results for the tests of the hypotheses. The qualitative analyses of open-ended questionnaire items and focus comments provided specific comments to reinforce the commonsense percep-

TABLE 12.2
Summary Results of Hypotheses

VM and Media Characteristics:	
H1. VM can reduce situational constraints.	Supported
H2. VM can provide information rich communication.	Supported
VM, Structural Effects, and Task Environment:	
H3. VM can better support the coordination of organizational tasks when there is a critical mass of other users.	Supported
H4a. A work unit's use of VM will positively influence individual work unit members' use of VM (horizontal differentiation effect).	Supported
H4b. This relationship will be stronger in less analyzable task environments.	Supported
H5a. A supervisor's VM usage will positively influence subordinates' usage (vertical differentiation effect).	Supported, but sequential effect
H5b. This relationship will be stronger in less analyzable task environments.	Not Supported; reversed
VM, Outcomes and Task Environment:	
H6a. The use of VM will lead to an improved ability to distribute and to obtain information.	Supported
H6b. This relationship will be stronger in less analyzable task environments.	Supported
H6c. This relationship will be stronger when individuals use VM more for messaging than for answering.	Supported
H7. These relationships will occur when controlling for effects of innovativeness, hierarchical level, and organizational tenure.	Supported; some effects of control variables

tion that VM can overcome constraints inherent in both mediated and interpersonal organizational communication. These constraints are particularly critical when tasks require coordination in the form of sequenced and timely communication among several individuals. The comments also showed that although there is particular concern that general use of voice mail may be too impersonal with respect to external customers, it can be used to great advantage in serving external clients when applied wisely. Furthermore, with increased experience and awareness of the proper use of VM internally, concerns about impersonalness decrease. Much more in evidence was the awareness that the typical alternatives—written memos, phone messages, or having the problem handled by someone not completely informed—are less rich means of communicating. VM can be used to maintain personal cues even though the process is asynchronous. Finally, the comments provided clear indications of the ways in which VM, especially messaging, can support management and coordination of work, such as through delegation, broadcasting, monitoring, and increased awareness of a project's progress. However, a critical mass of individuals involved in the coordinated task (such as processing a proposal) must have accounts on the VM system.

With respect to the quantitative analyses, the LISREL model for low analyzable environments best represents the theoretical model depicted in Fig. 12.1. Vertical differentiation (supervisor's VM usage) and horizontal differentiation (the average VM usage by one's work unit) strongly influences one's number of VM messages sent and received. Use of VM then directly predicts improved abilities both to obtain and to distribute information.

More general efforts to understand how and why individuals use different media in organizations may well be handicapped unless they consider both the task environment and influences of horizontal and vertical differentiation. Unless they take into account the extent to which tasks may require coordination and work unit communication, researchers may miss some of the contexts and consequences of intellectual technology. The power and parsimony of a structural approach, informed by theories of organizational contingency and media characteristics, is preferable to models dependent solely on an individual-level of analysis, and is theoretically appropriate for the study of coordination and collaboration of organizational work across different task environments. As a side note, using computer-monitored data provides highly reliable, and diverse, measures of communication system usage.

The number of VM messages sent influences the number of VM messages received, but not vice-versa, indicating that system usage generally is proactive. Users may often send messages to request information. This association could help explain the much stronger relationship between receiving messages and improved ability to obtain information, than between sending messages and improved ability to distribute information (primarily in low analyzable task environments). That is, obtaining information to conduct one's task or to coordinate tasks within a work unit is probably more important than distributing information. Regardless of task environment, use of VM for messaging rather than answering established a context for a significant positive relation between sending or receiving messages and improved communication.

Although horizontal differentiation is generally a strong predictor of the use of voice messaging, it is an even more powerful determinant in less analyzable environments, where VM is hypothesized to offer greater potential benefit because of its combination of greater social presence or information richness than written messages, and because it can overcome a variety of constraints to coordination and collaboration inherent in telephone or even face-to-face communication. However, system usage by the other members of an individual's horizontally differentiated work unit does not universally determine that individual's use of VM. VM usage by the work unit had no direct effect on receiving messages in high analyzable task environments, where information richness theory indicates that richer media should have no special advantage for performance. For the work unit to influence media usage, tasks should require or potentially benefit from characteristics of the media—in this case, where tasks require coordination and collaboration among work unit members to resolve communication problems of low analyzability.

Based on the preceding observations, a somewhat subjective scenario follows. VM is used asynchronously to request information from others within horizontally differentiated work units and across vertically differentiated organizational levels. The information returned may be in the form of a voice message, or in other more conventional forms (e.g., synchronous phone call, memo, etc.). The communication is more likely sequential, and initiated by the supervisor, in vertical relationships. The returned message increases one's ability to obtain information that, in turn, leads ultimately to an increased ability to distribute information. Due to the need for coordination and collaboration to establish common interpretations and shared information in low analyzable task environments, an ability to subsequently distribute information, perhaps to delegate a task to a set of subordinates or to integrate work unit liaisons, is highly salient.

One practical implication of these findings is that VM can apparently support tasks needing coordination, particularly in less analyzable task requirements. A related implication is that implementors should distinguish between voice answering and voice messaging, and encourage organizational members of the potential of messaging capabilities. Voice mail has great potential as a common, accessible communication tool, contingent on organizational structural factors and task requirements.

REFERENCES

Beswick, R., & Reinsch, N., Jr. (1987). Attitudinal responses to voice mail. *The Journal of Business Communication, 24*(3), 23–25.

Burgelman, R., & Sayles, L. (1986). *Inside corporate innovation: Strategy, structure, and managerial skills.* New York: Free Press.

Burns, T., & Stalker, G. (1961). *Management of innovation.* London: Tavistock Publications.

Chevreau, J. (1986). Voice technology gets vocal. *Canadian Datasystems, 18*(3), 76–79.

Crawford, D. (1986). New face of finance; All talk and action. *Wall Street Computer Review, 3* (11), 40–48.

Daft, R., & Lengel, R. (1986). Organizational information requirements, media richness, and structural design. *Management Science, 32*(5), 554–571.

Fayol, H. (1949). *General industrial management.* London: Pittman.

Fennel, K. (1986). Electronic mail: Putting the tag on phones. *ComputerData, 11*(10), 15.

Galbraith, J. (1973). *Designing complex organizations.* Reading, MA: Addison-Wesley.

Goldstein, M. (1986). Send a message, now! *Industry Week, 230*(2), 43–46.

Goodman, G., & Abel, M. (1987). Communication and collaboration: Facilitating cooperative work through communication. *Office: Technology and People, 3,* 129–146.

Hafner, K. (1986). Hello voice mail, goodbye message slips. *Business Week, 2951,* 80.

Henricks, M. (1985). Miraculous messaging. *Dun's Business Month, 125*(1), 90, 92.

Hiltz, S. R. & Turoff, M. (1978). *The network nation.* Menlo Park, CA: Addison-Wesley.

Huber, G. (1984). The nature and design of post-industrial organizations. *Management Science, 30*(8), 928–951.

Hurt, H., Joseph, K., & Cook, C. (1977). Scales for the measurement of innovativeness. *Human Communication Research, 4*(1), 58–65.

Katz, R., & Tushman, M. (1979). Communication patterns, project performance, and task characteristics: An empirical evaluation in an R&D setting. *Organizational Behavior and Human Performance, 23,* 139–162.

Keller, R. (1986). Predictors of the performance of project groups in R&D organizations. *Academy of Management Journal, 29,* 715–726.

Kiesler, S., Siegel, J., & McGuire, T. (1984). Social psychological aspects of computer-mediated communication. *American Psychologist,* October, 1123–1134.

Kondo, D. (1985). Voice mail system service and maintenance: What's hot, what's not. *Communication Age, 2*(2), 30–32.

Lawrence, P., & Lorsch, J. (1967). *Organization and environment: Managing differentiation and integration.* Boston: Graduate School of Business Administration, Harvard University.

Markus, M. L. (1987). Toward a critical mass theory of interactive media: Universal access, interdependence and diffusion. *Communication Research, 14,* 491–511.

Matthews, G. (1985). Bright future for corporate communications. *Telecommunication Products and Technology, 3*(6), 66, 68.

Moore, I. (1986). Cellular carriers to reap VS&F benefits. *Telephone Engineer and Management, 90*(15), 61–63.

Nicholson, R. (1985). Usage patterns in an integrated voice and data communications system. *ACM Transactions on Office Information Systems, 3*(3), 307–314.

Parker, M. (1987). *The practical guide to voice mail.* New York: McGraw-Hill.

Paznik, J. (1987). Voice mail: Pitfalls and promises. *Administrative Management,* March, 16–25.

Perrow, C. (1972). *Complex organizations: A critical essay.* Glenview, IL: Scott, Foresman.

Pfeiffer, G. (1986). A special delivery message for cellular. *Cellular Business, 3*(11), 16–24.

Pollack, B. (1985). Using voice mail is a easy as telephoning. *Management Technology, 2*(12), 10–14.

Pool, I. (1977). *The social impact of the telephone.* Cambridge, MA: MIT Press.

Reinsch, N., Jr., & Beswick, R. (1988). *Initial effects of voice mail: An abstract.* Paper presented to the Office Systems Research Association, Denver, CO.

Rice, R. E. (1980). Impacts of organizational and interpersonal computer-mediated communication. In Williams, M. (Ed.), *Annual review of information science and technology* (Vol. 15, pp. 221–249). White Plains, NY: Knowledge Industry Publications.

Rice, R. E. (1987). Computer-mediated communication systems and organizational innovation. *Journal of Communication, 37*(4), 65–94.

Rice, R. E., & Associates. (1984). *The new media: Communication, research and technology.* Beverly Hills, CA: Sage Publications.

Rice, R. E., & Bair, J. (1984). New organizational media and productivity. In R. E. Rice & Associates, *The new media: Communication, research and technology* (pp. 185–215). Newbury Park, CA: Sage Publications.

Rice, R. E., & Borgman, C. (1983). The use of computer-monitored data in information science and communication research. *Journal of the American Society for Information Science, 34,* 247–256.

Rice, R. E., Grant, A., Schmitz, J., & Torobin, J. (in press). Individual and network influences on the adoption and perceived outcomes of electronic messaging. *Social Networks.*

Rice, R. E., & Love, G. (1987). Electronic emotion: A content and network analysis of a computer-mediated communication network. *Communication Research, 14*(1), 85–108.

Rice, R. E., & Shook, D. (1990). Relationships of job categories and organizational levels to use of communication channels, including electronic mail: A meta-analysis and extension. *Journal of Management Studies, 27*(3).

Rice, R. E., & Shook, D. (1988). Usage of, access to, and outcomes from an electronic messaging systems. *ACM Transactions on Information Systems, 6,* 255–276.

Ruprecht, M., & Wagoner, K. (1986). Technological advances in the office of the future. *Modern Office Technology, 31*(5), 16–22.

Shook, D. (1988). *A structural equivalence and contingency theory perspective on media usage and communication performance: The case of voice messaging.* Unpublished doctoral dissertation, University of Southern California.

Short, J., Williams, E., & Christie, B. (1976). *The social psychology of telecommunications.* London: Wiley.

Stewart, C. (1985). *Voice messaging: An annotated bibliography of the literature.* Working Paper 85-02. Piscataway, NJ: AT&T Communications Technology and Productivity Research Center.

Thompson, J. (1967). *Organizations in action.* New York: McGraw-Hill.

Town, R. (1983). Voice store and forward, its evolution. *Interface '83 Proceedings, 11th Annual Interface Meeting, Miami Beach.* New York: McGraw-Hill.

Trevino, L., Lengel, R., & Daft, R. (1987). Media symbolism, media richness and media choice in organizations: A symbolic interactionist perspective. *Communication Research, 14*(5), 553–575.

Withey, M., Daft, R., & Cooper, W. (1983). Measures of Perrow's work unit technology: An empirical assessment and a new scale. *Academy of Management Journal, 26,* 45–63.

Woodward, J. (1956). *Industrial organization: Theory and practice.* London: Oxford University Press.

Teleconferencing as a Technology to Support Cooperative Work: Its Possibilities and Limitations

Carmen Egido
Bell Communications Research

Abstract

Teleconferencing systems and services are the main set of technologies developed thus far to support group work. Within this set of technologies, videoconferencing is often thought of as a new, futuristic communication mode that lies between the telephone call and the face-to-face meeting. In fact, videoconferencing has been commercially available for almost three decades. During this time, teleconferencing expectations in general have failed to realize themselves fully despite consistently brilliant market forecasts. Teleconferencing as a substitute for face-to-face meetings appears not to suffice. Furthermore, it is not the cure for ever-escalating business travel costs. Research and speculation about the lack of success of these technologies in the marketplace point to a variety of factors that lie beyond the scope of economic and technological analysis. This chapter reviews and analyzes existing literature that addresses these issues, particularly with respect to videoconferencing. In reviewing the teleconferencing experience we may draw from the many lessons it offers to avoid analogous pitfalls in the conception of other new technologies to support group work.

Teleconferencing is the use of electronic telecommunications to enable people to meet in spite of physical separation. Although it is often thought of as a new, futuristic telecommunication service, the concept is by no means a novel one. Taken to the extreme, it might be considered as old as the telephone, because, after all, a simple phone call constitutes an example of a teleconference. Even more narrowly defined to include more parties and/or communications media such as video and graphics, teleconferencing has been around for almost 3 decades. But over this time teleconferencing has failed to become much more than a revolutionary concept on the brink of success.

On the surface, the rationale behind teleconferencing, particularly video teleconferencing seems sound enough. Intuitively, it would seem that a video conference is the closest thing to "being there." Furthermore, there is solid justification in terms of "hard dollar" savings brought about by the potential reduction, if not elimination, of travel costs. However, there is increasing evidence that teleconferencing is not the communication mode that lies between the telephone call and the face-to-face meeting, and there are few examples of travel substitution directly attributable to teleconferencing. Furthermore, it is becoming increasingly clear that the success of these technologies is much more dependent on the nature of the application for which it is introduced than on system details or features.

Thus, the industry that developed around the teleconferencing concept in response to unanimously optimistic market forecasts of spectacular growth is facing dismal failure. In contrast to forecasts of the early 1970s, which predicted that a full 85% of all meetings would be electronically mediated by the end of that decade (Snyder, 1971), are current statistics that report that the number of videoteleconferencing facilities in existence worldwide amount to about 100 (including installations associated with teleconferencing vendors and telecommunications companies) (Beckmann, Ehlinger, & Macchia, 1985; Johansen, 1984; Noll, 1985; Tyson, 1987). Thus, teleconferencing, particularly videoconferencing, has become a synonym for marketing disaster, perhaps displaced only by the Coca-Cola fiasco of 1985. Curiously, however, predictions of large markets continue to emerge (Bohm & Templeton 1984; Frost & Sullivan, 1983; Lineback, 1982; Showker, 1982), and vendors continue to proclaim the virtues of teleconferencing at (face-to-face) conferences, seminars, and trade conventions.

There is already a substantial body of work, both systematic and speculative, aimed at analyzing the factors contributing to the failure of teleconferencing from a variety of standpoints. However, only recently has it become apparent that these factors lie beyond the scope of technological and economic analysis and include psychological and sociological factors. This chapter examples and reviews some of this work with a view toward understanding the discrepancy between the continuing optimism of marketing expectations and the current state of the industry. It is argued that the casting of electronic communication in the image of formal face-to-face meetings stands in the way of developing teleconferencing media to their fullest potential. At the very least, some basic assumptions about the role that teleconferencing is best suited to play are in need of reevaluation in light of what we know about how people work together.

After presenting an overview of teleconferencing media, this chapter focuses on some of the factors that have contributed to the general lack of success of these media. It then reviews the results of various studies aimed at evaluating video as a communications channel. Finally, the last two sections discuss the likely avenues for the success of videoconferencing, current trends toward office rather than conference room teleconferencing, and some factors that may potentially influence the acceptance of teleconferencing in general. In reviewing the teleconferencing experience, we may draw from the many lessons it offers to avoid analogous pitfalls in the conception of other new technologies to support group work.

OVERVIEW OF TELECONFERENCING MEDIA

Video Teleconferencing

The idea of providing video as a communications medium originated in the 1920s at Bell Laboratories. In those days television was conceived as an adjunct to the telephone. The first landmark demonstrations of television in 1927 and 1929 were demonstrations of a new point-to-point telecommunications medium, not of a broadcast medium as we know it today (Ives, 1930). At that time, television as a communications technology was clearly ahead of its time because available transmission facilities were not adequate to support the use of this technology.

Video teleconferencing dates back over 30 years. It was then intended to support large corporate meetings such as annual stockholders' meetings. Companies typically contracted with the Bell system for transmission facilities and television production organizations to supply cameras, microphones, and props, as well as video monitors and audio equipment at the receiving locations. Video teleconferencing was used only occasionally except by AT&T itself, who did not have to be concerned with the high cost of leasing terrestrial microwave facilities or establishing private microwave networks. The perceived success of AT&T corporate video teleconferencing meetings prompted the revival of the concept of point-to-point video communications through the development of the Picturephone.

Picturephone did not require the communication capacity of an NTSC television signal, which utilizes the same capacity in a microwave system as 1,800 analog telephone circuits. Rather, the 1 MHz of bandwidth needed to carry the Picturephone image could be transmitted over just three equalized twisted-pair wires. The bandwidth limitations of this system, however, precluded the reproduction of motion and fine detail (e.g., printed text).

In spite of these limitations, early market forecasts for the "picture telephone," first introduced publicly at the 1964 World Fair, were extremely enthusiastic. At that time it was predicted that replacement of the standard voice telephone by the picture telephone would take place by the early 1970s. Julius P. Molnar, executive vice-president of Bell Laboratories wrote in a special issue of *Bell Laboratories Record* (1969) devoted to the Picturephone:

> Rarely does an individual or an organization have an opportunity to create something of broad utility that will enrich the daily lives of everybody. Alexander Graham Bell with his invention of the telephone in 1876, and the various people who subsequently developed it for general use, perceived such an opportunity and exploited it for the great benefit of society. Today there stands before us an opportunity of equal magnitude—Picturephone service.

He continued in another article of the same issue:

> Most people when first confronted with Picturephone seem to imagine that they will use it mainly to display objects or written matter, or they are very much concerned with how they will appear on the screen of the called party. These reactions are only natural, but they also indicate how difficult it is to predict the way people will respond to something new and different. Those of us who have had the good fortune to use Picturephone regularly in our daily communications find that although it is useful for displaying objects or written matter, its chief value is the face-to-face mode of communication it makes possible. Once the novelty wears off and one can use Picturephone without being self-conscious, he senses in his conversation an enhanced feeling of proximity and intimacy with the other party. The unconscious response that party makes to a remark by breaking into a smile, or by dropping his jaw, or by not responding at all, adds a definite though indescribable "extra" to the communication process. Regular users of Picturephone over the network between the Bell Laboratories and AT&T's headquarters building have agreed that conversations over Picturephone convey much important information over and above that carried by the voice alone. Clearly, "the next best thing to being there" is going to be a Picturephone call. (Excerpt quoted by Martin, 1977, pp. 116–117)

But this enthusiasm met with disturbing reports of phenomena such as users' feelings of instant dislike toward parties they had never seen before, self-consciousness about "being on TV" (aggravated by distortions created by the camera's sensitivity to the infrared part of the spectrum), and resulting low acceptance. A special issue of the *London Economist* (1969) devoted to telecommunications talked about the Picturephone as "a social embarrassment" and describes conversing over it as "talking to a mentally defective foreigner."

Picturephone never really took off for a combination of reasons, including its cost and limited functional capability. Nevertheless, in the early 1970s attention shifted back to the related concept of video teleconferencing. Rising business travel costs spurred on the idea that most business meetings could be conducted over two-way television or similar systems.

A large number of demand modeling and attitude survey studies conducted in the early 1970s concluded that a large share of the total volume of business meetings are candidates for electronic mediation. Among the best known of the demand modeling studies are those performed by the Long Range Studies Division of British Telecom (see Harkness, 1973). Using trip data from a sample of 1,000 business meetings in the UK, these studies calculated that 41% of all business meetings involving travel could be conducted over narrowband teleconferencing systems with no loss of "effectiveness." The addition of a visual channel could accommodate another 9%. Paralleling these demand modeling studies, early attitude surveys also painted a rosy future for teleconferencing systems, particularly those that provide a visual channel. For instance, Snyder (1971) surveyed over 3,000 Bell Laboratories employees and found that 85% would be satisfied with a system that included audio and video for faces and graphics.

The sociopolitical climate of the early 1970s also stimulated much research and development effort on the topic of teleconferencing. Two major sources of concern heightened the interest in telecommunications technologies in general. The first of these was the deterioration of the quality of city life. Staggering crime statistics, poverty, disease, and violence were seen as products of high population density. The solution to the problem was envisioned as population dispersion into rural areas, with telecommunications as the means to that end (Goldmark, 1972a, 1972b).

The second factor contributing to the interest in telecommunications was the rising cost of long distance travel. Awareness of this factor was made distinctly acute by the energy crises of the 1970s. Separate studies conducted by AT&T, Coopers and Lybrand, Inc. (reported in Bohm & Templeton, 1984), and others done in the UK and Canada (reported by Kraemer, 1982) estimated that 75% of business travel is to meetings and 60% of these (45% of the total) are intracompany. Therefore, the Long Range Studies results previously mentioned could be translated as a total travel substitution level between 20%–30%. In terms of energy savings, Dickson and Bowers (1973) calculated that the energy expended in traveling by air is sufficient for 64 hours of videophone conversation between New York and California, and one gallon of gasoline contains enough energy to support 66 hours of local video connection.

Not surprisingly, the potential for substituting various forms of telework (neighborhood work centers, remote data terminals, teleconferencing) for intracity travel, and various forms of teleconferencing (audio, video, computer) for intercity travel became the subject of national and international policy discussions, with research peaking during 1972–1976 (Kraemer, 1982). Although the concept of a new dispersed rural society (Goldmark, 1972a, 1972b) did not materialize (urban renewal and suburbanization became the prevalent trends), enough impetus remained for teleconferencing on the basis of travel/energy substitution alone.

However, in spite of brilliant market forecasts, with rosy demand models and attitude surveys to back them, and the appearance of great activity generated by the flurry of (face-to-face) conferences, seminars, demos, and articles about teleconferencing, the 1984 installed base of videoconferencing systems was pitifully small. A recent estimate counts 210 systems in the United States, spread over some 75 companies, including telephone companies and videoconferencing system vendors who have an obvious interest in the technology (Tyson, 1987; see also Beckmann, Ehlinger, & Macchia, 1985; Johansen, 1984 for older but comparable estimates). Furthermore, as of January 1985, AT&T had closed down over half of its national conference rooms (Nelson, 1985).

Other Teleconferencing Media

Although the main focus of this chapter is video teleconferencing, it is worthwhile to briefly review alternative methods of teleconferencing. Aside from full and reduced motion video, there are several other teleconferencing media: computer, audio, and audiographic. The broad range of system subcomponents that provide these different communication modes can be mixed and matched into a myriad of distinct configurations. Few if any technical standards exist, particularly for videoconferencing technologies. As a result, some interested customers are paralyzed by the bewildering choice of teleconferencing formulas, and are choosing not to make purchase decisions until either the industry gravitates toward a uniform set of standards or there are enough system reviews to allow more informed decisions (Johansen, 1984).

Computer Conferencing

Computer conferencing stands in a class of its own among teleconferencing modes in that (a) it permits asynchronous (time shifted) communication, and (b) it relies on the written rather than the spoken word. It differs from electronic mail/messaging in that it provides shared files. Thus, computer conferencing users can read, modify, or otherwise contribute to a "dynamic" text file available to all participants. Multiple threads to a discussion may appear and lead to confusion because there is usually no organized way of turn-taking. (Johansen, Vallee, & Spangler, 1979). Computer conference meetings may be held over long periods of time, with participants making contributions in their own time. In addition, users are not restricted to any location (e.g., the confines of a meeting room); that is, conference material may be retrieved at home or while traveling. All correspondence may be stored as document files, and later edited and processed like any other computer files. In particular, it can easily be transformed into hard-copy records.

Another advantage of computer conferencing is its low cost. It does not require prime-time transmission facilities, and, furthermore, it may require minimal or no hardware expenditures because it may be compatible with equipment already in place for other purposes. Moreover, conferencing systems do not require any special meeting skills. In fact, some higher level managers use typists or secretaries to enter and retrieve conference material (Bohm, 1984).

Considerable research exits on computer conferencing, its evolution, uses, impacts on organizations, and cognitive implications. Among the most notable papers and books on the subject are those by Hiltz (1983), Hiltz and Turoff (1978, 1981), Kiesler, Siegel, and Maguire (1982), and Rice (1984, for a comprehensive review). These and other researchers have described a number of salient characteristics of the electronic print medium that offer various advantages and disadvantages for organizational interaction. First, due to speed limits imposed by the mechanics of computer conferencing, it takes longer to transmit a given amount of information via this medium than verbally (Johansen et al., 1979; Krueger & Chapanis, 1980; Hiltz & Turoff, 1978). Depending on deadline constraints, the communication delay introduced by this medium may, obviously, translate into either an advantage or a disadvantage. The printed medium also conveys less "social presence" and fewer affective cues (Short, Williams, & Christie, 1976). The impact of the reduction of human communication codes transmitted is controversial. For instance, some researchers have argued that removing affective cues enhances decision making by obscuring irrelevant factors such as physical attributes, status, and so forth (Jablin & Sussman, 1978), thereby reducing "groupthink" (Janis, 1972), and generally allowing "cooler," more rational discussions. On the other hand, others claim that removal of social and affective cues can give rise to (negative) emotional disinhibition rather than rationality during decision making (Barefoot & Strickland, 1982; Kiesler, Siegel, & Maguire, 1982; Hiltz, 1983), and nonverbal communication and social interaction of the type that occurs in elevators or at the coffee machine aids the transmission of implicit goals, values, and contextual clues.

But these two seemingly contradictory positions are in fact compatible if one considers differences in the spectrum of communicative tasks/objectives and their manifestation in meetings. Different applications (communicative tasks) are more or less amenable to computer mediation. For exam-

ple, routine communication (e.g., technical librarians sharing book purchase information to ensure complementary acquisitions) seems to benefit
from electronic mediation, whereas nonroutine communication tasks, e.g.,
handling crises, personal affairs, or issues with a high degree of uncertainty)
seem to lend themselves less well to formalized computer conferencing
procedures, and require shorter time frames and a different kind of organizational effort than this medium can provide (Kiesler et al., 1982).

Computer conferencing is currently popular among professionals who
use computers as work tools (Svenning & Ruchinskas, 1984). Judging from
the overwhelming success of electronic mail, there is good potential for
increased computer conferencing usage in the future (Steinfield, 1983).
Also, the growth of data networks and computer facilities, as well as the
increasing number of personnel with computer skills, may provide additional impetus for its future success (Rice, 1984).

Audio Teleconferencing

Audio teleconferencing is the most widely used and most familiar teleconferencing mode. In its simplest form, it involves using speakerphones at
different locations to allow group participation or using the three-way calling feature provided by current switching systems. In its more complex
forms, it involves dial-up arrangements through a telephone company operator or sophisticated bridging equipment at a central site to connect conferees into a "meet-me" style audio teleconference. Olgren and Parker
(1983) reported that 44% of regular business audio teleconferencing users
employ dial-up conferencing and 37% use meet-me bridging. The remaining 19% use only three-way calling and/or speakerphones (reported in
Svenning & Ruchinskas, 1984).

The ubiquitous availability of the telephone (over 400 million world-
wide as of 1983) contributes to audio conferencing its major strength. In
part because a special teleconferencing room is not necessary, audio teleconferences are cheap and easy to arrange with little notice or preparation.

However, audio teleconferences are limited in that sharing documents or
other graphic materials is difficult. Furthermore, for conferences involving
more than four or five participants, speaker order, speaker identification,
and sound quality also become serious problems (Chapanis, 1976).

Audiographic Teleconferencing

Audiographic teleconferencing is the second most popular and the fast-
est growing teleconferencing method (Bohm, 1984). Audiographic systems
can incorporate a wide range of devices that allow transmission of visual
materials over ordinary telephone lines, including telewriting devices (tab-
lets or electronic blackboards), facsimile machines, and remote slide pro-

jectors. The introduction of visual support for audio interactions drives audiographic meetings into specially designed rooms, but these are less complex and costly than those typically required for video teleconferencing. According to Olgren and Parker (1983), such systems are primarily used for operational-level meetings, such as project management and coordination meetings, staff meetings, technical presentations, and information updates.

FACTORS CONTRIBUTING TO THE FAILURE
OF VIDEOCONFERENCING

An analysis of teleconferencing and related literature points to two broad factors responsible for the discrepancy between videoconferencing market forecasts and current realizations. First, consider the inadequacy of needs assessment methodologies. Second, consider the questionable portrayal of videoconferencing as a direct replacement for face-to-face meetings. As we shall see later, the most successful videoconferencing systems currently in place depart significantly from this notion. These two factors are at least in part responsible for the unsuccessful marketing strategies used by teleconferencing vendors. As it turns out, many of the sales points used to encourage purchase decisions are the very points that militate against system usage.

The appropriateness of available methods for technology needs assessment has been questioned in the past (Elton & Carey, 1979; Short, Williams, & Christie, 1976). With respect to teleconferencing, the methodology is suspect on several counts. First of all, the results of surveys of potential users show wild variability that cannot be wholly attributed to experimental error or sampling population differences. For instance, although the Snyder (1971) study mentioned earlier predicted a potential 85% substitution of face-to-face meetings, a very similar study by Kollen and Garwood (1974, reported by Kollen, 1975) predicted only 20% substitution. The two surveys are nearly identical in format and methodology; both attempt to match hypothetical teleconferencing facilities (described to respondents in a section of the questionnaire) with descriptions of recent meetings (provided by respondents) in an effort to assess whether these facilities might meet respondents' meeting needs. However, the Kollen and Garwood study goes a step beyond assessing sufficiency of telecommunication devices for satisfying stated needs. Their survey explicitly asks respondents to indicate whether they would have used such devices instead of traveling to their meetings. The crucial distinction here is what technologists might offer to meet a perceived market need is not necessarily what target users might actually choose to use (see Moore & Jovanis, in press). Clearly, given the differences between the two results, there are more factors involved than a straightforward facilitation of the mechanics of a process that is candidate for electronic mediation or automation. Surprisingly, the difference between these studies seems to have been ignored, and both are often cited together simply as examples of positive market estimates (see e.g., Johansen, Vallee, & Spangler, 1979; Kraemer, 1982; Noll, 1985).

Nonetheless, there is also reason to suspect the results of both of these studies, and, for that matter, of any attitude survey or focus group study that expects participants to judge the utility of devices they have neither seen nor experienced. A verbal description of a novel system is open to many individual interpretations, and may bear little relationship to the actual experience of using the system. No less significantly, such a description is also subject to possible biases introduced by the assessor. Anyone aiming to assess potential needs is likely to find needs whether or not they exist (See Elton & Carey, 1979, for a description of this and other potential pitfalls of needs assessment research.)

Aside from the inherent difficulties and questionable methodology available for accurately assessing or foreseeing the size and needs of the teleconferencing market as a whole, we might also add that many teleconferencing vendors have misjudged the needs of individual client organizations. There are numerous examples of mismatches between users' needs at all levels (individual, corporate/organizational, and societal) and technology even at the stage of actual system implementation. Such mismatches are often the reason for the failure of many installations. So, for example, Johansen (1979) pointed out the importance of recognizing and accommodating the idiosyncrasies of the organizational culture of a user group. A group's culture sets the tone for its meetings, and the physical environment in which meetings take place is not only a direct reflection but a facilitator of this culture. As Johansen put it, a group of senior banking executives would hardly feel at home amidst the Spartan furnishings of a typical academic meeting room. Thus, many teleconferencing rooms that reflect the culture of the telecommunications vendor who designed them rather than that of their end-users quickly fall into disuse and become expensive fiascos.

Inadequate needs assessment is without doubt related to the apparently universal assumption that videoconferencing is a direct replacement for face-to-face meetings as we know them today.[1] Videoconferencing needs

---

[1]Many new automation technologies are designed to replicate existing procedures, with little thought given to the impact that these technologies will have on the way things are done. So, for instance, word processors have typically been designed for typists. They are not optimal for the originators/composers of text who might, for instance, find it useful to maintain a "history" of textual modifications (see Lippman, Bender, Solomon, & Saito, 1985 for a notable example of an editor designed for the text composer). However, new office technology has significantly changed work styles in that nonclerical workers now perform many functions

assessment and system design, as well as system evaluation (e.g., Duncanson & Williams, 1973), have been firmly founded on this basic assumption. Only recently have a few researchers begun to question this assumption as limiting and short sighted (Johansen, 1984).

Though the consensus has long been reached that teleconferencing is more appropriate for some kinds of meetings than for others, careful quantitative analyses of "target market" meetings have only just begun to emerge. The results of earlier laboratory-based and field studies (Champness, 1973; Christie, 1974, 1975; Christie & Holloway, 1975; Dutton, Fulk, & Steinfield, 1982; Noll, 1976) indicated that teleconferencing is best suited for regularly occurring meetings aimed toward the presentation or exchange of neutral information between colleagues in different locations.[2] However, it appears that the proportion of meetings that match that description is indeed very small. Noll (1985), for instance, surveyed organizations using a simple self-administered questionnaire to determine the proportion of target meetings, that is, those best suited for teleconferencing, out of the total number of all types of group meetings. Using the number of target-type meetings as a "rule of thumb" estimate of the total market for teleconferencing in a particular organization, he calculates that the market for two-way interactive teleconferencing is only about 4% of the total of all types of group meetings.

The nonsubstitution of travel by teleconferencing in itself also supports the notion that teleconferencing should not be regarded as a direct replacement for face-to-face meetings. Examining the "before and after" travel patterns of teleconferencing users we find, not a reduction in the amount of travel, but, rather, an increase in the number of meetings (Brancatelli, 1985; Johansen, 1984). Nonetheless, managers continue to perceive travel substitution as a direct benefit of selecting teleconferencing media (Fulk & Dutton, 1984), and many teleconferencing advertisements and marketing brochures continue to focus on travel substitution as a primary selling point.

The marketing strategy used by teleconferencing vendors reflects the limiting assumption that the technology is a substitute for face-to-face interactions and is often equally short-sighted. Though we now know the claim that teleconferencing reduces travel is unjustified, the potential reduction of travel budgets has been used as a sales point aimed at purchase decision makers. On the other hand, the reduced opportunity to travel is

---

delegated to clerical workers in the past. Another example, electronic mail, was initially little more than an electronic substitute for paper mail delivery, though it later evolved into the more interactive medium of computer conferencing.

[2]Note, however, that some researchers (e.g., Watzlawick, Beavin, & Jackson, 1967) hold that it may be over-simplistic to believe in the existence of any such low-risk interactions.

often viewed negatively by end-user executives (Johansen, 1984). Similarly, another commonly cited benefit is the idea that teleconferencing leads to more effective and efficient meetings. Ronald Bohm wrote in "The Executive Guide to Video Teleconferencing":

> Teleconferencing not only decreases the lead time for meetings, it also tends to make meetings more effective. A teleconference requires more planning than an "in person" meeting; consequently, shorter and more effective meetings are usually the result. Since personnel in two or more cities must be prepared for the meeting, more attention is devoted to the preparation of agendas, handouts, and presentation media. Less time is spent socializing because meetings are held more frequently with more accomplished in each meeting. In some cases the use of long-distance transmission seems to reduce the urge to waste time with small talk. (Bohm & Templeton, 1984, p. 3)

Efficiency claims such as this also turn out to be two-edged swords. First of all, managers easily recognize that there are much less costly ways of teaching their employees to conduct efficient meetings. Second, if preparation time is greater, meeting time may be reduced, but it is questionable whether there will be any savings in total time. But more importantly, it is precisely the reduced opportunity for informal, unofficial interactions that makes teleconferencing unattractive to politically savvy employees. It is often over informal chats outside of official meeting rooms that important information is transmitted and real decisions are made (Mintzberg, 1973).

Much systematic research has also been conducted to compare the effects of different communication media on various tasks such as problem solving, decision making, and information transmission (for reviews see Chapanis, 1980; Short, Williams, & Christie, 1976; Williams, 1977). Results generally point to the dubious value of adding a visual channel that allows visual contact between participants; performance does not improve significantly over that achieved with narrower bandwidths in either cooperative or conflictful situations.

In cooperative problem-solving situations where communication is noncontroversial, laboratory studies show no differences between audio alone and audio combined with video (Chapanis, 1976). In field experiments, video system users' reports confirm the laboratory findings (Johansen, 1984).

In conflictful situations, where participants are engaging in delicate negotiation, for example, system users report failures to arrive at agreement or completion of the communicative task (see Abel, chap. 18 in this volume). In fact, laboratory studies find the video channel to be detrimental in some cases, presumably because interpersonal variables are more likely to intrude on the task at hand (Short, 1974; Weeks & Chapanis, 1976). Similarly, studies of media effects on interpersonal perception suggest that the video channel can introduce irrelevant distractors that can interfere with the accuracy of interpersonal evaluations (Williams, 1975).

However, these results should not necessarily be taken to mean that teleconference systems should never include video capability. Visual contact among conferees does not add significant content in the information-theoretic sense, but it can provide a sense of social presence and mutual knowledge of the sort crucial for effective communication (Abel, chap. 18 in this volume; Krause & Fussell, chap. 5 in this volume). It also can add to its desirability or appeal if it is provided cheaply enough. There is, in fact, evidence that people in office environments would include video in the optimal information system design if they were not constrained by budgets. A 1982 survey by the Institute for the Future (reported in Johansen, 1984) found that about 50% of respondents would do so.[3] On the other hand, when asked to select optimal features for system design given a fixed, finite budget, only 15% of respondents chose video. Data such as these indicate that potential users realize the current limited utility of a video channel. However, people may show greater willingness to pay when new video-based services become available that increase the utility of having a video capability.

AVENUES FOR THE DIFFUSION OF VIDEOCONFERENCING

Even if the market for two-way interactive videoconferencing is in actuality very small, the study of the diffusion of innovations teaches us that the actual uses of many technologies are often different and/or broader than the applications envisioned by their inventors/designers (Dickson & Bowers, 1973). Furthermore, it teaches us that the diffusion of innovations can follow unexpected paths (Rogers, 1973). So, with respect to videoconferencing, the bulk of the anecdotal success stories that one finds in marketing documents and business reviews are largely related to special applications that go beyond direct substitution of face-to-face communication. These successful applications would, for the most part, not be possible without teleconferencing; face-to-face meetings in these cases are simply not practical (Fulk & Dutton, 1984).

There are indeed many examples of such successful applications. For instance, a number of companies, including Wang, Digital Equipment Cor-

---

[3]This result is not artifactual in the sense that everyone in the study did not select every option; only 13% did, in spite of the common belief that people will take as many features as they can afford.

poration, and Kodak, are making extensive use of their two-way videoconferencing facilities to train sales staff and services technicians distributed across the country (in fact, Wang is even linking their system with that of the Ford Motor Company to train Ford employees to use Wang equipment). The speed with which training can be delivered to large numbers of employees often gives these companies a competitive edge. For instance, when IBM announced in August 1985 that it would drop support for its System 34 software, Wang quickly set up a videoconference with sales people at 13 sites to disseminate this information and tell the sales force how to best use it to attract IBM customers.

Another example of a successful installation is the Boeing Company. In 1980, under the pressure of having to meet strict deadlines for the development of the 757 commercial aircraft, Boeing engineers jerry-rigged a two-way TV system to connect its airfield, engineering, and manufacturing facilities located within a 30-mile radius. Personnel at these locations foresaw a strong need for frequent interactions and no time to waste on interlocation travel. Teleconferencing was, and still is, seen at Boeing as the only way to meet ambitious schedules.

One last example of how teleconferencing can permit activities that would otherwise not be possible can be found at J. C. Penney's Dallas and New York headquarters. Penney takes advantage of its teleconferencing facilities at these locations to include in meetings junior executives whose travel budget would not allow for attendance. According to a member of J. C. Penney's systems engineering staff (personal communication), senior executives (who attend meetings in person) are able to call on more junior managers for consultation over the video link. In addition, Penney managers feel that attendance at these meetings is invaluable for the junior executives' own development.

For J. C. Penney, this application is just a small part of a company-wide effort to shift responsibility downward on the managerial scale. As another example of ways the company is using teleconferencing to achieve this goal, individual stores' senior buyers from around the country are now picking the styles they want via televised fashion shows arranged in and broadcast from New York. Before teleconferencing, merchandising specialists at the regional level would make frequent trips to New York and select merchandise to be sold in all the stores in their territories. Distributing this responsibility to middle managers in individual stores allows for more appropriate merchandise selection for each store.

Thus, the first question to ask given a view of teleconferencing as a supplement rather than a replacement for face-to-face meetings is what this technology allows us to do that we couldn't do otherwise. The next question to ask given the increase in communication to which teleconferencing can potentially lead is how to maximize the utility of this increase, and, relatedly, how to technologically enhance communication intensive functions that are already in place. To achieve these goals a thorough understanding is required of the kinds of communicative tasks that are commonplace in communication intensive domains, of the interaction dynamics that drive these tasks, and of the way people use their current communication tools. Thus, two types of studies are required. Detailed studies of collaborative work tasks are essential. In addition, evaluative studies of collaborations conducted over teleconferencing testbeds are invaluable. By itself, technology-driven research that evaluates the utility of various design features has poor chances of arriving at useful innovations; the space of possibilities is too great. On the other hand, task-driven research alone requires a great leap of imagination on the part of the researcher (and potential user), and as such, runs the danger of overlooking, among other things, crucial changes in the nature of the task or work style introduced by new technology.

Previous research on usage of and reactions to trial teleconference systems has already suggested some new directions for designers and marketers, who are now shifting their focus away from conference room teleconferencing toward office teleconferencing. The results of a 1-year study that monitored users of two portable audiographic office teleconference systems (Mosera & Springer, 1983a, 1983b; Springer & Mosera, 1982), led to the following recommendations for system design. The study found that users most frequently prefer office over conference room teleconferencing. Dedicated office systems (or at least systems that can be easily accessed and connected in a matter of minutes) permit spontaneous working-session style meetings of the type that are best as supplements for more formal face-to-face meetings. Office systems also allow conferees to be surrounded by their own resource material and/or colleagues. In cases where users indicated a preference for conference room teleconferences, reasons given had to do with (a) greater facility for assembling groups larger than three people, and (b) the fact that conference rooms typically have higher audio quality. Thus, Mosera and Springer recommended maximizing audio quality and providing two camera angle settings, one to capture individuals and another for small groups.

The study also concluded from users' responses that high-quality document transmission is an important system requirement. On the other hand, a video capability (not present in the trial system), particularly freeze-frame video, was not highly rated by users, presumably because most office teleconferences are working sessions among people who know each other fairly well. Full motion video was rated as somewhat more desirable.

Mosera and Springer's inferential data on the importance of audio and video quality for user acceptance are typical of what is available to date on this topic (at least in the public domain). Though responses to evaluative surveys commonly include complaints about the poor audio quality of tele-conferencing systems, there are no concrete data to define user accept-ability requirements. Anecdotally, it is worth noting that success of existing systems is spread over many types of systems varying widely in audio and video quality. So far, it would appear that the success or failure of telecon-ferencing systems is more closely tied to the nature of their intended ap-plication than to details of technical quality.

A survey conducted by the Institute for the Future in 1982 (reported in Johansen, 1984) constitutes an example of a more purely task-driven study. This study obtained data about workers' frustrations, which strongly indi-cated that store-and-forward capabilities would be highly valued. Re-spondents listed the following as major sources of frustrations in their day-to-day work life:

- too many interruptions
- difficulty reaching others
- time wasted at meetings
- communications too slow
- difficulty maintaining continuity in communications over time

The prediction has been borne out in the growing success of computer conferencing services and systems. Store and forward capabilities can po-tentially alleviate the problems associated with synchronized communica-tion over media that demand instant response and may augment the utility of teleconferencing systems. Innovative combinations of technologies such as this, as well as the integration of media in ways that will create more flexible and useful services (e.g., voice annotation of images) may expand the market for teleconferencing.

FACTORS THAT MAY INFLUENCE
THE ACCEPTANCE OF VIDEOCONFERENCING

So far, videoconferencing is not much more than a small conglomeration of "niche" markets each of which is being addressed by different vendors with different system formulas. However, there are a number of external factors that may positively influence its acceptance in the near future. Among these are organizational and social changes that may already be emerging as trends.

The decreasing cost of bandwidth, the proliferation of satellite commu-nications, and the emergence of cheaper, more convenient technologies and of new video-based services are often mentioned as factors that may increase the utility of a video capability (e.g., Springer & Mosera, 1982). In addition, market forecasters such as Frost and Sullivan (1983) predicted that increases in the number of installations and subscribers alone should have a positive influence because, as with most interactive technologies, the more people that have videoconferencing, the more useful it becomes.[4]

It is also possible that the current explosion in office automation systems, and the resulting attitudinal changes toward high technology, may open some avenues for related technologies such as teleconferencing. Some of these may be adopted as a by-product or side effect of general office automation, particularly as new employees enter the work force with greater computer and technological skills and orientation. Already, some of these effects are visible in the expansion of computer conferencing.

A severe fuel shortage could also have impact on teleconferencing. It is conceivable that people might desperately try to substitute telecommunications for travel should the latter be severely disrupted. This scenario is in the mind of many telecommunications managers, and many large companies are actually working on teleconferencing-based contingency plans. It is, at least in part, this fear that maintains the continuing level of interest in teleconferencing as reflected by the steady flow of articles on the subject in business magazines and periodicals. Concern is most evident in the hotel/motel industry, in which a growing number of corporations are hedging against the possible consequences of installing and promoting video teleconferencing facilities between hotel locations. In 1979 Holiday Inn started a nationwide network of more than 200 facilities in its motels. Marriott Corporation began offering video teleconferencing services in 1982, and Hilton Hotels Corporation followed in 1984 (Selz, 1984).

Another positive influence on the acceptance of teleconferencing may come from changes in organizational structures, particularly changes in managerial scales. Numerous recent business publications advocate the softening of managerial hierarchies and shifting responsibility to lower levels of management as the latest strategy for corporate success. Although there is as of yet no concrete evidence that such changes are actually taking place on a widespread basis, it is interesting to speculate on the effects such a trend would have on teleconferencing. Decentralized decision making in the form of project terms, for instance, may increase the proportion of working session style of meeting of the kind that is best suited for electronic mediation. Furthermore, a downward shift in responsibility places decision

---

[4]This prediction must be taken with caution, however. First, videoconferencing will probably be limited to business applications in the foreseeable future. With a few isolated exceptions (e.g., Wang-Ford teletraining) these applications are primarily intra-company, so the "critical mass" argument breaks down. However, a certain amount of diffusion is likely to occur as a result of companies emulating competitors who adopt the technology.

making in the hands of lower level managers with limited travel budgets. It is interesting to note that over one-third of the companies described in *In Search of Excellence* (Peters & Waterman, 1982) use teleconferencing on a regular basis.

CONCLUSIONS

To the present, videoconferencing has not met with widespread success except in limited niche markets. The reasons for its overall failure revolve around its misrepresentation as a substitute for formal face-to-face meetings and the current lack of real utility for a video capability. However, changes in the industry's overall focus, as well as various other external factors, may increase the acceptance of teleconferencing as a whole.

The shift toward office rather than conference room teleconferencing not only lowers its cost but also makes the technology more easily accessible for more spontaneous and informal types of communication that complement (rather than replace) face-to-face meetings. Furthermore, factors such as the increasing technical orientation of office workers, the proliferation of office automation technologies, and structural changes in the nature of managerial hierarchies may broaden the market for teleconferencing.

In the midst of these trends, it is difficult to predict the future of videoconferencing. What emerges clearly is the need for further research exploring how teleconferencing can allow users to do business in creative and innovative ways.

REFERENCES

Barefoot, J., & Strickland, L. (1982). Conflict and dominance in television-mediated interactions. *Human Relations, 35*(7), 559–566.

Beckmann, W. H., Ehlinger, J. C., & Macchia, D. (1985). At the frontier of information networking: Bellcore and the BOCs. *Exchange,* Nov/Dec, 7–13. Bell Communications Research.

Bohm, R. J. (1984). Video teleconferencing: A market trend and technology review. In Bohm & Templeton (Eds.), *The executive guide to video teleconferencing.* Dedham, MA: Artech House.

Bohm, R. J., & Templeton, L. B. (1984). *The executive guide to video teleconferencing.* Dedham, MA: Artech House.

Brancatelli, J. (1985). The problem with teleconferencing. *Frequent Flier Magazine,* January 61–64.

Champness, B. G. (1973). *The assessment of users' reactions to confravision II: Analysis and conclusions.* Communications Studies Group, University College London.

Chapanis, A. (1976). Interactive communication: Some findings from laboratory experiments. *Conference Record of the 1976 National Telecommunications Conference.*

Chapanis, A. (1980). *The human use of telecommunication systems.* Research report to the Office of Naval Research, Johns Hopkins University.

Christie, B. (1974). *Teleconferencing: Predicting the level of use.* Communications Studies Group, University College London.

Christie, B. (1975). *Travel or telecommunicate? Some factors affecting the choice.* Communications Studies Group, University College London.

Christie, B., & Holloway, S. (1975). Factors affecting the use of telecommunications by management. *Journal of Occupational Psychology, 48,* 3–9.

Dickson, E., & Bowers, R. (1973). *The videotelephone: A new era in telecommunications.* Report to the National Science Foundation from Cornell University.

Duncanson, J. P., & Williams, A. D. (1973). Video conferencing: Reaction of users. *Human Factors, 15,* 471–485.

Dutton, W. H., Fulk, J., & Steinfield, C. (1982). Utilization of videoconferencing. *Telecommunications Policy,* 164–178.

Elton, M. C. J., & Carey, J. (1979). *Implementing interactive telecommunications services.* The Alternate Media Center, New York University.

Frost & Sullivan, Inc. (1983). *The teleconferencing market in the U.S.* (Report No. 1112). New York: Frost and Sullivan, Inc.

Fulk, J., & Dutton, W. H. (1984). Videoconferencing as an organizational information system: Assessing the role of electronic meetings. *Systems, Objectives, and Solutions, 4*(2), 105–118.

Goldmark, P. C. (1972a). Tomorrow we will communicate to our jobs. *The Futurist,* April, 55–58.

Goldmark, P. C. (1972b). Communication and community. *Scientific American, 227,* 142–150.

Harkness, R. C. (1973). *Telecommunications substitutes for travel: a preliminary assessment of their potential for reducing urban transportation costs by altering office location patterns.* Unpublished doctoral dissertation, University of Washington, Seattle, WA.

Hiltz, S. R. (1983). *Online communities: A case study of the office of the future.* Norwood, NJ: Ablex.

Hiltz, S. R., & Turoff, M. (1978). *The network nation: Human communication via computer.* Reading, MA: Addison-Wesley.

Hiltz, S. R., & Turoff, M. (1981). The evolution of user behavior in a computerized conferencing system. *Communications of the ACM, 24*(11), 739–751.

Ives, H. E. (1930). Two-way television. *Bell Labs Record, 8.*

Jablin, F., & Sussman, L. (1978). An exploration of communication and productivity in real brainstorming groups. *Human Communication Research, 4,* 329–337.

Janis, I. (1972). *Victims of groupthink.* Boston: Houghton-Mifflin.

Johansen, R. (1984). *Teleconferencing and beyond: Communications in the office of the future.* New York: McGraw-Hill.

Johansen, R., Vallee, J., & Spangler, K. (1979). *Electronic Meetings.* Reading, MA: Addison-Wesley.

Kiesler, S., Siegel, J., & McGuire, T. (1982). *Does it matter if you're not all there? Social psychology of computer-mediated groups.* Pittsburgh, PA: Carnegie-Mellon University School of Social Sciences.

Kollen, J. H., & Garwood, J. (1975). *Travel/communication tradeoffs: The potential for substitution among business travelers.* Bell Canada Report.

Kraemer, K. L. (1982). Telecommunications/transportation substitution and energy conservation (Part 1). *Telecommunications Policy,* March, 39–59.

Krueger, G., & Chapanis, A. (1980). Conferencing and teleconferencing in three communication modes as a function of the number of conferees. *Ergonomics, 23*(2), 103–122.

Lineback, J. R. (1982). Video conferencing growing up. *Electronics*, September 22, 1982, 105–106.

Lippman, A. B., Bender, W., Solomon, G., & Saito, M. (1985). Color word processing. *IEEE CG&A*, June, 41–46.

Martin, J. (1977). *Future developments in telecommunications*. New York: Telecom Library.

Mintzberg, J. (1973). The nature of managerial work. New York: Harper & Row.

Molnar, J. P. (1969). Picturephone Service—A New Way of Communicating. *Bell Laboratories Record*, 47(5).

Mosera, M. A., & Springer, R. M. (1983a). *Interim report on the office teleconferencing trial—Holmdel to Denver*. Internal Memorandum for File, American Bell.

Mosera, M. A., & Springer, R. M. (1983b). *Extension of the office teleconferencing trial to a business environment*. Internal Memorandum for File, American Bell.

Moore, A., & Jovanis, P. (in press). Modelling media choices in business organizations: Implications for analyzing telecommunications-transportation interactions. *Transportation Research A*.

Nelson, M. (1985). Focusing on videoconferencing. *Insight (Bell Communications Research)* 2 (8), 8–13.

Noll, A. M. (1976). Teleconferencing communications activities. *IEEE Communications Society*, November, 8–14.

Noll, A. M. (1985). *Teleconferencing target market*. Unpublished manuscript, The Annenberg School of Communications, University of Southern California.

Olgren, C., & Parker, L. (1983). *Teleconferencing technology and applications*. Dedham, MA: Artech House.

Peters, T. J., & Waterman, R. H. (1982). *In search of excellence: Lessons from America's best run companies*. New York: Harper & Row.

Rice, R. E. (1984). Mediated group communication. In R. E. Rice & Associates (Eds.), *The new media: Communication research and technology*. Beverly Hills, CA: Sage Publications.

Rogers, E. M. (1973). *The diffusion of innovations* (3rd ed.). New York: Free Press.

Selz, M. (1984). Lights! camera! teleconferencing comes of age. *Florida Trend*, May, 86–92.

Short, J. A. (1974). Effects of medium of communication on experimental negotiation, *Human Relations 27*, 225–234.

Short, J., Williams, E., & Christie, B. (1976). *The social psychology of telecommunications*. London: Wiley.

Showker, K. (1982). Teleconferencing and the frequent traveler. *Frequent Traveler*, April 1982, 43–49.

Snyder, F. W. (1971). *Travel patterns: Implication for new communication facilities*. Bell Laboratories Memorandum.

Springer, R. M., & Mosera, M. A. (1982). *Synopsis of office teleconferencing research*. Memorandum for File, American Bell.

Steinfield, C. (1983). *Communicating via electronic mail: Patterns and predictors of use in organizations*. Unpublished doctoral dissertation, Annenberg School of Communications, University of Southern California.

Svenning, L. L., & Ruchinskas, J. E. (1984). Organizational teleconferencing. In R. E. Rice, & Associates (Eds.), *The new media: Communication research and technology*. Beverly Hills, CA: Sage Publications.

Tyson, J. (1987). Video teleconferencing is cutting costs while increasing the productivity of many companies. *Communication News 24*(2).

Watzlawick, P., Beavin, J., & Jackson, D. (1967). *Pragmatics of human communication*. New York: Norton.

Weeks, G. D., & Chapanis, A. (1976). Cooperative versus conflictive problem solving in three telecommunication modes. *Perceptual and Motor Skills, 42,* 487–512.

Williams, E. (1975). Medium or message: Communications medium as determinant of interpersonal evaluation, *Sociometry, 38,* 119–130.

Williams, E. (1977). Experimental comparisons of face-to-face and mediated communication: A review, *Psychological Bulletin, 84*(5), 963–976.

IV TECHNOLOGY FOR COOPERATIVE WORK

14

Technology and Groups: Assessment of the Empirical Research

Kenneth L. Kraemer
University of California, Irvine

Alain Pinsonneault
University of California, Irvine and École des Hautes Études Commerciales de Montréal, Québec

Abstract

In this chapter we analyze the empirical findings on the impacts of technological support on groups. We define and differentiate two broad technological support systems for group processes: Group Decision Support systems (GDSS), and Group Communication Support Systems (GCSS). We then present a framework and method for analyzing the impacts of such information systems on groups. We develop the framework from the literature of organization behavior and group psychology and apply it to the literature of MIS. We then review the empirical research and findings concerned with the impacts of GDSS and GCSS on groups, and we compare and contrast these findings. Finally, we conclude by discussing the implications of our analysis on the focus of attention and design of future research.

Five Major implications stem from our analysis: (1) there is a lack of research on some important "formal" factors of groups, (2) there is a paucity of research on the impacts of GDSS and GCSS on the informal dimension of groups, (3) there is a need to move away from laboratory settings to field study in organization settings, with "real" managers, (4) more research is needed on the stages in group development and on how they affect the impacts of GDSS and GCSS on groups, and (5) more research is needed to understand how the structure imposed by the technological supports affect group processes.

Historically, the study of group meetings has proven to possess both scientific and practical relevance. Scientifically, the study of meetings provides insight into group processes, and the relationship between group cohesion and task performance. Conceptualized as the essence of modern organizations, groups constitute a key basis for acquisition of knowledge on organizations. The practical relevance of these studies stems from the sheer amount of time managers spend in group meetings. *The Wall Street Journal* (June 21, 1988) reported that managers spend from 25% to 50% of their total work time in group meetings. With recent advances in computers, telecommunications, and management science techniques, serious efforts have been made to use technology to enhance this type of group performance. This chapter reviews and assesses the empirical research on the impacts of information technology used to support group processes.

This chapter has six sections. First we define and differentiate two broad types of technological support systems for group processes: *Group Decision Support Systems* (GDSS) and *Group Communication Support Systems* (GCSS). Next, we present a framework and method for analyzing the impacts of technological support systems on group processes and outcomes. We developed this framework from systematic review of relevant literature in group psychology and organization behavior and use it to review the empirical research and findings in MIS. We also analyze the studies concerned with the impacts of GDSS on groups, as well as the research concerned with the impacts of GCSS on groups. In addition, we compare and contrast the empirical findings on the impact of GDSS and GCSS on groups. Finally, we conclude by discussing implications of our analysis for future research.

TECHNOLOGICAL SUPPORT OF GROUP PROCESSES

Most of the literature concerned with technological support of group processes goes under the label of GDSS. Yet, there is no consensus in the literature on what exactly constitutes a GDSS. Qualitatively different information systems have been included in GDSS. Based on a previous review of existing aids for group decision making (Kraemer & King, 1988), and on other reviews of literature (Benbasat & Nault, 1988; Dennis, George, & Nunamaker, 1988; DeSanctis & Gallupe, 1987), it seems that there are basically two types of technological supports for groups: Group Communication Support Systems (GCSS) and Group Decision Support Systems (GDSS).

GCSS are information aids. They are systems that primarily support the communication process between group members, even though they might do other things as well. The main purpose of GCSS is to reduce communication barriers in groups. These systems basically provide information control (storage and retrieval of data), representational capabilities (plotting and graph capabilities, large video displays) such as those discussed by Zachary

(1986), and group "collaboration support" facilities for idea generation, collection, and compilation such as those discussed by Benbasat and Nault (1988). GCSS also include "Level 1" and "Level 3" supports of DeSanctis and Gallupe (1987).[1] Examples of GCSS are teleconferencing, electronic mail, electronic boardroom, and local group networks (Kraemer & King, 1988).

GDSS, on the other hand, are those systems that attempt to structure the group decision process in some way. GDSS can support members' individual decision processes through decision models. This basically corresponds to applying Decision Support Systems (DSS) to groups without supporting the group process per se. Here the technology supports decision processes of individuals working in a group. Examples of such systems are "What if" analyses, PERT, budget allocation models, choice models, analysis and reasoning methods, and judgment refinements such as those discussed by Zachary (1986). GDSS might also be in form of group decision process techniques supporting the group decision process itself. Examples of this support are automated Delphi technique, nominal group technique, information center, decision conference, and the collaboration laboratory described by Kraemer and King (1988). This corresponds to "Group 7: Structured Group Decision Techniques" of Benbasat and Nault (1988), and to "Level 2" support of DeSanctis and Gallupe (1987).[2]

A FRAMEWORK AND METHOD
FOR THE ANALYSIS OF IMPACTS

Framework For Analysis

We developed our framework for analysis from systematic review of research in organization behavior and in group psychology (Mitchell, 1978; Schwartzman, 1986; Steers, 1981; Zander, 1979). Based on that review, we conceptualized the relationship between technological support and group outcomes as involving four broad sets of factors concerned with: (a) the context, (b) the process, (c) the task-related outcomes, and (d) the group-

---

[1]Level 1 of the typology of DeSanctis and Gallupe (1987) are technological supports that improve the decision process by facilitating information exchange among members. Examples of Level 1 support are anonymous input of ideas and preferences, and electronic message exchange. Level 3 support is characterized by machine-induced group communication patterns.

[2]DeSanctis and Gallupe (1987) described Level 2 support of their typology as technological supports that provide decision modeling and group techniques aimed at reducing uncertainty and "noise" that occur in the group's decision process. Examples of Level 2 support are modeling tools, risk analysis, and multiattribute utility methods.

related outcomes of group interaction. Technological support, which is the focus of this analysis, is a contextual factor along with personal factors, situational factors, structure of the group, and task characteristics. The broad theoretical notion explains that technological support facilitates group process through enhancing group capabilities, removing barriers to group interaction, improving the group in its task, and building or reinforcing the social value of the group to its members through successful task performance. Thus, our framework and much of the MIS research, focuses on identifying the impacts of technological support on group process while controlling for the effect of the other contextual variables. Group process in turn influences task-related outcomes that conjointly with group process, affect group-related outcomes.

Contextual Variables

Contextual variables refer to factors in the immediate environment of the group rather than in the broader organizational environment. Five contextual variables appear to be important in the behavioral research on groups: personal factors, situational factors, group structure, technological support, and task characteristics.

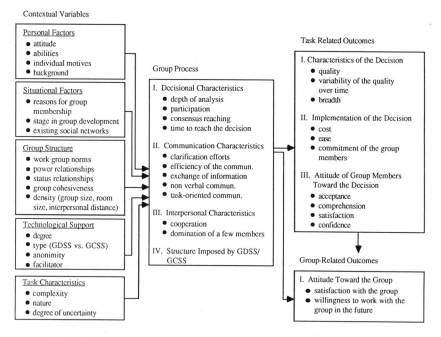

FIG. 14.1.   A framework for analyzing the impacts of GDSS and GCSS on group processes and outcomes.

Personal factors refer to the attitudes, behaviors, and motives of individual group members. Four personal factors have been found to affect group process in organization behavior: (a) The attitude that group members have toward working in groups and working with the members of the group; (b) the ability of the members to work in a group; (c) the individual motives, or hidden agendas of group members; and (d) the background of the group members, which includes previous experience in working with groups and other factors like education or specific knowledge.

Situational factors refer to the extent of existing social networks and relationships among members of the group and to the characteristics of the development of the group. There are three main situational factors found to be important in previous research. First are the reasons for group membership, which can be categorized as voluntary reasons (social needs, self-esteem) or involuntary reasons (e.g., superior's request) (Kemp, 1970). There is also the existing social networks between group members, which have a direct impact on the communication and the interpersonal dimensions of group process (Blau & Scott, 1962; Caudill, 1958). And finally, there is the stage of development of the group. Tuckman (1965) proposed a model in which groups evolve through four stages: (a) testing and dependence, where group members attempt to understand acceptable and unacceptable behavior and the norms of the group; (b) intragroup conflict, where members try to establish and solidify their position and also acquire influence over decisions made; (c) development of group cohesion, where members come to accept fellow members and the norms developed; and (d) functional performing, where the efforts of group members become mostly oriented toward task and goal accomplishment.

Group structure refers to patterned relations among members of the group. Five aspects of group structure have been found to influence group process in organization behavior and group psychology research (Cummings & Berger, 1976; Porter & Lawler, 1965): (a) work group norms (Festinger, 1950; Flowers, 1977; Hackman, 1976; Janis, 1972; McGrath, 1964), (b) power relationships (French & Raven, 1968; Mitchell, 1978), (c) status relationships between members (differentiation between the status of members) (Mitchell, 1978; Parson, 1949; Scott, 1967), (d) group cohesiveness (sense of oneness, group spirit) (Cartwright & Zander, 1968; Shaw, 1976), and (e) density of the group, which is a composite factor made of the size of the group, the size of the room, and the interpersonal distance between group members (Cummings & Berger, 1976; Paulus, Annis, Setta, Schkade, & Matthews, 1976; Porter & Lawler, 1965).

Technological support refers to what activities the GDSS and GCSS support and the extent of support they provide. Technological support includes four basic subfactors. The first is the type of support provided, whether it is a GCSS or GDSS, and if it is a GDSS, whether it is a decision model or a group decision process technique. The degree of support is also a factor. As stressed by DeSanctis and Gallupe (1987) and Benbasat and Nault (1988), this refers to how technological support, through its structure, capabilities, or technical characteristics, facilitates the generation of alternatives, the choice of alternatives or the negotiation over alternative generation or choice. The final two factors are the degree of anonymity the support permits, and whether a facilitator is part of the support.

Task characteristics refer to attributes of the group's substantive work. Three main factors were found to be important in organization behavior and group psychology. The degree of complexity of the task is one. Second is the nature of the task, for example, whether it is a financial task or a personnel task (Hofstede, 1968; Janis & Mann, 1977; Mintzberg, Raisinghani & Théoret, 1976; Pettigrew, 1973). A third is the degree of uncertainty associated with the particular task. For example, in decision making the uncertainty might relate to the consequences of the decision, or to the information provided to make the decision, or both (Bowman, 1958).

Group Process

Group process variables refer to characteristics of the group's interaction, and generally attempt to capture the dynamics of that interaction. We segmented group process into three categories: decisional characteristics, communication characteristics, and interpersonal characteristics.

Decisional characteristics basically refer to the ways decisions are made (Bailey, 1965; Davis, Strasser, Spitzer, & Holt, 1976; Olsen, 1972). This includes the depth of analysis (number of alternatives generated, and number and complexity of the criteria used to evaluate these alternatives), the degree of participation of the group members, the degree of consensus reached in making a decision, and the time it takes to reach a decision.

Communication characteristics include the clarification efforts made by group members in trying to better understand the alternatives, the problem, or the solution; the exchange of information between members (is there a tendency to withhold information?); nonverbal communication; and the degree of task-oriented communication between members (Argyris, 1975; Delbeq, Van de Ven, & Gustafson, 1975; Van de Van & Delbeq, 1974).

Interpersonal characteristics include the degree of cooperation in the group (Frenno, 1962; Goldman, Stockbauer, & McAuliffe, 1977; Levit & Benjamin, 1976; Okun & DiVesta, 1975), and the degree to which one or few members dominate the group processes (Caudill, 1958; Hollander & Julian, 1969; Michener & Burt, 1975; Vroom & Yetton, 1973).

The structure of these group processes (decisional, communication, and interpersonal), which has two dimensions, is also likely to affect the outcomes of groups. The degree of structure—how standardized and stable are the decision, communication, and interpersonal processes—is the first dimension. The second is the type of structure, or the extent to which the processes are hierarchically structured, whether formal or informal. The structure of group processes is important in MIS research because it is directly affected by technological supports.

Task-Related Outcomes

Task-related outcomes consist of three variables, each of which might be affected by technological support. The first variable is the characteristics of the decision. This includes the decision quality, the variability of the quality of the decision over time (or the consistency of group performance), and the breadth of the decision. The character of decision implementation is the second variable. This includes the cost of implementation, the ease of implementation, and the commitment of group members to implementation of the decision. Finally, there is the attitude of group members toward the decision. This includes the acceptance of the decision by the members, the comprehension of the decision, the satisfaction with the decision, and the confidence in the decision by the group members.

Group-Related Outcomes

Group-related outcomes include two main variables that might be affected by the technological support: The satisfaction of the group members with regard to the process and the willingness of the group members to work in group the future, whether in this particular group, or in other groups.

Method of Analysis

In order to examine what the research says about these foregoing sets of factors, we grouped the studies according to whether they focused on technological supports primarily aimed at reducing noise in decision processes (GDSS, Table 14.1) or at reducing communication barriers between members of a group (GCSS, Table 14.2). We further characterized the technological support by specifying whether it was a decision model (support individual decision process) or a group decision process technique (support group decision process), and whether it supported the generation of alternatives, the choice of alternatives, and/or the negotiation over alternative generation or choice. We also characterized the technological support by the degree of anonymity it permitted and whether or not a facilitator was part of the support. Based on information available in published articles and/or research reports, we then assessed how each study addressed the different variables in our framework. We determined the

TABLE 1

EMPIRICAL RESEARCH ON GDSS

AUTHORS (YEAR) (by school of 1st Author at the time of Publication)	Number of Groups — Experimental	Control	Size of Group	Type of Decisions	Goal of Research	Research Strategy
PERCEPTRONICS Steeb & Johnson (81)	5	5	3	complex political crisis	impact of gdss on decision quality	LAB EXP
SOUTHERN METHODIST UNIVERSITY Gray (83)	4	0	?	4 different decisions	impact of anonymity and gdss	LAB EXP impression
UNIVERSITY OF ARIZONA George et al. (87)			6	sales territories assignment	impact of leadership anonymity and gdss	LAB EXP
Nunamaker et al. (87)	7	0	6-22	different strategic planning		Field Study
Nunamaker (87)			5	planning		Case study

Column groups (rotated header):

- **CONTEXTUAL VARIABLES:** Number of Groups (Experimental, Control); Size of Group; Type of Decisions; Goal of Research; Research Strategy
- **INDEPENDENT VARIABLES**
  - Personal Factors: Attitude, Abilities, Motives
  - Situational Factors: Background, Group Membership, Stage in Group Development, Social Network
  - Task Characteristics: Complexity, Nature, Uncertainty
  - Group Structure: Group Norms, Power Relations, Status Relations, Cohesiveness, Group Size, Room Size, Physical Distance
  - Technological Support: IDP (Generate, Choose, Negotiate), GDSS GDP (Generate, Choose, Negotiate), Anonymity, Facilitator, Structure Imposed on the Process
- **INTERVENING VARIABLES**
  - DECISION — Decisional Characteristics: Depth of Analysis, Participation, Consensus, Time to Decide
  - PROCESS — Communication Characteristics: Clarification Efforts, Efficiency of Comm, Exchange of Info, Non-Verbal Comm, Task Comm; Inter-personal Charact: Cooperation, Domination by Few
- **DEPENDENT VARIABLES**
  - TASK OUTCOMES — Charact. of the Decision: Quality, Quality Variability, Breadth, Cost; Implementation of the Decision: Ease, Commitment, Acceptance, Comprehension
  - GROUP OUTCOMES — Attitude Toward the Decision: Satisfaction, Confidence; Attitude Toward Grp Proc: Satisfaction, Future Membership

Selected coded cells (INDEPENDENT VARIABLES):

Study	Attitude	Abilities	Motives	Background	Group Membership	Stage in Group Dev.	Social Network	Complexity	Nature	Uncertainty	Power Relations	Status Relations	Cohesiveness	Group Size	Room Size	Physical Distance	GDSS Generate	GDSS Choose	GDSS Negotiate	Anonymity	Facilitator	Structure Imposed
Steeb & Johnson (81)	?	C	?	?	?	1		H	C	H	?			C	?	?	X	X	X	?	C	NC
Gray (83)	NC	NC	NC	?	NC	2-3	H	M	NC	L	NC	NC	?	NC	?		X	X	X	?	?	?
George et al. (87)	Cr	Cr	Cr	Cr	Cr	?	Cr	L	M	L	X ?			NC	?		X	?	?	H	?	?
Nunamaker et al. (87)	NC	NC	NC	?	NC	?	?	H	NC	H	?	C	?	NC	C	C	X	?	?	H	C	?
Nunamaker (87)																						NC

Selected "+" entries (INTERVENING / DEPENDENT VARIABLES), predominantly Steeb & Johnson (81): Depth of Analysis +; Participation + +; Consensus +; Time to Decide +; Exchange of Info +; Non-Verbal Comm +; Cooperation +; Quality +; Breadth +; Satisfaction (toward Decision) +; Confidence +; Satisfaction (Grp Proc) + +.

382

TABLE 1 EMPIRICAL RESEARCH ON GDSS (Continued) AUTHORS (YEAR) (by school of 1st Author at the time of Publication)	Number of Groups							Attitude	Abilities	Motives	Background	Group Membership	Stage in Group Development	Social Network	Complexity	Nature	Uncertainty	Group Norms	Power Relations	Status Relations	Cohesiveness	Group Size	Room Size	Physical Distance	Generate	Choose	Negotiate	Generate	Choose	Negotiate	Anonymity	Facilitator	Structure Imposed on the Process	Depth of Analysis	Participation	Consensus	Time to Decide	Clarification Efforts	Efficiency of Comm	Exchange of Info	Non-Verbal Comm	Task Comm	Cooperation	Domination by Few	Quality	Quality Variability	Breadth	Cost	Ease	Commitment	Acceptance	Comprehension	Satisfaction	Confidence	Satisfaction	Future Membership
	Experimental	Control	Size of Group	Type of Decisions	Goal of Research	Research Strategy		Attitude	Abilities	Motives	Background														IDP Generate	IDP Choose	IDP Negotiate	GDP Generate	GDP Choose	GDP Negotiate																										
Jessup et al. (88)	5		4	university parking problem	impact of anonymity & proximity	LAB EXP		Cr	Cr	Cr	Cr	Cr	1		L	M	C	L			?	?	C	C				X			H	C	?					+																	+
	5																	C						C				X			C	C	?					+																	+
	5																							H				X			H	C	?			+	+			++															++
	5																							H				X			H L	C	?							++															++
Nunamaker et al. (88)	40	0	3-22	varied		Field Study		NC	NC	NC	NC	NC	?		?	?	NC	?		NC	C	?	NC	?	C				X	X	X	H L	NC	NC	+	+		+	+						-												++ +
Vogel & Nunamaker (88)	multiple		varied	varied		Multiple		NC	NC	NC	NC	NC	?		?	?	?	?		NC	?	?	C	?	C				X	X	X	?	NC	NC	+	+	+	-											+						+
OKLAHOMA STATE UNIV. Sharda et al. (88)	16	16	3	upper mgmt	multi product dec	LAB EXP		C	C	C	C	NC	?		H	M	C	M	NC	NC	NC	NC	C	?	?	X	X	X				?	C	?	o							o					+	-					o
NEW YORK UNIVERSITY Bui & Sivasankran (87)			3					C	C	C	C	?	1		High Low	C	M	C	?	?		?	C	?	?				X X	X X	X X	?	NC NC ?	NC NC NC	o +																		o + -
Bui & Al (87)	6	6	3	Selecting a regional director		LAB EXP																																																	

Column group headers (as printed across the top):

Spanning header	Covers
CONTEXTUAL VARIABLES	Number of Groups, Size of Group, Type of Decisions, Goal of Research, Research Strategy
INDEPENDENT VARIABLES	Personal Factors, Situational Factors, Task Characteristics, Group Structure, Technological Support
Personal Factors	Attitude, Abilities, Motives, Background
Situational Factors	Group Membership, Stage in Group Development, Social Network
Task Characteristics	Complexity, Nature, Uncertainty
Group Structure	Group Norms, Power Relations, Status Relations, Cohesiveness, Group Size, Room Size, Physical Distance
Technological Support	GDSS (IDP: Generate, Choose, Negotiate; GDP: Generate, Choose, Negotiate), Anonymity, Facilitator, Structure Imposed on the Process
INTERVENING VARIABLES — DECISION	Decisional Characteristics (Depth of Analysis, Participation, Consensus, Time to Decide)
DEPENDENT VARIABLES — PROCESS	Communication Characteristics (Clarification Efforts, Efficiency of Comm, Exchange of Info, Non-Verbal Comm, Task Comm, Cooperation, Domination by Few), Interpersonal Charact.
DEPENDENT VARIABLES — TASK OUTCOMES	Charact. of the Decision (Quality, Quality Variability, Breadth, Cost, Ease), Implementation of the Decision (Commitment, Acceptance, Comprehension, Satisfaction, Confidence)
DEPENDENT VARIABLES — GROUP OUTCOMES	Attitude Toward the Decision (Satisfaction), Attitude Toward Grp Proc (Satisfaction, Future Membership)

TABLE 2

EMPIRICAL RESEARCH ON GCSS

AUTHORS (YEAR) (by school of 1st Author at the time of Publication)	UNIVERSITY OF MINNESOTA — Gallupe et al. (88)	Zigurs et al. (87)	Watson et al. (88)	Poole et al (88)	INDIANA UNIVERSITY — LeBlanc & Kozar (87)

CONTEXTUAL VARIABLES

Variable	Gallupe et al. (88)	Zigurs et al. (87)	Watson et al. (88)	Poole et al (88)	LeBlanc & Kozar (87)
Number of Groups — Experimental	6 (gcss man)	30 (gcss man)	total 82	total 40 (gcss man)	1
Number of Groups — Control	6	30			0
Size of Group	3	3-4	3-4	3-4	?
Type of Decisions	marketing case	develop admittance criteria & choose	resource allocation	resource allocation	mgmt of vessel traffic
Goal of Research	impact gdss & task difficulty on quality	Impact gcss on influence behavior	resource impact gcss on behavior	resource impact of gcss on behavior	impact of gcss
Research Strategy	LAB EXP	LAB EXP	LAB EXP	LAB EXP	Longitudinal case study

INDEPENDENT VARIABLES

Variable	Gallupe et al. (88)	Zigurs et al. (87)	Watson et al. (88)	Poole et al (88)	LeBlanc & Kozar (87)
Personal Factors — Attitude	Cr	Cr	Cr	Cr	
Personal Factors — Abilities	Cr	Cr	Cr	Cr	
Personal Factors — Motives	Cr	Cr	Cr	Cr	
Personal Factors — Background	Cr	Cr	Cr	Cr	
Situational — Group Membership	Cr				
Situational — Stage in Group Development	2-3	3-4	3-4	3-4	4
Situational — Social Network	-M				
Task — Complexity	high / low	H	H	H	M
Task — Nature	C	C	C	C	
Task — Uncertainty	M	M	M	M	H
Group Structure — Group Norms		Cr	Cr	Cr	
Group Structure — Power Relations	?	Cr	Cr	Cr	?
Group Structure — Status Relations	?	Cr	Cr	Cr	?
Group Structure — Cohesiveness		C	C	C	?
Group Structure — Group Size	C	C	C	C	?
Group Structure — Room Size	C	C	C	C	
Group Structure — Physical Distance	C	C	C	C	C
Technological Support — GCSS Generate	X	X	X	X	X
Technological Support — GCSS Choose	C	X	X	X	X
Technological Support — GCSS Negotiate	C	X	X	X	X
Technological Support — Anonymity	?	?	?	?	?
Technological Support — Facilitator	NC	?	?	?	?
Technological Support — Structure Imposed on the Process	C	C	C	C	NC

INTERVENING VARIABLES

Variable	Gallupe et al. (88)	Zigurs et al. (87)	Watson et al. (88)	Poole et al (88)	LeBlanc & Kozar (87)
Decision — Depth of Analysis	+	+			
Decision — Participation	o	+		o	
Decision — Consensus	-		o	o	
Decision — Time to Decide	+	+			
Process — Clarification Efforts				o	
Process — Efficiency of Comm					
Process — Exchange of Info					
Process — Non-Verbal Comm			+		
Process — Task Comm					
Interpersonal — Cooperation	.				
Interpersonal — Domination by Few					

DEPENDENT VARIABLES

Variable	Gallupe et al. (88)	Zigurs et al. (87)	Watson et al. (88)	Poole et al (88)	LeBlanc & Kozar (87)
Task — Quality	++	o			+
Task — Quality Variability	+	o			
Task — Breadth					
Task — Cost					
Task — Ease					
Task — Commitment					
Acceptance					
Group — Comprehension					
Group — Satisfaction (toward Decision)			.		
Group — Confidence	.				
Group — Satisfaction (toward Grp Proc)	.				
Future Membership					

384

TABLE 2

EMPIRICAL RESEARCH ON GCSS (Continued)

AUTHORS (YEAR) (by school of 1st Author at the time of Publication)	Number of Groups (Experimental / Control)	Size of Group	Type of Decisions	Goal of Research	Research Strategy	Notes
CARNEGIE-MELLON UNIVERSITY Siegel et al. (86) #1	18 / 0	3	career choice	gcss & non-anonymous vs ftf	University Settings	
#2	12 / 0	3	career choice	anonymous vs non-anonymous	University Settings	
#3	18 / 0	3	career choice	simultaneous vs sequential simultaneous & email vs ftf	University Settings	

(This is a large rotated matrix table crossing CONTEXTUAL VARIABLES, INDEPENDENT VARIABLES [Personal Factors, Situational Factors, Task Characteristics, Group Structure, Technological Support], INTERVENING VARIABLES [Decisional Characteristics], PROCESS VARIABLES [Communication Characteristics, Interpersonal Characteristics], and DEPENDENT VARIABLES [Task Outcomes, Group Outcomes]. Cell entries include symbols such as Cr, C, L, NC, T, ?, O, X, SI, SE, H, +, and o across the various research variable columns.)

TABLE 2

EMPIRICAL RESEARCH ON GCSS (Continued)

AUTHORS (YEAR) (by school of 1st Author at the time of Publication)

NEW JERSEY INSTITUTE OF TECHNOLOGY
Turoff & Hiltz (82)

	CONTEXTUAL VARIABLES					INDEPENDENT VARIABLES — Personal Factors				Situational Factors			Task Charac.			Group Norms	Group Structure						Technological Support (GCSS)					Structure Imposed on the Process	INTERVENING — Decisional Characteristics				PROCESS — Communication Characteristics					Interpersonal Charact.		DEPENDENT — Task Outcomes (Charact. of the Decision)										GROUP OUTCOMES			
Row	No. of Groups (Exp / Control)	Size of Group	Type of Decisions	Goal of Research	Research Strategy	Attitude	Abilities	Motives	Background	Group Membership	Stage in Group Development	Social Network	Complexity	Nature	Uncertainty	Group Norms	Power Relations	Status Relations	Cohesiveness	Group Size	Room Size	Physical Distance	Generate	Choose	Negotiate	Anonymity	Facilitator	Struct. Imposed	Depth of Analysis	Participation	Consensus	Time to Decide	Clarification Efforts	Efficiency of Comm	Exchange of Info	Non-Verbal Comm	Task Comm	Cooperation	Domination by Few	Quality	Quality Variability	Breadth	Cost	Ease	Implementation	Commitment	Acceptance	Comprehension	Satisfaction (Attitude)	Confidence	Satisfaction	Attitude Toward Grp Proc	Future Membership
#1	8 / 8	5	artic survival	impact of gcss on quality decision	LAB EXP	Cr	Cr	Cr	Cr	Cr	1st	L	M	M	H	?	?	?		o	?	NC	X	X	X	?	?	o	+	+	-	+			-		+	+	-	o										+			
#2	6 / 6	5	artic survival	impact of gcss on quality decision	Field Exp	?	?	?	?	?	1st	L	M	M	H	?	x	x	o	o	?	NC	X	X	X	?	?	o			o									+													
#2	6 / 6	5		impact of gcss on quality decision	Field Exp	?	?	?	?	?	1st	L	M	M	H	?	x	x	o	o	?	NC	X	X	X	?	?	o			+									+													
#2										?	1st	L	M	M	H	?	o	o	o	o	?	NC	X	X	X	?	?	o			+									+													

Legend:

- **H:** High
- **M:** Medium
- **L:** Low
- **C:** Controlled
- **Cr:** Controlled (Random Assignment)
- **NC:** Not Controlled and Possibly
- **Blank:** Important — Not Relevant

- **+** Variable Increased
- **-** Variable Decreased
- **o** Variable Static
- **X** Variable Manipulated
- **?** Insufficient Data, May be Important

- **IDP:** Individual Decision Process
- **GDP:** Group Decision Process
- **GDSS:** Group Decision Support System
- **GCSS:** Group Communication Support System

Stage in Group Development:
1 = Testing and dependent
2 = Intragroup conflict
3 = Development of group cohesion
4 = Functional role related efforts

dependent and independent variables as well as the controlled and uncontrolled contextual variables in the studies. We did not include all the independent, dependent, and contextual variables addressed in MIS, but only those focused on by several studies and those found to be important in the organization behavior or group psychology literature.

Even with these limitations on the scope, our assessment provided a powerful and systematic approach to establish the knowledge accumulated to date. What is known, what is not known, where research efforts should be oriented, and what major weakness and threats to validity should be addressed stem clearly from such an analysis. For example, for any dependent variable, like decision quality, we can clearly and rapidly determine: (a) which studies found positive (+), negative (−), and no (0) relationship between technological support and decision quality; (b) whether there is a consensus among the findings of different studies; and (c) whether there are any contextual variables not controlled across studies that could offer alternative explanations to the findings.

In a literature review such as this one, the validity of a finding depends less on the quality of any one particular study, than on the diversity of contextual variables controlled and not controlled in the set of studies (Averch, Carrall, Donaldson, Kiesleng, & Pincus, 1972; Salipante, Notz, & Bigelow, 1982). Consequently, the more heterogeneous the distribution of uncontrolled contextual variables in a set of studies, the more valid the finding common to the set of studies. Our approach to reviewing the literature then is not as much to discuss each study in detail, but to focus on findings across a set of studies and discuss the similar and differential impacts of GDSS and GCSS on groups.[3]

IMPACTS OF GDSS ON GROUPS

As shown in Fig. 14.2, the research findings on the impacts of GDSS on groups are consistent both internally (i.e., within a set of variables like group processes, task-related outcomes, group-related outcomes), and externally (i.e., between sets of variables, such as between group processes findings and task-related findings).

Overall, GDSS affect group processes in three major ways. GDSS focus the efforts of group members toward the task or problem to be solved by the group. GDSS increase the depth of analysis, increase the task-oriented communication, and increase the clarification efforts. In addition, GDSS increase

---

[3]Readers who want to analyze each study further are encouraged to refer to Table 14.1 and Table 14.2 of this chapter, or to read Benbasat and Nault (1988) and Dennis, George, and Nunamaker (1988).

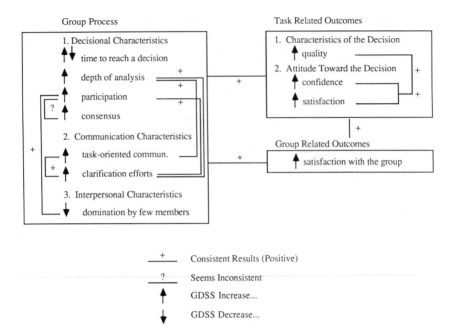

FIG. 14.2.   The impact of GDSS on groups.

the overall quantity of effort put in the decision process by the group, either by allowing more members to participate and/or the same number of members to apply more effort. GDSS were found to increase participation and decrease the domination of the group by one or few members. This is also consistent with greater clarification efforts caused by GDSS. Furthermore, GDSS increase consensus reaching. Although this appears inconsistent with the previous finding of increased participation, actually it is not. GDSS focus the efforts of the group members on the task to be solved (first finding), and, therefore, greater participation combined with a heightened focus of attention leads to higher consensus reaching.

How these impacts affect decision time is inconsistent. Research shows GDSS to both increase and decrease the time needed to reach a decision. This inconsistency might reflect the fact that GDSS increase participation thereby increasing the needed decision time; however, GDSS focus efforts on the task thereby reducing the needed decision time. Depending on which variable is more affected, GDSS might increase or decrease the needed decision time.

GDSS were also found to affect task-related and group-related outcomes. GDSS increase the quality of the decision and the confidence and satisfaction of the group members with the decision. They increase the group members' satisfaction with the decision process as well.

By focusing more efforts directly toward the task to be accomplished, GDSS increase the quality of decisions and the confidence and satisfaction of the members with the decision. These effects in turn lead to greater satisfaction of group members with the group processes. In the following pages, each of these findings is discussed in relation to major studies in the field.

Group Process

Depth of Analysis   Five studies focused on the impact of GDSS on the depth of analysis. Steeb and Johnson (1981), Gray (1983), Nunamaker, Applegate, and Konsynski (1988), and Vogel and Nunamaker (chap. 19 in this volume) found a positive impact, whereas Sharda, Barr, and McDonnell (1988) found no significant relationship between GDSS and depth of analysis.

Significantly, the type of decision does not appear to affect the positive relationship between GDSS and depth of analysis. This positive impact occurred with decisions ranging from complex political crisis (Steeb & Johnson, 1981) to strategic planning activities (Nunamaker et al., 1988; Vogel & Nunamaker, chap. 19 in this volume). Moreover, this impact was observed with decision process under varying degrees of uncertainty ranging from very high (Steeb & Johnson, 1981) to low uncertainty (Gray, 1983). The validity of this finding is reinforced by its generalized occurrence. The relationship was observed in studies with students (Gray, 1983; Steeb & Johnson, 1981) and with managers performing real managerial tasks (Nunamaker et al., 1988). However, it is important to note that the findings with managers are highly impressionistic and not based on controlled experiments.

Sharda and associates (1988) conducted the only study that did not find a positive relationship between GDSS and the depth of analysis. Unlike the other studies, this study used a decision model approach, supporting the decision process of individuals working in a group, not the group decision process per se. There seems to exist a synergy, which is an important part of the group process; this synergy can be enhanced by supporting the whole group process rather than each individual's decision process.

Task-oriented Communication and Clarification Efforts.   Along with an increase in the depth of analysis, research shows that GDSS increase task-oriented communication (Gray, 1983; Sharda et al., 1988) and clarification efforts of group members (Jessup, Tansik, & Laase, 1988; Nunamaker et al., 1988). There are two bases for this conclusion. First, all four studies found a positive relationship; no study obtained counter-findings. These findings are also consistent with the greater depth of analysis. Moreover, they seem generalized across multiple studies. The same results were observed with both students (Gray, 1983; Jessup et al., 1988; Sharda et al., 1988) and managers (Nunamaker et al., 1988). Also, groups of varying sizes support the same conclusion (Jessup et al., and Sharda et al., with groups of three or four members, and Nunamaker et al., with groups ranging from three to twenty-two members. Gray did not provide this information).

Although there is strong support for these findings, there are also notable limitations. Both findings were observed with managerial-planning decisions of medium complexity. Moreover, all four studies focused on the early stages of group development, when members try to establish group norms and typically focus their attention away from the task itself. The benefits of GDSS increasing task-oriented communication and clarification efforts might be minimal at the more advanced stages of group development, when members have already focused on the task. Furthermore, the structure imposed by GDSS on the group processes was not controlled in any study. Consequently, these results might be more indicative of structure rather than technological support itself.

Degree of Participation and Domination by a Few Members. There seems to be an inverse relationship between participation and domination. All studies that found a decrease in the domination structure of groups also found an increase in participation. However, it is unclear which one causes the other. It is undetermined whether a decrease in domination incites members to participate more, or by participating more, group members reduce the need and the opportunity for domination.

All four GDSS studies (George, Northcraft, & Nunamaker, 1987; Nunamaker et al., 1987; Nunamaker, Applegate, & Konsynski, 1988; Vogel & Nunamaker, chap. 19 in this volume) found a positive relationship between GDSS and the degree of participation of group members. Two of these studies also found a negative relationship between GDSS and domination (Nunamaker et al., 1987, 1988). There are three supports for these findings. First, all studies found the same relationship between GDSS and participation and domination. The findings are also consistent with an increase in clarification efforts (Jessup et al., 1988; Nunamaker et al., 1988). Moreover, they are valid for groups of varying size. The results were obtained in groups ranging from 3 to 22 members. It is also important to note that they were obtained from both students (George et al., 1987) and managers (Nunamaker et al., 1987, 1988; Vogel & Nunamaker, chap. 19 in this volume).

However, there is one serious threat to the validity of these findings, particularly to the increased participation. Most results are impressionistic in nature and were obtained in case studies with no control group (George et al., 1987; Nunamaker et al., 1987, 1988; Vogel & Nunamaker, chap. 19 in this volume). Moreover, the selection of participants of most of these studies might have been biased. The managers who go to a university setting to use computerized systems are likely to be very motivated, those who are not motivated, do not go there. Therefore, it is normal that participation in the group increases. In addition, the selection of participants was often done on a voluntary basis. Here again it might well be that the study attracted a very specific group of participants (those who enjoy using computer aids). This might positively bias the participation level of the subjects when they are assigned to computer-supported groups, and negatively affect their participation when they are not assigned. As a result, it is plausible that the control group and the experimental group of this study were not really comparable. In other words, participants might be predisposed toward using a computerized system by the mere fact of participating voluntarily in the experiment.

Decision Time. The findings on the impacts of GDSS on decision time are inconsistent. Bui, Sivasankaran, Fijol, and Woodbury (1987), Nunamaker (1987), and Vogel and Nunamaker (chap. 19 in this volume) found a negative relationship; Steeb and Johnson (1981) and Nunamaker and associates (1988) found a positive relationship; George and associates (1987) and Sharda and colleagues (1988) found no relationship. The finding of a negative relationship between GDSS and decision time is highly impressionistic, and is based on uncontrolled case studies (except Bui et al., 1987). One would expect that because GDSS increase participation, depth of analysis, and clarification efforts, GDSS would also increase the time needed to reach decisions. More research is clearly needed in this area.

Consensus Reaching. GDSS were also found to increase consensus reaching. Steeb and Johnson (1981), and Vogel and Nunamaker (chap. 19 in this volume) found a positive relationship; and George and colleagues (1987) found no relationship. This finding might seem inconsistent with increased participation and decreased domination; one would expect the consensus to decrease as more people voice their opinion and try to have their agenda supported by others. However, the relationship between GDSS and consensus might be explained by the fact that GDSS focus the attention and efforts of group members on task-related activities (increased depth of analysis, task-oriented communication, and clarification efforts) and therefore permit greater consensus even with increased participation.

Task-Related Outcomes

Decision Quality. Four studies that focused on the quality variable showed GDSS increased the quality of decision of group process (Bui et al., 1987; George et al., 1987; Sharda et al., 1988; Steeb & Johnson, 1981). This finding is consistent with the impacts of GDSS on group processes. All four studies also found a positive relationship between GDSS and decision quality. Moreover, an increased quality of decision was obtained in tasks of different complexity and uncertainty (Sharda et al., focused on tasks of medium complexity and uncertainty and Steeb and Johnson focused on tasks of high complexity and uncertainty). The potential weakness of this finding, however, is the lack of control the structure imposed on the group process. All studies were done on groups of three members, which limits the generality. Finally, the studies used groups in their early stages of development, when members typically do not focus on the task.[4] The gain from GDSS might be important for such groups, but not for groups in advanced stages who are already functional and task-oriented.

Confidence in Decisions and Satisfaction with Decisions. Consistent with the previously enumerated findings, Steeb and Johnson (1981), and Nunamaker (1987), we also found that GDSS increase the confidence of group members in decisions (Sharda et al, 1988 found no effect). Furthermore, Steeb and Johnson (1981), Nunamaker and associates (1987), and Vogel and Nunamaker (chap. 19 in this volume) found that GDSS increase the satisfaction of group members with the decision Bui and colleagues (1987) and George and associates (1987) found no effect.

The validity of these positive relationships, however, is questionable. Most results were obtained in case studies and are impressionistic by nature (Nunamaker, 1987; Vogel & Nunamaker, chap. 19 in this volume did not have control groups and did not carefully control variables.) Furthermore, the results of these studies might be biased by the fact that managers went to a university setting for their meetings. It is very possible that the mystique of the university setting made managers feel better with their decisions. The sample of participants might also be biased favorably toward using computers to make decisions by the mere fact of their coming to such a laboratory (the studies had no way of controlling such effects). And although Steeb and Johnson's study was conducted in a controlled laboratory setting, they did not control the effect of GDSS on the structure of group processes, which might well be the cause of greater confidence and satisfaction with the decision. The selection process itself might also have biased the results. Obviously, the findings are contradictory. Bui and associates (1987), George and associates (1987), and Sharda and associates (1988) found that GDSS have no effect on the level of confidence and satisfaction with the decision.

---

[4]George et al. (1987) and Sharda et al. (1988) did not provide this information; however, from the description of their research, they, like Steeb and Johnson (1981) seem to have focused on the very early stages of group development.

Group-Related Outcomes

Satisfaction with the Group Process. Steeb and Johnson (1981), Nunamaker (1987), Nunamaker and colleagues (1987, 1988), Jessup and associates (1988), and Vogel and Nunamaker (chap. 19 in this volume) found that GDSS increase satisfaction with the group process. George and associates (1987) found no such relationship; however, the increased satisfaction with the group process is consistent with the findings of higher consensus, better decision quality, higher confidence in the decision, higher satisfaction with the decision, and increased participation.

Discussion

Overall, it seems that GDSS research provides relatively consistent findings both within groups of variables (group process, task-related outcomes, and group-related outcomes) and across groups of variables. The research shows that GDSS (a) increase the depth of analysis; (b) increase the task-oriented communication and the clarification efforts; (c) increase the degree of participation and decrease the domination by a few members; (d) increase consensus among members of the group. These impacts seem to increase the quality of decisions, which in turn increase the confidence and satisfaction of group members toward the decision. Furthermore, the changes in group process and in the task-related outcomes increase the satisfaction of group members with the group processes.

However, four points need to be made. There is a lack of control for the effect of greater structure on group processes resulting from the technological support in most GDSS studies. This is particularly important because greater structure of the processes might cause changes in the group process variables and in the task- and group-related outcomes, rather than the GDSS. For example, Steeb and Johnson compared groups with no aid other than paper and pencil, with groups using GDSS support that provided computer-aided decision tree analysis. The positive relationship between GDSS and several group variables might not be an effect of the technological support, but rather the greater structure imposed on the group processes by the GDSS. Moreover, different types of GDSS might impose a very different form and degree of structure.

Furthermore, several GDSS studies do not monitor the potential effects of a facilitator (or do not provide enough information to determine if they did). A facilitator might affect group processes and outcomes in two ways: (a) intentionally, by playing an active role in planning, conducting, and facilitating the processes, or (b) unintentionally, by mere presence, which changes the atmosphere or the relationships between group members, or by being a good versus bad facilitator (i.e., being able or not being able to provide the information required by the group members). The unintentional effect may be particularly important with student participants. Students may perceive the facilitator as a professor evaluating them, which might influence their behavior.

Also, as discussed earlier, the selection process of many studies favor "computer prone" participants. These participants expect and want to use computer aids, but they also might be favorably biased in their estimate of the capabilities and of the impacts of computer aids on the group processes.

Finally, many GDSS studies focus on the very early stages of group development where group members try to establish and understand the norms of the group, try to define and defend their position, and try to obtain a basis of influence over the decision process. GDSS might have significant effects on groups at the early stages of development because it permits the members to focus more rapidly and intensely on the task itself. In a sense GDSS might decrease the time needed to arrive at the "functional" stage of group process and therefore permit technologically supported groups to outperform nonsupported groups. However, the vast majority of business meetings are composed of people who know each other very well and are used to working together in groups. Therefore most groups are at the later stages of group development, for which the current findings cannot be extended. Research is clearly needed on the relationship between technological support and the stages of group development.

IMPACTS OF GCSS ON GROUPS

We now turn to examine the research on communication support systems in relation to groups. As discussed earlier, GCSS focus on information aids rather than decision models per se. They primarily support the communication process between group members. As shown in Fig. 14.3, GCSS were found to have numerous impacts on group process and outcomes, most of which are consistent with one another. However, as is discussed later, these impacts are different from the impacts of GDSS.

Research shows that GCSS affect group processes in four major ways. GCSS increase the depth of analysis; they increase the total effort put in by the group members. GCSS were found to increase participation of group members and decrease domination of the group by a few members. Consistent with greater participation, GCSS were also found to decrease overall cooperation and consensus reaching. It appears that the increase in participation is not all channeled toward the task but also toward political behaviors. Finally, consistent with the previously listed impacts, research shows that GCSS supported groups take longer to reach a decision.

Research also shows that GCSS increase the quality of decisions. Although GCSS increase the quality of the decision, surprisingly they were

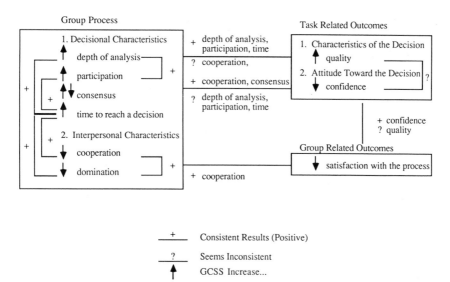

FIG. 14.3.   The impact of GCSS on groups.

discovered to decrease both the confidence of group members in the decision and their satisfaction with the process. This might be related to decreased consensus and cooperation among group members. GCSS may be efficient in terms of increasing performance of the groups (formal aspect) but not in terms of the interpersonal characteristics of groups (informal aspect). If these findings and the explanation advanced prove to be correct, it raises a serious question about the long-term future of GCSS. Each of these findings are discussed in relation to major studies in the field.

Group Process

Depth of Analysis.   Lewis (1982), Turoff and Hiltz (1982), Siegel, Dubrovsky, Kiesler, and McGuire (1986), and Gallupe, DeSanctis, and Dickson (1988) found a positive relationship between GCSS and depth of analysis. Interestingly, this finding was obtained in diverse type of decisions (arctic survival problem and career choice problem), and therefore, it does not seem to be dependent on the type of problem. Although all studies focused on problems of medium complexity, Gallupe et al. (1988) found no differences between high and low complexity problems; therefore, this should not affect the generality of the findings. Alternative explanations were well controlled in this set of studies. At least three studies (Gallupe et al., Lewis, and Turoff & Hiltz) controlled the degree of structure imposed by the GCSS, and the potential impacts of a facilitator was controlled in one study (Siegel et al.). However, results were identical in all these studies; apparently the facilitator did not have a critical impact on the relationship between GCSS the depth of analysis.

It is important to note that the positive relationship between GCSS and the depth of analysis was obtained with groups in the very early stages of group development. GCSS might permit groups at this stage to increase their focus on the task, or, in other words, to arrive at a functional stage faster than those not supported. However, the impact might be different in groups at more advanced stages of development. Consequently, the finding is not generalized across groups of varying levels of development.

Participation and Domination. Lewis (1982), Turoff and Hiltz (1982), Siegel and associates (1986), and Zigurs, Poole, and DeSanctis (1987) found that GCSS increase participation. Gallupe et al. (1988), and Poole, Holmes, and DeSanctis (1988) found that GCSS have no effect on the degree of participation of group members. Consistent with the positive finding, Lewis (1982), Turoff and Hiltz (1982), and Siegel and associates (1986) also found that GCSS decrease the domination by one or a few members of groups. Zigurs and colleagues (1987) and Watson, DeSanctis, and Poole (1988) found no relationship.

These two findings were valid for a wide variety of decisions. They are consistent with one another, and with the findings that GCSS decrease consensus and increase the time needed to reach a decision (discussed later).

It appears, however, that these findings might be limited to early stages of development. With the exception of Zigurs and associates (1987), the three studies that found a positive relationship between GCSS and participation focused on groups that were in early stages of development (Lewis, 1982; Siegel et al., 1986; Turoff & Hiltz, 1982). The studies that found no change focused on groups that were in advanced stages of development (Gallupe et al., 1988; Poole et al., 1988). Likewise, this pattern fits the findings on the dominance in groups. The studies that found a negative relationship between GCSS and domination by a few members (Lewis, 1982; Siegel et al., 1986; Turoff & Hiltz, 1982) focused on groups in early stages of development; the studies that found no relationship (Watson et al., 1988; Zigurs et al., 1987) focused on groups in later stages of development. This difference might reflect the fact that the change in the participation pattern and the structure of dominance is possible only at the beginning of group formation, but not later, when the pattern of participation and the structure of dominance is already established. GCSS do not make dominant groups or individuals "powerless," but seem able to prevent their emergence at later stages of group development, if they did not already emerge in the early stages.

Consensus and Cooperation. Gallupe et al. (1988) and Turoff and Hiltz (1982) found that GCSS decrease consensus, whereas Lewis (1982), Poole and colleagues (1988), and Watson and associates (1988) found no impact. When incorporating a feedback capability to the GCSS, Turoff and Hiltz (1982) found a positive relationship between GCSS and the consensus of group members. Two studies (Gallupe et al., 1988; Siegel et al., 1986) found GCSS to decrease cooperation. Poole and colleagues (1988), on the other hand, found no significant effect.

The research findings appear inconsistent with regard to the impact of GCSS on consensus and cooperation. However, this inconsistency may be explained by the development factor. In those studies that found a negative impact of GCSS on consensus and cooperation the focus was on groups in the early stages of development, whereas for those that found no relationship the focus was on latter stages of group development. This suggests that GCSS reinforce the existing structure of the group. When applied in early stages of group development, when the efforts of the members are oriented toward establishing position and power over the decision process, GCSS decrease consensus and cooperation. On the other hand, when applied in latter stages of group development, where there is an existing group structure and where the efforts of the members are mainly task-oriented, GCSS do not affect the consensus and cooperation between members.

Decision Time. There is a high consistency throughout the studies on the impact of GCSS on the time groups take to reach decisions. It was found by all studies (Bui & Sivasankaran, 1987; Gallupe et al., 1988; Siegel et al., 1986; Turoff & Hiltz, 1982) that GCSS increase the decision time. This is consistent with the other findings (increased depth of analysis, decreased consensus and cooperation).

Overall, the findings of the different GCSS studies concerning group processes are quite consistent. The research shows that GCSS increase the depth of analysis, increase participation, decrease the domination by a few members, and decrease consensus and cooperation. These changes in the group process apparently cause supported groups to require more decision time.

Task Related-Outcomes

Two of the findings obtained seem contradictory. Although GCSS increase the quality of decision, they decrease the group members' confidence in their decision.

Decision Confidence.   Zigurs and colleagues (1987), Gallupe et al. (1988), and Watson and colleagues (1988) found that GCSS decrease the confidence of group members in the decision, whereas Turoff and Hiltz (1982) found that GCSS increase it. Although decreased confidence is consistent with decreased consensus and cooperation, it is inconsistent with increased participation, increased depth of analysis, and increased decision quality.

Here again, the studies that found a negative relationship between GCSS and confidence in the decision focused on groups in advanced stages of development; the studies that found a positive relationship focused on groups on earlier stages of development. This suggests that GCSS decrease confidence when groups feel they can handle communication through already existing communication structures. In early stages, GCSS facilitate the focus of efforts on problems and seems to provide a support to the process that is needed. This explanation is supported by the negative relationship found in groups (Gallupe et al., 1988; Watson et al., 1988; Zigurs et al., 1987) with high existing social networks, and a positive relationship (Turoff & Hiltz, 1982), found in groups with low social networks.

Furthermore, the studies that found a negative relationship between GCSS and confidence used problems of medium to low uncertainty, whereas Turoff and Hiltz (1982), who achieved a positive relationship, used problems of high uncertainty. It seems that GCSS help groups that deal with decisions that might have high impacts on the group. As members of the group perceive their decision to have critical impact on themselves, there is a tendency for the group members to attribute greater responsibility to the computer support.

Quality of the Decision.   Lewis (1982), Turoff and Hiltz (1982), Bui and Sivasankaran (1987), Leblanc and Kozar (1987), and Gallupe et al. (1988) found that GCSS increase the quality of decision; however, Siegel and associates (1986) and Zigurs and colleagues (1987) found no relationship. It is significant to note that even if this finding seems inconsistent with some findings about group processes (like decreased cooperation), it is consistent with most other findings (increased depth of analysis, increased participation, increased time to reach a decision). Also, the positive relationship between GCSS and decision quality seems robust. It was found in very diverse types of decisions, at different stages of group development, and at different levels of uncertainty and complexity.

Group-Related Outcomes

Satisfaction with the Group Process.   Bui and Sivasankaran (1987) and Gallupe and associates (1988) found that GCSS decrease satisfaction with the process, whereas Lewis (1982) and Poole and colleagues (1988) found GCSS to have no effect. This negative findings seems to be highly correlated with the degree of consensus found in groups. Members of groups in which there was a low consensus were also found to have a low satisfaction with the process, not withstanding the quality of the decision. In addition, the studies that found a negative relationship between GCSS and satisfaction with the process used groups in early stages of development; studies that found no relationship used groups in later stages of development.

Discussion

Overall, the research on GCSS is consistent. The findings show that GCSS (a) increase the depth of analysis; (b) increase participation and decrease domination by a few members; (c) decrease cooperation; and (d) increase the time groups take to reach a decision. The greater depth of analysis, participation, and the increased decision time seem to increase the quality of decisions. The decrease in cooperation and consensus reaching seem to decrease confidence in the decision and satisfaction with the process.

Still, the following qualifying points need to be made. First, as in the GDSS studies, the selection of participants might bias the results obtained, particularly concerning increased participation. In addition, all the GCSS studies (except Turoff & Hiltz, 1982) used students, which highly limits the generality of the findings. Furthermore, all studies were conducted with small groups (typically three or four members). There are good reasons to expect that the findings would be different in larger groups. Also, Bui and Sivasankaran (1987) and Gallupe et al. (1988) showed that the degree of complexity of the task affects the impact of GCSS on groups. However, all studies on GCSS focused on tasks of medium complexity, and are therefore limited in their generality. Significantly, most studies do not account for the effect of the group's stage of development. This deficiency, although it might not be the only factor, seems to explain numerous apparent inconsistencies in the findings, and also limits the generality of the findings.

THE IMPACTS OF GDSS AND GCSS: COMPARISON AND CONTRAST

Our review of empirical research suggests that GDSS and GCSS have similar impacts on some aspects of group processes and outcomes, but opposite impacts on other aspects. GDSS and GCSS both increase the depth of analysis of groups, increase participation, decrease domination by a few members, and increase decision quality.

On the other hand, GDSS are found to increase consensus reaching, increase confidence in the decision by the group members, increase the satisfaction of group members with the process, and increase the satisfaction of the group members with the decision. GCSS are found to decrease consensus reaching and cooperation, increase the time to reach decision, decrease the confidence in decisions, and decrease the satisfaction of the members with the group process.

Our differentiation between GDSS and GCSS clarifies the findings of empirical research that otherwise seem inconsistent. When one analyzes the research without differentiating technological supports, one finds very inconsistent results. There are evidences of increased and decreased confidence in decisions, of satisfaction in decisions, and in the group processes. However, by grouping technological supports as either communication-related (GCSS) or decision-related (GDSS), the empirical evidences become consistent for each type of technological support. This suggests that GCSS and GDSS provide quite different support to groups and, consequently, have different impacts on them. The common impacts of GDSS and GCSS might be due to the similar support they provide facilitating communication between group members. The differential impacts might be due to the difference in support, GDSS supporting the decision process of groups.

Hence, it seems that GDSS and GCSS, by decreasing the communication barriers between group members, permit groups to channel the efforts of the members toward task-oriented activities and therefore increase the depth of analysis and decision quality. On the other hand, GDSS, by providing additional support to the group, increase the confidence members have in the decision, and increase their satisfaction with the decision and their satisfaction with the group process, whereas GCSS decrease these aspects. There are three potential explanations for this difference in impacts.

First, GCSS might not meet the expectations of the participants relative to their view of technologically supported group process. This might not only make them dissatisfied with the process and with the decision, but also decrease their confidence in the decision.

Our review of the research also shows that when GCSS are applied to groups in early stages of development (when there is no established communication network yet), GCSS increase the confidence of group members in the decision. However, when GCSS are applied to groups at more advanced stages of development (when communication networks are already established), GCSS do not seem to provide any perceived benefits, and consequently the confidence in the decision and the satisfaction with the group process decrease. On the other hand, members perceive that GDSS provides additional benefits at all stages of group development. This increases the confidence of the members in the decision, as well as their satisfaction with the decision and the group processes. It is important to note, however, that both GDSS and GCSS were found to increase the quality of the decision, and therefore the differential impact is in group members' perceptions of the process. This difference in perception is nonetheless important because, if group members feel that GCSS are not efficient, even harmful, the future of GCSS is threatened.

Or, perhaps the difference in impacts is due to the fact that GDSS focus group processes on the task and facilitate consensus. GCSS, although focussing efforts on the task, increase personally oriented communications. This decreases consensus and cooperation and decreases the confidence of group members in the process. It also decreases their satisfaction with the process and with the decision.

IMPLICATIONS FOR FUTURE RESEARCH

This review of empirical findings on the impacts of technological supports on groups has significant implications for both the focus of attention and the design of future research. Four points concerning the focus of future research arise from our review. It is important to note that most research effort is focused on a few factors of the formal dimension of group process, like decision quality, decision time, and depth of analysis. There is a lack of research on other important "formal" factors of groups, such as how technological support affects communication and interpersonal processes of groups and the impacts of technological support on decision implementation and on group-related outcomes.

In addition, there is a paucity of research on the impacts of technological support on the informal dimension of the group, such as power struggles, status establishment, and hidden agendas. Yet, as argued by Schwartzman (1986) and other behavioral scholars, and as reported in *The Wall Street Journal* (June 21, 1988), the informal dimension of groups might well be the most important of meetings.

Furthermore, the level of group development significantly affects how the technological supports affect group process, yet it is not taken into account in current research. This review shows that GDSS and GCSS have different impacts on groups, depending on whether they are applied to groups that are early or advanced in their developmental process. This factor, however, is not taken into account in present research, and its effect might have biased findings cumulated to date. More research is needed to better understand the impacts of the development factor on the success of GDSS and GCSS. Research in group psychology shows that important differences in group process can be expected between groups with and without meaningful history and future (cf. McGrath, chap. 2 in this volume).

Lastly, the structure imposed on group processes by the technological supports seems to have important effects on groups, but has not been investigated. This review shows that findings on how GDSS and GCSS affect groups are different whether or not the structure imposed by the technological support was controlled. This suggests that some impacts associated with the technological supports are in fact due to greater structure in group processes. More research is needed to clarify the importance of this effect.

One important point on the design of future research stems from our review. All GCSS studies were conducted with students in university settings. The GDSS studies were conducted with both students (Gray, 1983; Jessup et al., 1988; Sharda et al., 1988; Steeb & Johnson, 1981) and managers (George et al., 1987; Nunamaker, 1987; Nunamaker et al., 1987, 1988; Vogel, 1987; Vogel & Nunamaker, chap. 19 in this volume; Vogel et al., 1987), which provides greater external validity to the findings. However, the GDSS studies typically lack control over contextual variables and leave open many alternative explanations than the GCSS studies control. Also keep in mind that all studies, except Leblanc and Kozar (1987), were conducted in laboratory settings. Now that more group technological supports become more widespread and we have a basic understanding of how GDSS and GCSS affect groups, field studies in real organization settings are needed. Such field studies mean that researchers will have less control over contextual and independent variables than in laboratory settings. Therefore, they need to carefully identify and report the context in which the study was conducted. For this, Table 14.1 and Table 14.2 can be used as guidelines. The most important factors stemming from our review are: size of the group, type of the decision, complexity of the decision, group's development stage, reasons of members for joining the group, power and status relationships between group members, group's density, degree of anonymity, structure of group processes, and presence and quality of a facilitator.

REFERENCES

Argyris, C. (1975). Interpersonal barriers to decision-making. In *Harvard business review, on management* (pp. 425–445). New York: Harper & Row.

Averch, H. A., Carroll, S. J., Donaldson, T. S., Kiesleng, H. J., & Pincus, J. (1972). *How effective is schooling? A critical review and synthesis of research findings.* Santa Monica: CA: The Rand Corporation.

Bailey, F. G. (1965). Decisions by consensus in council and committees. In M. Banton (Ed.), *Political systems and the distribution of power* (pp. 1–20). London: Tavistock.

Benbasat, I., & Nault, B. R. (1988). An evaluation of empirical research in managerial support technologies: Decision support systems, group decision support systems, and expert systems. Unpublished manuscript, University of British Columbia, Faculty of Commerce and Business Administration, Vancouver, British Columbia.

Blau, P. M., & Scott, W. R. (1962). *Formal organizations.* San Francisco: Chandler.

Bowman, M. J. (1958). *Expectations, uncertainty, and business behavior.* New York: Social Science Research Council.

Bui, T., & Sivasankaran, T. R. (1987). *GDSS use under conditions of group task complexity.* Monterey, CA: The U.S. Naval Postgraduate School.

Bui, T., Sivasankaran, T. R., Fijol, Y., & Woodbury, M. A. (1987). Identifying organizational opportunities for GDSS use: Some experimental evidence. *DSS-87,* 68–75.

Cartwright, D. P., & Zander, A. F. (Eds.). (1968). *Group dynamic, research and theory.* New York: Harper & Row.

Caudill, W. (1958). *The psychiatric hospital as a small society.* Cambridge, MA: Harvard University Press.

Cummings, T. G., & Berger, C. J. (1976). Organization structure: How does it influence attitudes and performance? *Organization Dynamics, 5*(2), 34–49.

Davis, J. H., Strasser, G., Spitzer, C. E., & Holt, R. W. (1976). Changes in group members' decision preferences during discussion: an illustration with mock juries. *Journal of Personality and Social Psychology, 34,* 1177–1187.

Delbeq, A., Van de Ven, A., & Gustafson, D. (1975). *Group techniques: A guide to nominal and delphi processes.* Glenview, IL: Scott Foresman.

Dennis, A. R., George, J. F., & Nunamaker, J. F. Jr. (1988). *Group decision support systems: The story thus far.* Tucson, AZ: MIS Department, College of Business and Public Administration, University of Arizona.

DeSanctis, G., & Gallupe, R. B. (1987). A foundation for the study of group decision support systems. *Management Science, 33,* 589–609.

Festinger, L. (1950). Informal social communication. *Psychological Review, 57,* 271–282.

Flowers, M. L. (1977). A laboratory test of some implications of Janis' group-think hypothesis. *Journal of Personality and Social Psychology, 35,* 888–896.

French, J., & Raven, B. (1968). The bases of social power. In D. Cartwright, & A. Zander (Eds.), *Group dynamics.* New York: Harper & Row.

Frenno, R. F., Jr. (1962). The house appropriations committee as a political system: The problem of integration. *American Political Science Review, 56,* 310–324.

Gallupe, R. B., DeSanctis, G., & Dickson, G. (1988). Computer-based support for group problem finding: An experimental investigation. *MIS Quarterly, 12*(2), 277–296.

George, J. F., Northcraft, G. B., & Nunamaker, J. F. (1987). *Implications of group decision support system use for management: Report of a pilot study.* Tucson, AZ: College of Business and Public Administration, University of Arizona.

Goldman, M., Stockbauer, J. W., & McAuliffe, T. G. (1977). Intergroup and intragroup competition and cooperation. *Journal of Experimental Social Psychology, 13,* 81–88.

Gray, P. (1983). Initial observation from the decision room project. In G. P. Huber (Ed.), *DSS-83 Transactions,* Third International Conference on Decision Support Systems, June 27–29, Boston, MA, Transactions, 135–138.

Hackman, J. R. (1976). Group influence on individuals. In M. D. Dunnette (Ed.), *Handbook of industrial and organizational psychology.* Chicago: Rand McNally.

Hofstede, G. H. (1968). *The game of budget control.* London: Tavistock.

Hollander, E. P., & Julian, J. W. (1969). Leadership. In E. F. Borgatta (Ed.), *Social psychology: Readings and perspectives* (pp. 275–284). Chicago: Rand McNally.

Janis, I. (1972). *Victims of groupthink.* Boston: Houghton Mifflin.

Janis, I. L., & Mann, L. (1977). *Decision making.* New York: Free Press.

Jelassi, M. T., & Beauclair, R. A. (1987). An integrated framework for group decision support systems design. *Information and Management, 13,* 143–153.

Jessup, L. M., Tansik, D. A., & Laase, T. D. (1988). *Group problem solving in an automated environment: The effects of anonymity and proximity on group process and outcome with a group decision support system.* Manuscript submitted for publication.

Kemp, C. (1970). *Perspective on Group Process.* Boston: Houghton Mifflin.

Kraemer, K. L., & King, J. (1988). Computer-based systems for cooperative work and group decision making. *Computing Surveys, 20,* 115–146.

Leblanc, L. A., & Kozar, K. A. (1987). *The impact of group decision support system technology on vessel safety.* Bloomington, IN: School of Management, Indiana University.

Levit, A. M., & Benjamin, A. (1976). Jews and Arabs rehearse Geneva: A model of conflict resolution. *Human Relations, 29,* 1035–1044.

Lewis, F. L. (1982). *Facilitator: A micro computer decision support system for small groups.* Unpublished doctoral dissertation, University of Louisville.

McGrath, J. E. (1964). *Social psychology: A brief introduction.* New York: Holt, Rinehart & Winston.

Michener, H. A., & Burt, M. R. (1975). Components of "authority" as determinants of compliance. *Journal of Personnel Psychology, 31,* 600–614.

Mintzberg, H., Raisinghani, D., & Theoret, A. (1976). The structure of "unstructured" decision processes. *Administrative Science Quarterly, 21,* 246–275.

Mitchell, T. R. (1978). *People in organization.* New York: McGraw-Hill.

Nunamaker, J. F. (1987). *Collaborative Management Work.* Unpublished manuscript, University of Arizona.

Nunamaker, J. F., Applegate, L. M., & Konsynsky, B. R. (1987). Facilitating group creativity: Experience with a group decision support system. *Journal of Management Information Systems, 3*(4), 6–19.

Nunamaker, J. F., Applegate, L. M., & Konsynski, B. R. (1988). Computer-aided deliberation: Model management and group decision support. *Journal of Operations Research,* forthcoming.

Okun, M., & DiVesta, F. (1975). Cooperation and competition in coacting groups. *Journal of Personality and Social Psychology, 31,* 615–620.

Olsen, J. P. (1972). Voting, "sounding out" and the governance of modern organizations. *Acta Sociologica, 15,* 267–283.

Parson, T. (1949). *Essays in sociological theory: Pure and applied.* New York: Free Press of Glencoe.

Paulus, P. B., Annis, A. B., Setta, J. J., Schkade, J. K., & Matthews, R. W. (1976). Density does affect task performance. *Journal of Personality and Social Psychology, 34,* 248–253.

Pettigrew, A. M. (1973). *The politics of organizational decision-making.* London: Tavistock.

Poole, M. S., Holmes, M., & DeSanctis, G. (1988). Conflict management and group decision support systems. *Proceedings of the Second Conference on Computer Supported Cooperative Work,* Portland, Oregon.

Porter, L. W., & Lawler, E. E. (1965). Properties of organization structure in relation to job attitudes and job behavior. *Psychological Bulletin, 64,* 23–51.

Salipante, P., Notz, W., & Bigelow, J. (1982). A matrix approach to literature review. In B. M. Staw & L. L. Cummings (Eds.), *Research in organizational behavior* (pp. 321–348). Greenwich, CT: JAI Press.

Schwartzman, H. B. (1986). The meeting as a neglected social form in organizational studies. In B. M. Staw, & L. L. Cummings (Eds.), *Research in organizational behavior* (pp. 233–258). Greenwich, CT: JAI Press.

Scott, W. G. (1967). *Organization theory*. Homewood, IL: Irwin.

Sharda, R., Barr, S. H., & McDonnell, J. C. (1988). Decision support system effectiveness: A review and an empirical test. *Management Science, 34,* 139–159.

Shaw, M. E. (1976). *Group dynamics: The psychology of small group behavior*. New York: McGraw-Hill.

Siegel, J., Dubrovsky, V., Kiesler, S., & McGuire, T. (1986). Group processes in computer-mediated communication. *Organizational Behavior and Human Decision Processes, 37,* 157–187.

Steeb, R., & Johnson, S. C. (1981). A computer-based interactive system for group decision-making. *IEEE Trans., 11,* 544–552.

Steers, R. M. (1981). *Introduction to organizational behavior*. Santa Monica, CA: Goodyear.

Tuckman, B. W. (1965). Development sequence in small groups. *Psychological Bulletin, 64,* 384–399.

Turoff, M., & Hiltz, S. R. (1982). Computer support for group versus individual decisions. *IEEE Transactions on Communications, COM-30* (1), 82–90.

Van de Ven, A., & Delbeq, A. (1974). The effectiveness of nominal, delphi and interacting group decision-making processes. *Academy of Management Journal, 17,* 605–621.

Vogel, D., Nunamaker, J., Applegate, L., & Konsynski, B. (1987). Group decision support systems: Determinants of success. *DSS-1987,* 118–128.

Vroom, V. H., & Yetton, P. W. (1973). *Leadership and decision making*. Pittsburgh: University of Pittsburgh Press.

Watson, R. T., DeSanctis, G., & Poole, M. S. (1988). Using a GDSS to facilitate group consensus: Some intended and unintended consequences. *MIS Quarterly, 12*(3), 463–478.

Zachary, W. (1986). A cognitively based functional taxonomy of decision support techniques. *Human-Computer Interaction, 2*(1), 25–63.

Zander, A. (1979). The psychology of group processes. *Annual Review of Psychology, 30,* 417–451.

Zigurs, I., Poole, M. S., & DeSanctis, G. (1987). *A study of influence in computer-mediated decision making*. Minneapolis, MN: MIS Department, Curtis L. Carlson School of Management, University of Minnesota.

15

Hypertext and Collaborative Work: The Example of Intermedia

George P. Landow
Brown University

Abstract

Hypertext, by blurring the distinction between author and reader, allows, encourages, and even demands new modes of reading, writing, teaching, and learning. Because hypertext permits a reader both to annotate an individual text and also to link it to other, perhaps contradictory texts, it destroys one of the most basic characteristics of the printed text—its separation and univocal voice. In so doing it creates new understanding of collaborative learning and collaborative work. These themes are developed in a description of Intermedia, the networked hypertext system developed at Brown University by its Institute of Research in Information and Scholarship.

HYPERTEXT, COLLABORATIVE WORK, AND THE HUMANITIES

Intermedia, the networked hypermedia system developed at Brown University by its Institute of Research in Information and Scholarship (IRIS), allows, encourages, and even demands new modes of reading, writing, teaching, and learning. In so doing it creates new understanding of collaborative learning and collaborative work. Hypertext changes the relation of teacher and student and of author and reader (Yankelovich, Meyrowitz, & van Dam, 1985) just as it also changes the relationship of text and commentary (or the relationship of one text to other texts) (Landow, 1988a). All

407

these changes contribute to changing notions of authorship and authorial property.

Hypertext, a term coined by Theodor H. Nelson in the 1960s, refers to text in an electronic medium designed to be read nonsequentially. One can easily comprehend what is meant by nonsequential reading if one recalls how one proceeds through a scholarly or technical article. The reader begins at the top of the text, encounters a number or symbol that indicates the presence of a footnote, endnote, or bibliographical citation outside the main body of text, and then leaves it to investigate this material. Articles and books in the humanities often contain extensive discussion of issues, presentations of additional evidence, and statements of indebtedness to other authors or disagreement with them. All writing that makes use of reference conventions, however, leads the reader to exit the main text, consider additional material, and return to it. In some cases, material contained in the referenced section leads the reader outside the particular article or book entirely, and the reader may investigate other printed texts before returning to the original one. Imagine if one could simply touch the reference symbol and the indicated additional text appeared. Then imagine if one could touch the title of a work or body of research data mentioned in that additional text and it appeared, too. That is hypertext.

According to Nicole Yankelovich, one of the designers of Intermedia, a hypertext system is "both an author's tool and a reader's medium." It permits authors or groups of authors "to *link* information together, create *paths* through a corpus of related material, *annotate* existing texts, and create notes that point readers to either bibliographic data or the body of the referenced text" (Yankelovich, Meyrowitz, & van Dam, 1985, p. 18). Intermedia is a *networked hypermedia system.* It is *hypermedia* and not just hypertext, because it links images, graphic documents, and sound to text. It is *networked* because individual workstations join together to share a large body of information, thus making material created or modified at any one workstation available at all others.

Before looking at Intermedia and discussing in detail how it encourages collaborative work, let us examine the various forms that such collaboration might take. The word, which derives from the Latin for *working* plus that for *with* or *together,* conveys suggestions of working side by side on the same endeavor. I suspect that most people's conceptions of collaborative work take the form of two or more scientists, songwriters, or the like continually conferring as they pursue a project in the same place at the same time. I have worked on an essay with a fellow scholar in this manner. One of us would type a sentence, at which point the other would approve, qualify, or rewrite it, and then we would proceed to the next sentence. Far more common a form of collaboration, I suspect, is a second mode described as *versioning* (Morrell, 1988), in which one worker produces a draft that another person later edits by modifying and adding. The first and second forms of collaborative writing tend to blur, but the distinguishing factor here is the way versioning takes place out of the presence of the other collaborator and at a later time.

Both of these models require considerable ability to work productively with other people, and evidence suggests that many people either do not have such ability or do not enjoy putting it into practice. In fact, according to those who have carried out experiments in collaborative work, a third form proves more common than the first two: the *assembly-line* (Morrell, 1988) for segmentation model of working together, according to which individual workers divide up the overall task and work entirely independently. This last mode is the form that most people already engaged in collaborative work choose when they work on projects ranging from programming to art exhibitions.

Networked hypertext systems like Intermedia offer a fourth model of collaborative work that combines aspects of the previous models. By emphasizing the presence of other texts and their cooperative interaction, networked hypertext makes all additions to a system simultaneously a matter of versioning and the assembly-line mode. Once on Intermedia, a document no longer exists by itself. It always exists in relation to other documents in a way that a book or printed document never does and never can. Two principles derive from this crucial shift, which in turn produce this fourth form of collaboration: (a) any document placed on Intermedia (or on any other networked system that supports electronically linked materials) potentially exists in collaboration with any and all other documents on that system; (b) any document electronically linked to any other document collaborates with it. The examples provided in the following pages will make clear how collaboration takes place on Intermedia.

According to the *American Heritage Dictionary of the English Language, to collaborate* can mean either "to work together, especially in a joint intellectual effort" or "to cooperate treasonably, as with an enemy occupying one's country." The combination of labor, political power, and aggressiveness that appears in this dictionary definition well indicates some of the problems that arise when one discusses collaborative work. On the one hand, the notion of collaboration embraces notions of working together with others, of forming a community of action. This meaning recognizes, as it were, that we all exist within social groups, and it obviously places value on contributions to that group. On the other hand, collaboration also includes a deep suspicion of working with others, something both aesthetically as well as emotionally engrained since the advent of romanticism, which exalts the idea of individual effort to such a degree that it often fails to recognize or even suppresses the fact that artists and writers work collaboratively with texts created by others.

Most of our intellectual endeavors involve collaboration, although we do not always recognize it. The rules of our intellectual culture, particularly those that define intellectual property and authorship, do not encourage such recognitions, and furthermore, information technology from Gutenberg to the present—the technology of the book—systematically hinders full recognition of collaborative authorship. Intermedia and other hypertext systems, however, emphasize the collaboration suppressed by other technologies of cultural memory. Thus, even though print technology is not entirely or even largely responsible for current attitudes in the humanities toward authorship and collaboration, a shift to hypertext systems may well change them. If we can make ourselves aware of the new possibilities created by these changes, at the very least we can take advantage of the characteristic qualities of this new form of information technology.

Networked hypertext systems characteristically produce a sense of authorship, authorial property, and creativity that differs markedly from those associated with book technology. Intermedia changes our sense of authorship and creativity (or originality) by moving away from the constrictions of page-bound technology. In so doing, it promises to have an effect on cultural and intellectual disciplines as important as those produced by earlier shifts in the technology of cultural memory that followed the invention of writing and printing (Bolter, 1988; McCluhan, 1962).

By blurring the distinction between authors and readers as well as between teachers and students, networked hypertext systems create powerful shifts in the politics of reading (Landow, 1989a; Yankelovich, Meyrowitz, & van Dam, 1985). One corollary of this change appears in the radically different notions of authorship and authorial property generated by networked hypertext systems. Throughout this century the physical and biological sciences have increasingly conceived of scientific authorship and publication as group endeavors. The conditions of scientific research, according to which many research projects require the cooperating services of a number of specialists in the same or (often) different fields, bear some resemblances to the medieval guild system in which apprentices, journeymen, and masters all worked on a single complex project. The financing of scientific research, which supports the individual project, the institution at which it is carried out, and the costs of educating new members of the discipline, nurtures such group endeavors and consequent conceptions of group authorship. In general, the scientific disciplines rely on an inclusive conception of authorship: anyone who has made a major contribution to finding particular results, occasionally including specialized technicians and those who develop techniques necessary to carry out a course of research, can appear as authors of scientific papers. Similarly, those in whose laboratories a project is carried out may receive authorial credit if an individual project and the publication of its results depend intimately on their general research. In the course of graduate students' research for their dissertations, they may receive continual advice and evaluation. When the student's project bears fruit and appears in the form of one or more publications, the advisor's name often appears as coauthor.

Not so in the humanities, where graduate student research is supported largely by teaching assistantships and not, as in the sciences, by research funding. Although an advisor of a student in English or Art History often acts in ways closely paralleling the advisor of the student in physics, chemistry, or biology, explicit acknowledgements of cooperative work rarely appear. Even when a senior scholar provides the student with a fairly precise research project, continual guidance, and access to crucial materials that the senior scholar has discovered or assembled, the student does not include the advisor as coauthor. Part of the reason for the different conceptions of authorship and authorial property in the humanities and sciences, it is clear, derives from the different conditions of funding and the different discipline-politics that result.

Technology, specifically page-bound print technology and the attitudes it supports, is also responsible for maintaining exaggerated notions of authorial individuality, uniqueness, and ownership that often drastically falsify the conception of original contributions in the humanities and convey distorted pictures of research. The sciences take a relatively expansive, inclusive view of authorship and consequently of text ownership. The humanities take a far more restricted view emphasizing individuality, separation, and uniqueness—often at the expense of creating a vastly distorted view of the connection of a particular text to those that have preceded it. Neither view possesses an obvious rightness. Each has on occasion proved to distort actual conditions of intellectual work actually carried out in a particular field.

Whatever the political, economic, and other discipline-specific factors that perpetuate noncooperative authorship in the humanities, print technology has also contributed to the sense of a separate, unique text that is the product—and hence the property—of one person, the author. Intermedia and other networked hypertext systems promise to change all this, in large part because they do away with the separation of one text from all others that characterizes the book. As McCluhan (1962) and other students of the influence of print technology on culture have pointed out, modern conception of intellectual property derive both from the organization and financing of book production and from the uniform, fixed text that characterizes the printed book. Printing a book requires a considerable expenditure of capital and labor, and the need to protect that investment contributes to notions of intellectual property. But these notions would not be possible in the first place without the physically separate, fixed text of the printed book. Just as the need to finance printing of books led to a search for the large audiences that in turn stimulated the ultimate triumph of the vernacular and fixed spelling (McLuhan, 1962, pp. 229–33), so, too, the fixed nature of the individual text made it possible for each author to produce something unique and identifiable as property.

Hypertext, which links one block of text to myriad others, destroys that physical isolation of the text as well as the attitudes created by that isolation. As Walter J. Ong (1982) pointed out, books, unlike their authors, cannot be challenged:

> The author might be challenged if only he or she could be reached, but the author cannot be reached in any book. There is no way to refute a text. After absolutely total and devastating refutation, it says exactly the same thing as before. This is one reason why "the book says" is popularly tantamount to "it is true." It is also one reason why books have been burnt. A text stating what the whole world knows is false will state falsehood forever, so long as the text exists. (p. 79)

Because hypertext systems permit a reader both to annotate an individual text and link it to other, perhaps contradictory texts, it destroys one of the most basic characteristics of the printed text—its separation and univocal voice. Whenever one places a text within a network of other texts, one forces it to exist as part of a complex dialogue. Hypertext linking, which tends to change the roles of author and reader, also changes the limits of the individual text.

As I have pointed out elsewhere, electronic linking radically changes the experience of a text by changing its spatial and temporal relation to other texts (Landow, 1989a). Reading a hypertext version of Dickens's *Great Expectations* or Eliot's *The Waste Land*, for example, one follows links to predecessor texts, variant readings, criticism, and so on. Following an electronic link to an image of, say, the desert or wasteland in a poem by Tennyson, Browning, or Swinburne takes no more time than following one from a passage earlier in the poem to one near its end. Therefore, readers experience these other, earlier texts outside *The Waste Land* and the passage in same work as if they existed equally distant from the first passage. Hypertext thereby blurs the distinction between what is "inside" and what is "outside" a text. It also makes all the texts connected to a block of text collaborate with that text.

CONTEXT32 AND INTERMEDIA

For the past two years Intermedia has supported the teaching of four English courses plus one each in biology, anthropology, political science, and the Program in Liberal Medical Education. Recent publications by other members of IRIS have described the design, underlying theories, and development of Intermedia (Meyrowitz, 1986; Yankelovich, Haan, Meyrowitz, & Drucker, 1988), and I have similarly described its use in English courses (Landow, 1987a, 1989a). Undergraduate and graduate students in English employ *Context32*, that part of the Intermedia-based corpus specifically dedicated to humanities courses, to supplement assigned readings. The full corpus at present contains 4,700 electronically linked documents in various forms, and *Context32* contains 2,000 documents. The Intermedia system and the body of documents it links make up the largest as well as the most fully developed hypertext and hypermedia system thus far used for teaching at the college and university level.

Context32 consists of a mixture of primary materials, study guides, and questions to individual works, summaries of state-of-the-art scholarship ("Dickens Biography") introductions to basic critical concepts ("Satire," "The Sonnet"), and original scholarly and critical contributions ("Feminist Views of the Literary Canon," "Biblical Typology"). These essays contain biographies of individual authors, brief essays on literary technique, both general and specific (e.g., "Narration and Point of View" and "Imagery in D. H. Lawrence's 'Prussian Officer'"), and discussions of nonliterary topics related to more than one author (e.g., "Social Darwinism," "Ages of Technology," "Biblical Typology," and "Freud and Freudianism"). Most essays contain questions that refer students back to the reading, ask them to apply their newly acquired information to an included portion of text, or encourage them to follow links to other files.

In addition to these text documents, *Context32* also contains graphic documents in various forms, including digitized reproductions of paintings, maps, photographs, architectural drawings, and the like. Furthermore, using InterDraw, the graphics editor in the Intermedia system, we have created many index diagrams. These graphic presentations of intellectual relationships, one of the most educationally important parts of *Context32,* serve as directories or overviews that inform the user about various information on individual authors, works, and topics, and also include links that provide quick access to that information. By surrounding an individual phenomenon, say, Tennyson's poem *In Memoriam* (Fig. 15.1), Alexander Pope, or Victorianism (Fig. 15.2), with a range of phenomena, including biographical information, contemporary science, and history, these overview diagrams immediately enforce one of the main educational points of the course—that any literary or other phenomenon exists surrounded by relatable contributing phenomena. This graphic presentation simultaneously shows existing links, thus directing the reader to more information, and cultivates the habit of making such connections, thus developing a particular intellectual skill. *Context32* also contains graphic representations of literary influence and interrelations that take the form of diagrams of vector forces. Unlike over-

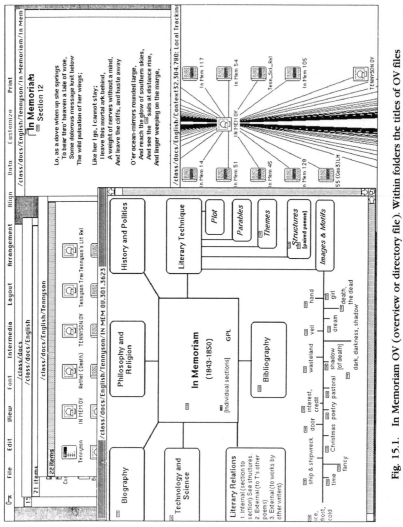

Fig. 15.1. In Memoriam OV (overview or directory file). Within folders the titles of OV files appear in full caps to make them easier to locate. The Tennyson folder appears above (and behind) the overview, and the local tracking map, which shows what documents link to the active window (here the overview), appears on the right.

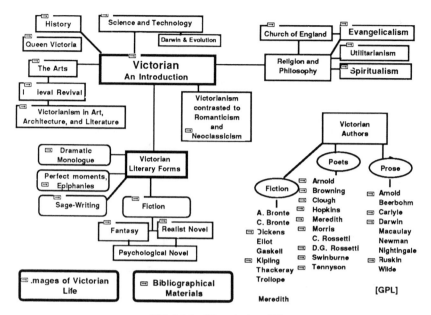

FIG. 15.1.   Victorianism OV.

view files, literary relation files and similar analyses of complex historical and cultural phenomena emphasize unidirectional flow of forces.

EXAMPLES OF COLLABORATIVE WORK
FROM INTERMEDIA

In the early days of developing and using Intermedia and *Context32*, the reader's shaping of the text and choice of linkpaths provided the only form of student collaborative work that concerned us. The four graduate or postdoctoral students and I who created the materials that constituted the first version of *Context32* worked collaboratively, of course, but only in ways characteristic of traditional group projects. Each person wrote documents on a set of authors and topics, also gathering graphic materials. Acting in the manner of the editor of an encyclopedia or anthology, I then co-ordinated the materials and made them conform to house style. Once we reached the stage of putting documents on Intermedia, some of the contributors modified materials created by others and linked them to their own creations. To this point, the Intermedia materials were the product of the five original contributors alone. However, ever since students in the English 32, *Survey of English Literature, 1750 to the Present,* used *Context32,* their collaboration has proved increasingly important. As I have explained elsewhere, the first assignment in each course that uses Intermedia is intended to acquaint the student with the nature of the system and the materials it contains (Landow, 1989b). After instructing students to open an overview file and follow various links, the assignment asks them to record what they encounter and then asks for suggestions of additional links or materials. Another part of the assignment asks the students to choose a passage from the week's reading to append to one of the maps or other graphic documents. Somewhat to our surprise, these assignments had the happy effect of convincing a substantial portion of the class that they had control over the material and could contribute to it. Students in English 32 therefore continued to offer proofreading corrections, suggestions for links, and requests for additional materials throughout the semester. And in fact, after students expressed the view that discussions of technical devices, such as imagery and narration, worked best with specific proof-texts, we created new materials for later readings. In addition to the clearly demonstrated student attitude of participation and collaboration in shaping the materials on Intermedia, we also discovered several students who took matters into their own hands and, after receiving permission (and passwords), began to make their own links as well as obvious corrections (e.g., moving links that had been labeled mistakenly or correcting typographical errors).

The following semester, when *Context32* supported English 61, an upperclass seminar in Victorian poetry, the fourteen students enrolled in this course used it to work in a more intensively collaborative manner than the students in English 32. They created documents, and some entered them on the system themselves and also made links. Observing students from an upperclass course reading and benefiting from materials created by those in another class convinced me that I should attempt an even more elaborate experiment in collaborative hypertext with graduate students, some of whom had begun to use Intermedia to prepare for their qualifying examinations. Therefore, the following term, when *Context32* again supported the teaching of the Survey, I also used it for my graduate seminar in Victorian literature, whose six members contributed to the *In Memoriam* project described later.

On Intermedia the student makes four kinds of contributions to *Context32,* each of which involves collaborative work: (a) reading, in which the reader plays a more important role in shaping the reading path than does the reader of a book; (b) creating links among documents present on the system; (c) creating text documents (and linking them to others); and (d) creating graphic documents (and linking them to others). Contributors to the system have produced graphics documents by adding digitized images, such as maps or reproductions of pictures, and by using InterDraw to create concept maps with varying degrees of text. Student users have both created entirely new concept maps in the form of overview or literary relations files and used earlier ones as templates, making minor modifications and changing the texts.

Collaborative work on Intermedia takes many forms, one of the most interesting of which illustrates the principle that one almost inevitably works collaboratively whenever creating documents on a multiauthor hypertext system. One day when I was linking materials to the overview (or directory) file for Graham Swift's *Waterland* (1983), I observed Nicole Yankelovich, Project Coordinator at IRIS, working on materials for a course in arms control and disarmament offered by Richard Smoke of Brown University's Center for Foreign Policy Development. These materials, which were created by someone from a different discipline for a very different kind of course from mine, filled a major gap in *Context32*. Although my coauthors and I had created materials about technology, including graphic and text documents on canals and railroads, to attach to the science and technology link in the *Waterland* Overview (OV), we did not have the expertise to create parallel documents about nuclear technology and the antinuclear movement, two subjects that play a significant part in Swift's novel. Creating a brief file on the subject of *Waterland* and nuclear disarmament, I linked it first to the science and technology section in the *Waterland* OV and then to the timeline that the nuclear arms course materials employ as a directory file (Fig. 15.3). A brief document and a few links enable students in the introductory survey of English literature to explore the materials created for a course in another discipline. Similarly, students from that course can now encounter materials showing the effects on contemporary fiction of the concerns covered in their political science course. Intermedia thus allows and encourages collaborative work, and at the same time it encourages interdisciplinary approaches by making materials created by specialists in different disciplines work together—collaborate.

It is important to note here that hypermedia linking automatically produces collaboration. Looking at the way the arms control materials joined to those supporting the four English courses, one encounters a typical example of how the connectivity that characterizes Intermedia transforms independently produced documents into collaborative ones. When one considers the arms control materials from the point of view of their originator, they exist as part of a discrete body of materials. When one considers them from the vantage point of a user of Intermedia, their status changes: As soon as they appear on the Intermedia system, these and all other documents there exist (a) as part of a larger system and (b) in relation therefore to other materials on that system. By forming electronic pathways between blocks of texts, Intermedia links actualize the potential relations between them.

The way Intermedia changes both our notions of collaborative work and our experience of it appears in student contributions to *Context32*. The

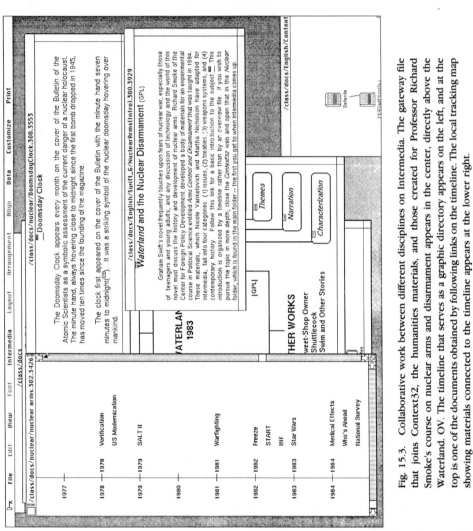

Fig. 15.3. Collaborative work between different disciplines on Intermedia. The gateway file that joins Context32, the humanities materials, and those created for Professor Richard Smoke's course on nuclear arms and disarmament appears in the center, directly above the Waterland. OV. The timeline that serves as a graphic directory appears on the left, and at the top is one of the documents obtained by following links on the timeline. The local tracking map showing materials connected to the timeline appears at the lower right.

most basic kind of contribution to Intermedia—and the most fundamental—is the addition of a link, something students are encouraged to do by an
assignment due a few days after each course begins. Introductory exercises
require them to explore the Intermedia materials by following links and
then to suggest others. Students have to link a text from the first week's
reading in Graham Swift's *Waterland* to one of several maps intended to
illuminate that novel. Figure 15.4 exemplifies this simplest form of link, for
here Daphne Beal, a student in the survey of English literature (English 32),
has chosen a passage from the week's reading to append to a map of English
transport 1760–1930.

The next most complex form of contribution to Intermedia involves
creating a document, either text or graphic, and then linking it to existing
documents on Intermedia. Emma Leheny thus collaborated with the system
and its many other authors when she added the following document entitled "What do maps of railroads and canals tell us about the novel?" to the
Waterland folder and then linked it to a file that contains both a picture of
Chirk Acqueduct and a map of the waterway system in 1789:

> The Cricks of the Fens are occupied with business related to the river. The
> picture of the acqueduct [reproduced on Intermedia] . . . is reminiscent of
> the opposing forces of human power and nature in *Waterland*. The acqueduct
> is the result of a massive human effort to control the course of water. Similarly,
> Henry Crick [the narrator's father] is the lock-keeper of the river, the lock
> being a seemingly absurd human attempt to control the river. For the most
> part, the people of the Fens do seem in control, but nature overpowers them
> when the river overflows, drowns them, and destroys their crops. An impor-
> tant theme in the novel is that the water, like all nature, has power over
> people. As Tom Crick tells his students, "When you work with water, you have
> to know and respect it. When you labour to subdue it, you have to understand
> that one day it may rise up and turn all your labours to nothing."

The student has created her own text, which includes a quotation from the
work in question, rather than simply link something in *Context32* to another text. Thus this form of collaboration represents a more complex
contribution than that exemplified by Beal. (In practice, however, they
proved similar: because the entire text of *Waterland* does not appear in
Intermedia, one has to add a passage from it to the one to which one wishes
to make a link, just as one has to write one's own text and then link it to
preexisting documents. In a more complete hypertext corpus, such as that
exemplified by the *In Memoriam* project described later, one simply links
the blocks of texts from complete works to one another, connecting, say,
the description of Miss Havisham in Dickens' *Great Expectations* to one of a
similar character in Swift's *Waterland*.)

Two things about these student contributions demand comment. First,

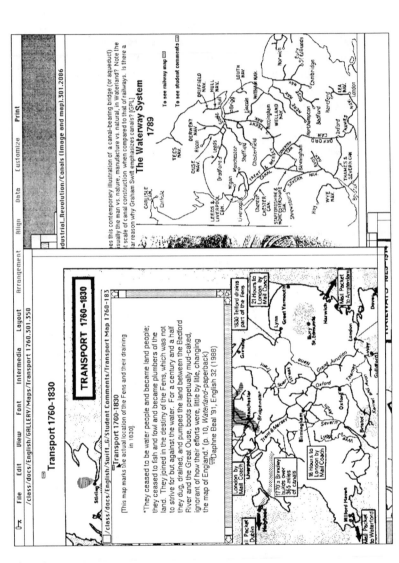

Fig. 15.4. The student has here overlaid the map of canals opened in the previous stage of the exercise with one entitled "Transport, 1760–1830." A brief document composed of text quoted from Swift's *Waterland* in turn overlays this map; this file, which Daphne Beal '91 created, exemplifies the kind of student annotation and contribution that Intermedia encourages.

presented by means of print technology, as they are here, they at first seem separate, discrete documents created as student exercises that do not collaborate with anything else. But as part of *Context32* on Intermedia, they exist in different form and are experienced differently, because they link to other documents, qualifying and supplementing them.

Second, these student documents mingle with those created by faculty members. They therefore represent a radical departure from current modes of learning and scholarship. We encourage our students to think independently, and some of us even prompt them to challenge our pet theories and interpretations. Occasionally, in our books and articles we thank students for having helped us formulate these theories in the pressure of discussion or for having uncovered some interesting bit of evidence. But we do not publish their comments in our books. Intermedia, however, enables student–faculty collaboration by including a large number of links and documents created by students. Whereas few students can contribute general essays or much in the way of original scholarly research, all can contribute links and many can produce valuable graphic and text documents that supplement those that are faculty-created. These documents can add materials not included previously, qualify existing approaches, and even simply contradict existing presentations of individual topics.

All four literature courses require students to create their own versions of overview or literary relations documents. "Tennyson's 'Lady of Shalott': Literary Relations" (Fig. 15.5) by Laura M. Henrickson, a student in my graduate course, represents such an attempt made early in the semester to create an Intermedia-style concept map based on those present in the system. The six boxes graphically present this particular text's relations to those by earlier authors. Several of the individual boxes link to additional materials, and the entire concept map links to another view of the poem created by a student in my undergraduate seminar. In what ways, then, does this document exemplify collaborative work? First, it adds something new to *Context32*'s Tennyson materials. Moreover, it links to various documents on one particular poem, "The Lady of Shalott," thereby working together with them. In addition, one of those documents to which it links, another concept map, was created by a student in an undergraduate course, and Henrickson's document therefore exists related to one produced by an undergraduate student. It is worthwhile to emphasize this point, because professors do not ordinarily collaborate with students, nor do graduate and undergraduate students. I have observed graduate students reading documents written by freshmen and freshmen reading works created by advanced graduate students. I have also observed students at widely differing places in their academic careers creating links to documents produced by those at different academic levels. Intermedia, in other words, allows collab-

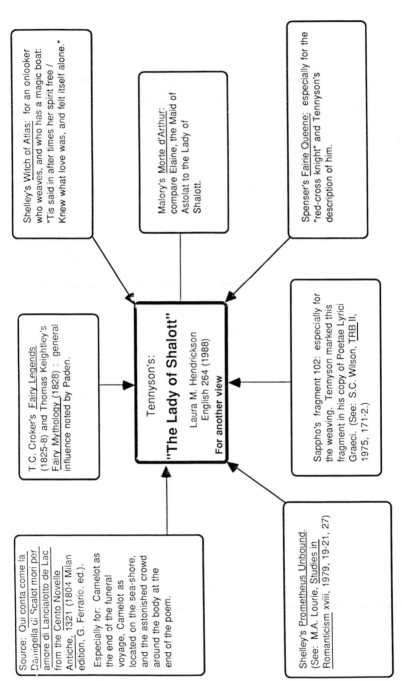

Shelley's Witch of Atlas: for an onlooker who weaves, and who has a magic boat: "Tis said in after times her spirit free / Knew what love was, and felt itself alone."

Malory's Morte d'Arthur: compare Elaine, the Maid of Astolat to the Lady of Shalott.

Spenser's Fairie Queene: especially for the "red-cross knight" and Tennyson's description of him.

T.C. Croker's Fairy Legends (1825-8) and Thomas Keightley's Fairy Mythology (1828) : general influence noted by Paden.

Tennyson's:

"The Lady of Shalott"

Laura M. Hendrickson
English 264 (1988)
For another view

Sappho's fragment 102: especially for the weaving. Tennyson marked this fragment in his copy of Poetae Lyrici Graeci. (See: S.C. Wilson, TRB II, 1975, 171-2.)

Source: Qui conta come la Damigella di Scalot mori per amore di Lancialotto de Lac from the Cento Novelle Antiche, 1321 (1804 Milan edition, G. Ferrario. ed.).

Especially for: Camelot as the end of the funeral voyage, Camelot as located on the sea-shore, and the astonished crowd around the body at the end of the poem.

Shelley's Prometheus Unbound. (See: M.A. Lourie, Studies in Romanticism xviii, 1979, 19-21, 27)

Fig. 15.5. "Tennyson's 'Lady of Shalot': Literary Relations," by Laura Hendrickson.

oration not only among those of equivalent academic rank or status, but also among those of widely different rank or status.

THE *IN MEMORIAM* PROJECT

The *In Memoriam* project, which employs all the forms of collaborative work described thus far, takes advantage of the capacities of hypermedia to do things virtually impossible with book technology. In particular, the dual capacity of hypertext to record relations between text blocks and allow readers quickly to navigate these links offers enormous possibilities to the humanistic disciplines. As an experiment in collaboration to determine precisely how one goes about creating, maintaining, and using hypertext to study the internal and external connections implicit in a major literary work, the members of the graduate seminar and I placed a particularly complex poem on *Context32* and then linked to it (a) variant readings from manuscripts, (b) published critical commentary, as well as (c) that by members of the seminar, and (d) passages from works by other authors. Tennyson's *In Memoriam,* a radically experimental mid-Victorian poem, perfectly suits this experiment, in part because in its attempt to create new versions of traditional major poetic forms from 133 separate sections, each a poem that can stand on its own it makes extensive use of echoing, allusion, and repetition, all of which are perfectly suited to hypertext linking.

The *In Memoriam* project made use of documents created as an exercise for the undergraduate seminar in Victorian poetry that directed students to take a single section of Tennyson's *In Memoriam* and "show either by an essay of no more than two pages (typed) or by a one-page diagram its connections or relations to other sections of the poem." Kristen Langdon's "Relations of In Memoriam 60 to Other Sections" (Fig. 15.6), which relies on a wheel diagram in which blocks of text connect by spokes to a center, reinvents the Intermedia concept map by making a more concrete use of it. Langdon demonstrates how Tennyson enriches his straightforward, simple diction by linking individual phrases, such as "dark house," "some poor girl," and "sphere," to other sections of the poem. This author's decision to link partial blocks of text to a complete one and avoid generalizing statements or summaries distinguishes her approach from most previous material on the system. Her solution to the assignment, which was paralleled by those of several other students, manages to convey on one page or screen information that would take many more words in an essay format.

Between January and April 1988, the six members of the graduate seminar added links and documents to the body of materials already on-line. In addition to the 133 sections of the poem, the students in the course encountered several dozen files on the poet and his other poems, as well as relevant

In 60 concern is more for passing of the friend and the earthly loss; Compare: 95:33-36 "So word by word, and line by line/The dead man thoughed me from the past."

116:15-16 "Less yearning for the friendship fled / Than some strong band which is to be."

129:9 "Strange friend, past, present, and to be"

environmental description reflects speaker's mood:

7:1-2. "Dark house, by which once more I stand/Here in the long . unlovely street

No. 119 shows same setting with happier mood, thus reflecting a change of attitude. [follow for discussion by R. Fletcher] ▭

Others around the girl of 60 and women of 97 question her position in love:

97:13-16 "Their love has never past away. . . . Whate'er the faithless people say."

BUT with spritual awakening in 95, he can see friendship in both present and future terms (Cp 116, 129)

60

He past, a soul of nobler tone;
My spirit loved and loves him yet,
Like some poor girl whose heart is set
On one whose rank exceeds her own.

He mixing with his proper sphere,
She finds the baseness of her lot,
Half jealous of she knows not what,
And envying all that meet him there.

The little village looks forlorn;
She sighs amid her narrow days,
Moving about the household ways,
In that dark house where she was born.

The foolish neighbours come and go,
And tease her till the day draws by;
At night she weeps, "How vain am I!
How should he love a thing so low?"

▭ 9:18 "Till all my WIDOW'D race be won"

85:113 "My heart, tho' WIDOW'D, may not rest"

52:13 "So fret not, like an idle GIRL"

97:7 "And of my spirit as a WIFE"

(In 48 and 49, sorrow is identified as "she" when the speaker is overwhelmed by sorrow. Likewise, knowledge and wisdom are females in 114)

Imagery of circles and spheres:
61:3 "With all the CIRCLE of the wise"
63:11-12 "The CIRCUITS of thine ORBIT ROUND"

97:31 "She knows but matters of the house"

Fig. 15.6. "Relations of In Memoriam 60 to Other Sections," by Kristen Langdon '88.

materials on Victorian religion, science, history, and art. Students from the undergraduate seminar had created approximately a dozen graphic or text documents and linked them to individual sections of *In Memoriam*. I had already created an overview file (Fig. 15.1) for the poem itself, basing it on the one for Tennyson, and to this file student consultants, room monitors, and I linked individual sections and a few of the relevant motifs.

In the course of the next few months the members of the graduate seminar added more than a hundred documents, each commenting specifically on one or more sections of the poem and on one another's work. The first assignment for the project required them to create five documents to

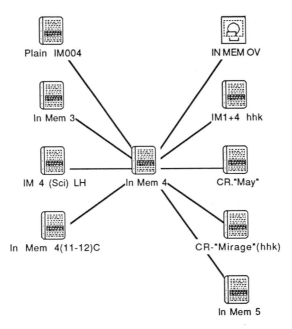

Plain IM004

IN MEM OV

In Mem 3

IM1+4 hhk

IM 4 (Sci) LH

In Mem 4

CR."May"

In Mem 4(11-12)C

CR-"Mirage"(hhk)

In Mem 5

FIG. 15.7. Local Tracking Map for the fourth section of *In Memoriam* (In Mem 4). The active file appears at the center of the linked files. On the left, the top icon represents a clean copy of the poem without any link markers in the text. Since particular phrases in the preceding (In Mem 3) and following (In Mem 5) sections ink to this one, icons indicating them appear (at upper left, second from the top, and lower right). Third from the top on the left appears the icon indicating an essay on the allusion to contemporary geology in section 4, and the last item on the left indicates commentary on lines 11–12. In Memoriam OV appears at the top right, and below that appears the icons for an essay comparing sections 1 and 4, two poems by Rossetti, and the already mentioned earlier section 5.

The number of words required to explain these documents suggests how much more efficient are the Intermedia tracking maps as a means of quickly conveying such information.

append to individual sections of the poem. Each week members of the seminar read the contributions of others, added more documents, and then made links. The final assignment directly involving the *In Memoriam* project required each student to put on-line the texts of poems by another poet, Christina Rossetti, that had obvious relevance to individual sections of Tennyson's work. Members of the class had earlier added texts from work by writers other than Tennyson, and this assignment was intended to explore hypertext presentation of interauthor relations in specific terms. The local tracking map (Fig. 15.7), which represents the documents linked to whichever open document is active, shows those connected to a single section of *In Memoriam.*

Although the project has just begun, it already rivals in size and complexity the first version of *Context32.* Working independently and yet together, the members of the seminar have created a presentation of a major nineteenth-century literary work that makes obvious many of its internal and external relations. Equally interesting, graduate students in English have worked collaboratively in a manner rare in their discipline, and because their work has taken the form of contributions to Intermedia, those who follow them will have access to what they have created.

CONCLUSION

One can argue, of course, that all writing inevitably follows this form of collaboration however much book-bound technology hides or obscures it. Such is precisely the argument made by Roland Barthes and other structuralists who continually emphasize that each speaker or writer manipulates a complex semiotic system containing layers of linguistic, semantic, rhetorical, and cultural codes with which one always collaborates. Unlike book technology, hypertext, however, does not hide such collaborative relationship. Even if all texts (however defined) always exist in some relation to one another, before the advent of hypertext technology, such interrelations could only exist within individual minds that perceived these relations or within other texts that asserted the existence of such relations. The texts themselves, whether art objects, laws, or books, existed in physical separation from one another. Networked hypermedia systems, in contrast, record and reproduce the relations among texts, one effect of which is that they permit the novice to experience the reading and thinking patterns of the expert. Another result of such linking appears in the fact that all texts on a system like Intermedia potentially support, comment on, and collaborate with one another. To repeat what I said in the first section: Once placed on Intermedia, a document no longer exists alone. It always exists in relation to other documents in a way that a book or printed document never does and never can. From this follows two corollaries. First, any document placed on Intermedia (or on any other networked system that supports electronically linked materials) potentially exists in collaboration with any and all other documents on that system. Second, any document electronically linked to any other document collaborates with it.

Intermedia is the outstanding example of a system in which the whole is far greater than the sum of its parts, for each works synergistically with others. The idea that any text placed on Intermedia potentially collaborates with any other and that any link between texts in fact makes them work collaboratively may take some getting used to. Can technology so radically change the status and conditions of work? Can technology so challenge established notions of writing, authorship, and authorial property? Yes. The technology of printing and book production clearly created current notions of grammar, fixed orthography, national languages, copyright, and so on, so one should expect that a technology that again shifts the relations of author, reader, and work would again have equally powerful effects.

To create a document or a link on Intermedia is to collaborate with all those who have used it previously and will use it in future. The essential connectivity of Intermedia encourages and demands collaboration. By making each document in *Context32* exist as part of a larger structure, Intermedia places each document in what one can term the "virtual presence" of all previously created documents and their creators. This electronically created virtual presence transforms individual documents created in an assembly-line mode into documents that also exist as if they had been produced by several people working at the same time. In addition, by permitting individual documents to contribute to this electronically related overarching structure, Intermedia also makes each contribution a matter of versioning. In so doing, it provides a model of scholarly work in the humanities that better records what actually takes place in such disciplines than traditional book technology.

ACKNOWLEDGMENTS

Intermedia is the culmination of two years of intense effort by a large team of developers at IRIS led by Norman Meyrowitz. I would especially like to thank Nicole Yankelovich, our Project Coordinator, for her continual resourcefulness, tireless effort, and unfailing good humor as well as for her assistance with this chapter. I would like to thank David Cody, Tanuja Desai, Laurelyn Douglas, Glenn Everett, Suzanne Keen Morley, Kathryn Stockton, and Robert Sullivan for their contributions to *Context32*. Finally, I wish to thank the students in my graduate seminar in Victorian literature—Maryanne Ackershoek, Chatchai Atsavapranee, Mark Gaipa, Laura Henrickson,

Helen Kim, and Mark McMorriss—for their contributions to the *In Memoriam* project.

The work described in this chapter was sponsored in part by a grant from the Annenberg/CPB Project and a joint study-contract with IBM.

REFERENCES

Bolter, J. (1988). *Writing space: Computers in the history of literacy.* Unpublished manuscript.

Landow, G. P., Cody, D., Everett, G. Stockton, K., & Sullivan, R. (1986). *Context32:* A web of English literature. Providence, RI: Institute for Research in Information and Scholarship, Brown University.

Landow, G. (1987a). *Context32:* Using Hypermedia to Teach Literature. Proceedings of the 1987 IBM Academic Information Systems University AEP Conference. Milford, CT: IBM Academic Information Systems, 30–39.

Landow, G. (1987b). Relationally Encoded Links and the Rhetoric of Hypertext. *Hypertext '87* (pp. 331–344). Chapel Hill, NC: Department of Computer Science, University of North Carolina.

Landow, G. (1989a). Hypertext in literary education, criticism, and scholarship. *Computers and the Humanities, 23,* 173–98.

Landow, G. (1989b). Course assignments in Hypertext: The example of Intermedia. *Journal of Research on Computing in Education, 21,* 349–65.

McLuhan, M. (1962). *The Gutenberg galaxy: The making of typographic man.* Toronto: University of Toronto Press.

Meyrowitz, N. (1986). Intermedia: The architecture and construction of an object-oriented Hypermedia system and applications framework. *OOPSLA '86 Proceedings* (pp. 186–201). Portland, OR.

Morrell, K. (1988). Teaching with *Hypercard* An Evaluation of the Computer-Based Section in Literature and Arts C-14: The Concept of the Hero in Hellenic Civilization. Perseus Project Working Paper 3, Department of Classics, Harvard University.

Ong, W. (1982). *Orality and literacy: The technologizing of the word.* London: Methuen.

Yankelovich, N., Meyrowitz, N., and van Dam, A. (1985). Reading and writing the electronic book. *IEEE Computer, 18,* 15–30.

Yankelovich, N., Landow, G., & Cody, D. (1987). Creating Hypermedia materials for English literature students. *SIGCUE Outlook, 19,* 12–25.

Yankelovich, N., Haan, B., Meyrowitz, N., & Drucker. (1988). Intermedia: The concept and the construction of a seamless information environment. *IEEE Computer, 21,* 81–

16

Supporting Collaboration with Advanced Multimedia Electronic Mail: The NSF EXPRES Project

Gary M. Olson
The University of Michigan

Daniel E. Atkins
The University of Michigan

Abstract

Most scientific reports and scientific grant proposals in particular are collaboratively written. Most proposals are also multi-media, with equations, figures, tables, graphs, and photographs frequently supplementing the text. Some way of sharing editable, multi-media documents in electronic form could be very useful in the creation and submission of scientific documents, especially where the collaborators are not colocated. EXPRES is a research and development project, funded by NSF, to create an architecture, in the form of a prototype of a next generation information technology environment, that can support the electronic creation, submission, and review of research proposals. The greatest technical challenge in this work is creating an interoperable system that allows the interchange of editable documents produced using a wide range of software on a wide range of workstations.

Collaborative work is central to modern science and engineering. In most empirical sciences, research is conducted by teams of investigators rather than by solitary individuals. The frontiers of science and technology usually consist of problems that are best attacked by interdisciplinary teams. International competition for ideas and technology favor collaborative efforts. The expense of specialized equipment such as space telescopes, supercomputers, and particle accelerators necessitates the sharing of facilities and their supporting resources, requiring coordination and cooperation. Large interdisciplinary research centers are now common in many fields. Indeed, our entire system of federal support for science and engineering is

429

based on community evaluation of the content of science and collaborative decision making about what kinds of science to support. Thus, at all levels, from the conduct of science to its administration and funding, groups of individuals participate in the process, aided where possible by modern communication technologies.

Electronic mail is one of the newer communication technologies. Whereas it has been used extensively in some scientific fields, it is scarcely known in others. But with the spread of high-quality networks and the availability of personal workstations with good mail systems running on them, electronic mail is rapidly emerging as a significant tool for scientists and engineers. Common Lisp, a regularized version of the most common programming language in artificial intelligence (AI), was developed almost exclusively through the use of electronic mail (Steele, 1984). This ensured broad participation in the setting of standards by the AI community. In 1987, electronic mail played a significant role in the dissemination and interpretation of data associated with a newly discovered supernova among an international community of astronomers.[1] Key observations and interpretations unfolded over a period of days, and astronomers from all over the world were able to participate via electronic mail. Kiesler and Sproull (personal communication) studied the use of a commercial electronic mail service among physical oceanographers, an international research community scattered across the world. This community has made effective use of a simple commercial system, finding that the reliability and the simplicity of the system were much more important than elaborate features. Though there are no reliable numbers on how widespread the use of electronic mail is among scientists and engineers at present, our limited surveys suggest it is used still by only a minority. But this can be expected to change rapidly over the next few years as the cost barriers fall, its functionality improves, and word of the many advantages spreads.

What are the advantages offered by electronic mail as a collaborative tool? At least on good days, it is a quick way to communicate. When the networks between points are all operating, e-mail can go between distant spots in a matter of minutes. As an asynchronous medium, e-mail can be sent and received at the convenience of the participants. This can eliminate such annoying phenomena as "telephone tag." Distribution lists make it as easy to send multiple copies as single copies. Electronic mail can be conveniently archived, to be organized, searched, and even edited for collaborative purposes. Bulletin boards and conferences are extensions of electronic mail that make group communication easier, faster, and better organized.

Most electronic mail is restricted to the sending and receiving of only character information. This, of course, is extremely useful. But for many

---

[1]We thank Morris Aizenman of the National Science Foundation for allowing us to examine the collection of messages that were exchanged during this period.

purposes one would like to be able to send much more. Scientific and technical documents contain such things as mathematical equations, tables, photographs, and drawings. Such specialized objects as spreadsheets can be used to present scientific data or, in the case of a proposal, a budget. And, once this bridge has been crossed, a variety of other forms of information unthinkable in paper documents can be included in electronic ones: video, audio, animations, and complicated networks of associations like hypertext.

Consider the example of grant proposals. Leslie Olsen and colleagues (Olsen, Beattie, Brinkerhoff, Kmenta, & Santucci, 1988) examined the content of a random sample of 125 proposals to the National Science Foundation during fiscal year 1986, drawn from five major research universities. These proposals represented the full range of science: 24% were from the physical sciences, 23% the biological sciences, 22% engineering, 17% mathematics and computer science, and 15% social science. In this sample, 70% of the proposals involved collaboration in planning, writing, or reviewing. Of those involved in working on such collaborative proposals, 26% were geographically dispersed, meaning not in the same building. How did dispersed collaborators work together? All of them (100%) used face-to-face meetings at some point in the collaboration. In addition, 48% used the regular mail, 28% used phone calls, and 16% used electronic mail.[2] In the entire sample, 54% used overnight mail at some point, either for submitting the proposal or for draft-passing.

Two-thirds of the proposals had items other than straight text: 43% had equations, 38% had figures, 34% had tables, 26% had graphs, 9% had photographs, and 7% had other specialized things (e.g., maps). In fiscal year 1986, the vast majority of the proposals were written with the aid of a word processor. Only 2% had all of their drafts done on a typewriter. Over half of them (56%) had their final draft done on a laser printer.

Several salient features emerged from this survey. First, proposal preparation is already a highly collaborative activity. It is the exception for a proposal to be planned, written, and submitted to NSF with only one person ever seeing it. Many of the collaborators in the activity of proposal planning and writing are geographically dispersed. In addition, proposals are multimedia, with the typical proposal containing much more than just text. And furthermore, many proposals exist in electronic form at some point during their generation.

These features would seem to describe an opportunity for technological intervention. Electronic sharing of plans and drafts ought to make it easier for collaborators, particularly those who are geographically dispersed, to work together. Most proposals exist in electronic form at some time during their preparation anyway. However, because of the highly multimedia char-

---

[2]A similar survey during fiscal year 1987 found that 38% were using electronic mail, suggesting that the rate of change in the use of e-mail is very rapid during this period.

acter of proposals, normal character-oriented electronic mail is inadequate. Some way of sharing editable, multimedia documents in electronic form would appear to be very useful to the scientific and engineering community. The entire process of planning, writing, submitting, processing, reviewing, and evaluating NSF proposals is of course a complex one, involving many persons and organizations. Creating a technology that might assist in this process is only one step. For the technology to work, it must fit into the operational and organizational milieu in which this entire process takes place. If the past is any guide, these problems are often larger than the technological ones.

In this context of growing electronic mail use and increasing technological opportunities, the National Science Foundation launched the EXPRES project.[3] EXPRES is a research and development project to create an architecture, in the form of a prototype, of a next-generation information technology environment that can support NSF and its science and engineering constituency in the creation, submission, and review of research proposals. The specification includes consideration of the operational environment and the personnel in the review chain, including investigators, administrators, clerical staff, program managers, and reviewers. To this end, the development of the technology is tightly coupled with a structured deployment experiment to obtain user involvement and provide feedback to the designers. EXPRES is an effort to provide a software platform that will support experimentation by the broader collaboration technology community. Furthermore, recognizing that the scientific community will continue to use heterogeneous hardware and software, the EXPRES project has placed a premium on developing interoperable software that can be used by the broadest possible number of users. Interoperability, making the software available on a wide range of workstations, as well as allowing interchange with much related software, is a large technical challenge.

In the remainder of this chapter we review the general goals of the EXPRES project, describe in detail the kind of software being developed as part of UM EXPRES, outline the efforts to deploy and evaluate this software, and offer some general comments about the role of a tool like this for the support of collaboration.

THE NSF EXPRES EXPERIMENT

The general goal of the EXPRES project is to explore new roles for information technology in facilitating scientific communication and collaboration. Technical documents (proposals, reports, manuscripts) are increasingly

---

[3]EXPRES is an acronym for EXPerimental Research on Electronic Submission.

produced in electronic form by the NSF research community, so electronic proposal submission was selected as the initial application on which to focus the research and development. The project is to evolve a functional prototype of a system for proposal preparation and submission, and to test it with real users. To do this, a broad range of issues must be considered: the software to allow creation and exchange of documents, the workstation and networking infrastructure to support transmission, and the social and organizational issues involved in changing routine practices in several bureaucracies.

At the outset it was assumed that EXPRES would have to operate in a heterogeneous information technology environment, where the interchange of documents would have to occur across diverse equipment, operating systems, and editing applications. Vendor neutrality is an important goal for EXPRES. NSF made awards to two institutions, Michigan and Carnegie Mellon, with two different compound document editors so that the task of document interchange between them could be explored experimentally. Another premise proposed that current document preparation systems did not sufficiently support rich media objects and further work on "compound document" editors was necessary.

Although transmission of facsimile or page description ("formatted") representations of documents would satisfy the requirement for getting a multimedia proposal to Washington, the EXPRES project focuses on the more ambitious goal of creating and interchanging formatted and revisable documents. This choice was made recognizing that an electronic document intended for human interaction via a workstation could be a much richer structure than a document intended only for rendering on paper. With such a system, active spreadsheets with all the underlying equations could be included instead of a static table. A static figure could become an animation. Sound and video clips could be included. All of the underlying structure of particular objects in a document is transmitted, so that every part of the document is editable by all recipients.[4]

The revisable document also provides a platform for a much richer space of options for creating and editing a compound document authored by collaborators. Group collaboration can be done through rapid draft passing in an asynchronous fashion or synchronously across a wide area network. Copies of revisable documents can be active at all the meeting sites, consequently only editing commands rather than full screen updates would need to be transmitted across the network.

In sum, the broad goal of the EXPRES project is to explore multimedia,

---

[4]Full editability by all recipients conflicts with the need for security. Clearly, someone submitting a proposal to NSF does not want to lose control of its content. These important issues have, for the moment, been deferred by the EXPRES project participants.

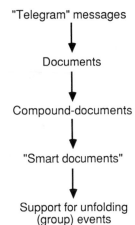

"Telegram" messages

Documents

Compound-documents

"Smart documents"

FIG. 16.1.   The evolution of elec-   Support for unfolding
tronically shareable objects.   (group) events

scientific document preparation and interchange by individuals and groups working with heterogeneous, distributed computing environments. NSF proposal preparation and submission is a task selected to help focus the work and force consideration of all components of the systems: hardware, software, and the procedures and practices of the individual and organizations.

To us, the EXPRES project is a key piece in the evolution of technology to support collaboration. Figure 16.1 shows some of the dimensions of this evolution. One way of looking at this is to see us moving from being able to share telegram messages toward the sharing of increasingly complex, even intelligent objects. Another view is to see us moving from individual workstations that support solo work to networks of workstations supporting the group process. This is enabled both by the creation of an appropriate hardware infrastructure, in terms of networks and powerful workstations, and an appropriate software technology.

ADVANCED MULTIMEDIA MAIL:
THE EXAMPLE OF UM EXPRES

We focus on the University of Michigan EXPRES project to illustrate the characteristics of a multimedia mail system and how it is shaped to be functional, usable, and interoperable.[5] We further describe the Carnegie Mellon system when we explain how the two systems will achieve document exchange.

---

[5]The University of Michigan EXPRES project consists of a team of players: several organizations at the University itself, Bolt Beranek & Newman Laboratories, and ArborText Inc. Throughout this chapter, the phrase UM EXPRES Project refers to this entire team of players.

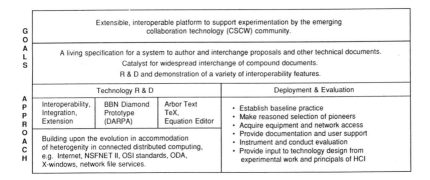

FIG. 16.2.   Overview of UM EXPRES goals and approach.

Figure 16.2 shows an overview of the UM EXPRES goals and approach. At the highest level, the objective is to participate in the development of tools to support collaboration quite generally. As indicated earlier, this is being done by developing a living specification, in the form of a prototype, for the way NSF could conduct its business in the future. In meeting the goal mentioned earlier, the UM EXPRES project is attempting to create an extensible, interoperable platform to support experimentation by the collaboration technology community. Thus, the project consists of a blend of technology research and development to evolve the technology and a deployment and evaluation component, which provides specifications based on current practice, and deploys successive versions of the prototype for purposes of evaluation and feedback.

The overall goal of the technology research and development for UM EXPRES is to create an integrated, extensible, workstation-based environment for multimedia documents. The general parameters of this task have been shaped jointly by NSF and the two EXPRES awardees, Carnegie Mellon and the University of Michigan. EXPRES technology is to run under the Unix operating system, and is to be available on as many Unix workstations as possible. Indeed, some form of access from non-Unix workstations would also be desirable, because many NSF proposals are currently prepared on either DOS or Macintosh machines.[6] The software must support the creation, modification, and exchange of multimedia documents appropriate to the NSF mission. To the extent possible, all of these activities must be carried out supported by standards, so that the technology can be made available to the widest possible audience of users. We now turn to the details of how these goals are being met by the UM EXPRES project.

---

[6]Olsen et al. (1988) found that even in fiscal year 1986 53% of the computers used in proposal preparation were DOS or Macintosh machines. These figures are, if anything, higher now.

The overall goal of creating an environment for handling multimedia documents can be broken into several parts. First, we need to provide support for the preparation of such documents by individuals and groups. This requires both an editing environment and a means of importing constituent parts of documents from other sources. We also need to provide an electronic mail capability, so that documents can be exchanged for the purposes of annotation and revision, and can of course be submitted electronically through the appropriate administrative channels to the NSF. And, although the goal is to minimize the role of paper, for the foreseeable future users of such a system will want to be able to print their documents according to the high standards that have evolved from personal computer desktop publishing systems and widespread laser printers. Finally, one needs to support all of the standard filing and retrieving processes required for working with such documents in a networked workstation environment.

Compound Document Editor

The UM EXPRES Project has developed a compound document editor through the merging and refinement of the products of three groups of developers. The core editing system is based on Diamond, a Unix-based multimedia editing and mailing environment developed by Bolt Beranek and Newman Laboratories, Inc. (Thomas, Forsdick, Crowley, Schaaf, Tomlinson, Travers, & Robertson, 1985). This system allows the user to create, edit, and mail electronic documents containing structured text, graphics, images, spreadsheets, and even voice. Developers at the University of Michigan's Center for Information Technology Integration (CITI) are working with BBN to expand and modify Diamond to fit the needs of the EXPRES project. This work includes basic system enhancements, new media types, and translation programs that allow users to import portions of a document from popular personal computer programs. Another key part of UM EXPRES is the TeX formatting and printing capability provided by ArborText, Inc.

Version 2.0 of UM EXPRES software is based on version 3.2 of the Diamond system, and runs on Apollo, DEC, IBM, and Sun Unix workstations, using the X window environment, version 11.[7] The system's multimedia editor can be used by either a menu-and-mouse style of interface, or a keyboard-based set of commands. The menus are arranged by task level; the user selects the type of object to be entered (text, graphics, images, etc.), which automatically presents the next level of menu at that point in the document. When editing an existing document, the menu is appropriate to

---

[7]The X window system has been developed at MIT's Project Athena, and is a candidate for a standard system for handling all of the interactions between a program and the input/output devices such as display screen, keyboard, and mouse (see Scheifler & Gettys, 1986).

the region in which the cursor rests. Thus, when the cursor rests in text, clicking the mouse produces a text editing menu. When the cursor rests in an image, an image editing menu appears. This seamless editing allows for easy transitions between the different media types. Figure 16.3 shows a screen from an editing session selected to show the variety of media types.

The text editor has preprogrammed formats for entering structured text (such as indented examples or bibliographic style) and lists (such as enumerated or itemized lists). The list option has useful features, such as automatic renumbering when a new item is entered into an existing list, and automatic changes in header symbol when lists are embedded in other lists. These features can be modified by the user to create a customized formatting set. New types of structures can be created by modifying existing ones, the names of which are then automatically saved into the menu for use in that particular document. Plain ASCII text can be read from a Unix file into an EXPRES document and then manipulated and formatted as needed. Structured text from such popular word processing programs as Microsoft Word and WordPerfect can be imported with only a small loss in structure.

Graphics and images are also available. Graphics consist of structured drawings composed of separate elements like lines, circles, and boxes. The

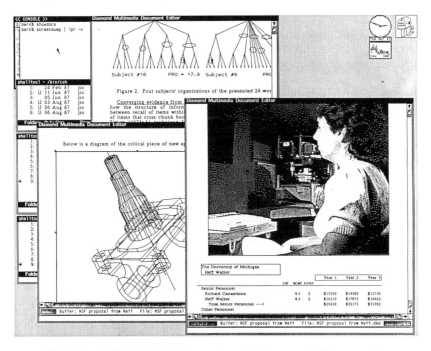

FIG. 16.3.   A UM EXPRES editing session, showing several different media types.

elements preserve their identity within the graphic, which allows them to be moved, scaled, rotated, duplicated, and deleted. The UM EXPRES graphics editor functions in a manner similar to the popular MacDraw program. Images, on the other hand, are digitized, bit-mapped objects, analogous to MacPaint drawings. A user can create an image with a set of painting and drawing tools provided with the editor. An image can be scanned into a Unix file and read into an EXPRES document, where it can be edited. Thus, drawings or photographs can be included in a document. Developers at CITI have implemented a feature that permits input from a video tape or video camera to be frozen, digitized, and read into a file. Both MacDraw and MacPaint files, as well as IGES engineering drawings, can be read into a document using import programs developed at CITI. High-quality gray scale images will be available in a later release, and it would not be difficult to extend the system to include color as well.

The spreadsheet function is useful for creating tables, budgets, and even charts based on numerical data. The UM EXPRES system contains a standard set of spreadsheet capabilities, all easily accessed via menus or keyboard commands. This portion of the system is similar to the popular Lotus 1-2-3 spreadsheet program, and indeed, spreadsheets prepared with Lotus can be imported directly into an EXPRES document. Line, bar, and pie graphs can be drawn from spreadsheet data, and these drawings can then be edited using the image tool set.

It is important to note that this system is extensible. A framework exists in which new media types can be added to the basic document repertoire provided by the core system. Several new media types are already nearly developed and ready to include in UM EXPRES. One is a new electronic forms media type to handle institutional and NSF cover sheets. Although this media type will provide some standard forms, the user will also be able to design custom forms with a special forms editor. Once created, the custom form can be stored and copies recalled and filled out as needed. In turn, the data contained in these electronic forms will be extractable for use in institutional data bases, like those maintained at NSF or university research offices.

Another media type to be included in UM EXPRES shortly is an equation editor developed by ArborText. This editor allows one to create and edit complex mathematical expressions. The display of the expressions is automatically scaled, so that as one creates or copies various parts they are rendered appropriately. Figure 16.4 shows an example of an equation created with this editing system.

The mail portion of UM EXPRES is currently based on the widely used SMTP mail protocol. This is the standard mail transport format for electronic mail on the major national networks. A multimedia document can be mailed to other UM EXPRES users, where it remains fully editable, using the

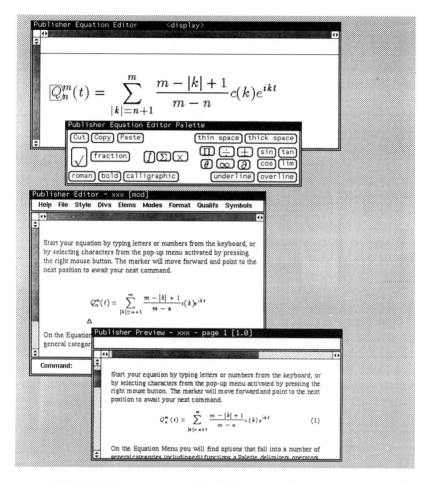

FIG. 16.4.   An equation created with the UM EXPRES equation editor.

same electronic mail addresses as are used for text-only mail. A text-only version can be mailed to collaborators who do not have UM EXPRES software. The text-only version of course loses all of the special formatting information, as well as pictures, drawings, spreadsheet structure, and other nontext media.

A UM EXPRES document can be printed at any point during its preparation on a standard PostScript printer.[8] For professional looking, publication-

<hr />

[8]PostScript is the de facto standard for so-called page description languages. It is a language for representing the special information necessary for producing formatted output on a device like a printer. Most widely used high-quality printers, such as the Apple LaserWriter, use PostScript.

quality page layout, documents will soon be able to be formatted and printed using TeX. TeX (Knuth, 1984) is a powerful formatting language that produces publication quality results. It can be used to produce documents on popular laser printers as well as phototypesetters. It supports capabilities that can be used to produce non-English characters or technical symbols, tables, and equations. Documents can be previewed before they are printed.

Interoperability

The world of Unix workstations is a heterogeneous one. No single workstation dominates. For example, in 1987 the market shares for Unix workstations were Sun 25.5%, Apollo 18.5%, DEC 17.8%, Hewlett Packard 17.2%, Silicon Graphics 3.9%, IBM 3.8%, and others 13.3%. Similar heterogeneity characterizes the software packages that people use. A key feature to the success of a project like EXPRES is to ensure, insofar as possible, that the broadest possible community has access to the technology. This is the theme of interoperability. Numerous mechanisms are in place or under development to encourage this to happen.

As already mentioned, from the outset the project sought to have the software running on a number of different hardware platforms. Five information technology vendors joined the project to assist in this effort: Apollo, Apple, DEC, IBM, and Sun. This has been achieved through the porting of the software to the workstations of multiple vendors using the X windows environment, version 11 (Scheifler & Gettys, 1986). At present, UM EXPRES runs on four different sets of Unix workstations: Apollo, DEC, IBM, and Sun. The client–server model of X also provides a way to gain access to EXPRES software from non-Unix workstations. This model allows for the separation of the software that handles the basic functionality of the system (called the client code) from the software that handles the interactions with input and output devices like display screens, keyboards, and mice (the server code). An X server running on an Apple Macintosh, for example, could access the client code that is running on a full-function workstation, using a local area network for the server and client to exchange information. This would make it possible for a user to open up an EXPRES window on their Macintosh and edit a multimedia document, even though the basic EXPRES software itself did not run on the Macintosh. The portability of code under X's client–server model allows a general solution to hardware interoperability.

Within the UM EXPRES project we have also provided accessibility via the import of media objects from non-EXPRES applications. We mentioned many of these in passing as we described the core media types of the EXPRES system.

Another dimension of interoperability in UM EXPRES is the link to the

TeX system for previewing and printing formatted documents. TeX is a widely used system in the scientific and technical community. A UM EX-PRES document can be output as a TeX file, and a variety of standard TeX macros can be included. A TeX user could then edit this file within a TeX editing package, and print high-quality page layouts.[9]

Mail interoperability is provided currently through the use of SMTP mail transport. This is the same electronic mail system used for regular text-only internet mail. UM EXPRES developers are also working on providing X.400 mail capability as soon as reliable mailers based on this standard become available.[10]

A primitive form of multimedia document exchange is possible through the interchange of PostScript page descriptions. A PostScript representation of a multimedia document can be placed in a file and then included in a regular text-only mail message to a recipient, who can then print the document locally. Of course, unlike EXPRES, such a document does not carry its editable structure with it. But it does allow a facsimilelike exchange of complex documents. Such PostScript exchange of documents is being investigated in the EXPRES project as an intermediate step toward the full EXPRES solution of the exchange of editable documents. Many document preparation systems currently output PostScript, and Postscript can handle a wide range of media (e.g., images, drawings, tables), thus it is presently feasible for a broad range of scientists and engineers to prepare PostScript versions of their proposals and submit these to the National Science Foundation. This would allow much of the handling of such proposals to proceed electronically.

The most ambitious component of interoperability in the EXPRES project is the exchange of revisable compound documents between the UM EXPRES and CMU EXPRES systems based on the emerging Office Document Architecture (ODA) standards (International Organization for Standardization, 1988). To place this aspect of the project in perspective, let us examine the present situation. One can create a multimedia document using UM EXPRES, on any of several Unix workstations, and send it to another user of UM EXPRES using standard internet connectivity. The recipient can then edit the document, if desired, and send it back to the originator. But what if one wants to send a document to someone who does not have UM EXPRES software? At present, one can (a) sent a text-only version, which loses both the structure in the text and any nontext media type; (b) send a PostScript version that the recipient can print locally, but not edit; or (c) send a paper version. No particular multimedia editor is likely to become a standard, so if

---

[9]At present, there is no feature allowing a TeX file to be converted into a UM EXPRES document.

[10]X.400 is a new international standard for a more powerful mail transport mechanism.

we are to obtain widespread document interchange capability, some standard way of handling such complex documents must be found.

At the outset of the EXPRES project, all of the principals involved from NSF, CMU, and the various elements of the UM project examined in detail the options for achieving such document interchange, and agreed to pursue this goal through the emerging ODA standards for multimedia documents. There are two models through which this could be done. One is to have the multimedia editor use an ODA representation as its native document format. In the case of the CMU and UM EXPRES systems, other document formats already existed, and it would have taken a large effort to redo this part of each system. An alternative was to build translation routines that take whatever document format the originating system uses and build an ODA representation of this document. This is what would be sent via electronic mail to a recipient, who would then use another translation routine to change the ODA representation into the format used by the recipient's multimedia editor. This enormously simplifies the exchange problem, at least conceptually, because instead of having to build n^2 translation routines to take each format into each format, one only needs to build $2n$ translation routines, one in each direction between ODA and the format used by a particular editing system.

In reality, the problem is much larger than this. First, ODA is at present an incomplete standard. It is still under development, and many "content architectures" of multimedia documents are not covered yet by the ODA standard. This means that the EXPRES developers must work closely with the ODA community to help set standards in the areas not yet covered. In the worst case, EXPRES developers will have to proceed with a tentative representation for those areas not covered by ODA, and hope that these tentative solutions will emerge as the ODA way of doing it. This is why it is so important to work closely with the standards community in proceeding with this problem.

In addition, at least within EXPRES, the two systems—CMU and UM— already contain many features that are either not currently addressed by ODA or may never be addressed by it. Thus, in going from, say, a UM EXPRES document to ODA, there will be some loss of structure. For example, as is common in many such editing systems, UM EXPRES allows the user to develop style sheets that define a recurring set of formatting options. Thus, a user might define the style "quotation" that consist of text that is indented one inch from both left and right margins, single-spaced, and in italics. In UM EXPRES such styles can be defined in relation to other styles. Another style called "important quotation" might be defined as the "quotation" style with the additional feature that it appears in bold face. This nesting scheme allows features to be inherited. If I change "quotation" from single-spacing to double-spacing, the nested style "important quotation" will also acquire this characteristic. There is no provision within the ODA framework for handling such nesting of style sheets. Should such a feature be supported or not supported in ODA? What will get lost in the translation process, and how costly is this? Inevitably, the proliferation of systems leads to a diversity of features, and it is inevitable that only a portion of these will ever be addressed by the standards. This problem will remain far beyond EXPRES.

Furthermore, ODA is not yet a widely used standard, primarily because it is still under development. The UM and CMU EXPRES teams are hoping to influence the acceptance of ODA as a standard in this area by their efforts. If successful multimedia document exchange can be demonstrated, others who are developing editing systems in this arena may be influenced to participate in the ODA movement, either by using ODA as a native representation or by building the appropriate translators so they can participate in document exchanges in the same way as UM and CMU EXPRES. To help this process along, EXPRES developers have built an ODA toolkit that will assist other developers in building the translators needed for a particular system. More detailed discussions of ODA and its role in EXPRES appear in Giuffrida (1988) and Rosenberg, Sherman, Marks, and Giuffrida (1988).

Figure 16.5 summarizes in pictorial form the various dimensions of interoperability we have been discussing. As this picture makes clear, a serious effort has been made to ensure the broadest possible access to the UM EXPRES system.

Extensions and Enhancements of This Technology

The present versions of the UM and CMU EXPRES software represent only a beginning toward providing a useful, powerful set of collaboration tools based on the electronic exchange of multimedia documents. There are at least four areas of extension worth mentioning.

New Media Types

There are many other media types that would be useful to include. Both UM and CMU EXPRES software are extensible, so that new media types can be added, including custom ones for very specific needs (e.g., musical notation).

Animation. CMU EXPRES currently has a rudimentary animation capability. More powerful and easy-to-use animation tools would make it possible to include dynamic representations of objects in a document.

Video. Similarly, a real-time video media object would be an obvious extension of the present image capability.

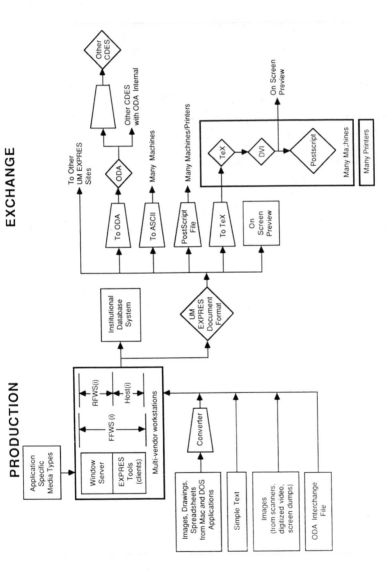

FIG. 16.5. Dimensions of interoperability in the UM EXPRES system. The left side of the figure shows the variety of sources of information that can be assembled into a UM EXPRES document. FFWS refers to full-function workstation, RFWS to reduced function workstation. The right side of the figure shows the many different ways in which a UM EXPRES document can be exchanged. CDES refers to compound document editing system, ODA to office document architecture (see text for discussion), and DVI is the name given to the device independent representation of a TeX file.

Voice. The Diamond editing system contains a simple voice feature, wherein one can include brief voice clips in a document, and play them back under user control. This is useful for such tasks as annotating a document. It could also be the basis for including sound tracks along with animations or video.

More Complex Document Architectures

Both the UM and CMU EXPRES systems at present support fairly traditional, linear document structures. However, there is considerable interest at present in new document architectures, such as hypertext or hypermedia (Conklin, 1987). The transition from paper-based document exchange to electronic exchange is best effected by keeping the traditional, linear document architecture during the transition phase. In part, this is to let users adapt to a modest-sized change, and in part, this is in recognition of the fact that for some considerable time the paper-based and electronic traditions will have to coexist. But as the hypertext and hypermedia ideas become better established, their incorporation into multimedia electronic mail is an obvious extension.

Advanced Document Management

Malone and his colleagues (Malone, Grant, Lai, Rao, & Rosenblitt, 1987; Malone, Grant, Turbak, Brobst, & Cohen, 1987) experimented with software that takes techniques from artificial intelligence and applies them to the routing of electronic mail. This allows one to sort and filter incoming mail according to a sophisticated set of principles. One interesting offshoot is the notion of an "anyone" server. Here, for mail that may be of interest to unknown individuals, one addresses it to "anyone," and each individual's mail filtering routines examine such mail for possible relevance or interest. These ideas, and extensions of them, seem obviously useful in the context of multimedia documents, and there is no reason why either the CMU or UM EXPRES systems could not be equipped with such features. These might be particularly useful in the context of NSF proposal handling, allowing the automatic routing of proposals to their proper program offices.

Simultaneity

At present UM EXPRES allows a limited degree of real-time, simultaneous conferencing. Each participation in the conference has a document of interest loaded in their system, and as they work together, moment-by-moment updates are sent back and forth between the two sites. This can be useful when this is coupled with a telephone or video link. Thus, two participants could negotiate a budget that is contained in an EXPRES spreadsheet by observing at two sites the what-if reasoning for which the spreadsheet is so ideally suited. More powerful support for this mode of interaction is clearly needed. For instance, a workstation that allowed one to have a video link to one's collaborators in a window along with various objects of interest in other windows might offer a powerful integration of communication technologies. To us, these are all part of the vision of the collaboration technologies down the road from EXPRES.

THE USE OF ADVANCED MULTIMEDIA MAIL: DEPLOYMENT AND EVALUATION OF UM EXPRES

Creating a collaborative tool is only one part of altering actual practice. The tool must be accepted and propagated. One key to this is having a tool that meets the user's needs. We can anticipate much of what this will be from an evaluation of prior document handling and communication tools. UM EX-PRES investigators have surveyed present practices among typical PIs and at university research offices (Olsen, Beattie, Brinkerhoff, Kmenta, & Santucci, in preparation). The UM EXPRES software has developed to fit perceived needs on the part of the scientists and engineers who are served by NSF. Many of the developers of this system are themselves just such users. However, any new technology must undergo a period of testing and refinement before it is ready for a more general release. Thus, an essential phase in the UM EXPRES project is the deployment and evaluation as a collaborative tool among carefully selected test sites. Once we have verified that we have a functional and usable system, a wider deployment is possible.

Full support of the electronic submission and review of NSF proposals requires many organizational and cultural changes. The full chain of activities shown in Fig. 16.6 involves many people from different segments of the submitting research organization and the foundation itself. For the EX-PRES software to fulfill all parts of this, many changes must be made in how regular work proceeds. We are under no illusions about the difficulties involved. An important part of the project is the assessment of current practice and the education of the many participants in the characteristics and advantages of this new technology. Fortunately, changes are already taking place in parallel with the EXPRES project that should make this transition easier. Several programs within the foundation have begun to experiment with limited electronic submission of proposals and reviews. Another EXPRES-related project at the foundation is working to make possible the routine electronic submission of administrative cover sheets, abstracts, and budgets, items of information that at present often have to be repeatedly keyed in to various administrative data bases.

Even before we are able to use EXPRES to support the full transmission of

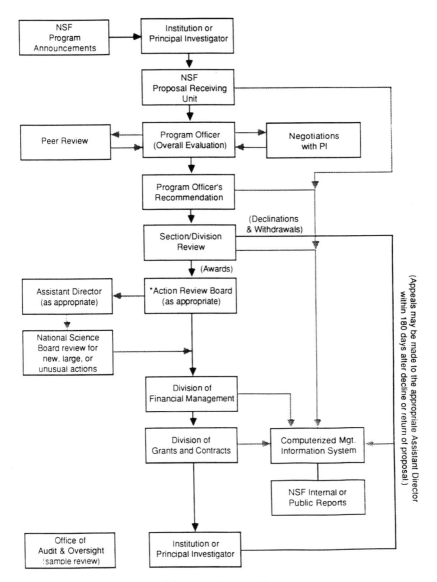

FIG. 16.6   The NSF proposal process.

proposals to NSF, we are gathering experience with its use as a collaborative tool among scientists and engineers. UM EXPRES 1.0, an initial version of the software that ran only under the Suntools environment, has been in use among the EXPRES project staff for some time, and we have learned much about its usefulness. A small deployment of version 1.0 to selected external sites, including the National Science Foundation itself, has further added to our experiential base. However, our efforts to deploy and evaluate the UM EXPRES software more widely have depended on the availability of version 2.0, which is the version that runs under X windows and is available on the workstations of all of the supporting vendors. We are carrying out an expanded but still limited deployment of this version.

Potential Difficulties for the EXPRES Project

EXPRES is an ambitious project, with an interrelated set of complex technical, social, and organizational goals. Can they be achieved? Already, our limited deployment and evaluation of EXPRES suggests some possible obstacles to success. We group our discussion into three classes.

Design and Building of the System

Both the UM and CMU EXPRES systems are complex. Much of this complexity arises because of the many functions the software includes, and some of it is because the Unix environment in which the systems are being built is inherently more difficult than those environments (e.g., IBM PC, Macintosh) designed explicitly for new or occasional users. Furthermore, these complex systems are being developed in research environments, without the enormous capitalization of commercial software development. This makes it very difficult to get the systems to the point where they are free of pitfalls and bugs. Yet these problems could interfere with the acceptance and use of what might otherwise be good systems. The idea of EXPRES may be exactly right, and the systems may have the right intentions, but the project could fail because of the enormous difficulty in crafting a technology that users will actually use. Indeed, to the extent that the core technical problems in EXPRES such as interoperability are more difficult than anticipated, it will be even harder to ensure that the system will have user acceptance.

Social Processes Involved in Making the Technical Decisions Needed for Interoperability

As part of the effort to build interoperable systems, EXPRES participants have made a series of technical decisions that will have a large bearing on the propagation of the system. Some of these were made by the National Science Foundation when they issued an RFP for the EXPRES project. For instance, the RFP stipulated that the software be developed for the Unix environment, that it run on many different vendors' machines, that the exchanged documents be editable, and that the documents be multimedia. The EXPRES participants themselves decided to use the X windows environment, SMTP mail, and ODA. In each of these cases, the decision has consequences for the use and acceptance of the resulting technology. Moreover, in the examples of the X windows environment and ODA, the larger technical community is still in the process of defining, evaluating, and accepting these, and EXPRES dependency on them both depends on and influences the broader technical community. The social and even political processes involved in making these technical decisions often have little to do with technical merit. Furthermore, the technical milieu can change quickly as a result of market forces and other nontechnical causes, leading to a different view of things by the time a complex system is ready for wider use.

Introducing New Technology into Existing Practice

There are many challenges in introducing any technology into existing environments. In the case of EXPRES, the entire process of preparing, submitting, and evaluating NSF proposals shown earlier in Fig. 16.6 involves a variety of individuals and organizations. There are the scientists and engineers themselves, along with their graduate students and supporting clerical staff. There are the administrative and research offices at universities that must process the proposals before they are sent to Washington. These organizations are usually no where as technically advanced as certain portions of the scientific and engineering world. At NSF, there are further administrative steps as well as the substantive review supervised by at least one program manager. For the most part, the people involved at all of these various steps have only recently begun to use personal computing for word processing and electronic mail. Introducing a technology that uses the Unix operating system, advanced workstations, and complex, high-functionality software is a major challenge. We have already found in our early deployment of UM EXPRES that introducing a major new technology into an established bureaucracy like the NSF or a university research office is not at all easy. For instance, at NSF we had to hire a full-time Unix expert to be on site because there was no Unix expertise present to oversee the installation and support of the advanced workstations used in EXPRES. Our early experience with university test sites also revealed that the EXPRES software requires a computing infrastructure that is only beginning to emerge in many parts of the scientific world. Furthermore, there is often resistance to changing practices that work well. When the changes in practice are accompanied by a major change in the supporting technology, the challenge is all the greater.

Conclusions

Multimedia electronic mail is one of a number of emerging software tools to support collaboration (see other examples in CSCW 86, 88; Grief, 1988). The EXPRES project is especially important because of its stress on interoperability. The computing and communication world will continue to be heterogeneous for some time to come, and efforts like EXPRES to attack this problem head-on are critical if we are to benefit maximally from the empowerment of groups that is possible through the use of the networked world of information technology that is presently arriving at all of our doorsteps. EXPRES both demonstrates the feasibility of technical solutions to a range of important questions, and explores the patterns of use that need to be understood in order to have this technology accepted by appropriate user communities.

ACKNOWLEDGMENTS

The EXPRES Project is supported by the National Science Foundation through cooperative agreement ASC-8617699. The views expressed in this chapter are those of the authors, and should not be construed as the position of the National Science Foundation. The authors thank Judy Olson, Neff Walker, Dave Rodgers, Harry Stevens, and Bob Kraut for their comments on earlier drafts of this chapter.

REFERENCES

Conklin, J. (1987). Hypertext: An introduction and survey. *IEEE Computer, 20,* 17–41.
CSCW '86. *Proceedings of the Conference on Computer-Supported Cooperative Work.* Austin, TX, December 1986.
CSCW '88. *Proceedings of the Conference on Computer-Supported Cooperative Work.* Portland, OR, September 1988.
Giuffrida, F. (1988). ODA as a translation medium. UM EXPRESS working paper.
Greif, I. (Ed.). (1988). *Computer-supported cooperative work: A book of readings.* San Mateo, CA: Morgan Kaufmann.
International Organization for Standardization. (1988). *(ISO 8613) Office Document Architecture (ODA) and interchange format.* Internation Organization for Standardization (ISO).
Knuth, D. E. (1984). *The TeXbook.* Reading, MA: Addison-Wesley.
Malone, T. W., Grant, K. R., Lai, K-Y., Rao, R., & Rosenblitt, D. (1987). Semi-structured messages are surprisingly useful for computer-supported coordination. *Transactions on Office Information Systems, 5,* 115–131.
Malone, T. W., Grant, K. R., Turbak, F. A., Brobst, S. A., & Cohen, M. D. (1987). Intelligent information-sharing systems. *Communications of the ACM, 30,* 390–402.
Olsen, L. A., Beattie, R. R., Brinkerhoff, W., Kmenta, D., & Santucci, R. (1988). *Processing*

sponsored project proposals at twelve universities. UM EXPRES working paper, University of Michigan.

Olsen, L. A., Beattie, R. R., Brinkerhoff, W., Kmenta, D., & Santucci, R. (in preparation). *Baseline studies of current practice: Methods and some significant results.* UM EXPRES working paper, University of Michigan.

Rosenberg, J., Sherman, M. S., Marks, A., & Giuffrida, F. (1988). *Translating among processable multi-media formats using ODA.* Manuscript in preparation.

Scheifler, R. W., & Gettys, J. (1986). The X window system. *ACM Transactions on Graphics, 5,* 76–109.

Steele, G. (1984). *COMMON LISP reference manual.* Bedford, MA: Digital Press.

Thomas, R. H., Forsdick, H. C., Crowley, T. R., Schaaf, R. W., Tomlinson, R. S., Travers, V. M., & Robertson, G. G. (1985). Diamond: A multimedia message system built on a distributed architecture. *IEEE Computer, 18*(12), 65–78.

17

Visual Languages For Cooperation: A Performing Medium Approach To Systems For Cooperative Work

Fred Lakin*
Stanford University

Abstract

When people employ text and graphic objects in communication, those objects have meaning under a system of interpretation, or visual language. *Visual languages for cooperation* are graphical representations for group work such as brainstorming or cooperative task structuring. A visual language for cooperation can give group members a way to visualize an aspect of group work so they can better understand and perform it. If a computer system could interpret expressions in such a language, then it could participate in the group's work. This chapter describes a computer graphics system that can process visual languages for expressing the structure of group work, thus providing a way for computers to understand and assist intellectual teamwork.

The iterative work cycle of design, discussion, and presentation that characterizes the daily activity of design engineers is a particularly rich example of intellectual teamwork. This activity typically combines both individual and group work; it incorporates discussion of ideas and reactions to preliminary designs; and it involves construction of text-and-graphic presentations, including both printed documents and visual displays. At present, moving through this cycle requires people to use a variety of technologies to support their individual work and their communication with each other, ranging from notes hastily jotted on a piece of paper to sophisticated computer-aided design (CAD) tools. In this chapter, I describe my efforts to produce a computer-based tool to support activities like these that will permit people to move back and forth from working alone to working with other people,

*e-mail: lakin@csli.stanford.edu

using a single piece of software for creating and modifying text and graphics and for communicating with each other.

The tool I am designing is called **vmacs**[TM,1] which stands for visual macros (a macro is a short program; thus **vmacs** is a collection of short programs for manipulating visual objects; also, the interface style was inspired by a text editor called **emacs**). In the next section, I present a scenario showing how the members of an engineering design team might do the kind of work described earlier using tools currently available. This scenario is a way of specifying the nature of the problems **vmacs** is designed to solve.

MONDAY AT WORK: SCENARIO ONE

Mandy Bateman, a senior staff member for Analysis Associates, a large engineering consulting firm, is working at her desk at 9:30 A.M. on a Monday morning. She leads a team of engineers who are working to design a telescope, and is preparing to present their work at a meeting with the client on Friday. She plans to present 15 viewgraphs that illustrate her team's design ideas; after the presentation, the client will be given paper copies of the transparencies, along with a five-page report describing the work in more detail.

At the moment, Mandy is transcribing handwritten notes into a word-and-graphics processor at a personal workstation; mostly she is working on the artwork for the viewgraphs. Occasionally, her work on the slides prompts an idea for a revision in the report and she shifts to working on the text of the report. The word-and-graphics processor she is using to prepare the viewgraphs and the report allows her to cut and paste material from one to the other. As she works on a diagram, a question arises about a part of the project being handled by Tom, another team member. Mandy exits the word-and-graphics program, logs onto Analysis Associates' inter-office e-mail system, and looks through the project message file.

Unable to find the answer to her question, she telephones Tom; during the conversation she cradles the phone between her shoulder and her head so that her hands are free to type the information Tom gives her into the report. At the end of the conversation, he mentions a relevant CAD drawing that he has made. Unfortunately, the CAD/analysis system is incompatible with the software she is using, so the drawing cannot be directly inserted into the report. Remembering this, she calls Tom back and asks him to copy the drawing into the word-and-graphics processor manually, and to bring a disk with the image on it to the team meeting at 10:30 a.m. Then Mandy

---

[1]**vmacs** is a trademark of the performing graphics company.

works for a few more minutes, copying the rest of her ideas from her paper notes into the files containing the viewgraphs and the report.

At 10:25 A.M., Mandy has completed rough versions of each of her viewgraphs and quickly makes acetate copies of them; she also makes multiple paper copies of the draft of the report, and hurries off to the meeting. When she arrives, Tom hands her the disk of the copied CAD drawing. She starts the meeting by projecting the first viewgraph on the screen, and a lively discussion of the planned presentation ensues. Moving back and forth between overhead projector and whiteboard, Mandy begins to record people's comments. As the ideas appear on the board, group members comment on them further, and the meeting turns into a general brainstorming session. Mandy tries to write down all the comments, but simultaneously recording ideas and rehearsing the presentation becomes too difficult, so Tom takes over as recorder at the whiteboard.

As the discussion unfolds, brainstorming about the presentation of the project leads to new ideas about technical details in the project, and the team attempts to thrash out several new design ideas. A question arises about a technical detail, but, to answer it, they need a drawing that is stored in George's files. These files are not accessible from the meeting room; moreover, George doesn't remember exactly which drawing it is. The technical discussion particularly affects the work of two team members—Tom and Laureen—and they request copies of the notes from the whiteboard.

After 20 minutes Mandy points out that it is 11:30 and they need to get back to reviewing the presentation. In the next half hour, she works through the remainder of the transparencies; Tom is recording ideas for changes in virtually every slide. At noon, Mandy ends meeting and gives each member a copy of the written report to mark up and return to her by 3 P.M. After the rest of her team has gone, Mandy spends another 20 minutes copying the accumulated notes from the whiteboard (including both feedback on the presentation and the technical discussion) into her notebook. She then picks up the notebook, the transparencies, and the disk with Tom's CAD drawing and returns to her own office at 12:30 P.M.

Back from lunch at 1:30 P.M. Mandy searches through her meeting notes for ideas that are worth incorporating into the presentation. The notes lead her to make substantial changes in both the artwork and the report, and she also adds the redrawn CAD image from Tom's disk to the presentation artwork. This drawing is so informative that Mandy decides to include it as one of the figures in the report, which she easily does. Just as Mandy finishes her work on the presentation, Laureen drops by with suggestions for revisions in the written report. Mandy had forgotten about the team's reactions to the report, but now wonders where the revisions from the other three team members are. She calls them to say that she would like the revisions before they go home. It is now 3:15 P.M. She begins to look through the revisions Laureen has suggested to determine which ones to use in the final report.

Observations About Scenario One

Mandy spent most of her time on Monday interacting with people and manipulating text-and-graphics, often at the same time. We can describe Mandy's activity on Monday in more detail in terms of three functional needs: *text-and-graphic performing, group<—>individual mode switching,* and *technical task switching.* We can also describe her activities on Monday as almost incessant media changing, from paper to computer text-and-graphics to overhead projection to whiteboard to paper to computer text-and-graphics again (whew!). We will find the frequent media changing to be a direct consequence of the demands of the three functional needs.

The generation and manipulation of text and graphics is a *text-graphic performance.* During her work day, Mandy functioned as a text-graphic performer in the four different media listed above. Calling her a performer points out that she needs the same sort of agility and responsiveness in the tools she uses as a musician seeks in an instrument; ideally, she would like a system that can provide immediate response in support of her every improvisational whim as she expresses her ideas. In this respect, paper and whiteboard are superior to traditional computer systems, which is one reason why she used each of them on certain occasions during the day.

Another important aspect of Mandy's work is *group<—>individual mode switching.* Sometimes she works as an individual, sometimes as a member of a group, and sometimes the distinction is moot. For instance, while working alone in her office, she calls Tom on the phone, continuing to use the computer as she talks with him. Has she suddenly become a group member? Regardless of how we classify this particular episode, we see that such social mode switching occurs many times during her day, and that each switch requires a different medium for text-graphic manipulation. Overhead projection and whiteboard, for instance, are group media, and the others are not. It is especially important to this chapter to note that after changing media she is often manipulating exactly the same material as she was before the change.

A third aspect of Mandy's Monday is *technical task switching.* Over the course of the day, she prepares artwork, writes reports, carries out CAD analyses, sends and receives e-mail messages, participates in group discussions, and manages the activities of her team. These various tasks—and the special support needs of each—are yet another reason why she must change media as often as she does.

But what if a single medium could assist Mandy as she moved through her day's sequence of tasks and interactions? That medium would have to support her as a text-graphic performer, offering her agility for spontaneous performances. And that same medium would also have to support her as she switched social modes and technical tasks. For a number of years, I have been working on text-and-graphic tools for groups that will provide this kind of flexibility and adaptability. The latest system is called **vmacs**, and the working prototype shows promise as a medium that can meet these needs. In this chapter, I describe **vmacs** in more detail, and, at the end of the chapter, I present another version of Mandy's Monday demonstrating how the group's work patterns change when Mandy and her team use **vmacs**.

THE ORIGIN OF vmacs

The **vmacs** system, in its current form, is based on research that began in the early 1970s with the design of a series of non-electronic text-graphic performance systems for working groups. The first system grew out of my observations that groups of designers often wrote and drew together as part of thinking about a problem, but that the media they used for this purpose were far from ideal. Even when the designers used big pads of paper, only a few people at a time could see them; flip charts on a wall were too small, and black boards did not support color, high resolution or saving of images. The solution was the Wall Scroll (Figs. 17.1 and 17.2), a system for dispensing large sheets of paper that could be used for "group graphics" (Lakin, 1971a).

Later, I attempted to make it possible to weave text and graphics together; this "text-graphic loom" was to be a tool that groups could use to develop and display concepts (Lakin, 1971b). The idea was to create a workspace that a single individual could operate, while one or two others viewed the material and told the operator how to manipulate it. The design solution meeting these specifications was the "vacuum board"—a vertical surface drilled with small holes on a one inch grid and a quiet fan pulling air through them. The low suction was sufficient to hold pieces of paper against the vertical surface, while allowing them to be moved easily on the surface. This "vertical desk" could be used to display and manipulate pages in manuscripts under construction. The vacuum board technology was augmented with three ring binders for long term storage and a slide projector for limited group display. The resulting environment was dubbed the "Concept Workspace"; a sketch of it is shown in Fig. 17.3.

Subsequently, I designed another system in an effort to make the flexibility of the "Concept Workspace" available to larger working groups. The system (shown in Fig. 17.4) used 5″ × 8″ cards with a waxed strip on the back allowing them to stick to the wall (similar to a product later marketed

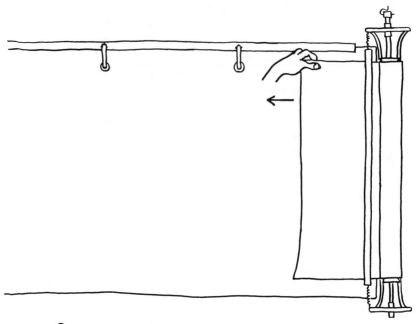

Pulling Paper Across

gresp upper corner of paper with left hand
as shown and pull paper across, moving 'C'
rods out of the way with right hand as
they are encountered; all height adjustments
of paper must be made while paper is moving.

FIG. 17.1.   The "Wall Scroll," a large sheet paper dispensing system for use
by groups.

as "Post-Its.")[2] This technology was first developed by Porter and Verger
(1974); my system extended their ideas by adding movable line networks
and color overlays. A five part strategy evolved to make it possible to use
this Group Card medium for group problem solving (Lakin, 1974a):

1. Generate cards
2. Use juxtaposition to show relation of cards
3. Add color overlays to show relation of cards
4. Add connecting lines to show relation of cards
5. Shuffle cards around on the wall to shorten or remove connecting
   lines where possible, using juxtaposition to show connection instead.

---

[2]"Post-Its" is a trademark of 3M.

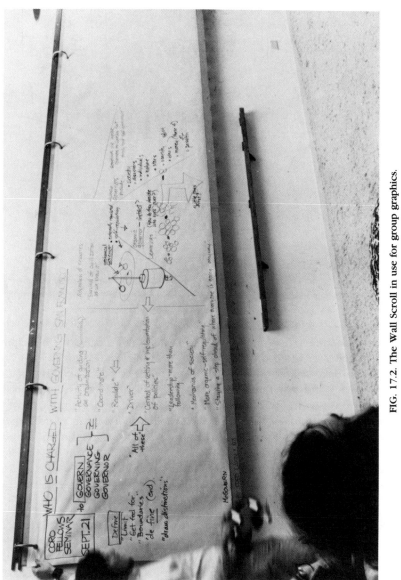

FIG. 17.2. The Wall Scroll in use for group graphics.

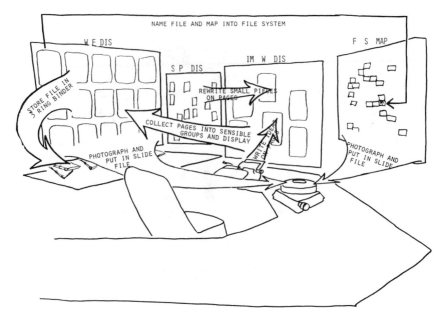

FIG. 17.3.   Sketch of a "Concept Workspace" using vaccum boards to provide easy shuffling of vertically-displayed paper pieces.

This technique (shown in Fig. 17.4) was very successful in helping groups to generate and organize large numbers of ideas (Lakin, 1974b), but, as we shall see, lacked much of the functionality and flexibility of the systems that I and other researchers working in related areas (Landow, chap. 15; Olson & Atkins, chap. 16 in this volume) are developing now. In the following section, I review the basic properties of the sort of tasks these systems are designed to support as a prelude to the description of **vmacs.**

TEXT-GRAPHIC ACTIVITY ANALYSIS

To do text-graphic analysis, we want to formalize the perspective of an analytic outsider viewing text-graphic activity for the first time. I have used this approach (Lakin, 1986b) to analyze the image manipulations that take place over time on a blackboard and similar group display devices. On the one hand, this method is concerned with the people using the blackboard, treating them as performers of text-graphic activity. On the other hand, the method also finds it useful at times to bracket (consciously and carefully ignore) the social context of the performance and concentrate solely on the

FIG. 17.4. Problem definition session using manipulable cards to brainstorm, then organize.

movement of the text-graphics themselves.[3] This method has been applied to examples of text-graphic activity such as those presented in Scenario One and the non-electronic systems described above; the method reveals the following features of text-graphic performances:

1. *Chronological:* If we were to come upon a text-graphic performance, what might strike us first is that it is a dynamic phenomenon, unfolding in time: *something is moving.*

2. *Text-Graphic:* Because these performances unfold over time, we are able to observe how objects precipitate out of them. Static frames from the examples show the kind of images that are being manipulated: text and graphics in spatial arrangement. As a general policy, we don't want to say whether any particular object is text or graphics until we must.

3. *Manipulatory:* A third feature of these performance activities is that they involve manipulation. It's because of manipulation that the text-graphics change over time (and in changing, we can see what the pieces of text-graphics *are*). Manipulation includes generating, moving, modifying and erasing text-graphic objects. We observe that sometimes operators want to manipulate small sections of a display, whereas at other times they want to manipulate groups of objects as a unit (most apparent in the manipulable cards).

4. *Performed:* Working group graphics are performed *by* an operator *for* a group. This fact helps characterize the operation of the medium, and the nature of the medium being operated. There is a performer, and there are consumers of the performance. The consumers are there to watch the images, which endure as a physical product of the group's work—an explicit group memory.

5. *Fast:* The agility of text-graphic manipulation is paramount; it can be measured in text-graphic manipulations per second. Leisurely illustration will not do; the group will get bored or distracted. Loss of a minute may mean loss of an idea. Oddly enough, old fashioned paper-based media still set the standards for agility. Figure 17.2 is the final frame from a Wall Scroll paper graphics performance; it only took the operator 18 minutes to make this image, roughly 5 or 10 times faster than computer-based media can currently be operated (Lakin, 1986b).

6. *Unstructured:* Except for the manipulable card system, which restricts the size of images, the media in the three previous examples do not restrict the kind of objects that can be written or drawn on them; nor do

---

[3]Actually, this method of study is akin to old-style linguistics, which should be seen in contrast to newer approaches such as the study of situated language at the Center for the Study of Language and Information at Stanford University.

they restrict the temporal order in which images are created. Thus, any kind of image can be created—from diagrams to paragraphs to LISP code to cartoons to matrices—regulated only by the purpose and style of the operator.

7. *Structured:* Both spatial and temporal structures can be observed in the text-graphic manipulation found in the examples. For instance, in Fig. 17.2, we can see a formal spatial schema that might be called "vertical list of text lines with hollow arrows to show relations." Such a system limits the kind of text-graphics one may create and their arrangement while at the same time giving them special meaning; it is a visual language.

8. *Reflective:* Text-graphic manipulation for working groups can be reflective: that is, a text-graphic performer can use a piece of text-graphics to refer to some aspect of a text-graphic performance. The performers in Fig. 17.4 made competing plans for the reorganization of the display as part of their performance. The plans were themselves pieces of text-graphics each of which diagrammed a possible way to reorganize the display.

In addition to specifying the attributes of text-graphic performances, it is useful to consider the properties of these performances in relation to the activities and goals of the group. Several authors have commented that having a common display often aids face-to-face task groups. Ball and Gilkey (1971) coined the term *explicit group memory* to point out that the display provides a lingering representation of the task state. Graphical imagery seems to tap a powerful kind of conceptualizing: "visual thinking" (Arnheim, 1969; McKim, 1972). The social dynamics of the working group may change for the better. Professional display operators such as Brunon (1971), Doyle and Straus (1976) and Sibbet (1976) pointed out that orienting group meetings around a visual stimulus prevents the concepts under discussion from being controlled by the verbally and/or politically dominant; instead, more of the group's members tend to participate in idea generation and evaluation.

A COMPUTER MEDIUM
FOR PERFORMING TEXT-GRAPHICS

vmacs™ is a performance-oriented graphics editor designed to support the features of text-graphic performance previously described. As a first goal, vmacs is intended to directly facilitate the kind of visual activities that takes place on the Wall Scroll. The text-graphic moves in such performances are a major challenge for a computer medium because of the panoramic graphics, the extreme agility requirements, and the embedded special visual languages. Designed initially as a performing medium for spontaneous improvisation, **vmacs** offers individual performers maximum agility in making text and graphics do what they want. Like paper, **vmacs** displays come in varying sizes: for instance, the 1,000 by 800 pixels it controls can be presented on a workstation for an individual or on a wall screen for groups. With a wall-size display, **vmacs** can provide support for face-to-face meetings by using the wall space as if it were a large sheet of electronic paper. Unlike paper, however, **vmacs** offers powerful ways of getting text and graphics to behave, such as dragging and erasing.

In general, **vmacs** gives the performer two kinds of manipulative control—manual and automatic. Manual control provides for agility in the hands-on interface and automatic control provides for program-directed processing of visual objects. Figure 17.5 shows how agility and processing are related through the text-graphic logic in **vmacs.** In this figure, we see that design of a performing medium starts with the human, a "front-in" approach. And because the interface hooks directly to a primitive text-graphic logic out of which more complex applications are built, the approach is also "bottom-up."

Performing Medium and Processing Medium

How can **vmacs** help groups beyond simply providing an electronic blackboard? That is, how can a performing medium such as **vmacs** supply the other functionalities needed to support cooperative work? The answer is, **vmacs** is not only a performing medium, but also a medium for automatic processing of visual objects. These two aspects of **vmacs** will be in constant contrast as the system is revealed in more detail. But at the same time, there is a necessary interplay between the two if **vmacs** is to be a single system that can meet the complex needs of groups such as Mandy and her team. In its first aspect, **vmacs** is a *performance-oriented graphics editor;* in its second aspect, **vmacs** must be able to handle the special processing required by *visual languages for cooperation.* Such visual languages are themselves a powerful tool for groups, and they are even more powerful if they can be processed in a performance graphics editor. In the following paragraphs, we see how these two aspects codetermine the **vmacs** system. (See Lakin, Wambaugh, Leifer, Cannon, & Sivard, 1989).

When people employ text and graphic objects in communication, those objects have meaning under a system of interpretation or visual language. Visual languages for cooperation are graphical representations for forms of group work such as brainstorming or cooperative task structuring; these languages permit group members to visualize some aspect of their work which, in turn, may permit them to understand it better or perform it more effectively. If a computer system can also interpret expressions in such a language, it can participate in the group work. That is, the computer can

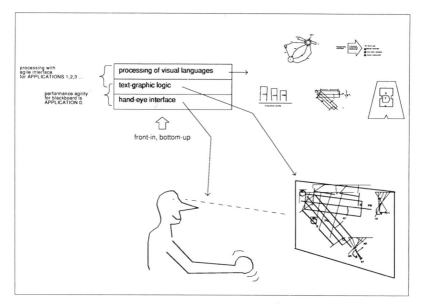

FIG. 17.5.   Front-in, bottom-up structure of the **vmacs** graphics editor for cooperative work.

understand the visual language expression and perform useful and appropriate actions to assist in the work the expression represents. The traditional way to achieve computer processing of expressions in visual languages is to employ a special purpose editor that is "hard-wired" for a particular language (syntax-driven). Hard-wired or syntax-driven editors achieve graphical agility and interpretive power, but at the expense of generality. Such editors limit the user's freedom; she can't spontaneously arrange text and graphics however she chooses. This is, of course, undesirable, because it conflicts with our other idea of creating a performance-oriented graphics editor.

Writing and drawing on a common display area often assist working groups in their tasks. For example, face-to-face groups have long enjoyed the richness of graphic communication found on blackboards. Emulating the spontaneous image manipulations that take place over time on a blackboard demands a performing medium that permits live manipulation of text and graphics. In such a performing medium, the fit between the tool and its human users must be so close that operators feel as if they have their hands directly on the text-graphics themselves; a performance editor must be both fast and general purpose. However, there is a problem with general purpose editors because although users can write and draw anything they want, they can't do anything with the drawing, such as process it as an expression in a visual language, which conflicts with our first idea.

The solution to this conflict is a performance-oriented graphics editor that can also do visual language processing. Initially designed as a general purpose medium for performing live text-graphics, **vmacs** gives the performer manual control over the behavior of objects on the screen. **vmacs** also provides the performer with automatic control of the behavior of visual objects, wherein programs process them and return results without user intervention. Taken together these two forms of control mean that **vmacs** is really two media in one—a performing medium for generating visual language expressions and a processing medium for analyzing the expressions thus generated. This combination of performance agility and processing power gives **vmacs** users the freedom to simply create text and graphics, and, then subsequently, to have the system interpret those objects and perform some useful action. Automatically handling expressions from visual languages for cooperation is an example of such interpretation.

DETAILS OF vmacs

According to the **vmacs** litany, it provides "performance agility plus processing power." But what is performance-grade agility? Agility can be gauged in text-graphic manipulations per second. **vmacs** achieves agility through a touch-typing interface with no waiting for menus (Lakin, 1986b). And processing power means that **vmacs** has the ability to interpret a spatial arrangement of text-graphic objects as an expression in a visual language and then take appropriate (assistive) action. Processing a visual expression in **vmacs** occurs in two stages: parsing and semantics. Parsing is the recovery of the underlying syntactic structure from the spatial arrangement of the elements; that structure is then used in the semantic stage, where procedures deal with how the parsed expressions carry meaning and the appropriate actions. Spatial parsing and semantic processing is discussed in more detail in Lakin (1980c, 1986a, 1987).

Many computer graphics systems offer processing of visual languages, but the editors in these systems are "hard-wired" for a particular visual language. The advantage of **vmacs** is that processing is supported in the midst of general purpose blackboard activity. The relation of processing to this activity is shown in Fig. 17.6. Blackboard activity is live and spontaneous, general and unstructured—a kind of "conversational graphics." In contrast, an expression in a particular visual language is highly structured according to the rules for laying out phrases in that language. The most natural way for expressions in visual languages to occur is embedded in conversational graphics. These expressions can be viewed as locally coagulated lumps in the more general text-graphic stuff ("text-graphic oatmeal")

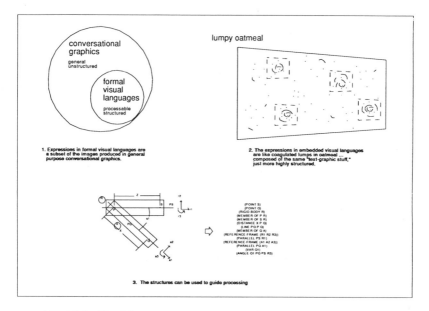

FIG. 17.6. Visual language expressions are often embedded in conversational graphics, like coagulated lumps in oatmeal.

generated during blackboard activity. **vmacs** has the capability to process such lumps when they occur in the midst of conversational graphics.

As an example of special processing for a particular kind of lump, consider the conversationally generated text-graphics in Fig. 17.7. Part of the visual oatmeal has formed into a special purpose diagram. This particular expression is in a visual language used to represent the dynamics of rigid bodies (Brown, 1988). When processed, the expression is first automatically translated into text forms as in Fig. 17.8. The text forms describe the features of the diagram that an engineering expert system need to analyze rigid bodies; the text forms are automatically loaded into the expert system to be employed in guiding analyses requested by the user.

A Libertarian Editor

vmacs is a general purpose graphics editor. The operator simply creates text-graphic objects wherever and whenever she desires. The operator may later choose to have the system process some of those objects under particular systems of interpretation (a visual language), but then again she may not. An arrangement of text-graphic objects can be perfectly useful to a working group just as they are, without further processing. In fact, there

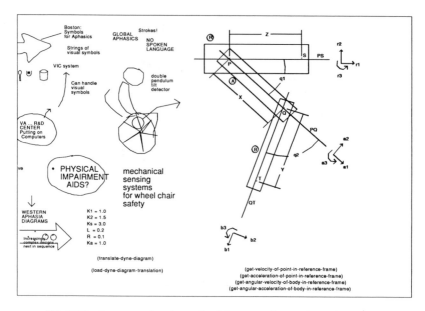

FIG. 17.7. An expression in a visual language for mechanical engineers which can be processed by **vmacs**.

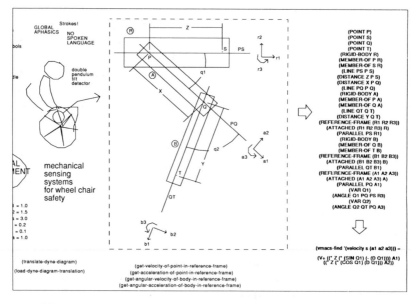

FIG. 17.8. Result of processing the visual language expression from Fig. 17.7 for representing the dynamics of rigid bodies.

may not be any particular, specifiable (to a computer) system of interpretation for those objects.

The point is, there will always be tension in text-graphic performing between specifiable formal structure and the lack of it—images may start out looking like one thing and end up as another. The change may have been the performer's intention all along, or she may have changed her mind in midstream. **vmacs** supports this feature of working group graphics by being general purpose; this is different from other systems that allow processing of visual objects, but at the expense of syntax-directed editing, forcing the user to choose a single system of interpretation for the images before they can be created. In contrast, **vmacs** is libertarian: every graphic act not prohibited is permitted.

A consequence of the **vmacs** approach is the freedom to use different visual languages in the same image, as is typical of blackboard use. Equally important, as mentioned earlier, is the flexibility to create objects in no particular visual language. **vmacs** supports new and different styles of performance before we understand them well enough to build special tools. This freedom allowed **vmacs** to be used to create expressions in the five visual languages presented in this chapter. The expressions were created simply as patterns of text-and-graphics before **vmacs** could do anything special with them.

Single Operator

vmacs is currently operated by one person at a time; that is, mouse and cursor from only one person affect the screen. This is not unlike a blackboard in a meeting situation, typically operated by one person at a time. The issue of cooperated displays is orthogonal to the issues of agility and processing. The individual's experience of the interface will be the same— hand-eye controls, text-graphic logic, and visual languages used—whether there is more than one person controlling the screen or not. An analogy can be made to the cars with dual controls that are used to teach driving. The controls are the same whether there is one set, two sets, or even more. The thrust of the current research is to find a set of controls that can supply the agility, and to figure out the computational support behind them to supply the processing of visual languages.

Once developed, the basic **vmacs** interface paradigm can be extended to include multiple operators. This requires finding a way around the machine dependence that most schemes for cooperation seem to require. One approach to cooperation is to start with multiple cursors and multiple access to the same screen, carefully measure the inevitable resulting manipulation collisions, and then based on these measures advance to some better scheme, perhaps in directions such as those being developed in the Colab project (Stefik et al., 1986, 1987).

Group Tool or Individual Tool?

vmacs can also be used very successfully to perform standard office computing tasks such as text-editing, page-layout, and sketching in an individual
workspace (**vmacs** doesn't know or care what the physical size of the
display is or how many people are watching the screen). There is great
advantage in being able to use the same basic tool in both group meetings
and in the individual workspace. Professional workers such as Mandy routinely shift back and forth between individual work and work in groups. Life
is much simpler if the same tool can be used in each situation, if the same
hard-eye reflexes and concepts work in each situation, and if the same
documents can be manipulated in each situation. My approach is to first
provide people with the manual agility and computer processing to make
text-graphics do what they want in support of thinking, and then later
specify the difference between use for individual work and use for group
work in terms of that system. In a sense, the visual languages for cooperation
presented here are actually a way of using **vmacs** to specify the structure of
use for group work.

A Bottom-Up Tool

The **vmacs** user interface is connected directly to a simple yet powerful
text-graphic logic, which cannot initially do very much by itself, but functions as a kit or foundation out of which other applications can be built. At
this stage in our understanding of group and individual needs, such a "bottom-up tool" seems appropriate. It closes off few avenues, and allows exploratory programming and rapid prototyping for a variety of specialized
capabilities.

   Through the extended capabilities described in this chapter, **vmacs** can
provide users with many of the functionalities cooperative groups need.
However, it may not yet be the tool for every user. Although powerful,
bottom-up tools (such as **emacs** and LISP in their respective domains of
text-editing and symbol manipulation) have a reputation for being somewhat harder to learn. They can be compared to manual transmissions in
automobiles, which give the driver much more control over the behavior of
the car than automatic transmissions, but at the price of more complexity.
This greater complexity means that some users may not feel at home in the
bottom-up **vmacs** interface. But **vmacs** was designed as a high performance
interface to function with the agility and power necessary for a performance
medium; at this stage in interface science, increased complexity during
early stages of use seems to be the necessary price for higher performance.
   Nonetheless, **vmacs** should not be relegated to the realm of computer
fanatics too quickly. Millions of people who are not performance car enthu-

siasts do learn to drive cars with manual transmissions, and people do learn to use moderately complex computer systems every day with a minimum of training. Secretaries across the nation have learned to use **emacs,** a moderately complicated, but powerful text processor, and LISP is taught as the first programming language at at least one major university (MIT). In actuality, the difficulty of learning **vmacs** for the casual user remains to be seen. As the user community widens, more data will be available; a number of people with neither **emacs** nor LISP background are now satisfied **vmacs** users. It is also a research goal to use the text-graphic processing of **vmacs** to assist the beginning user, making it easier to learn.

Because **vmacs** can be used as both an individual workspace and as a group medium, it offers the advantage of integrating these two domains. The concepts and reflexes used to operate **vmacs** are similar across applications; for example, **vmacs** allows the traditionally individual tasks of electronic messaging and text-editing to be done in the same system used for group work. Thus, as a practical matter, the user need not learn two or more separate systems; despite frequent social-mode switching, users can conduct all their work within a single medium. Furthermore, as a theoretical position, I oppose the separation of group work from individual work— trying to enforce that distinction always leads to trouble in the long run.

vmacs is also designed as a measuring medium (Lakin, 1983), keeping a symbolic history list of all user sessions. By analyzing such data, social and visual researchers may be able to discover general principles about ways humans manipulate text and graphics to do group and individual intellectual work. Insofar as scientists succeed in this quest, **vmacs** can be made both easier to use and more powerful for specific applications. Some of the principles discovered may provide the basis for rules which the text-graphic engine can use to guide automatic assistance, helping beginners to use **vmacs** on the one hand and providing more knowledgeable domain specific aid to groups on the other.

Implementation

vmacs combines the generality and agility of **emacs** with LISP-like processing of visual objects. The name **vmacs** indicates that the interface was inspired by **emacs** (Stallman, 1981), is meant to coexist with **emacs,** can be thought of as a collection of visual macros bound to keys and mouse buttons, and is basically a general purpose editor that can be specialized for particular applications (like LISP mode in **emacs**). **vmacs** is for people who spend a great deal of time using ("living in") their graphics editor. In the interest of speed and to avoid visual clutter, the primary functions are not invoked by menu. **vmacs** is written partly in the PAM graphics language, which provides text-graphic objects, manipulations of them, and computing with text-graphic forms (Lakin, 1980a, 1980b, 1980c). **vmacs** and PAM are implemented in ZetaLISP running on a Symbolics 36xx. Figures 17.5 through 17.16 were all done in **vmacs**.

An important note on **vmacs** to understand its use: visual objects are displayed on a *page*; the page may be larger than the screen and scrolling is provided. Multiple pages are available, but only one page is visible at a time. Currently **vmacs** does not do multiple windows for two reasons: first, there are often more efficient ways to achieve the functionality of windows, and, second, windows are not well enough understood text-graphically at this time to be processed as objects on the screen.

Processing Visual Languages for Cooperation in vmacs

Five visual languages are presented in this chapter: PROOF-MARKS, BRAIN-STORM-ORGANIZER, TEXT-GRAPHIC-QUERY, VISUAL-MAIL, and TASK-STRUCTURE. At the time of the initial draft for this chapter, none of the visual languages defined here could yet be processed in **vmacs**. But experience with the nine other visual languages implemented thus far (six are pictured in Fig. 17.9) has shown that the most difficult part of setting up a visual language system is in initially defining the language and how it will work. Second, it appears that the new visual languages presented here can all be implemented quite easily in **vmacs**.

The first point is important: visual languages for cooperation are for the benefit of both human and computer. They will benefit the humans first (remember phrases in the languages can be constructed in **vmacs** before they can be processed), but to do so they must be well-designed. In a sense, this chapter is partly an exercise in graphic design: to invent five new visual languages. As an operational definition of visual language, we say: *A visual language is a set of spatial arrangements of text-graphic symbols with a semantic interpretation that is used in carrying out communicative actions in the world.* Visual languages for cooperation are to be comprehended by humans and processed by computer. Humans get a way of visualizing an aspect of group work that can help them understand and perform it, and the computer gets text-graphic objects arranged according to rules that allow it to process them as expressions.

The second point is also important: experience has shown that formal visual languages used by humans, languages designed to be explicit and unambiguous, are quite easy to process using the facilities in **vmacs**. In this sense, **vmacs** is a toolkit for visual language processing. In the 3 months between the first and second drafts of this chapter, working prototypes for the VISUAL-MAIL and TASK-STRUCTURE languages were implemented. They are discussed in more detail later.

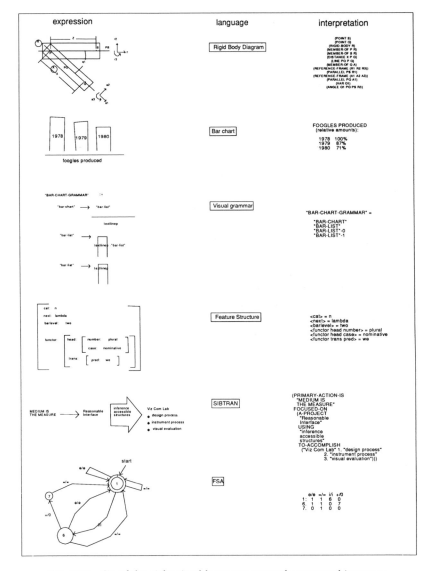

FIG. 17.9. Six of the eight visual languages currently processed in **vmacs**.

EXTENDED FACE-TO-FACE MEETING SUPPORT

The previous section described some capabilities of **vmacs** for supporting face-to-face meetings, namely its performance-grade agility in functioning as an electronic notepad or blackboard. But there are other specialized functions that face-to-face groups find useful. In this section, we translate two of these functions into definitions of visual languages that both humans and computers can understand.

Join Authoring With the PROOF-MARKS Language

As a simple example, let us take joint authoring. Assume that a group of five is composing a document together. Marking up a document offers a visual language for this, allowing the changes and alternatives to be viewed at the same time as the original text (Fig. 17.10). The text editor in **vmacs** allows us to compose paragraphs on the screen. As the group reworks the paragraphs, any changes that all members agree to can be edited into the text immediately. But many suggestions will need to be seen in comparison to the original version before they are accepted by the group. If they are edited into the text, however, the original version will be lost. In this situation, **vmacs** allows use of the traditional visual language of marking up a rough draft, with crossouts, connecting lines to proposed new wordings, arrows to indicate rearrangements of sentences and paragraphs, and marginal annotations as to the rationale for changes.

Up to this point, the group has been using the visual language to help it write the document, putting the graphic devices on the **vmacs** screen, but

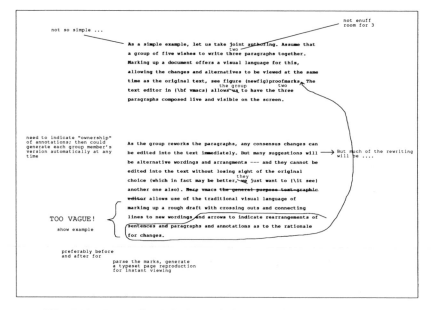

FIG. 17.10.   Paragraphs marked up with the processable PROOF-MARKS visual language for group authoring.

has not used **vmacs** to process those symbols. However, any time the group wants to see how its changes would affect the finished document, **vmacs** could parse the text and graphics and generate a typeset page reproduction to allow instant viewing of that particular rewrite. **vmacs** could also use the same procedure to generate a paper copy. We call the system thus described the PROOF-MARKS language. The purpose of this language is to generate alternative text-only paragraphs from the text-plus-graphics expressions in the language. We return to this system again in the course of the chapter, showing how the power of other visual languages can work in concert with it.

Group Idea Generation Using the BRAINSTORM-ORGANIZER Language

Another useful tool for face-to-face groups is the manipulable card technique described earlier. Again, we view this graphic technique as a language for humans to use manually on **vmacs,** and then later define a processor to interpret that language. In employing the language, users must voluntarily restrict themselves to generating text pieces as "cards" that are 13 character by 4 line pieces of text, or simple graphics that fit into the same rectangular area. Then the five-part strategy for using the Group Card medium can be employed in **vmacs,** substituting enclosing shapes for color overlays, thus creating an expression in the brainstorm-organizer language (Fig. 17.11).

1. Generate cards initially.
2. Use juxtaposition to show relation of cards.
3. Add enclosing shapes to show relation of cards: major point, double box; minor point, single box; special notice, jagged box.
4. Add connecting line to show relation of cards.
5. Shuffle cards around on the screen to shorten or remove connecting lines where possible, using juxtaposition to show connection instead.

When processing is implemented for the BRAINSTORM-ORGANIZER language, **vmacs** will be able to contribute by performing step 5 automatically. It would first follow the connecting lines to find related groups, and then rearrange pieces to remove or shorten the lines. Figure 17.11 is a transcription of the card patterns on the wall in Fig. 17.4. It uses additional elements not defined in the BRAINSTORM-ORGANIZER language, namely the circular enclosing line with subdividers and arrows, but the processor can be written to ignore everything enclosed by a line, thus making that graphic element a "NO-OP" in BRAINSTORM-ORGANIZER. Later the processor could be extended to consider the enclosed objects as a group and shuffle them as a unit.

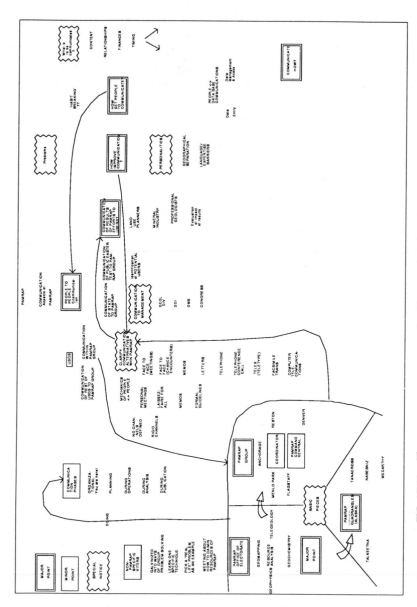

FIG. 17.11.   The BRAINSTORM-ORGANIZER visual language based on the manipulable cards method in Fig. 4.

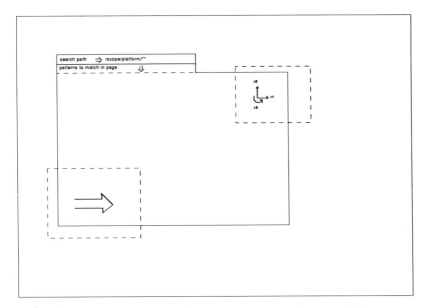

FIG. 17.12.   An expression in the TEXT-GRAPHIC-QUERY language defining a
set of visual pages for retrieval.

STORAGE AND RETRIEVAL OF TEXT-GRAPHICS

Storage and retrieval is essential when the **vmacs** medium is used over
weeks or months. The simplest storage mechanism is to name text-graphic
pages and write them out onto disk; the pages are then retrieved by name. A
visual directory page facilitates this process by listing all the page names and
allowing the user to select a page to be retrieved.

A more sophisticated retrieval mechanism would allow the user to retrieve pages by content. Content-directed retrieval might proceed by having the user write and draw an expression in the TEXT-GRAPHIC-QUERY[4]
language that would then be used as a pattern to filter a set of pages and
select a subset for perusal. Figure 17.12 shows such a visual query form,
which could be submitted to the page filing system as a guide for retrieving
a set of pages. The interpretation of the TEXT-GRAPHIC-QUERY form and the
matching against the contents of visual pages in storage can be easily accomplished by using text-graphic processing abilities already in **vmacs**;
however, further development work is needed to make it possible to retrieve information at an acceptable speed.

Content-directed text-graphic retrieval would be useful in almost every

---

[4]TEXT-GRAPHIC-QUERY is a trademark of the performing graphics company.

aspect of **vmacs** use. For example, a group doing joint authoring with the PROOF-MARKS language would generate multiple versions over time. It would often be easier to remember a version by distinctive graphic marks on the page than by name, in which case a TEXT-GRAPHIC-QUERY expression would be the appropriate way to retrieve it.

NON-FACE-TO-FACE COMMUNICATION

As other authors in this volume have observed (Bikson & Eveland, chap. 10; Finholt, Sproull, & Kiesler, chap. 11; Kraut, Egido & Galegher, chap. 6 in this volume) tools that allow group members to communicate and share documents or other artifacts even when they are not meeting face-to-face can be important aids to intellectual teamwork. **vmacs** facilitates communication between dispersed users in a variety of ways.

The most basic communication facility is simply mailing text-graphic pages from one group member to another. Any standard mail system can be used because **vmacs** images are stored as ASCII characters. Figure 17.13 shows the first **vmacs** page that was mailed over the ARPANET from one **vmacs** user to another. At that time manual effort was required to prepare the page for mailing, but since then the procedure has been automated.

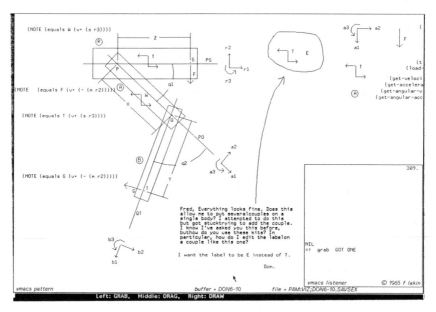

FIG. 17.13.   A **vmacs** page which was mailed over the ARPANET.

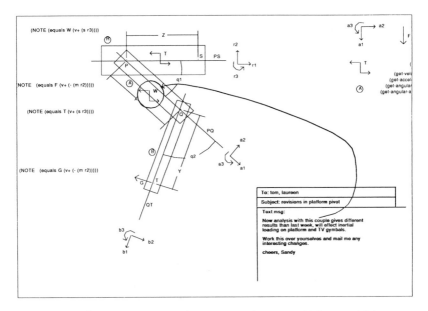

FIG. 17.14.   An expression in the VISUAL-MAIL language which can send the
enclosing **vmacs** page to the addressee.

Figure 17.14 shows an expression in the VISUAL-MAIL™[5] language which,
when processed, sends the **vmacs** page containing it to the addressee.

VISUAL MAIL would be very handy in a community of **vmacs** users. Once
again joint authoring is a good example, where different marked-up versions
of a manuscript could be mailed between group members. As the VISUAL-
MAIL system evolves, it can acquire all of the features of textual mail. Message filtering is one such feature that is very powerful. Malone, Grant, Lai,
Rao, and Rosenblitt (1986) point out that teleconferencing can be implemented as a kind of message filter. The same underlying text-graphic processing power in **vmacs** that does visual language interpretation can also
support visual message filtering, and a related capability would allow group
members to use TEXT-GRAPHIC-QUERY on their VISUAL-MAIL files.

ADMINISTRATION OF COOPERATIVE TEAMWORK

Group projects can be structured in many different ways. Whatever that
structure happens to be, the group needs to know about it and be kept
abreast of its evolution during the course of the project.

---

[5]VISUAL-MAIL is a trademark of the performing graphics company.

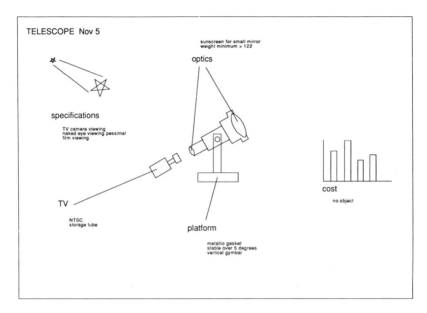

FIG. 17.15.   The early stage of a task structure diagram (for a telescope design group) is stored on a communally accessible "base page."

Diagramming Task Structures

Groups such as the one described in Scenario One can use **vmacs** as individuals to work on their respective parts of the project, and they can also use **vmacs** together in group meetings. For instance, when they meet, they might want to look at a **vmacs** page summarizing the project task structure as shown in Fig. 17.15. This diagram lives on the "base page," and shows the five parts of a telescope design project, who is in charge of each part, and key points in the progress of each part.

As work progresses, each team member will generate other **vmacs** pages relating to their part—that is, they will be doing their design work using **vmacs** as a personal computer medium. When individuals create a new page, they would add a pointer to it on the base page (Fig. 17.16). This pointer is simply the name of a file where the page is saved so that other team members can look at it if they wish. Also, any change in the status of each part would be noted in its summary on the base page. Thus the base page serves as a "blackboard" through which the group members communicate (in a sense similar to the way cooperating software agents communicate through a less literal blackboard in certain artificial intelligence systems).

By convention, only one team member at a time can modify the base page (this convention could be supported by software that locks the base page file to prevent modifications by other members during that time). Also, all team members have read-only access to the pages of any other members for which pointers are listed on the base page. Thus, at any time, each team member has an up-to-date top level snapshot of the current status of the project—in particular, the state of the other parts that interact with his or her part and where to find out more detailed information about them.

The TASK-STRUCTURE Language

The previously described scenario describes a way of visually representing group task structure; a major use of this representation is to show the names of other visual files related to the task for manual retrieval. It would be nice, however, if the user could simply point at a file name and the file would be retrieved. What would it take for such assistance? All that is required is to define a visual language for laying out base pages so that assisting procedures will know how to find the information they need about underlying directory structure in order to locate the named file. But the human team members, in order to perform their manual file retrieval, are *already* using a convention for laying out the base page that shows directory membership of files (the "/scope.dir" etc. headings for each list of files in Fig. 17.16). Text-

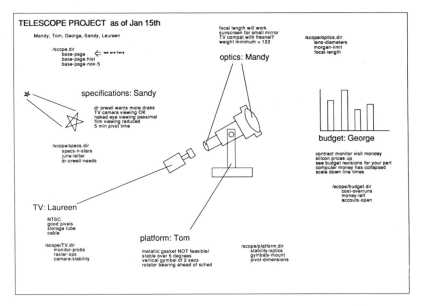

FIG. 17.16.   The TASK-STRUCTURE language shows the status of an evolving project, and can be used to retrieve other pages with more detailed information.

graphic processing in **vmacs** can take advantage of what the humans are already doing, using the spatial regularities of their convention in order to find the requisite information for automatic retrieval, thus turning the base page into a graphical directory to other pages. We can think of this now as the TASK-STRUCTURE language for expressing the page infrastructure of group projects; a prototype of this language is currently running.

MONDAY AT WORK:
SCENARIO TWO WITH vmacs

It is once again 9:30 A.M. Monday morning. Mandy Bateman is at her desk working on Friday's presentation for the client. The presentation still consists of about 15 viewgraphs describing the telescope project, along with a five-page written report to be given to the client.

At the moment, Mandy is using **vmacs** to work on the artwork for the viewgraphs. Because **vmacs** has sufficient agility for spontaneous writing and drawing, she does not need to prepare rough drafts of artwork on paper and transcribe them into the computer; she now composes all text-and-graphic documents, from first cut to last, directly in **vmacs**. Occasionally, her work on the slides prompts an idea for a revision in the report, and she switches to that page in **vmacs**, and works on it for a while. A **vmacs** user can have many different pages available during a session, each one a keystroke away. She can freely cut and paste material from one to the other because both artwork and report are being created in **vmacs**.

As she works on a diagram, a question arises about a part of the project being handled by Tom, another team member. Mandy has a vague visual memory of a particular drawing of Tom's on which **vmacs** had done CAD-style analysis. **vmacs** supports special technical contexts by allowing special processing for visual images used in those contexts. In Tom's case, **vmacs** processed a drawing of part of the telescope system and utilized it as a visual interface to mechanical engineering analysis software (Fig. 17.7). Mandy thinks the analysis might be relevant to the presentation on Friday. She goes to another page in **vmacs** on which there is a diagram in the TASK-STRUCTURE language (Fig. 17.16). This diagram shows her both the current organizational structure of the project team and the technical status of the project itself. Parts of the diagram list the **vmacs** files used by each team member in day-to-day work.

She finds the file directory for Tom's part of the project and uses the TEXT-GRAPHIC-QUERY language to construct a visual query expression (Fig. 17.12) containing the key features of the remembered drawing; **vmacs** will match the query against all the files in that directory. Mandy looks through the four candidate diagrams which the query returns, and finds the right drawing. She copies Tom's drawing into a fresh **vmacs** page of her own and makes some minor changes. Then she asks **vmacs** to reinterpret the drawing, thus reanalyzing the system it represents in terms of rigid-body mechanics. **vmacs** computes the answer and inserts it into the page with the drawing as pieces of visual text (Fig. 17.8). Indeed, she sees that the drawing plus analysis do sum up much of the project, so she includes it in both the artwork for the presentation and also as a figure in the report.

It is now 10:00 A.M.—time for the meeting about Friday's presentation. (Note the meeting time is a half hour earlier than in Scenario One.) There is a large screen video projector for the **vmacs** terminal in the meeting room and the artwork for the presentation can be shown directly as **vmacs** pages, so there is no need to make transparencies. Also, as we shall see later, there is no need to make paper copies of the written report to distribute to the other team members. Mandy hurries off to the meeting. (Even with great tools, one is always a little late.)

The four other team members are already seated in the meeting room by the time she gets there. She greets Tom, and tells him about the CAD drawing she pulled from his **vmacs** files. He says that's fine. She starts the meeting by projecting the first slide onto the large **vmacs** screen, and a lively discussion of the planned presentation ensues. The team's feedback on the artwork is varied, comprehensive, and useful. Some of the suggestions are simple and obviously for the better, so Mandy makes the changes on the image as the group views it. Other suggestions will take more time and thought, so she starts a new **vmacs** page that will serve as a note-page to record them. The rehearsal of the presentation continues in this fashion for a while: the next **vmacs** image is put up on the screen, Mandy delivers the few sentences that explain it, and then a few more minutes are spent modifying the artwork and putting additional notes on the note-page.

One of the team members then points out that Friday's meeting with the client will be in this room. This is good news, because it means that they can use **vmacs** and the large screen projector for the presentation. This realization prompts other changes in the artwork, and activity on the note-page for the presentation becomes more and more animated. Everyone in the group can see the feedback as it is recorded, and they interact with each other's ideas further. In fact, the meeting turns into a general brainstorming session about the entire presentation; Mandy writes down all the ideas as they are spoken. Now and then she uses connecting lines and enclosing boxes to organize the rapidly accumulating information on the note-page. These graphic devices are known to **vmacs** as part of the BRAINSTORM-ORGANIZER visual language (Fig. 17.11). Later, **vmacs** can use them to process the brainstorming activity captured on the note-page, helping Mandy to find patterns in the text-and-graphics generated by the activity. After a while,

Mandy asks Tom to take over at the **vmacs** console. Even with the agility of **vmacs,** trying to run the meeting and record the group's ideas at the same time is too much for one person.

As the discussion unfolds, brainstorming about the presentation *of* the project leads to some new ideas about technical details *in* the project. The focus has shifted from the form to the content of the presentation; the team wants to thrash out one of the new design ideas on the spot. Mandy gives the OK, allowing them 15 minutes. Thanks to **vmacs,** the team will be able to switch contexts and do "real work," dealing with actual technical details in the meeting room (a major change from Scenario One). Each team member uses **vmacs** for day-to-day work, consequently all the relevant design documents and analysis tools are available immediately through the **vmacs** outlet in the meeting room.

The first step is to display the project structure diagram on the screen; it provides access to the working files of each team member. The technical detail they want to work on is in Sandy's part of the project; Sandy takes over the **vmacs** console and constructs a TEXT-GRAPHIC-QUERY to locate the relevant drawing. He finds the drawing, makes the suggested changes, and invokes the rigid-body analyzer on the modified diagram. The team is now fully switched to hardcore engineering mode: they use the meeting room as if it were one of their offices (and, in fact, it is; they often work together in this meeting room, using the big screen for face-to-face collaboration).

After 20 minutes Mandy points out that it is 11:10 A.M. and they need to get back to reviewing the presentation. The new work the team has accomplished on Sandy's part of the telescope impinges directly on other aspects being handled by Tom and Laureen. Both people request copies of Sandy's modified drawing, so he quickly adds a VISUAL-MAIL header to the drawing and mails it to them (Fig. 17.14) before relinquishing the **vmacs** console.

Mandy then proceeds through the remainder of the slides; Tom is again making changes in virtually every slide based on the group feedback. It is now 11:45 A.M. Mandy starts to declare the meeting over, but before the first team member can make it out the door, she remembers the draft of the written report that she wanted them to review. She persuades them to sit back down for 15 minutes of "group authoring." She projects the draft of the report onto the screen and they go over it from the beginning, one paragraph at a time. Mandy has arranged the screen so that the text is in a triple-spaced column with very wide margins, leaving lots of room for putting in additional text, crossouts, and arrows.

As the group reworks the paragraphs, they agree on some changes and those are edited into the text immediately. But most of the suggestions are alternative wordings and arrangements, not necessarily better but choices that should be considered. These, of course, cannot be edited into the text without losing sight of the original version; instead, the team needs to be able to contemplate several possibilities at the same time. When marking up the draft in this manner, they are using the PROOF-MARKS language (Fig. 17.10).

They work on the draft of the report in this fashion until a general revolt stops the proceedings at 12:05 P.M. Mandy is pleased; they have gotten through the first two pages, including the all-important overview. Now she lets the team leave, thanking them for a good meeting and the help with the report in particular. After the others have gone, Mandy spends an extra minute at the **vmacs** console making sure all the modified pages are saved onto disk. She also uses VISUAL-MAIL to send a copy of the marked-up report to each team member with a note saying that any additional work they want to contribute will be appreciated but is not required. She leaves the meeting room at 12:07. (Note the time saving over Scenario One. Preserving the information generated at the meeting is far quicker in **vmacs** than manually transcribing the information from whiteboard onto paper).

Back from lunch at 1:30 P.M., Mandy sits down at her **vmacs** terminal and retrieves the note-page from the morning's meeting. She reworks the page by hand for a couple of minutes, moving pieces of text around and adding more connecting lines. Then she copies the whole image into a new page and runs the BRAINSTORM-ORGANIZER visual language processor on the copy to see what patterns **vmacs** can expose in the text-and-graphics. The organizer's processor reshuffles the pieces in the image to shorten or remove connecting lines where possible, using spatial juxtaposition to show connection instead. Because having related pieces next to each other is visually simpler than a spaghetti network of lines connecting pieces, such reshuffling makes it easier to see relations among the pieces.

Looking at the reorganized brainstorm image, Mandy realizes that two sections of the presentation are really the same topic from different perspectives. She then finds the relevant artwork for the presentation and modifies it accordingly. This in turn suggests other changes and she settles in to preparing the final artwork/slide sequence for the presentation, referring to the brainstorm image from time to time. She works continuously on the artwork for almost an hour. (Note more time savings over Scenario One: First, Mandy does not have to transcribe the team feedback back into computer from paper; and second, many of the suggested changes to the artwork have already been made, having been done on the spot in the meeting.)

She is interrupted by the arrival of visual mail from Laureen, who has sent a further reworking of the draft for the written report. This prompts Mandy to turn her attention to the report, and she sets up two **vmacs** pages so that she can compare Laureen's draft with the version as it was at the end of the meeting. The drafts were both modified using PROOF-MARKS, so **vmacs** can help her with the comparison. For each draft, **vmacs** processes the graphic devices of the marking-on-the-draft visual language and produces a clean copy to look at in a new **vmacs** page. The clean copy incorporates all changes indicated by crossouts, inverted V's for phrase insertions, and arrow patterns for sentence rearrangements. Going back and forth between the marked-up drafts, with alternative phrasings all present at the same time, and the various clean copies allows Mandy to more readily compose the final report.

(Note, finally, another change from Scenario One: Mandy doesn't have to phone reluctant team members to inquire about their versions of the report. She has already gotten 20 minutes of work on the draft from each of them during the meeting. Any additional work from people like Laureen she can gratefully accept, and the rest of the team is grateful to be left alone, having discharged their required duties.)

CONCLUSIONS

Visual languages for cooperation are formalized graphical representations for different kinds of group work such as brainstorming or cooperative task structuring. A visual language for cooperation assists group members by giving them a way of visualizing an aspect of group work so they can better understand and perform it. Formal visual languages like these have the feature that the text-and-graphics in expressions are carefully laid out in spatial arrangement according to well-defined rules.

vmacs is a graphics editor intended for use as a performance medium that supports the spontaneous generation of text-and-graphics, including expressions in visual languages for cooperation. **vmacs** is also a processing medium for interpreting expressions in visual languages. By taking advantage of the well-defined spatial regularity in such expressions, **vmacs** can first parse them to recover underlying structure and then employ that structure to guide semantic interpretation and perform useful actions. In this way, the visual language expression becomes a means for the computer to understand and assist intellectual teamwork.

The visual languages for cooperation described in this chapter serve two masters, being both comprehended by humans and processed by computer. But to take full advantage of the power of these languages, their use must be embedded in a computer system for doing everyday work. As a performance medium, **vmacs** is first and foremost a comfortable place for a knowledge worker to spend her day. It has a good fit as she goes about the business of manipulating text-and-graphics in various guises and modes. The **vmacs** performance medium is general purpose, so it can follow and support her as she crosses and recrosses the boundaries of categories such as individual agent, group member, report writer, artwork sketcher, public presenter, technical task performer, and electronic mail communicator. To support intellectual teamwork, a system must support the members of the intellectual team in all of their work.

REFERENCES

Arnheim, R. (1969). *Visual thinking.* Berkeley, CA: University of California Press.

Ball, G. H., & Gilkey, J. Y. (1971). Facilitation and explicit group memory: Their application in education. Menlo Park, CA: SRI International. (IR & D No. 183531-409).

Brown, D. R. (1988). *Knowledge-based engineering analysis.* Unpublished doctoral dissertation, Design Division, Mechanical Engineering Department, Stanford University.

Brunon, J. (1971). Group dynamics and visual thinking. *Journal of Architectural Education,* (3).

Doyle, M., & Straus, D. (1976). *How to make meetings work.* Richfield, CT: Wyden Books.

Lakin, F. (1971a). *Wall Scroll hardware in use at meeting of the CORO fellows.* San Francisco, CA, September 21.

Lakin, F. (1971b). *The text-graphic loom.* Unpublished manuscript, Stanford University.

Lakin, F. (1974a). *Facilitating cognitive group display: A behavioral approach.* Unpublished manuscript, Stanford University.

Lakin, F. (1974b). Facilitation at the US Geological Survey, Menlo Park, CA, May 3.

Lakin, F. (1980a). A structure from manipulation for text-graphic objects. *Proceedings of SIGGRAPH '80.* Seattle, WA.

Lakin, F. (1980b). Diagramming a project on the electric blackboard. Videotape for SIGGRAPH '80. Seattle, WA.

Lakin, F. (1980c). Computing with text-graphic forms. *Proceedings of the LISP Conference.* Stanford, CA: Stanford University.

Lakin, F. (1983). Measuring text-graphic activity. *Proceedings of GRAPHICS INTERFACE '83.* Edmonton, Alberta.

Lakin, F. (1986a). Spatial parsing for visual languages. In S. Chang, T. Ichikawa, & P. A. Ligomenides (Eds.), *Visual languages* (pp. 35–85). New York: Plenum.

Lakin, F. (1986b). A performing medium for working group graphics. *Proceedings of the Conference on Computer-Supported Cooperative Work,* Austin, TX.

Lakin, F. (1987). Visual grammars for visual languages. *Proceedings of AAAI-87,* Conference of the American Association for Artificial Intelligence, Seattle, WA.

Lakin, F., Wambaugh, J., Leifer, L., Cannon, D., & Sivard, C. (1989). The Electronic Design Notebook: Performing Medium and Processing Medium. *THE VISUAL COMPUTER: International Journal of Computer Graphics, 5,* 214–226.

Malone, T. W., Grant, K. R., Lai, K., Rao, R., & Rosenblitt, D. (1986). Semi-structured messages are surprisingly useful for computer-supported coordination. *Proceedings of the Conference on Computer-Supported Cooperative Work,* Austin, TX.

McKim, R. H. (1972). *Experiences in visual thinking.* Belmont, CA: Wadsworth.

Porter, E. H., & Verger, M. D. (1974). *Interactive planning system.* Unpublished manuscript, Los Angeles, CA.

Sibbet, D. (1976). Introduction to group graphics. *The Corospondent,* CORO Foundation Northern California Public Affairs Quarterly, Summer.

Stallman, R. (1981). EMACS: The extensible, customizable self-documenting display editor. *MIT AI Memo,* 519a, March.

Stefik, M., Bobrow, D., Lanning, S., & Tater, D. (1986). WYSIWIS revised: Early experiences with multi-user interfaces, *Proceedings of the Conferences on Computer-Supported Cooperative Work,* Austin, TX.

Stefik, M., Foster, G., Bobrow, D. G., Kahn, K., Lanning, S., & Suchman, L. A. (1987). Beyond the chalkboard: Computer support for collaboration and problem solving meetings. *Communications of the ACM, 30*(1), 32–47.

18

Experiences in an Exploratory Distributed Organization

Mark J. Abel
*U S WEST Advanced Technologies**

Abstract

Between 1985 and early 1988, a research project was conducted within the Xerox Palo Alto Research Center (PARC) to understand the needs of geographically distributed organizations and to build technology that would help distributed organizations function. To provide a testbed, one computer research organization at Xerox PARC was intentionally split between existing facilities in Palo Alto, California and new facilities in Portland, Oregon. A major goal of this exploratory effort was to force the twenty to twenty-five computer researchers in this organization to build and integrate technology to support collaboration over the distance between Palo Alto and Portland. The resulting technology was a combination of computer technology with always-available cross-site video and audio.

This chapter discusses the lab's cross-site experience. To provide a backdrop for this discussion, the paper first describes the motivations, setting and technological support for this distributed organization experiment. The chapter then presents a discussion of the author's and other lab members' cross-site experiences.

MOTIVATIONS

In late 1984, Adele Goldberg and others in the System Concepts Lab (SCL) at Xerox PARC decided to pursue an exploratory effort to build and integrate technology for the support of distributed organizations. They felt that technical and organizational trends would be coming together in the 1990s

---

*Formerly with Xerox PARC-Northwest.

to provide both the capability and the marketplace for systems that support geographically distributed work groups.

In the technical arena, the lab saw that the merging of computing and communications technology would eventually allow the emergence of interpersonal computing systems. In other words, by combining the capabilities of high bandwidth telecommunications and computer networks with faster, more intelligent, and cheaper computing systems, systems that greatly enhanced human-to-human interaction would eventually be feasible and affordable. Such interpersonal computing/communications systems have since come to be known as "Groupware" (Johansen, 1988) or "Computer-Supported Cooperative Work", (CSCW, 1986).

In the organizational arena, it became clear to SCL leadership that organizations of all sorts were becoming more geographically distributed. For example, the emergence of a competitive global marketplace is causing corporations to disperse sales offices, research and development capabilities, manufacturing, and marketing. A company might have their headquarters in New York City, their research and development facilities in Silicon Valley, Boston, and Munich, their manufacturing capability in Mexico and Taiwan, and their sales and marketing force all over the world. SCL's leadership (and other leaders in the business and research communities) felt that economically viable systems to support such distributed problems could be made available in the 1990s.

Finally, in SCL's pioneering work in personal computing (e.g., Smalltalk), lab members' need for new computing tools and capabilities had helped foster the creation of prototype systems. In other words, lab members' needs had provided a "forcing function" for the creation of new personal computing technology. Lab leadership decided to try to create such a forcing function for technology to support distributed organizations. They created a geographically distributed organization by establishing a second SCL facility in Portland, Oregon about 600 miles from the lab's existing facilities in the Palo Alto, California research center. It was hoped that this separation would provide a forcing function and a laboratory testbed for the prototyping of support systems for distributed organizations.

THE SETTING

The Organizational Environment

The System Concepts Laboratory, the birthplace of Smalltalk, was one of three computer research labs at the Xerox Palo Alto Research Center. Historically, SCL did research in object-oriented systems, user interface design, and personal computing environments.

The lab established the remote Portland facility in May 1985. A research group was established, primarily in Portland, to focus on collaborative systems to support geographically distributed work (see Goodman & Abel, 1986, 1987 for more details). In addition to the collaborative systems project, other continuing projects investigated shared object-oriented databases and programming environments, and the support of group design work over time. Geographic and personnel boundaries between these projects were somewhat fluid. Researchers in both sites sometimes worked on multiple projects and projects often cooperated on particular pieces of technology.

The lab maintained a permanent staff of between twenty and twenty-five, including researchers, managers, and support staff. The lab staff also usually included some visiting scientists, students, and consultants. In general, about a third of the lab members worked in Portland and about two thirds of the lab members worked in Palo Alto. With one exception, the Portland-based lab members were all hired form outside of Xerox PARC.

There were two levels of formal management in the lab. A lab manager who worked primarily in Palo Alto ran the entire lab. During the period of this exploratory effort, either three or four area managers reported to the lab manager. Each area manager had between one and seven researchers and support staff reporting to them. In general, an area manager was responsible for a project area. One area manager resided in Portland and also acted as the Portland site manager. The other area managers resided in Palo Alto. Over the course of this exploratory effort, all the area managers and the lab manager supervised at least one staff member at the other site.

The Physical Setting

The physical layout of SCL's "pod" in the Palo Alto Research Center was important to the way SCL functioned over the years. The main feature of the SCL pod at PARC was a large comfortable commons area. The Palo Alto commons area was a large carpeted area (33 by 40 feet) containing couches, lunch tables and chairs, book shelves, some technical information, some technical toys, and a few computers. One of its main features was a floor to ceiling whiteboard at the front of the room. The commons area provided a comfortable environment for lab get-togethers and informal interactions.

A number of researchers' private offices were arrayed around this rectangular commons area and opened into it. If researchers left their doors open, they could hear a great deal of what happened in the commons. In addition to the doors, most offices had floor to ceiling glass walls/windows facing the commons area. This allowed researchers to see much of what happened in the commons. It also allowed those in the commons to see into researchers' offices.

The physical layout of the Portland site was designed to mirror the already established Palo Alto site. The Portland commons area, offices, and furniture were all carefully chosen to resemble their Palo Alto counterparts. Many people who visited the Portland site after being in the Palo Alto site first, remarked that "the Portland site feels a lot like Palo Alto."

SUPPORT FOR
THE DISTRIBUTED ORGANIZATION

Basic Facilities: Telephone and Internetworking

For many years, computer researchers at Xerox PARC have employed individual workstations connected via Ethernet † as a basic research platform. In addition to providing advanced programming environments, networked workstations provided access to internet features like electronic mail and file servers. Electronic mail was in common usage throughout Xerox PARC (and throughout Xerox Corporation). By the end of summer 1985, all of the Portland-based researchers also had workstations running an advanced programming environment, Smalltalk-80 ††, with the availability of electronic mail and other internet features. To provide these features, the Portland workstations were connected to a local 10 Mbps Ethernet, which was gatewayed to Palo Alto initially via a 9.6 kbps data line and later via a 56 kbps data line.

This arrangement allowed a regular electronic mail (e-mail) flow within the distributed laboratory. The difference in geographic location was absolutely transparent in the e-mail world. For example, to send mail to Palo Alto lab member Dave Robson one sent to 'Robson.pa,' whereas to send to Portland lab member Mark Abel one sent to 'Abel.pa' regardless of the sender's location. To send to the entire lab, one simply used a distribution list name. In the author's opinion, this shared e-mail space and the equality of the e-mail world helped enhance the feeling of lab unity despite the lab's geographic distribution.

Initially, the only other electronic connection between Palo Alto and Portland was via telephone lines. For cross-site group meetings in offices and conference rooms, we used normal telephone lines with half duplex (i.e., only one way at a time) speakerphone endpoints. For cross-site meetings in the commons areas, we generally used speakerphones with handheld mikes because the acoustics of the large open rooms rendered the speakerphones' built-in mikes almost useless. To allow document sharing, the lab used fax machines or computer network tools.

Shared Cross-site Space: "Video Walls"

Research by Allen (1977) at MIT, and Kraut and associates (chap. 6 in this volume) at Bellcore, pointed out the importance of physical proximity in research and development organizations. Proximity allows frequent com-

---

† registered trademark of Xerox Corp.
††registered trademark of ParcPlace Systems, Inc.

munication and low-cost unplanned interaction, both of which facilitate the emergence and maintenance of personal/working relationships.

In an attempt to simulate physical proximity across the 600 miles between the Portland and Palo Alto sites, the lab established a "shared cross-site audio/video space." This shared space was established by providing a two-way audio/video connection between the Palo Alto commons area and Portland commons area that was always on. This technology was sometimes characterized as looking through a "video wall" or "video window" to the other site. Figure 18.1 shows a conceptual drawing of the shared cross-site commons space. Fig. 18.2 shows a photograph of the shared cross-site commons space as seen from Portland.

This shared audio/video space provided a constantly available, cross-site facility for drop-in interactions. The shared cross-site commons area also allowed researchers working around the commons to keep in touch with the other site. For example, from many offices around the Portland commons one could see and hear the activities in the Palo Alto commons and vice versa. The shared audio/video space also supported scheduled cross-site meetings like weekly lab meetings, project meetings, and managerial staff meetings.

Audio and Video Facilities
for the Cross-site Shared Space

To control transmission costs, the always-on cross-site audio and video connections were of limited quality, for example, rapid motion in the video was blurred, details of facial expression were sometimes difficult to discern via the video, and the audio was "telephone quality." The cross-site video was transmitted via a 56 kbps channel using a technique called video compression. Standard full motion NTSC video (i.e., U.S. standard broadcast video) would have required over 1,000 times as much bandwidth (i.e., information-carrying capacity) as the video compression technology that we used. The compressed video signal had lower resolution, less color information, and significantly less ability to follow motion than a standard video signal. The video endpoints were consumer quality NTSC video cameras for input and consumer quality 19-inch monitors for video output. Initially the audio was provided by a pair of centrally located standard speakerphones connected by a standard phone line. The audio and the video were not synchronized with each other.

Later the system was improved by adding 40-inch rear projection monitors for video output in both commons areas and AT&T Quorum †††linear array microphones as the endpoints for cross-site audio. The Quorum microphone did an outstanding job of covering the large commons areas. However, the Quorum system was still a half-duplex system based on speakerphone technology with a limited frequency range, and lack of audio directionality.

---

††† registered trademark of AT&T

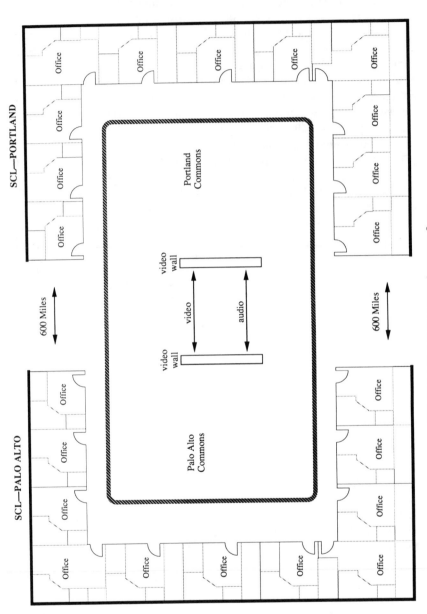

FIG. 18.1. Shared Cross-Site Commons Space

FIG. 18.2.   Meeting in Shared Commons Space (As Seen from Portland)

Computer Controllable Video Network

As we experienced the cross-site video in the commons areas, we began to want to use it and control it from offices and other locations. To fill this need, we installed and built a computer controllable video switching network that spanned most locations in both SCL sites. From any network station in the cross-site environment, users were able to control video connection. Control of the cross-site video network from offices allowed lab members to simulate several standard same-site activities remotely, for example, looking around for a particular colleague, meeting and giving tours to visitors, stopping by someone's office to initiate an impromptu meeting, or looking out into the commons or down hallways over the course of the day.

This video network was constructed by outfitting offices, conference rooms, and other areas with cameras, monitors, audio equipment, and wiring. The video cameras and monitors at each site were connected to the site's computer-controllable video switch. The Portland and Palo Alto video switches were connected to each other via the compressed cross-site video. Networking software was built to allow transparent, distributed, and coordinated control of the video switching equipment from any workstation in our environment. Eventually, we had a cross-site video network including ten video sources and destinations in Portland, and twenty video sources and destinations in Palo Alto.

Travel

Although the majority of cross-site interaction took place through the cross-site electronic infrastructure, there was some travel between the two sites. On the average, SCL researchers travelled to the other site one to two times per year for a visit duration of about four days. SCL managers travelled to the other site about five times per year for an average visit duration of about two days.

EXPERIENCES

This section describes the cross-site experiences of the author and other members of the lab. The intent is to provide a set of experiences and impressions that capture, even if informally, the essence of the practical daily use of this technology. Observations of this sort can be useful in the improvement of the technology itself, in the understanding of how to apply the technology, and in providing insights into the likely consequences of using such technology.

Many lab members contributed cross-site experiences and impressions to our collection, primarily by sending electronic mail to a repository established for this purpose. In addition, the author kept a personal journal of cross-site experiences. Key excerpts from these experiences and impressions are used to support the general discussion in this section (note: to protect individual privacy, all names have been removed from these excerpts). These excerpts are delineated by indentation and use of a different font, for example,

> Excerpts and quotes from our collection of experiences appear in this manner.

In the following subsections we summarize the lab members' cross-site experiences and impressions regarding (a) organizational issues, (b) social issues, and (c) cognitive and physical issues. In general, the author has tried to relate the lab's consensus opinion on these issues. However, different people often had different impressions of working in our distributed environment. In cases where lab members' opinions differed significantly, the author has tried to present the range of opinion on the issue.

Organizational Issues

The operation of our distributed organization was affected in a number of ways by its distributed nature and the cross-site technology used to support it.

Short, Williams, and Christie (1976) talked about group cohesion in individual teleconferencing meetings. One of the goals of our exploratory effort was to see if, over time, a two-site distributed organization supported by technology could function as if it were a single-site organization. The lab tried to function as if it were a single-site organization. We held weekly cross-site lab meetings. Most of the projects in the lab involved researchers at both sites. All managers in the lab had at least one direct report at the other site. Occasionally lab members at the two sites even had lunch together via the cross-site technology.

Many of our experiences support the notion that we were one group. For example, other site visitors were often treated as "locals":

(Four Portland-based lab members) were having a technical discussion and brainstorming session in a Portland common area. (A Palo Alto based lab member) arrived on a (physical) visit from Palo Alto. He had not visited Portland in person for over six months. He happened to arrive during this technical discussion. Almost without missing a beat and without almost any "introduction protocol," the Palo Alto based lab member joined this brainstorming session. As the discussion wound down after about fifteen minutes, the Portland folks realized that (the Palo Alto based lab member) had arrived in person, and welcomed him.

The five lab members felt enough like part of the same group that there was no need for extensive social protocol (e.g., hi, welcome to Portland) and the Palo Alto person could just join right in. In addition, this Palo Alto lab member had enough shared knowledge about the project to join in effectively. Again, although these people interacted over the link frequently, they had not been together physically for over 6 months and had never worked together on a regular basis in the same physical location.

People even became so accustomed to the shared cross-site space that they even found themselves occasionally looking for a local person at the other site:

"I'm going office to office looking for (another Palo Alto person) because he's wanted on the phone. A dozen people have seen him 'over there' or going 'that way' in the past three minutes, but none of the pointers lead to (him). His briefcase is still in his office, there are no feet in either stall in the restroom. I'm doing one more loop around the atrium and heading back toward my office, thinking "now is there anywhere I haven't looked", when I pass the open door of the conference room. I slow my pace slightly to scan the empty room, turn my head back forward to continue down the hall, then my motor system snaps my head back around in a double-take just a moment before the verbalization gets to consciousness: 'I didn't check Portland.' "[1]

Lab members also noticed that our environment both inhibited and supported cross-site information flow. (Organizational information flow is considered to be a critical factor in organizational success by some organizational theorists; see Galbraith, 1973.) For example, the video link allowed one of the Palo Alto-based managers to develop a feeling of who was working with whom in Portland:

> (A Palo Alto based manager) has a good feeling of who's working with whom in Portland by watching the Portland video. For example he mentioned that Portland researcher A and Portland researcher B were working closely together and Portland researcher C was no longer working as much with them. This was exactly correct.

Unfortunately the information flow between the sites was not as good as within a site. People in Portland often did not know things that were almost common knowledge amongst Palo Alto lab members—PARC political gossip. The sites also sometimes did not communicate in other ways. The following comments from a Palo Alto-based manager describe a short impromptu research exploration ("the color activity") that collected enthusiastic contributors in Palo Alto but none in Portland.

> "This week's color activity pointed out to me that we lack a sufficient mechanism for communicating enthusiasm. The color work involved the color machine in the Palo Alto commons, with at least six programmers (most of whom joined some time into the project), and with at least 3/4 of the PA people dropping in for demos and other kibbitzing. If our communication channel were more like the hallway, we would have also enrolled some number of programmers and some numbers of drop-ins from Portland. As far as I know, all we accomplished was sending the code to Portland, and getting it demoed there, but none of it was together with PA people. . . . I am not sure what we can or should do to enable packet gusto."

In summary, the lab members felt that this distributed lab functioned as if it were one organization. Portland and Palo Alto lab members felt like they were part of the same entity despite the 600-mile gap between the sites. Our experience also showed that although some information flowed between the sites, some types of cross-site information flow were limited.

---

[1]Excerpts in "double quotes" are direct quotes from lab members or visitors. Unquoted excerpts are the author's descriptions as derived from observation or other's descriptions.

Social Issues

In cross-site social interaction we noticed that (a) many social protocols governing interaction had to be altered in cross-site situations, (b) while it was difficult to initiate relationships via the cross-site link, once established via face-to-face interaction, cross-site relationships sometimes grew and developed, (c) making certain types of decisions sometimes required face-to-face interaction (i.e., the link was inadequate), and (d) the presence of cameras and microphones that acted as remote "eyes and ears" sometimes impacted privacy.

Social interactions are governed by the standard social protocols of the culture in which the interaction takes place (Hall, 1959; 1966). Knowledge of the context provides participants with a set of rules or protocols to follow in an interaction (e.g., this is a formal business meeting at Xerox corporation in the United States, so I'm supposed to act in a certain way). Verbal and nonverbal cues exchanged between meeting participants control the progression through various scenarios (e.g., everyone has quizzical looks on their faces, so I better go back and explain that again). These cues help control turn-taking behavior, conversational repair mechanisms, meeting entry, meeting exit, consensus mechanisms, and so forth (Krauss, Garlock, Bricker, & McMahon, 1977).

In communicating via any medium, even face-to-face, these cues can be lost, misunderstood, and so forth. In communicating via the cross-site media infrastructure, required cues were often lost or altered. For example, visual cues might have been lost because the person in question was out of camera view. Due to the quality and size of the video display, subtle gestural cues or changes in posture might have been less noticeable over the video than they would have been face-to-face. Verbal cues were sometimes lost due to the half-duplex audio or because the quality of the audio prevented their detection.

Standard social rules and protocols were therefore sometimes rendered inoperable in cross-site situations because of this loss of information. In many cases, we were able to compensate for these altered or missing conversational cues by altering or adapting social protocols and procedures to this new environment. For example, we learned quite early that conversational turn-taking in our large cross-site meetings was not as easy as it was in single-site meetings. We adapted to this by occasionally asking people at the other site if they had anything to add, or watching the other site's video very carefully for gestural and postural indications that someone wanted to speak. Over time the group learned to handle many cross-site situations:

"We have become sensitized to the different social protocols of the link. For example, we have adapted to the technology in giving cross-site demos in the following ways: 1. wearing bright colors to give more cross-site presence, 2.

preparing ahead of time because glitches are much more difficult to deal with over the link (the communication mechanism and demo are using the same channel), 3. trying not to move too much so that the video compression doesn't dominate the conversation, 4. doing things "on cue," 5. speaking loudly, and choosing carefully when to speak, etc."

When social protocols were not yet established/adapted for certain cross-site situations, confusion, awkwardness or what we called "video rudeness" sometimes resulted:

A Xerox Corporate VIP came to PARC and visited each lab. SCL's visit included a short presentation by each area manager. The Portland-based area manager's presentation via the link was first. After the end of his presentation and as the next presentation was beginning, most of the Portland contingent left to go to an off-site meeting without saying anything (i.e., without valid exit protocol). At the same time, the first Palo Alto manager began his presentation with a video tape that wasn't transmitted to Portland. The remaining Portlander saw a blank screen and could hear almost nothing. Thinking that the Portland folks were being intentionally excluded, and not wanting to interrupt, the remaining Portlander went to his office, leaving an empty couch in video view. When the videotape was completed in Palo Alto, the Portland image returned to the Palo Alto monitor showing an empty couch. To Palo Alto, it appeared that Portland had given their presentation and then just left, showing no interest in the Palo Alto presentations. In other words, it appeared to Palo Alto that Portland was being extremely rude. It affected the rest of the meeting because the empty Portland couch was constantly in view. From Portland's perspective, it appeared that Palo Alto had intentionally excluded them by turning off Portland's "eyes and ears." So it appeared to Portland that Palo Alto had been rude.

A particularly important social cue that was affected by our video environment was eye-contact. Eye contact provides a number of the nonverbal cues that control interaction (Hall, 1959, 1966; Krauss et al., 1977). Our experience indicates that eye contact was important in interaction over video as well. (The major television networks also feel that video eye contact is important. Television announcers and newspeople usually read things using teleprompter technology, which allows a speaker to read something while looking directly into a camera.)

In our experimental video environment, we occasionally had cameras and monitors positioned such that "video eye contact" was not maintained (e.g., when person A looks at the person B's video image, the camera looking at person A and providing B's view of A may be looking at the side or back of person A). Almost universally when this occurred, people felt uncomfortable:

"I attended a meeting in the Palo Alto conference room this morning by Video. The camera was placed at one end of the room and the monitor at the other. This had an interesting effect. Whenever I said anything all the heads I could see turned away from me. Of course they were turning to see me on the monitor so rationally there was nothing rude about it. But I felt much more comfortable when (a Palo Alto lab member) moved the camera near the monitor."

After a few of these incidents, we tried to provide video eye contact whenever possible by placing cameras and monitors very close to each other. This allowed users to look approximately into the camera while they were looking at the monitor.

Another important cross-site social issue involved the development of working relationships between geographically distributed lab members. In team environments the ability to do productive work is affected by the working relationships between work group participants. Our experience indicates that relationships were difficult to initiate via the link. People didn't feel that they had really met one another until they came together in person:

(A visitor) met (two of the Portland researchers) over the video from Palo Alto. The next day she was in Portland physically. Someone said "Well at least you met (the two Portland researchers) via the video before you came up." The visitor emphatically said, "I hadn't really met them until I met them in person in Portland!"

Our experience supports Short, Williams and Christie's (1976) findings that getting to know someone over electronic media can be problematic.

Once cross-site relationships had been established via face-to-face interaction, people were able to work together cross-site and enhance their cross-site personal and working relationships. For example, the author, who was based in Portland, worked closely at times with Palo Alto lab members Steve Harrison, Kim McCall, and Sara Bly. The author eventually became friendly with each of them. Other lab members developed similar cross-site relationships. Geographically distributed lab members rarely visited each other in person, interacting primarily via the cross-site technology.

Just as our cross-site link seemed inadequate for initiating relationships, our experience showed inadequacies in the support of certain other types of cross-site interaction. For example, settling particularly divisive issues sometimes required face-to-face interaction. One five-person project team (three in Portland, two in Palo Alto) was unable to resolve some critical design issues after working together for several months via the cross-site technology. They decided that they had to come together face-to-face. They met for 3 days of intense design discussions in Portland and settled their critical design questions. One Palo Alto-based team member's description was as follows:

> "Halfway through the process (the other Palo Alto team member) and I journeyed up to Portland for three days of intensive discussions. I think these played a valuable role both on the technical end (the state of the discussion was such that it really felt like certain issues were ready to "crystallize" or at least "gel") and also for building our personal feelings for each other (bonding is a pretty overused term these days, but there was definitely some kind of bonding going on during these intensive all-in-the-same-room sessions). . . . To me it seems there is something indispensable about face to face contact in those situations where you want someone to 'disconnect' from their position on a solution or from their view of a problem just long enough to really get in touch with your view or position. Somehow, it seems harder to get this kind of temporary disconnection to happen in the more formal setting of a (video) meeting, or via e-mail. . . . Somehow when we were all in the same room together it seemed easier to get this back and forth (discussion) to happen than over the (video)."

This team accomplished some important tasks by meeting face-to-face that they had bee unable to accomplish via the cross-site technology.

Another interesting social issue in our environment was privacy. Whenever the author has described the SCL media environment, someone invariably asks, "Wasn't lack of privacy a problem?" Within a trusted group like SCL, video privacy was not a major problem. Social protocols developed for use of the video mirrored those for face-to-face interaction. For example, when wandering around via video, people generally didn't look in on someone for extended periods without their knowledge, just as people would not generally enter someone's office surreptitiously and watch them without their knowledge. Furthermore, people had several mechanisms to prevent others from looking in on them when they desired privacy. Actually, for the author, audio privacy was more important than video privacy. In other words, the author kept his camera on to allow people to enter his video space, but kept his microphone off so that he had explicit control over who entered his audio space. (Note that standard telephone protocol works this way too.)

From a system design and human interface perspective, we talked about potential privacy designs a great deal. Often privacy traded off with accessibility in system design. In other words, one person's access impinged on another's privacy. Two human interface features were added to our system to try to cope with the privacy issue. One was George Goodman's "Big Brother Detector." This was a set of eyes on the computer interface that opened when someone looked at you and closed when you were unobserved. Another privacy feature was "peek." In the interface "peek" allowed only a 5-second glance into someone's office. This was to simulate "sticking your head in someone's door to see if they're available." People also had the option of turning off their cameras or putting the lens cap on their office cameras to keep people out of their video space.

We also proposed a number of other privacy designs. Many people liked the idea of using the "door metaphor" to represent whether or not something was private. In our environment a closed door normally symbolized "I'm busy or in a private conversation right now and I prefer not to be disturbed." By building software into our system we could have created a "virtual door" that represented one's desired level of privacy. We also considered putting detectors in doorways so that a closed physical door would cause one's virtual door to be closed too.

In any event, although we realized privacy would be a major concern in applying such technology in most settings, our prototype system did not include much privacy protection. As soon as one considers applying this technology across organizational boundaries or in less trusting groups, mechanisms for providing control over the privacy of one's space will probably be required.

In summary, we noticed a number of significant social issues in our distributed environment, including issues involving social protocols, the initiation and development of personal and working relationships, the inadequacies of the link for certain types of interaction, and privacy.

Cognitive and Physical Issues

Our experience highlighted a number of cognitive and physical issues in our distributed environment: (a) people often felt the "presence" of remote individuals, (b) some aspects of our system were felt to be limiting or distracting, and people were able to adapt to many of these limitations, and (c) people tended to orient to audio output rather than video output.

Short, Williams and Christie (1976) discussed the "social presence" of remote individuals in teleconferencing meetings. In our cross-site media environment, lab members often felt the presence of people at the other site. This manifests itself in many ways. Sometimes an action visible to the other site was enough to provide a feeling of remote presence. Sometimes it was the sound of someone's cough at the other end that reminded one that there were other-site participants in a meeting:

> The lab manager in Palo Alto was speaking at the beginning of the meeting explaining the meeting's purpose. He was speaking in a normal conversational tone. Then a cough was heard from Portland. The lab manager immediately began speaking in a louder more "public" speaking voice (the "I'm talking over the audio to Portland voice").

Over time, certain lab members were able to establish a strong presence at the other site. For example, one Palo Alto lab member had such a strong and continual presence in Portland via the link that Portland lab members thought he had visited Portland in person before he actually visited:

> "(Another Portland-based lab member and I) were talking about which Palo Alto lab members had been to Portland site (physically) and which people had not yet been here. At first, we were certain that (a particular Palo Alto lab member) had been here, but as we carefully checked the travel records and thought about it, we realized that he had actually never been physically present in the Portland site."

These Portland lab members and the Palo Alto lab member had worked closely together for several months via the link. The frequent interaction over the link actually gave the Palo Alto lab member a significant "Portland presence" in the minds of the two Portland-based researchers.

On the down side, a number of equipment limitations in our system were recognized. The limitations imposed by video compression, the half-duplex audio arrangement, and the lack of synchronization of the audio and video signals were all noted as distracting and limiting by system users. Lab members and other regular system users adapted to most of these limitations and rarely commented on them (after an initial novelty period). The major continuing problem was the half-duplex audio that limited interactive discourse. First-time users were especially sensitive to system limitations and almost always commented on them. Our experience showed that within the first half hour of system usage, users generally adapted to most of these limitations.

Our experience also indicated that the video sometimes didn't provide an accurate picture of other-site people and places. In general, this was noted by people who had first seen the person or place in question via video:

> A (new Palo Alto-based researcher) joined the lab. She worked with the Portland people over the link for a few months and had not yet met (a particular Portland-based researcher) in-person. When she finally did meet (this Portland researcher) she was surprised at how short he was in person. She thought he was much taller from the "video impression" she had of him.

Another example is described in these comments from a consultant who worked at the Portland site for about 6 months before his first in-person visit to Palo Alto. Until this visit, his impressions of the Palo Alto physical layout and many Palo Alto lab members were obtained via the cross-site video:

"The SCL (Palo Alto) commons and office space viewable on (video) looked completely different in person: the commons were much larger than I had thought, yet the couch seemed smaller. (Video) gave me no clear perception of where the computers were located in the room. Even the shape of the commons area and the presence of pillars was not clear to me before the trip. The (Palo Alto lab members) that I had met only on (video) seemed different in person. My pre-trip perception of their faces and individual traits did not match reality that well. I had problems matching faces to names. On the other hand, I found talking to (the Portland people) via (video while in Palo Alto) to be easy and very natural."

During the course of experimenting with our environment, we noticed another audio/video artifact that was (at least to me) surprising. When we separated audio and video output, we found that people oriented to the audio:

A Portland researcher and his two year old son were in the Portland commons talking to a Palo Alto researcher in the Palo Alto commons. The video output (large screen display) and audio output (Quorum microphone/speaker system) were about ten feet apart. The Portland researcher was introducing his son to the Palo Alto researcher. The Portland researcher pointed his son toward the Palo Alto researchers' picture on the monitor and explained that "there's (the Palo Alto researcher)." As soon as the Palo Alto researcher spoke, the little boy went over to the Quorum box, turning his back on the monitor where the Palo Alto researcher's picture was, and spoke directly to the speaker where the Palo Alto researcher's voice was coming from. Again the Portland researcher pointed out to the little boy that the Palo Alto researcher's picture was on the monitor and again, as soon as the Palo Alto researcher spoke, the little boy turned his back on the picture and dealt only with the audio box. The two year old clearly believed that someone's presence is "where their voice comes from."

Such reactions were by no means limited to small children:

"A Palo Alto researcher and I were chatting via office-to-office video. The audio was via a speakerphone in my office. The audio box and video box are physically far apart in my office. I found myself talking to the audio box, where (the Palo Alto researcher's) voice was, rather than to his image on the monitor."

Our experience supports Johansen's (1984) conclusions that audio is much more important to videoconferencing users than video.

In summary, our experiences pointed out a number of interesting cognitive and physical issues: the remote presence phenomena, particular limitations of our environment, and people's ability to adapt to many of them, the video not providing an accurate picture of other-site people and places, and people's orientation to audio rather than video.

SPECULATIONS ON OUR EXPERIENCES

In the previous section, we presented a number of cross-site issues derived from the lab's experiences. This section presents some additional information based on the author's informed intuition regarding our cross-site experiences. Although most of these opinions are unsubstantiated in any formal sense, this additional information may be useful to others involved in constructing or studying collaborative systems. This additional section is presented in the spirit of Fred Brooks' (1988) plenary address at CHI'88 where he said that "any data is better than no data."

Our experience showed that there was a sense of group cohesion in our distributed lab despite the 600-mile gap between the sites. Personal and working relationships were able to grow between distributed lab members. How were these things possible? We might speculate that they were possible primarily because we were able to simulate physical proximity to some extent via technology. In particular, the cross-site shared audio/video space and the ability to wander the other site via video allowed us to simulate many informal same-site interactions. For example, it was quite common for conversations to spring up in the shared commons space discussing the weather, someone's family, or a technical issue. As Allen's (1977) work would predict, this frequent informal interaction over time allowed cross-site personal and working relationships to grow. It allowed the lab to become a more cohesive unit. One of our experiences indicated that the simulated physical proximity provided by the shared space was a major reason that the lab felt this organization oneness. This quote came from a Palo Alto lab member after we lost our video link for several days due to an equipment problem:

> "I . . . have missed the link, and have already started to think of Portland as one might expect a remote lab to be thought of—a group of people who are intellectually known to exist, but that's it. At least with the (video), I felt like we had a kind of common back fence over which to chat."

As discussed earlier, the link seemed to support the growth of relationships over time but not their initiation. Why not? The author believes that this may have been due in part to the limited resolution of the compressed cross-site video. When meeting someone for the first time, people focus very carefully on facial features and other small details of a person (e.g., how tall a person is, how heavy a person is, etc.) to help fix that person in their minds (Krauss et al., 1977). This was difficult to accomplish between our two sites. For example, we documented cases in our environment where cross-site counterparts who had only met over the link had trouble recognizing each other's faces when they later met face-to-face. The limited resolution of the compressed video must have contributed to this problem. One could test this hypothesis by repeating some of our explorations using a higher quality video connection. As discussed previously, the video sometimes also didn't provide an accurate picture of other-site people (i.e., their height or weight) and this may have contributed to the recognition problem as well.

Another problem of perception that the author feels influenced many cross-site interactions involved how people perceived distances over the link. Short, Williams and Christie (1976) discussed the possibility that interacting over telecommunications facilities may distort an interaction by imposing a particular inter-site distance level. Hall (1959; 1966) pointed out that in a given culture, there are normal comfortable distances for particular types of interactions. The author feels that the cross-site link sometimes imposed distances that simply did not match the norm for an interaction. For example, for a small group meeting held in one physical location, Hall claimed that the normal distance between meeting participants would be about 4 to 12 feet. For such a meeting our technology might have imposed a distance level between the two ends of the link which was say, 20 feet. It's easy to see how such a cross-site meeting might feel awkward to meeting participants. One could understand if this meeting split into two separate camps that could not come to a joint consensus. We encountered these situations in our environment at one time or another. The author believes that in designing a video system for distributed work, an attempt should be made to constantly match distance level to the cultural norms for a particular type of interaction (see Hall, 1959; 1966 for more discussion of normal distances).

CONCLUSIONS AND DIRECTIONS
FOR FUTURE WORK

The author is in the process of establishing another distributed organization experiment (at U S WEST Advanced Technologies). We plan to base this work on the lessons learned from this exploratory project in distributed organization support at Xerox PARC. We learned a great deal from this effort.

The author believes that the application of shared spaces and the general focus on informal interaction were key aspects of the PARC effort. The geographically distributed System Concepts Lab, supported by the shared space technology and the ability to wander the other site via video, was able to function to a large extent as if it were a single-site organization. The lab was able to develop a sense of group cohesion. Lab members were able to develop cross-site relationships. The author believes that this was due in large part to the shared cross-site audio/video space (i.e., the always-on audio/video connection between the two commons spaces), the computer-controllable video network, and a strong internetworking (e.g., electronic mail) environment.

We will work to extend the shared spaces concepts of the PARC experiments. We hope to extend the simulated proximity provided by audio and video to include entire information spaces. For example, people should be able to electronically share and browse books and journals, records of previous meetings, electronic mail, videos of their children, the evening news broadcast, and so forth. Artificial intelligence technology might be applied to help navigate through this communications and information environment.

The exploratory effort at PARC also pointed out a number of problems and areas for improvement in the cross-site technology. For example, the author believes that the low quality of the compressed cross-site video contributed to our inability to initiate cross-site relationships. The half duplex audio clearly inhibited interactive discourse across the link. We plan to use better quality cross-site video and full duplex audio in the new environment.

Looking at Portland–Palo Alto social interaction also points out areas for future work. We plan to build the next system to allow a variety of privacy schemes. Our next environment will take into account the social protocols of interaction and the verbal and nonverbal cues that control these protocols. Providing video eye contact will be a priority. It is also the author's belief that an attempt should be made to constantly match the system's imposed distance level to the cultural norms for a particular type of interaction.

We also plan to pursue a number of new experiments in both the behavioral and technical domains. On the technical side, we will also be investigating how the telephone network of the future might best support collaboration over space and time. We plan to investigate various collaborative tools (e.g., shared cross-site drawing, shared computing contexts, remote device control) and new input/output metaphors (e.g., helmet displays).

In the behavioral domain, we see a number of interesting new experiments to try. We would like to understand the needs of distributed organizations. Therefore we plan to compare a distributed organization with a nondistributed one (in our case, this will probably be a before and after comparison). We plan to eventually extend collaboration technologies to support non-research and development organizations (e.g., marketing organizations, upper management). This will allow us to evaluate the (possibly) different needs of such organizations. We want to investigate using these technologies between different types of organizations (e.g., between engineering and manufacturing or between engineering and marketing). We eventually plan to focus these technologies on other domains besides distributed organizations. We may try to prototype a next-generation distance education environment. One could also easily imagine applying such technologies to remote sales, remote consulting, or even the home of the future. Each domain will provide new behavioral issues to investigate.

We also will focus some energy on comparing the environment that we construct with the PARC environment. This may help us determine if the results from the PARC effort are extensible to other organizations. In other words, it may help us determine which behavioral impacts are related to particular aspects of the PARC system design, and which impacts are simply inherent in any system used to support a geographically distributed organization.

ACKNOWLEDGMENTS

The author would like to thank Stu Card and Dave Robson of Xerox PARC, Steve Reder of the Northwest Regional Education Lab, and Bob Johansen of the Institute for the Future, for their significant contributions to this work. Margi Olson of NYU, Sara Bly of Xerox PARC, George Goodman, formerly of Xerox PARC, Steve Bulick of U S WEST Advanced Technologies, and many other colleagues at Xerox PARC and U S WEST Advanced Technologies also provided helpful input. Finally the author would like to thank Paul Bauer at U S WEST Advanced Technologies for allowing the author to complete this work on U S WEST time.

REFERENCES

Allen, T. J. (1977). *Managing the flow of technology: Technology transfer & the dissemination of technical information within the R & D organization.* Cambridge, MA: MIT Press.
Brooks, F. (1988). Plenary address: Grasping reality through illusion. *Proceedings of CHI'88,* May 1988, Washington, D.C.
Galbraith, J. (1973). *Designing complex organizations.* Reading, MA: Addison-Wesley.
Goodman, G. O., & Abel, M. J. (1986). Collaboration research in SCL. *Proceedings of the Conference on Computer Supported Cooperative Work,* December 1986, Austin, TX.
Goodman, G. O., & Abel, M. J. (1987). Communication and collaboration: Facilitating cooperative work through communication *Office: Technology and People, 3,* 129–145.
Hall, E. T. (1959). *The silent language.* Garden City, NY: Doubleday.
Hall, E. T. (1966). *The hidden dimension.* Garden City, NY: Doubleday.

Johansen, R. (1984). *Teleconferencing and beyond: Communications in the office of the future.* New York: McGraw Hill.

Johansen, R. (1988). *Groupware: Computer support for business teams.* New York: Free Press.

Krauss, R. M., Garlock, C. M., Bricker, P. D., & McMahon, L. E. (1977). The role of audible and visible back-channel responses in interpersonal communication. *Journal of Personality and Social Psychology, 35,* 523–529.

CSCW '86. *Proceedings of the Conference on Computer Supported Cooperative Work* December 1986, Austin, TX.

Short, J., Williams, E., & Christie, B. (1976). *The social psychology of telecommunications.* New York: Wiley.

Design and Assessment of a Group Decision Support System

Douglas R. Vogel
Jay F. Nunamaker
University of Arizona

Abstract

Although decision researchers and students of group processes have identified many kinds of errors and biases in group decision making, it remains an important and frequently-occurring aspect of life in most organizations. This chapter describes a system designed to counter communication and information processing problems in group deliberation and choice. It focuses on the design and use of an advanced group decision support system (GDSS) first installed at the University of Arizona, and subsequently, at other academic and industrial sites. The authors describe the behavioral realm in which the system is intended to operate, design features, and users' reports about their experiences with the system.

Group deliberation and decision making are examples of a particularly important kind of intellectual teamwork. In most organizations, group decision making goes on at both high and low levels, and encompasses strategic, operational, and technical issues. There is considerable evidence, some of it cited in other chapters, that group decision making is often suboptimal, not only because of the cognitive limitations of the decision makers, but because of difficulties in group dynamics that arise during the evaluation and selection of alternatives. The systems described by Kraemer and Pinsonneault (chap. 14 in this volume) are the result of efforts to overcome these difficulties. As their chapter indicates, there are a variety of forms of group decision support systems (GDSSs); they differ on a number of dimensions including cost, number of users that can be accommodated, whether users must be co-located or can be geographically dispersed, and the sort of support provided for the group's activities.

In this chapter, we describe the group decision support system facilities designed and first installed at the University of Arizona. These facilities incorporate leading-edge hardware and software and trained group facilitators in physical surroundings designed to maximize comfort, visibility of display media, and opportunity for multiple kinds of interaction. Our main goal here is to create a detailed picture of the elements of the system and the way it operates. To provide a context for this technical description, however, it may be useful to have in mind some examples of the kinds of groups who might want to use such a system. Consider, for instance, examples such as a group of high-level university administrators developing long-term institutional strategies, community betterment groups attempting to specify plans for local economic development, or senior executives in a division of a large, multinational firm defining divisional objectives. Typically, groups such as these and the others who have used our labs specify a question or set of issues that provides a focus for their discussion and proceed through a series of steps involving some combination of idea generation, deliberation, and selection of alternatives, depending on the goals of the group and the nature of the issue. Each step of this process is supported in some way by the various elements of the GDSS.

Our technical description provides a basis for a discussion of the reactions of real-world decision makers who have used our labs as a forum for working on important organizational problems, as well as the research activities that we and our colleagues have undertaken to try to understand the impact of these systems on group deliberation and decision processes. It becomes evident that accumulating a body of sound, empirically based knowledge in this area is a very difficult enterprise, involving, as is the case in other areas of research about groups, the multiple complexities that derive from variations in tasks and group composition, and from the multidimensional nature of group effectiveness (cf., Hackman, 1983; McGrath, chap. 2 in this volume). Nevertheless, we believe that the rather considerable commitment of research energy and other resources required to carry out this enterprise is justified by its potential to contribute to our understanding of an important type of distributed cognition (Hutchins, chap. 8 in this volume) and by the practical importance of its potential to improve highly consequential group decision processes such as those described earlier.

GDSS TECHNOLOGY

The elements of Group Decision Support System technology are an appropriately designed facility, hardware, software, and a trained facilitator. Each of these elements is important for successful GDSS implementation. Furthermore, attention to the relationships between these elements is important to insuring that the GDSS is effective and compatible with the needs and goals of its users.

Facility Design

Facility design includes the physical organization of the technology, and other design features (i.e., lighting, seating, etc.) of the room in which the group decision making takes place. The layouts of the two facilities in operation at the University of Arizona are shown in Figs. 19.1 and 19.2. The smaller facility contains 16 workstations and the larger contains 24; each of these workstations can accommodate one or two individuals. Thus, these facilities can be used for groups ranging from relatively small committees to fairly large assemblies. Both labs include small adjoining rooms that are helpful for presenter preparation, conferences, and breaking a larger group into subgroups. Both are temperature-controlled and sound-proofed to minimize external distractions. In addition, the workstations are designed so that users seated at the terminals can see the display media at the front of the room easily, and can turn in their seats to speak directly to other members of the group during discussion periods.

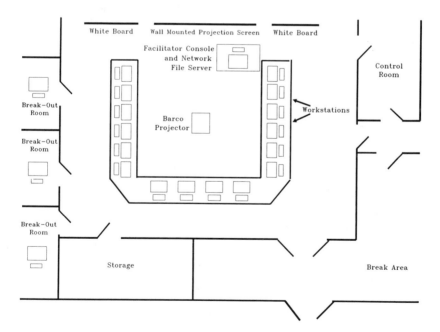

FIG. 19.1. University of Arizona Group Decision Support System with 16 workstations.

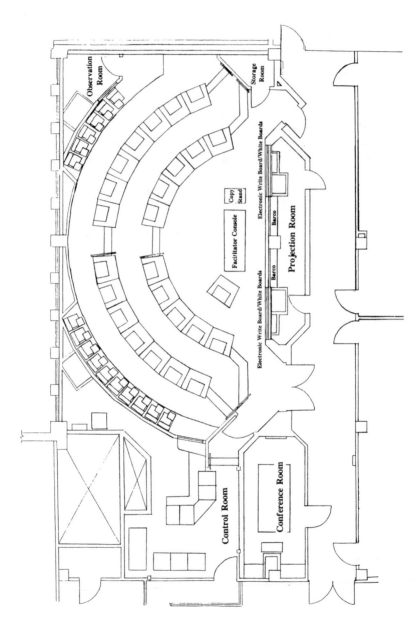

FIG. 19.2.   University of Arizona Group Decision Support System with 24 workstations.

Hardware

The hardware includes the individual workstations, linked by a central file server in a local area network, as well as the presentation media. The workstations are hard-disk based so as to enhance system performance and minimize the disruption associated with the use of floppy disks. High resolution color graphic terminals are used to provide sharp, clear screen displays. Group members can use either template-designated function keys or mice to interact with the system.

A high bandwidth local area network (LAN) is used to maintain high levels of performance in transmitting text between individual group members. The central file server assists in the coordination and management of input from individual decision makers and acts as a source of "organizational memory" from session to session.

The presentation media support a wide variety of visual modes, including overhead transparencies, 35 mm slides, videotapes, and hard-copy projection, and also provides teleconferencing capability.

Software

A broad spectrum of computer programs is used to guide the activities of the group and its facilitator. In general, software in GDSSs can be designed to support idea generation, issue organization, consensus formation through prioritization and voting, policy development, information system specification and systematic evaluation of plans, as well as presentation of individual and group output.

Underlying our efforts is the software design premise, groups should not be artificially constrained or forced into a fixed procedure or set of tools. Rather, to encompass the needs of different groups facing a variety of complex problems, the software must be both comprehensive and flexible. Modules need to be generic, but easily customized to meet special group needs; it should be possible to combine them in a variety of ways to support a particular group's purpose. Our goal has been to create software that is not merely "user friendly" but "user seductive" as a way of encouraging individual involvement in group decision-making sessions.

In our labs, individual tools can be used in combination with knowledge bases that link together the work products of multiple sessions, make it possible to import data from organizational files, and provide the opportunity for feedback and analysis from multiple perspectives as illustrated in Fig. 19.3. Any given group may use a number of tools, each with a specific purpose. The following paragraphs provide a description of some of the various pieces of software used to support groups in our labs at the University of Arizona.

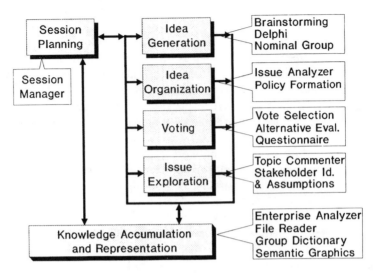

FIG. 19.3.   Plexsys Group Support System.

Session Director is a program that helps the facilitator or group leader select the tools to be used in a session and suggests an appropriate sequencing of steps within a session. Default order, times, and output reports are listed, which may be modified at the group's discretion. The Session Director generates an agenda that drives the activation of new software programs, or tools, as the group proceeds through a session. The Session Director also coordinates the transfer of information from one program to another to provide integrated support for various group activities. Additional support is provided for coordinating information between group sessions.

Electronic Brainstorming (EBS) supports idea generation, allowing group members to both enter comments simultaneously and anonymously and to share information on a specific question. In EBS, participants begin by entering a comment in response to the question on their individual computer screen; those initial comments are then randomly distributed to other members of the group via the local area network. Subsequently, group members can enter "comments on comments" as they receive files containing the ideas and observations of other participants. Typically, this process continues for 30 to 45 minutes. Other tools supporting idea generation are modeled after Delphi and nominal group techniques.

Issue Analyzer helps group members identify the key items produced during the idea generation process and consolidate them into a smaller set. In the identification phase, individuals select topics that merit further consideration by the group and can also append supporting comments from the idea generation session to those topics. It is also possible to integrate external information such as corporate financial reports, budgets, policy statements, and information about competitors' practices. After the selection of key issues by individuals, the lists are consolidated and may be further reduced in face-to-face discussion. The result is a manageable set of ideas and comments that can provide the basis for further discussion, or, depending on the group's goals, may be treated as a set of alternatives in a voting procedure.

Voting provides a variety of prioritizing methods including agree/ disagree, Likert scales, rank ordering, and multiple choice. The program is designed so that all group members can cast private, anonymous ballots. The accumulated results can be displayed in a graphical or tabular format. We have also designed a program to support multiple criterion decision making that presents a list of alternatives and a set of criteria arranged in a matrix format; in this program, criterion weighting can be varied to obtain a sensitivity analysis. Summary statistics and information about the degree of consensus are also provided.

Topic Commenter uses an identified list of topics in a multiwindow format to guide structured group discussion. Individual group members can respond to any or all of the topics in whatever order they desire, enabling members to work at their own pace. Additionally, the participants can examine the comments made by other group members. Topics can be further decomposed, as necessary, into subtopics for comment. In addition, this program permits users to contribute asynchronously and from geographically dispersed sites; thus giving this type of tool the attributes of a decision room without walls.

Policy Formation supports the group in developing a policy statement or mission through iteration and group consensus. A related program is a *Stakeholder Identification and Assumption Surfacing* tool, which supports systematic evaluation of the implications of a proposed policy or plan. Stakeholders who could potentially affect or be affected by a plan or policy are identified by the group. Assumptions and feelings these stakeholders may have regarding the plan or policy are recorded by the group members. Stakeholders' assumptions are then rated on several dimensions and graphically analyzed.

Session Dictionary can be used to help the group establish a glossary of words and phrases containing the group's agreed on "definitions"; thus, this program can help to provide a valuable record of the group's understanding of its own activity that can be useful in future sessions or in its day-to-day activities. Additional programs help link shared understandings of this type to new groups by extracting key ides from sessions, integrating them with related information from other sessions and storing them for later retrieval.

These tools can be arranged in whatever way seems most appropriate given the needs of particular user groups. The output derived from use of these programs acts as an "organization memory" as groups return for additional sessions or as new members or groups seek to build on the results of previous sessions.

Facilitation

When we first began to conduct GDSS sessions, facilitators had to be sophisticated about the technology itself to assist users with the hardware and software. More recently, higher levels of technological integration, automated support for "backroom" functions and software to provide facilitator guidance (i.e., the Session Director noted earlier) have made it possible to shift attention to managing the session itself. In particular, expert systems can be used to guide the selection of tools to meet group needs and can also be used to assist facilitators during the session by monitoring and directing their activities.

We have also found that it is particularly important to meet with the group leader or key group members prior to the initial automated session. This allows us to establish the best match between the information-processing goals of the group and the automated support tools described earlier. It also makes it possible for us to clarify the role of automated support with group members, thus establishing an appropriate set of expectations.

GDSS RESEARCH AND DEVELOPMENT

In this section, we draw on a taxonomy of management information systems research and development activities developed by Vogel and Wetherbe (1984) to organize our discussion of our technical achievements, the research we and others have done to examine the impact of our GDSS and others like it, and some of the research and development activities that might be undertaken to solve problems in this area. The major categories in this taxonomy are software engineering, laboratory and field research, theoretically guided mathematical simulations, and conceptual analysis. Most, but not all, of the completed work we describe has been conducted in our labs; other investigations have taken place at organizations where we have established research connections. This section is organized to first present a description of our initial development activities, followed by a brief discussion of the research that we have undertaken and, subsequently, problems we've identified that create opportunities for further development.

Designing the System

Software Engineering

As the description of our system indicates, we and our colleagues have done a substantial amount of software engineering. For example, Applegate (1986) used prototype development to design, implement and evaluate the technical feasibility of automated support for electronic brainstorming. More recent software engineering has focused on the development of se-mantic-guided interfaces; these interfaces enable the user to specify the meaning of the relationship between individual pieces of data (i.e., consists of, will lead to) and can help users access and incorporate information stored in knowledge bases during group deliberations (Valacich, Vogel, & Nunamaker, 1988). The semantic-guided interfaces provide a visual framework that supports directed perusal of the knowledge base.

We are currently developing a semantic-guided graphics system to create, examine and modify models drawn from databases of various sorts. The system employs a familiar financial spreadsheet user interface and displays information from the knowledge base in a high resolution graphic format. Additional software engineering research focuses on the integration of multiple criterion decision-making models with existing Arizona GDSS software (Hong, Vogel & Nunamaker, 1987). In general, our GDSS software engineering efforts use a systems approach, focusing on adaptability for users as group composition and group needs change, and the provision of an organizational memory that permits users to identify and retrieve significant information.

Empirical Evaluation

Case Studies

From the development activities already described, we have moved into providing support for various groups of real-world decision makers. These sessions have proven to be a valuable source of reactions to the system, as each group provides us with an opportunity to obtain an in-depth evaluation of GDSS capabilities. These case studies may focus on a single session or may, instead, take a longitudinal approach. Although there are, of course, many threats to validity associated with case studies as a research method (Campbell & Stanley, 1966; Cook & Campbell, 1979), accumulated case studies can provide a rich source of qualitative data that can be used to generate hypotheses about the effects of particular GDSS features and the applicability of GDSSs as a function of task and organizational characteristics. We have now conducted a large number of GDSS sessions involving participants from many different kinds of organizations, both in our own lab and in a similar lab installed at one site of a large, multinational corporation. Here, we briefly describe two of the case studies conducted in our lab, and also describe, in a general way, some of the sessions we have conducted at the other site.

In the first, the CEO and twelve key members of a health care organization used the University of Arizona GDSS facilities to formulate strategic plans for confronting the increasing turbulence in the health care industry (Vogel & Nunamaker, in press). They met for two sessions, each lasting about three and a half hours. During these sessions they used a number of the tools previously described, including Electronic Brainstorming, Issue Analyzer, Voting, and Stakeholder Identification and Assumption Surfacing. In the first session, they focused on identifying and prioritizing key health care issues. In the second session, they tried to determine how a fixed amount of resources might be allocated over the projects that the group had identified in the first session. In these sessions, we observed how much time group members spent on each of the subparts of the process and also collected feedback from the participants about their reactions to the process. In addition, we interviewed them four months after the session to find out whether any of the ideas they developed during these sessions had actually been implemented.

The participants reported great satisfaction with their use of the GDSS and claimed that their productivity during the work sessions was greatly increased by the alterations in group communication patterns produced by the system. They reported that they were able to generate more ideas, were more creative, and were better able to reach consensus when using the GDSS than in their ordinary, unsupported group meetings. One group member commented that they had accomplished as much in one morning as they would normally accomplish in two days, given the same task. These reported process gains were attributed to the anonymity provided by the GDSS, which allowed ideas to be freely expressed. Follow-up reports indicated that a number of the ideas developed during these sessions had been implemented, and others were undergoing further review, prior to implementation.

A second recently completed case study involved a Fortune 1000 electronics corporation. The CEO and thirty members of his executive team and support staff used our GDSS facilities for a three day session that included electronic brainstorming, issue identification, and rank ordering of alternatives, as well as oral presentations supported by the display media discussed earlier. During these sessions, the group worked at establishing corporate performance expectations, defining directions for new product development and making the related resource allocation decisions, evaluating divisional plans and budgets, and specifying ways corporate objectives were to be accomplished. The group reported that the computer-supported sessions were particularly helpful in establishing a stronger sense of understanding and agreement among a larger group of participants than had been achieved in past unsupported sessions.

As noted earlier, the software we have developed at the University of Arizona has also been installed at one site of a large, multinational corporation in a room specially constructed for research purposes. Group facilitators and maintenance personnel have been trained by the University of Arizona faculty and staff, and internal procedures have been established for preplanning and reporting. The software has been used for problem solving in a variety of areas including handling of shop orders, production control, formulation of product strategies, discussion of advancement opportunities, and development of internal information systems. Typically, about ten people participate in each of these sessions; participants have included top-level executives, as well as plant foremen and line personnel. On-line pre- and postsession questionnaires allow participants to report their reactions to the automated process and their views about how it compares to unsupported, face-to-face meetings in terms of time spent in planning and project duration. These data are routinely transmitted to University of Arizona researchers.

The results to date have been very positive. Participants report that reliance on the GDSS in planning and problem-solving meetings has brought about significant reductions in the number of such meetings required, as well as in project calendar days. Users have expressed high levels of satisfaction with the system, praised the fairness and comprehensiveness of the process, and indicated that they would be willing to participate in a similar process in the future. Group members consistently reported that the computer-aided process is better than the unsupported process in terms of ideas generated, generation of commitment to a particular plan or project, fairness, achievement of project goals, and efficiency. The facility has never been advertised, yet is now fully booked based on word-of-mouth reports of successful use.

In conjunction with five other institutions using University of Arizona software, we are currently working to standardize instruments to capture data from GDSS sessions at each of the various sites. A data collection and analysis module has been developed that will support research by providing demographic information about individuals, subjective evaluations of the experience, and information about session dynamics, including use of specific software programs and time spent with each. In addition, the development of a longitudinal "research memory" will facilitate comparisons across studies, including meta-analytic investigations, and can also provide information about the value of GDSSs. By accumulating data across multiple GDSS sessions, eventually we will be able to explore questions about the impact of the system in a way that will, to some extent, counteract the epistemological difficulties associated with "one shot" case studies (Campbell & Stanley, 1966).

Laboratory Experiments

The presence of a state-of-the-technological-art GDSS such as ours on a university campus creates an outstanding opportunity to conduct controlled studies comparing computer-supported group deliberation and decision making to ordinary face-to-face sessions, as well as to examine the impact of variations in specific features of the GDSS. A number of such studies have been undertaken in our lab. For instance, Jessup, Connolly and Galegher (1988) examined the effect of anonymity on group process and outcome when using a GDSS. In their study, student subjects were asked to generate solutions to the (very real) campus parking problem. Their results provide modest confirmation of our intuitions about the value of anonymity, and of the favorable comments regarding the value of an opportunity to contribute anonymously obtained in our case studies. Compared to subjects whose comments were identified, groups who were able to work anonymously tended to be more probing and critical of each other's ideas. In this investigation, there was, however, no effect of anonymity on the number or rated quality of the solutions produced by the groups.

In a second study, Jessup, Tansik and Laase (1988) pursued the question of the effects of anonymity and also explored how physical proximity affects group deliberations. In their investigation, group members working together in a decision room were more satisfied with the process and more likely to focus on the positive aspects of each other's ideas than those who were physically dispersed, and group members working under anonymity reported higher levels of perceived system effectiveness than did group members whose contributions were identifiable. Individuals who could participate anonymously were also more likely to report that their session was more productive than previous unsupported group problem-solving sessions than were those whose comments were identifiable. Groups working under the anonymous, dispersed condition generated the most, and shortest, comments. These groups worked in a mode much like traditional brainstorming, making quick, short comments. Groups working under the identified, face-to-face configuration generated the least and longest comments. These groups worked in a mode more like a natural discussion, producing fewer and more well-formulated comments. These effects on the nature of the comments can be seen as evidence of the effects of the "cuelessness" induced by computer-mediated communication (Sproull & Kiesler, 1986).

A third investigation in this area (Connolly, Jessup & Valacich, 1988) also examined the effects of anonymity, this time in connection with a manipulation of the evaluative context of the discussion. That is, group members were prompted (by the actions of a confederate) to be either challenging and critical in their reactions to each other's comments, or to look for the merit in each other's ideas and seek to build on them. These researchers did find an effect of anonymity, such that anonymity was associated with generating more and better solutions for this problem. The evaluative context manipulation also had an effect on the quality of the discussion such that the groups operating with a more critical orientation produced more and better solutions. It is interesting to note, however, that self-reports of satisfaction with their experiences were inversely correlated with these performance measures. Although the anonymous, critically oriented groups performed most effectively, the identified, constructively oriented groups reported higher levels of satisfaction. These results point to the value of laboratory investigations where performance can be reliably assessed, independent of the subjective reports of users. They also give emphasis to McGrath's argument (chap. 2 in this volume) that the impact of advanced communications technology is likely to depend on the development of social norms (i.e., defining a problem-solving orientation that fosters effective use) to govern its use.

New Possibilities

Surveys

In addition to examining the impact of GDSSs, we and other researchers have used survey research methods to determine the extent of GDSS penetration in corporate settings, as well as to identify opportunities for new GDSS applications. For instance, Straub and Beauclair (1988) conducted a survey of 135 organizations and determined that GDSSs are gradually being incorporated into information system portfolios. In particular, they noted that GDSS application seems to fall into three major categories: planning, administrative and data analysis tasks, each relying on a different form of GDSS. They concluded that organizations are increasing their commitment to GDSSs especially in situations where opportunities for integration of computer conferencing and electronic mail exist. A recent University of Arizona survey is an additional example of the sort of application-seeking investigation already mentioned. In this survey we sought information that might help us develop management systems to overcome the delays and cost overruns characteristic of large-scale software development projects. We are currently analyzing these data, and expect that they will yield substantial valuable information about opportunities for the application of GDSSs.

Mathematical Simulation

Numerous opportunities exist to create mathematical models or simulations of the operation of GDSSs in different environments. For example, electronic brainstorming as implemented at the University of Arizona involves the interchange of $n + 1$ files, where n is the number of group members. (A file in this sense is equivalent to a sheet of paper; group members write in the file to add their comments to those of other members.) The extra file is provided to allow group members to work at their own speed and still have a file waiting for immediate use when a group member finishes a comment.

Our experience with electronic brainstorming, including monitoring of file use, suggests that periods of extreme nonrandomness can occur in file interchange between group members. Consequently, a group member may not see all of the files during a session and/or may see a small group of files an abnormally high percentage of the time. We are currently working to create a mathematical model of electronic brainstorming that would enable us to determine whether including additional files (i.e., more than $n + 1$) or revising the exchange protocol based on frequency of access by group members would allow us to achieve a more effective file distribution. The statistical profile regarding distribution of files and amount of time spent with each file by individual group members could be used to gain an appreciation of file dynamics, which could then be confirmed with live groups.

Additional simulation studies could address some of the system integration problems associated with the design of increasingly sophisticated GDSSs. For instance, technological characteristics such as the network bandwidth required to import information from external knowledge bases or to use the network to transmit screen images among participants within a session can, to some extent, be modeled and systematically investigated. The former problem might arise when users want to incorporate statistical or other data into their deliberations, rather than relying on argumentation. The latter problem becomes more important as communication is extended beyond the decision room environment to include people in remote locations in the group discussion.

Conceptual Analysis

In addition to seeking new applications for GDSSs and carrying out additional research to examine their impact, we are defining new areas for future GDSS developments. These developments rest on enlarging the conceptual realm of GDSSs to encompass additional features of the decision-making situation. For example, we are interested in the role of the facilitator and in the properties of the decision problem.

With regard to the first problem, we are currently considering the development of expert systems to apply captured facilitation expertise in GDSS sessions. This involves capturing facilitation expertise effectively, validating captured expertise, and integrating that expertise in a system that can be used appropriately by less experienced facilitators. Solving these problems presents formidable difficulties. First, the capture of expertise is complicated by the necessity to consider phases of GDSS support involving preplanning sessions with groups as well as the monitoring of feedback from group members during a session often involving visual clues to group dynamics. Moreover, validation of captured expertise requires the capacity to test the system on groups similar in size, composition, and focus to those that the system was based on and, furthermore, providing a means of real-time delivery of expertise to assist a less experienced facilitator without adversely affecting the group process requires a system that is comprehensive, easy to use, and can be adapted to groups with different needs and goals.

Methodological Synergism

The research and development activities we have described make it clear that there are many interesting issues associated with GDSSs that remain to be dealt with. New developments in hardware and software are needed to make the systems faster and more flexible, and more research is needed to clarify their impact. Our approach has been to strive for synergism, developing new programs as the need for them becomes apparent, and collecting data about the impact of both existing and proposed support tools in a variety of ways.

One example of this sort of synergism between GDSS research projects is that our observation of difficulties in organizing the output of electronic brainstorming sessions led to software engineering efforts resulting in the Issue Analyzer tool. This tool in turn has been used extensively in case and field studies to assist groups in planning and decision-making tasks, as well as in experimental studies evaluating the impact of integration of external information into the context of group deliberations (Vogel, 1988). This experience, in turn, has prompted the development of additional software engineering support of better user interfaces and more comprehensive integration of knowledge base capabilities (Valacich, Vogel, & Nunamaker, 1988).

An additional example of synergism between studies has its starting point in problems sensed in group brainstorming sessions in case and field studies involving anonymity, proximity, and participation as a function of group characteristics and tasks. The laboratory experiments described addressing anonymity, evaluative context, and proximity accompanied by software engineering support for various approaches to brainstorming have assisted in achieving a better understanding problems in these areas. Mathematical simulation and exploration of the impact of geographically remote group support as well as surveys about the need for technological support in particular task environments are expected to provide additional insight into the problem area. The application of these empirical methodologies will, ultimately, result in new software designed to make the best use of human and technological capacity. To further explicate the direction of our own future work, and to provide an impetus for others to join in our efforts, we present a number of hypotheses, developed through informal observation, that can provide the basis for additional research and development efforts.

Over the past three years, we have conducted hundreds of group sessions varying in size from 3 to 31, covering a variety of tasks and topics with a wide spectrum of group-member characteristics. Through this experience, we have identified several issues or factors that seem to be important determinants of ways people interact with GDSSs and affect group processes and outcomes. It is, perhaps, not too surprising that the list we have generated re-presents the familiar variables that have been found to influence work in nonautomated groups, as well (McGrath, 1984). We present them here as an indication of the kinds of questions and issues that should be considered in the design of future GDSSs and in research about the impact of those systems.

Group Size

Group size may be an important determinant of the actual and perceived value of GDSSs. As size increases in unsupported groups, participation rates become increasingly skewed and, typically, group discussion becomes increasingly inefficient. However, it is our impression that GDSSs have the potential to reverse this trend; it appears that as groups become larger, the system's capacity to support distributed participation and increase the efficiency of group discussion become more apparent. Members need not "wait their turn" to contribute to the question or problem before the group. Larger groups seem to appreciate the structuring associated with automated support, which keeps the group from becoming "bogged down" as well as the efficiency achieved through simultaneous human and machine parallel processing. Members tend to individually "buy in" and support the group solution with enhanced confidence that problem or question issues have been sufficiently explored. The potential of GDSSs for rationalizing deliberation and decision making with large groups deserves careful research attention.

Group Tasks

As is the case with unsupported group interaction, the nature of the task facing the group may affect the nature of its interactions and the nature of the tools it needs to do its work. Thus, features of a GDSS and the particular GDSS tools used should be matched to the task at hand and responsive to group characteristics and dynamics. For instance, groups whose members already have a high degree of knowledge about the problem and potential solutions in common may find it possible to start with issue organization rather than idea generation. Anonymity may be important to groups when sensitive issues are being discussed that can easily be confounded with personalities in the group but less so for routine, nonthreatening tasks. Or, when voting is warranted, the group (in conjunction with the leader or facilitator) might want to select member weighting and issue scaling appropriate to the question or problem under discussion. Again, investigations in which group characteristics, features of the task and features of the GDSS are systematically varied are in order.

Group Dynamics

Many aspects of group functioning depend, of course, on the quality of the interpersonal relationships and the status distribution of group members, and these variables also seem to interact with the various features of GDSSs. For instance, it appears that use of a GDSS tends to both heighten and diffuse conflict within the group. On the one hand, conflict is heightened as group members become more blunt and assertive in their comments. Members tend to express themselves more forcefully and are often not as polite when communicating through the system as they are in person. (See also Sproull & Kiesler, 1986 for similar observations.) On the other hand, many of our users report that the comments of others seem less threatening when presented on a computer screen than in a face-to-face encounter. These observations present an interesting paradox, in need of further exploration and clarification, but the potential of GDSSs as a tool for resolving conflict as yet has received little direct study. This is, then, another area that might be fruitfully explored in future GDSS research.

ACKNOWLEDGMENTS

We are grateful to Jolene Galegher for helpful editorial comments on an earlier version of this manuscript.

REFERENCES

Applegate, L. (1986). *Idea management in organization planning.* Unpublished doctoral dissertation, University of Arizona.

Campbell, D. T., & Stanley, J. S. (1966). *Experimental and Quasi-experimental design for research.* Skokie, IL: Rand McNally.

Connolly, T., Jessup, L. M., & Valacich, J. S. (1988). *Idea generation using a GDSS: Effects of anonymity and evaluative tone.* Unpublished manuscript, University of Arizona.

Cook, T. D., & Campbell, D. T. (1979). *Quasi-experimental design: Design and analysis issues for field settings.* Skokie, IL: Rand McNally.

Hackman, J. R. (1983). The design of work teams. In J. W. Lorsch (Ed.), *Handbook of organizational behavior* (pp. 315–342). Englewood Cliffs, NJ: Prentice-Hall.

Hong, I., Vogel, D., & Nunamaker, J. (1987). A knowledge-based DSS for supporting ill-structured multiple criterion decisions. *Proceedings of the 22nd Annual Hawaii International Conference on System Sciences.*

Jessup, L. M., Connolly, T., & Galegher, J. (1988). *The effects of anonymity on GDSS group process in an idea-generating task.* Unpublished manuscript, University of Arizona.

Jessup, L. M., Tansik, D., & Laase, T. D. (1988). Group problem solving in an automated environment: The effects of anonymity and proximity on group process and outcome with a group decision support system. *Academy of Management Best Paper Proceedings,* Anaheim, CA.

McGrath, J. E. (1984). *Groups: Interaction and performance.* Englewood Cliffs, NJ: Prentice-Hall.

Sproull, L., & Kiesler, S. (1986). Reducing social context cues: Electronic mail in organizational communication. *Management Science, 32,* 1492–1512.

Straub, D., & Beauclair, R. (1988). *GDSS technology in practice.* MISRC Working Paper 88-03, University of Minnesota.

Valacich, J., Vogel, D., & Nunamaker, J. (1988). A semantic guided interface for knowledge-base-supported GDSS. *Proceedings of DSS-88.* Boston, MA.

Vogel, D. (1988). The impact of "messy" data on group decision making. *Proceedings of the 21st Annual Hawaii International Conference on System Sciences.*

Vogel, D., & Nunamaker, J. (in press). Health service group use of automated planning support. *Administrative Radiology.*

Vogel, D., & Wetherbe, J. (1984). MIS research: A profile of leading journals and universities. *DATABASE,* Fall, *16,* 3–14.

Author Index

Subject Index